NINTH
INTERNATIONAL SYMPOSIUM
ON THEORY AND PRACTICE IN TRANSPORT ECONOMICS

MADRID, 2nd-4th NOVEMBER, 1982

TRANSPORT IS FOR PEOPLE

INTRODUCTORY REPORTS
AND
SUMMARY OF THE DISCUSSION

THE EUROPEAN CONFERENCE
OF MINISTERS OF TRANSPORT [ECMT]

The ECMT is an inter-governmental organisation independent from OECD, but its Secretariat is attached, from an administrative point of view, to that of the OECD, which distributes its publications.

The European Conference of Ministers of Transport (ECMT), established by a Protocol signed in Brussels on 17th October 1953, constitutes a forum for the Ministers of Transport of 19 European countries[1]. The work of the Council of Ministers is prepared by a Committee of Deputies.

The purposes of the Conference are

 a) to take whatever measures may be necessary to achieve, at general or regional level, the most efficient use and rational development of European inland transport of international importance;
 b) to co-ordinate and promote the activities of international organisations concerned with European inland transport, taking into account the work of supranational authorities in this field.

Major problems which are being studied by the ECMT include: transport policy; the financial situation and organisation of railways and road transport; problems concerning inland waterway transport and combined transport; development of European trunk lines of communication; problems concerning urban transport; the prevention of road accidents and co-ordination, at European level, of road traffic rules and road signs and signals; traffic trends and long-term traffic forecasts.

Moreover, the ECMT organises Round Tables and Symposia. Their conclusions are considered by the competent organs of the Conference, under the authority of the Committee of Deputies, so that the latter may formulate proposals for policy decisions to be submitted to the Ministers.

In addition, the ECMT is equipped with a computerised Documentation Centre to which inquiries concerning transport economics may be addressed.

---

1. Austria, Belgium, Denmark, Finland, France, Germany, Greece, Ireland, Italy, Luxembourg, the Netherlands, Norway, Portugal, Spain, Sweden, Switzerland, Turkey, the United Kingdom and Yugoslavia (associated countries: Australia, Canada, Japan, United States).

Publié en français sous le titre :

NEUVIÈME SYMPOSIUM INTERNATIONAL
SUR LA THÉORIE ET LA PRATIQUE DANS
L'ÉCONOMIE DES TRANSPORTS

TABLE OF CONTENTS

INTRODUCTORY REPORTS

SUMMARY OF THE DISCUSSIONS

4

ASSESSMENT OF
SOCIETY'S TRANSPORT NEEDS
MOBILITY OF PERSONS

Dr. P. CERWENKA
PROGNOS AG
Basle, Switzerland

SUMMARY

1. INTRODUCTION

In order to give an immediate first impression of the many-faceted and contradictory nature of the "mobility" problem area, this paper begins with two striking quotations. The first is attributed to the theologian Romano Guardini, who died in 1968, "Most people don't know where they want to go, but they want to get there as quickly as possible". The second is taken from a doctor's contribution to a report on the environment [1], "the atavistic burning desire within us to conquer space and time ... is precisely, not just a fashionable and changing trend, but a deep-rooted heritage of our species".

The first quotation can safely be categorised as an aphorism. This type of maxim is generally considered to be about 50 per cent truth, which is already a fairly high percentage. The second quotation, on the other hand, is a well-founded statement, though it cannot be proved and there is in fact no way of bringing any proof using scientific methods. Only indications to support the statement, which thus becomes a hypothesis, can be provided. As soon as we start groping our way towards the support or refutation of the hypothesis, defining, examining and interpreting specific qualitative and quantitative indicators and categories to understand and describe this "atavistic burning desire within us to conquer space and time" and its concrete manifestations and characteristics with all their consequences, we unexpectedly find ourselves plumb in the middle of the "mobility" issue with which we are concerned here and which has become for many a serious subject for research and for others a happy hunting ground for profitable speculation. One of the tasks of the former can and should be to expose the speculations of the latter.

Science and forecasting have long been inseparably bound together in noteworthy ambivalence. Unlike physics, which is concerned with the laws of dead matter and the relationships between its components, research into mobility necessarily has to include man and his personal freedom of decision and thus also unpredictability. The concept of "social physics" was coined (by Auguste Comte) as early as 1822 for this hazardous enterprise [2].

It is my personal conviction that the original causes of mobility - like so many other subjects of research - will virtually never be completely understood and analysed and therefore certainly not precisely forecast, but man in his multiple aspects and freedom of action plays a predominant role. Despite this view, it is entirely possible to observe human behaviour and its more or less marked recurrent patterns and recognise certain "laws" within it which are certainly not absolute, but which have a certain (frequently even measurable) probability of being valid over a given period.

An important issue in social physics is behavioural stability in general and the question of at what level of aggregation it is established. By and large, human behaviour can be divided into three such tiers of aggregation, which can best be illustrated by the questions:

- Whether?
- In what quantity?
- In what quality?

Let us take a simple example, i.e. eating:

- the question at the highest tier, namely whether people have to eat, is absolutely indisputable. The answer "yes" is true for all peoples and all times. Behaviour at this level of aggregation is absolutely stable so that it is possible to talk of a "law" or constantly recurring behaviour pattern.
- Turning now to the intermediate tier - in what quantity, it is clear that this question itself has to be differentiated, for example with the questions "how much" and "how often". The answers to these have to be further differentiated: a distinction has to be made between people doing heavy manual work and the unemployed, between babies and adults, healthy people and the sick, etc. etc. Nutritional scientists have developed an important indicator, however, to describe this quantity - kilo calories per person per day. There is still no deterministic value for this indicator, valid for all peoples and all times, however. It is given by reference to the above-mentioned categories and, what is more, for each category there is a certain range of variation. For the subject which concerns us here, mobility, the two keywords "category" (or segment) and "range of variation" (or scatter) are significant. It can be seen that the classical "law" concept is already at this level of aggregation highly relative and blurred. The quantitative data indicated are nevertheless helpful, useful and of great importance for the practical life of the individual and the organisation of an economy;

- Moving on to the lowest level of aggregation, quality, the number of possible questions grows in such an explosive fashion that in order to keep the picture useful and accessible to human comprehension, a selection of important questions has to be made, such as: hasty or leisurely eating? Lying, sitting or standing? What kind of food? Raw or cooked? How concentrated? Liquid or solid? Etc. etc. Opinions can also be very different as to which questions are regarded as important. The selection of questions will in any case always depend on the particular task involved. For our study of mobility, it should be remembered that qualities can be made accessible to analytical treatment mainly by creating further categories (segments), though there are frequently difficulties of demarcation: for example, up to what viscosity is a food considered liquid and from what viscosity as solid? In these questions it is apparent that a quantity, "viscosity" is being used to describe a quality, "liquid" or "solid". I considered it imprudent at this level of aggregation to talk of laws of behaviour in the classical sense, i.e. stable, universally applicable behaviour, as with many people this would lead to completely misleading expectations.

It can be seen from this example that there is a sharp boundary only between the highest tier of aggregation and the next, while the boundary between quantity and quality cannot be drawn clearly and unambiguously and depends on the state of research. The magic formula of replacing quantity by quality, which has often been heard recently as a slogan precisely in the transport field, with the aim of appearing as environment-conscious as possible, thus cannot stand up to scientific analysis.

When laws of human behaviour are discussed, then in addition to the already-mentioned relativisation there is a further important aspect to take into account, that of periodicity or - more specifically - the scalar spread of the stability. Human behaviour may be stable in the short term, it may - as can be seen in mobility behaviour in particular - be cyclical according to time of day, week or year, but it is also capable, in particular through technological innovations such as the car or television, of changing suddenly and probably irreversibly, entailing a whole series of unsuspected consequences.

In this introductory chapter a further important factor in human behaviour must be taken up, one which is of particular significance in the field of mobility, but is at the same time very difficult to pin down and therefore extremely difficult to translate into policy action. This is the most remarkable merging of want and requirement, liking to and having to, purpose and constraint.

9

For a long time, particularly during the phase of explosive growth in car ownership, the debate was always confined to the need for mobility. This standpoint is based on the idea that mobility is an independent need, an end in itself, a value as such. Any attempt to frustrate the meeting of this need - for example through introducing speed limits on motorways - was indignantly opposed in Germany at the time and shot at by the German Automobile Club (ADAC) with the slogan "Free driving for free citizens". Everything has now gone strangely quiet about this slogan and the selfsame German Automobile Club is publishing brochures on the design of pedestrian precincts and pedestrian-only residential areas under the title "Safety for the pedestrian" [3][4].

The car, as still the number one status symbol for many people [according to one newspaper report, getting a car is a bigger event in family life in the German Democratic Republic than birthday, confirmation and wedding put together(1)] has, through the free decision of individuals to fulfil the equally atavistic burning desire for a house in the country, created a scattered settlement structure, and the former freedom has unexpectedly become a constraint; people have become dependent on the car. Indeed, each family generally needs two cars in order to counter the undesirable social consequences of the oh-so-longed-for house in the country, apparent in such expressions as "grass widow" or "dormitory town". The journey from the house in the country to work in the town now has to be made in the very car that made the house in the country possible in all cases where there is no acceptable alternative. The "like to" has suddenly changed into "have to", a tyranny of unsuspected permanence, as settlement structures can only be changed in the very long term. The full weight of the constraint is now slowly becoming felt with rising energy prices.

In the "mobility" problem area, it is necessary to distinguish between four categories of participation or non-participation:

- wanted mobility (associated idea: a drive in the country);
- enforced mobility (associated idea: commuter);
- wanted immobility (associated idea: stay in a monastery);
- enforced immobility (asssociated idea: stay in hospital).

It may be remarked in passing that - for example through a road accident - wanted mobility can very quickly become enforced immobility.

---

1. Süddeutsche Zeitung, 21st-22nd November, 1981, p. 120.

In addition to the two polarities of want and requirement which are so important to mobility and between which in fact no fixed boundary can be drawn, two others need to be looked at and included in the discussion: supply and demand. In general terms, transport can be regarded as a market in which there is interaction (albeit very difficult to pin down) between supply and demand. Unfortunately this interaction in no way corresponds with the idealised conditions postulated for a perfect market (perfect competition between sellers, perfect information for buyers about the services and costs of alternative supplies, large number of sellers, etc.).

Briefly, two consequences of the interrelationship between supply and demand in the field of mobility must be considered:

- the existence of a transport infrastructure (supply) does not necessarily generate a demand for mobility. To take a concrete example, opening a canal does not in itself necessarily mean that it will be used, in particular if there are more attractive alternatives. A careful distinction always needs to be made between wishful thinking and sober forecasting;
- the non-existence of a transport infrastructure does not necessarily mean that there is no demand for mobility. Again giving an example, if there is no bridge over a fairly long reach of a river, this by no means implies that the people on the two sides of the river do not wish to meet one another.

The examples may seem trivial in the extreme, but both these logics are obviously constantly disregarded in planning and policymaking. The proof is there for anyone driving through the country with his eyes open to see: either existing bottlenecks in large towns are avoided by building inconvenient by-passes or else lonely boulevards are built to arouse demand in no man's land.

Overall mobility is thus the resultant of a very complex and hard-to-grasp interplay of:

- human wants (demand for mobility);
- constraints, which mainly stem from different land uses and their spatial distribution and the restrictions on people's time and money;
- technological and economic potential for bridging space (transport supply).

The wants could also be called the "software", and the constraints and transport supply the "hardware" of the transport market.

11

2. CONCEPTS

After that deliberately somewhat full introduction, which was intended to give some understanding of the problem and a first idea of the concept of "mobility", it is now necessary to define, differentiate and narrow down the expression "mobility" for analytical purposes. That is the purpose of this chapter.

So what actually is mobility? In everyday speech it means simply the ability to move. In transport economics though the concept has undisputedly earned a permanent place, it is unfortunately not always uniformly defined. In the earlier example of eating, in which the quantity of kilo calories per person per day was singled out as the characteristic indicator; in a classical approach to mobility the "number of journeys per person per day" can be assigned this function. (In classical transport planning the parameter was also called "traffic volume".) This parameter - just as in the earlier example - is, however, only one (though, as it happens, very convenient and easily comprehensible) descriptive parameter which by no means exhaustively covers the mobility phenomenon.

In a study carried out by this Institute for the Federal Minister of Transport, Bonn, mobility was defined as follows [5] (p. 6). "Mobility [in the most general form] is essentially a measure of the ability or capacity, the technical, economic and physical capability of individuals and groups to move and bridge distances ... In the most restricted and frequently-used form, mobility is seen in the last analysis as a measure of actual changes of location, of effective demand for transport services. Such changes of location mainly, and almost exclusively, lead to problems when they are accomplished using motor vehicles and are concentrated in space and time. It was thus in the first place only natural ... that for transport planning purposes mobility has so far been understood and used almost exclusively as the number of journeys per unit of time and population by persons using cars or public transport."

In a later study, also carried out by this Institute for the Federal Minister for Transport, Bonn, mobility was considerably more firmly established in an interdisciplinary approach, but became less convenient in its analytical contours [6] (p. 61): "Mobility is currently a much-discussed behavioural phenomenon which plays a part in the discussion of labour and housing market policies, social and educational policies as well as in transport policy. 'Mobility' means in general readiness and ability to undertake social and spatial 'changes of location' ... In the short term these locations are fixed as objective framework conditions, however. Mobility then means readiness and ability to move between fixed locations, such as home and place of work ... in order to perform location-specific activities."

If we follow this train of thought it may now help to explain and justify what is meant by "mobility of persons" as used in the title of this paper. Attention must be drawn to a peculiarity and ambiguity in the concept of mobility, which becomes clear with increasing carownership levels and increasing wealth: as mentioned above, mobility - especially in the social policy field - is regarded as readiness to change location (move house, for example). In transport economics, on the other hand, mobility is readiness and ability to bridge the distances between the fixed predetermined locations of different functions (such as being at home and working). Close observation now reveals diametrically opposed tendencies in these two phenomena: as soon as somebody has satisfied the "atavistic burning desire" for a house in the country, he becomes as a rule immobile in the demographic sense (it is no accident that we call land and houses "immovable assets". Unlike "movable" assets they cannot be shifted and the same seems to be increasingly true of their owners, who cling to their house in the country.) In the transport economics sense these property owners are nevertheless forced as a rule to become more mobile, since after their move they generally have to accept a longer journey to work and are therefore dependent on the car. We shall call the first type of mobility resettling or migratory mobility, and the second type, with which we are concerned here, simply "mobility" for the sake of convenience. Unless expressly stated otherwise, the word will always mean "mobility of persons" in the transport economics sense, as in the title of this paper. Goods transport is dealt with in Topic 1(b) of this Symposium.

The statement that as a rule mobility increases when somebody moves into his house in the country is at first not necessarily consistent with the choice of "number of journeys per person per day" as an indicator of mobility, as the number of journeys per day can certainly remain unchanged after a move. As a rule the distance certainly will change, however, and thus either the time taken for the trip or the speed will increase. In order to give an overall understanding of mobility, studies always ought to include at least the following three indicators:

- number of trips per person per day (trip frequency);
- distance of each trip (trip length);
- time taken for each trip (trip duration) or speed.

It must be stressed, however, that there are considerable practical difficulties in the way of this desirable goal, some financial, but others of a more fundamental nature. (For example, all surveys of trip distances that I know of are based on respondents' estimates and can therefore be considerably different from the distance

13

actually covered. This naturally means that the data about speed, which is calculated from these distances, are also inaccurate.)

In order to be able to compare statements made in different studies and as a basis for joint discussion, it is necessary to define the concepts unambiguously and uniformly. The following conventions have been agreed:

- A ride (in passenger transport) is defined as a person's change of location with the help of a conveyance. (Rides on a bicycle are not to be forgotten here!);
- A journey on foot is defined as a person's change of location outside the home on foot. (For a long time such journeys were totally disregarded in transport planning.);
- The common term covering both rides and journeys on foot is simply "trips". An independent trip which it is useful to record in planning is characterised by the fact that its points of origin and destination are formed by specific independent activities. This classification is important, but also gives rise to certain problems as it is also necessary to decide what constitutes "independent" activities. As a rule, for example, filling up at a filling station does not count as an independent activity. (In the case of a shopping expedition on foot - when there is no fixed destination and no previously determined order of shops - it can be compared to a Brownian movement of molecules with scarcely identifiable individual movements, so that delimitation is virtually impossible.) Finally, it is generally agreed that trips are only recorded if they take place within the public traffic area, as only these are relevant to planning;
- Finally, trip chains are sequences of several rides and/or journeys on foot within a certain time period (e.g. a day) where there are breaks of different lengths in order to perform specific activities between the individual trips.

In considering car transport, a careful distinction has to be made for planning purposes between a "person trip" and a "car trip". These two parameters are linked via car occupancy rates. (In this paper we are only concerned with person trips which will simply be called "rides".)

In comparing mobility figures from surveys in different studies, difficulties arise as not all specifications are explicitly formulated so that they sometimes have to be reconstituted with considerable difficulty. The most important specifications are:

14

- definition of the groups of people covered (children under a certain age are often not included);
- definition of the period of the survey or period of
  validity (frequently work day mobility only is
  examined);
- definition of the survey area or area of validity;
- definition of the representativeness and size of
  the samples surveyed;
- definition of the reliability of different characteristics surveyed (as already mentioned, distances
  are as a rule based on respondents' estimates);
- definition of the exact demarcation criteria when
  populations are broken down into "homogeneous behaviour" groups.

3. NOTES ON THE HISTORY OF PERSONAL MOBILITY AND OF RESEARCH INTO THE TOPIC

Obviously it is impossible in the context of a single
contribution to a symposium to give a comprehensive and
detailed history, complete with sources, of the development of human mobility in all its aspects and manifestations and nobody will expect it, although it would be a
most interesting and rewarding task. Some approaches do
in fact exist (e.g. [7]). To sum up in very general
terms, the history of mobility up to the railway age could
be described as almost exclusively the history of both war
and trade. Travel in the modern sense was probably "enjoyed" only by an infinitely small minority of the population and this "enjoyment" was associated with extraordin-
ary exertion, cost and danger. Just how difficult travel
must have been is hinted at by the German word "Elend",
which now means wretchedness or misery but originally
meant nothing other than foreign or strange.

To my knowledge, all relevant studies are concerned
more with the history of transport modes, infrastructures
and goods transport than with the mobility that concerns
us here. So it is virtually never possible to establish,
for example, how many kilometres a day were covered by an
average Roman in classical antiquity on foot, on horse-
back, or in a litter (probably nobody would be very interested anyway). It is almost certainly true, however,
that historical migrations of peoples, which we all heard
about at school, took place in a much more leisurely
fashion than our modern holiday nomadism, which often
starts the moment the bell rings at the end of the last
school period.

A very striking overview of the development of mobility in Germany is given by Figure 1 [8]. Mobility in
this case is defined as the number of kilometres covered
per person per year (other than on foot).

Figure 1 seems to confirm up to the hilt the thesis
of the "atavistic burning desire within us to conquer
space and time": the advent of new technologies each time
caused a jump in mobility and on the historical scale no
saturation can be recognised, as it must be borne in mind
that the vertical scale in Figure 1 is logarithmic, not
linear. The question must nevertheless be asked whether
on the basis of new technologies this trend can be extrapolated with similar growth rates in the future or whether
there is not perhaps some limit to man's natural physical
and psychological capacity. In my opinion the question

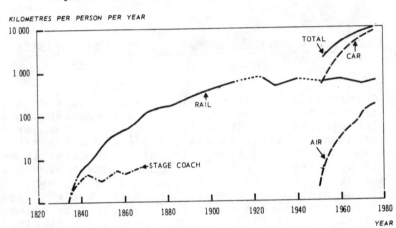

Figure 1 DEVELOPMENT OF MOBILITY IN GERMANY [8]

has to be asked, but it is scarcely possible to give a
satisfactory answer at present. One attempt states
that [9] (pp.38-39), "no practical upper limit can be set
to possible transport demand ... The long-term demand
curve for transport services is an unusual one, perhaps
unique among major consumption patterns: no end point is
discernible." A similar statement is found in [8]
(p. 125): "on the whole no tendency to saturation can be
found in the 150 year time series, only life cycles and
the importance of individual transport modes ...".

The complete spectrum of answers ranges from the
hypothesis that man will further develop his brain in such
a way that he can adapt to any situation, even to the
end-of-the-world scenario, with man himself as the cause
through constantly and inexorably increasing speed. At
least one thing appears certain to me, namely that the
proponents of these extremely different views have too
little interchange of ideas, so that opposing arguments
are never properly registered, let alone processed. In
addition, here as in other fields, there is a need for
much more interdisciplinary work, greater effort to find a
common language and hence greater exposure of charlatan-
ism. We must learn to distinguish much better between

what we know to be and to some extent certain and what we only hope or fear.

Now if we leave the historical time scale and turn to that of our own life time, we can see straight away that obviously a basic human need is to meet other people, exchange ideas, in other words to cultivate contacts with others. To do this, however, it is necessary to bridge space in time. This drive to bridge space is by no means a discovery of our age, but in the present century as never before we are technically in a position - with all its advantages and disadvantages - to yield to this impulse.

Mobility is today on every tongue and is a recurring theme in the media. It is a prominent characteristic of the dynamic, successful, modern man, whose lifestyle is fundamentally different from the contemplative, introverted, static life of many past epochs. There have been times - and it should not be entirely forgotten - in which, for example, a monk spent a substantial part of his life in one and the same place copying handwritten books by hand in solitude. His living and working space was his cell, which he seldom left. The situation was similar with the farmer, his wife and workers. They formed a virtually autonomous social and economic community. These rigidly-enclosed structures were not broken down until the age of industrialisation and division of labour.

Let us now consider this concept of the "division of labour", as this is certainly one of the important reasons for increased mobility. (The vastly increased division of labour as a result of industrialisation coincided with the invention of the railway, and this was most probably no accident, so that the argument about whether division of labour or the invention of the railway was the reason for increased mobility is pointless.)

The principle of the division of labour is that the manufacture of a product is broken up into individual operations in such a way that each can be accomplished rapidly and in large quantities and therefore at low cost. In many cases this means that not all steps in the process are accomplished in the same room, the same building, the same town, or even the same country. The manufacturing process is not only broken down as regards structure and staff, but individual processes can under certain circumstances be carried out in totally different places. To simplify, according to the relentless laws of economics this happens only when the sum of the cost of production of individual parts in different places, plus transport and assembly is not greater than the cost of production otherwise would be. This is only one side of the problem of division of labour, however, which I shall call the material (product-related) component. The other side concerns the human (man-related) component: as in

the case of mobility, so with division of labour the question arises of the psychological ability to tolerate monotony in work. I shall return to this - in my opinion -
very important aspect for the future development of
mobility.

The development of the division of labour and the new
jobs that result is to be seen in close interrelationship
with the development of telecommunications. Both developments will certainly have an enormous influence on mobility. Models which take, for example, car ownership as
the main or even only "descriptive parameter" for mobility
(e.g. [10]), will necessarily fail as planning instruments
because the famous "other things being equal" stipulation,
i.e. the constancy of all not explicitly included variables, will be even less realistic than it is already because of the difficult energy situation. With regard to
telecommunications, however, the essential thing is to
study in good time - that means before the technological
and economic conditions for it are actually fulfilled -
how people actually imagine their world of work would be
in the ideal case. To give an idea of the ambivalence and
lack of knowledge about such ideas, I would like to put
forward two contradictory quotations, which are admittedly
already rather old, but whose incompatibility in my
opinion has still not yet found any satisfactory explanation. This appears so difficult mainly because almost all
of us have prejudices on the subject, and anybody who
hears the two following quotations will probably react for
or against quite emotionally according to his or her own
history.

In his, at the time, famous and frequently repub-
lished book "My Life and Work" which appeared in 1923,
Henry Ford says [11] (pp. 122- 123): "I have so far not
been able to establish that repetitive work does anybody
any harm. Armchair experts have certainly often assured
me that repetitive work has harmful effects on body and
soul, but our research contradicts this. We had one worker who had virtually nothing more to do, day in day out,
than make a certain treading movement with one foot. He
thought the movement was making him lopsided. Medical
examination showed this was not so but he was of course
given another job in which other sets of muscles were
brought into action. A few weeks later he asked for his
old job back."

The Austrian writer Franz Werfel, in his speech entitled "Realism and Sincerity" on 6th May, 1931 to the
Cultural Association in Vienna said [12] (p. 10): "Now
what does the worker's reality look like? He stands in
the machine shop and makes one and the same tailorised
movement six times a minute, for eight hours. Is there
anything more unreal, less worthy of man, more hellish?

Not because of the hard work - a farmer works a lot harder - but because of the irreality, the abstractedness of this work, the factory is a hell."

Now, disregarding the fact that in Ford's case the worker concerned was obviously switched from one type of monotony to another, Werfel was a sensitive intellectual, in Ford's eyes an armchair expert, and Ford was a pragmatic industrialist, in Werfel's eyes the owner of a hell. Probably "objective" social scientists would be able to approach this problem somewhat freer of prejudice, but is there such a thing as an objective social scientist? And indeed can there be?

Turning now to the development of methodological instruments for examining mobility, without quoting individual sources the following overall tendencies can be recognised.

The beginnings of mobility research in connection with transport problems in the German-speaking countries go back roughly to the 60s (e.g. [13], [14], [15]). The term "mobility" was not used at that time however. The target parameter relevant to planning was then known as traffic volume and was to a large extent concerned with commuter rides by private car.

The ultimate goal of these investigations was almost exclusively to determine traffic load in terms of "vehicles per hour" in order to design roads. The investigations were accordingly virtually always made by engineers. So far as I know, social scientists - at any rate in Europe - had virtually no interest in this type of mobility. What is more, investigators contented themselves to a large extent with the single dimension "number of rides per person per day". Journeys on foot and the two other dimensions named above (i.e. trip distance and duration or speed) were to a large extent ignored. The dependence of transport volume on the land-use structure was scarcely recognised. It was a matter of relatively simple procedures, mainly linear regression, which are now considered to be static and pragmatic. The approach was phenomenological rather than aimed at causal analysis. These procedures nevertheless served well at the time, but methods, as well as the objectives and investigations and the problems themselves have changed.

Since about 1975, mobility studies in the German-speaking countries have been more specific and, at last, even interdisciplinary. A corollary of this seems to me that in many investigations each minor change in survey methods was given a new and resounding, marketoriented name, and these new names now give the impression that the philosopher's stone to "explain" the phenomenon of mobility has been found. I consider that somewhat more modesty is called for here. I shall not go into the many

19

nuances and intermediate phases of methodological development, but go directly into a description of the present situation.

The present situation and also indications of the path to be taken in the future seems to me to have been first sketched out in an article by Hägerstrand under the humorous title "What about people in regional science?" which came out in 1970 and has since become famous [16]. In this article, he not only anticipated as a theoretical concept the main lines of thought of the generation of models now generally known as "individual behaviour models" or (somewhat misleadingly) as "disaggregated behaviour-oriented models", whose conversion into concrete plans is a problem we are still chewing over and breaking our teeth in the process - but, even at that time went still farther, not making the individual as such the primary object of investigation, but recognising the significance of the coordination of the interweaving daily timetables of individuals interacting with one another. Two aspects of Hägerstrand's approach seem to me particularly significant and innovative:

- The first is the recording of daily timetables of persons closely interacting with one another in the form of space/time diagrams (e.g. as "graphic household diaries"). An example for a four-person household is given in Figure 2, which is taken from a later publication by Hägerstrand [17]. Various "stations" indicating spatially distinct activity locations are shown on the horizontal axis, the vertical axis showing the time of day.
- The second aspect is made understandable by an interpretation of Ortega y Gasset, who defines a thing as the set of conditions that make it possible [18] (p. 82). Hägerstrand bases himself on a complementary idea according to which mobility could be defined as the residual value of an "action space" left to us by three types of framework conditions or constraints [16]:

    - capacity conditions (limited time and money budgets);
    - interactive conditions (obligation to meet someone at a particular time in a particular place);
    - conditions arising from socially agreed rules (laws, standards, customs, etc.).

If we observe the above two end points in the evolution of methodological instruments to date from the relative distance of our own particular disciplines, we find a pattern which is also to be seen in many other fields of study: development from simple, highly formalised and easy-to-use methods and procedures to ever-greater branching into more complex structures, which serve more as procedures to promote awareness and understanding than as

concrete planning instruments for use by the authorities.
(The electronic data processing explosion may well have
made a substantial contribution to this development. We
now find that computing speed and the rate of production
of output exceeds our physiologically conditioned speed of
understanding and interpretation, so that we are often
confronted with a mountain of computer results and simply
do not know where to start. In the striking phrase of the
philosopher Günther Anders, we can now produce more than
our minds can grasp.)

Even with the latest generation of complex procedures
for recording and describing the phenomenon of mobility it
is generally still not (yet) possible to design a specific
individual measure in the field of transport infrastructures; this does not even seem to be their aim, but they

Figure 2 **A GRAPHIC DIARY OF A FOUR-PERSON HOUSEHOLD**

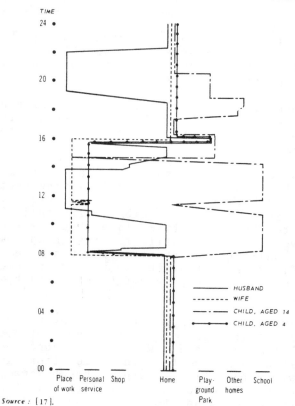

Source : [17].

do help to give insight. It is sobering to realise that
the famous "other things being equal" (generally not explicitly stated) of the first generation of procedures
scarcely ever applies. In addition, the modern instruments are integrating mobility into man's overall interactive behaviour pattern. Rühl [19] (p. 20), for example,
recommends that: "... model building should be based on

21

the theories of the behavioural sciences and not on mathematical considerations, as is now often the case."

At this point in my considerations, an observation by the philosopher Jean Gebser occurred to me, which is already somewhat dated (1960) and at first sight appears to have nothing to do with research into mobility, but on closer examination reflects the development of this research very precisely. Gebser himself calls his observation "new reality". It is characterised by the following three aspects [20] (p. 26):

"1. The former, mainly quantitative approach was replaced by a qualitative one, or complemented by it;
2. the former classification of the world into systems to a large extent collapsed; today we think and live in a world of structures, the difference between system and structure being expressed in the fact that
3. the predominantly static view towards which the systematising approach is always inclined was replaced by a more functional and hence structural approach.

These three new and mutually conditioning approaches, which put the accent on the qualitative, structural and functional aspects, have afforded new insight into the nature of things."

The parallel (though with a time lag) with mobility research can be demonstrated by the following statement made in 1980 [6] (p. 112): "The findings stress ... the necessity, to shift this discussion increasingly from the quantitative to the qualitative plane, because the quality of the observed activities still remains an unknown, as do the possible qualitative advantages which accrue from extending the field of action; the answer is extremely difficult to find and probably cannot be provided by transport economics alone."

There may be some disappointment at my not yet having presented any actual figures. In the sense of Gebser's "new reality" I am here and now primarily concerned with determining structural and functional relationships and not so much with presenting figures (though some will in fact be given in the following two chapters). Figures are, of course, by no means to be despised, but they need to be preceded by an insight into the "new reality".

It may now be objected that the "new reality" does not, for example, offer any help to the road planner in the field, as when all is said and done he does need to know how many lanes to provide on a given section, how long the traffic light cycle has to be and how long the light has to remain green to prevent traffic chaos, etc.

The "new reality" of mobility research cannot, at the present stage, give any information on this. But it can enable a completely new approach, which, continuing the chosen analogies, may be expressed as follows: the traffic light installation whose programme has to be determined, may become meaningless if, for example, there is a better arrangement of living and working places, if the town land-use structure is changed, if working hours are made more flexible or are better staggered with respect to one another, if a low-traffic zone is established and public transport made more attractive, if new distribution systems for providing households with daily needs are established, in other words if the complete chain of all determinants which influence mobility are gone through with a fine toothcomb. This means that, as already indicated, the "new reality" fits the phenomenon of mobility into the overall pattern of interactive human behaviour and thus makes it possible at the planning stage to include very radical and comprehensive alternatives. These are often known as town renewal or conversion schemes and mean that in no case can they still be managed or judged by the representatives of one single discipline; traditional boundaries between the professions have to be broken down.

It is now realised that mobility is not to be understood as a concept which can be represented simply by scalar dimensional figures, but as a complex structure of relationships the description of whose characteristics by a number of numerical values can be no more than a rough guide. The aim of this chapter and the preceding one was to give some understanding of this complex structure of relationships. The two following chapters are intended to present some of the numerical findings that constitute this rough guide.

4. SOME CURRENT FINDINGS ON THE MOBILITY OF PERSONS

First the qualifications "some" and "current" need to be briefly elucidated. One must be aware that it is always possible to bring together and present only a certain selection of findings, and even this selection - if the truth is to be told - is often fairly fortuitous. "Current" is intended to mean that the findings presented below to some extent correspond with the latest survey situation and are thus relevant to planning. The chapter relates exclusively to findings from Germany which are mainly based on the "Continuous survey of traffic behaviour (KONTIV)" carried out for the Federal Minister of Transport during the period July 1975 to June 1977. The survey did not include the transport behaviour of children under 10, foreigners and soldiers.

23

It is of course natural - in the truest sense of the word - to begin with findings produced by one's own organisation. I too shall adopt this practice. Accordingly, some important results of certain studies carried out by PROGNOS are presented first. This is followed by some other findings. The main emphasis throughout is on the presentation of the three important quantitative mobility indicators: trip frequency, distance and duration.

Findings of the "Mobility in passenger transport" study [5]

The basic data for this study was provided by surveys carried out under the KONTIV project between July and December 1975. Table 1 shows total trip frequencies for each day of the week and the percentage of trips for the different purposes. Trip purposes are usually determined according to the activity (A) at the destination of a walk or ride. These were classified as:

- A_1: home
- A_2: work
- A_3: business (bank, post office, etc.)
- A_4: education
- A_5: service (carrying passengers)
- A_6: shopping
- A_7: leisure (recreation)

Table 2 shows the frequency distribution of trip distances for different transport modes and the average distance for each mode. Only the weekdays Monday to Friday are included and it should also be borne in mind that all distances are based on informants' estimates.

Table 3 shows the frequency distribution of trip duration and average durations. Here again only the weekdays Monday to Friday are covered.

Combining the data on average trip distances and durations, an average speed can be calculated. Table 4 shows the results.

Finally, it is also instructive to present the frequencies of characteristic trip chains, whose links are designated by specific activity destinations (A_1 to A_7). Some quite typical sequences can be determined. Table 5 shows the trip chains (also known as trip patterns) in order of frequency. (Here again, only the weekdays Monday to Friday are covered.)

Findings from the study "Mobility opportunities of different population groups in passenger transport" [6]

The basic data for this study were mainly the KONTIV data for the survey month of September 1975. The main aim

Table 1

TRIP FREQUENCIES ACCORDING TO DAY OF THE WEEK AND PURPOSE

	MON	TUE	WEDS	THURS	FRI	SAT	SUN	MON-FRI
No. in sample	4,034	3,728	3,662	3,668	3,656	3,769	3,746	18,740
Total No of trips	11,319	11,012	10,752	10,795	10,719	9,974	6,582	54,597
No. of trips per person per day	2.81	2.95	2.94	2.94	2.93	2.65	1.76	2.91
Percentage of trips for each purpose								
Home	43.5	41.4	41.7	41.9	42.1	43.6	44.7	42.1
Work	17.4	17.6	16.9	16.6	15.8	5.0	1.6	16.9
Business	5.1	5.5	5.4	4.7	4.5	1.7	1.1	5.0
Education	6.7	6.8	6.3	6.5	6.1	4.0	0.2	6.5
Service	1.7	2.0	2.0	2.0	1.9	1.1	0.7	1.9
Shopping	14.3	14.8	14.9	15.3	17.1	20.4	2.1	15.3
Leisure	11.3	11.9	12.9	13.1	12.5	24.4	48.7	12.3
Total	100.0	100.0	100.0	100.0	100.0	100.0	100.0	100.0

Source: Derived from [5].

25

of the study was to identify by appropriate segmentation
of the total survey population social groups which, in
terms of their mobility behaviour, were as homogeneous as
possible in themselves and also as sharply distinguished
from one another as possible. Segmentation into the 10
social groups listed in Table 6 was shown by cluster
analysis to be significant and suitable for the purpose.
(The number of people included in each case is also
shown in Table 6.)

Table 7 shows that, in car availability which is to
some extent an indicator of the mobility opportunities
open to a person, there are fairly clear differences
between individual segments.

Table 8 shows the main mobility indicators:

- Trip frequency (journeys per person per day);
- Daily trip distance (km per person per day);
- (Single) trip distance (km/trip);
- Daily trip duration (minutes per person per day);
- (Single) trip duration (min/trip);
- Speed (km/h);

for each of the social groups. The table includes only
mobile persons, i.e. those who made at least one trip outside the house (on foot or otherwise) on the survey day.
(The percentage of mobile persons is also shown in Table 8
so that mobility indicators may be calculated for all persons in the segment concerned if necessary.)

With regard to modal split, there are clear differences between the segments. The figures are shown in
Table 9.

Findings from the study "Development of an individual
behaviour model to explain and forecast workday activity
patterns in urban areas" [21]

The aim of this study was to identify the actual
mobility-determining factors and determine the extent of
their influence. The basic data was provided by surveys
carried out under the KONTIV project for the months of
September and October 1976. Here again, only the weekdays
Monday to Friday were included.

Mobility was taken to be an imposed or desired
instrument to link specific activities in the course of
the day. Activity frequency and trip frequency are thus
closely related. The determining factors and the rough
structure of their arrangement and their influence on the
mobility indicator "trip frequency" can be seen in
Figure 3.

26

Table 2

FREQUENCY DISTRIBUTION OF TRIP DISTANCES ACCORDING TO MODE

Distance	Total trips			Foot			Cycle			Car			Public transport		
	abs.	%	cum. %	abs.	%	cum. %	abs.	%	cum. %	abs.	%	cum. %	abs.	%	cum. %
over to 1 km	16,076	29.38	29.38	11,101	74.87	74.87	2,581	35.90	35.90	2,353	9.41	9.41	41	0.53	0.53
1 " 2 km	8,130	14.86	44.24	2,415	16.29	91.16	2,165	30.12	66.02	2,874	11.50	20.91	676	8.78	9.31
2 " 3 km	5,274	9.64	53.88	805	5.43	96.59	1,102	15.33	81.35	2,643	10.57	31.48	724	9.40	18.71
3 " 4 km	3,209	5.86	59.74	227	1.53	98.12	523	7.28	88.63	1,963	7.85	39.33	487	6.32	25.03
4 " 5 km	2,862	5.23	64.97	122	0.82	98.94	285	3.96	92.59	1,746	6.98	46.31	709	9.21	34.24
5 " 6 km	2,313	4.23	69.20	32	0.22	99.16	148	2.06	94.65	1,563	6.25	52.56	570	7.40	41.64
6 " 7 km	1,624	2.97	72.17	30	0.20	99.36	117	1.63	96.28	1,069	4.28	56.84	408	5.30	46.94
7 " 8 km	1,636	2.99	75.16	12	0.08	99.44	84	1.17	97.45	1,083	4.33	61.17	457	5.94	52.88
8 " 9 km	766	1.40	76.56	11	0.08	99.52	24	0.33	97.78	561	2.24	63.41	170	2.21	55.09
9 " 10 km	1,711	3.13	79.69	13	0.09	99.61	69	0.96	98.74	1,160	4.64	68.05	469	6.09	61.18
10 " 15 km	3,500	6.40	86.09	24	0.16	99.77	64	0.89	99.63	2,739	10.92	78.97	673	8.74	69.92
15 " 20 km	3,076	5.62	91.71	17	0.11	99.88	20	0.27	99.90	1,904	7.62	86.59	1,135	14.74	84.66
20 " 25 km	1,551	2.47	94.18	-	-	99.93	4	0.06	99.96	948	3.79	90.38	392	5.09	89.75
25 " 30 km	875	1.60	95.78	6	0.05	99.97	2	0.03	99.99	632	2.53	92.91	235	3.05	92.80
30 " 35 km	480	0.88	96.66	-	-	99.97	1	0.01	100.00	380	1.52	94.43	99	1.29	94.09
35 " 40 km	387	0.71	97.37	1	-	99.97	-	-	100.00	265	1.06	95.49	121	1.57	95.66
40 " 45 km	226	0.41	97.78	-	-	99.97	-	-	100.00	169	0.68	96.17	57	0.74	96.40
45 " 50 km	192	0.35	98.13	1	-	99.97	-	-	100.00	135	0.54	96.71	56	0.73	97.13
50 km	1,030	1.87	100.00	4	0.03	100.00	-	-	100.00	814	3.29	100.00	221	2.87	100.00
Total	54,718			14,828			7,189			25,001			7,700		
Average distance	7.20			0.97			2.06			10.84			12.21		

Source: [5].

27

Table 3

FREQUENCY DISTRIBUTION OF TRIP DURATIONS

Trip duration	Total trips			On foot			Other		
	absolute	%	cum. %	absolute	%	cum. %	absolute	%	cum. %
Under 5 mins.	10,042	18.24	18.24	4,331	29.31	29.31	5,711	14.18	14.18
5 to 10 mins.	12,427	22.58	40.82	3,891	26.33	55.64	8,536	21.20	35.38
10 to 15 mins.	10,213	18.55	59.37	2,698	18.26	73.90	7,515	18.66	54.05
15 to 20 mins.	5,285	9.60	68.97	1,279	8.66	82.56	4,006	9.95	63.99
20 to 25 mins.	2,137	3.88	72.85	363	2.46	85.02	1,774	4.41	68.40
25 to 30 mins.	6,109	11.10	83.95	1,213	8.21	93.23	4,896	12.16	80.56
30 to 40 mins.	2,510	4.58	88.53	235	1.59	94.82	2,275	5.65	86.21
40 to 50 mins.	2,327	4.23	92.76	234	1.58	96.40	2,093	5.20	91.41
50 to 60 mins.	1,619	2.94	95.70	180	1.22	97.62	1,439	3.57	94.98
60 to 70 mins.	418	0.78	96.48	38	0.26	97.88	380	0.94	95.92
70 to 80 mins.	414	0.75	97.23	39	0.26	98.14	375	0.93	96.85
80 to 90 mins.	403	0.73	97.96	53	0.36	98.50	350	0.87	97.72
90 to 100 mins.	73	0.13	98.09	3	0.02	98.52	70	0.17	97.89
over 100 mins.	1,065	1.91	100.0	220	1.48	100.00	845	2.11	100.0
Total	55,042	100.00	-	14,777	100.00	-	40,265	100.00	-
Average trip duration (mins.)	19.4			13.5			21.5		

Source: Derived from [5].

28

Table 4

AVERAGE TRIP DISTANCES, DURATIONS AND SPEEDS

Mobility indicator	Total trips	On foot	Other
Average trip distance (km)	7.20	0.97	9.88
Average trip duration (min)	19.4	13.5	21.5
Average speed (km/h)	22.3	4.3	27.6

Table 5

TRIP CHAINS (PATTERNS) IN ORDER OF FREQUENCY

Ranking	Trip pattern	Frequency		
		abs	%	cum %
1	$A_1+A_2+A_1$	3,260	20.6	20.6
2	$A_1+A_6+A_1$	1,602	10.1	30.7
3	$A_1+A_4+A_1$	1,542	9.8	40.5
4	$A_1+A_4+A_1+A_7+A_1$	531	3.4	43.9
5	$A_1+A_7+A_1$	499	3.2	47.1
6	$A_1+A_2+A_1+A_7+A_1$	459	2.9	50.0
7	$A_1+A_2+A_1+A_6+A_1$	446	2.8	52.8
8	$A_1+A_6+A_1+A_7+A_1$	368	2.3	55.1
9	$A_1+A_2+A_7+A_2+A_1$	318	2.0	57.1
10	$A_1+A_6+A_1+A_6+A_1$	315	2.0	59.1
11	$A_1+A_4+A_1+A_6+A_1$	230	1.5	60.6
12	$A_1+A_6+A_6+A_1$	228	1.4	62.0
13	$A_1+A_2+A_6+A_1$	199	1.3	63.3
Other patterns (No. 14-1178)		5,802	36.7	100.0
Total		15,799	100.0	-

Source: Derived from [5].

The most important finding is that the major factors determining activity frequency are:

- job
- sex
- social status (as measured by the highest level of education reached)
- age
- car availability.

Table 6

SEGMENTATION INTO SOCIAL GROUPS WITH HOMOGENEOUS BEHAVIOUR

Seg-ment	Short description	Persons	
		abs.	%
I	Wage-earners living alone	43	1.6
II	Wage-earners from households with young children	225	8.6
III	Other wage-earners	978	37.5
IV	Schoolchildren and students	477	18.3
V	Apprentices	99	3.8
VI	Housewives with young children	137	5.3
VII	Other housewives	371	14.2
VIII	Pensioners from wage-earner households	91	3.5
IX	Pensioners from pensioner households	141	5.4
X	Unemployed	45	1.7
	Total	2,607	100.0

Source: Derived from [6].

Combining the factors job and sex into the following segments:

- S_1: housewives with children under 10
- S_2: other housewives
- S_3: male pensioners
- S_4: female pensioners
- S_5: Males in full-time employment
- S_6: females in full-time employment
- S_7: females in part-time employment

proved to be useful, in other words it explained of itself a large proportion of the differences in behaviour. Within individual segments, social status is the dominant influencing factor in all cases, but this status effect is not equally strong in all segments.

30

Table 7

CAR AVAILABILITY ACCORDING TO SOCIAL GROUPS
WITH HOMOGENEOUS BEHAVIOUR

Segment		Car availability			Total
		None	Limited	Full	
I	Wage-earners living alone	41.5	9.8	48.7	100.0
II	Wage-earners from households with young children	16.1	53.9	30.0	100.0
III	Other wage-earners	25.9	41.8	32.3	100.0
IV	Schoolchildren and students	88.4	8.1	3.5	100.0
V	Apprentices	91.0	9.0	-	100.0
VI	Housewives with young children	38.7	51.1	10.2	100.0
VII	Other housewives	65.0	29.0	6.0	100.0
VIII	Pensioners from wage-earner households	81.3	13.2	5.5	100.0
IX	Pensioners from pensioner households	71.4	14.3	14.3	100.0
X	Unemployed	42.2	35.6	22.2	100.0
	Total	50.5	30.9	18.6	100.0

Source: [6].

It is most marked in segments S_2 (housewives without young children) and S_4 (female pensioners). In the case of adults, under otherwise equal conditions the activity level tends to fall with increasing age. The influence of car availability on activity frequency is slight.

Table 10 shows some important mobility indicators broken down according to the seven segments defined above. (Mobile persons are again those who made at least one trip on the survey day. Only activities which took place outside the home were counted.)

Table 8

MOBILITY INDICATORS FOR MOBILE PERSONS ACCORDING
TO SOCIAL GROUPS OF HOMOGENEOUS BEHAVIOUR

Segment	Percentage of mobile persons	Mobility indicators for mobile persons					
		Trip frequency (trips per person per day)	Daily trip length (km per person per day)	Trip length (km/journey)	Daily trip duration (min per person per day)	Trip duration (min/trip)	Speed (km/h)
I	97.7	3.83	27.2	7.1	82.2	21.5	19.9
II	92.9	3.95	27.9	7.1	73.1	18.5	22.9
III	92.3	3.59	26.4	7.4	74.3	20.7	21.3
IV	91.9	3.36	16.1	4.8	66.4	19.8	14.5
V	90.1	3.05	24.2	7.9	85.0	27.9	17.1
VI	75.9	3.94	17.2	4.4	56.7	14.4	18.2
VII	70.6	3.17	10.8	3.4	52.8	16.7	12.3
VIII	56.0	2.90	9.9	3.4	57.8	19.9	9.3
IX	68.1	3.67	12.4	3.4	59.9	16.3	12.4
X	66.7	2.73	20.5	7.5	49.6	18.2	24.8
Total	85.3	3.47	21.0	6.1	68.5	19.7	18.4

Source: Derived from [6].

32

Table 9

MODAL SPLIT BY SOCIAL GROUPS OF HOMOGENEOUS BEHAVIOUR

Seg- ment	Modal Split (%)					
	Foot	Cycle	Car (driver)	Car (passenger)	Public transport	Total
I	26.2	6.1	43.6	1.3	17.9	100.0
II	22.1	5.2	59.7	4.4	8.4	100.0
III	16.3	7.9	57.1	6.6	11.8	100.0
IV	30.7	28.8	7.1	7.8	24.6	100.0
V	17.1	26.2	6.5	10.9	38.2	100.0
VI	42.8	12.0	29.1	11.7	4.0	100.0
VII	49.6	19.9	16.1	12.5	8.0	100.0
VIII	52.5	11.1	9.9	5.6	16.0	100.0
IX	56.5	7.7	15.8	8.1	12.0	100.0
X	24.2	8.8	51.1	3.8	12.1	100.0
Total	27.3	13.1	37.0	7.4	14.1	100.0

Source: Derived from [6].

Figure 3   STRUCTURE OF MOBILITY-DETERMINING FACTORS

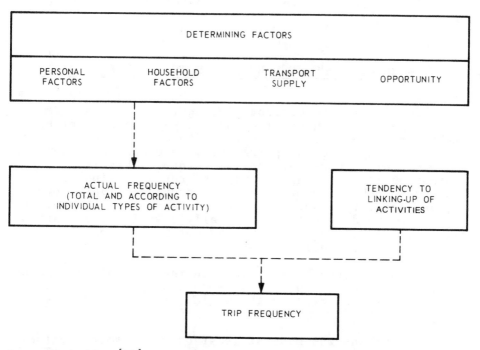

Source : Derived from [21].

Findings from the study "Traffic analysis and forecasts for Greater Hanover" [22]

This study was designed to record and analyse current (1980) mobility behaviour in greater Hanover, i.e. the German town of Hanover itself and its surrounding area, and to estimate demand-side mobility reactions to changed transport supply conditions.

The basic data were provided by surveys made specifically for this study in spring 1980 in all communities in the greater Hanover area. Only mobility behaviour on weekdays from Monday to Friday was studied.

Tables 11, 12 and 13 show trip frequencies, distances and durations recorded during this study, for each weekday.

Once again the average speed can be determined from the averages for trip distance and duration. These figures are shown in Table 14.

Finally, a time series comparison was made between the figures obtained in the KONTIV project in 1975 in greater Hanover and the 1980 figures. The proportion of mobile persons(2) as a percentage of all persons (1976: 74 per cent, 1980: 74.4 per cent) and average trip frequency (1976: 2.56 journeys per person per day, 1980: 2.61) showed little change, their variation remaining within the limits of chance. (Comparisons of trip distances and durations were unfortunately not made in the study named.)

5. SOME FINDINGS ON TRENDS IN MOTOR-POWERED MOBILITY

In addition to current findings, it is always very useful for the planner, i.e. anyone who wants to or has to make provision for the future, to know past trends in certain planning-relevant parameters, in order to be able to draw useful conclusions for the future. This is also my intention in this chapter. In the research studies required for this, however, a basic problem is very soon encountered; time series trends for mobility-relevant indicators are documented practically only for that part of effective mobility demand met by motor vehicles, whether private car or public transport.

This has long been a thorn in the side of the planner aiming at a comprehensive all-mode transport concept. Thus in all countries of the world motor vehicles are

---

2. Persons who made at least one trip (outside the house) on the survey day concerned.

34

Table 10

MOBILITY INDICATORS FOR MOBILE PERSONS

Segment	Percentage of mobile persons	Mobility indicators for mobile persons				
		Activity frequency (activities per person per day)	Trip frequency (trips per person per day)	Daily activity duration (min. per person per day)	Daily trip duration (min. per person per day)	Trip duration (min./per trip)
1	74.2	2.25	3.99	142.3	49.8	12.5
2	71.0	1.78	3.24	139.8	54.9	16.9
3	64.2	2.04	3.45	183.5	73.5	21.3
4	59.8	1.70	3.06	158.2	60.4	19.7
5	94.2	2.47	3.90	538.6	76.6	19.6
6	92.9	2.15	3.51	489.6	69.0	19.7
7	87.9	2.13	3.82	285.6	61.0	16.0
Total	83.3	2.19	3.66	355.6	66.6	18.2

Source: Derived from [21].

Table 11

TRIP FREQUENCIES ACCORDING TO DAY OF WEEK IN GREATER HANOVER (1980)

Mobility on survey day	Total	Monday	Tuesday	Wednesday	Thursday	Friday
Basis	10,321	2,151	2,134	2,057	2,015	1,964
	%	%	%	%	%	%
Percentage of persons on survey day:						
- did not leave home	25.6	26.0	28.3	25.1	25.0	23.6
- left home	74.4	74.0	71.7	74.9	75.0	76.4
of which:						
. one trip	0.4	0.3	0.5	0.3	0.5	0.5
. two trips	28.0	26.9	28.0	30.1	26.8	27.9
. three trips	6.8	6.6	5.8	6.5	7.7	7.4
. four trips	20.8	21.9	19.8	21.1	21.1	20.3
. five trips	5.4	5.0	5.1	4.9	6.0	6.1
. six trips	7.4	8.3	7.5	5.8	7.0	8.4
. seven trips and over	5.6	5.0	5.0	6.2	5.9	5.8
	100.0	100.0	100.0	100.0	100.0	100.0
- Average number of trips for mobile persons	3.50	3.53	3.48	3.43	3.55	3.53
- Average number of trips for all persons	2.61	2.61	2.50	2.57	2.66	2.70

Source: Derived from [22].

36

Table 12

TRIP DISTANCES ACCORDING TO DAY OF WEEK IN GREATER HANOVER (1980)

Trip distance	Total	Monday	Tuesday	Wednesday	Thursday	Friday
Basis	26,901	5,621	5,330	5,277	5,368	5,304
	%	%	%	%	%	%
Under 500 metres	8.1	7.9	8.4	7.3	8.4	8.4
500 m to 1 km	10.9	11.3	11.0	10.4	11.5	10.3
1 km to 2 km	16.2	15.8	16.6	15.5	16.4	16.9
2 km to 5 km	23.9	23.1	25.6	23.4	24.6	23.0
5 km to 10 km	16.3	16.8	14.3	17.4	14.8	18.3
10 km to 15 km	9.0	9.0	8.6	9.4	9.0	9.0
15 km and over	12.3	11.8	12.5	13.6	11.8	11.8
No data on distance	3.3	4.3	3.0	3.1	3.5	2.3
	100.0	100.0	100.0	100.1	100.0	100.0
Average distance per trip (km)	6.9	6.5	7.2	7.4	6.8	6.8

Source: Derived from [22].

37

Table 13

TRIP DURATION ACCORDING TO DAY OF WEEK IN GREATER HANOVER (1980)

Trip duration	Total	Monday	Tuesday	Wednesday	Thursday	Friday
Basis	26,901	5,621	5,330	5,277	5,368	5,304
	%	%	%	%	%	%
under 5 minutes	3.1	3.7	3.0	2.9	2.8	2.9
5 to 10 minutes	15.7	14.5	15.5	16.4	16.3	15.8
10 to 15 minutes	19.2	18.6	19.6	18.7	19.5	19.9
15 to 30 minutes	30.5	30.3	29.9	29.6	29.7	32.9
30 to 45 minutes	14.4	14.6	13.3	14.7	14.8	14.7
45 to 60 minutes	4.4	4.2	4.6	4.7	4.2	4.2
over 60 minutes	4.9	4.5	5.5	5.1	5.2	4.4
No data on trip duration	7.8	9.5	8.7	7.9	7.5	5.2
	100.0	99.9	100.1	100.0	100.0	100.0
Average duration of a trip (min)	21.3	21.1	21.4	21.7	21.4	21.1

Source: Derived from [22].

Table 14

AVERAGE TRIP DISTANCES, DURATIONS AND SPEEDS
IN GREATER HANOVER (1980)

Mobility indicator	Total	MON	TUES	WEDS	THURS	FRI
Average trip distance (km)	6.9	6.5	7.2	7.4	6.8	6.8
Average trip duration (min)	21.3	21.1	21.4	21.7	21.4	21.1
Average speed (km/h)	19.4	18.5	20.2	20.5	19.1	19.3

Source: Derived from [22].

subject to compulsory registration, but this applies to
bicycles in only very few countries. Furthermore, for
general economic reasons - so that every precious drop of
taxation is collected - all industrialised countries also
keep very careful records of the amount of motor fuels
used, whereas the fuel used by cyclists and walkers is
stored in the human body and cannot be recorded at all.
Finally, in Germany, Austria and Switzerland for example
there is permanent automatic metering of traffic flows on
certain parts of the main road network, but here again
cyclists are ignored.

These shortcomings should not be any reason for
ignoring the recordable indicators for representing
"motor-powered mobility" however. A selection of such
indicators is given below, but it must be borne in mind
that we are dealing only with varyingly relevant mobility
indicators, not with mobility itself, which - as I have
emphasized more than once - is a complex behavioural phenomenon and cannot be defined in the form of a single
value. The indicators discussed below can nevertheless
provide some slight help in certain planning tasks.

An indicator which until very recently was completely
dominant in mobility studies, and to a certain extent
still is, is density of car ownership, i.e. number of cars
per thousand population. The very recent challenge to
this dominance can be explained as follows [23] (p. 95):
"The availability of a car turns out to be much less
'mobility-increasing' by comparison with the effect of the
job than is generally claimed. This false conclusion is
the result of the frequently used ... analysis procedure
in which only the difference in mobility between persons
with and without access to a car is considered. As the
present analysis clearly shows, mobility effects which
originally depend on other factors, in particular those

grouped together here under the heading 'job', are ascribed to car availability."

Table 15 shows car ownership density (cars and related vehicles per thousand population) in Germany for the period 1950 to 1981. The "OBS." column lists the actual (observed) figures; the "REGR." column contains the results obtained from a regression model based on a three-parameter Gompertz function. These results are extrapolated to the year 2000. The "RES." column lists the residues (difference between regression values and actual values). The procedure described in [24] was used here and for determining the 90 per cent confidence interval for the forecasts. The information contained in Table 15 and the 90 per cent confidence interval for the forecasts to 2000 are shown in graph form in Figure 4.

A further indicator for trends in "motor-powered mobility" is petrol consumption. This can be misleading for mobility-relevant passenger transport output, however, mainly for two reasons:

- petrol consumption reflects vehicle/kilometres and not person/kilometres. Changes in car occupancy levels would also have to be taken into account if it were desired to convert petrol consumption trends into passenger transport output trends;
- technological progress means that specific fuel consumption per kilometre is constantly falling. This effect would also have to be taken into account if use were to be made of the above-mentioned analogy.

Table 16 shows annual petrol consumption for the period 1970 to 1980 in Germany and Switzerland. The respective indices (base year 1970) are also shown.

Figure 5 is a graph of the indices showing the difference between trends in Germany and Switzerland.

A more direct indicator of "motor-powered mobility" in Germany - though only for travel on trunk roads (motorways and main roads outside built-up areas) - is given by average daily traffic volume (vehicles per 24 hours) derived from permanent metering. Obviously this also only gives traffic volume in terms of number of cars, not persons. What is more, in addition to cars it naturally includes goods transport using lorries and all other motor vehicles. Nevertheless, it gives a certain insight into trends in "motorpowered mobility". The trend is shown in Figure 6.

Even allowing for the above-mentioned reservations, trends in average daily traffic volumes are further distorted as indicators of trends in transport output because the total length of the trunk road network has changed in

Table 15

CAR OWNERSHIP DENSITY IN THE FEDERAL REPUBLIC OF GERMANY

SURVEY DATA	CAR OWNERSHIP DENSITY (cars, etc. per 1,000 pop.)		
	OBS	REGR.	RES.
1.7.1950	10.8	10.5	-.3
1.7.1951	14.2	13.9	-.3
1.7.1952	18.6	18.0	-.5
1.7.1953	23.0	23.0	.0
1.7.1954	28.2	28.9	.7
1.7.1955	33.3	35.7	2.3
1.7.1956	40.3	43.4	3.1
1.7.1957	48.2	52.1	4.0
1.7.1958	57.0	61.7	4.7
1.7.1959	67.2	72.3	5.1
1.7.1960	81.0	83.7	2.7
1.7.1961	95.1	95.9	.8
1.7.1962	111.5	108.9	-2.6
1.7.1963	127.3	122.5	-4.8
1.7.1964	142.8	136.6	-6.1
1.7.1965	158.2	151.3	-6.9
1.7.1966	174.3	166.3	-8.0
1.7.1967	185.6	181.5	-4.1
1.7.1968	196.2	197.0	.9
1.7.1969	209.2	212.6	3.3
1.7.1970	229.7	228.1	-1.5
1.7.1971	246.7	243.6	-3.1
1.7.1972	260.3	258.9	-1.4
1.7.1973	274.7	274.1	-.7
1.7.1974	279.5	288.9	9.4
1.7.1975	289.5	303.4	14.0
1.7.1976	307.6	317.6	10.0
1.7.1977	326.1	331.3	5.2
1.7.1978	346.0	344.7	-1.3
1.7.1979	367.4	357.5	-9.9
1.7.1980	376.7	369.9	-6.8
1.7.1981	384.8	381.8	-3.0
1.7.1985	*****	424.4	***
1.7.1990	*****	467.0	***
1.7.1995	*****	499.0	***
1.7.2000	*****	522.5	***

Source: Calculated according to [24].

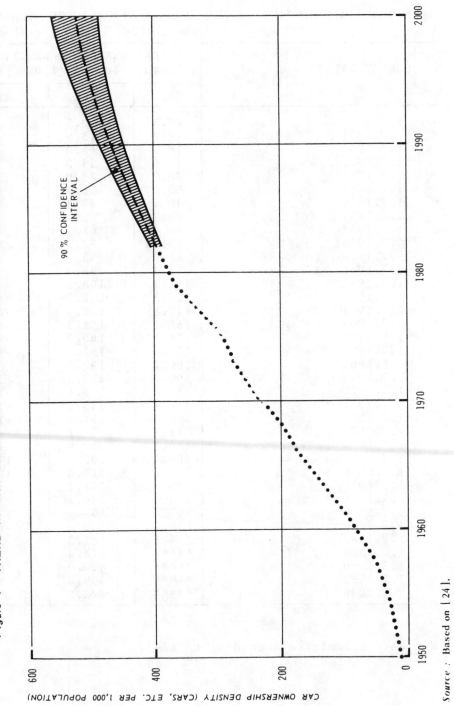

Figure 4 TREND IN CAR OWNERSHIP DENSITY IN THE FEDERAL REPUBLIC OF GERMANY

90 % CONFIDENCE INTERVAL

CAR OWNERSHIP DENSITY (CARS, ETC. PER 1,000 POPULATION)

Source : Based on [24].

42

Table 16

PETROL CONSUMPTION IN THE FEDERAL REPUBLIC OF GERMANY
AND SWITZERLAND

Year	Germany		Switzerland	
	Quantity (1000 t)	Index (1970 = 100)	Quantity (1000 t)	Index (1970 = 100)
1970	15,492	100	2,065	100
1971	17,205	111	2,307	112
1972	18,130	117	2,416	117
1973	18,508	119	2,462	119
1974	18,048	116	2,420	117
1975	19,474	127	2,413	117
1976	20,583	133	2,409	117
1977	21,809	141	2,548	123
1978	23,015	149	2,573	125
1979	23,307	150	2,560	124
1980	23,721	153	2,709	131

Data sources: [25][26].

the course of time. Table 17 therefore shows average
daily traffic volume (DTV), total length of road and an
index (base year 1975) derived from the product of the two.

The number of persons carried by public passenger
transport and the number of passenger-kilometres covered
in Germany are given as a last indicator of developments
in "motor-powered mobility". Table 18 shows trends in
public passenger transport(3) excluding the railways (the
corresponding index is based on 1970) and trends in the
associated average ride distance. Table 19 shows the comparable figures for railway passenger transport.

It can be seen from the two tables that the average
public transport ride distance remained fairly stable over
the period 1970 to 1980.

Finally, it is appropriate to compare the average
public transport ride distance of 12.21 km in 1975, as
shown in Table 2, with the values given here. Calculating
an average from Tables 18 and 19 for all public transport,
(50,614 + 37,727)/(6,641 + 1,079) = 11.4 km, and comparing
this figure with the 12.21 km mentionedin Table 2, it can
be seen that these two values, determined by completely
different methods, lie very close to one another.

---

3. Excluding occasional transport.

43

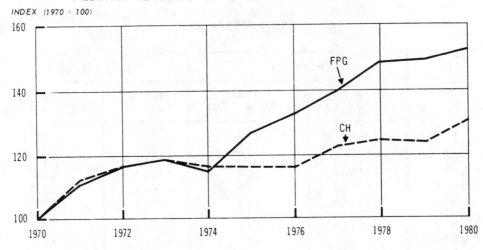

Figure 5 **INDEX OF PETROL CONSUMPTION IN THE FEDERAL REPUBLIC OF GERMANY AND SWITZERLAND**

Table 17

TRANSPORT OUTPUT INDEX OF TRUNK ROADS IN THE
FEDERAL REPUBLIC OF GERMANY

Year	Motorways			Main roads outside built-up areas		
	DTV (vehi-cles/24h)	Total length (km)	Index (1975 = 100)	DTV (vehi-cles/24h)	Total length (km)	Index (1975 = 100)
1975	25,422	5,981	100	6,000	25,411	100
1976	27,001	6,324	112	6,075	25,400	101
1977	28,793	6,573	124	6,394	25,328	106
1978	29,120	6,870	132	6,601	25,172	109
1979	29,443	7,161	139	6,590	25,124	109
1980	30,014	7,293	144	6,688	25,142	110

Data source: [27].

6. CONCLUSION AND OUTLOOK

In its original significance, the magic word "mobi-lity" covers a broad spectrum of ideas and fantasies. The fact is that for a long period of human history mobility had quite magical, mythical significance: we only need to think of the ritual/religious dances of peoples we still today arrogantly designate as "primitive". The "irration-al" element in mobility should not be forgotten in the present age of high-technology mobility, since psychology

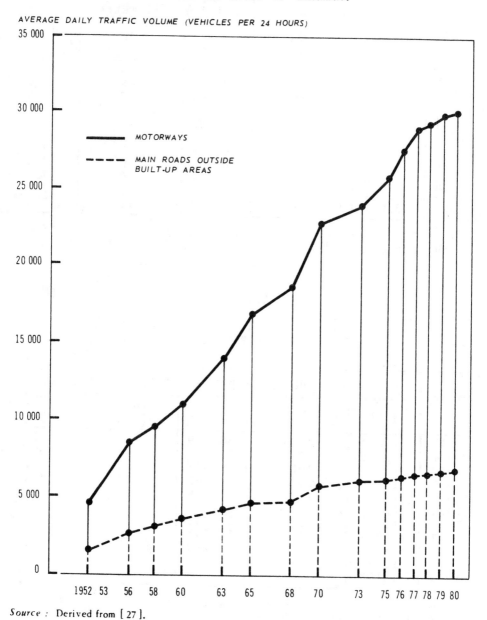

Figure 6 **TREND OF AVERAGE DAILY TRAFFIC VOLUME IN THE FEDERAL REPUBLIC OF GERMANY**

AVERAGE DAILY TRAFFIC VOLUME (VEHICLES PER 24 HOURS)

MOTORWAYS

MAIN ROADS OUTSIDE BUILT-UP AREAS

Source : Derived from [27].

Table 18

TRENDS IN PUBLIC TRANSPORT IN THE FEDERAL REPUBLIC OF
GERMANY EXCLUDING RAILWAYS

Year	No. of passengers		passenger-kilometres		Average ride distance (km)
	Mill.	Index (1970 = 100)	Mill.	Index (1970 = 100)	
1970	6,096	100	45,123	100	7.4
1971	6,279	103	47,429	105	7.6
1972	6,346	104	48,305	107	7.6
1973	6,508	107	49,759	110	7.6
1974	6,590	108	50,182	111	7.6
1975	6,641	109	50,614	112	7.6
1976	6,463	106	49,718	110	7.7
1977	6,383	105	49,253	109	7.7
1978	6,376	105	48,982	109	7.7
1979	6,484	106	49,883	111	7.7
1980	6,621	109	50,628	112	7.6

Data source: [28]

Table 19

TRENDS IN RAILWAY PASSENGER TRANSPORT IN
THE FEDERAL REPUBLIC OF GERMANY

Year	No. of passengers		passenger-kilometres		Average ride distance (km)
	Mill.	Index (1970 = 100)	Mill.	Index (1970 = 100)	
1970	1,054	100	38,129	100	36.2
1971	1,053	100	36,892	97	35.0
1972	1,053	100	39,638	104	37.6
1973	1,093	104	39,765	104	36.4
1974	1,124	107	40,568	106	36.1
1975	1,079	102	37,727	99	35.0
1976	1,025	97	36,451	96	35.6
1977	1,029	98	36,543	96	35.5
1978	1,049	100	36,798	97	35.1
1979	1,085	103	38,016	100	35.0
1980	1,108	105	38,358	101	34.6

Data source: [28]

confirms that it still appears to be active [29]
(p. 136): "Road traffic seems to have become a playground
where man seeks to invest claims on experience, that he is
increasingly unable to invest in other fields of life
which are becoming more and more devoid of emotion".

Ritual dances may have been the beginning of the need
for mobility (all other movements, such as hunting or
flight are rather to be counted as enforced mobility). At
first the manifestations of mobility were for a long time
limited by the insurmountable limits of physical
strength. Gradually this was supplemented by animal
power. The great change in the manifestations and extent
of mobility did not appear until the invention and use of
technological transport modes which were no longer dependent on human or animal resources for their energy supply. Undreamed of travel possibilities were opened up.

Now it is clearly a psychological law that human
wants grow with possibilities. Both wants and possibilities in the field of mobility have had a mutually ampli-
fying effect and led to mankind's space-time diagram
basically and radically changing in the course of history. At least for the age of the technological transport
modes, something like the following phenomenon can be observed (I avoid the expression "demonstrated"; these observations are to be seen not as facts but as hypotheses):

- The time budget that individual persons use for
  purposes of bridging space per unit time (day or
  year) turns out to be extraordinarily stable [30]
  (p. 8): "Despite massive changes in spatial organisation caused by modern transport developments,
  our society has proved so adaptable that the average expenditure of time for changes of location
  outside the house have changed but little."
- Quite obviously, the daily or yearly journey distance per person is to be seen as the really available parameter in mobility behaviour. In the
  course of time - looked at on the historical
  scale - this has in fact increased enormously
  (cf. Figure 1).
- The conclusion to be drawn from these two observations is evident; the key to the compatibility of
  the two hypotheses is speed. The constant increase
  in speed through technological progress has greatly
  extended the radius of action while travelling time
  has remained the same.
- It could on the other hand be claimed that increasingly speed should as a rule lead to savings on
  travelling time and thus to increased time remaining available to alternative activities. This
  hypothesis may be regarded as disproved: savings
  in travelling time are usually again converted into
  mobility in another place at another time [30]
  (p. 8).

47

Thus - greatly simplifying - mobility is finally reduced to the dimension of speed. Today, speed is still -
or perhaps I should say more than ever - capable of sending us into a state of intoxication. The longing for
speed, the atavistic burning desire for it, is such that
whole industries devote themselves to manufacturing speed
and speed is becoming purely and simply the symbol of progress. The faster, the more powerful. One only has to
think, for example, of the two superpowers' race to the
moon.

At the same time it is becoming apparent that travel
in itself is losing a great deal of its independent significance and to an increasing extent the only interest is
in the destination. This is probably also partly due to
the fact that at high speed the associated perceptual intensity and multitude of experiences can no longer be processed by the mind of the traveller. As early as the
first decade after the invention of the railway the following aphorism appeared in Silesia [31] (p. 5): "One no
longer travels, one arrives."

Mobility or speed is frequently - either implicitly
or quite openly - associated with the idea of freedom.
Witness the slogan I have already referred to: "Free
driving for free citizens". Technology, which is now trying to develop all possible and impossible social processes to a demoniacal pitch, has given us the ability to
rapidly expand our field of action. But what is freedom?
In my understanding it does not just mean the freedom of
use of every new product - and I regard mobility as a product. For me freedom is an individual decision process
with an ethical dimension which may be called responsibility. It obliges us before using a thing to test whether
it is useful and whether it serves man. In this respect I
would refer to the title of the general topic of this Symposium: "Transport is for People". I believe that in
future we shall have to be increasingly careful to ensure
that - in our fascination with the technologically feasible or the business advantages to be gained - we do not
let the production of mobility get out of hand, as has
already happened in the field of armaments production.
(The power of weapons too rests on the speed built into
them: the faster the weapon the more powerful it is.) It
is essential that we keep open the option to have transport go on serving people; we must prevent people becoming
the slaves of transport.

According to my scientific understanding, philosophical questions cannot be answered using scientific
methods alone. Here I would go along with Einstein's
statement that science can only determine what is, not
what ought to be [32]. This distinction seems to be
important because everything which carries the label
"scientific" arouses great expectations and it should be
possible to attribute a high degree of reliability and

48

validity to a scientific statement. Unfortunately, however, the label "scientific" has been and is still being much misused. A very old example from the transport field may illustrate how difficult it is to separate reality from wishful thinking, i.e. what is from what ought to be: When the building of the first German steam railway commenced (between Nürnberg and Fürth, opened on 7th December, 1835) the high medical council in Bavaria declared [33] (p. 7), "operating steam train services should be prohibited in the interest of public health. The rapid movement would indubitably cause brain disorders; even watching a train hurtling along could cause this damage ...".

To conclude, it will have been noticed that my intention in this contribution was to promote a global understanding of the phenomenon of personal mobility. This explains my many excursions into philosophy. Engineers - and I am an engineer - are inclined either to avoid philosophical excursions or to apologise for them. I have deliberately not obeyed either of these two "rules", because I am convinced that engineers - somewhat on the model of Leonardo da Vinci ought once again to see their activity far more generally, with more appreciation of its consequences and hence more responsibility than many do today. Such a global approach would perhaps free the engineering profession from the now very indiscriminately applied charge of "technocracy".

BIBLIOGRAPHY

[1] Möse, J.R., Zusammenfassendes Gutachten über das projektierte Bundesstrassennetz im Raume von Graz aus umwelthygienischer Sicht. Graz, 1974.

[2] Comte, A., Plan der wissenschaftlichen Arbeiten, die für eine Reform der Gesellschaft notwendig sind. Carl Hanser Verlag, München, 1973 (Reihe Hanser 131).

[3] Allgemeiner Deutscher Automobilclub (ADAC), Sicherheit für den Fussgänger, Vorschläge für die kommunalen Bemühungen um die Verkehrssicherheit. Ergebnisse und Schlussfolgerungen aus dem Städtewettbewerb 1975. Hrsg.: Bundesminister für Verkehr, Bonn, und ADAC, München, o.J.

[4] Allegemeine Deutscher Automobilclub (ADAC), Sicherheit für den Fussgänger II - Verkehrsberuhigung. Erfahrungen und Vorschläge der Verkehrsplanung in Städten und Gemeinden und Schlussfolgerungen aus dem Städtewettbewerb 1977. Hrsg.: Bundesminister für Verkehr, Bonn, und ADAC, München, o.J.

[5] Hautzinger, H.; Kessel, P., Mobilität im Personenverkehr. Forschungsauftrag der PROGNOS AG, Basel, durchgeführt im Auftrag des Bundesministers für Verkehr, Bonn. Forschung Strassenbau und Strassenverkehrstechnik, Heft 231, Bonn, 1977.

[6] Hautzinger, H.; Kessel, P.; Baur, R., Mobilitätschancen unterschiedlicher Bevölkerungsgruppen im Personenverkehr. Forschungsauftrag der PROGNOS AG, Basel, durchgeführt im Auftrag des Bundesministers für Verkehr, Bonn. Forschung Strassenbau und Strassenverkehrstechnik, Heft 310, Bonn, 1980, S. 59-118.

[7] Schulz-Wittuhn G., Von Mensch zu Mensch - 16000 Jahre Verkehr. Verlag Julius Cramer, Köln, 1957.

[8] Frenzel, D., Verkehrsmittel der Zukunft - Technologische Trends und Konzepte für die Verkehrssysteme von morgen. In: Der Bürger im Staat, 30 (1980), Nr. 2, S. 124-127.

[9] Thomson, J.M., Grundlagen der Verkehrspolitik. Verlag Paul Haupt, Bern und Stuttgart, 1978.

[10] Kessel, P.; Hautzinger, H., Verkehrsmobilität: Meinungen - Analysen - Prognosen. In: Zeitschrift für Verkehrswissenschaft, 47 (1976), Nr. 1, S. 31-44.

[11] Ford, H., Mein Leben und mein Werk. Paul List Verlag, Leipzig, 1923.

[12] Werfel, F., Realismus und Innerlichkeit. Paul Zsolnay Verlag, Berlin - Wien - Leipzig, 1931.

[13] Schütte, K., Ein Beitrag zur Vorausschätzung des Verkehrsaufkommens von städtischen Wohngebieten. Dissertation, Technische Hochschule Braunschweig, 1966.

[14] Drangmeister, K., Das Kfz-Verkehrsaufkommen von Wohngebieten unter besonderer Berücksichtigung der Spitzenverkehrszeiten. Strassenbau und Strassenverkehrstechnik, Heft 64, Bonn, 1967.

[15] Ruske, W., Stochastische und deterministische Modelle zur Errechnung des Verkehrsaufkommens aus Strukturmerkmalen. Dissertation, Rheinisch-Westfäflische Technische Hochschule Aachen, 1968.

[16] Hägerstrand, T., What about People in Regional Science? In: Papers of the Regional Science Association, 24 (1970), p. 7-21.

[17] Hägerstrand, T., The Impact of Transport on the Quality of Life. In: Fifth International Symposium on Theory and Practice in Transport Economics. Athens, 22nd-25th October, 1973. Volume 1 (Introductory Reports), ECMT, Paris, 1974.

[18] Ortega y Gasset, J., Betrachtungen über die Technik. Deutsche Verlags-Anstalt, Stuttgart, 1949.

[19] Rühl, A., Strategy Studies for Urban Transport in the Netherlands. In: Transportation Research Record, No. 775 (1980), pp. 17-21.

[20] Gebser, J., Alte und neue Wirklichkeit. In: Wege zur neuen Wirklichkeit, S. 9-30. Verlag Hallwag, Bern, 1960.

[21] Prognos AG; Socialdata GmbH, Entwicklung eines
     Individual-Verhaltensmodells zur Erklärung und
     Prognose werktäglicher Aktivitätsmuster im
     städtischen Bereich - Stufe 2. Untersuchung im
     Auftrag des Bundesministers für Verkehr, Bonn.
     Basel - München, 1980.

[22] Brög, W.; Erl, E.; Förg, O.G. et al., Verkehrsanalyse
     und -prognose Grossraum Hannover. Untersuchung der
     Socialdata GmbH, München, durchgeführt im Auftrag
     des Zweckverbandes Grossraum Hannover. München,
     1981.

[23] Wermuth, M.; Der Einfluss des Pkw-Besitzes auf Fahr-
     tenhäufigkeit und Wahl des Verkehrsmittels. For-
     schung Strassenbau und Strassenverkehrstechnik,
     Heft 265, Bonn, 1978.

[24] Cerwenka, P., Methoden langfristiger Prognosen,
     gezeigt am Beispiel der Pkw-Motorisierung. Stras-
     senbau und Strassenverkehrstechnik, Heft 179, Bonn,
     1975.

[25] Mineraloelwirtschaftsverband e.V., Jahresbericht 1980.
     Hamburg, o.J.

[26] Bundesamt für Statistik, Schweizerische Verkehrs-
     statistik 1978, 1979, 1980. Bern, 1979, 1980, 1981.

[27] Heidemann, D.; Wimber, P., Jahresauswertung 1980 -
     Langzeitzählstellen. Strassenverkehrszählungen,
     Heft 19, Bonn, 1981.

[28] Statistisches Bundesamt, Statistisches Jahrbuch 1980,
     1981 für die Bundesrepublik Deutschland, Verlag W.
     Kohlhammer GmbH, Stuttgart und Mainz, 1980, 1981.

[29] Spörli, S., Psychologie des Autofahrens. Herder,
     Freiburg - Basel - Wien, 1974 (Herderbücherei Band
     499).

[30] Heinze, G.W., Mobilität und Verkehrsmittelwahl. In:
     Personennahverkehr - Verkehrsbedürfnisse und Trans-
     portmittel. Vorträge anlässlich des Seminars der
     Forschungsgruppe Berlin, 6./7. Oktober 1980, S.
     7-13. Hrsg.: Daimler-Benz AG, Stuttgart-
     Untertürkheim, o.J.

[31] Schadendorf, W., Zu Pferde, im Wagen, zu Fuss -
     Tausend Jahre Reisen. Prestel Verlag, München,
     1959.

[32] Einstein, A., Science and Religion. In: Science,
     Philosophy and Religion, a Symposium, pp. 209-214.
     Published by the Conference on Science, Philosophy
     and Religion in Their Relation to the Democratic
     Way of Life, Inc., New York, 1941.

[33] Stemplinger, E., Von berühmten Aerzten. R. Piper &
     Co. Verlag, München, 1938.

TOPIC 1A

ASSESSMENT OF
SOCIETY'S TRANSPORT NEEDS

MOBILITY OF PERSONS

Mr. A. RÜHL
Mr. A. BAANDERS
Miss J.M. GARDEN
Ministry of Transport and Public Works
Netherlands

SUMMARY

1. INTRODUCTION

Assessment of society's needs the mobility of persons, is a topic of formidable dimensions, especially as we are asked to consider not only the current situation but also future trends. This paper tries to deal with the essential elements of the subject.

Our first objective is to describe alternative methods that could be used to establish the transport needs of society. Beginning at the individual level of analysis is a principle of fundamental importance since it recognises that society's transport needs are built up from people, in all their great diversity. It also leads to a need to distinguish the priorities which individuals attribute to activities and the level of satisfaction which they currently experience.

Assuming that transport needs and their importance can be identified, consideration is given to the manner in which society can meet them. Attention is drawn to the many factors which limit satisfaction and to some of the consequences of decision making practices which reinforce the position of some groups within society while neglecting to equally recognise the needs of others. It is suggested that improved understanding of individual needs is likely to raise further questions about inequalities in society arising from the unequal satisfaction of travel needs. Modified means of assessment are required which can take more account of the priorities of individuals and recognise the weak position of some groups in society in comparison with others.

The growth of car use and concentration of investment in infrastructure necessary to support that use, has eroded the position of those who have to rely on walking, cycling and public transport. Unless there is an attempt to redress the balance more in their favour, it seems likely that those without access to cars will be unable to obtain a reasonable degree of satisfaction of their transport needs.

To establish the needs of individuals and to assess the priorities which should be attributed to them is a difficult task. However, it is a challenge which has been set in recent years by decision makers who have asked increasingly searching questions about the effects of policies on people and their likely responses. This paper tries to accept that challenge and suggest where our attention should be concentrated in terms of future effort.

2. SOCIETY AND ITS CONSTITUENTS

It is necessary to begin with a brief consideration of the meaning of society. Within the context of this discussion the term will be used generally to cover groupings ranging from the level of Europe down to the level of village or neighbourhood. Our concern will be directed towards the individuals who make up these various social communities and the means by which their needs can be established. However, because we are concerned with all the needs of society, consideration will also be given to organisations and their functioning. This distinction needs to be drawn because the needs of the latter are not always synonomous with those of the sum of individuals.

It seems clear that the assessment of society's transport needs is potentially as many sided as its constituent parts. What are the needs? How should they be identified and/or measured? Who has them and with what intensity and how are they distributed geographically and socially? These are questions so broad reaching in their generality that it is necessary to adopt a strategy for approaching them within the context of this report, which will reduce the topic to manageable proportions while still allowing us to consider the underlying conceptual problems of need.

Given that any society is the sum of different types of individuals, households and organisations in varying situations, we propose to adopt a series of examples and through them consider the merits of alternative means of establishing needs. The following examples will be used for discussing the approaches.

Through these fragments of society, consideration will be given to defining, describing and valueing society's needs for transport.

The urban handicapped

Consider a handicapped person of working age living in an urban area.

The rural family

Consider a rural family living in a mountainous area.

The industrial enterprise

Consider an industrial enterprise dependent on low wage earning, semi-skilled or unskilled labour whose premises are located on the fringe of an urban area.

The suburban mother and children

Consider a mother with three children of six, eight and fourteen years old, living in a suburban environment.

The inner-city retailer

Consider a retailer in an area which has suffered from a decline in the density of employment and population and is experiencing competition from out of town shopping centres. The quality of the environment is poor, parking is restricted and public transport services are handicapped by operating in congested circumstances.

3. WAYS OF DEFINING NEED

3.1. The concept of need - need and demand

Before an assessment of transport needs can be given, it is necessary to discuss first what need actually is. The notion of need should also be related to another concept of (transport) economics, i.e. demand.

Need can be described as a feeling that one wants to have something with some degree of intensity. Thus a transport need is the feeling that one wants to make a journey, or to send goods. Transport needs are therefore those journeys which individuals, households and organisations attach importance to. It is a concept related to both users and possible users of the transport system.

In contrast, demand is a concept related to the market. For each traffic link between two places, a given quality of service and price will determine demand and thus the number of journeys that people will make. As early as the 5th ECMT Round Table, the relation between demand and need was defined as follows: "Demand being understood as the real need satisfied by the market."[1] Demand is always related to a real or hypothetical supply but need is independent of supply.

_____

1. Schneider Dr. W.L. and Precht Dr. G., Elaboration of Models for Forecasting Demand and Need in the Transport Sector, report on the 5th Round Table on transport economics, 1969.

For commercial operators, information about demand is sufficient if it allows them to reach decisions about what services to offer at which prices. Their requirements are that they should be able to establish the likely demand in each of the alternatives under consideration. Knowledge of needs will only be relevant insofar as it increases understanding of the way in which demand will change.

However, public authorities and other organisations which consider wider interests should obtain information about needs and the degree to which they are satisfied for each individual, household or organisation. It is only in this way that they can appreciate to what extent actual travel that takes place satisfies travel needs and the extent to which the degree of satisfaction experienced may be different for both people and organisations.

Thus while demand is a concept of economics and can be explained by economic science, need is considered by economics as given and therefore other sciences should be used to determine what the needs are. In practice, this is seldom done.

3.2. Delimitation of need

As has been said earlier, needs indicate some degree of intensity. A journey can be thought of as being a transport need if it represents a certain degree of importance. These qualifications do not imply that need cannot include trips that can be labelled as a luxury, e.g. a holiday trip to a faraway destination can be considered very important for personal well-being. However, clearly some delimitation of need is necessary.

A visit to one's parents or to a friend living 500 km away may be felt to be important but it will not lead to a useful appreciation of transport needs if we take account of such a wish to pay a visit every other Tuesday evening, because other people whose parents live locally have such regular habits.

Unlike demand, need is independent of supply. However, it is not useful to include in transport needs, journeys for which the provision of an adequate supply is not technically feasible, or only by using vehicles that are not normally available, e.g. supersonic aircraft or helicopters.

Journeys that are feasible but do not belong to a normal pattern of behaviour, like weekend trips to America, are not very relevant either. A reasonable delimitation should be sought for but, when in doubt, it will always be better to include journeys rather than excluding them.

61

Policy decisions about the provision of transport services and infrastructure imply that only certain needs can be satisfied and others only partially or not at all. Therefore the assessment of needs cannot stop at simply enumerating them. It is also necessary to value their relative importance. For systematic reasons the evaluation of needs will first be discussed for individual people, households or organisations and then for society as a whole. In the sections which follow only the ranking of needs for individuals will be discussed. The wider assessment of groups of individuals or organisations and their needs within society will be discussed at a later stage.

3.3. The assessment of individual needs

In economic theory, it is generally assumed that decision makers can place their needs in an order of ranking, based on their degree of importance and that they are willing to pay a higher price for the satisfaction of a need, the more important it is. An available budget can then be allocated in such a way as to give the highest possible satisfaction.

In passenger transport, however, there are a number of reasons why this simple scheme can only be applied in part. These can be explained through the following reasoning.

- Transport needs are derived from wanting to undertake activities in different places. Satisfaction is derived from the activities while the travel will be considered as the cost of undertaking them.
- Many activities are subject to time constraints and therefore cannot easily be substituted.
- People sometimes have an idea about a "reasonable" price to be paid for a journey of a certain type, e.g. a taxi or a firstclass only train may be ruled out for even very important journeys because the price is thought to be unreasonably high in comparison with private cars, public transport or second-class train services respectively.
- Needs and the importance attached to them vary over time.

The above arguments imply that the prices that people are willing to pay cannot serve as indicators of the importance of needs without additional information. Also, it should not be assumed that journeys which cease to be made when supply conditions change, reflect a reduction in their importance. It may well be that in the changed situation no alternatives are available which fit the pattern of the need. Other indications of the relative importance of different transport needs are therefore required.

3.4. Approaches to the assessment of needs

The following approaches have been developed as three rather different means of establishing needs. It is recognised that these approaches are by no means definitive and that discussions are likely to yield many further ideas and variations. While each is considered separately, it is also possible that they could be used in parallel.

1. The ubiquitous supply approach

Transport needs are derived from the journeys that would be made if, for all people, the supply conditions between places were to be improved to the same level as the best quality that is normally available, given the type of link.

2. The reference group approach

Transport needs are all journeys that must be made to maintain a reasonable level of activities. In this approach, what is reasonable is derived from the level of activities which we find for people without transport constraints.

3. The direct questioning approach

Again transport needs are all journeys that must be made to maintain a reasonable level of activities. In this approach, what is reasonable is derived from what individuals say they consider to be appropriate for people like themselves.

4. THE UBIQUITOUS SUPPLY APPROACH

4.1. The principles of the approach

In most cases travel is not undertaken for its own sake, but in order to take part in certain activities at the destination end. The journey itself can be considered as a cost of undertaking these activities. This disutility should be more than compensated for by the utility of the activity if the journey is to be considered worthwhile. The higher the disutility of travel, the less likely it is that a particular journey will be made.

The disutility of travel can be expressed in a generalised cost, this will include with the money costs of undertaking a journey, all the negative elements of the journey, each multiplied by an appropriate coefficient to convert them into monetary units. As most of the negative elements are measured by their duration (in vehicle time, walking time, waiting time, etc.) the coefficients are generally labelled as values of time.

Generalised cost is normally associated with a particular way of making a journey and can be different for an individual person according to route, mode of transport, time of day and party size. In circumstances where it is possible to make a journey in different ways, all the relevant generalised costs should be taken into account. This can be done by considering them all and then taking the minimum value. However, a better method is to apply a mathematical transformation which results in a combined value being calculated which is less influenced by a relatively unattractive way of making a journey and more so by an attractive means.

In general, transport supply is determined, for each type of journey, by technical factors, geographical conditions, economic circumstances and transport policy. These will cause generalised costs of travel and generalised accessibility (that is the generalised cost of travelling to destinations of a certain type) to vary between places. For each type of journey, however, it is possible to define a maximum level of supply or a minimum level of generalised cost that can be expected. For journeys between cities this can be based on the use of motorways or intercity rail services; in mountain areas on ordinary roads, buses and/or narrow gauge railways; in towns or walking, cycling, car driving and the use of buses or trams. All these modes of travel will be assumed available to all people, except for those under the minimum age for driving licences, who will be excluded from driving but not from travelling as a car passenger. For all journeys the system of prices and taxes applicable to the country under consideration, including levies for the use of infrastructure, will be included in generalised costs.

Transport need can now be defined as the number and length of journeys people would make if the maximum level of supply were available for all possible trips of a certain type. Needs are of course not the same for all persons and appropriate differentiations will have to be made according to professional status, household structure, social class, etc.

4.2. Determining needs

A technical process to determine transport needs within this approach could make use of transport demand forecasting models. Normally these models are used to provide forecasts of demand for existing supply conditions, or changes to supply conditions that are under consideration, e.g. the construction of a motorway or a new railway or the introduction of a road pricing scheme. The models use very differentiated data on the quality of service (measured in generalised cost or disutility), differentiated according to, amongst other things, origin and destination pairs, mode of transport and availability of modes.

In the approach for defining transport need, quality of service is only differentiated according to type of link (interurban, intraurban, rural) and by person type, i.e. above or below 18 years of age. The very complicated networks for different modes associated with such demand models can be replaced by two simple networks representing the combined disutility of all modes. One will include all modes and the other will exclude car driving for those people below driving age. On this basis the models will produce estimates of travel need as it follows from the supply conditions which have been defined.

There are two ways of making the above calculations. A full application of the forecasting process provides matrices of needs, that can be compared to actual or forecast demand. A simpler process is an application of the so-called sample enumeration method,(2) which calculates the need for passenger transport of a limited number of individuals, who have first been sampled, and for whom data on their actual travel have been collected. This last method shows immediately the difference between actual travel and travel need for each member of the sample.

It should be noted that travel need does not normally include all trips that are actually made. In many cases people want to go to certain places, but because they cannot get there in a reasonable way, decide to go elsewhere. These "second best" trips are part of transport demand, not of transport need.

4.3. The five examples

Let us now consider what would be the likely results of applying this approach to each of the five examples.

The urban handicapped

Transport need will be based on the normal trip pattern of a person living in the urban area who has no

---

2. Daly A.J., van Zwam H.H.P, "Travel Demand Models for the Zuidvleugel Study", PTRC summer annual meeting 1981.

constraints in travelling on foot, by bike, as a car driver or on public transport. It will not include trips made possible by specific transport services provided for handicapped people but will allow for these services if they are considered as being comparable with the private car. Unusual trips which the handicapped person may have to make as a result of his or her handicap, e.g. to a re-habilitation centre, will not be included.

The rural family

In a country where mountain valleys have well-kept, surfaced roads and secondary railways or good bus services, transport needs will be extensive. However, if the modes to be normally relied upon are of lower quality, e.g. relying on foot, animal traction or jeep, then the needs as defined by this method will be accordingly lower.

The suburban mother and children

For this example the models will perform worst. Children of six and eight are usually left out of travel demand models, as they do not travel long distances on their own. Also the linkages between journeys of different people, e.g. mother and child and the time constraints for individual activities are neglected.

The industrial enterprise

For journeys to work the pattern of need will be less influenced by the existing public transport system than by the means of calculating demand. Careful inspection of the calculations is likely to show that the daily arrival of the number of workers that the firm can employ is the result of the balancing factors calculated in the model to equalise the number of workers arriving in each zone with the number of jobs. The influence of the quality of the public transport system will therefore largely be ignored. Also, business traffic is frequently neglected as a special travel purpose and therefore whether it can be included or not will depend on the nature of the data available.

The inner-city retailer

In this case the process can be expected to work well, at least when the number of customers arriving in each shopping zone is not introduced as a constraint, but determined by accessibility of the shopping area. Need will then be calculated as the number of shoppers arriving when accessibility is good, and demand as the number of

arrivals under present conditions of parking and public
transport. The effect of depopulation of town centres
will be the same in both cases.

5. THE REFERENCE GROUP APPROACH

5.1. The principal assumptions

This is the first of two possible approaches which
try to establish the amount of travel necessary for individuals which would allow them to maintain a reasonable
level of activities. It is assumed that there are groups
of people who, within reason, are free to enjoy activities
without being unduly inhibited by difficulties in the use
of transport. Such constraints on the use of transport
might be caused by a lack of suitable supply of transport,
personal physical difficulties or isolated housing locations. This is not to say that they might not aspire to
do more things than they do now, but that the sort of
limitations mentioned above do not cause them to renounce
any important activities. This group is termed the
reference group and because, within reason, they have no
constraints on their activities because of travel difficulties, it is assumed that their needs are being met by a
reasonable level of activities (i.e. reasonable given the
local social and geographical conditions). Similarly it
is assumed that other people in less fortunate circumstances (referred to as the target group) aspire to the
same activity level, but are unable to reach this simply
because of travel difficulties. The principle of the
approach is therefore that reasonable levels of activities
for people with transport constraints can be inferred from
the pattern of activities of people who enjoy much greater
freedom. The approach is based on comparisons between
target groups and reference groups. The word "level",
which is used throughout, indicates both the amount and
the composition (pattern) of activities.

5.2. Method of measurement

The procedure for measuring transport needs would
require the following steps and assumptions.

1. A number of groups must be identified. The group
   of people whose needs we want to establish will be
   called the "target group". The members of this
   population will be equal in the attributes that we
   assume determine their level of activity, with the
   exception of the transport constraints. The people with the lowest transport constraints will be
   the "reference group".
2. The activity level of the reference group should
   be measured. It should be equal to or higher than

the activity level of the group we want to measure
and it will be assumed that the differences can be
explained by the transport constraints.
3. The activity level of the reference group should
   be transposed to the target group and the locations which the latter would choose for their
   activities should be identified.
4. The amount of travel should be derived from the
   activity locations and the frequency of visits to
   each one. This amount of travel indicates the
   transport need for the target group. The difference between the actual existing level of activities and the reasonable level as measured will
   then indicate the extent of potentially unsatisfied need.

5.3. The importance of constraints

Three categories of constraint can be discerned:

1. Physical constraints: the extent to which physical health or handicaps make the use of a transport mode difficult, e.g. public transport,
   bicycle.
2. Supply constraints: the extent to which there is
   no suitable means of transport available to the
   individual at a price he can afford.
3. Locational constraints: the extent to which the
   spatial pattern of activity opportunities cause
   them to be far from the individual's home (e.g. in
   rural areas with low settlement densities, or in
   big cities with little open air recreational space
   or in suburbs with few employment opportunities).

We shall assume that societal values imply a hierarchy of
values in terms of the importance of these constraints.
Physical constraints will be considered the most serious
and least acceptable. This is because people who experience such constraints cannot change their own circumstances. Clearly transport policy should pay particular
attention to unsatisfied needs which are caused by physical constraints on individuals. The second category, the
supply constraints, are also properly the concern of transport policy, but to a lesser degree. Public transport
services cannot be provided at all places and at all
times. Taxi services or private cars cannot be paid for
by all people. However, cheap transport is not the only
solution to this problem; changes in the income distribution are another one.

    The third category, that of the locational con-
straints, is of less importance because it contains an
element of free choice. Many families choose to live in
low density areas; moreover, living in those places has a
number of real advantages that urban areas lack. There

are, however, still limits to the acceptability of this constraint, as is shown by the fact that many people deplore the depopulation of certain rural areas, caused by the inhabitants trying to overcome the locational constraints by moving to more densely populated areas, where more activity opportunities are available within a reasonable distance.

5.4. Some problems of measurement

The procedure has a number of problems associated with it which will be discussed under three headings:

- the choice of the reference group;
- the two-way relationship between transport and activities;
- the amount of detail that should be used in comparing the two groups.

5.4.1. The choice of reference group

It should be noted that activity patterns vary considerably between individuals. The reasons for these differences can largely be explained by economic, social and cultural factors; by time, money and effort constraints and, last but not least, by personal tastes. Because of this variance, due care should be given to choosing groups of people who in as far as possible are alike in all but their transport constraints. The selections of the reference group will inevitably entail value judgements. The approach is normative with ideally both groups being compared having equal attributes except for the transport constraints. In practice this is of course impossible both because there are few people without some degree of transport constraints, and because the number of attributes that influence the level of activities of each individual is so very large.

5.4.2. The relationship between transport and activities

The level of activities that is thought to be reasonable in our society is in part determined by the existence of transport constraints, e.g. it is not thought reasonable that someone living in a rural area, far from a large city, be able to participate daily in such typical urban activities as shopping in a large department store. The inhabitant of the rural area will have a reasonable activity pattern which is different from an urban dweller. His economic, social and cultural attributes may also be different because of the existence of a transport constraint, i.e. the greater distance between the location of activities. This example shows that not only do the personal attributes influence the activity level and pattern but that also the transport constraints influence the attributes. This two-way relationship between activities and transport implies that some element of the transport constraint should be incorporated in the attributes used in the first step of the measuring procedure. The extent of constraints experienced by the reference group will be the result of value judgements exercised in choosing the group.

5.4.3. The amount of detail in the comparison

The comparison between the group of people whose needs we want to establish and the reference group can be made at all kinds of levels, varying from very aggregate data giving only rough indications to very detailed descriptions of the activities and relevant factors. Because it is essential to make relevant comparisons between people, a rough selection of groups based on few variables would have little value as only a crude image of the needs of the target group would be derived. However, as has been said, there are a great many difficulties in finding comparable groups and there will be very real limitations on the extent to which detailed comparisons are possible. A just balance has to be sought between too much or too little detail. This will apply to the following elements:

- the attributes of the people that we will use to define the target group and the reference group;
- the number of activity categories to be used in defining the level of activities;
- the number of location categories;
- the way in which transport will be measured;
- the number of constraint categories.

5.5. The five examples

Let us now consider the application of the approach. The people from the examples are each seen as being part of a target group within which the transport constraints vary, but the other relevant attributes (assumed to determine the level of activity) are the same. The reference group is the part of the target group for whom there are no transport constraints or for whom these are very low.

The urban handicapped

Our urban handicapped will have a certain social and cultural status resulting from his or her family background and education. It should be possible to identify a group of urban dwellers who form a social group to which our handicapped person rightly belongs, or would do so if

it were not for his or her handicap. This then is the
target group as referred to above. The reference group
will be formed by members of the target group who have the
lowest transport constraints. In a number of target
groups this will be people who own a car. Certainly they
will not be handicapped and will have no physical or men-
tal difficulty in making trips by foot, bicycle or public
transport. In many cases, because they are urban dwellers, these will be people whose level of out-of-home
activities are high in comparison to the average for the
country. Our handicapped will be far below that level,
which means there will be a large gap between their actual
transport demand and transport need as derived from the
activity pattern of the reference group. Some care will
have to be taken in comparing the activities of the reference group and the handicapped.

The rural family

As in the first example, a social group should be
defined to which our rural family belongs. The most
important constraint for rural families is the locational
constraint. Activity opportunities are generally far from
home and are not high in number or quality. Rural dwellers have therefore in most cases a very particular activity pattern which differs markedly from urban patterns.
As the rural family in our example lives in a mountain
area, the activity opportunities are very unevenly spread
over the area. Most of them will be located in the valleys, where the best transport links will also be found.
Families living in these valleys will therefore have much
lower transport constraints than those living on the mountain slopes. Valley families who have direct access to
the main transport routes will thus be chosen as the reference group. The family living higher up the mountain
will have a lower level of activities than that of the
reference group, and there will thus be an unsatisfied
need for transport. The better the quality of transport
available generally, the smaller the unsatisfied need will
be. If our family lived in a flat rural area the activity
opportunities and the transport facilities would be spread
more evenly. The difference between the reference groups
and the families that were worse off would then be much
smaller. As a consequence the unsatisfied transport needs
would also be less.

The suburban mother and children

Transport needs of this example include trips to be
made by the mother or the older child to accompany the
younger children to activities they cannot go to on their
own. The necessity of accompanying children, especially
to very regular activities like school, will to some extent depend on the quality of the transport facilities in

the suburban area and on the location of the activity opportunities. In some areas it might be safe to let children of 6 and 8 walk and cycle locally or even use a bus
service on their own. In other areas parents will consider this far too dangerous.

The range within which the children are allowed to
enjoy independent activities will be related to their
age. For the youngest this range will be very limited,
while the eldest will have far greater individual freedom. Given all of these factors, the reference group
should consist of families living in suburbs with a high
degree of segregation between foot and cycle paths and
roads for other traffic. Such conditions exist in a number of suburbs in Western Europe (in most cases fairly
recently built). The reference group should also have
good public transport to the central city and a private
car should be available if that is normal in the target
group.

Measuring the needs in this way, we shall find that
in the absence of safe walking and cycling facilities,
there will be important unsatisfied needs for our suburban
mother and children.

The industrial enterprise

The industrial enterprise in this example is situated
on the edge of an urban area and is not very accessible by
public transport. The transport needs of the enterprise
are the needs of the people who visit it. They fall into
two categories, those who work there or (in the case of
vacancies) would work there, and those who visit to do
business. Those visiting to deliver or take away goods
are not considered here because they are concerned with
freight traffic.

The target group, of which our firm is part, consists
of all firms in the same trade and of similar size.
Because the problem is the accessibility of this firm, the
reference group will have firms with much better accessibility. If we consider the accessibility of the
employees, it is likely that only some will have cars, but
that most will be dependent on public transport. As this
is of poor quality, some jobs may remain unfilled, even
though there is unemployment in other parts of the urban
area. Under these circumstances the activity level of the
enterprise is lower than it would be if the transport
facilities were otherwise. Comparison with the reference
group will show this, and unsatisfied need for transport
is thus identified. It should be noted that there is an
important difference between this and the ubiquitous supply approach in this respect. Most traffic models distribute all workers over all jobs, so that problems such as
this would be obscured by the latter approach.

Looking next at business visitors, we will find that they travel mostly by car. The location at the edge of the urban area makes access easy. Even if they arrive by train or airplane, they will usually have no financial constraint on using a taxi. It does not seem likely that we will find an important difference in business visits between our enterprise and the reference group. This means that there will not be a substantial unsatisfied transport need in this respect.

The inner-city retailer

The inner-city retailer in our example is located in an area which is gradually running down. The population is decreasing or being replaced with people whose spending power is lower. Traffic congestion and parking problems make accessibility by car poor. While public transport may have relatively high frequencies and network densities, it suffers from congestion and unattractive stations and stops. The needs of the retailer are primarily concerned with the trips of his clients to his shop, but also with the trips by his employees and by sales representatives.

In this analysis the retailer is part of a target group of shops of similar size and in the same trade. The reference group will consist of shops around which, within a given radius, there are more potential clients, or the same number with a higher spending power. Accessibility by car is better and by public transport at least as good, with perhaps a better environment and thus with more pleasant stations and stops.

Some shoppers may come on foot or by bicycle, but the range of these modes is limited and fewer people now live locally in the area which thus emphasises the importance of other modes. Those shoppers purchasing large goods, or large quantities of shopping, will be concerned to use their cars, but may be discouraged by the poor facilities, so that fewer of them patronise the inner-city area than patronise the shops in the reference group. This will indicate an unsatisfied transport need. The inner-city retailer may also find that it is difficult to recruit suitable staff because of the poor accessibility, and that sales representatives complain that it costs them more time and thus they do less business than they would otherwise.

6. THE DIRECT QUESTIONING APPROACH

6.1. The method

As has been said earlier in the discussion of need, it is a concept based on individuals and the importance which they attach to travelling to particular activities. In the reference group approach, the activity levels that are considered reasonable for people with transport constraints are to be inferred through comparison with the activity patterns of those who do not have transport constraints. Thus, while the approach can be used to establish norms, they are derived from people whose backgrounds are similar but whose circumstances differ from those of the target group. There are, however, other means of arriving at reasonable levels of activities which have a more direct relationship with the individual.

The approach described here is based on the argument that the best judge of what constitutes an important need is the individual himself. Thus people should be asked about their wants, in relation to their personal circumstances, in order to establish what would be their desired level of activities. The objective would be to try and discover the intensity of people's feelings about their travel needs and the reasons for them. The emphasis of the approach is thus what individuals think to be important.

In order to try to overcome biases in judgements about what would constitute a reasonable level of activities, caused by exaggerated self-interest, special wishes or modesty, individuals would be asked to consider their needs in relation to others in similar circumstances in their community, the idea behind this being that it would encourage them to reach a view about what could be considered reasonable for people like themselves. It is anticipated that relating their own experience to what they know of family, friends or neighbours should lead to a responsible and realistic judgement. It should be noted that, as with the reference group approach, comparisons should be made between people with comparable backgrounds so that behaviour differences caused by social or cultural differences, do not lead to unrealistic comparisons.

One of the advantages of the approach is that through discussions it should be possible to explore views about constraints and the manner in which they influence activities and the individual's attitude towards them. Such information is of importance when later trying to establish the best means of meeting the needs which have been identified. In developing the method for application, psychological measurement techniques might have a role to play in quantifying the intensity with which people feel their needs.

Another aspect of the approach is that it would allow the differences between individuals, who are being considered as a group, to be identified. This could be valuable when considering the development of policies. Such information might indicate that a policy which treated people as though their needs were alike might be less successful than one which could discriminate between different sorts of help which would best meet different sorts of need. Given the interest that has been shown in recent years in minority groups and the recognition that average people are not a realistic representation of society, this aspect of the approach seems particularly relevant to this discussion of needs.

6.2. The five examples

Let us now consider the possible application of this approach using the five examples which effectively can be seen as presenting policy case studies.

The urban handicapped

Individual handicapped people would be asked for an assessment of their reasonable level of activities and to explain their satisfaction or frustration relative to their individual circumstances. In asking them to consider the "reasonableness" of their level of activities and for people like them, they could be encouraged to compare their situation with other handicapped people whose circumstances were known to them and also with non-handicapped people whose age and interests were similar. They should be encouraged to explain their degree of freedom or dependence on others for help in meeting their needs for activities which they value or would value if they could overcome the transport constraints of their particular situation. An additional source of information would be to question those closely involved with disabled people, e.g. doctors.

It is likely that the responses will differ considerably with individual circumstances. Those heavily dependent on others will presumably have rather different responses from those who are handicapped but capable of living an independent life. The nature of particular handicaps may physically preclude certain activities for some individuals but not for others. The responses of these individuals about their own experiences but also their knowledge of other handicapped people will undoubtedly contain very important descriptive information which is likely to indicate that the reasonable level will vary with the nature of the handicap and individual circumstances. This would seem to demonstrate the value of the approach in relation to policy making since it would indicate where the priorities lie for different sorts of handicapped people and warn against treating them as a homogenous group.

The rural family

In keeping with the individual level of approach, all members of families would need to be asked about their needs in relation to a reasonable level of activities. The family and how it functioned would be central to the study but this would need to be built up on the basis of individual explanations and descriptions of needs. As with the handicapped the identification of satisfaction or frustration would need to be established together with its relationship to the available transport opportunities.

The object will be to establish the views of members of the family about their situation and whether they consider that they benefit from a reasonable level of activities given their local area. The approach allows various factors to be taken into account, e.g. living in isolated areas will imply that some activities may be difficult to reach because they are distant and therefore cost both considerable time and money. Also public transport is generally less frequent than in more populated areas and at certain times bad weather may make the journey hazardous. If the individuals life style is adapted to such constraints, in their judgements about their needs relative to their opportunities to satisfy them they are likely to acknowledge that there are difficulties inherent in the location in which they live and that so long as their basic needs are met for essential activities then they would consider that reasonable given their circumstances. Others may feel much more frustrated by constraints. Under these circumstances they may well feel that their needs are not met fully because they cannot maintain what they consider to be a reasonable level of activities to ensure a fulfilled way of life. A direct approach to the individuals concerned would allow such attitudes to be explored so that the effects of the limitations on activities could also be considered, e.g. pressure on young people to leave their villages and live and work further away, feelings of isolation amongst an ageing population, etc.

The industrial enterprise

In this application of the approach emphasis is placed on the reasonableness of accessibility of individuals to a place of work. If a high turnover of staff is evident or difficulty encountered in recruitment, then it will be important to establish whether there is a relationship between difficulties in satisfying a potential need to reach the site and the apparent unattractiveness of the work opportunities. The employer or personnel responsible for recruitment would be asked to define their needs in relation to their employees in some detail. This will include the type of worker which they require together with any available information on where such people who are seeking employment tend to be located within the local area and thus where they would be likely to be travelling from. A further question is what are the working hours and does any flexibility exist given the nature of the production process. They would then be asked for their judgement of whether their needs were reasonably met given their location and the location of the potential workforce. They would be encouraged to consider the experience of other employers in the area and whether they encountered similar difficulties in maintaining their workforce and whether it was commonly felt that there were accessibility difficulties.

In this example it would be difficult to judge the role of other external factors such as low wages and bad employment conditions in limiting the attractions of working for the employer in question. Information would be required from other sources in order to establish the importance of such factors.

The suburban mother and children

In this example it would perhaps be most appropriate to begin by asking the children about the nature of their activities and whether they feel frustrated at not being able to do all that they would like and perhaps not as often as they would like to. With the younger children it would be valuable to try to establish the extent to which their activities are limited by the need to be escorted and whether or not this is specifically related to road safety problems.

In discussing a reasonable level of activities with the mother, one could begin by considering the extent to which her activities are limited by those of her children. If she spends a lot of time acting as an escort it would be useful to try and establish whether this is because of traffic circumstances locally or for other reasons.

It is likely that a mother's views on a reasonable level of activities will be limited by the time available to her once she has accommodated the demands of her children. She may for example desire to have a part-time job but find it impossible because taking and collecting her children from school leaves her with insufficient time to make this feasible. Using this approach one will try to understand the extent to which the constraints on the mother's activities are a function of being a responsible mother or whether they could to a certain extent be reduced through policy measures, e.g. making road crossings safer for children to use, or introducing very low speed restrictions in residential areas.

The inner-city retailer

A retailer needs customers to patronise his shop. Thus for him it is important that the attractions of the shopping location should not be diminished by difficulties of access caused by road congestion, lack of parking space and an unpleasant environment for the users of public transport. The retailer can be asked to describe in detail his customers and their needs not only in reaching his premises but also in carrying away their purchases. His needs are therefore likely to relate to the location and comfort of the public transport facilities, the location, cost and extent of parking available, the condition and width of the pavements and the safety and ease of crossing the streets. All such factors can contribute to whether or not a particular location is seen as attractive for the activity of shopping or not.

7. CONSTRAINTS ON SATISFYING NEEDS

7.1. Types of constraints

There is a limit to the degree to which transport needs can be satisfied. This limit is set by a number of constraints, which fall into three categories:

- economic or financial constraints;
- political constraints;
- external constraints.

The economic or financial constraints relate to the limits that exist in any society to pay for the satisfaction of transport needs. Most transport is paid for in part by the users and in part by the public authorities. The economic welfare of a country determines to a large extent the transport supply it can afford.

The fact that transport is paid for partly by the users and partly by the authorities introduces a political dimension. By political constraints, we mean the degree to which a society is prepared to use public funds to pay for certain transport services. Spending money to satisfy a personal need is something an individual may or may not decide to do. Spending public funds to satisfy the needs of some people is a collective decision, the costs are not borne by those who profit. This mutual solidarity, the willingness to pay for those who are worse off, has its limits. Large variations can be seen between European countries in this respect, e.g. in the proportion of total public transport cost paid by the travellers, or in the proportion between highway investment and maintenance cost, and the taxes and tolls paid by car users.

The external constraints form a different category. They arise from the fact that if an individual satisfies a transport need, it is possible that this lowers the satisfaction of someone else. This may be the transport need of someone else, when congestion occurs. When many people travel in the same place at the same time, quality elements like speed, comfort or safety often fall.

It is also possible that the satisfaction of transport needs of some people lowers the satisfaction of non-transport needs of other people. This happens when scarce resources are used in the process, the scarcity of which is not reflected in the prices paid. Land may be needed for infrastructure, which cannot be used for other uses. This is principally a problem in densely settled areas. Energy resources are needed to move vehicles, and this may be constrained by conservation policies. Finally, the movement of most types of vehicles causes the emission of noise and of air, soil and water pollutants. All these external effects can be seen as the costs of one group of people satisfying their needs at the expense of others.

A clear example of this is provided by airports, which meet the needs for fast long-distance travel. Many people living near an airport will not have this need but their enjoyment of their home environment will be reduced as a result of others receiving satisfaction. A compromise will sometimes be reached whereby night flights are forbidden and noise abatement procedures applied to day-time arrivals and departures.

A common feature of all external effects is that they do not constrain the use of transport services automatically. Measures by the public authorities are needed, and these can take the form of direct regulations (like maximum noise emissions from cars) or the form of economic disincentives (like a pricing system based on social costs).

In many cases, cars are the most flexible means of satisfying needs. They are, however, the mode which is being increasingly affected by external constraints and regulations associated with them. It is perhaps ironic that the mode which was seen as being the ideal for meeting all needs in the past is now seen as reducing satisfaction for users and non-users, as the population of car users increases. Indeed with more congestion and less freedom resulting from necessary traffic control measures, the level of satisfaction offered to users themselves is being reduced.

7.2. The five examples

We conclude this consideration of the constraints on the satisfaction of need with some remarks related to the needs of the individuals in the examples.

The urban handicapped

Meeting the needs of the urban handicapped will be dependent on the nature and the severity of their condition. It may be that further adaptations to a car may make driving possible, or that limited changes in the design of the public transport system will make it more accessible; greater attention to dropped kerbs and to the surfaces of pavements may make walking easier. If the handicap is more severe, special services or extensive changes to the fixed plant and rolling stock will be more appropriate solutions. Special services are likely to be the most practical solution for that part of the handicapped who cannot be helped to use the existing system. Where new systems are being built they should be constructed in a manner to maximise accessibility. The extent to which the needs of the handicapped are satisfied is primarily dependent upon the political constraints. The extent of commitment of the non-handicapped will determine the amount of public funds that are made available for these solutions. As the handicapped are relatively few in number, the satisfaction of their needs will not cause important external problems for other members of society, though they themselves may be constrained by the external effects of other people's travel.

The rural family

For the rural family living in the mountains, the best way to satisfy travel needs will be to own a car. This, too, is subject to economic constraints. The alternative is in most cases the provision of bus services, which in many places will require a subsidy. The importance of external constraints in this environment is likely to be negligible.

The suburban mother and children

An important element in the satisfaction of both the mother and her children, is the possibility for the children to move about safely on their own. For the fourteen year old this may be less of a problem than for the younger children. If the suburb is not designed for a complete segregation between pedestrians and cyclists on the one hand, and motorised traffic on the other, as is the case for most suburbs in Europe, then the mother is likely to restrict the movements of the younger children. The constraints on such provisions are economic, political and spatial. Also new towns are frequently criticised for the layout of cycle and foot paths which tend to increase the distance between two points, frequently with the roads being the shortest means of reaching the local shops.

If the economic constraints permit, then the provision of a car will partially solve the problem in terms of reducing the amount of time a mother must spend on escort duties. Increasing car use in suburban areas does, however, bring with it congestion and energy and pollution problems.

The industrial enterprise

In order to improve access to the industrial enterprise by the work force, additional public transport services may be necessary. If public resources are too limited as a result of economic or political constraints, then special work buses subsidised and organised by the employer himself may be an alternative. A further alternative would of course be to raise wages sufficiently, so that all employees can afford to drive to their place of employment. However, all pressures which increase the use of private cars for the journey to work have external effects. Increased congestion, pollution, noise and the use of space and energy would result from meeting this need in this way.

The inner-city retailer

Providing good access for inner-city shoppers requires good public transport facilities, an environment in which it is safe and easy to walk or cycle, and parking which is conveniently placed. Unfortunately economic, political and spatial constraints make it difficult to find really adequate solutions within the inner-city area. Compromise solutions frequently imply bus and pedestrian-only streets and, if the area is being redeveloped, it may be possible to reduce on-street parking and replace it with parking garages. Economic and political constraints are, however, frequently powerful in these circumstances, and the effects of the external factors increase with every additional car borne shopper.

8. ASSESSMENT IN SOCIETY

8.1. The setting of priorities

It is likely that in the light of more information about the needs of individuals and the priorities which they would attach to them, assessment of the needs of groups of people and organisations could be somewhat modified.

Existing inbuilt mechanisms for allocating priorities result in some needs being met and others not. While we may accept that all needs cannot be met, an issue of importance is the distribution of satisfaction over the population. If information about needs indicates that some people are being implicitly discriminated against, such that highly valued trips and activities cannot take place or only with the greatest difficulty, then we should examine more closely the mechanisms that are used to set priorities and consider how they may be adjusted.

8.2. A market policy

The normal working of a market economy implies that supply is determined by demand, i.e. when a sufficient number of people wish to purchase certain goods or services and are prepared to pay a price sufficient to cover their provision, then this will take place. Satisfying one's needs under these circumstances, implies that it is not enough for one individual to have a desire, there must also be others who have the same or similar needs. This is particularly relevant in transport, where services are not transferable from the space where they are produced and infrastructure also has a fixed location. Private transport has advantages over public transport in this respect, as the services are produced individually, while public transport needs a certain number of passengers in order to be remunerative. Those requiring special services will be less well off whether they are special in the sense of routing, timing or the equipment of the vehicles, because there are fewer of them which raises the cost per trip.

On the basis of a market economy many needs will remain unsatisfied and in particular those which deviate from a standard pattern. Private transport is much better adapted to meeting these non-standard needs than public transport. However, in some circumstances the slow modes will be impeded by facilities for motorised traffic, e.g. wide fast roads or roundabouts. A general conclusion is that people who cannot satisfy their needs with one of the private modes will be at a considerable disadvantage.

8.3. Steering policies - infrastructure

More than a century ago, many countries became involved in policies affecting the development of infrastructure: building nationwide road and rail networks. In some instances this was in places where demand did not materialise sufficiently in order to justify the extent of the investments. Over time this improved the position of most people with regard to the availability of routes; however, the quality of the services offered remained highly variable.

8.4. Steering policies - services

Later on policies began to be developed which had a direct influence on the services which were available. These policies particularly related to the provision of public transport services. They enabled public transport to be supplied in situations where it could not be provided on a remunerative basis. Sometimes the deficits were financed by cross subsidisation and sometimes by specific subsidy. This had considerable implications with regard to the extent to which needs could be met and had the potential to improve the ability of public transport to meet the needs of those who depended upon it. A service policy when properly applied can be directed towards particular needs in society provided that appropriate information is available to guide it.

8.5. Categories of need

As has been said in the introduction to this paper, investigating needs is a formidable task and the approaches which have been sketched here are still vague and as yet incompletely developed for application. However, we are not wholly without knowledge or imagination. The challenge is to try to work with incomplete information while developing the techniques for improving it. It is clear that people need to travel whether they live on a busy route or in a remote location and whether or not they own a car. When travel opportunities are poor for some and extensive for others, there are good reasons for assuming that needs are satisfied to different degrees.

Of importance in the discussion of priorities is the recognition that the amount of resources required to satisfy needs is highly variable. The satisfaction of some needs also helps in creating resources. This applies in the case of journeys made in the course of work and also to a certain extent to journeys to work. Satisfaction of these needs is beneficial to society as soon as the amount of resources generated or value added is higher than the amount of resources used. In such cases the mechanism applied for establishing priorities should guarantee that such needs are satisfied. When, in the case of the industrial enterprise, it is not possible to fill all vacancies, or if there is a high turnover of labour to the extent that production is inefficient, then a service policy should be introduced which will allow appropriate transport facilities to be created. This should happen even if the normal working of the market mechanism would not make this possible. Another example which is on the fringe of goods and passenger transport, is the rural family. If they were having such difficulty in reaching their market centre that it was endangering their livelihood, then it could be argued that their needs should receive extra priority.

It has already been suggested in the discussion of constraints, within the context of the reference group approach, that the type of constraints influencing people's relative satisfaction should be taken into account when considering priorities in meeting needs. For this reason special attention should be given to people in circumstances which are not a matter of free choice. The handicapped whose physical difficulties make it impossible for them to use public transport are one example but those with very low incomes could similarly be considered in this category.

At a more general level it should be possible to identify essential activities which are relevant to everyone, e.g. journeys to shops, schools and medical facilities. Journeys for social and recreational purposes are commonly thought to be less important but this may not be a realistic reflection of personal priorities if one considers that few would maintain that people can exist happily without social contacts or recreational opportunities. It is likely that their importance is far from negligible and indeed is likely to be growing in importance as leisure time itself increases.

The direct questioning approach to needs could be particularly valuable in helping to evaluate the significance and value placed on these activities by individuals. This information could be used in the further development of service policies, which should try to ensure that adequate support is given to such activities in terms of the locations and times of day at which they take place.

8.6. Demand-based assessment

As has been said, within the market mechanism, demand normally determines supply. However in transport, decisions are frequently made which do not reflect market pricing, e.g. the use of infrastructure is not normally charged for, as is done for other services. In the case of roads, usually these are provided free of charge, with special taxes on vehicles sometimes being considered as a counterpart. Thus investments in such infrastructure to provide enough capacity for future traffic are decided upon without application of the test of willingness to pay.

The comparison of financial revenue and cost in the market system can be developed into a comparison of social benefits and costs. If this extension is applied only to road infrastructure because, as has been explained, the normal price mechanism fails there, then this constitutes a bias in assessment which reinforces the advantage of private transport already inherent in the market mechanism.

In policy discussions the concept of potential demand is sometimes brought forward, that is demand that would materialise if an appropriate supply were available. In demand-based assessment, potential demand is only consi- dered in relation to specific changes in supply, e.g. new infrastructure or better services, but not as an overall measure of transport need.

Another aspect of evaluation based on demand is rela- ted to cost benefit calculations. Here demand for business travel is valued far higher than journeys for private purposes. This means that built into the assess- ment are values which give a low priority to journeys made by children, or older people who are no longer employed.

8.7. Need-based assessment

Earlier in this report it was said that need is rela- ted to people or organisations whereas demand is related to the market. Assessment based on satisfaction of needs should consider how far needs of individuals are met, and whether it is possible for each of them to meet the most urgent needs first. Infrastructure and service policies as sketched above are not based on information about the actual needs and implicitly rest upon the premise that needs are evenly spread over the population and that therefore supply should do the same. In doing so they disregard differences in need and constraints upon using certain sorts of vehicles.

A needs-based approach could be developed, to derive from a careful study of activity and travel patterns and people's desires, a type of supply of transport that would make it possible for most people to arrive at a reasonable level of satisfaction of their needs. A study of this sort has recently been undertaken in Germany(3). This resulted in the development of a minimum pattern of public transport services that would enable inhabitants of rural areas, without access to cars, to satisfy at least their most essential travel needs. The exact nature of the ser- vices would then be related to local conditions taking account of the geographical structure and size of popula- tion. For villages beyond a certain size conventional buses would provide the basic form of service; for

---

3. Heinze G.W., Herbst D. and Schühle U., Mindestbedienungsstandards für den OPNV ländlicher Räume, Akademie für Raumplanung, Hannover, forthcoming.

smaller villages or dispersed housing, demand-responsive services or taxis would be preferred.

It is possible that a policy directed towards the satisfaction of the most essential travel needs for all people (i.e. including the handicapped or those living in isolated locations) could still make use of the market mechanism as a decision-making tool for other needs. It would need to be extended to include the social costs of congestion or nuisance caused to non-users of the transport system. Excessive nuisance could be prevented by rules affecting the construction and use of vehicles and the construction of infrastructure itself, e.g. construction of a new road or rail link crossing a nature reserve would be prohibited entirely. Working with social costs would mean that any transport need that helps to create more resources than it uses will be satisfied and also those consumer needs for which one is prepared to pay the full economic cost.

8.8. The choices

All those responsible for framing transport policies are faced with difficult choices with regard to the priorities which are set. It may perhaps be helpful here to identify some of the questions which need to be asked and answered when considering the problem of needs in society.

1. Should needs be satisfied only if the individuals concerned are willing to pay the economic costs of doing so? Or should a fairer distribution of satisfaction be taken as a fundamental principle accepting that this implies subsidisation?
2. Should a minimum level of facilities be guaranteed irrespective of cost up to a certain cost level or not?
3. Should society allow freedom in the satisfaction of need, providing that people are willing to pay the full economic and social cost, or will limits be drawn on the basis of negative effects on others?

It is not the object of this paper to suggest answers to these questions, or to many others that might be put, but only to suggest in which ways transport needs might be taken account of in policy decisions, i.e. the policy makers' wish to care about people's needs. In that case, it is time to switch at least some of the efforts traditionally given to demand studies to the study of needs.

9. FUTURE TRENDS

9.1. How did we view the future?

Thoughts about the future in terms of what we hope for and expect to happen, if translated into policies, can affect what actually occurs. Sometimes, however, views are relatively quickly modified and so things turn out very differently from what was expected. It is perhaps instructive to briefly cast our minds back and consider the ways in which views have changed in recent years, before we look forward to what we now anticipate will occur.

If we try to recall how the future looked some 20 years ago, we may remember that its main characteristic was an increasing reliance on mechanisation and the potential of new technology. It was anticipated that the role of public transport would be mainly confined to long distances, e.g. using express trains and aeroplanes and, in the large urban areas, underground railways would replace trams and buses thus freeing the road space for cars. Technologies like magnetic levitation were expected to produce trains of far greater speed and this and other technological developments could be used for unmanned "people movers" where demand was too low for the higher capacity underground services. At its extreme this type of thinking led to a view of society in which the traditional modes, reliant on human energy, would be largely replaced. The private car and hightechnology public transport systems would meet the needs of the future.

The ideal was seen as being a situation in which people could get into their cars in their own garage, open the doors from the car, drive to the parking garage of an airport and board an aircraft without ever having to suffer the dangers of fresh air. Thus it was expected that transport needs would be satisfied in comfort if not at low cost. Other needs would of course be created by the new options open to people and by the changing organisation of human life which required more space and thus longer distances between activity locations. Little consideration was given at first to needs, including the newly created ones, that could not be catered for in this way. People without driving licences were completely overlooked and presumably would need to be driven everywhere or stay at home. Recently there has been a trend towards a more human concern for the sort of lives which people wish to lead in society. This is exemplified by the recent attention given to the existence of so-called minority groups or the "transport disadvantaged", as they are sometimes called. This is in contrast to the image of the average traveller frequently used in the considerations of decision makers, whether they be in public authorities or transport companies. This image is based on a majority who usually have a car available, no luggage or children to impede their progress, are fit and at ease in airports and railway stations. It is only comparatively recently that it has been argued that there is no such majority but that rather travellers are made up from many sorts of minority groups.

With regard to the needs of the minorities which were considered, sometimes solutions were found that could be relatively easily and cheaply implemented and in these cases helpful policies were adopted. More often the conclusions reached were that costly solutions were required in order to give substantive help and in these cases such needs remain inadequately met.

9.2. How does the future of the past look today?

Thanks to a considerable rise in incomes, the car fleet in most countries has expanded even more than was expected. The speed of travel has not, however, grown as anticipated especially in urban areas where considerable development of the road system could not keep up with rising levels of traffic.

Rising incomes have also of course had an important influence which can be seen for example in the increasing number and length of holiday journeys. This need has partly been met by car journeys but also by increases in air travel and, to a variable degree, by longdistance train and short-sea routes.

Thus demand for public transport also grew in some places although it fell considerably in others. Some countries succeeded in maintaining reasonable levels of public transport services and others have let services deteriorate and/or prices rise.

The general availability of cars has led to considerable growth in the amount of travel, demonstrating needs that were not previously considered. Some additional travel need has undoubtedly been created as a result of the changing location of activities which in many cases has raised them above walking or cycling distances.

Needs for travel have risen for everybody and many of these new needs will have been satisfied. Whether unsatisfied needs have risen is uncertain but we may assume that inequality in degrees of satisfaction has risen considerably, especially in those countries where public transport is now of low quality and/or high fares. The independence that cars have brought to many has reduced the safety and freedom of others.

We seem to have reached a point now, and this symposium is indicative of that, when more attention should be given to the needs of people in all their great diversity.

The majority good is no longer a sufficient standard and divergence from a standard pattern is to be expected rather than excluded. The traditional approaches still look at vehicles rather than the people in them and at financial rather than social values. When they do allow for variations in the utility of travel they are considered as "random errors" rather than being representative of real differences in values.

9.3. Speculations about today's future

Indications about future trends in transport needs are necessarily speculative. It is not possible to know what people will find important in the future, we can only project forward from what they think to be important today. Nevertheless, there is always a tendency for some people to be trend-setters for others and we shall try to find types of behaviour from which we can possibly generalise. However, transport needs also depend to an important extent on people's personal circumstances, i.e. age, household structure, geographical location, income and type of employment. Some information is available which suggests the way in which the structure of society is changing but the direction of change is always easier to predict than the speed or degree to which it will be significant. What can be said is that population growth in most European countries is diminishing and as a consequence the age structure is growing out of equilibrium so that we expect fewer children and a higher proportion of elderly people in our society.

Household structure is also changing and single or two adult households without children and single adult with children households are becoming more common. The ensuing changes in patterns of travel need are as yet poorly understood.

The density of housing is diminishing, not only through the smaller size of households, but also because of the growth in space occupied by dwellings. Also the scale of many activity centres, e.g. schools, shops and hospitals has grown as facilities become more centralised, which has an impact on travel distances. Other factors likely to influence needs are the increasing average level of education together with increases in leisure time, both of which we may assume will induce growth in travel needs which are likely to have even less of a standard pattern.

Meeting needs in the future will also to some extent be constrained. Certainly it will be impossible to provide enough road space for all cars, particularly in the cities. Financial constraints also show every sign of increasing in importance as the cost of both public transport and motorised private transport rise. This is likely to cause private households, business organisations and public authorities to be far more concerned about the way in which they use their resources for transport.

For private households it is likely that future car ownership will not grow as rapidly as has been the case in many countries. Indeed the ownership of a car need no longer be a stage that begins with a minimum age and income and ends only when driving is no longer possible. More and more people may own cars at some stage of their lives but may be without at some stages as well. This would mean that even if the car fleet is approximately constant, there will be flows into and out of the group of car owners that will compensate each other. It may well be that renting a car perhaps for weekend trips will become a more attractive option. Certainly more people who may once have been car owners may turn more to public transport and the non-motorised modes. It is important that the difference in the quality of travel offered in terms of the ability to meet needs by these alternative means should not be so low that they cannot be reasonably satisfactory alternatives.

Within the political framework of each country, decisions have to be reached about whether to satisfy the needs of those interest groups with the strongest financial backing or whether the goal should rather be, if not to equalise, then at least to give each individual user a fairer share of satisfaction. The former approach may concentrate resources on roads and well patronised public transport links, allowing services that are less well used to deteriorate or be priced so high that they are beyond the reach of many potential users. The latter idea would spread resources over more people concentrating on the provision of a minimum level of transport facilities everywhere and only allocating additional resources as the needs arise.

Both policies are not strictly speaking separate since elements of each can be combined. Priorities do, however, have to be set and this is the responsibility of political bodies; a symposium such as this can only show what issues are at stake.

10. CONCLUSION: TOWARDS RECOGNISING THE NEEDS OF ALL PEOPLE

The market mechanism should continue to play an important role as a regulator for the provision of transport services and infrastructure. This can both relate to the acquisition and use of private vehicles and public transport. There is no reason not to permit the market to satisfy needs providing the economic cost of doing so is borne by the users. In the transport literature and at

90

earlier meetings, much has been said about letting prices reflect economic costs, but much needs to be done in this respect.

The market strongly favours situations of high demand or (but preferably and) low cost. Many needs therefore are likely not to be satisfied when the market is left to work on its own, and this situation has been recognised by many national, regional and local authorities, and also by the Council of the European Communities, through Regulation No. 1191/69 which explicitly lays down that public transport services could be provided where the market did not justify this, in order to guarantee a "sufficient supply of transport facilities".

The broad approach of this paper has been to suggest that policies should be based on information about the needs of individual people or groups of people (households or organisations). The three approaches sketched are seen as ideas which have elements within them which could be potentially useful for deriving or inferring information about needs. It is suggested that for the future a highly differentiated level of information gathering will be required, but that this should lead to the development of policies which are better related to the needs of the individuals who make up society.

Looking towards future needs and the resources available to satisfy them, a number of subjects can be identified which require further attention and deeper investigaton:

- Consideration of the needs of people who are handicapped, live in isolated circumstances, or lack access to some transport modes.
- The investigation of minimum levels of provision related to essentially important activities for isolated areas, off-peak periods in suburban areas, etc.
- Special attention to the transport needs of children.
- Travel patterns and needs associated with particular household structures, e.g. the single parent family.

From this report it is clear that we are only at the beginning of assembling information about transport needs and their relative importance. Much needs to be done in this field, nevertheless, and policy makers should start to make use of both information and conceptual ideas which are available now. Work in many places is starting to yield new information but a combined effort of commitment and imagination is required in order to realise the objective of relating policies to the needs of individuals in society.

TOPIC 1B

ASSESSMENT OF
SOCIETY'S TRANSPORT NEEDS

GOODS TRANSPORT

Mr. N. HAIGH
Institute for European
Environmental Policy
Bonn, Paris, London

Mr. C. HAND
University of Reading
United Kingdom

1. INTRODUCTION AND SUMMARY

The argument of this paper can be stated quite simply and in a couple of sentences: that policies and long-term plans for goods' transport in Europe have, with relatively few exceptions, been based on the assumption that environmental constraints are peripheral or simply do not exist; that despite inadequate studies it can be shown that such constraints are already at work and having an effect; and that to ignore them (or pay lip service to them) will not only result in increasing damage to the environment but will result in the pursuit of transport policies and of more general economic policies which time will prove to have been misguided.

This paper is therefore not just an argument that it is desirable for environmental protection to be taken more seriously in the development of transport policies: it is an invitation to transport policy makers to examine their own self-interest and not allow themselves to be taken unawares.

Such an argument immediately raises questions about the nature of the new policies that are needed if the argument is correct. A broad objective and some tentative suggestions are made but it would be premature - as well as presumptuous - to begin to offer detailed solutions before there is general acceptance that there are indeed environmental constraints which cannot simply be overcome by technical means. Until there is acceptance of this argument, there will be little incentive to adopt any solution put forward unless by chance it operates in the immediate self-interest of the country doing so. Nevertheless some ideas are put forward for further studies which will help to establish the existence and nature of the environmental constraints and provide the raw material for formulating new policies.

The paper is structured around a triplet of questions concerning society's needs, questions which looked at in one way are simply different words with the same meaning but which looked at in another way can produce quite different answers:

- What do we need?
- What do we want?
- What can we have?

What do we need?

Transport has traditionally been regarded as a servant of the rest of the economy with the volume of goods' transport reflecting the level of economic activity. Tonne-kilometres of freight and Gross Domestic Product (GDP) have indeed been remarkably closely correlated in many countries for many years so that the question "what does society need in the way of goods' transport?" has been easily answered by reference to the level of economic activity. Forecasters have simply taken the officially anticipated levels of Gross Domestic Product (GDP) and have calculated the volume of goods' transport accordingly. When projected even a short period ahead, the volume of lorry traffic becomes very large. This is discussed in Chapter 2.

What do we want?

Does society want this volume of goods' traffic, especially when it goes by road? The answer provided by social surveys is clear - people do not like lorries because they are noisy, smelly, intrusive and frightening. The growth in the use of the heaviest lorries has become a matter for concern in several countries so much so that the United Kingdom Government in 1979 appointed an inquiry - the Armitage Inquiry - into the causes and consequences of the growth in the movement of freight by road. The report of the Inquiry in advocating an increase in permitted lorry weights did so not just because it saw economic benefits but also as a way of slowing the increase in vehicle-kilometres which it recognised as environmentally undesirable. Chapter 3 describes the environmental effects of lorries and Chapter 4 describes various measures to reduce them. The examples given are largely from the United Kingdom but show that the overall lorry problem must be getting worse as vehicle-kilometres increase.

What can we have?

Whether we need or want more goods' movement this third question introduces the energy constraint. Is a policy of reducing dependence on oil consistent with a policy of expanding goods' transport, especially oil consuming road transport? The oil argument reinforces the environmental argument that increasing vehicle-kilometres should be discouraged: that it should be an object of policy to stabilize or reduce the movement of freight by road and that the forecast increases should be regarded as a warning of something to be avoided rather than as something to be fulfilled.

2. THE GROWTH OF ROAD FREIGHT

2.1. The Dominance of the lorry

Transport history is full of examples of different modes being superseded by others - carts phased out by canals, canals yielding to rail, rail being complemented and dominated by road. We cannot be sure that alternatives to road transport will not emerge but, for the foreseeable future, it is road transport which predominantly meets the needs of Government, industry and consumers alike.

The environmental consequences are severe but it is important to be clear as to how roads managed to take the dominant share of all goods' movement. Knowing the factors behind this state of affairs is the first step towards influencing them in the name of some environmental or social goal.

The performance of a transport mode can be measured through various indicators such as total tonnage or tonne kilometres which gives due weight to the distance travelled by the goods and so provides a better indicator of environmental impact. While both can be used to indicate the importance of road transport to the economy, trends in goods lifted and tonne kilometres may not necessarily coincide. In fact, in Great Britain especially, it has been the case that tonnage lifted has fallen while tonne kilometres have continued to increase. Two separate explanations are required for these two phenomena. Though many of the reasons for the growth in tonnes lifted apply equally to tonne kilometres, they are still sufficiently different to be treated separately.

To begin with, the factors causing road transport to be the dominant mode as regards tonnes lifted will be sketched. From Table 1 below, it will be appreciated that the lorry plays an important role in many West European countries.

Table 1

TONNAGE BY MODE OF TRANSPORT 1978

Country	Road	Rail	Water	Pipeline	% of total
France	76	13	5	6	
W. Germany	78	11	8	3	
Italy	91	3	0.2	6	
U.K.	85	10	0.3	4.7	

Source: Armitage Inquiry, Table 12.

97

Italy and Great Britain stand out in the significance of road transport to their economies while France and West Germany put greater reliance on their inland water and rail systems. Part of the explanation lies in the greater distances between cities in France and Germany which favours rail since it is cheaper per unit cost over longer distances and is also less compromised by restrictions on drivers' hours. France and Germany also operate controls over the quantity of road freight.

Looking more closely at the British experience, there is an apparent paradox. As Table 2 shows, the tonnage of goods lifted by lorries has shown a slight decrease since 1968 but this has not adversely affected its share of the transport market which increased from 72 per cent to 83 per cent between 1953 and 1979, while rail saw its fortunes decline, reflected in an absolute and relative decrease in goods lifted.

Table 2

TONNAGE BY MODE OF TRANSPORT IN THE U.K. 1953-1979

	Million tons			% share	
	1953	1968	1979	1953	1979
Road	875	1680	1480	72	83
Rail	289	208	166	24	9

The important feature is the overwhelming dominance of road transport. Conventional wisdom suggests this is due to consumer demand which was interpreted by industry and resulted in them choosing road transport as best fitting requirements. In the past it was the railway which helped industrial dispersal with industries finding it advantageous to locate next to the railway in order to maximise throughput at their depots and to allow easy communication (Hamer 1978). These were the days when labour was cheap and manufacturers wielded more power than retailers (Department of the Environment 1973). Little care was taken over the presentation of the goods delivered which quite often arrived in tea chests. Delays were common and the standard of service low. Since then the retailer has required improvements in the quality of goods as regards their appearance, regularity and dependability of delivery time, all of which has meant an ever increasing role for the lorry to play. Industry has become more specialised. These specialist demands are not best met by the traditional rail system and it is the lorry which has proved itself more capable, being able to meet the need for new storage, handling techniques, delivery scheduling, bulk breaking, quality control and display systems which these new demands entail. In a competitive world, speed and reliability are valued and it is the lorry which is better able to guarantee delivery times.

In all this, it might be thought that the cost of transport plays a significant role in determining the modal split. Conventional wisdom does not subscribe to this view (Bayliss 1973). Though minimum transport costs may be a policy actively pursued by some firms, it is unlikely to be as rigorously applied as it might be, firms preferring instead to compromise this goal for the sake of the service advantages the lorry affords: reliability, flexibility and efficiency. The cost of transport has never been the chief explanation for distribution by road transport though it may be a factor in competition between modes over long hauls.

A further advantage of the lorry in terms of the quality of service it achieves is that it is not a monopoly industry and is sufficiently fragmented so that a shipper does not have to rely on any one haulier.

The railway also sometimes works to the benefit of road. Although not repeated in other West European countries where the maintenance of an extensive rail network has often been Government policy, something like 7,800 km of railway track were abandoned in 1963 in Great Britain (Fullerton 1974). Admittedly the lines which were closed were the least intensively used but this has still meant a loss of traffic. British Rail, apart from this, has pursued its own policies to break even which has meant concentrating on the bulk, long distance movement of materials such as oil, coal, building aggregates, iron ore and cement. Consequently the number of rail heads has declined from 6,114 in 1956 to 600 in 1970. Potential users of the railway suddenly found themselves abandoned and had no choice but to use the road system.

Factors of geography have also conspired to give the lorry the major share of the transport market. Railways are best served by a network of towns that are widely spaced apart because of the price, and speed, advantages it is able to offer on long hauls. So countries where the distance between cities is high have a greater proportion of their freight moved by rail. These conditions are met in the case of France and West Germany.

Macro changes in economic structure have also played a role in determining the modal split. As incomes rise relative to prices, proportionately more money is spent on luxury items and consumer durables rather than on food and clothing. Production of these more refined consumer goods consequently increases and it is these goods such as electrical equipment, computers and, to some extent, cars which have, until recently, shown the fastest rates of growth in the manufacturing sector. It is also these industries which have invariably chosen the lorry to meet their transport requirements. Being high value goods in relation to their weight, the need to minimise transport costs has never been overwhelming. For example, transport costs amount to only 1-2 per cent of the final cost of computer equipment. Since computers and electrical equipment are made of a great variety of components, many disparate freight movements are generated which are best handled by the flexible lorry, while the final delivery to retailer could not go any other way.

There are additional reasons why the lorry has acquired the lion's share in the goods' market. One of these revolves around the fact that heavy goods' vehicles do not pay their full track costs. In most European countries, the money to maintain and build roads has come from excise duty on fuel, tax on new vehicles and through the price of a new vehicle licence. Controversy has arisen, however, that the amount of damage inflicted by heavy goods' vehicles is not adequately reflected in the amount of tax they pay. Critics of the lorry are also concerned that the failure of Governments to charge lorry operators even a notional amount for the social and environmental costs they impose may have artificially boosted the incentives to use the lorry. Calculating these costs such as noise, vibration and accidents is notoriously difficult but many are of the opinion that any charge is better than no charge.

Another factor is that entry to the road haulage business has always been easy and the option of starting a road haulage firm is open to most people. The capital outlay is not excessive. One lorry will do and somewhere to keep it, which is not difficult since local authorities have often been lax in allowing lorry operating centres in environmentally unsuitable areas. The haulier is not required to make any significant outlay for the infrastructure he uses and there has never been any question of beneficial scale economies in the road haulage industry so that a firm with just one lorry can be as profitable as a large firm. This ease of entry into the road haulage business has no doubt contributed to the growing share of the freight market being held by the lorry.

These trends have also been literally fuelled by years of cheap and available energy. It is still true to say that the real cost of oil is no more than it was in the 1950s. Though increases in the price of oil since the 1973 crisis have been marked, this has still not been able to exercise restraint on the growth of road freight.

Government attitudes have equally played a significant role in promoting the growth of road freight. One need only refer to the policy of most West European countries to build motorways as being a spur to road freight. Similarly, the increase in the permitted dimensions of

100

lorries has played its part. Furthermore, the EEC's principle of free movement of goods by means of a customs'
union where all restrictions are removed is an obvious in-
citement for long distance freight movement. One has only
to quote the case of Great Britain whose trade with its
EEC partners has increased sharply - an increase from
2.7 million tons by RO-RO across the Channel in 1970 to
11.5 million by 1977 (Freight Transport Association 1979).

2.2. Travelling further?

It is difficult, when examining the environmental effects of lorries, to ignore the fact that the average
lorry today is heavier than yesterday. Figures for the
United Kingdom in Table 3 below show that while overall
the number of goods' vehicles over 1.5 tons has recently
fallen, the number of goods' vehicles above 8 tons has
grown something over 400 per cent over the last 15 years.

Table 3

GOODS' VEHICLES IN BRITAIN: BY UNLADEN WEIGHT 1950-1979
In thousands

Over	Not over	1950	1960	1970	1979
1.5 tons 3 tons 5 tons 8 tons	1.5 tons 3 tons 5 tons 8 tons	364 401 65 15 2	757 348 186 41 11	933 197 234 132 55	1153 167 142 114 121
All lorries over 1.5 tons		483	585	620	544
All goods' vehicles		847	1342	1552	1697

Source: Armitage Inquiry Table 1.

Not surprisingly, the growth in the heaviest goods'
vehicles consisting largely of articulated lorries with
four axles or more and vehicles with drawbar combinations
has meant that these vehicles have increased their share
of the road freight market. It is significant, for instance, that vehicles below 1.5 tons in Britain count for
60 per cent of the total goods' vehicle population but
only contribute 3 per cent of the total ton-mileage and
5 per cent of the total tonnage. Lorries heavier than
16 tons account for 90 per cent of the ton-mileage compared to 30 per cent in 1958. This in fact marks an absolute as well as a relative increase in the importance of
the work done by larger vehicles.

What is not in doubt is the fact that ton miles by
road has increased over the last few years (Table 4).

101

Table 4

TON MILEAGE IN THE U.K.: BY ROAD AND RAIL 1953-1979
Thousand million ton miles

	1953	1963	1973	1979
Road	19.7	35.1	55.3	64.0
Rail	22.8	15.4	15.7	12.2

Combining Tables 2 and 4 the picture then is one of lorries travelling further despite a fall in the tonnage of freight circulating in the road market. This actual decrease in tonnage is fairly recent but before that, there had been several years where the amount of freight lifted had been stable. Tonnage lifted is not apparently correlated with GDP. In 1922 the average lorry travelled 22 miles but by 1979 this had doubled to 43 miles, most of this increase occurring since 1963. Another feature of recent years has been for vehicle miles to rise but not by the same magnitude as ton miles. An explanation for this is that the growth in vehicle miles is largely due to the increased distance travelled by the largest lorries. All these figures point to the increasing importance of the heaviest goods' vehicles in terms of their numbers, the distances they travel, the share of the tonnage and ton mileage they account for. It is these that cause the most environmental disturbance.

Taking the analysis a few steps further, a case can be made that the increased size of lorries has in fact generated the increase in ton miles. Looked at like this, it is not surprising that the heaviest lorries have taken the lion's share of the rising ton-mileage market since they in fact initiated the rise in the first place. The reasons are less to do with the make-up of the road haulage industry and more to do with structural changes in the nature of industry and retailing. In a competitive world, industrialists and retailers are constantly seeking ways to minimise their costs. This desire may be precipitated by the presence of rival companies, putting a premium on innovation and cost minimisation, or it may be part of the "progress ethic" of the firm. For whatever reason, industry has seen it in its best interest to concentrate its production in particular areas and to make each of its factories a specialist in the production of particular goods. The result has been fewer, more geographically concentrated factories which often generate more freight movement, especially if the process of concentration takes the firm further away from its customers and suppliers. Freight movement may also be increased between the various plants of the same company as components and semi-finished items pass between the specialised factories. These trends are well documented in, for example, the car

102

industry and the brewing industry. From the transport cost point of view, this move by industry may seem fool-hardy. In many cases, the cost of transport has risen substantially. Viewed from the perspective of the total cost structure of the firm, this move has probably meant an overall decrease in the company's outlays. This is be-cause land and labour make up the biggest components of the firm's cost profile. Concentrating production means that land and labour can be released where the factories are closed while at the same time considerable scale eco-nomies can be reaped at the location where the industry is now concentrated. It may appear that transport has little to do with these changes but this is not so. Indeed, the option to concentrate in some cases may be solely due to the existence of larger lorries permitted by law and capa-ble of carrying heavier loads. Heavy lorries, though not offsetting completely the increased cost of transport these industrial location changes entail, do allow very economical rates over long distances. One may be able to carry in five 32 ton lorries what formerly would have needed eight or ten 24 ton lorries, thereby saving on fuel and labour. Time is also saved in loading and unloading as it takes longer to load eight 24 ton lorries than to load five 32 ton ones. The existence of heavier lorries and the benefits they yield have then to be very much taken into account in the location and marketing strate-gies of firms.

Retailers and distributors have not been slow either to realise the advantages afforded by heavier vehicles. Traditionally, in the past, distributors operated up to 50 depots to meet the needs of their consumers. Now the norm is 20 depots or fewer. Instead of servicing shops from depots close by, the trend is now for lorries to come fur-ther. The whole of the south of England may be served from one depot in London. The number of warehouses has thus fallen dramatically and, with it, the labour and land commitments of the organisations concerned yielding useful economies in much the same way as happened in the case of manufacturers. Bigger warehouses mean more economies of scale and more than offset the increased transport bill of running lorries over longer distances. Again this trend is partly due to having the option of using heavier lor-ries which minimise costs.

So it seems the heavy goods' vehicle has been very instrumental in generating an increase in ton mileage. But there are other independent reasons for the rise in ton miles. Some of these stem from the reasons given al-ready for the dominant position of the lorry in the freight market. Foremost among these perhaps has been the construction of high grade motorways which extend the dis-tances a driver can manage in a day without infringing the laws on driver's hours. Others include regional policies and the political creation of larger markets (EEC).

2.3. Forecasts

Forecasters, like prophets, have their critics and have often been wrong but the need for some sort of forecast is widely felt for future planning even though the forecast may turn out to say more about the assumptions of the forecaster than what will actually happen. The Annex lists those ECMT countries who replied to a questionnaire and said they had freight forecasts.

It seems to be a central principle of lorry forecasting that there is a link between GDP and tonne kilometres. The methodology used in Great Britain in 1974 (TRRL 1974) took assumptions about GDP to the year 2000 using high, medium and low growth hypotheses and translated them into forecasts of ton miles by means of a ratio which was empirically derived from trends in the past and in other West European countries. This led the forecasters to claim that ton miles in the future would increase in proportion to 2/3 the GDP. As the report claimed, this was to take account of the slow decrease of the ratio of ton miles to GDP which was occurring at the time and was expected to continue more strongly in the future. Reasons for supposing this revolved around the fact that there would be an increase in the proportion of services to GDP and services do not generate as much freight as industry. The report also suggested that environmental considerations or high energy prices might intervene.

Once the ton mile forecasts had been arrived at, this was somewhat arbitrarily divided up among the different modes, road naturally getting the biggest share. Then to estimate future vehicle miles, the number of ton miles was divided by the average carrying capacity of future lorries and then divided by load factor, the latter two measures being derived on the basis of past trends extrapolated into the future. From this, estimates of how much of the work will be done by lorries above 32 tons can be calculated and so forth. Recently the techniques used have become more sophisticated. GDP is disaggregated into seven commodity types and the output for each is calculated. Then a forecast is made of the ratio of tons carried to tons produced or consumed, known as the handling factor. The proportion that will be apportioned by the road sector is then estimated and then average distances each commodity is moved is forecast to give a value for ton miles. Using forecasts of the future composition of the goods' vehicle fleet and the quantity of work vehicles of different gross vehicle weights are likely to perform, the tonne mile forecasts are translated into heavy goods' vehicle traffic. Obviously some critical assumptions which border on inspired guesses have to be made. Even using this improved method, there is still the use of a ratio between the amount of goods produced and the amount of transport they require which is open to great variation. Experience has shown that these models are very sensitive to assumptions about economic growth. If the rate of economic growth differs marginally from that forecast, it can completely upset the predictions.

Of perhaps greater interest, however, is the picture of the future which these forecasts portray. Unlike forecasts of car use, there is no ceiling or "saturation level" for the lorry forecasts: they go up for as far ahead as anyone can see. Looking at the forecasts which were produced for the Armitage Inquiry, the picture is not a settling one. If small lorries are included, an overall increase of 7 per cent in lorry miles is forecast between 1978 and 2000 on a high growth hypothesis and a 4 per cent decrease on a low growth hypothesis. This looks acceptable enough but if one separates out the larger categories of lorry for closer scrutiny, the picture becomes rather different. Assuming that existing maximum lorry weights do not change, and based on the low growth hypothesis, a 53 per cent increase in lorry miles for vehicles above 25 tonnes is forecast between 1978 and 2000. The implications of this for the environment are considerable and if this looks bad enough, the high growth forecast is even worse: here a 71 per cent increase is anticipated.

If anyone thinks that a 53 per cent or 71 per cent increase in heavy lorry miles will not create unacceptable environmental problems, he should ask himself what increase will create them, because the forecasts only stop at the year 2000 for convenience: there is no suggestion as to when the trend finally stops.(1)

Similar results are likely to be found in the forecasts in other countries. The EEC Freight Forecasting Study 1979 also points to increasing journey lengths by assuming that freight movement between Member States will continue to grow faster than within individual countries. The EEC forecast suggests a threefold increase in international freight between 1974 and 2000, even on a low growth hypothesis, and this has been used by the Commission - COM(79)550 - to argue for an EEC infrastructure fund to overcome the "bottlenecks" standing in the way of the trend - a clear case of a forecast influencing a policy. The EEC forecast also makes no suggestions as to when the trend will stop.

However speculative these forecasts, they present scenarios of what might happen. Some might argue that this is what society wants and that these trends should be encouraged. In economic analysis, society's needs are couched in terms of consumption and prosperity. Lorries

_____

1. This has inspired a reductio ad absurdum. Extrapolating the official forecasts it emerges that by the year 2025 the whole population in Britain will have become lorry drivers (Adams 1981).

are the supposed servants of the economy and of the general public, the life blood which brings the things people value and need. Whether people do need goods beyond what is required for subsistence is a philosophical question and hard to answer. People will say they want these goods but whether they want them to come over longer distances and in bigger vehicles is a little easier to answer and the answer is almost certainly "No". The Armitage Inquiry established by the British Government in 1979 to consider the "causes and consequences of the growth in the movement of freight by road" put it like this (para. 138):

> "On the basis of existing policies it seems likely that lorries would have greater adverse effects on people and the environment over the next decade and probably up to the end of the century, principally because of the large increases expected in the mileage done by the heaviest lorries. There would be a particularly sharp deterioration (in environmental conditions) for certain people and certain places. We have already concluded that the present effects of lorries are unacceptable. The future prospect confirms our view that action must be taken to reduce the effects of lorries on people and the environment."

3. THE ENVIRONMENTAL EFFECTS OF LORRIES

3.1. Quantifying the "lorry problem"

Is there in fact a "lorry problem" - as it is sometimes referred to - or is it the invention of oversensitive environmental groups with no grasp of the importance of the lorry to the economy in the real world? Are their views shared by a sufficient number of the general public to warrant it becoming a political issue? And will this concern be a factor in influencing the forecast increase of road freight in the long term?

The difficulty of dealing with the lorry problem in theoretical fashion is that this is contrary to the nature of the lorry problem itself which is characterised by its direct impact on "flesh and blood" people and how they feel. Furthermore, the lorry problem is made up of a series of problems such as noise, vibration, fear and visual intrusion, all of which are related to the extent of lorry use, some of which are related to the size of the lorry while others vary according to the location and time where they are experienced. One of the most serious difficulties in assessing the effects produced by lorries is that they cannot be easily combined to yield a total

figure of lorry nuisance. Such a gross figure - which the
Armitage Inquiry hoped could be found - would allow comparisons to be made between places and would permit the
monitoring of the problem over time. The very disparate
nature of the nuisances caused by lorries however makes
quantification difficult. It would involve asking whether
10 accidents per annum could be calculated in the same
currency as 88 decibels (A) (L10) for 18 hours. Or
whether so much black smoke was of equivalent nuisance
value as 10 seconds delay to pedestrians trying to cross a
road blocked by parked lorries. Any final lorry nuisance
value is bound to be subjective.

Another difficulty in generalising about the lorry
problem is that it varies in time as well as space. A
residential area, for example, might be free of lorries
all day but attract overnight parking, which causes annoyance and loss of sleep in the morning when the lorries
start up. Where the lorry is perceived can also be important in assessing whether it is a nuisance or not. Lorries running on purpose-built roads on industrial estates
may not be so harshly viewed as lorries passing through an
unbypassed historic market town. Feelings and attachments
to a colourful High Street in an old historic centre may
be very strong and the slightest damage caused by a lorry
might excite adverse comment. In areas where the environment is valued less and people have lower expectations,
lorry nuisance is not ranked so highly.

Social surveys, therefore, have limitations because a
problem intensely felt by a few people through their sen-
ses will not be easily comparable with problems intellectually understood. A recent survey of public opinion in
Britain (Marplan 1980) for example showed that 26 per cent
of the population surveyed saw lorry traffic as a serious
problem. As can be seen from Table 5, this did not rank
as highly in their minds as problems of violence and drug
addiction, but it is difficult to know what inference to
draw from this.

Table 5

THE NUMBER OF PEOPLE CONSIDERING CONTEMPORARY ISSUES TO
BE "VERY SERIOUS"

Problem	% of people calling it "very serious"
Violence/vandals	76
Drug addiction	45
Road congestion	39
Road accidents	39
Alcoholism	38
Air pollution	26
Lorry traffic	26
Noise	21

When asked how much the lorry contributes to noise, air pollution and road accidents, the following results were obtained. These suggest that, while people do recognise the importance of the lorry in the movement of goods, people still consider the lorry as a major contributor to these problems (Table 6).

All of these difficulties render the overall quantification of the lorry problem awkward if not impossible. Lack of a suitable measurement technique or lack of a consensus among the general public has not precluded efforts to curb the nuisance caused by lorries. The Heavy Commercial Vehicles (Controls and Regulations) Act 1973 in Britain, giving powers to local authorities to reduce local lorry restrictions, was precipitated by the increased public awareness of the lorry problem. So also has been the difficulty experienced by the British Government in increasing lorry weights. It would seem then that politically speaking, sufficient people are concerned to warrant policies and Government action.

Table 6

THE NUMBER OF PEOPLE WHO CONSIDER THAT THE LORRY PLAYS
A MAJOR ROLE IN PRODUCING SOCIAL ILLS AND BENEFITS

Effect	% of people who consider the lorry plays an important role
Efficient goods distribution	83
Bad road surfaces	80
Availability of a variety of goods	77
Noise	68
Air pollution	62
Employment	61
Road accidents	44

3.2. Noise

While it is difficult physically to measure sound because of its different frequencies, it is even more difficult to correlate this with some measurement of annoyance. Annoyance is a form of mild anger (Weinstein 1976) and anger has no known or universally accepted unit of measurement. Any assessment of annoyance must consequently be subjective by means perhaps of an attitude scale. For example, "0" might mean "not annoyed in the slightest" while "5" might signify "highly annoyed". Whatever the scaling system used, it is bound to be fraught with problems. People may vary in how they interpret their feelings and may give them different names. Much of the difficulty also stems from the fact that it is an awkward task putting one's feelings into words (Lowenthal 1971). Thus it is no easy job to correlate sound measured in no-nonsense decibels with more "soft" data of an attitude survey. Perhaps more important, however, it is impossible to find a level above which "sound" becomes "noise", i.e. unwanted, and therefore annoying. Thresholds of noise tolerance vary considerably among individuals and also within the same individual. Sound experienced when one is in a particular emotional state or in a different place or at a different time may or may not be noise. No magical figure exists. One cannot simply claim that 70 or 75 or 80 decibels is the right level to choose. Indeed, it has even emerged that overall annoyance may be lower where noise is objectively higher. Clifford Sharp cites a case where people living on a road with an average noise intensity of 75dB(A) were less dissatisfied than people living on a road with 61dB(A) on average. One could argue that it is the peaky nature of noise that causes annoyance. Two lorries per day on a quiet road may cause as much nuisance as a hundred lorries per hour on a busy road since lorries on quieter roads cause more peaks in the overall noise level. In recognition of this tendency, researchers commonly use the L10 method to measure annoyance. This is the noise level exceeded for 10 per cent of the time and although not perfect, it has been found to correlate well with annoyance (TRRL 1973).

It is not contested that individual lorries make more noise than individual cars. Heavy goods vehicles make between 88 and 92 decibels of noise, light goods vehicles between 79 and 81dB(A). Since lorries are individually more noisy than cars, it follows that a flow of traffic with a high proportion of lorries in it percentage-wise will produce more noise than a traffic flow consisting merely of cars but the effect will depend on whether the traffic is free flowing or not. According to the Department of the Environment in Britain, lorries are nine decibels noisier than cars in free flow situations but 17 decibels noisier when the traffic is congested. This reflects the greater noise lorries make when they accelerate from a stationary position. Cars, on the other hand, make more noise at higher speeds than when they accelerate. It follows then that roads with traffic lights and other impediments to the traffic flow will encourage more lorry noise than other straighter roads. Gradients also make lorries work harder and produce more noise. A lorry travelling at 30 miles per hour makes nine decibels more noise when on a 1 in 20 gradient. Lorries, therefore, serve to increase total traffic noise, though the actual contribution varies according to the physical nature of the road and the traffic flow. Diminishing marginal returns apply to these rules of thumb, however. The Greater London Council (1979) suggest:

"In narrow streets with low traffic flows - between 100 and 200 vehicles per hour - a relatively small increase in the number of lorries would lead to an appreciable deterioration of their reasonably quiet and pleasant environment... In streets with heavy traffic flows - between 2,000 and 3,000 vehicles per hour - a truly large increase in the number of lorries would be needed to further erode the poor environmental conditions prevailing there due to the high levels of noise, air pollution..."

Much empirical work has been done to examine the nature of lorry noise in typical working conditions. The Transport and Road Research Laboratory (TRRL) in Britain have done a number of surveys of lorry noise in towns (TRRL 1973a and 1973b). In their report on Newbury, a small town in the south east of England, the following results emerged to corroborate the points made above (TRRL 1973b). Of the 5,000 vehicles that were measured, 24 achieved peaks of 85dB(A) of which 12 were medium or heavy goods vehicles. Looking at the percentage of each class of vehicle that reached 80dB(A), it transpires that 0.44 per cent of cars and light goods vehicles, 24.6 per cent of buses but 71.4 per cent of heavy goods' vehicles reached this level. Thus it is particularly the lorries which cause the peaks in the noise profile and since people are often more annoyed by the "peaky" nature of noise, it would not be surprising if people were more prone to blame the lorry as opposed to the car for noise nuisance.

Moving away from the minutiae of noise measurement in specific situations it is pertinent to make the point that objective noise measurement may not be as important as subjective impressions. If sufficient people speak out against lorries to local councillors and to national and international politicians, the question of noise can become a political issue. So even if no precise agreement can be reached on what noise levels are tolerable, the fact that some people are complaining and lobbying politicians is reason enough for action.

The most direct expressions of annoyance are the findings of attitude surveys. One of the largest of these is the work of the Social and Community Planning Research carried out in the United Kingdom in 1972 but not published until 1978. This was a national survey and revealed that 9 per cent of the total population was "quite a bit" or "very much" annoyed by traffic noise. Unfortunately, this does not indicate to what extent it is the lorry which is the malefactor. One can only assume the lorry plays no small part in stimulating this 9 per cent of the population to speak out against noise. Examining more local studies, however, reveals a different response from the national figure.

Among the most readily available of these have been three studies undertaken by the TRRL in Britain (TRRL 1973a, 1973b, 1978). To take Ludlow as an example (TRRL 1978), this is a small "typical", English market town which at the time of the survey had no by-pass despite being a route focus, although one has now been built. All traffic had to pass the centre of the town. The result is a much greater dissatisfaction with noise than was recorded nationally. As Table 7 below shows, most groups of people in Ludlow High Street were affected and annoyed by noise as well as other traffic problems.

Table 7

THE OPINION OF PEOPLE IN LUDLOW HIGH STREET AS REGARDS TRAFFIC PROBLEMS

	Pedestrians	Shop Workers	Office Workers	Residents
Noise	17	60	46	52
Vibration	6	20	23	21
Danger	68	20	0	10
Dirt/dust	3	15	9	9
Smoke & fumes	8	5	0	11
Visual appearance	1	0	0	1

Source: Table 4, TRRL 1978.

With regard to other traffic problems, noise was the most frequently mentioned by three of the four groups, ranking above danger or fumes. While many people thought that traffic in general contributed most to other problems, noise was attributed to the lorry alone.

Further light is shed by two other surveys, one relating to Putney in London (TRRL 1973a) and a second report which documents conditions in Newbury and Camberley, two towns in the south east of England. Here it was found that many residents found traffic noise in the house a nuisance, especially when it stopped people going to sleep, woke them up or interfered with listening to records or the radio. People were more apt to blame lorries for their inconveniences although, in Camberley, motor cycles and cars were appraised as more bothersome.

What emerges from these studies then is that many people, whether pedestrians, residents or workers, find noise a nuisance in shopping streets and that, more often than not, it is the lorry which is seen to be most at fault. Such local hotbeds of feeling may be watered down at the national level but they can be very live local

issues. Although the political response to such feelings
has been remarkably weak, it has resulted in some Government research to quieten lorries (see Chapter 4).

3.3. Vibration

Houses and people shake as heavy traffic rumbles past
outside their front doors. Despite the plausible relationship between vibration and structural damage, there is
as yet no empirical evidence of how or if traffic induced
vibration does promote the failure of building materials
although it is clear that people do not like vibration.
On the question of vibration, the discussion must proceed
with caution.

There is little doubt, however, what the causes of
vibration are. Firstly, there is ground borne vibration.
This occurs when there are irregularities in the road surface and wheels bump over them. Secondly, there is air-
borne vibration. This consists of low frequency "noise"
emanating from the engine and exhaust system. These sound
waves are especially associated with lorries working under
heavy loads. Low frequency noise is more difficult to in-
sulate against than higher frequencies so vibrations are
frequently very noticeable inside buildings which may indeed amplify them. Larger engined lorries produce more
vibration than smaller ones and it has been these larger
lorries that have increased in number over the last 10
years.

If one can talk with confidence about the causes of
vibration, this is not so with its effects which can also
be divided into two: effects on people and effects on
buildings. Taking people first, it is considered that
vibration of 2.5mm/s is sufficient to annoy people. This
is the level when people's sensory organs are able to de-
tect the vibration caused and to respond to it. What
little evidence there is suggests that air-borne vibration
may be more annoying to people than ground-borne vibration. This is because ground-borne vibration is generally
of a lower frequency. It has also been posited that
vibration experienced by the body is more annoying to
people than the vibration of buildings. Nevertheless, as
everyday experience of traffic, rattling windows and shak-
ing ornaments on mantlepieces give rise to considerable
irritation for residents on main roads. Whether all these
effects are damaging to physical health or man's sense of
well-being is not known. It is still reasonable to say
that vibration does nothing to enhance life on a main road.

There is uncertainty about the effects of vibration
on structures. It is admitted that vibration may cause
cracks in the plaster but how vibration might affect the
fatigue of building materials is simply not known, nor is
it known to what extent structural damage is done. It is

thought, however, that ground-borne vibration is more important than air-borne vibration in this context. What little research has been done on this subject was reviewed by the Civic Trust (Civic Trust 1979). It is clear that architects responsible for the maintenance of historic buildings believe that traffic vibration speeds their decay.

Whatever the scientific ignorance as to the effects of vibration, opinions are often more clear cut among members of the general public. In a recent survey undertaken by one of the authors in Barnstaple, North Devon, the question of vibration prompted some very hostile reactions. People pointed to cracks in ceilings, porches and retaining walls, attributing the blame uncompromisingly to traffic and more specifically lorries. Housewives described how ornaments in china cabinets or on mantlepieces take on lives of their own, move, making it necessary to move them back into their old position in the morning. On a national scale in Britain, surveys indicate that slightly fewer people are disturbed by traffic vibration than by noise but that more people, 8 per cent, view vibration as a "very serious" problem (Social and Community Planning Research 1978). Again, as with noise it is the local effect and reaction that is the most revealing.

It transpires from the TRRL studies alluded to earlier that vibration is a source of considerable annoyance to people working in shops or offices or living on the main road. In Ludlow, for example, when respondents were asked specifically about vibration, 50 per cent of shop workers, 31 per cent of office workers and 33 per cent of residents were "very much bothered". The findings are replicated elsewhere. In Putney, 59 per cent of residents said that traffic frequently made the house vibrate. Fewer than 20 per cent, however, were able to cite particular instances where vibration had caused cracks in walls and ceilings or made ornaments fall off mantlepieces. In Barnstaple, vibration was the most frequently mentioned problem people experienced in the home from traffic. It was also the effect most likely to generate anti-lorry feeling since most sufferers blamed the lorry for their inconvenience. Much of the hostile feeling may revolve around the extra perceived cost and effort of repairing cracked walls and ceilings. For some this might mean a decline in the real value of the house. For others, it might mean a decline in the subjective value of the house, depressing the value perhaps below the level of expected or desired utility. Sometimes it might prompt people to move house. Homes are worth more than money to their occupants. They represent repositories of fond and bitter memories of the past. They remind the occupier of who he is and give him a lasting sense of security and identity. Longer standing residents may even feel that the house is part of themselves, a mirror image of their character and reinforcing their sense of worth and well-being.

113

Vibration and traffic nuisance threatens this peace and stability. To damage a house is to "damage" its occupant psychologically. The sense of well-being the home provides should not be underplayed nor should anyone try to underplay the damaging effect lorries may have.

The picture regarding vibration then is disturbing on four counts. Firstly, it is worrying that so little is known about the effects of vibration. Secondly, it is disturbing that so little research is planned into the question of vibration. Thirdly, it is disturbing that the main cause of vibration, the heavy goods' vehicle, is likely to increase in its damaging effect as more axle weights approach the maximum weight and as lorries undertake longer journeys. Fourthly, it is a worrying feature that little is known as to the ways vibration may harm people. If the home is as important as literature suggests it is, then the cost of vibration may be as much psychological as economic.

3.4. Accidents

The effect of noise and vibration on human health may not be clear cut. With road accidents there is no excuse for ignorance. Accident victims are the most disadvantaged group of all, the people who experience the environmental disbenefits of the lorry at its worst. If life is something to be held precious, then there is no room for complacency on the question of road safety and accidents. If anywhere it is here that questions of economics should be buried and a more human face shown.

Each year 6,000 people are killed on the roads in Britain. This represents the largest single cause of accidental death and is especially preoccupying due to its toll on young lives. Hard economics fail to capture the amount of grief and suffering this causes. Lorries have played a big part in this. Of the 349,795 accidents on United Kingdom roads in 1978 6.7 per cent involved lorries (Armitage 1980). Expressed in terms of the number of accidents per hundred million vehicle miles travelled, lorries were involved in 134 while other motor vehicles caused 256. This seems to suggest that lorries are safer than cars. What is more, the individual rate for lorries fell by 43 per cent between 1970 and 1978 while other vehicles only recorded a 19 per cent decline. Lorries are tending then to become safer over the years, but it would be fairer to present the figures in terms of accident per tonne lifted rather than by distance travelled.

For fatal accidents, the lorry has a less distinguished record. When lorries are involved in accidents with pedestrians or motorists, the result is very often a fatal one. To take the example of the pedestrian, 1 in 10 of pedestrian accidents are fatal when it involves a car.

114

The odds narrow to 1 in 5 when a lorry is involved. Similar considerations apply to cars when in collision with other cars as opposed to lorries. As a whole, 15.6 per cent of the 6,831 fatal road accidents on British roads in 1978 involved a lorry.

One group most at risk from lorry accidents, yet standing to gain least from any safety improvements, are pedestrians. While the use of better brakes, underrunners and energy absorbing guards might reduce the severity of accidents to car occupants, they are less likely to help pedestrians. As the Armitage Inquiry (para. 282) observes on the subject of improved brakes:

"... No doubt there are also some accidents between lorries and other road users, such as pedestrians and cyclists, in which better brakes would be of assistance. But often the lorry driver does not see the pedestrian or the cyclist until too late, as in the case where the cyclist is alongside the lorry. For these road users, a collision with a lorry travelling at any speed, however slow, is likely to be very serious. So, while better brakes will help road safety, the improvement is likely to be limited".

So far, the argument has dwelt on people directly affected by accidents. While it is true that most people do not directly experience a road accident, it is also true that the majority is aware of the problem of road accidents and their effects. Everyone knows there is a probability of them being involved in an accident. The social surveys already referred to bear this out. In Camberley, for example, pedestrians ranked "danger crossing the road" as the most bothersome aspect of the High Street (TRRL 1973b). In Newbury, it ranked third, while in Putney it came fourth (TRRL 1973b, 1973a). The blame is not attributed solely to the lorry. Pedestrians tend to blame all vehicles equally but the point still remains that people are very aware of the dangers of lorries.

Environment is very important in making people notice the dangers of traffic. As with noise, it is the narrow, often historic and usually interesting places which are the most dangerous. Narrow roads and pavements mean that lorries frequently have to mount the pavement in order to let other vehicles pass. There can be few more frightening aspects of everyday life than a big lorry lurching over the pavement and casting a pall of gloom, smoke and noise over any pedestrian who happens to be passing by. The experience is distinctly unpleasant. Sometimes it can be fatal. There are tales of pedestrians being crushed by lorries. Such accidents focus the attention of the local population on the lorry problem and can arouse very strong local opposition.

Lorries, though they may not be objectively as dangerous as cars in terms of the number of accidents caused, look more dangerous to pedestrians. Fear is often the result of these encounters between man and lorry. This is particularly so for elderly people who are not so mobile as they used to be and may be anxious about crossing a road where there is a high proportion of heavy vehicles. Mothers with young children may be similarly worried about the damaging potential of heavy lorries. So even if people are not directly involved in lorry accidents, they are still aware of the risks. And most people know that railways are very much safer: for every one death caused by railways in the European Community, 1,292 occurred on the roads.

3.5. Air pollution

Lorries are often thought to contribute excessively to levels of air pollution. This is particularly so in urban areas where the effects of lorries are generally more noticeable. A heavy lorry emitting plumes of black smoke is obviously degrading the environment but looks can be deceiving because, while lorry emissions may be more noticeable, visibility does not correlate with toxicity and a stronger case can be made out against car exhausts. Though less visible, car exhausts contain far more carbon monoxide and hydrocarbons than do the diesel engines of lorries while car emissions of nitrogen oxide and aldehyde are also significantly higher. Of course, no pollution is "good" pollution but it is definitely true to say that lorries are not as harmful as cars in this respect. One factor is that diesel engines produce no lead.

In the Armitage Inquiry, it was suggested there were three types of smoke. White smoke is the first type and occurs during start-up and warm-up, consisting of unburnt and partially burnt fuel particles, though it does tend to disappear as the engine gets warmer. Its effects are unpleasant as it is odourous and lachcrymatory. Secondly, there is blue smoke produced by high-mileage worn engines and due to unburnt lubricating oil. Lastly and more seriously, there is black smoke which is the most visible, smelly and objectionable type. It consists of particles of carbon as a result of incomplete fuel combustion brought about perhaps by a faulty or worn engine. As such, lorries emit four times the quantity of particulates as cars do and these are three times as black as an average urban particulate of a given weight. In London, lorries are particularly significant in generating smoke and of the 34 per cent of the smoke attributable to motor vehicles, 80 per cent comes from lorries (Department of the Environment 1980). Lorries are thus high smoke generators and must be held responsible for much of the staining and soiling that occurs to buildings in cities.

116

One of the problems with controlling smoke is that it is difficult objectively to measure it. Objectivity is often a guarantee that something will be given attention. If precise numbers cannot be attached nor simple cause-and-effect mechanisms discovered, the factor is less likely to be accorded the importance it may deserve. This deficiency was recognised in the Armitage Inquiry, where it was recommended that legal standards for smoke emission should be established, the forerunner to this being the setting up of an objective method to measure smoke.

While measuring the concentration of smoke may yet prove possible, measuring odour, however, may prove more difficult. Social surveys bear out the point that people do not like lorry fumes. In Ludlow (TRRL 1978a) for example, 25 per cent of shopworkers in the main street were "quite a lot" or "very much bothered" by traffic fumes and smoke, the lorry being singled out as particularly annoying in this respect. On average, people in the other towns expressed similar annoyance. The survey undertaken by one of the authors in Barnstaple confirms this. Indeed, dissatisfaction with fumes was the single most important characteristic of the lorry that people objected to. The sense of smell, it seems, is more easily offended than either eye or ear.

3.6. Visual intrusion

The road haulage industry is, by its nature, a highly visible industry. It is sometimes described as a heavy engineering industry carried on outside people's homes without their consent. Heavy lorries can present unattractive sights as they pass along narrow country lanes or thread their way through historic urban streets. They seem out of scale with the surrounding buildings, a modern human artifact clashing intrusively with the timeless artifacts of the past. Or the problem may lie in residential areas where parked lorries impinge on the pleasant environment of a housing estate and detract from its amenity. These occasions may be intensely local but they nevertheless conjure up anti-lorry feeling.

Much of the difficulty in generalising about visual intrusion stems from its subjective nature. Visual intrusion is connected with matters of aesthetics and these are notoriously difficult to categorise or make judgements about. It has been suggested that more of a consensus can be reached by approaching the question of aesthetics from a different angle. Instead of asking what people find beautiful, it is more fruitful to ask what people find ugly (Kates 1966). People and cultures are more entrenched in their opinions of what constitutes a bad view and it is reasonable to suppose that lorries fall into this category today. Subjective as visual intrusion may be, there can be few who would not wish to see the disappearance of lorries from their environment.

If one relies on people's judgements and opinions expressed in social surveys to prove the importance of visual intrusion, then one will be disappointed. No social surveys hitherto published have revealed that visual intrusion is a significant factor of people's annoyance or that it is a major problem associated with lorries. Pedestrians and residents alike are very low-key when asked whether they find traffic or lorries unsightly. This may be due to the fact that some do not adequately understand the term "visual intrusion" or that other factors such as noise and fumes may be a proxy for it. Indeed if one asks whether people would prefer to see the road without lorries, the answer is invariably in the affirmative and often accompanied by some comment as to the self-evidence of this. Even if these answers are a little ambiguous to interpret, there are still many who are sensitive to the aesthetic quality of their town and are concerned about the presence of heavy lorries. For them the lorry is an unwelcome intruder in an otherwise pleasant environment and the sooner it is removed, the better. Whereas there may be technical solutions to noise and perhaps vibration, there is no way that the bulk of a large lorry can be conjured away.

3.7. Damage to buildings

Lorries by virtue of their weight, speed and size often damage buildings and structures but unfortunately there are no aggregate statistics on the amount of such damage. Many incidents go unreported or happen so frequently that home-owners become phlegmatic or apathetic and accept them as part of life on a busy road without lodging any complaint. The evidence shows, however, that these instances of damage are quite numerous and can be serious.

Lorries have a particular propensity to damage parts of buildings which protrude. This means that porches and balconies are especially vulnerable (Civic Trust 1969). Goods' vehicles also tend to damage the corners of buildings if these happen to be close to the road and are prominent. Then there are buildings which do not possess any particularly vulnerable feature but which are on a dangerous piece of road. Thus houses on sharp bends or hills may incur excessive damage from vehicles whose brakes fail or which lose manoeuvrability when trying to take corners too fast. Lorries with brake defects or sleeping drivers have been known to career into the fronts of buildings on gradients. The damage can be very extensive and very expensive to repair. Whole facades may have to be rebuilt and costly restoration work undertaken. No data is available to indicate the costs of these repairs to house-owners and insurance companies but they cannot be negligible. Other damage which is caused is often smaller in nature but may be a persistent problem of, for example, a lorry continually scraping a wall. Very often, the owner of the building will lose any urge to maintain the house since any efforts are swiftly nullified. This is more serious when it happens to buildings of historic or architectural interest as no amount of money can recreate exactly the original fabric. Such occurrences are also more likely to arouse anti-lorry sentiment among local people.

Coupled to the actual damage sustained to a building, there is the matter of the resident's peace of mind. If a lorry crashes into someone's living room, it tends to stick in the memory and become a niggling source of worry that it could happen again with more serious consequences for life and limb. Nothing is more likely to convert somebody from a passive stance towards lorries to an openly hostile one than if that person has had first hand experience of the damaging power of lorries. It is also a poignant experience for anyone living next-door to think that it could happen to them and also to know somebody to whom this has happened. Vague dangers and threats always take on a more real guise if they have befallen close friends or neighbours.

Concern is not only voiced at the damage caused by heavy goods' vehicles to private property. Public buildings and landmarks are equally at risk. Very often, these public-owned artifacts are as jealously protected as an individual's property and if any lorry should chance to damage one of these, an outcry can be substantial. Narrow historic bridges are especially vulnerable. Parapet walls are frequently disturbed and there are instances where masonry dislodged by lorries has fallen onto a main railway line and held up services. As well as the problems of falling masonry, there are also problems of lorries trying to use bridges of insufficient head-clearance. Again, if the bridge carries a railway line, there is the possibility of a serious accident (British Rail 1979).

Besides bridges, lorries have also shown slight respect for walls, scaffolding and trees. Though these instances appear trivial from a distance, they can be very important to local people attached to their local environment. So too the destruction caused to paving stones and grass verges can cause consternation to local amenity groups. It is difficult to keep towns and villages with attractive amenities when there is constant erosion of them by lorries. Every group could point to examples in their area which have spoilt some of the enjoyment of living in a town and undermine civic pride. No easy remedy exists to this problem: remedial measures such as the erection of crash barriers and warning signs can be as disfiguring as the damage they are trying to prevent.

3.8. Delay and frustration

It is one of the central theories of psychology that all behaviour is goal-directed and that if this behaviour is frustrated, the individual experiences annoyance or some other subconscious form of disturbance. Obviously, the degree of annoyance varies with the importance of the goal at a particular time. Some goals allow latitude in the time they can be fulfilled if the individual is in no hurry. If, however, the individual is pressed for time, any minor threat to the fulfilment of the goal will generate annoyance. The commuter who is late for his train and gets caught in a traffic jam serves as a good example. People doing their shopping in the High Street are also subject to inconveniences which can frustrate them, not least of which is the amount of traffic on the road or the number of vehicles parked at the kerb. In this lorries are often no worse than cars or buses but people may perceive them as contributing unduly to the delays as they move around on foot.

This delay and frustration caused by lorries is exemplified by the importance people attach to it in the various social surveys. In the study of Barnstaple, "difficulty in crossing the road" emerged as the second most frequent criticism of the lorry, a problem specifically mentioned including the discourteous behaviour of some lorry drivers. Much of the difficulty may be more imagined than real. "Causing an obstruction" was another effect people in Barnstaple noticed, this reflecting the problem of parked lorries, especially articulated ones, outside supermarkets and furniture shops. These lorries parked at the kerb make it difficult and dangerous for pedestrians to cross the road. They also restrict freedom of movement on the pavement, an affect compounded in situations where pavements are narrower since pedestrians are unable to step into the road to allow others to pass. These features, so much part of walking along a busy street may seem trivial but can nevertheless build an impression in people's minds about lorries.

Lorries are also blamed by motorists for causing them delays. Parked lorries for example cause delay to other road users. A survey undertaken in Paris in 1971 (Roudier 1976) revealed that 23 per cent of lorries were double-parked and though they were not long in making their deliveries, this can mean significant time losses for other road users. Indeed, a lorry parked for 2.5 minutes can produce a total 20 to 30 minutes' delay for other road users if it is a single lane road with 0.08-0.15 vehicles per second. Obviously the length of time parked is an important variable and it is also significant to remember that the larger more obstructive lorries often stay longer, especially at larger shops such as supermarkets and furniture shops.

3.9. Miscellaneous social costs

To bring this consideration of lorry problems to a close, one can briefly cite a few more social costs of having large vehicles in close proximity to the places where people work, live and walk. One characteristic touched on earlier is the power the lorry has to instill fear in people. This was brought up in relation to accidents and visual intrusion but it is also worthy of consideration as something existing in its own right. A nationally conducted social survey found that fear of traffic was a feeling subscribed to by 30 per cent of the people asked (Social and Community Planning Research 1978). Though this refers to all traffic in general lorries undoubtedly contribute proportionately more than their numbers, especially as they carry dangerous loads and look more threatening.

Under this catch-all umbrella of miscellaneous social costs, one can also note that lorries cause blight to areas. These are typically inner city, arterial roads which have a run-down, decaying aspect. Nobody is willing to invest in the area or improve the quality of the environment so that buildings look unkempt, poorly maintained and dirty. Obviously, the presence of heavy traffic may not be the main cause of the dilapidated appearance of these areas but neither is it a beneficial effect.

Lorries can also depress the quality and appearance of buildings when in wet weather the tyres throw up water and dirt. Residents frequently complain about this, especially housewives who have the thankless task of keeping windows, doorsteps and paintwork clean.

Busy roads act to sever communities. The psychological barrier with few points to cross can disrupt the establishment of friendship patterns with people on the other side of the road. This can circumscribe the range of movement and area of play opportunities to young children as parents may forbid them crossing the road for reasons of safety. Similarly, elderly people may suffer unduly as they are unable to negotiate the steps at subways and footbridges or may fear that their inability to cross the road quickly puts them at risk. The results of this are hard to gauge accurately but they are important to the people involved.

3.10. The picture completed

The picture of the lorry problem is now complete or at least sufficient to give an outline of the sorts of effects the lorry has. Cataloguing the effects of the lorry is the easiest way to comprehend them but it is important to see how they all contribute to the aggregate impression. In real life, though one effect may rank uppermost

it is the total impression of the lorry that counts so
that the whole is worth more than the sum of the parts.
People dislike lorries for a variety of reasons, all mutually reinforcing and individually discernible but it is
probable that the overall subjective impression will
colour opinions more than any single effect. The "lorry
problem" cannot be cured by dealing with only parts of it.

4. THE PROSPECT FOR IMPROVEMENT

An outline of the environmental effects of lorries
must be balanced by an outline of the measures which can
be taken to reduce these effects. Short of discouraging
lorry use, they fall under two headings:

- improving lorries;
- getting lorries away from settlements.

Lorries can be improved by making them quieter, reducing
the vibration and fumes they produce and by making them
safer. It is possible that lorries could be made to look
a little less intrusive though bulk is hard to hide. Some
effects are inherent in the lorry and nothing can be done
about them: even if lorries were as quiet as cars or indeed silent, fume free and generated no vibration, people
would still be frightened of them. Since noise is one of
the most frequently mentioned causes of lorry nuisance and
is a problem which surely is susceptible to technical
solution, it is instructive to look at progress in this
field.

In 1969/70 the lorry problem reached the political
agenda in the United Kingdom as a result of a much publi-
cised proposal to increase lorry weights. One political
response to the widespread criticism of heavy lorries
which was then voiced was the Quiet Heavy Vehicle (QHV)
launched in 1971 by the United Kingdom Government's Transport and Road Research Laboratory (TRRL). The QHV project
was designed to prove that practical diesel-engined articulated lorries of the heaviest kind (over 200 hp) could
be produced with external noise levels some 10dB(A) lower
than 1971 levels [i.e. down to about 80dB(A) so that lorries would be "as quiet as cars"], and to indicate the
relationship between cost and noise level (TRRL 1979). By
1978 a Foden/Rolls Royce demonstration vehicle designed to
pull 38 tonnes (350bhp) had been built to production standards and emitted 80dB(A). The engine, gearbox, fan,
cooling system, and exhaust had all been redesigned. In

1981 the QHV was being tested in operating conditions to discover whether operating costs are higher than normal. It is expected that the purchase price will be 8 to 10 per cent more than the standard vehicle of the same weight and power. The prospect of a commercially available vehicle is nevertheless a long way off and the United Kingdom Government has just decided to launch a QHV 90 project to achieve this during the 1990s.

In 1977 the EEC Council of Ministers, apparently on a German initiative, declared its intentions of achieving 80dB(A) for lorries by 1985. This declaration was made at the same time as a Directive was agreed setting the maximum lorry noise at 88dB(A). In reply to a European Parliamentary Question on 5th August, 1980 (OJ C236/12 15.9.80), the Commission reaffirmed its commitment to the target of 80dB(A) by 1985. The Commission stated that only in the United Kingdom was there a prototype lorry of the heaviest category which met the target, although a much lighter lorry (130hp) emitting 77dB(A) was on the market in Germany. One year later (OJ C240/20 18.9.81) the Commission had effectively admitted that it was unlikely that the target of 80dB(A) would be achieved by 1985.

The making of a Council declaration setting a target in 1977 followed by remarkably little action by EEC Member States, by the Commission and by lorry manufacturers so that it is highly unlikely that the target will be met has inevitably generated cynicism among environmentalist bodies that only lip service is being paid to the issue. The QHV cost £1.25 million and this sum can be compared with £40 million spent on technology to quieten the Concorde aircraft technology which even though it was never used would have benefitted far fewer people than the reduction of lorry noise. It is obvious that the inertia of Governments and industry is considerable and undoubtedly lorry noise reduction will require major efforts in the coming years. These efforts will have to be undertaken by all lorry manufacturing countries if EEC legislation is not to be blocked by an individual country trying to protect its own industry.

On vibration, progress is even less visible. Some research has been conducted in the United Kingdom by the TRRL into the causes of vibration, and some inconclusive research has been conducted into its effects, but all work now seems to have stopped. To reduce airborne vibration involves a reduction of the low frequency noise emitted by lorries. This means setting a limit on the dB(C) rather than the dB(A) scale - since the "C" scale takes into account lower frequencies than the "A" scale. To reduce ground vibration requires either smoother roads or better suspension design. It is not known what work is being done in these fields, but the little progress on noise - a subject where the technical possibilities are at least

understood - does not offer much encouragement for more
difficult subjects like vibration.

There are three methods of getting lorries away from
people:

- road building;
- rebuilding settlements;
- local controls over lorry movements.

The housing stock in Europe is now being rebuilt at a
rate of not more than 2 per cent per annum so the theoretical scope for rebuilding settlements to minimise disturbance by lorries is small and can be largely ignored.
Much greater emphasis has been placed on road building -
both completely new roads and motorways, and bypasses - as
a means of getting lorries away from people, although this
has always been a secondary reason for road buildings, the
primary reason being to speed the flow of traffic. But
the massive amount of road building in the last twenty
years has not kept pace with the growth of lorry traffic
so that even towns which have been bypassed find that
traffic has picked up again and many towns and villages
lying on trunk roads have yet to be bypassed. It is not
possible in the space available to discuss fully the possibilities for road building but a recent survey in
England (Civic Trust 1982 to be published) is instructive. This shows that only about 25 per cent of the 693
settlements with populations between 500 and 150,000 lying
on the 8,000 miles of roads most used by lorries have by-
passes. Although there are plans to bypass a further 142
of these settlements (about 20 per cent) some of these
plans are unlikely to be achieved before the end of the
century and for 284 settlements (about 40 per cent) there
are no plans at all. These are all settlements lying on
roads proposed as a lorry route network in 1976 and omit
the many other settlements lying on roads which are also
heavily used by lorries. It would be extremely instructive to see similar surveys carried out in other European
countries. Assuming that the English experience is at
least to some extent representative of other countries of
Europe, the general conclusion must be that even an extensive programme of road building will leave large numbers
of settlements on major roads still troubled by growing
use of heavy lorries by the end of the century. Road
building has, in any event, been cut back in many countries because of attempts to cut public expenditure and,
of course, there is growing opposition to road building on
other environmental grounds. As in so many other spheres,
a choice has to be made between two environmental evils.

Bypasses do not solve the problems in large conurbations for two reasons; the larger a town the smaller the
proportion of through traffic to local traffic, and the
more difficult it becomes to build a true bypass anyway.
The solution most often advocated in large towns is the

compulsory transshipment of goods from large lorries to
smaller lorries for delivery, and the Annex shows that
this is compulsory in some countries. The arguments
against transshipment are nearly always expressions of
self-interest from manufacturers and retailers who would
be inconvenienced. If there are economic penalties to
compulsory transshipment, then, for that reason, it becomes a natural subject for the EEC in its concern to remove distortions to competition. The EEC can approach the
issue as a matter of environmental policy or of transport
policy, and since the recent proposal on combined transport - COM(80)796 - holds the promise that environmental
considerations are beginning to shape transport policy it
may well be that the Directorate-General for Transport
will want to consider the subject.

The Annex also shows that most countries have local
restrictions or weekend bans designed to control the environmental effects of lorries. Comparative studies of
these restrictions, as well as of transshipment policies,
could well be instructive, particularly of the effects
that they are said to have on transport costs.

In conclusion, it can be said that although there are
prospects for both technical improvements and for separating lorries from settlements, the forecast growth in
heavy lorry traffic may well be outstripping the improvements. Certainly a significant number of places can expect a steady deterioration in environmental conditions
over the years.

5. THE ENERGY CONSTRAINT

That transport is a significant consumer of oil is
borne out by the statistics: transport consumes 25 per
cent of final energy in the EEC (European Parliament
1980). While this might not sound too drastic, it is the
figure for oil which is most illuminating for the transport sector accounts for 40 per cent of the oil consumed
within the EEC. This must be seen in the context of considerable variation about the norm. In Luxembourg, for
example, only 12 per cent of final energy consumed finds
its way into the transport sector while it is 34.1 per
cent in Greece. Differences there may be but this cannot
disguise the fact that energy consumption in the road
transport sector has shown a tendency to rise in recent
years. The magnitude of this was 37 per cent between 1968
and 1978 in Great Britain in the road freight industry so
that road freight now accounts for 26 per cent of the

125

total transport energy consumed and 5 per cent of total
oil consumed in the United Kingdom. As a result of the
increase in the real cost of oil in the 1970s, the proportion of a road haulier's costs attributable to energy
costs has risen from 2 per cent to 20 per cent since
1970. Up until 1970, the real cost of oil had been falling and the incentives for using this cheap, available and
flexible energy resource were obvious. Indeed this is one
of the reasons for the meteoric growth of the road freight
sector and conversely may yet be the reason for its decline. No-one can predict with any confidence the future
of world energy supplies and yet, without such predictions, it is impossible to know how road haulage might
develop in the future.

Not least of the difficulties is the political nature
of oil and who controls it. Absolute scarcity may not be
the issue where there is a powerful cartel like OPEC whose
policy has been recently to maintain production levels
while allowing increasing demand to push up prices. In
addition, OPEC countries have not been afraid to use their
power to impose price rises of their own. With 56 per
cent of the known oil resources in the hands of the Middle
East (Foley 1981), the political nature of oil and its uneven distribution remains. Simply calculating the size of
known resources and matching this with consumption rates
is insufficient as a way to predict future changes in
energy, yet it is the only method which can claim to be
objective. Even estimating the quantity of oil resources
in the world is a hazardous task. Academics tend to be
very sceptical of oil forecasts made by the major oil companies as they underexaggerate the probable amounts of oil
in the world. Actual oil reserves may be up to nine times
the figures given by the oil companies who are keen to
preserve conditions of near panic so as to be able to
raise oil prices without arousing the interest of the tax
man. So for these reasons, academics have preferred to
make their own estimates. An attempt to reconcile different estimates of the actual amounts of oil available
comes to around 2,000 billion barrels (Foley 1981). If
one assumes production will double every 8-9 years and
that consumption describes a 7.5 per cent per annum
growth, the oil depletion curve will peak in the 1990's
after which it will gradually decline. However optimistic
one might care to be - and in 1981 there was a decline in
oil consumption in Europe - there is still the unpleasant
fact to be faced that oil will one day run out. Synthetic
oil may then be manufactured from coal but it will certainly be expensive.

There are optimists who believe that technology (e.g.
fast breeder reactors, fusion power) will eventually provide abundant energy sufficiently cheaply to enable porta-
ble fuel (hydrogen perhaps) to be manufactured so that
energy will never be a constraint on road transport. That
is only a possibility and commercial fast breeders are

25 years away and fusion probably 50 years. Since one
cannot say when there will be oil shortages or significant
price rises but that one or other of these are also possibilities, it is prudent to assume that one or other will
happen and to plan accordingly. There are, of course,
technical improvements to be made and these fall under two
headings, though each has its limitations:

- improvements to vehicles;
- the switch to less energy consuming modes.

Today's motor cars consume 10 per cent less petrol
than did cars 10 years ago, and manufacturers offer the
prospect of a further 10 per cent saving by 1985. One
estimate (Leach 1979) is that lorries will be 20 per cent
more efficient by the year 2000 as a result of improvements including: minimising external projections; avoiding tyre drag; better maintenance and engine improvements. Savings of this order of magnitude are useful but
only counteract to some extent the increased fuel consumption implicit in the forecast growth of vehicle kilometres.

Savings could also be made by switching to less
energy consuming modes. Assuming that each mode runs at
50 per cent capacity, an articulated lorry with a two ton
or over payload running on a motorway would consume
0.046kgce/ton-kilometre if it was carrying commercial
goods, while its consumption rate would be 0.062kgce/
ton-kilometre if the goods were of an industrial nature
and 0.09kgce/ton-kilometre if the lorry were operating
under urban conditions (European Parliament 1980). In
comparison, the railway uses 0.019kgce/ton-kilometre while
inland waterways achieve 0.016kgce/ton-kilometre. Using
these average figures, it has been calculated that railways could be used for just 30 per cent of the journey and
still yield energy savings than if the journey were undertaken all the way by road.

Average figures, of course, conceal some important
variations. They take no account of variable load factors
so that under some conditions when the train has a low
load factor, a heavy lorry might be more energy efficient. Furthermore, the calculations do not include the
consumption of energy in the manufacturing of rolling
stock, the maintenance of infrastructure, though in truth
these do not alter the energy advantages of railways and
inland waterways. It must also be recognised that energy
and time are used when the freight is transshipped from
the rail to the road or vice-versa although, again, this
does not tip the balance in favour of the lorry. More
fundamental problems to the transfer of freight from road
to rail lie in the fact that there are certain duties that
the railway is unable to perform. Most importantly these
include the final delivery stage which, unfortunately, is
the type of lorry operation which consumes the most energy.

Even assuming that there is no intervention in the market to favour rail or water against road, the most promising prospect for the transfer of freight lies in the freight forecasts themselves. If the tendency for freight to travel further continues, then the advantages of rail for long hauls will make it more attractive with time (the average length of haul by lorry in the United Kingdom increased from 22 miles in 1953 to 30 miles in 1968 and 43 miles in 1979). However, even if this shift were to take place, it would still not represent an absolute reduction in energy use - merely a reduced rate of increase of energy consumption.

The theoretical conclusion is simple. If what is required is to stabilize or even reduce the total consumption of oil in freight transport, then it must become an object of policy to stabilize or reduce the total volume of road freight.

It may be objected that, despite the fact that transport accounts for 40 per cent of oil consumed within the EEC, it is the motor car that accounts for most of it and that freight accounts for only a small proportion of total oil consumed (about 5 per cent in the United Kingdom). The argument is that as a premium user freight will always be protected, e.g. by rationing oil for cars, and that therefore oil shortages will not act as a constraint on freight. This is possible but it may be that the objective of stabilizing or reducing freight movement will be achieved in any event: any shortage of oil or high prices will so depress the economy that much less freight will be moved anyway.

Various means to effect energy savings in transport were discussed at a recent ECMT Round Table (Baron 1981) and one suggestion was intervention in the price of oil. The possibility of "adjusting the transport market so as to favour energy saving modes" on the grounds that the current market price for oil products does not reflect their full value in the long term has also been put forward by the EEC Commission as a suggestion - COM(79)550 - though in a rather tentative way.

If a flattening of the graph of freight forecasts is the end which will be achieved anyway, there is no reason why it should not be discussed seriously as an objective of policy rather than waiting for it to happen.

An artificial raising of energy prices for transport will merely anticipate what is to come about but it has the advantage that it can be done in a controlled way giving operators the chance to adjust and plan accordingly. Any sudden increase in oil prices can then be cushioned by reducing the tax element, thus avoiding sudden and damaging disruptions. Such a policy could only be adopted by agreement between countries to prevent distortions to competition so that the arguments for it have to be very well established and understood. No-one can pretend that this will be easy.

6. CONCLUSION

In December 1976 the German Minister for Transport, Herr Gscheidle, wrote a letter to the Ministers of Transport of the other EEC countries. He was explaining why Germany had taken a restrictive view of an increase of the quota for international lorry movements. Herr Gscheidle's letter provides almost a summary of this paper. He talked about a road network being progressively overloaded and he talked about how there would be less money available in the future for road building. He went on:

"Furthermore, the extension of the road network is not only a question of money, it is becoming increasingly difficult in our country - nearly everywhere densely populated - to find routes for new roads, because residents oppose them. New roads and resulting traffic affect the environment through noise pollution and congestion. It is rather difficult to quantify the resulting external costs but they are considerable. Added to this, there are the high accident figures. I would also mention the energy problem."

Herr Gscheidle's letter demonstrates that environmental constraints have indeed been recognised at the highest level. This was five years ago but the recognition has not yet been sufficiently widespread for general objectives of policy to be reformulated. All forecasts of freight movement (see Annex) show an ever increasing volume of road freight, and the authors know of no explicit statement of policy that it would be desirable for the rising graph of freight transport to be flattened.

Perhaps the nature of environmental constraints has not been demonstrated convincingly enough. There is still too much loose talk about the possibilities for technical improvements, e.g. noise and for road building with sufficiently rigorous study of the possibilities. The Annex shows that in many countries there are official reports on the environmental problems of lorries and that social surveys have been made on the extent of those problems. The authors have not been able to study these reports and social surveys in the time available so this is an obvious field for further study. A review of the existing reports

129

and social surveys - rather than relying on material largely from one country as in the present paper - might well identify areas where more information would be helpful to establish the argument or modify it.

Another possibility is that a policy of curbing the growth of road freight runs counter to the culture in which most transport planners and policy makers have been brought up: it has, after all, almost been axiomatic that demand for transport will increase and that it is a transport planner's job to supply and plan the facilities for it. In such a climate it becomes easy to forget that transport is not an end in itself but only a means to an end and that it may be necessary to pursue other means for a given end when circumstances change.

The confusion between means and ends used to occur in the field of pollution. Earlier this century, it was simply assumed that industrial production went hand in hand with the generation of pollution, whereas we now know that industrial production can increase while pollution decreases. Every country now has a policy of stabilizing and reducing pollution, and the "standstill principle" is a concept well understood in pollution policy and has a place in EEC environmental policy. Similarly, it was until recently assumed that energy consumption was an indicator of prosperity and that control of total energy demand was not a matter for public policy. It has not been shown (Leach 1979) that GDP can increase while total energy consumption remains static or decreases and the objectives of policy are now changing. At the recent Venice Summit the EEC heads of Government called for a lowering of the energy coefficient: the ratio between energy consumed and industrial output. Since then the very concept of the energy coefficient has been called into question.

The main conclusion of this paper then is that we need to make a similar shift in our assumptions about road freight: that we need to work towards a policy objective for freight transport that would aim to stabilize or reduce the environmental effects of freight movement. In the absence of a refined indicator of these effects we can, in the meanwhile, state more crudely that vehicle-kilometres of the heaviest lorries should be stabilized.

Once this objective is generally accepted, as a first step at least as a basis for general discussion, consideration can move to the means for doing so. That would be the subject of another paper but some possibilities arise from the analysis in Chapter 2 of this paper.

It is long distance road freight that is growing most and it is this that is carried out in the heaviest lorries which are the ones that present environmental effects at their worst, particularly when they pass through unbypassed towns. Indeed the figures for the United Kingdom show no overall growth in freight lifted but rather an increase in the distance over which freight is moved. If measures could be taken to stabilize the growth in this sector of the freight market, then we would be moving towards the new objective.

Intervention in the price of oil has already been mentioned as one tool. Herr Gscheidle's letter quoted above referred to another. The Minister was explaining his Government's opposition to the liberalisation of lorry movements within the EEC. In doing so he used a wholly new argument because capacity controls (or quotas) have traditionally been used to protect state investments in the railways and to protect the established haulier against unfair competition. The environmental and energy saving arguments used by Herr Gscheidle have not hitherto been used as justification for capacity controls on lorries. This point has been confirmed by the authors who wrote to all ECMT countries asking the question whether capacity control of road freight had ever been justified for environmental reasons.

Replies were received from:

Belgium	Netherlands
Denmark	Spain
Finland	Sweden
France	Switzerland
Greece	West Germany
Ireland	

In no case did the replies suggest that capacity controls have been justified for environmental reasons. Perhaps the question was badly phrased because even West Germany - despite Herr Gscheidle's letter - claimed that environmental protection was not a justification for capacity controls. Yet such controls obviously work. Officials from the U.K. Department of Transport in giving evidence before a House of Lords' Committee concerning the EEC's proposals for combined transport - COM(80)796 - attributed the decline in use of the German Rollende Landstrasse system by British hauliers to the increase in the quota for lorry journeys that had been issued by the German authorities (House of Lords 1981).

Is it not possible that a policy tool, widely used and well understood, and which was invented for one reason has now assumed a wholly new importance for a wholly new reason? To accept the new reason would be of course to reverse the policy of liberalisation of freight movement that some countries and the EEC have pursued for many years. But the policy of liberalisation was a policy formulated before environmental and energy constraints were recognised. Times have now changed: transport policy makers have wholly new problems to contend with.

131

BIBLIOGRAPHY

1. Adams, John., 1981. Transport Planning: Vision and Practice, Routledge & Kegan Paul.

2. Armitage, A., 1980. Report of the Inquiry into Lorries, People and the Environment, HMSO.

3. Baron, P., 1981. Transport and Energy, ECMT Round Table 52.

4. Bayliss, B.T., 1973. Demand for Freight Transport, ECMT Round Table 20.

5. British Railways Board, 1979. Memorandum on the Inquiry on Lorries, People and the Environment.

6. Civic Trust, 1969. Heavy Lorries.

7. Civic Trust, 1979. Heavy Lorries - Nine Years On.

8. Civic Trust, 1982 (to be published). Bypass Study.

9. Department of the Environment, 1973. Lorries and the World we Live in.

10. Department of the Environment, 1980. Inquiry on Lorries, People and the Environment.

11. European Parliament, 1980. Public Hearing on Energy Saving in the Transport Sector, Committee on Transport.

12. Foley, G., 1981. The Energy Question, Penguin.

13. Freight Transport Association, 1979. Evidence to the Armitage Inquiry into Lorries, People and the Environment.

14. Fullerton, B., 1974. Development of British Transport Networks, Oxford University Press.

15. Greater London Council, 1979. Lorries and the Environment. Report of the Controller of Planning and Transportation, PC 498.

16. Hamer, M., 1978. A Load on Your Mind, Transport 2000.

17. House of Lords, 1981. First Report, Select Committee on the EC, Session 1981-82. Combined Transport.

18. Kates, R., 1968. The Pursuit of Beauty in the Environment, Landscape 16 (2), p. 21-24.

19. Leach, G., 1979. A Low Energy Strategy for the U.K. IIED.

20. Lowenthal, D., 1971. Assumptions behind the Public Attitudes. In H. Jarret "Environmental Quality in a Growing Economy".

21. Marplan, 1980. Marplan Survey of Public Opinion on the Lorry.

22. Roudier, J., 1976. Freight Collection and Delivery in Urban Areas, ECMT Round Table 31.

23. Sharp, C., 1973. Living with the Lorry.

24. Social and Community Planning Research, 1978. Road Traffic and the Environment.

25. TRRL, 1973a. Urban Freight Distribution: a Study of Operations in High Street, Putney, LR 556.

26. TRRL, 1973b. Urban Freight Distribution: Studies of Operations in Shopping Streets at Newbury and Camberley, LR 603.

27. TRRL, 1974a. Forecasts of Vehicles and Traffic in Great Britain: 1974 Revision, LR 650.

28. TRRL, 1978. Environmental Effects of Traffic in Ludlow, Salop. SR 245.

29. TRRL, 1979. Quiet Heavy Vehicle (QHV) Project, SR 521.

30. Weinstein, N., 1976. Human Evaluations of Environmental Noise. In K.H. Craik and E.H. Zube (ed) "Perceiving Environmental Quality".

Annex

RESPONSE TO QUESTIONNAIRE

A questionnaire was sent on 16th October, 1981 by the authors on behalf of the ECMT Secretariat to national experts whose names were provided by the Secretariat. Eight replies were received and are tabulated on the following page. Seven countries failed to reply.

The questionnaire was as follows:

1. Are there published forecasts of freight movement (particularly road freight) in your country?

2. Have there been any official studies or reports on the environmental problems caused by road freight (e.g. similar to the Armitage Report in the United Kingdom)?

3. Have any officially sponsored social surveys been carried out on public attitudes to road traffic and, in particular, road freight (e.g. to what extent is the public troubled by traffic noise and is the problem increasing)?

4. What kind of measures have been adopted by Government, regional authorities or local authorites to control the environmental effects of lorries, e.g.:

   a) local restrictions by zone or by time of day;
   b) national restrictions by time, e.g. weekend bans;
   c) compulsory transshipment into small lorries for delivery in towns;
   d) measures to encourage long distance travel by railways.

The replies are presented schematically on the next page.

Annex

	Freight forecasts	Report on environ. problems	Social surveys	Local restrictions	National restrictions	Compulsory transshipment	Measure to encourage long distance rail
Austria							
Belgium							
Denmark							
Finland	Yes	No					
France			Noise only	Yes	No	*	Yes
Greece	No	No	No	Yes	No	No	No
Ireland	Yes	Yes	No	Yes	No	No	No
Italy	*	*	*	Yes	Yes	Yes	Yes
Luxembourg			(No questionnaire sent)				
Netherlands	Yes	Yes	Yes	Yes	No	No	No
Norway	Yes	*	Noise only	*	*	*	*
Portugal							
Spain							
Sweden	Yes	Yes	Yes	Yes	Yes	Yes	Yes
Switzerland	Yes	Yes	Yes	*	*	*	Yes
Turkey			(No questionnaire sent)				
United Kingdom	Yes	Yes	Yes	Yes	No	No	No
W. Germany							

* Indicates that either the official contacted was unable to help or else the literature sent was inconclusive.

135

TOPIC 1B

ASSESSMENT OF
SOCIETY'S TRANSPORT NEEDS

GOODS TRANSPORT

M. E. QUINET
Service d'Analyse Économique et du Plan
Paris, France

M. R. MARCHE
Institut de Recherche des Transports
Arcueil, France

M. C. REYNAUD
Service d'Analyse Économique et du Plan
Paris, France

SUMMARY

INTRODUCTION

The close link between transport and economic activity has always been recognised. A smooth flow of goods
is considered a pre-condition for a country's prosperity.
The great French historian Fernand Braudel stresses this
link with the words "Transport is the natural conclusion
of the production process. If it accelerates, all goes
well or better".

Historical analyses have brought out this interrelationship in all periods. The Roman Empire was based on
good land and sea links. The economic upsurge of the
Renaissance enabled the great voyages of discovery to be
made which in their turn prolonged the upward trend. In
the 19th Century, the industrial revolution was accompanied by the growth of transport, the most striking example being the advent of the railways. The period after
the Second World War was marked by both vigorous economic
growth and the rapid development of transport.

Over the past ten years or so the economic world has
changed - what was at first taken to be a short-term economic crisis has turned out to be structural change
characterised by much slower growth, inflation and unemployment. How is transport adapting to this new environment? What is the nature of its new links with economic
activity?

Light can be thrown on these questions from the different angles constituted by the analytical tools used by
researchers and academics and these tools can be used to
examine recent quantitative and qualitative trends.

They can be divided into three categories, each of
which is the subject of a chapter in this report:

- descriptive analysis of traffic statistics and
  their characteristics;
- quantitative modelling, i.e. the search for econometric relationships explaining traffic volume and
  modal split;
- study of transport organisation and its development.

Before developing these different aspects, however, two prefatory remarks are called for on the scope and limits of the following discussion.

First, there can be no question of such a brief report claiming to be exhaustive and take account of all studies and analyses in the field. Those mentioned appear by way of example, which by no means implies that those left out are devoid of interest.

Second, because of the authors' nationality, the report presents mainly French experience and findings, in particular as regards the descriptive analyses of statistics and the study of transport organisation.

1. GOODS TRANSPORT VOLUME: CHARACTERISTICS OF ITS STRUCTURE AND DEVELOPMENT

The aim of this first chapter, devoted to transport demand, is to bring out the facts on the basis of the available figures. It is intended to describe the situation of domestic and international transport and the relative shares of the different modes with the twofold aim of demonstrating the importance of the transport sector and giving an initial idea of the role of the factors determining both the volume of demand and its modal split. In the main, statistics used are readily available world and European data, but the illustrations based on more detailed statistics are limited to France.

1.1. Measuring transport volume

First of all it is worthwhile recalling the units of measurement used or available and the nature of the existing statistical sources (see Annex for further details).

1.1.1. Units of measurement

As far as transport operators are concerned, the quantity of freight is naturally measured by weight, or more exactly mass, in tonnes, quintals or kilogrammes, but this measurement varies considerably according to what is involved: net or gross weight; actual or chargeable tonnage.

Simply adding up tonnages generally gives a somewhat inadequate measurement of transport activity:

- especially where in the field studied transport distances vary greatly or change over time as a result of changes in the geographical pattern of trade;
- also because (even disregarding transport within manufacturing or storage firms) a transport operation very often takes the form of a "transport chain", using a succession of different modes, which leads to double counting in the measurement of freight movements.

It is therefore advantageous to use tonne-km (or tonne-miles for seaborne transport), though the range of concepts covered by this definition needs to be

141

emphasized, since tonnage may be gross or net, actual or chargeable and distance, too, may be actual or chargeable.

Carriers' receipts, however, are not directly dependent on tkm:

- while tariffs are often, at least in principle, "linear" according to distance, they generally include a substantial fixed component;
- tariffs and rates vary with the nature of the goods, packing and size of shipment.

The result is that:

- to define an "economic volume" of transport activity it would be necessary to calculate receipts at constant prices or to weight tkm by constant average unit prices for different relatively homogeneous categories of freight;
- trends in tkm give only a very rough indication of trends in this economic volume because of changes in the structure of freight transport as regards the nature of the goods and distance.

Finally, it should be noted that the physical volume of vehicles or containers, or more exactly the relationship between physical volume and permitted payload may be more of a constraint than permitted payload itself in the case of low-density goods. As this volume/payload relationship varies with transport mode and even from one type of vehicle to another within each mode, this supply side factor can influence modal choice.

1.1.2. Statistical sources

Statistical sources are varied and hence supplement one another. However, despite the efforts made to improve them, both in individual countries and by international organisations, there are gaps in the data and the degree of accuracy is not uniform. By and large:

- tonnages and tkm for sea, air, rail and inland waterway transport are generally fairly well-known thanks to the data provided by carriers;
- the same cannot be said of road transport, for which the administrative documents used for statistical purposes are often piecemeal, so that countries carry out sample statistical surveys which can cause problems regarding the field covered, or uncertainty associated with statistical sampling errors when detailed analysis is required;
- in the case of international transport, foreign trade statistics drawn up by customs services supplement transport statistics: they provide cross-checks for tonnages and also permit an

142

estimate of tkm (on the basis of origin, frontier point and destination of shipments) and, above all, provide data on the value of the goods carried: however, the data relating to transport are sometimes imprecise (as regards origin or destination and mode) and there may be no statistics on transit traffic.

1.1.3. Definition of domestic and international transport

The activity of domestic transport networks covers both purely domestic traffic (origin and destination of the traffic flow within the country) and the carriage of goods involved in international trade: imports, exports and transit traffic. Explaining transport volumes as a function of the economic activities of producer or consumer sectors is obviously much clearer if a distinction is made between purely domestic transport and the different categories of international transport.

A distinction is therefore made in the present report between "internal" and "external" transport (see Table 1.1.).

Table 1.1.

DEFINITION OF INTERNAL AND EXTERNAL TRANSPORT

Purely domestic transport		Internal transport
Domestic leg of transport involved in foreign trade (imports and exports)	(- with break of (bulk in sea (ports (	
	(- without break (of bulk	External transport
International transit traffic		

1.2. Trends in domestic and international transport

What is the effect of increasing specialisation of economies and growing international trade on transport activity? Before examining the international trade share of the activity of domestic transport networks and, more generally, the "diffusion" of transport, it is only natural to mention the broad upstream trends in world production and trade. As already mentioned, the value of goods and the cost of transport differ greatly as between raw

143

materials and manufactured products; in addition, the demand for these different categories of goods evolves differently, so that an attempt must be made to distinguish between them.

In this and following sections, the time series have been analysed so as to locate changes in trend. Rather than adding to the bulk of this report by including numerous graphs, the conclusions have been summarised with the aid of tables. It will be seen that the time series used generally end in 1980 or even 1979 or 1978; it would obviously have been interesting to take the most recent years into account, but the relevant statistics are not readily accessible.

1.2.1. Trends in world production

The statistics published by UNO [1](1) enable trends in the main indicators of world production for the period 1960 to 1978 to be analysed:

- GDP (gross domestic product) less services, with agriculture shown separately;
- main components of industrial production: manufactured articles (output of manufacturing industry) and main products of extractive industries (crude oil and natural gas, coal, ores).

In the period 1960 to 1978, two distinct trends can be identified: 1960-69 and 1969-78. It is in fact worth noting, as shown in particular by the work of CEPII (Centre d'Etudes Prospectives et d'Informations Internationales) [2](2):

- that the trend in world demand for the different sectors of manufacturing industry (excluding agro-food industries) changed direction in 1970;
- that the years 1977 and 1978 roughly continue the new trend from 1969 to 1976.

It is therefore justifiable to describe developments in terms of two distinct periods (1960-69 and 1969-78), for which Table 1.2. shows annual growth rates.

----

1. The figures in square brackets refer to the bibliographical references.
2. The data on world demand are taken from the CEPII world data bank (excluding Eastern countries): CHELEM (Harmonized accounts on trade and the world economy). Based mainly on UN statistics, this data-bank contains in particular, besides socio-economic aggregates by geographical area, international trade between 32 areas for 70 categories of products and world demand for 54 categories of product regardless of area (in two broad production chains: agro-chemicals and metallurgy).

Table 1.2.

TRENDS IN WORLD PRODUCTION (1960 to 1978)

AGGREGATES	1975 weighting		Average annual growth (%)	
	GDP excluding services	Industrial production	1960-1969	1969-1978
GDP excluding services	100		5.7	4.3
of which: Agriculture	11.9		1.5	2.1
Industrial Production				
Extractive industries of which:		13.1	5.6	3.3
- crude oil and natural gas		8.9)	8.3	4.5
- coal		1.8)11.8	0.6	0.2
- metallic ores		1.1)	5.0	1.0
Manufacturing industry		31.1	6.9	4.7
Electricity, gas and water		5.8	8.5	6.0
Total		100	7.0	4.6

Points to note are:

- given the slower growth in basic products, growth in manufacturing industry (which is close to that of industrial production) is slightly higher than that of GDP excluding services;
- there is a considerable slow-down, as between the two periods, in manufacturing and extractive industries, while the modest growth of agricultural production continues(3).

The trends obviously differ from one area of the world to another(4). Here we shall consider only the products of manufacturing industry [1]. Table 1.3. shows:

---

3. It should be noted that the increase in the volume of production of products based on agriculture is slightly more rapid than that of agricultural value-added in GDP: 2.3 and 2.4 per cent per annum for the two successive periods.
4. See also: OECD, Interfutures [3].

Table 1.3.

TRENDS IN THE PRODUCTION OF MANUFACTURING
INDUSTRY (1960-1978)

Region of the world	1975 weighting (industrial production)	Annual average growth rate (%)	
		1960-1969	1969-1978
Centrally planned economies	26	9.1	8.1
Market economy countries	74	6.7	3.6
of which: - developed countries	64	6.6	3.2
- developing countries	10	7.8	6.8
World Total	100	6.9	4.7

- the slight fall in growth rates in market economy developing countries and centrally planned economies;
- the more marked slowdown in developed countries.

1.2.2. Trends in world trade

The curves showing trends in the volume of world trade of market economy countries (volume index of exports, base year 1970) [1] are similar to the production curves, but the growth rates are much higher (see Table 1.4.): although the weighting structure is somewhat different (product values as opposed to value added), this clearly illustrates the internationalisation of trade. In particular, between 1969 and 1978, the exports of manufactured products increased by 7.0 per cent per annum on average while the production of manufacturing industry increased by only 3.6 per cent per annum.

1.2.3. Increasing share of international trade in domestic traffic

In the developed countries, the tendency to locate heavy industry near seaports may lead to reduced domestic transport of imported raw materials, but the growth of international trade in other products may far outweigh this possible reduction and transport statistics ought to show the increasing share of international traffic (imports, exports and transit) in the transport output (tkm) of domestic networks and hence in carriers' earnings.

Table 1.4.

COMPARATIVE TRENDS IN THE VOLUME OF WORLD TRADE AND
PRODUCTION OF MARKET ECONOMY COUNTRIES (1963-1978)

Aggregates	Average annual growth rate (%)	
	1963-1969	1969-1978
World Trade: Volume Index		
All products	9.5	6.4
of which:		
- Food and raw materials	3.9	4.9
- Fuels	8.6	3.7
- Manufactured products	11.7	7.0
Volume of Production		
- GDP excluding services	5.8	3.8
- Basic products	2.2	2.4
- Manufacturing industry	6.5	3.6

We would have liked to estimate these trends for the European countries, but unfortunately we came up against the difficulty mentioned above (see paragraph 1.1.3.) of assessing the share of international trade in internal transport. Even for France it has so far been possible to make a clear distinction here only in the case of rail traffic [4].

Despite this fragmentary view of the situation, Table 1.5 clearly illustrates the phenomenon for the period 1971 to 1980:

- international freight rose from 35 to 39 per cent of total tkm;
- with an overall increase in tkm of 2 per cent there was a significant decrease in domestic traffic (-4 per cent) and a marked rise in international traffic (+13 per cent: foreign trade up 7 per cent and transit up 45 per cent).

1.2.4. The "diffusion" of transport: methodological approaches

Distinction in the statistics between domestic and international transport is obviously to be encouraged since it is necessary to clarify the relationship between economic activity and transport, but in itself this distinction is not enough for an analysis of the relationship between transport and space because the different

147

Table 1.5.

TRENDS IN SNCF FREIGHT TRAFFIC (1971-1980)
(SHIPMENTS OF AT LEAST 3 TONNES)

| Type of Traffic | Tonne-kilometres | | | | Percentage change 1971-1980 |
| | 1971 | | 1980 | | |
	billion tkm	%	billion tkm	%	
Internal traffic of which:	46.9	74.3	45.9	71.1	- 2
- domestic	40.8	64.7	39.3	60.9	- 4
- foreign trade	6.1	9.6	6.6	10.2	+ 8
External traffic of which:	16.2	25.7	18.7	28.9	+ 15
- foreign trade	12.6	20.0	13.5	20.9	+ 7
- transit	3.6	5.7	5.2	8.0	+ 45
Total of which:	63.1	100	64.6	100	+ 2
- domestic traffic	40.8	64.7	39.3	60.9	- 4
- international traffic	22.3	35.3	25.3	39.1	+ 13

countries are of very different sizes and each needs to be
sub-divided into an appropriate number of regions.

In other words, it is necessary to analyse the structure of inter-regional, domestic and international trade
as regards both levels and trends, taking account of the
nature of the goods in order to situate them in the relevant production, distribution and consumption chains.

The first studies of this type were carried out in
France in 1978-1979 [5], and were concerned mainly with
trade:

- between the 21 regions of France for the years
  1971-1976;
- between these 21 regions and each of six EEC countries for the same years;
- between the 10 German Länder for the years
  1969-1971.

In these studies, the diffusion of transport, as
regards both level and trend, is shown by statistical indicators of relative dispersion in the distribution of
inter-regional flows according to their size (tonnage), in
particular by the coefficient of variation (standard devi-
ation/average), a high level of diffusion corresponding to
a relatively low dispersion.

The results which are instructive, concern:

- the level of diffusion, which varies according to the nature of the product (food products, semi-finished goods, finished goods) and transport mode;
- a tendency during the 1970s towards greater diffusion as time went on, corresponding to the downswing phase of the long Kondratieff movements and which one might be tempted to interpret in this period of slowing growth as an effort by firms to optimise their supplies or seek new markets.

It must not be forgotten, however, that trends in the statistical distribution of transport flows reflect at the same time changes in the pattern of the regional location of production and consumption as well as changes in the internal structure of trade.

Application of these diffusion analyses is obviously to be encouraged through:

- extending geographical coverage;
- extending the time series using the data now available for the most recent years(5);

Table 1.6.

TRENDS IN SURFACE FREIGHT TRANSPORT FOR SIX EEC COUNTRIES
(1970-1979)
(Belgium, France, Germany, Luxembourg, Netherlands, United Kingdom)

| Transport mode | Tonne-kilometres | | | | Percentage change between 1970 and 1979(%) |
| | 1970 | | 1979 | | |
	billion tkm	%	billion tkm	%	
Rail	179	34.0	168	27.7	- 6
Inland waterway	101	19.2	103	16.9	+ 2
Pipeline (oil products)	6	1.2	12	1.9	+ 89
Road (national transport)	240	45.6	324	53.5	+ 35
of which:					
- other	145	27.6	190	31.4	+ 31
- own account	95	18.0	134	22.1	+ 41
Total	526	100	607	100	+ 15

5. It would obviously be interesting to try to find out whether or not there was diffusion in the period preceding 1970 (Kondratieff upswing phase), but the trade matrices which can be drawn up are probably limited.

- methodological aspects: separation of location and trade effects, more suitable subdivisions as regards both geographical area and the nature of the goods.

1.3. Trends in continental transport

This section is simply intended to recall the main trends in the markets for the different transport modes for the European countries (limited to the EEC).

1.3.1. Increasing share of road transport

Table 1.6. drawn up on the basis of statistics published by the Statistical Office of the European Communities [6], shows the trends in the four main surface transport modes for six EEC countries(6).

In the first place it should be stressed that the data on road transport, obtained by means of sample surveys, are generally limited to national (internal) traffic and generally exclude vehicles with a small payload (under 1t or 3t), which leads to underestimating:

- the road share of the transport market and, probably, the growth of road transport (probably due to faster growth of external traffic);
- hence the volume and, above all, the growth of surface transport as a whole.

We would draw attention to:

- the stagnation since 1970 of railway and waterway traffic and since 1975 of oil product transport by pipeline;
- the very vigorous growth of road transport: up 28 per cent between 1965 and 1970, 16 per cent between 1970 and 1975, 17 per cent between 1975 and 1979;
- an (underestimated) overall increase for the four modes of 2 per cent between 1970 and 1975 and 13 per cent (an annual average of 3.2 per cent) between 1975 and 1979.

1.3.2. Own account and other road transport

Since transport is an integral part of the activities of production and distribution, it is quite understandable

---

6. The majority of the data are not available for Denmark, Ireland and Italy. Some estimates have had to be made to fill gaps in the data for the six countries covered.

that many firms should carry their own goods: for the six EEC countries studied, own account transport amounted to 41 per cent of road tkm in 1979(7).

Table 1.6. shows that between 1970 and 1979 own account grew more rapidly than other road transport, but (see Table 1.7.):

- for the six countries as a whole the own account share fell between 1965 (42.2 per cent) and 1970 (39.5 per cent), reached the 1970 level again in 1975 (39.3 per cent)(8) and increased significantly in 1979 (41.2 per cent);
- the own account share varies from one country to another and the trends differ somewhat.

1.3.3. The development of complete trainloads in rail transport

The data for internal transport in France [4], from 1971 to 1980 (see Table 1.8.) show that:

- rail tkm fell slightly (2 per cent), while road transport increased by 44 per cent;
- complete trainloads (or more exactly shipments of at least 480 tonnes) increased by 16 per cent while SNCF "wagon groupings" (3 to 480 tonnes) fell by 13 per cent, the share of shipments of at least 480 tonnes increasing from 37 to 44 per cent of SNCF traffic;
- the combined "rail/road" share of shipments of at least 480 tonnes remained virtually the same: 16.3 per cent in 1971 and 15.3 per cent in 1979;
- the greatest increase (based on the data also given regarding distance covered) was in distances over 150 km, but the trend remained the same as regards shipments over 480 tonnes.

How are these results to be interpreted:

- how much is due to changes in the make-up of the goods to be transported (see paragraph 1.5.2.)?
- what has been the influence of changes in the quality of service?

The fact is that during the 1960s the SNCF made efforts to improve the quality of service by facilitating

---

7. The own account share falls rapidly with distance (see para. 1.5.1.). It should be noted that the distinction between own account and other is not always simple, particularly because the hire of vehicles with or without driver is widespread in certain countries (e.g. France).
8. Having been lower in 1973 (38.6 per cent).

Table 1.7

TRENDS IN THE OWN ACCOUNT SHARE OF ROAD FREIGHT
TRANSPORT IN SIX EEC COUNTRIES (1965-1979)
(Tonne-kilometres, internal transport)

Country	Own account + other					Own account as % of tkm			
	tkm 1979		Changes in tkm (%)			1965	1970	1975	1979
	Billion tkm	%	1965-1970	1970-1975	1975-1979				
Germany	97.8	30.2	+ 19	+ 12	+ 24	37	38	41	41
Belgium	9.9	3.1	+ 42	+ 8	+ 1	64	60	55	58
France	94.6	29.2	+ 43	+ 26	+ 21	46	39	40	44
Luxembourg	0.3	0.1							
Netherlands	17.0	5.2	+ 39	+ 24	+ 10	36	32	32	33
United Kingdom	104.6	32.2	+ 24	+ 12	+ 10	43	40	37	39
Total for the six countries	324.2	100	+ 28.1	+ 16.1	+ 16.6	42.2	39.5	39.3	41.2

the carriage of large shipments. In addition to complete trainloads of bulk goods, "block trains" or specialised complete trains were developed, running directly between origin and destination and thus by-passing marshalling yards: special trains for fresh vegetables, block trains of containers or rail/road trailers, car carriers, etc.

It should also be noted that seeking a higher quality of service through shorter transport times led, in the case of wagon groupings, to a substantial decrease in the ordinary service (tkm down 30 per cent between 1970 and 1979) to the benefit of the rapid service (tkm up 38 per cent between 1970 and 1979).

1.3.4. Development of combined transport

The statistics available for France enable the trends in SNCF tkm to be followed for both domestic and international traffic [7]:

- for road vehicles on wagons, i.e. combined rail/road transport in the strict sense of the term, operated by Novatrans;
- for containers and transcontainers, operated by the CNC (Compagnie Nouvelle de Conteneurs).

In the case of transporting road vehicles on wagons:

- the old URF (Union of European Railway-owned Road Services) technique, which was dominant in the early 1960s has gradually declined: about 10 per cent of tonnage in 1975, 1 per cent in 1981;
- the "piggyback" (ordinary semi-trailers on wagons) and "swap body" systems developed steadily, as shown by Table 1.9. which includes Novatrans international traffic;
- over the whole of the rail network there was an increase in tkm of 82 per cent between 1975 and 1980, an annual average of 12.7 per cent.

CNC operations include transporting sea containers to ports and domestic or international continental container or swap body traffic, (international business being handled by the Intercontainer Company). There was an overall increase of 58 per cent in CNC rail tkm between 1975 and 1980, an annual increase of 9.6 per cent.

1.4. Sea and air transport

1.4.1. General trends in seaborne transport

Characteristic trends of world seaborne trade in tonne-miles from 1965 to 1980(9) are as follows:

---

9. Data published by the OECD [8] according to Fearnleys [9]. The 1980 figures are estimates.

153

Table 1.8.

TRENDS IN INTERNAL RAIL AND ROAD TRANSPORT IN FRANCE
(1971-1980)

(Shipments of at least 3 tonnes)

Transport mode	Distance < 150 km tkm			Distance ≥ 150 km tkm			All distances tkm		
	1971 %	1980 %	Percentage change 1971-1980	1971 %	1980 %	Percentage change 1971-1980	1971 %	1980 %	Percentage change 1971-1980
Rail(*)									
- wagon groupings(**)	33	22	- 38	66	59	- 12	63	56	- 13
- over 480 tonnes	67	78	+ 10	34	41	+ 18	37	44	+ 16
Total	100	100	- 6	100	100	- 2	100	100	- 2
Rail	13.2	10.2	- 6	56.6	44.6	- 2	43.9	34.7	- 2
Road	86.8	89.8	+ 27	43.4	55.4	+ 59	56.1	65.3	+ 44
Total internal transport of which:	100	100	+ 23	100	100	+ 25	100	100	+ 24
- rail over 480 tonnes	8.9	8.0	+ 10	19.5	18.3	+ 18	16.3	15.3	+ 16

(*) Including rail/road combined transport (Novatrans).
(**) Shipments under 480 tonnes.

Table 1.9.

TRENDS IN NOVATRANS PIGGYBACK AND SWAP BODY TRAFFIC
(1971-1981)

Technique	Mt-km 1981	tkm (%)			Coefficient of interest(*)	
		1971	1976	1981	1971-1976	1976-1981
Piggyback	1699	96.1	92.7	62.9	1.39(6.8)	1.20(3.8)
Swap body	1002	3.1	7.3	37.1	3.36(27)	9.0(55)
Total	2701	100	100	100	1.45(7.7)	1.78(12.2)

(*) Figures in brackets: annual average rates of increase

- total seaborne trade increased but little between
  1974 and 1980 (up 2 per cent), because of stagnation in crude oil, oil products and iron ore;
- growth since 1974 nevertheless remains substantial
  for coal, grain and other products.

Table 1.10 shows trends between 1975 and 1980 and
also provides data on tonnages and hence average distances.

It should be noted that:

- total tonnes increased more than total tonne-miles
  (average annual growth 3.6 per cent as against 1.7);
- in the case of "other products", growth between
  1975 and 1980 (annual average about 5.5 per cent
  for both tonnes and tonne-miles) is connected with
  the increase in the volume of world trade in manufactured products for market economy countries between 1969 and 1978 (average annual increase 6.4 per
  cent; see Table 1.4).

Finally, the increase in world seaborne trade
(17,675 billion tonne-miles or 32,700 billion tkm in 1979,
up 15 per cent between 1975 and 1980) should be compared
with world freight transport by rail: 6,600 billion tkm
in 1979, up 9 per cent on the 1975 figure [1].

1.4.2. Development of roll-on roll-off and container
       traffic

During the sixties and up to about 1975, the vigorous
growth of seaborne transport led to a substantial increase
in the size of ships carrying bulk cargoes: tankers, ore

carriers, bulk carriers, and combination carriers (oil-ore and oil-bulk-ore carriers) [10].

In the general cargo sector there was considerable development of specialised ships and also an increase in size: ro-ro (roll-on/roll-off) and container (lift-on/lift-off) ships.

Mention should also be made of the more recent appearance of barge-carrying ships, but these are scarcely used except when the transport chain can use inland waterways at both ends of the sea leg.

Taking Europe as an example, ro-ro traffic developed first on short links - cross channel transport of accompanied cars and road transport vehicles or links between mainland France and Corsica - and has also spread to international coastal trade particularly in the Mediterranean. It also exists on deep-sea routes, but then often using mixed ro-ro/container ships (Atlantic Container Line, Europe-Pacific and Indian Ocean Traffic).

So far as we know, there is no world-wide statistical coverage of ro-ro transport. We would simply recall that cross-channel traffic is well-known thanks to the studies carried out for fixed-link projects and the growth of the sector can be illustrated by total ro-ro tonnages loaded and discharged in French mainland ports [12, 13].

- 17.2 million tonnes in 1980;
- despite a slackening in 1980, the annual average growth rate was 12.3 per cent over the period 1975-80 (up 78 per cent).

As regards the development of container traffic, still in French mainland seaports, the corresponding figures are:

- 10.3 million tonnes in 1980;
- an increase of 170 per cent between 1975 and 1980, i.e. an annual average growth of 22.0 per cent.

1.4.3. Trends in the pattern of deep-sea routes

The route taken by transport chains using seaborne transport and, in particular, the port used, depends not only on the proximity of the port to the origin or destination of the goods, but above all on the transport supply characteristics for the whole chain: total price and quality of service.

It is well known that the hinterlands of different national and foreign seaports overlap and it should be remembered that certain areas quite naturally tend to use

Table 1.10.

TRENDS IN WORLD SEABORNE TRADE (1975-80)

Cargo	Tonne-miles 1980 billion	Tonne-miles 1980 %	Tonne-miles Percentage change 1975-80(*)	Tonnes 1980 million	Tonnes 1980 %	Tonnes Percentage change 1975-80(*)	Average distance (miles) 1975	Average distance (miles) 1980
Crude oil	8,650	51.8	- 3(-0.5)	1,420	39.1	+12(2.4)	7,030	6,090
Oil products	920	5.5	+ 9(1.7)	245	6.8	+ 5(1.0)	3,630	3,760
Iron ore	1,510	9.0	+ 3(0.5)	310	8.5	+ 6(1.2)	5,040	4,870
Coal	870	5.2	+40(7.0)	172	4.7	+35(6.3)	4,890	5,060
Grains	1,070	6.4	+46(7.8)	185	5.1	+35(6.2)	5,360	5,780
Other products(**)	3,690	22.1	+31(5.6)	1,300	35.8	+31(5.5)	2,820	2,840
Total	16,710	100	+ 9(1.7)	3,632	100	+19(3.6)	5,040	4,600

(*) Figures in brackets: annual average rate of increase.
(**) Estimate.

foreign ports: for example, Eastern France is linked to Benelux ports through the Moselle and the Rhine [14].

It should also be noted that the hinterland of certain continental European ports, and especially Rotterdam, also extends to the United Kingdom. This transit between short-sea shipping across the Channel or the North Sea and deep sea routes was brought out by the 1978 survey by the National Ports Council [15]: this type of "transshipment" of United Kingdom deep sea shipping (excluding fuels) amounted in 1978 to 7.4 per cent of imported tonnage and 5.3 per cent of exported tonnage, these figures rising to 15.5 and 9.6 per cent for containers and 52.4 and 31.1 per cent for ro-ro (road transport vehicles).

These findings show clearly how specialised shipping services (ro-ro and container ships) can influence transport chains and it would obviously be very interesting to be able to assess the impact on these chains of the tendency of shipowners operating large unit-load vessels to limit the number of ports of call at each end of the voyage and make extensive use of land bridges.

1.4.4. Development of air freight

On the world level air freight transport remains modest as compared with seaborne transport, but the goods carried are generally of very high unit value. World air freight [1] (excluding mail):

- was only 23.6 billion tkm in 1978 as compared with over 30,000 billion tkm for sea transport (see paragraph 1.4.1);
- increased by a factor of 2.23 (tkm) between 1970 and 1978, i.e. an average annual increase of 10.5 per cent.

1.5. An example: the rail and road transport markets in France

This section describes some more detailed analyses of road and rail markets by the IRT (French Transport Research Institute). These analyses cover French internal transport as defined above (see paragraph 1.3.3.).

1.5.1. The influence of distance and type of freight

The data presented here are limited to medium and long-haul traffics (excluding transport within departments or between neighbouring departments, i.e. more or less distances of less than 100 km)(10); in the case of rail

---

10. In the SITRAM databank distances are not comparable between modes (see paragraph 1.1.). Therefore:

(Continued on next page.)

transport, only wagon groupings (shipments between 3 and 480 tonnes) are taken into account.

Figure 1.1. shows market shares as a function of distance for all freight(11). It can be seen that as distance increases:

- the SNCF share of total rail and road transport increases;
- the own account share of road transport decreases;
- the rapid service share of SNCF traffic increases.

For most products (according to the NST classifications), the rail share of all common carrier transport (rail + non-own account road, according to the statistical processing of way bills), increases as a function of distance. Regressions were carried out, particularly of the type:

$$\ln (T_1/T_2) = a \ln (d/400) + b(12).$$
Figure 1.2. shows the results(13).

There is no relationship between coefficients a and b, but arranging the results in a triangular form is in itself very informative:

- the goods which appear in the right-hand corner of the triangle, corresponding to high values of a (marked influence of distance on modal split) and values of b close to zero (market share of each mode substantial at around 400 km), are goods whose value is relatively low, density frequently high and which are often carried in bulk: grains, straw, non-ferrous minerals, dairy products;

(Note 10 continued from previous page.)
- a single geographical area has been used in a matrix of departments of origin and destination;
- a single reference distance has been used for each mode, based on an average distance for each pair of departments calculated according to the chargeable road distance which is close to the actual road distance.
11. Source: SNCF and sample survey of road freight transport.
12. b indicates the market shares for a distance of 400 km, approximately the average distance; a is the coefficient of elasticity of T_1/T_2 as a function of distance.
13. The rectangles indicate the precision of the estimate ($\pm$ standard deviation for the estimators of a and b). The results are most precise for the analysis of public carrier transport in view of the high sampling rates used for the way bills (3/10). The analyses cover traffics for which the reference distance is over 220 km.

Figure 1.1

SNCF (WAGON LOAD) AND ROAD MARKET SHARES ACCORDING TO
DISTANCE (1977)

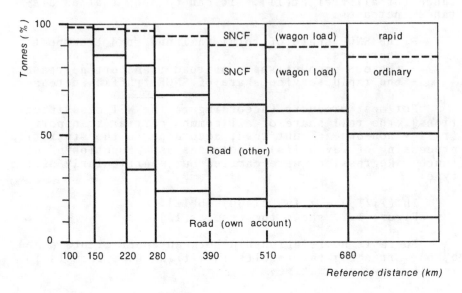

- NST classification 9 (manufactured articles) and
  other relatively high-value goods (fruit and
  vegetables, drinks) are less sensitive to distance
  (relatively low value of coefficient a) with very
  variable market shares (high dispersion of b).

1.5.2. Trends in the structure of the goods transported

It has already been seen (paragraph 1.3.3.), that
over the period 1971-80 road traffic increased while SNCF
traffic fell slightly. It is important to try to determine the factors which caused this and in particular the
possible impact of changes in the structure of freight
traffic, as regards the nature of the goods and the transport distance.

Table 1.11. [4] shows the trends for 13 major categories of freight.

A fall in the rail share can be seen for each category, but if the pattern of freight traffic had been the
same in 1980 as in 1971 it can be calculated that the rail
market share would have been 47 per cent in 1980 instead
of 44.6 per cent (as against 56.6 per cent in 1971).
This structural effect certainly appears relatively

160

Figure 1.2

INFLUENCE OF DISTANCE ON THE MARKET SHARES OF PUBLIC CARRIERS
(SNCF WAGON LOADS; ROAD HAULAGE EXCL. OWN ACCOUNT) (1977)

In (rail tonnage / road tonnage) = a In (d / 400) + b

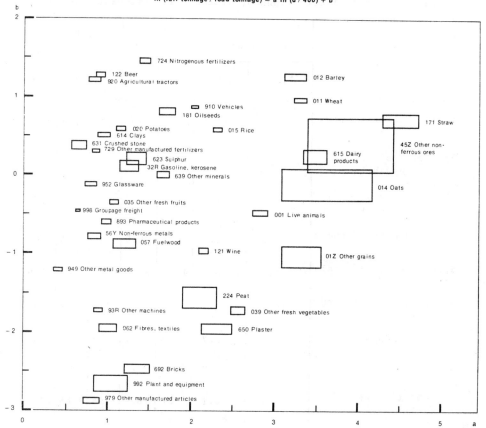

insignificant as regards these 13 categories of goods: it could actually be more important, but to prove this the analysis would have to use more homogeneous freight categories. Work is continuing in this direction, analysing trends at the level of NST items (trends during the period 1971-1980 of the coefficients a and b discussed above for the year 1977).

1.5.3. The search for models to explain modal split

The influence of distance on the rail/road modal split certainly reflects the influence of transport costs: the comparative cost of the two modes or the importance of transport costs in the price of the good. Interpreting modal split as a function of transport prices is very difficult, however, because:

Table 1.11.

TRENDS IN INTERNAL SNCF AND ROAD TRAFFIC BY SECTOR
(1971-1980)
(Shipments of at least 3 tonnes, distance 150 km, based on tkm)

Sector	Rail + road 1980		Rail share (%)		1980 index (1971 = 100)		
	billion tkm	%	1971	1980	Rail + Road	Rail	Road
1. Agricultural raw materials	9.4	10.0	45.7	42.1	135	124	144
2. Perishable agro-food products	6.5	6.9	30.1	14.3	134	64	164
3. Non-perishable food products	11.3	12.0	48.4	34.6	141	101	179
4. Solid mineral fuels	2.6	2.8	94.2	89.0	86	81	161
5. Ores & scrap metals	2.7	2.8	93.1	87.6	88	83	159
6. Sands, gravels and building materials	10.7	11.4	59.0	48.1	119	97	150
7. Oil products	6.3	6.7	72.3	63.1	111	97	149
8. Chemicals	7.2	7.6	53.0	44.1	133	110	158
9. Conditioners and fertilizers	5.8	6.1	90.4	78.3	98	85	222
10. Iron, steel and non-ferrous metals	8.2	8.7	65.7	58.6	113	101	136
11. Vehicles, mechanical & electrical engineering products	7.2	7.7	34.4	22.1	140	90	166
12. Other manufactured goods	8.5	9.0	34.8	20.7	127	75	154
13. Groupage freight, containers, combined transport	7.8	8.3	45.1	45.9	173	176	170
Total	94.2	100	56.6	44.6	125	98	159

- first, it is difficult to assess the actual price
of transport, even on average, for NST items (effective tariffs, price of terminal hauls by road in
the case of rail transport);
- second, the quality of service certainly has an
influence.

It is therefore very likely that the development of
models relating to modal split will need in future to
adopt a disaggregated approach based on sample shipments,
these being placed in the logistic chain. This will need
appropriate surveys to be made and the first phase, of a
methodological nature, has just been started.

2. GOODS TRAFFIC MODELLING

Once the actual situation has been observed and
analysed by means of the available statistics, the normal
scientific procedure is to try to explain the phenomena,
bring out the constant features and determine laws. This
research will naturally be given a quantitative dimension
through trying to build a model in the mathematical sense
of the term.

This approach was adopted long ago in the field of
passenger transport but it was only much later that efforts began to be made to analyse freight transport along
these lines.

2.1. Different types of model

Models can be classified according to different
criteria.

The first criterion is geographical: certain models
apply to each particular link, each line of communication
taken separately; others only make sense for a region or
country.

According to a second, comparable distinction, certain models are micro-economic, i.e. attempt to reflect
the behaviour of individual agents and reproduce their
decisions, others are macro-economic in the sense that
they try to explain trends in aggregates at the level of a
group of agents (industrial sector, geographical area,
etc.).

A third distinction can be made between explanatory
and descriptive models; the second reflect relationships
observed in the past without the nature of the causal link
between the parameters analysed appearing very clearly;
the first on the other hand are based on technical functions or hypotheses regarding the behaviour of agents or
groups of agents in order to determine the relationships
between the parameters investigated.

163

Analysis can also cover transport demand as a whole or take account of modal split.

Apart from these classifications which are very general and could apply to many fields other than freight transport, a distinction more pertinent to the present problem stems from the epistemological approach; from this standpoint, a distinction is made between:

- models concerned solely with transport demand, disregarding supply conditions;
- models based on the overall equilibrium between transport supply and demand;
- finally, models concerned with the analysis of individual behaviour.

It is this distinction that guides the structure of the present chapter. Besides it being appropriate to the problem concerned, it follows fairly faithfully the development of scientific thought in the field; it also corresponds to an increasing order of difficulty in obtaining the required statistics; finally, it satisfactorily matches up with the other classifications mentioned. The table below, though greatly simplified, shows this interrelationship.

Type of model / Classification	Demand analysis	Supply and demand equilibrium	Explanation of behaviours
Geographical coverage	Country or region; not by link	By country or region; not by link	By link
Micro or macro-economic	Macro-economic	Macro-economic	Macro-economic
Explanatory or descriptive	Slightly explanatory	Mainly descriptive	Explanatory
Modal split or not	Fairly poor reproduction of modal split	Imperfect reproduction of modal split	Permits the analysis of modal split

2.2. Demand analysis

Certain studies carried out in France are fully representative of this type of analysis where the aim is to establish a connection between transport volume and level of economic activity.

2.2.1. Description of the French studies

The reference documents on this subject are:

164

- the PRETRAM (freight transport forecast) model [17];
- the TRIMAR (international freight transport) [18];
- studies undertaken by the French railways to forecast freight traffic for all modes [19].

Though the studies are very different, the underlying philosophy is the same. Freight traffic may be expressed in tonnes or tonne-kilometres. According to the case it may be domestic or international traffic. Different relationships are established, either global (covering all types of freight) or by sector of activity; the indicators used may be either the value added of the sector or an indicator of quantitative output (e.g. steel or grain tonnages).

When these relationships are used for forecasting, they are generally supplemented by qualitative assessments based on specialist knowledge of the market analysed. This means that certain changes such as technological progress or the relocation of large plants in oligopolistic sectors can be taken into account.

2.2.2. Some results

As shown by the following examples, the econometric quality is satisfactory, since coefficients of correlation are considerably higher than 0.90 and are even in the order of 0.98 in the majority of cases.

PRETRAM:

- Correlation between the indicator of general economic activity and total freight traffic excluding hydrocarbons.

$$Y = 0.115 \ X \ 47.222 \quad R^2 = 0.9825$$
$$\quad (11.4) \quad (8.1) \quad DW = 1.2291$$

Y : total freight traffic excluding oil
X : traded GDP

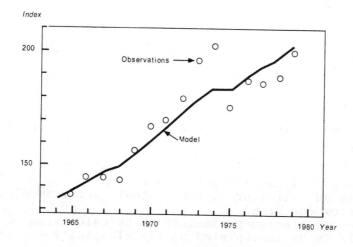

165

- Explanatory equation of building materials carried
  by road (tkm)

$Y = 0.0557 X - 1.367 \quad R^2 = 0.9622$
$\quad (19.5) \qquad (-2.6) \quad DW = 1.9354$

Y : building materials carried by road (tkm)
X : production of sands and gravels (tonnes) period
    1967 - 1979 - transport of fertilizers
    (a) Total traffic

$Y = 0.0177 X_1 + 3.219 \times 10^{-3} X_2 + 4.360 \times 10^{-4} X_3 + 2.117$
$\quad (2.0) \qquad\quad (0.872) \qquad\qquad\quad (4.5) \qquad\qquad\quad (2.6)$

$R^2 = 0.8909$
$DW = 1.8944$

Y : Total fertilizer traffic (tkm)
X_1 : Index of potash production (1970 = 100)
X_2 : Index of chemical industry production (1970 = 100)
X_3 : Production of compound fertilizers ('000 tonnes)
    Period 1963 - 1979
    (b) SNCF traffic

$Y = 0.0167 X_1 + 3.775 \times 10^{-4} X_2 + 1.121$
$\quad (2.1) \qquad\quad (4.1) \qquad\qquad\quad (1.4)$
$\quad R^2 = 0.7438$
$\quad DW = 1.8285$

Y : Fertilizers carried by the SNCF (tkm)
X_1 : Index of potash production (1970 = 100)
X_2 : Production of compound fertilizers ('000 tonnes)
    Period 1963 - 1979
    (c) Road traffic

$Y = 0.0168 X_1 - 0.490$
$\quad (36.8) \qquad (-9.9)$
$\quad R^2 = 0.9890$
$\quad DW = 1.8917$

Y : fertilizers carried by road (tkm)
X_1 : chemical industry production (1970 = 100)
    Period 1962 - 1979

TRIMAR

- Explanation of the imports of various products by road

$Y = 0.0129 X_1 - 1.336$
$\quad (41.8) \qquad (-10.8)$
$\quad R^2 = 0.9926$
$\quad DW = 1.7156$

Y : Imports of various products by road
X_1 : Total French imports by volume
    Period 1965 - 1969

SNCF studies

These studies by sector are based on a relationship
of the form

$P = a I^b$
    where P is total traffic in tkm
    I is an indicator of the economic activity of the
    sector concerned
    a and b are two parameters to be calculated
    b is to be interpreted as the elasticity

The regressions relate to the period 1967 - 1980.

2.2.3. Limits of this approach

Satisfactory as the results appear to be, the fact remains that these models have their limits.

Sector	Elasticity b (b)	In a		a	R^2
1. Agricultural and food products NST: 0-1	1.4205 (0.08311)	- 5.86657		0.00283	0.9605
2. Solid mineral fuels NST: 2	1.5615 (0.06575)	+ 2.56210		12.9630	0.9758
3. Oil products NST: 3A - 3B	0.6847 (0.04857)	+ 6.55664		703.901	0.9342
4. Minerals and building materials NST: 6A	0.97805 (0.05997)	- 1.43746		0.23753	0.9500
5. Ores and metals NST: 4A - 4B 5A - 5B	1.0860 (0.10431)	- 1.02631		0.35833	0.8856
6. Chemicals and fertilizers NST: 6B - 7 - 8A - 8C	0.6787 (0.03428)	2.37920		10.7963	0.9703
7. Transport equipment, agricultural equipment, metal goods and manufactured articles NST: 8B - 9A - 9B - 9C - 9D	1.0645 (0.06525)	- 3.28649		0.03738	0.95685
Total	0.7686 (0.06442)	+ 1.89232		6.63476	0.92225
Total excluding energy products All NST except 2 - 3A - 3B	0.8393 (0.06653)	+ 0.80237		2.23082	0.9300

First, their forecasting ability is not great; this is connected with the natural limits of this type of approach: by and large, the parameters involved have increased fairly regularly in the past; their correlation is thus to some extent fortuitous and does not necessarily correspond to a causal relationship, and could well be disproved in the future. A second reason for the limited forecasting capacity of these models lies in the nature of the explanatory variable. This may be either a physical quantity or a value added. Obviously the best explanatory variable is the physical quantity expressed in tonnes, for example, but the easier parameter to forecast is very often value added. There are no medium or long-term forecasts, in France at any rate, of the physical quantities representative of the activity of economic sectors.

This type of model is also limited as regards the field of application. They can explain and hence forecast traffic for a given country or region, but are totally inoperative where it is a matter of determining traffic over a particular link, for example between two towns or two regions. Their powers of geographical discrimination are very limited.

These models can also be assessed according to the forecasting horizon they permit. In this regard, in the very short term, i.e. the horizon of a few months, the economic relationships implied by the models concerned do not have the time to operate and such models are not very useful. They work best in the medium term, in the range from one to a few years.

At the long-term end of the scale, say over five years, structural changes generally invalidate the models.

This is particularly apparent in the correlation between total freight traffic and traded GDP. A market fall in this correlation can be seen after 1973. This phenomenon is quite common in crisis periods, as shown by Patrice Salini [21].

Period	Elasticity	R^2
1901 - 1913	1.01	0.974
1919 - 1938	0.70	0.795
1948 - 1965	0.52	0.943
1966 - 1977	0.27	0.431

In this analysis covering a very long period, the elasticity calculated is that for French rail traffic. Elasticity is low, but this is because rail transport was for a long period the only option available to the production sector and the coefficient of correlation, or rather its square R^2, measures the quality of the fit obtained between these two variables over the period considered. It can be seen that this quality falls sharply in the periods of crisis 1919-38 and 1966-77.

This probably reflects the introduction in crisis periods of new mechanisms which upset the simple relationship between production and transport. This probably applies in the first place to stocks, which can be managed differently, but also to changes in buying and marketing policy. It appears that during crisis periods the rationalisation of production leads heavy industry to choose locations which cut down overall transport distances (e.g. steel works by the sea) while, conversely, light industry tends to seek cheaper suppliers further

afield and the need to sell more makes them seek more distant clients. Knowledge of average transport distances
and their trends is in line with this interpretation, as
are the studies [5] mentioned in Chapter I on the
diffusion of transport in the downswing phase of
Kondratieff cycles.

What is more, the overall relationship between production and transport does not appear stable over time.
The long period analyses by P. Salini already mentioned
[21] show that elasticity has decreased over time during
the 19th and 20th Centuries. This is shown by the graph,
where it can be seen that as compared with a constant
elasticity curve the deviations show a long-term trend for
elasticity to fall.

Finally, as their name indicates, these models are
solely demand models. Transport supply is not taken into
account, or rather comes in only indirectly. Service
quality, transport times reliability and above all cost
are disregarded. This disadvantage is perhaps not very
serious when trying to estimate total traffic for a country, since the transport share of the total cost of products is generally low, in the order of 3 to 10 per cent.
A change in transport cost will not have much effect on
the price of goods and will therefore not affect the
volume of trade very much; in short, the elasticity of
overall transport demand is low with respect to supply
characteristics. But this observation immediately needs
to be qualified. First, it is true only in the short
term; faced with a rise in transport costs, shippers
modify their organisation, their storage locations, distribution and supply systems and this will have an effect
on tonne-kilometres if not on the actual tonnage transported. Second, if the average transport share of total
cost is low, this is not true in international trade which
in volume terms is mainly goods of low unit value for
which transport costs may account for a substantial percentage of total cost. Under these conditions a change in
transport costs is not without repercussions on the volume
of activity of the sectors concerned and there may be a
rapid change in sources of supply and consequently in the
pattern of traffic flows. Finally, and above all, the
absence of supply characteristics makes these models ill-
suited for accounting for modal split. In fact, as shown
by the examples mentioned, modal split is assumed to depend on time, the share of each mode changing ineluctably,
generally according to laws of a logistic nature. This
crude interpretation accounts reasonably well for the past
trends, but obviously is mainly of an explanatory nature.
For this reason, there are reasons to doubt the value of
forecasts derived from such a model.

Thus, despite its econometric precision, the model
based on demand analysis has its limits (no geographical
precision, absence of supply conditions, inability to

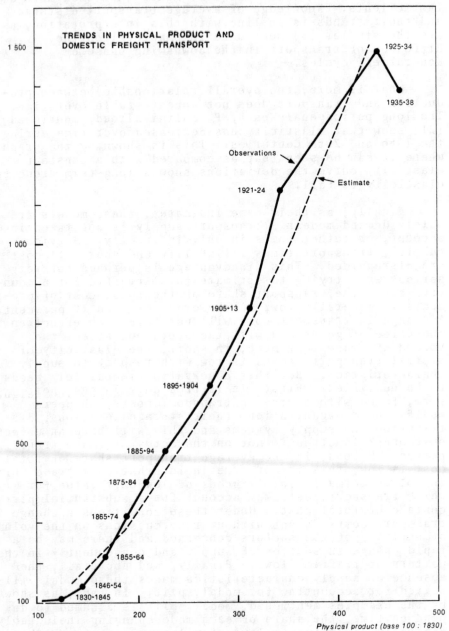

t-km (base 100 : 1830)

TRENDS IN PHYSICAL PRODUCT AND
DOMESTIC FREIGHT TRANSPORT

1 500

1 000

500

100

1925-34
1935-38

Observations

Estimate

1921-24

1905-13

1895-1904

1885-94

1875-84

1865-74

1855-64

1846-54
1830-1845

100   200   300   400   500

Physical product (base 100 : 1830)

account for modal split, instability of its parameters in
the long term). There is therefore reason to question the
reliability of an approach which tries to explain transport volume solely through production indicators and to
turn instead to research based on the equilibrium between
supply and demand.

2.3. Equilibrium between supply and demand

The work that best illustrates this method and which is used as a basis for discussion here is that carried out by the Netherlands Transport Institute for the Commission of the European Communities [22 and 23].

The aim of this research was "the preparation of estimates of Community infrastructure requirements for merchandise traffic on principal routes (road, rail and inland waterway) in the years 1985 and 2000".

These terms of reference highlight the nature of the improvements to be made on the previous demand models: these concern geographical precision (transport volume has to be forecasted link by link and no longer globally for the whole of an area if infrastructure requirements are to be determined), and modal split (traffic for each mode has to be known).

To meet this objective the Netherlands Institute has developed a model, or rather a series of consecutive models, very similar to those traditionally used to analyse passenger traffic.

2.3.1. General description

The block diagram taken from the reference text shows the structure of the models. As regards domestic freight, there is:

- a production and attraction model which connects the demand for transport by commodity group to the economic activity of the country; this model is not unlike the preceding demand models;
- a distribution model which divides the total volume of transport among the different possible destinations. These models give the total volume of transport by geographical link, town to town or area to area. Gravity models are well-known in passenger traffic theory; generalised costs are taken into account, bringing into play transport time, cost and distance in the form of weighted means for each transport mode. These variables constitute the argument in the traditional resistance function in traffic models, the best known form being:

$$\frac{1}{c\alpha} ;$$

- a modal split model which divides the above total traffic among the different modes. Modal split is assumed to be determined by three explanatory variables:

171

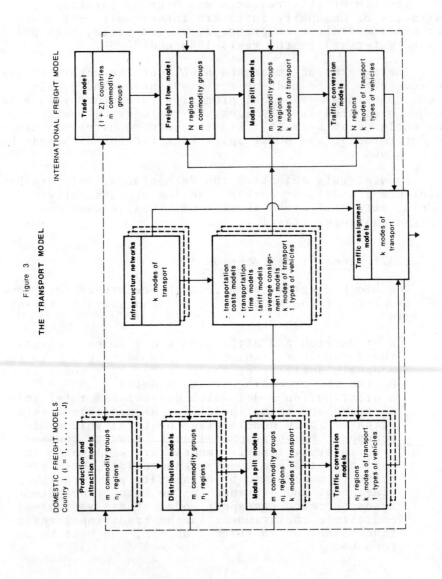

Figure 3

THE TRANSPORT MODEL

INTERNATIONAL FREIGHT MODEL

Trade model
(1 + Z) countries
m commodity groups

Freight flow model
N regions
m commodity groups

Modal split models
m commodity groups
N regions
k modes of transport

Traffic conversion models
N regions
k modes of transport
1 types of vehicles

Infrastructure networks
k modes of transport

- transportation costs models
- transportation time models
- tariff models
- average consignment models
k modes of transport
1 types of vehicles

Traffic assignment models
k modes of transport

DOMESTIC FREIGHT MODELS
Country i (i = 1, ... J)

Production and attraction models
m commodity groups
n_j regions

Distribution models
m commodity groups
n_j regions

Modal split models
m commodity groups
regions
n_j regions
k modes of transport

Traffic conversion models
n_j regions
k modes of transport
1 types of vehicles

. transport cost
. transport time
. transport volume,
the three factors influencing modal split in the
order shown;
- a traffic conversion model. This type of model is
meaningless in passenger traffic studies, but is
essential here: it converts the tonnages and
tonne-kilometres provided by the preceding models
into vehicle movements. This conversion depends on
the volume of the transport market, a factor
already introduced in the modal split model, but
also on the size of vehicles and the relative proportions of laden and unladen journeys.

Finally, it should be noted that for the sake of
logical consistency there should be feedback between the
distribution and modal split models. The distribution
model in fact introduces the weighted mean transport cost
for each commodity group and this weighted cost depends on
modal split.

2.3.2. Main findings

Of the many findings resulting from this study, it
would appear interesting to give some examples of traffic
forecasts and the elasticities of transport volume with
respect to supply conditions.

There are scarcely any points of comparison against
which to judge these elasticities, but they nevertheless
appear very plausible as to order of magnitude.

2.3.3. Scope and limits

As described above, these models appear satisfactory. They form a logical sequence: what quantities are
to be transported? Where? By what modes? In what vehicles? This sequence of questions seems well-organised.

What is more, they fill many of the gaps found in
demand models.

The geographical analysis is finer - they determine
traffic link by link, not just by region or country.

Finally, the results depend on transport supply, i.e.
infrastructure capacities, transport costs, transport
times. Transport supply does not influence the volume of
goods to be carried, however, which means that according
to the model economic activity does not depend on
transport quality, but this assumption, though probably
open to question in the long term, seems correct in the
short term. Supply does, however, come into the
determination of destinations (distribution models) and
above all modal choice.

THE DEVELOPMENT OF DOMESTIC FREIGHT TRANSPORT PER COUNTRY
(in million tonnes, index 1974 = 100)

Country	1974	1985	2000/(2%)	2000/(3%)
Belgium	391 (100)	524 (134)	648 (166)	941 (241)
Denmark(1)	14 (100)	21 (150)	28 (200)	47 (336)
France	1,974 (100)	3,136 (159)	3,919 (200)	5,946 (301)
United Kingdom	1,939 (100)	2,664 (137)	3,350 (173)	5,638 (291)
Ireland	92 (100)	127 (138)	148 (161)	214 (233)
Italy	1,099 (100)	1,484 (135)	1,736 (158)	2,591 (236)
Luxembourg	20 (100)	24 (120)	31 (155)	43 (215)
The Netherlands	422 (100)	535 (127)	652 (154)	934 (221)
Germany(1)	557 (100)	636 (114)	872 (157)	1,388 (249)
Spain	1,659 (100)	2,232 (135)	2,636 (159)	3,595 (217)
Total study areas	8,167 (100)	11,384 (139)	14,020 (172)	21,337 (261)

1. The freight transport figures for Denmark are not
complete, while for Germany freight transport under 50 km
is not recorded.

These satisfactory aspects, however, should not be
allowed to hide the difficulties encountered in using
these models.

First, the accuracy of the findings is limited - the
parameters used in the models can be estimated only - with
a fairly large margin of error. When these models are
used to reproduce the past, the traffics calculated
deviate substantially from the recorded figures. This is
not really surprising, because already in the case of
passenger traffic, sequential models and their gravity
specifications were but a poor representation of the real
situation, and in the case of freight transport there are

TONNES AND TONNE/KM BY MODE OF TRANSPORT FOR INTERNATIONAL TRANSPORT
(1974 = 100; tonnes in millions, tonne/km in thousand millions)

	1974		1985		2000/(2%)		2000/(5%)	
	Absolute	Index	Absolute	Index	Absolute	Index	Absolute	Index
Rail transport								
Tonnes	91.2	100	124.9	137	191.5	210	254.2	498
Tonne/km	46.9	100	72.4	154	116.8	249	287.2	612
Road transport								
Tonnes	117.3	100	263.7	225	466.0	397	1,121.5	956
Tonne/km	53.5	100	128.0	239	233.2	436	596.3	1,115
Inland waterway navigation								
Tonnes	190.8	100	327.4	172	567.9	298	1,490.6	781
Tonne/km	66.1	100	114.3	173	198.9	301	531.7	804

	30 per cent increase in real road transport costs	30 per cent increase in real rail transport costs
Change in the volume transported by:		
- Road	- 12 %	+ 7.4 %
- Rail	+ 24 %	- 25 %
- Inland waterways	+ 1 %	+ 3.7 %
Corresponding price elasticities(*)		
- Road	- 0.41	+ 0.25
- Rail	+ 0.80	- 0.83
- Inland waterways	+ 0.02	+ 0.12

(*) Ratio between the change in the relative value of transport volume to the change in the relative value of costs.

added difficulties associated with the state-of-knowledge of this field.

In the majority of countries the fact is that there are deficiencies in the freight transport statistics. Sometimes it is such or such a mode which is particularly poorly understood, generally road traffic (see Chapter 1), sometimes it is empty back hauls; combined transport is everywhere very poorly understood as regards its nature and function, so that its modelling is particularly defective. All this makes it particularly difficult, both to construct complete models, particularly for international traffic, and to assess these models and compare their results with reality, because this reality is itself very poorly understood.

But the very prevalence of this statistical inadequacy is food for thought. If we lack reliable data of the required type, is it not because basically the problem has been poorly or inadequately stated and the quantities usually measured are not necessarily the right ones? This question links up with another concerning the insufficiently explanatory nature of the models described. At first sight these models appear logical and consistent, but while they are a definite advance on demand-based models, they remain above all descriptive - they are not based on a detailed analysis of agents' behaviour, as is proved by the fact that they are at macro-economic level. While the choice of variables and the way in which they operate appears intuitively correct, it must be recognised on reflection that this intuition is not supported by any precise and rigorous reasoning. All in all, once again it is much more a matter of a descriptive model than an explanatory one. For this reason, despite the value of these models and the undoubted advance that they represent, their forecasting capability and accuracy remain limited. In order to go further, it is necessary to start on a different basis and analyse individual behaviours.

2.4. Modelling individual behaviours

The analyses which have been developed in this direction find their culmination and most sophisticated expression in a study by the MIT (Centre for Transportation Studies)[24]. This is based on the disaggregated models developed at MIT by M. Manheim and M. Ben Akiva, in which the variable to be explained is the individual decision, here that of the firm with a transport operation to carry out, either to obtain its raw materials or to distribute its finished products.

2.4.1. Description of the method

The original feature of this freight transport model is that it treats as part of a single decision-making

176

process not only the transport operation itself, i.e. the choice of destination and mode, but also the whole policy of moving and storing goods, or, in the terminology now becoming accepted, the firm's logistic policy. The decision admittedly does not involve the volume of production nor the location of factories and plants, and in this sense the model can be considered as intermediate between short and medium term. To this extent, it may appear more restrictive than some of the previous models in which the volume to be transported could vary according to economic activity and was implied by it: but it is also wider in that it covers the whole logistic policy. All in all, it appears different, more precise and more logical.

In the case of raw materials supplies, the most important costs involved are:

- purchase price;
- administrative costs associated with ordering;
- handling and packing costs;
- transport costs;
- financial cost of the goods being immobilised during transport;
- financial cost of storage (interest on the working capital required to finance the stock);
- cost of possible exhaustion of the stock.

The firm tries to minimise the sum of these costs.

Two types of model can be developed on this basis.

In the first, which could be called deterministic, it is assumed that the various costs are perfectly known or at least are so judged by the decision-maker, who chooses the lowest cost solution. The decision is thus an all or nothing one according to the value of the parameters.

The second model is probabilistic: it is assumed that the different costs are poorly known by the decision-maker and contain a random element. The model then determines, according to the value of the parameters, not a decision but the probability of a decision. Using certain traditional hypotheses on the nature of the random factors affecting costs, well-known mathematical formulae are derived, such as the logit or probit models.

The most convenient is the logit formula:

$$\text{Pr (imq)} = \frac{e - \mu \ W^\circ \ imq}{\sum_{i'm'q'} e - \mu \ W^\circ \ i'm'q'}$$
$$i'm'q' \ \Sigma \ A$$

Where

i   : place of origin of the good transported
m   : mode
q   : size of shipment
μ : a parameter representing the variance of the random factors affecting the costs
W° imq   : the observable and certain part of the logistic cost of the decision corresponding to para- meters i m and q.

W° i'm'q' is a linear combination of the parameters listed above.

The model whose general structure has just been described presents several attractive features. First, it is based on a reasonable hypothesis regarding the decision-maker's behaviour from which it directly derives. It is based on a proven principle: logit-type models are already widely used in passenger traffic studies and for modelling many other choice situations.

2.4.2. Some results

Models of this type do in fact lead to satisfactory concordance between calculated and observed values.

The originators of the model have tested it on several types of data and a presentation of some of the results obtained is not without interest.

First, the sign of the coefficients corresponds to what might be expected - in particular, the coefficients relating to cost are negative. The most important variables are the transport characteristics and the financial expenditure - an equally plausible result.

In addition to the coefficients relating to financial costs there can be an implicit interest rate perceived by the shipper, this rate being distinctly higher than the actual interest rate.

It is also possible to derive coefficients of fit of the elasticities. The following table shows some of these elasticities for different sectors and different transport modes.

Transport cost elasticities

For a load equivalent to a full vehicle.

	Rail	Road	Air	
1. Fertilizers	- 1,045	- Houston-Chicago - 1,143	- 5,000 t/year - 5,087	
2. Pharmaceutical products		- Los Angeles-Boston- 0,0001	- 1 t/year - 0,002	
3. Textiles	- 0,011	- Boston-Martford - 0,006	- 100 t/year - 0,003	

178

In the absence of percentages for comparison, it is difficult to judge the absolute values of these elasticities, but they can be considered not unreasonable and, above all, the differences seen between each of the three cases are correct.

This analysis also has the merit of bringing out the influence of new factors such as size of shipment or the different logistic cost parameters.

2.4.3. Limits of the analysis

But this enrichment is also the cause of further problems - where are these additional data, these factors which are not available in any general statistical system, to be found? The gaps in the statistical apparatus, already regrettable in the case of supply/demand equilibrium models, appear even more glaring here. They can be filled only by means of special surveys among shippers.

A further factor complicates both the analysis and the observation of the actual situation. This results from the heterogeneous nature of the transport market which needs to be reduced to improve the accuracy of the model. The question then arises as to what the most pertinent segmentation is for transport decisions and in particular modal choice. The common sense answer is supported by analysis of the concrete data available which brings out three factors: unit value of the good, transport distance and the utilisation flows of the good concerned, but these factors are badly covered by the usual statistics.

It can therefore be seen that disaggregated models are scarcely adapted for general use. They do not constitute a universal tool for dealing with each concrete case of choosing infrastructures or fixing operating or tariff policies.

Their big advantage is to open up the prospect of improving knowledge in the long term. They will make it possible to determine the most pertinent statistics, which are not the most common and usual ones.

Their main shortcoming, however, is methodological. These models are based, as the authors admit, on short-term analyses. They in fact assume stability as regards all the long-term variables concerning the firm's volume of activity, its location and the nature of its production.

Disaggregated models can therefore not take account of medium- and long-term structural change like those discussed above which from 1973 caused a break in the relationship between transport volume and the level of economic activity.

It may indeed be asked whether the analysis of these medium- and long-term developments is at present capable of being modelled mathematically.

The fact is that at the 5-10 year horizon where such an analysis has to be placed the interactions are so numerous and so complex and qualitative change becomes so important that quantification seems both beyond our capability and not very appropriate.

*

*　　　　*

On the basis of these considerations, an attempt can be made to indicate the broad lines that future research into explaining freight transport should take.

First of all it is necessary to bring out the parameters pertinent to the main choices regarding transport and the factors governing these choices by refining and generalising the analysis of the agents involved in transport, in the first place shippers, but also auxiliaries and carriers, this analysis to include transport decisions as far as possible in the overall policy of the firm.

It will then be necessary to analyse the statistics compiled on this basis, this analysis probably being fairly qualitative in nature, somewhat along the lines of those described in Chapter I, but based on more sophisticated and more relevant statistical data.

Such analyses would provide answers to the usual and traditional questions regarding modal choice. It must also be hoped that they would throw light on medium and long-term trends.

Since they do not yet exist, this last point is merely a matter of conjecture, but it is founded on such a broad base of facts and observations that it is permissible to venture someway along the path indicated, which passes via the analysis of trends in transport organisation.

3. TRENDS IN TRANSPORT ORGANISATION

Analysis of the main trends which have marked recent years and of the limits of modelling suggests that the field of investigation in the search for the phenomena governing developments in the transport sector needs to be extended.

There has always been a temptation to regard transport as a relatively autonomous sector whose underlying trend follows its own internal logic; very often considerations of the freight transport problem have lacked the horizontal, intermodal dimension.

Today's more socio-economic approach enables new consistencies in the trends of this sector to be discovered; transport is the reflection of interdependence between regions, firms and individuals so that it might almost be asked what its specific nature is.

Be this as it may, transport always plays a strategic role both for economic agents in their market activities and for the authorities in their policies for economic and social relations.

In the case of firms, recognition of the role of transport is demonstrated by their increasing concern with the logistics of the movement of goods.

In the case of the authorities, discussion of transport was long limited to the structuring effects of infrastructures without sufficient attention being paid to the operation of complete transport chains.

This concluding chapter is not intended to propose a new approach to the transport problem but simply to raise certain issues, as far as possible illustrated by examples which appear indicative of trends in the transport sector.

Recent trends in transport organisation are characterised mainly by the appearance of logistic policies in firms, recognition of the transport chain logic and attempts to control the shipment of products.

3.1. Emergence of logistic policies

In a context of slower growth and greater competition on national and international markets, rationalising all transport, storage and handling operations appears to be a new source of productivity increases and hence a factor in competitiveness. It has destroyed the stable transport/production relationship as described in Chapter 1.

A logistic policy can not only reduce the cost of transporting goods but also accelerate the turnover of capital: as was seen in the preceding chapter, these parameters are still difficult to quantify but they already appear to be determinant in industrial and agricultural policy.

The French national accounting system does not permit the cost of transport in intermediate consumption to be assessed with any precision. In particular, expenditure on own-account transport is not shown separately.

Very rough overall estimates suggest a transport share of something over 10 per cent in intermediate consumption, this figure ranging from about 2 to over 20 per cent depending on sector.

Difficulties are also encountered with estimating transport statistics in foreign trade and a series of studies of the role of transport in international competitiveness has been started in France, involving both quantitative studies to evaluate costs and analyses of transport operating mechanisms and market organisation.

The very broad estimates made to date give an order of magnitude of 15 per cent for the transport share of the value of products traded with other countries. Once again this figure is an average of very diverse situations, ranging from raw materials, in which the value added by transport services is sometimes higher than the initial value of the product itself, to very sophisticated high-value products.

Transport operations in the strict sense of the term also need to be seen in relation to all the logistic operations which control packaging, storage, handling and distribution to keep pace with production rates.

Without trying to precisely define the field covered by logistics, it concerns a substantial share of the national value added, estimated by trade sources at something in the order of 20 to 30 per cent.

All these estimates justify firms' concern with logistic problems which sometimes even leads them to modify their management structure.

In addition, two major factors have reinforced this awareness since the mid-70s:

- the high interest rates of recent years, which heavily penalises immobolised capital - and the interest rates perceived by operators are probably even higher than the actual rates, as seen in Chapter 2;
- technical possibilities connected with progress in computing and more particularly micro computers which make it possible to implement the information systems necessary for keeping track of goods and managing administrative and financial documents.

With the development of trade and increased complexity of transport operations there is increasing need for a "transport organiser" function to co-ordinate and organise the shipment of products according to increasingly diverse criteria and procedures.

3.2. The logic of the chain

A transport chain for shipping a particular good is a series of operations comprising services very often supplied by different firms. The accent is not just on the operation of each link, but the co-ordination of the whole.

International trade, in particular involving seaborne transport, provides examples of chains involving a great variety of carriers, agents, etc.

An interesting example of this chain logic is found in the analysis of port hinterlands. In the carriage of various goods, the distribution of flows within a given country is generally determined not by the criterion of surface distance or cost of land transport, but by the sea transport and port organisation.

Thus the overseas areas traded with are a very important factor determining the areas of influence of French ports. First, it is possible to distinguish foreign areas for which the attraction of a single port (or group of ports) extends to the greater part of the country: this is the case of the United Kingdom as regards the "medium-sized" channel ports.

In trade with Northern Europe, the large ports such as Le Havre, Dunkirk, Rouen have greater dominance over the medium-sized channel ports.

In the case of South American and Indian Ocean trade, the hinterland of Marseilles and to a certain extent Bordeaux exercise a stronger attraction in the South of France.

Finally, the case of links with Africa is really the only one where the port hinterlands correspond closely with the "natural" hinterlands(14) and where the influence of Benelux ports is very weak.

The differences can really be explained only by the quality of shipping services to the different ports, which is known to be relatively homogeneous in the case of French ports and West Africa.

All these observations are confirmed in the case of container traffic where "equalisation" practices have been developed by shipowners who try to concentrate traffic on a limited number of ports in order to increase the turn-around of ships and therefore offer rates for the land leg according to the origin (or destination) of the goods in France, regardless of the port which will actually be used.

---

14. Hinterlands defined according to the criteria of land distance or cost of land transport.

3.3. Controlling transport chains

A transport chain may be controlled upstream by the industrial firm, carrier or transport auxiliary or downstream by the distribution firm.

Efforts to obtain this control may result from a desire to impose a logistic policy on the operation of the chain, and thus impose a transport organisation in line with particular interests or to strengthen a commercial position on the market.

Control may be total or partial depending on whether it is exercised over all or part of the chain. It takes various forms ranging from very tight integration of the whole chain to simply using to advantage the operating rules of the market.

Thus, within a single sector, that of large-scale distribution, very different systems of control can be seen. These correspond in fact to diametrically opposed marketing philosophies and it is interesting to study them. Several types of organisation are found among the biggest distribution companies, in particular(15):

- the goods go via a depot belonging to the producer - and thus a part of his logistic system - then, generally, via a distributor's warehouse before being delivered to the retailer (about 20 per cent of distribution).
- the goods go directly to the distributor's warehouse (about 80 per cent of distribution).

Even retailers which hitherto had not worked out a policy of integration with the transport chain are increasingly linking up with warehouses which deliver complete lorryloads. This in fact raises a problem of marketing policy to the extent that the buyers who formerly had great freedom in ordering are now forced to be more disciplined.

With the concentration of points of sale over the past twenty years or so there have often been conflicts between producers with a network of depots and distributors setting up, with their warehouses, a competing logistic system extending upstream in the chain.

The tendency towards concentration of points of sale has apparently not resulted in an improvement of the rail share of the market.

---

15. This analysis summarises a number of conclusions emerging in particular in the work of J. Colin of the CRET (Aix-en-Provence) and SAE Studies [26 to 32].

The system of goods going via a producer's depot is becoming proportionately less important as compared with direct delivery to a warehouse. But the rail share of delivery to depots is often higher because of the nature of the shipments (bigger and less frequent) even though the number of hypermarkets with warehouses served by rail has increased.

It nevertheless seems that the competitive conditions of road and rail are fairly even for deliveries to a large number of warehouses, even though the advantage is generally with road transport. This means that if road haulage conditions become more restrictive (e.g. driving hours), it is very likely that the railways will substantially increase their share of this type of traffic.

It is also to be noted that:

- warehouses are all too often not linked to the rail network;
- the network of inter-regional warehouses (often about ten covering France) is on the whole badly served by rail.

The above system involving only the producer and distributor can become more complicated with the appearance of transport sector operators (carriers or transport auxiliaries) who get involved in the distribution network such as, for example, a road haulier who groups the regional depots of several producers in a single centre. This centre may be supplied by rail, but local distribution of the different products is by road.

It should in fact be stressed that as regards transport the concentration of operations and firms is not the only trend and that more indirect forms of control in a market where regulation through competition is difficult are equally constraining.

There are economic reasons which justify a certain specialisation of activities in this field, thus enabling firms of more modest size to impose themselves or at least to survive.

This specialisation may be either technical, for a particular type of product or handling (e.g. food products, cold chains, etc.), or geographical to the extent that the activities connected with transport need particular conditions of location in the regions in France. Furthermore, in trade with other countries, knowledge of the practices and regulations and the existence of durable commercial contracts to guarantee continuity of the transport chain are also a factor in the specialisation of activities.

In the case of large firms, recognition of the need for a certain specialisation is reflected in the adoption of relatively decentralised management systems in order to be able to respond to needs.

It has introduced a certain limit on the diversity of activities; diversification into sectors controlled by trading partners may be justified in order to know the competitors better, but the greater part of activity generally remains concentrated on a well-defined service.

This specialisation is brought out by surveys among firms which show that diversification of activities rarely exceeds 25 to 30 per cent of turnover.

Specialisation leads to subtle control mechanisms which the introduction of computerisation and new management methods make even more difficult to identify.

Control strategies are developing based on operations management, whether it be a matter of information relating to goods movements, financial movements or simply administrative formalities more or less independent of the physical control of the goods.

An example taken from international transport illustrates rather well the degree of sophistication that control mechanisms may reach in a difficult context where a firm has to ship exports to about twenty countries every week. Such a diversity of flows prohibits strict control of the chains and means that specialist agents have to be used for the different areas. In this case the control mechanisms are based on continuous reappraisal of the choice of agents, with requests accounts in the form of a "progress schedule" of the product, and the development of a transport document, a kind of specification circulated to all distribution centres and ex-post examination of transport costs. The company keeps informed of the prices and tariffs in force and performs the administrative operations itself.

Finally, in the development of transport control attention must be drawn to two important trends which have marked recent years:

1. A gradual change in the balance of power between producers and distributors in favour of the latter. Control over the movement of goods is thus shifting from upstream to downstream with a relatively greater dispersion of decision centres;
2. Vigorous marketing activity by shipping companies who, with the development of containerisation, are approaching shippers directly to obtain freight and increase their control over the complete transport chain. "Equalisation" practices are one of the consequences of this movement and for many

shipowners the container is considered part of the ship's hold, which in fact raises legal problems which have yet to be resolved.

3.4. General conclusions

Each of the instruments of analysis described in this report has its own contribution to make. Simple and descriptive observation of traffic data brings out the areas in which certain modes have the advantage and shows trends and developments. Mathematical modelling, despite the difficulties associated in the first place with the availability of statistics, throws light on the factors which explain traffic and in particular modal split. It also shows that modal choice is here but one factor in a decision-making process which concerns the whole logistic system including storage and the location of suppliers and customers. These considerations lead on naturally to the concept of transport chains and the problem of the struggle for their control.

As could be expected from examination of the past, changes in the economic environment have repercussions on freight transport.

In the first place, it can be seen that there is a change in the elasticity of transport volume with respect to the volume of production. Ex-post observations on the period following 1970 seem to indicate an elasticity somewhat less than unity whereas it was previously in the vicinity of unity. It also seems that in difficult periods firms rationalise their management by restricting transport volumes and distances. This also tends to raise doubts about the value of the elasticity concept in explaining and forecasting traffic.

Considerable changes are also taking place in the pattern of modal split, indicating that the type of service, own-account or other in the case of road transport, ordinary or rapid service in the case of railways, are important factors in shippers' choices and decisions.

The most recent developments in modelling show the advantage of taking into account the whole of the firm's logistic problems, a concept which also emerges from a study of trends in transport organisation, in which a diversification of road transport operations can be seen with the development of semi-trailer and swap body systems and the appearance of diversification on the part of shippers, each of whom pursues his own strategy, not only as regards type of transport but also and especially in the integration of transport in the firm's general logistic policy. This attitude is admittedly still limited to the minority of shippers, but there is reason to think that it is an active one, likely to spread.

187

It is impossible not to be struck by the resemblance between this development and trends in passenger transport. There too, there is a certain break in the link with economic growth and a diversification of modes, particularly in urban and peri-urban areas.

It is probable that, very broadly speaking, the quantitative development of transport is behind us on both the supply and demand sides. The major infrastructural gaps have been filled and vehicle performance is not likely to improve dramatically. Mobility will increase at a lower rate for both passengers and freight.

The future is to be seen in terms of diversification: diversification in needs and transport resources, the latter being more finely adjusted to demand. In short, and this clearly shows the close links between transport and economic activity, the shift from the quantitative to the qualitative characteristic of the present period is also found in the transport field.

Annex

MEASURING TRANSPORT VOLUME: ADDITIONAL NOTES

1. Units of measurement

a) Net and gross weight

Net weight may exclude packing altogether or include the original packing. Gross weight can include the material used to make up unit loads, e.g. pallets and also containers and even, in certain cases the transport vehicle itself such as semi-trailer, complete road train or railway wagon.

In general, particularly in the data published by the Statistical Office of the European Communities (Eurostat), the "foreign trade" statistics are net weights (excluding packing), while "transport" statistics use various interpretations of growth weight.

b) Chargeable tonnage

Charging by weight is generally according to the bracket on the tonnage scale within which the shipment falls, so that the conventional rule of "pay for" may mean that the actual tonnage is replaced by a chargeable tonnage corresponding to the lower limit of the next higher bracket.

For example, in the French "compulsory road transport charging" an actual tonnage between 13 and 15 tonnes is replaced by a chargeable tonnage of 15 tonnes.

c) Chargeable distance

In French domestic transport, for example:

- the chargeable distance by road is close to the actual distance;
- the SNCF chargeable distance, which can vary from - 20 to + 30 per cent with respect to the shortest rail route, is on average close to the road distance for distances over 700 km, but is about 10 per cent longer over short distances (200 to 500 km).

d) Tariff structure according to distance

For example, the French "compulsory road transport charging" includes a fixed component approximately equal to 160 km.

e) The relationship between useful capacity and permitted payload

There are few statistics available on this subject. In France, it is planned to carry out surveys to improve knowledge in the field, particularly for articulated road vehicles.

2. Statistical sources

Sample surveys on the activity of road transport vehicles are often limited to vehicles of a certain minimum payload (e.g. 3 tonnes in France) but, above all, they generally cover only vehicles registered in the country concerned.

3. Definition of domestic and international traffic

Foreign trade statistics are particularly valuable because they cover the whole transport chain corresponding to the trade chain from the country of origin to the country of final destination. It can happen, however, that the transport chain covers two trade links. For example, in the case of imports, the surveys by the United Kingdom National Ports Council make a distinction between the country of origin and the country of export (consignment). Thus, for example, among the goods imported from North America and transiting via continental European ports, some correspond to re-exports by continental European importers.

On the other hand, the transport statistics frequently cover only the known link of the chain in the case of transshipment between modes:

- transport flows by rail or inland waterway generally take no account of feeder services or terminal hauls by road; this may lead to an underestimate of international transport in the case of rail or waterway delivery to the frontier and road delivery to the foreign frontier area;
- seaborne transport statistics drawn up by shipping companies or ports may be limited to the loading and discharge ports;
- when trying to compile statistics of international transport of goods carried within the country, if there is transshipment at the frontier in particular

in a sea port, it is not always known whether the transport operation is entirely domestic or international; this is the case for France, for example, for road transport statistics based on the TRM (Transports Routiers de Marchandises) sample survey and, to a certain extent, waterway transport.

On this last point it should be stressed that (in France) in the case of combined land/sea transport (in the broad sense of the term):

- containers are considered as having a "transshipment" or "break of bulk" in the ports;
- by contrast, ro-ro traffic (road vehicles on ro-ro ships) and railway wagons on train ferries are considered as having no break of bulk.

The fact that it is not always possible to distinguish between the two categories of internal transport is less of a problem for analysing modal split (distribution between transport networks on the domestic transport system) than for analysing the relationship between economic activity and transport.

In the case of internal transport of goods involved in foreign trade, however:

- the correct analysis of modal split cannot totally disregard the whole of the chain because it is at this level that the choices regarding the port and onward transport are frequently determined;
- comparative trends of the different domestic modes cannot be interpreted without taking account of trends in external transport (ro-ro ships, train ferries, etc.).

Finally, it should be noted that the output of transport networks in a given country is generally produced by both domestic and foreign transport firms (concept of flag).

BIBLIOGRAPHY

[1] UN Statistical Yearbooks (in particular 1979/80, published in 1981).

[2] CEPII - Economie prospective internationale - No. 1, January 1980: Spécialisation et adaptation face à la crise.

[3] OECD - Interfutures Facing the future: towards mastering the probable and managing the unforeseeable, 1979.

[4] Groupe interministériel "SNCF après 1982" - Potentiel transportable et trafic ferroviaire voyageurs et marchandises à l'horizon 1995 - April 1982.

[5] Gouvernal, Elisabeth and Hanappe, Paul; Association Développement et Aménagement - La diffusion dans l'espace des flux de transport de marchandises - 1979.

[6] Eurostat - Annuaire Statistique: transports, communications, tourisme (in particular: 1978-79, published in 1981).

[7] Département des Statistiques des Transports (Ministère des Transports) - Annuaire Statistique (in particular: 1980 results, published in 1981).

[8] OECD - Maritime Transport 1980.

[9] Fearnleys, Oslo - Review 1980.

[10] CERLIC, IRT - Etude du marché des frets maritimes pour le transport des minerais et du charbon - December 1978.

[11] Rapport du Groupe de travail sur la liaison transmanche - Manche: Quelles liaisons? La Documentation française - April 1982.

[12] CERLIC, IRT - Le roulage maritime - November-December 1978.

[13]   Direction des Ports et de la Navigation Maritimes
        (Ministère de la Mer) Statistiques (in particular
        1980, published in 1981).

[14]   Département des Statistiques des Transports
        (Ministère des Transports) - Comment évaluer la
        part du trafic maritime né de notre commerce
        extérieur qui échappe aux ports français (in
        particular: results 1978, October 1980).

[15]   National Ports Council - in particular: United
        Kingdom International Freight Forecasts to 1988
        (1980) and Bulletin 15 (July 1980).

[16]   IRT - Journée GRECO Transports (25th March, 1982)
        - Répartition des transports interrégionaux
        intérieurs de marchandises entre le chemin de fer
        et la route (to be published).

[17]   Chatard, Dominique and Salini, Patrice: Le modèle
        PRETRAM" - SAE report - 1980.

[18]   Chatard, Dominique, Hayat, Ruth and Reynaud,
        Christian: "Le modèle TRIMAR" - SAE report - 1981.

[19]   Stencilled document SNCF - "Note sur le disponible
        transportable marchandises" - March 1982.

[20]   Reynaud, Christian: "Modèle macro-économique
        sectoriel de transport de marchandises"
        - Communication au PTRC - 1981.

[21]   Salini, Patrice: "Les transports et les cycles
        longs" - Doctoral thesis to be published.

[22]   Stencilled Note VII/417/79 - "Résumé et Commen-
        taires des résultats de l'étude de prévision des
        transports de marchandises dans la CEE" - CEE.

[23]   Study report NVI - 'La prévision des transports de
        marchandises dans la CEE" - 1979.

[24]   Chiang, Roberts, Ben Akiva: "Development of a
        Policy Sensitive Model for Forecasting Freight
        Demand" - MIT - 1980.

[25]   Gray, R: "Behavioral Approaches to Freight
        Transport Modal Choice" - Plymouth Polytechnic -
        1979.

[26]   Lengrand, Colin: "Formation au sein de l'entre-
        prise de stratégies logistiques tendant à maîtriser
        les flux physiques de marchandises" - CRET - April
        1980.

[27] Transport de marchandises et logistique (Communications par thème dans le cadre du CRECO "Transport et espace") - CRET - May 1981.

[28] Reynaud, Christian, Callamand, Henry: "Les auxiliares de transport et la logistique" - SAE - December 1981.

[29] Domenach, N: "Etude monographique de l'organisation transport d'une grande entreprise de distribution française" - SAE - January 1981.

[30] Domenach, N: "Etude monographique de l'organisation française de biens de consommation durables" - SAE - 1980.

[31] Domenach, N: "La chaîne de transports de fruits et légumes" - SAE - 1980.

[32] Laurin, P: "Les problèmes commerciaux et logistiques dans la distribution des produits sidérurgiques - Leur impact sur les transports" - SAE - September 1979.

194

TOPIC 2A

MANAGEMENT OF FIRMS
TO SATISFY TRANSPORT NEEDS

GOODS TRANSPORT BY ROAD

Dipl. Volksw. H.H. BINNENBRUCK
Bundesverband des Deutschen Güterfernverkehrs (BDF) e.V.
Frankfurt, Germany

SUMMARY

1. INTRODUCTION

In the transport economy it is commonplace that the shipment of goods is not an end in itself but is necessary to maintain production and consumption. It is a precondition for the economic division of labour without which economic growth and social well-being can scarcely be conceived. Goods transport - and this applies to road haulage just as much as to railways or inland waterways - is necessarily involved in the production plans and consumption decisions of both industry and the public. This is basically what determines and justifies goods transport.

In line with this view, goods transport is to be expected when the necessity arises on the grounds of production and consumption. The present topic is not concerned with the necessity, however, but with the transport needs which have to be satisfied. Is the production or consumption-conditioned necessity for goods transport already a transport need, or does the transport need trigger off the necessity for goods transport?

1.1. The market economy standpoint

In a market economy system this question is easily answered - it is the transport needs which mainly determine the necessity for goods transport. What follows will therefore be based on the market economy system. This means, however, nothing other than that in the final analysis the demand determines, by weighing up the economic advantages, whether transport takes place and what modes are considered. This means at the same time that transport demand has a certain supremacy and can dictate what managers in the transport industry have to do. This supremacy, however, is of practical significance only when demand can choose between different transport modes or even systems.

1.2. Business results and competition

It is in this possibility of choice that the particular appeal of the topic lies. Its challenge to the management of road transport firms to satisfy transport needs makes economic sense when for the managers concerned this is associated with entrepreneurial success. It is in fact not just a question of whether the existing management is in a position to meet present and future transport demand "necessities" - they first of all have to be recognised. It is more a question of providing means for satisfying transport needs which best take into account - more than all others - the wishes of transport demand.

This aspect is very important because it makes clear that the topic tacitly implies competition as the guiding mechanism in the above-named possibilities of choice. This is what gives an objective basis for judging the question of whether transport needs can be considered as satisfied. In a market economy system this can be assumed to be the case if somebody or some system has done better than the others and has come out on top in economic competition as entrepreneur or system.

1.3. The example of Germany

It is intended to examine more closely what general and specific prospects open up here for road haulage, using the example of German domestic and border-crossing shipments as being representative of a developed, pluralistic industrialised society.

2. TRANSPORT DEMAND TRENDS AND THE EMPHASIS ON TRANSPORT NEEDS

Presenting the most important features of transport demand developments succinctly means a certain concentration of aspects and problems. Transport events in a developed industrialised country such as Germany, where business plans and decisions are dominated by the principles of a welfare-oriented competitive market economy system can be so incredibly different and take so many forms that trends can be described only in a summary, abstract form. What could not be said about transport needs?

2.1. Fundamentals of past and future trends

In recent decades the transport market has given increasing importance to road haulage, whose significance to the economy as a whole is now greater than that of the railways and inland waterways. Almost 80 per cent of all the goods which have to be moved in Germany to supply industry and the public or remove waste products are carried by road. Road haulage accounts for almost 50 per cent of total transport output (see Annex, Table 1).

In foreign trade and the trans-frontier division of labour too, road haulage has continuously expanded. In the European Community its volume has grown more quickly than that of other carriers (see Annex, Table 2). It obviously receives a demand preference in international transport comparable or similar to that in domestic transport.

2.1.1. Quantitative demand structure

The structure of its transport output is varied, however. Road transport is given special priority in demand for the shipment of food, drink and tobacco and animal feeds, investment goods and all types of consumer goods[1]. It has also increased its market share against the railways in the carriage of sands and gravels and chemical products and against inland waterways also in the carriage of iron and steel products (see Annex, Table 3). This reflects the suitability of lorry transport for large groups of goods and products[2]. The advantages of road transport technology mainly derive from the fact that vehicle sizes, types and equipment can be adjusted to the different technological requirements of the goods carried. This potential for technological adjustment does not yet seem to be exhausted. A further advantage of the lorry is ease of operation.

2.1.2. Aspects of the distance structure

It should be pointed out that in the domestic transport system the lorry clearly dominates over the shorter distances. Surprisingly enough, however, the railways too carry a large proportion of their transport volume over relatively short distances. In Germany, 43 per cent of the amount of goods carried by rail are shipped over distances of less than 50 km. The volume of goods involved is nevertheless very small compared with that carried by local road transport (see Annex, Table 4).

The overall trend is for transport volume to increase over the shorter distances, or in other words long-haul transport is falling as a percentage of total transport volume while the transport volume over short and medium hauls up to 200-300 km is increasing. In the conurbations there is probably now virtually no alternative to the lorry which carries over 90 per cent of all goods in some heavily built-up areas. A general impression of this is given by Figure 1, which shows the daily transport balance of an average large town in the Rhine-Ruhr area.

It is now usual for a large town to help supply the surrounding area. The volume of goods coming in is smaller than that going out. In this example, 91,900 tonnes flow into the town area each day and 93,100 tonnes are distributed in the surrounding districts. About two-thirds, i.e. over 60,000 tonnes, are moved within the town area in industrial and commercial traffic - without taking into account weight losses and gains.

199

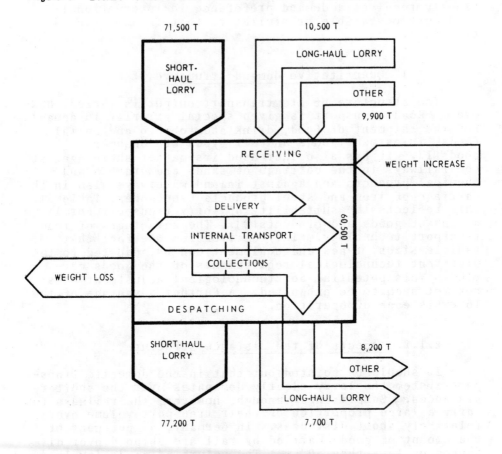

Figure 1   DAILY TRANSPORT BALANCE OF AN AVERAGE LARGE TOWN

71,500 T   10,500 T

SHORT-HAUL LORRY

LONG-HAUL LORRY

OTHER

9,900 T

RECEIVING

WEIGHT INCREASE

DELIVERY

INTERNAL TRANSPORT

60,500 T

COLLECTIONS

WEIGHT LOSS

DESPATCHING

SHORT-HAUL LORRY

OTHER

8,200 T

LONG-HAUL LORRY

77,200 T   7,700 T

2.1.3. Present situation

The internal relations of town delivery traffic have as yet been little researched. The trend in overall transport demand with the marked relative growth of local goods traffic brings delivery services in the conurbations very much to the fore.

This means that certain initial conclusions can be drawn:

- Goods transport demand clearly shows in many areas a considerable affinity for the lorry. This is a constant feature and the assessment will probably remain true in the future. The volumes of raw materials and basic feedstocks are falling in relative terms while both investment and consumer goods are showing an increased preference for road transport.

200

- In domestic goods transport, the absolute volume of
  traffic over the shorter distances has increased
  more rapidly than that of long-haul traffic over
  more than 300 km. The majority of transport events
  take place in localities close to the consumer, so
  that goods transport in the conurbations is moving
  to the forefront of demand trends.
- It is at present not possible to make any such
  statements in the case of trans-frontier road
  haulage.

2.2. The relationship between transport demand and the problem of the economy as a whole

In industrialised societies, the demand for and pro-
ducton of goods transport services runs roughly parallel
to trends in GNP.

Both with regard to domestic demand for goods of all
types (including imported goods) and with regard to
foreign demand, all branches of the transport industry can
count on a further increase in transport volume. The
leading economic indicators for goods transport nevertheless show that the rate of growth of transport demand will
slow down. Structural changes in transport demand also
mean that the situation will be different for the different types of transport. The production of certain goods
will probably even cease altogether.

With the expected slowing of economic growth, markets
will become buyers' markets to an even greater extent than
hitherto. Buying habits and the public's need for goods
in the consumer area to a large extent determine investment and the division of labour. This has its effects on
the receiving side of goods transport because this is
where buying power is most concentrated.

2.2.1. Population and market

Population trends are considered in relation to the
leading indicators of goods transport under this heading:

- Population numbers:
  Falling birth rates can lead to a reduction in the
  total population of certain economies, but at the
  same time mobility as expressed in migratory movements, to some extent beyond national frontiers, is
  increasing.
- Internationalisation:
  The progressive integration of Europe is being
  accompanied by international migration. Some
  changes in buying habits are to be expected, but
  they will generally not be of major importance. On
  domestic markets the sales outlets for imported

goods will become stabilized. In the case of
Germany it is expected that a share of imported
goods will rise from the present 25 per cent to
40 per cent by 1990.
- Regional distribution:
Concentration of the population in conurbations encourages transport flows over the major axes between conurbations, and also leads to increased
local distribution traffic in the centres themselves. An increase in direct liner transport over
medium distances is to be expected.
- Buying habits:
A high standard of living means that people have
high demands as regards supplies. They require the
proper quality and quantity of goods of all sorts
at all times and in all places. This claim is a
vital aspect of competition in production and
trade. The supply function takes precedence over
the transport function.
- Distance between home and work:
The tendency for greater distances between home and
work is increasing the average transport distance
for goods and products and hence the overall costs
of distribution. In order to meet the supply requirements and at the same time counteract the
tendency for distribution costs to rise, the trade
sector has set up central self-service markets,
large stores and distribution centres. In the consumer area, in addition to lorry transport services, pick-up traffic using private cars should
often also be taken into account.

2.2.2. Real incomes

Characteristic features for assessing transport demand arise from trends in real incomes. Over the past
decade, value-added in the transport sector was considerable and had an effect on GNP. The value share of transport in the creation of GNP increased. Lorry transport
has a substantial share in the creation of value in the
economy as a whole. Increased cost-consciousness in the
distribution of goods can be seen in the way incomes are
used. Budget expenditure is being examined more thoroughly than hitherto to see what competitive advantage can be
bought with it.

2.2.3. Decision structures

A third aspect connected with the major features of
the economy as a whole is the decision structure in production and trade. Transport demand is obviously taking a
new direction as regards quality. Past transport decisions as to what vehicles were to be introduced and what
tasks were allotted to them are being examined to see

whether the future costs of handling transport tasks are economically justifiable. This involves not only the supply requirements of the receivers of the goods, but also the competitive situation and state of development of suppliers. Of practical significance is the question of whether the claims regarding the detailed distribution of goods can go on being satisfied in a comprehensive and complex fashion or whether some of the depots and distribution warehouses as well as delivery services will have to be given up for cost reasons. They would have to be replaced by more direct transport from the place of production or a central distribution depot to the receiver.

- At the same time the vehicles and associated transport organisation have to comply with a number of tasks and wishes arising from marketing and the logistics of supply. Basic considerations here are costs, in particular in insurance, claims, loading and discharging activities and also the need to minimise the costs of having capacity available. All this means a need for: careful handling of goods, security against accidents and theft, rapid loading and discharging, meeting deadlines and general respect of the environment.

2.3. Problem analysis and trends

The reasons for the qualitative reorientation lie in the problems of the economy as a whole. Because of its great volume, and its close relationship with economic trends, road transport is particularly affected by any problems here. The present problems are well-known so that it probably suffices merely to mention the main headings. The consequences, however, need some comment (see Figure 2).

In considering general economic trends, the problem of escalating energy costs undoubtedly plays a major role. But the increased influence of environmental protection requirements on locational and industrial policy influences not only production but also transport decisions. In the plans of economic agents there is an increasing tendency to exploit innovation and develop new technologies in order to improve technical and institutional structures. This also includes the question of how to reverse the former tendency to exaggerated division of labour or how to eliminate uneconomic and unproductive components of the industrial structure. Underlying this is the constant striving for higher productivity and better economic efficiency.

These trends in economic planning are characteristic of a general need for an overall system which takes full account of external factors.

Figure 2. PROBLEM ANALYSIS FOR THE OVERALL ROAD HAULAGE SYSTEM

PROBLEM SITUATION (from the standpoint of the economy as a whole)	MARKET DEMAND (Options)	MARKET SUPPLY (Functions)	EXTERNAL CONDITIONS (Restrictions)
- ENERGY CONSERVATION	- TRANSPARENCY OF GOODS MOVEMENTS	- STORAGE (stocking-up, buffer stocks, working on commission)	- TECHNICAL
- ENVIRONMENTAL POLLU-TION	- BEST POSSIBLE ARRANGE-MENT AND ALLOCATION OF TRANSPORT CAPACITY FOR SHIPPING GOODS	- FORWARDING (negotiation, organisation, dispatching, transshipment)	- STRUCTURAL
- IMPROVING THE TECHNICAL AND INSTITUTIONAL STRUCTURE (exploiting innovation)	- SCHEDULING THE TRANSPORT PROCESS	- CARRYING (negotiation, organisation, dispatching, transshipment)	- FINANCIAL
- IMPROVING PRODUCTIVITY	- MANAGEABLE, HUMANE AND USER-FRIENDLY SYSTEMS	- PORTS/TERMINALS (modal transfer)	- LEGAL
- ELIMINATION OF UNECONO-MIC FRAGMENTATION IN THE ORGANISATION OF WORK	- HIGH DEGREE OF ORGANIS-ATIONAL FLEXIBILITY	- ANCILLARY SERVICES (customs clearance, pack-ing, stowing, chartering capacity, regulating and organising the transport, insurance, monitoring, financing)	- PSYCHOLOGICAL (accep-tance of change)
	- POSSIBILITIES FOR DIVISION OF LABOUR (using comparative advantages)		

204

As regards its contribution to the economy as a whole, lorry transport has so far not exhausted its many qualities and maintains a constant value. It is nevertheless faced with the task of recognising the quality profile of transport demand, i.e. the subtle transport needs which arise and meeting their specific requirements.

2.4. Prospects for combined transport

All carriers try to adjust to changes in the structure of transport demand requirements.

In long-haul goods traffic there is a dominant trend on both rail and road to extend direct, single-destination traffic, maintain or even improve the journey speeds achieved and promote unit loads as far as possible. This includes combined transport, which has been jointly developed and extended by road transport firms and the railways. This is one means of increasing the capacity utilisation and improving the turnround of vehicles engaged in long-distance transport. In all countries, combined goods transport is considered to be a solution to the general economic problem in that it contributes to improving the transport system. Is this transport economy view correct, however? Does the extension of combined transport not neglect the satisfaction of the economy's local transport needs? Does examination of the economy as a whole not show that the real demand of industry and the public on the management of transport firms stems from the growth of short- rather than long-haul transport?

The answers to these questions are certainly not the same in trans-frontier traffic as in domestic traffic. In the first place, it is necessary to work out for just domestic goods transport how and when in the overall transport demand the individual transport desires of industry and the public actually appear.

2.5. Characteristics of individual transport needs and the challenge to the management of firms

Given the general economic constraints which have just been outlined but whose effects on the financial situation and income levels in economic life have as yet been taken into account, it will be useful as a first step to determine the options which can be considered in trying to master the economic challenge. This may suggest possible decisions and reactions to the management of firms, wherever they may be located in the transport system.

Where is the emphasis in the actual individual needs hidden behind the visible structural changes in goods transport demand?

2.5.1. Supplying goods

Pride of place is taken by goods supply which, at the lowest possible price and the highest possible quality of service, is intended to meet the requirement of the economy as a whole that at all times and in all places all products will be available in the quantity desired. This implies a function which contains a transport function and a rationalisation function.

Goods supply

Transport function   Rationalisation function

The transport demand desire line is very much marked by the supply requirement. In a pluralistic society and an economy based on the division of labour, the supply requirement on the national level is divided into an almost infinite number of individual requirements and locations. In addition to the quantitative requirement there are qualitative differences which first and foremost affect type of transport demand. To give some ideas, we might mention packing, temperature, breakdown of deliveries and size of shipments, reliability, punctuality, security, etc. The structure of the supply function thus naturally depends on transport, i.e. the vehicle, transport time, distance and route. The organisation of goods transport and the other services necessary to meet these requirements also determine the degree of rationalisation of the quality of supply. This concerns essentially the linking of the different transport phases and activities, in particular the structure of transport relations, the fulfilling of orders and providing other services.

a) General requirements

With regard to the costs and quality of the goods supply, it can be seen that both industry and consumers over the past 10 to 15 years have required increasingly integrated services containing very varied components. Goods supply is thereby understood as a logistic problem which - in accordance with the great variety of goods carried - calls for distinct systems tailored to the different categories of requirement:

- Better customer service through bringing together the goods on a single order from several sources and making a single delivery.
- Customer instructions, i.e. forms of packing and transport tailored to specific ranges of goods.
- Short transport and transshipment times - even in fringe areas - with a fixed timetable even though the volume of goods fluctuates considerably from day to day (regularity of service).

- Reliability in carrying out the order (repeated delivery if the receiver is absent, uniformity of services and representation over the whole of the delivery area).
- Flexible short-term adjustment to additional service requirements.
- Individuality of transport, i.e. taking orders directly from the customer in the context of a general service supply.
- Appropriate vehicles.
- Loading possibilities or handling equipment at each loading and discharging point.
- High quality of delivery services and security of transport (from theft, damage, misdirection).
- Employment of staff familiar with their customers wishes; minimal staffing.
- Favourable transport costs, simple and transparent accounting system for both shipper and receiver, differentiated cost allocation (price determination) with respect to different services to help the supplier choose the optimal service mix.

In Germany, the goods supply transport demand profile is shown in Figure 3. It is clear that reliability and punctuality are top of the list. Then follows the desire for advantageous costs, i.e. economy and short transport time. Transport duration does not just mean the speed of the transport operation, however, but also the respect of deadlines. Of roughly equal ranking are the desires for better customer service, frequent trips and good loading, discharging and transshipment facilities (see Figure 3 for details).

In 1981 the desire profile of several market leaders in the forwarding sector of road haulage were reassessed and the results show that there had been significant shifts. Figure 4 shows that customers are prepared to pay only for rapidity and transshipment possibilities, even though reliability and security are decisive factors in customer service and winning new customers and frequency and reliability of service are important factors in competitiveness.

b) A unified view

Given the relatively high ranking of the speed, reliability and customer service requirements, the precision of the service organisation must be improved even further if the supply is to correspond to transport needs. But this means nothing less than that the planning and carrying out of goods transport operations needs to be regarded globally, with a view to connection and integration, recognising that all the individual jobs, subfunctions and steps are mutually determined.

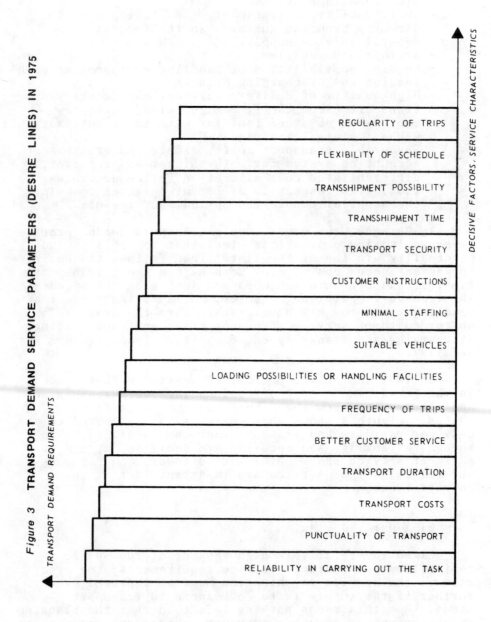

Figure 3 TRANSPORT DEMAND SERVICE PARAMETERS (DESIRE LINES) IN 1975

TRANSPORT DEMAND REQUIREMENTS

DECISIVE FACTORS, SERVICE CHARACTERISTICS

REGULARITY OF TRIPS

FLEXIBILITY OF SCHEDULE

TRANSSHIPMENT POSSIBILITY

TRANSSHIPMENT TIME

TRANSPORT SECURITY

CUSTOMER INSTRUCTIONS

MINIMAL STAFFING

SUITABLE VEHICLES

LOADING POSSIBILITIES OR HANDLING FACILITIES

FREQUENCY OF TRIPS

BETTER CUSTOMER SERVICE

TRANSPORT DURATION

TRANSPORT COSTS

PUNCTUALITY OF TRANSPORT

RELIABILITY IN CARRYING OUT THE TASK

Figure 4. TRANSPORT DEMAND SERVICE PARAMETERS (DESIRE PROFILE) 1981

Service parameter Ranking	Assessment(1)			
	Commands a price in the market	Important for winning customers	Necessary to maintain competitiveness	Of general importance
a) Transport duration	x		xx	
b) Service frequency			xx	
c) Reliability		xx	xx	
d) Regularity				x
e) Punctuality		x	x	
f) Security		xx	x	
g) Adaptability			x	
h) Logistic service		x		
i) Network density				
j) Loading facilities				x
k) Type of vehicle			x	x
l) Transshipment possibilities	x			
m) Scheduling flexibility			x	
n) Transshipment time			x	

1. xx denotes a particularly important service parameter.

209

This unified view leads to a systems supply approach. Road haulage thus appears as a total system in which a great number of very diverse components are united with one another in its superstructure and infrastructure. In addition to transport networks, firms and installations and actual carrying capacity, communication appears as a means of integration. As in the past, personnel management systems, operating systems and premises are necessary (see Figure 5).

The total road haulage system has not yet been comprehensively and intensively analysed from the standpoint of the logistic requirements of the economy as a whole. So far, the conclusion has emerged from trends in transport demand and its specific needs, that for the best goods supply the individual operations from production to the consumer area need to be closely and economically linked with one another. This means in the first place technological and operational requirements. There is a lack of knowledge of the organisational and institutional links.

There are nevertheless already transport policy approaches which draw lessons from demand trends. To meet the claim of the economy as a whole for the best possible goods supply, a transport management system is to be developed which will facilitate the necessary linkages and make possible the necessary institutional arrangements.

c) Formation of supply and transport chains

The unified approach has now been adopted to a relatively large extent in road haulage. In all European countries suppliers and consignees have built up a suppply and transport system. In the 1970s in particular, own-account traffic grew more rapidly than carriage for third parties. This is an indication of the existence of thoroughly integrated "transport chains" from shipper to consignee.

In addition, however, systems have developed which do not use just one single transport mode. There has been a long history of co-operation between road and rail transport in lorry feeder and collection traffic to and from goods stations. The development of the container has added new technologies which have extended the possibilities for integrated transport chains using different transport modes and systems (see Figure 6).

The possibilities existing today for meeting the functional requirements of goods supply through building systems and transport chains (using road and rail only) are shown in Figure 7.

210

Figure 5. TOTAL ROAD HAULAGE SYSTEM

Transport supply components

	INFRASTRUCTURE	FIRMS, FACILITIES	TRANSPORT CAPACITY	COMMUNICATION SUPER-STRUCTURE	COMMUNICATION INFRA-STRUCTURE
Land	· Traffic regulation · Safety equipment · Bridges, tunnels, crossing · Routes	· Loading areas · Transshipment bays · Garages, yards, workshops · Stores · Stations · Terminals · Ports	· Vehicles · Superstructures (including containers) · Transshipment systems · Types of transport	· Documents and forms · Routines · Computer programs, telephones, etc.	· Telecommunications · Data transmission (including satellites)
Equipment Operating Systems Management Systems					
Personnel					

Road haulage (short- and long-haul)

211

Figure 6 **THE POSSIBLE TRANSPORT CHAINE**

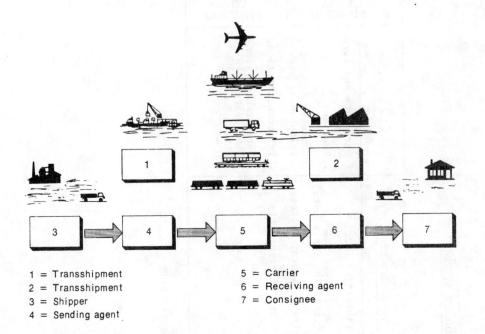

1 = Transshipment
2 = Transshipment
3 = Shipper
4 = Sending agent

5 = Carrier
6 = Receiving agent
7 = Consignee

In these transport chains there are different technological variants with smaller and larger transport units
which facilitate loading, discharging and transshipment.

This does not exhaust all the possibilities for forming transport chains, however.

2.5.2. Transport function

Goods delivery and pickup in large towns and conurbations is becoming increasingly difficult. This trend can
also be seen in medium towns and nodal communities. There
are many reasons for this: loading and unloading areas,
parking and stopping bans on lorries, one-way streets,
pedestrian areas, bans on through traffic for heavy vehicles, deviations, road works, low-noise areas, etc. There
are also restrictions on transport and loading times and
all these factors may imply longer distances or a less
than optimal choice of route. Because of narrow streets,
relatively small delivery vehicles must often be used, and
these are less economic than larger ones. Direct deliveries to individual town shops, stores and firms using
large long-haul vehicles are scarcely possible as traffic
regulations in the towns no longer allow them.

- Waiting times for vehicles at the delivery platforms of stores, in the street or on company

Figure 7 PRESENT LAND TRANSPORT CHAINE

N°	Shipper	Vehicle	Dep. terminal	Vehicle	Arr. terminal	Vehicle	Consignee
1	B	short-haul lorry	U	road train with fixed body	U	short-haul lorry	E
2	B	short-haul lorry	U	covered goods wagon	U	short-haul lorry	E
3	B	short-haul lorry	U	DB-wagon + container	U	short-haul lorry	E
4	B	semi-trailer + container	ZL	DB-wagon + container	U	short-haul lorry	E
5	B	semi-trailer + container	ZL	DB-wagon + container	TE	semi-trailer + container	E
6	B	covered goods wagon			U	short-haul lorry	E
7	B	short-haul lorry	U			covered goods wagon	E
8	B	short-haul lorry	U			semi-trailer + container	E
9	B	semi-trailer + container			U	short-haul lorry	E
10	B	semi-trailer + container			TE	semi-trailer + container	E

KEY

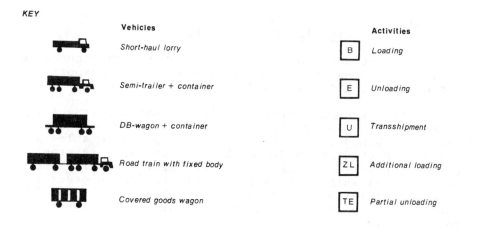

Vehicles

- Short-haul lorry
- Semi-trailer + container
- DB-wagon + container
- Road train with fixed body
- Covered goods wagon

Activities

- B — Loading
- E — Unloading
- U — Transshipment
- ZL — Additional loading
- TE — Partial unloading

premises have increased substantially in recent years. Waiting times of up to four hours to unload 800 or 1,000 kg are no rarity. It is becoming increasingly difficult to keep to the regulation hours for driving staff.
- The consignee provides less and less help with unloading. Driving staff have to do an increasing amount of loading and warehousing work.
- The time limits on loading and delivery have become shorter. It is often necessary to make several trips without being able to hand over the goods. Sometimes there is even refusal to accept non-standard consignments.
- Sometimes consignees in the same street have different loading or delivery times so that a pre-scheduled delivery cannot work.
- Conditions in traffic to and from container terminals are also deteriorating. Traffic congestion at peak periods has become so bad that train departures frequently cannot be met[3].
- There is frequently no time or a lack of the required facilities for forming shipments suitable for containers or piggyback transport, so that it is increasingly difficult to make up unit loads.

Finally, a very special problem should be indicated: the great majority of all deliveries in the conurbations take place between 8 and 11 a.m. (see Figure 8). This is true of all the larger towns. On week days, 50 per cent of deliveries have already been completed by 10.30 and as early as 9.30 a.m. in the food, drink and tobacco sector[4].

2.5.3. Rationalisation function

The more unfavourable traffic conditions become, the greater the need for rationalisation. The transport and system chains are only as good as their weakest links.

With its nodal point traffic concept and its city parcel traffic the railways are trying to improve the supply of combined transport possibilities. Timetables are aimed at providing an overnight service for a substantial proportion of the goods carried by rail. Container traffic combines shipments in long-haul traffic in order to cover great distances rapidly. The piggyback system is another form of combined transport which has expanded considerably.

This tranport supply, however, does little to further rationalisation where it is most urgently required. On the contrary, the concentration in long-haul traffic creates a quality gap between it and local traffic and increases rationalisation pressure there (the time taken for transport from Köln to Düsseldorf is less than that of

214

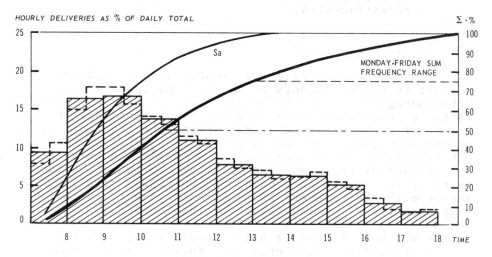

Figure 8 **LOCAL DELIVERIES ACCORDING TO TIME OF DAY**
(Average weekday)

a delivery within Köln). What is now actually being done
for short-haul goods transport? What tasks arise for the
management of firms in the transport system?

3. TASKS AND PROBLEMS FOR FIRM MANAGEMENTS

3.1. Basic assessment

The tasks coming under the heading of road haulage
traffic management constitute only part of the problem as
it concerns the economy as a whole, even though it is one
of the most important. The options open to managements
are very much influenced by the demand trend towards
transport chains and the logistic approach. They include:

- the greatest possible transparency of the flow of
  goods in order to be able to have control at all
  times and in all places;
- the best possible scheduling and allocation of
  freight capacity in order to achieve the highest
  possible productivity, i.e. best possible use of
  vehicles and operating time;
- scheduling of deliveries and respect of these
  schedules;
- systems which fit the requirements of a humane
  working life and are user-friendly;

215

- great organisational flexibility, i.e. the possibility of fulfilling individual wishes at any time;
- use of the comparative advantages of different systems, in particular different transport modes and infrastructures.

3.1.1. Definitions

The above examples of management aspects and options suggest that the concepts of "traffic management" and "firm management" need to be defined. Traffic management is to be understood as the overall management task in the transport economy, aimed at satisfying the transport needs of industry and consumers in the best possible way through offering a favourable combination of price and service quality and at the same time assuring the continued existence of the transport economy. Within this "traffic management" the task of "transport management" is to be responsible for running firms and institutions,

- which carry out transport operations,
- are active, as agents, for forwarders and goods transport organisers,
- maintain and run warehouses and/or transshipment facilities and
- plan, build and maintain transport links, nodal points and networks suitable for goods transport.

Like any other manager, the transport manager has to deal in the first place with all the influences arising from the direct business relationships of his firm. At the present time, however, taking into account the market situation as regards demand and deciding on the employment of inputs make much greater demands on managers than a few years ago.

The basic features of transport demand trends have been outlined, but it should also be mentioned that this demand can also be subject to rapid change on a regional basis in that it can shift beyond national boundaries to other countries or can emerge from foreign countries.

Figure 9 shows the general profile of management tasks.

3.1.2. Criteria

The first task of transport management in the present qualitative reorientation of transport demand should be to gear the service supply to the requirements of transport chains and systems. This view arises from the fact that in short-haul goods transport where covering distance is not so important as the time factor, the available time will in future carry greater economic weight than at

216

Figure 9. TRANSPORT MANAGEMENT TASK PROFILE

CONSTRAINTS	STRESSES	EFFECTS
DEVELOPMENTS WHICH CHANGE THE COMBINATION OF FACTORS IN PRODUC-TION AND DISTRIBUTION	OUTCOME (EFFECTS) OF PROCESSES ON DIFFERENT STAGES OF DECISION-MAKING AND OPERATIONS	ADJUSTING THE STRUCTURE AND LEVELS OF INPUT/OUTPUT PARAMETERS
- Dearer energy	- Energy conservation	- Rationalisation of production and distribution
- Social requirements	- Optimal use of oper-ating time	- Change in the divi-sion of labour
- Environmental pro-tection	- Non-polluting tech-nologies	- Search for techno-logical alternatives
- Financial restric-tions	- Reduction of expen-diture (costs)	- Supply of services able to provide links (co-operation)

217

present. The time per kilometre - distributed over the frequency of trips, i.e. the availability of the vehicle - is vital in determining the profitability of the transport operation and whether the goal of a business success can be achieved. While in long-haul transport the amount of goods carried per kilometre remains the determining factor for transport services and freight rates, in transport chains and systems what matters is the best possible utilisation of the capacity employed. There are thus two vital factors: time and the ability of the service to link up with other services or requirements. Business success no longer depends solely on transport capacity being sold, deliveries being made and specific tasks carried out, but increasingly on the services involved being capable of integration in the customer's requirements and the system into which the collection and delivery of goods are organised.

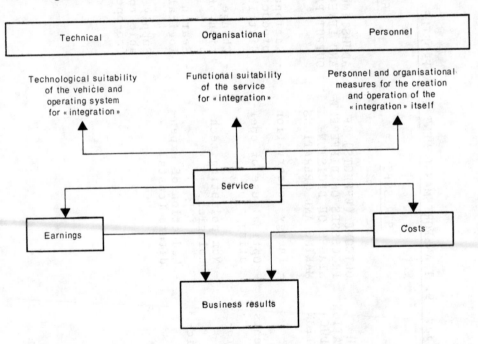

3.1.3. Internal and external costs

This examination has to take into account the fact that business success is achieved not only on the basis of internal costs, but must also include the external costs caused by road transport such as infrastructure costs, environmental costs, etc. These external costs have to be fully covered by earnings if a positive result is actually to be achieved from the standpoint of the economy as a whole. Obviously the development of transport systems tends at the same time to keep the external costs low and save on internal costs.

3.2. Analysis of firms' structure and tasks

Assessing the basics of management tasks quickly reveals the present economic stress situation for road
transport, namely the need for:

- energy conservation;
- optimal use of operating time;
- non-polluting technology; and
- reduction of expenditure (costs).

The mastery of these tasks would be no problem from the
standpoint of the economy as a whole if road haulage firms
could already satisfy transport needs globally and in detail. A number of serious questions remain from the
standpoint of management structure however.

3.2.1. Structural weaknesses

The vast majority of firms running own account or
commercial road transport are very small. With the exception of some Eastern countries the number of firms is very
high everywhere, the majority of them having very few
vehicles. There are nevertheless also large concerns and
state-owned undertakings with large fleets of vehicles.
It can generally be assumed, however, that the industry is
made up of a large number of private firms (see Annex,
Tables 5 and 6). The structure of the road haulage industry is thus very heterogeneous.

Whatever actual management tasks may arise, the number of supervisory staff in the many small and medium
firms is very small and constitutes a particular structural problem. Firms are limited in their range of action
by organisational factors. Management is under constant
pressure to take decisions and is so burdened by day-to-
day operations that there is scarcely any time for management analyses, basic accounting and assessment of the
firm's activities.

- Management has all-round responsibility, so that a
  single person has to look after several tasks and
  activities at the same time.
- No management, however, can in the long run plan,
  co-ordinate and control such varied functions as
  buying, running transport operations, visiting customers, managing staff and ensuring the liquidity
  situation all at the same time without making
  serious mistakes.
- What is more, road transport services are to a
  large extent of a craft nature, requiring personal
  involvement, ability and presence.
- Of particular importance, however, is the time
  capital, which as a rule is very limited in small
  and medium firms. Instead of systematic management

219

of the firm and operations, improvisation is often
the dominating organisational principle. Experience takes the place of a management system. As
yet there is still no specialised management training for the road haulage sector.

It should not be concluded, however, that the lack of
time, the principle of improvisation, the personal nature
of services and the small number of supervisory staff in
small and medium firms means that they operate badly. On
the contrary, a small firm can make do with a simple
organisation if it delivers a simple product. Firms with
a sophisticated form of organisation can have advantages
in data collection and analysis. Large firms can econo-
mise on fixed costs, but they also have important competitive disadvantages because personal contact with the
market and personal control over operations and the satisfying of customers' individual transport needs is reduced. These structural peculiarities of the road haulage
industry prove to be weaknesses when goods supply is
handled by means of transport chains.

3.2.2. Problem-oriented weaknesses

Given the existing transport chains and in order to
extend transport systems, customers increasingly want to
prescribe general recommendations for the transport operation, including prior announcement to the consignee, time
of delivery, opening times of loading platforms, exchange
of pallets and other logistic conditions. Such co-
ordination will increase the "integration" capability of
services.

Similar considerations apply for the operation of
other transport chains such as overseas container traffic,
combined road/rail traffic, forwarder/groupage traffic on
the roads, road/air freight traffic, etc. According to
type of goods and the system of organisation the requirements may be very different.

3.2.3. Technological adjustment

A further aspect is consideration of the national
vehicle stock. This has grown over the course of history,
evolving with changes in the supply of the goods vehicle
industry.

The lorry is relatively young as compared with railway and inland waterway transport. Its technology, however, has now reached a stage which makes it possible to
determine an optimum vehicle stock for the economy as a
whole. This means that transport management should select
and use the vehicles having the lowest fuel consumption.
The opportunities offered by lorry technology should be

used here: to adjust not only the size of vehicle, but also the type and engine efficiency to energy policy requirements.

3.2.4. Management shortcomings

The weaknesses in firms' internal organisation lie in:

- the lack of a fully developed cost and production accounting system, and
- lack of a selective marketing concept.

Management planning and action is generally based on the data contained in the commercial accounts, but since these are shaped by the requirements of commercial and tax law, the information which can be derived does not cover all aspects necessary for business success. This severely restricts the possibility of having demand-oriented management.

3.2.5. Legal conditions

Finally, it should also be pointed out that in Europe there are legal and technical regulations governing lorry operation which affect not only the structure and level of costs, but also operating time. They can as a rule not be changed in the short term and are thus regarded as constant by firm managements. The regulations cover not only driving conditions and hours, thus influencing scheduling and flexibility of operation, but also market access and the area in which vehicles can be employed.

3.3. Assessment of practical measures

The structural, problem-oriented and management weaknesses in road haulage might give the impression that on the whole it is faced with such great economic problems that the industry cannot master them using its own resources alone.

In this connection it is worth recalling that in most countries road haulage, in contrast to other transport modes, has so far experienced no structural crisis. It is clear that the heterogeneous firm and service structure in road haulage does reflect transport demand.

A practical goal for management would therefore be to help build transport chains and systems aimed at improving the supply of goods and reducing costs.

ORGANISATIONAL POSSIBILITIES FOR RATIONAL ENERGY USE IN ROAD HAULAGE

PROPOSAL	CONSERVATION MEASURES	SAVINGS POTENTIAL	COMMENTS/PROBLEMS
1. Changes in behaviour	a) Energy-saving driving through establishing a catalogue of rules including such things as: no driving at high revs, avoidance of sudden accelerations, correct tyre pressure	a) Up to 15 per cent	a) Costs-benefits: Very favourable. Problems: Driver motivation. Explanation of the relationship between driver behaviour and fuel consumption, driver training, seminars, counselling
	b) Fuel and performance monitoring through appropriate systems	b) Up to 10 per cent	b) Costs-benefits: Not yet known as systems generally not yet introduced in practice. Problem: Very expensive. Introduction of a continuous information system covering vehicle use and performance; improved transport management in industry, trade and the transport industry
2. Trip planning	Optimisation procedures to minimise distances, maximise the capacity loading of vehicles and minimise loading and discharging times	Up to 25 per cent according to fleet size	Costs-benefits: favourable, not only as regards fuel consumption. Problems: Requires suitable managers. Introduction of trip planning methods and optimisation procedures.
3. Fleet rationalisation	Formation of the optimal fleet size from the cost standpoint	Varies according to firm	Costs-benefits: Favourable. Problems: Implies co-operation between shippers and carriers
4. Higher freight utilisation	Avoidance of empty return journeys and detours	Varies according to firm	Costs-benefits: Favourable. Problems: Implies interregional co-operation in the transport economy; creation of an inter-regional information system to exchange shipments

TECHNICAL POSSIBILITIES FOR RATIONAL ENERGY USE IN ROAD HAULAGE

PROPOSAL	CONSERVATION MEASURES	POTENTIAL SAVINGS	COMMENTS/PROBLEMS
1. Constructual measures exluding changed engine performance	a) Reduction of wind resistance through rounding-off angles/wind deflector and spoiler/aerodynamic shape	a) On long hauls up to 5 per cent/wind deflector up to 8 per cent	a) Costs-benefits: Favourable/ no practical problems/ instruction useful for fleet managers and drivers
	b) Reduction of rolling resistance by improving the rolling properties of tyres	b) Not known exactly, as no systematic research results available	b) Necessary: Investigation of rolling properties on different road surfaces
			Problems: Noise emission, road holding and braking performance and track holding
2. Instructional measures including changed engine performance	a) Optimisation of engine and transmission design through changing the gear ratios or adjusting the transmission ratios	a) Up to 5 per cent	a) Costs-benefits: Favourable
			Problem: Introduction of automatic transmission in lorry transport
	b) Exhaust gas turbo-charging in diesel engines	b) Up to 8 per cent	b) The development of exhaust gas turbo-charging also reduces environmental pollution; engines are more or less fully developed and already tested in practice
3. Increased capacity utilisation of commercial vehicles	a) Regular maintenance	a) Up to 5 per cent	a) Costs-benefits: Unfavourable if fuel conservation only is considered: staff need to be motivated to carry out inspections: systematic procedures are necessary and are already available in practice
	b) Larger units and raising of the maximum permissible weight for lorries	b) Up to 8 per cent	b) Overall optimisation of vehicle dimensions, permissible all-up-weight, transport speed and road area occupied are all to be re-examined: only then can costs-benefits be assessed
4. Technological self-monitoring possibilities	Fuel-flow metering, revolution counter, if possible with indication of the most fuel-efficient-range	Not known at present	Costs-benefits: At present not yet assessable from the economic standpoint
			Problem: Driver motivation

223

3.3.1. Energy conservation

The many technological and organisational possibilities for rational energy use in road haulage indicate that fuel consumption can be expected to go on being reduced. This does not, however, necessarily mean a fall in costs (see table below). The reduced fuel consumption can merely compensate for part of the cost increase due to higher prices.

Possible alternatives which could replace road haulage transport services without using oil products do not appear any more energy-efficient from the standpoint of the economy as a whole. The alternative to the lorry is often substantially more expensive.

3.3.2. Optimal use of operating times

In the context of a logistic approach, there are a number of rationalisation possibilities as regards making optimal use of the available operating time. These include trip optimisation, the proper choice of vehicle size and economic use of the freight capacity. It turns out, however, that improving turn-round in local transport through trip optimisation or the introduction of shuttle services or reducing the number of loading and unloading points improve the transport structure and service output in rare cases only, because the time thus saved is wasted elsewhere.

On the other hand, reducing waiting times during the vehicle operating period brings about an actual productivity increase (see Figure 10).

A pre-condition is co-ordination with consignees in order to achieve the shortest possible loading and discharging times. This implies improving handling conditions, which can be achieved by using swap bodies and containers as well as through modernising handling procedures - as already mentioned.

Management also has to take into account periods when the vehicle is out of service for maintenance, repair or preparation for a specific transport. Here too, there are rationalisation possibilities: pre-planning, scheduled vehicle servicing and maintenance.

3.3.3. Environmental pollution

The growth of lorry traffic in conurbations has necessarily brought about a sharp increase in emissions. In many countries the legal regulations on noise abatement have been tightened, but without any consideration of the broader logistic context. At the same time, the transport

Figure 10 POSSIBILITIES FOR TRANSPORT RATIONALISATION THROUGH INCREASING THE PRODUCTIVE OPERATING TIME OF VEHICLES

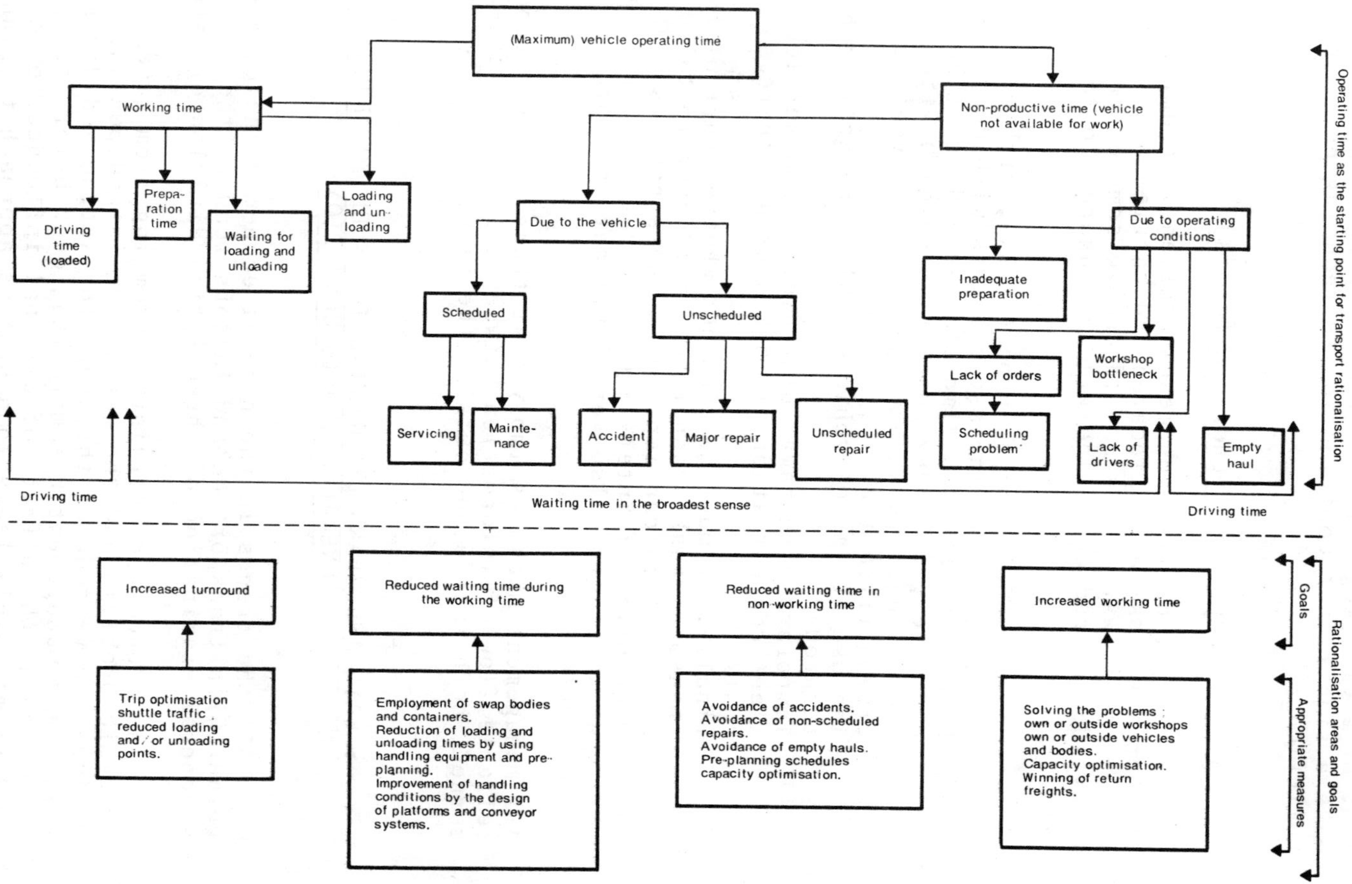

Operating time as the starting point for transport rationalisation

Rationalisation areas and goals

Goals | Appropriate measures

(Maximum) vehicle operating time

Non-productive time (vehicle not available for work)

Due to operating conditions
- Empty haul
- Workshop bottleneck
- Lack of drivers
- Inadequate preparation
- Lack of orders
- Scheduling problem

Driving time

Due to the vehicle

Unscheduled
- Unscheduled repair
- Major repair
- Accident

Scheduled
- Maintenance
- Servicing

Waiting time in the broadest sense

Working time
- Loading and unloading
- Waiting for loading and unloading
- Preparation time
- Driving time (loaded)

Driving time

Increased working time

Solving the problems:
own or outside workshops
own or outside vehicles
and bodies.
Capacity optimisation.
Winning of return freights.

Reduced waiting time in non-working time

Avoidance of accidents.
Avoidance of non-scheduled repairs.
Avoidance of empty hauls.
Pre-planning schedules
capacity optimisation.

Reduced waiting time during the working time

Employment of swap bodies and containers.
Reduction of loading and unloading times by using handling equipment and pre-planning.
Improvement of handling conditions by the design of platforms and conveyor systems.

Increased turnround

Trip optimisation
shuttle traffic.
reduced loading
and/or unloading points.

225

industry has been more than ever restricted by uneconomic traffic regulations. Low-noise lorries and the development of a city logistics system for large conurbations can make a significant contribution to reducing environmental pollution.

3.3.4. Reducing expenditure (costs)

Fleet rationalisation means constantly examining whether all tasks are allocated and carried out in the best possible way. This should enable some expenditure to be avoided or reduced. Individual measures to this end are:

- A new grouping of transport tasks, with orders being selected, inelastic orders with deadlines being converted to time-elastic orders without deadlines, delivery quantities being unified and simplified. This can lead to higher vehicle capacity utilisation.
- The use of larger vehicles which can achieve better turnround.
- Temporary withdrawal of vehicles from service; fleet concentration if this does not increase fixed costs.
- Finally, it must be examined whether part of the transport tasks cannot be handed over to third parties if this can improve business results. This is a question of inter-firm co-operation in road haulage, a factor also very important in another context.

All management measures imply that there exists a good and reliable flow of information between all parties concerned, both inside and outside the firm.

4. WAYS AND MEANS OF MEETING THE NEED TO ADJUST TO GENERAL ECONOMIC CONDITIONS

All the trends in the general economic indicators together with transport demand factors lead to the need for a general examination of the existing division of labour.

The economic constraints - stemming from general economic problems and the world-wide interdependence of nations - have reduced the scope for action and decision-making and management has more than ever before to take into account the effects of external influences on individual firms. This leads to a systems approach to planning, with all internal and external parameters being included.

The road haulage industry, mainly consisting of small firms, is thus faced with a particular problem. Transport proper is becoming part of a logistic chain including such functions as warehousing, transshipment operations, delivery organisation and supply planning. Competition is leading to the increasing appearance of "systems" on the supply side of the market in order to meet this "logistic demand". The managers of transport firms must now decide how to adapt the businesses for which they are responsible to these developments. Some possible approaches are given below.

4.1. Alternative choices

- Specialisation: selective orientation towards transport needs can provide the opportunity for firms and businesses to specialise and tailor their service supply to the requirements of transport chains and systems for specific groups of customers, types of goods or transport links. Management needs to be aware, however, that this not only brings the advantages of semi-monopolistic positions in certain market segments (incentive to monopolise), but also substantial risks due to greater dependence on markets and short-term economic trends.
The entrepreneur has to be in a position to be able to fulfil the individual wishes of customers, particularly in the case of special transport operations. This implies being able to keep an eye on all the firm's activities, but the optimal firm size has not yet been found and in any case, large firms have more opportunity than small ones to develop a specialisation.

- Firm expansion: concentration and large firms should not be regarded as a cure-all, however. Running a road haulage firm needs a "craftsman's touch", as it is only through personal attention that the individual and general service capabilities can be fully exploited. This is easier in small and medium firms than in large ones. Large firms have certain cost disadvantages as compared with small ones and also suffer from certain structural weaknesses in management as the supervisory staff responsible for different functions are not all equally competent. On the other hand, large firms can impose their pricing system on the market far easier than small ones.

- Co-operation: fully committed management, i.e. readiness to help customers solve their goods supply and distribution problems, which are subject to constant change, is an important prerequisite for successful survival in a competitive situation. Solving logistic problems involves planning beyond the limits of the firm and requires a capacity to

227

co-operate. Because of the general interrelation-
ships in the economic system, the capacity to co-
operate needs to be developed in several directions:

. between transport firms and their customers,
   whether they be shippers, consignors or
   consignees;
. between different transport undertakings, whether
   this be in the context of combined transport or
   where break of bulk is involved, as even here an
   attempt must be made to implement the concept of
   a thorough-going transport chain.

All the different possibilities for co-operation are
open to small and medium road haulage firms and they can
also join together in co-operative associations or systems. This decision is of particular importance, as the
managers of such firms are in much closer direct contact
with individual customers than are the managers of large
firms.

4.2. Improving the conditions

There should no longer be any doubt that transport
demand as a whole has significantly increased the requirement for co-operation in goods transport. Managements
have clearly not yet exhausted the possibilities of co-
operation as a policy instrument.

We now need to examine whether the conditions for
co-operation between individual firms and groups of firms
are in line with the market trends and whether they are in
need of improvement. A distinction needs to be made between improvements:

- for the transport user;
- for transport firms;
- for co-operation itself.

4.2.1. Rationalisation of distribution procedures for the transport user

The problem of goods distribution in conurbations has
been posed from the standpoint of "city logistics". The
idea suggests itself, more than ever before, that an infrastructure supply should be built up in the form of
goods distribution centres. These are transport and trading centres, which as a logistic system are tailored to
the transport needs of a conurbation and in which forwarders, transport firms, warehouses and other service undertakings are located. Their service supply can thus be
produced and used in both individual and co-operative
forms (see Figure 11).

228

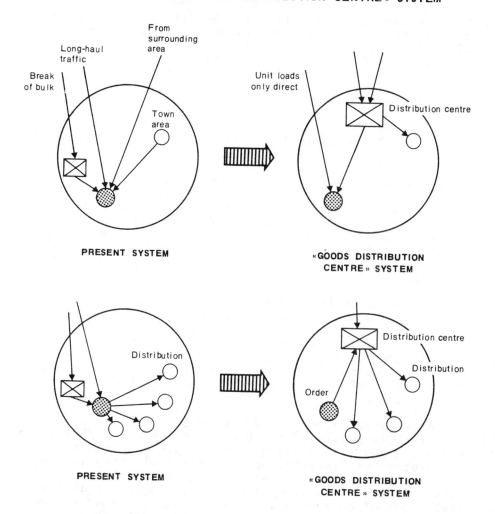

Figure 11 COMPARISON OF PRESENT GOODS DISTRIBUTION METHODS WITH THE «GOODS DISTRIBUTION CENTRE» SYSTEM

Note:

In the goods distribution centre system, combined transport and all shipments involving break of bulk pass through a goods distribution centre organised as a co-operative facility with its own infrastructure.

A pre-condition for this is that there should be a free flow of information between all parties involved in the transport and operating system. This is by no means always the case, however, so that an improvement in computer-based systems would also substantially improve the conditions for transport firms.

229

4.2.2. Changing the division of labour in transport firms

Obviously, co-operation in the distribution of goods also has its advantages for transport firms. They can obtain higher capacity utilisation, co-ordinate trip and route plans with one another, specialise in specific types of customer or transport link and produce a market-oriented logistic supply in the context of transport chains.[5]

4.2.3. Technological progress to aid co-operation (integration capability)

A number of investigations show that the information available to consignors and consignees for the organisation of logistics and transport do not in fact at present correspond to their needs. This is particularly true at a time when the degree of organisation in the transport sector is increasing and the structure of the transport system is becoming increasingly unamenable to improvisation[6].

Transport chains, transport systems and combined transport have very often contributed to rationalisation, but have also made the world of transport more complicated. A lack of communication has appeared in many areas and this now has to be overcome through increased use of computer-based methods[7]. Information and communications technology is of great assistance here and the needs can now be clearly identified (see Figure 12).

A decisive factor in improving co-operation will be whether it is possible to achieve problem-free information processing and transmission from one place to another. This problem of "interfacing" is incredibly complicated, as is the business and service structure of the road haulage industry itself. It appears, however, that the development of communications technology could solve these interface problems so that the actual conditions for co-operation will be substantially improved.

From among these developments, management has to recognise and exploit the right innovations. Here it should be taken into account that in road haulage, scheduling and operation cannot generally be separated into two levels, though this is relatively easy to achieve in large firms. Scheduling in particular needs computer support as cheap data transmission would provide many opportunities for assisting with this task. In small and medium firms, the driver co-operates and takes over part of the scheduling task during the transport operation. Information transmission and processing systems extending beyond the firm need to be developed here. This implies not only the extension of radio-controlled services, but also the

230

Figure 12. COMPUTER-BASED TASKS IN GOODS TRANSPORT

Function	CHANGE OF LOCATION							COMMERCIAL FUNCTIONS					MARKETING			
	Commission and sort	Load	Store	Marshall	Transship	Unload	Drive	Information	Booking	Contract and conditions	Invoicing and payment	Profit and loss accounting	Market research	Advertising	Customer service and counselling	Supply structure
Collection of all input data — *Change of data concerning*	+	+	+	+	+	+	Location of vehicle; routing trip planning; personnel loading; environment	+	+	+	+	+	Data collection concerning market situation	+	+	+
Preparation of all information — *with scheduling rules*	+	+	+	+	+	+	Context, e.g environment, vehicle, driver, goods, optimisation of economic and technical conditions	+	+	+	+	+	+	+	0	+
Output of all results — *in the desired planning context*	+	+	+	+	+	+		0	+	+	+	+	+	+	+	+

Transship note: Combined transport; formation of unit loads; general forwarding activities

Output row note: External context, results of projections, e.g. of liner services

231

existence of a radio network suitable for long-haul traffic.

In the case of border-crossing traffic, it would be useful to facilitate the flow of information through a satellite communications system.

4.3. Training for firm and transport management

The question is often raised whether small and medium transport firms are actually in a position to maintain their supply for transport chains in the long term. Such firms not only have a very small number of supervisory staff, but also appear little suited for transport systems because of their principle of organisation and their "craft" nature. The view is put forward that however hard management may try, the structural and problem-oriented weaknesses will always make it impossible for such firms to adjust in good time and to a sufficient extent to developments in demand and markets.

This view is invalidated by experience. Management is definitely in a position to learn from developments and make use of economic and technological progress. There are also simplified management systems to support them and link the advantages of improvisation with those of "scientific management". This implies, however, that the entrepreneur and senior staff in road haulage receive constant training and further training. This is not easy because managers have no time to devote to further training.

A great deal has been written about the introduction and financing of further training measures and also about main present-day management concerns (ranging from worker motivation to the monitoring of results). To date, however, there has been no intensive discussion to help improve the practical methods of implementation. It is no doubt very difficult to bring the different structures of transport firms into a single training concept. The different external contexts in individual countries also play a role and influence the extent and intensity of management education. This should not, however, prevent management training from being promoted beyond national boundaries.

The involvement of transport in the economy as a whole requires increasingly interdisciplinary management training, and this applies equally to personality formation.

Finally, one aspect of ever-increasing practical importance is that management has to consider the development of infrastructures and the opportunities thus opened up. This means a comprehensive transport management in which planning authorities and administrations also help to satisfy transport needs.

232

BIBLIOGRAPHY

[1] H. Baum,
Der Güterverkehr in den 80er Jahren - Prognosen und
ihre wirtschaftlichen Voraussetzungen in:
Entwicklungstendenzen des Güterverkehrs und der
Nutzfahrzeugindustrie in der Bundesrepublik
Deutschland in den 80er Jahren, Schriftenreihe des
Verbandes der Automobilindustrie e.V. (VDA), Heft 31,
Frankfurt/M., 1981, S. 15.

[2] Bundesminister für Verkehr,
Das Nachfrageverhalten der verladenden Wirtschaft im
Güterverkehr der Bundesrepublik Deutschland - Eine
ökonometrische und demoskopische Analyse,
Schriftenreihe Heft 43, Hof/Saale, o.J.

[3] H.H. Binnenbruck,
Organisatorische und technische Rationalisierungsmög-
lichkeiten in den Schwerpunkten des Güternahverkehrs,
in: Transportkette Nr. 30, Studiengesellschaft für
den kombinierten Verkehr e.V., Frankfurt/Main, 1980,
S. 35 ff.

[4] W. Schwerdtfeger,
Städtischer Lieferwerker, Veröffentlichungen des
Institutes für Städtebauwesen, Heft 20, Braunschweig,
1976.

[5] H. Hölterling,
Neue Formen des Stückgut-, Sammel-und Verteilerver-
kehrs, in: Transportkette Nr. 28, Studiengesellschaft für den kombinierten Verkehr e.V.,
Frankfurt/M., 1979, S. 19 ff.

[6] G. Schweitzer,
Informatik im Güterverkehr, Forschungsvorhaben im
Auftrag des Bundesministers für Forschung und
Technologie, DV 7987/0 Karlsruhe, 1980.

[7] H.H. Binnenbruck,
Informationsssystem und dispositiver Faktor im
Straßengüter- und Huckepackverkehr in:
Transportkette Nr. 37: Informations-fluß in
Transportketten, Studiengesellschaft für den
kombinierten Veekehr e.V., Frankfurt/M., 1982.

STATISTICAL ANNEX

Table 1.

GOODS TRAFFIC IN GERMANY BY TRANSPORT MODE
(including border-crossing traffic)

Transport mode	Goods carried						Transport output (tkm)						
	1979		1980		1981		1979		1980		1981		
	Million t.	%	Million t.	%	Million t.	%	Billion tkm	%	Billion tkm	%	Billion tkm	%	km
	1	2	3	4	5	6	7	8	9	10	11	12	13
Road haulage													
Long-haul goods	141.8	4.3	140.3	4.3	138.5	4.6	40.8	15.7	40.9	16.1	40.6	16.5	29
Long-haul furniture	0.6	0.0	0.6	0.0	0.6	0.0	0.2	0.1	0.2	0.1	0.2	0.1	339
Long-haul own-account transport(3)	95.5	2.9	99.6	3.1	100.4	3.3	16.8	6.5	17.5	6.8	17.7	7.2	176
Long-haul using foreign vehicles	55.9	1.7	57.7	1.8	58.0	1.9	20.9	8.1	21.4	8.4	21.7	8.7	374
Total long-haul	293.8	8.9	298.2	9.2	297.5	9.8	78.7	30.3	80.0	31.3	80.2	32.5	270
Short-haul commercial(2)	915.0	27.7	900.0	27.7	840.0	27.7	21.7	8.4	21.3	8.3	20.0	8.1	24
Short-haul own-account(2)	1 385.0	42.0	1 355.0	42.0	1 260.0	41.5	23.5	9.1	23.1	9.0	21.5	8.7	17
Total short-haul	2 300.0	69.7	2 255.0	69.7	2 100.0	69.1	45.2	17.4	44.4	17.4	41.4	16.8	20
Total road haulage	2 593.8	78.6	2 553.2	78.9	2 397.5	78.9	123.9	47.8	124.4	48.7	121.7	49.4	51
Railways													
Deutsche Bundesbahn(1)	337.5	10.2	331.9	10.3	314.3	10.3	67.1	25.9	65.7	25.7	62.6	25.4	199
Non-State owned railways	33.9	1.0	32.4	1.0	31.7	1.0	1.1	0.4	1.1	0.4	1.1	0.4	35
Total railways	371.4	11.3	364.3	11.3	346.0	11.4	68.2	26.3	66.8	26.1	63.7	25.8	184
Inland waterways													
German craft	130.8	4.0	126.4	3.9	119.1	3.9	27.5	10.6	27.7	10.8	26.8	10.9	225
Foreign craft	115.7	3.5	114.6	3.5	112.3	3.7	23.5	9.1	23.7	9.3	23.2	9.4	207
Total waterways	246.5	7.5	241.0	7.4	231.4	7.6	51.0	19.7	51.4	20.1	50.0	20.3	216
Pipelines	87.6	2.6	76.1	2.4	62.7	2.1	16.0	6.2	13.1	5.1	11.2	4.6	179
TOTAL	3 299.3	100.0	3 234.6	100.0	3 037.6	100.0	259.1	100.0	255.7	100.0	246.6	100.0	81

1. Including surface traffic (excluding road haulage) and exchange traffic with non-state-owned railways:
1979: 40.6 million tonnes, 1980: 38.0 million tonnes.
2. Estimate by DIW, Berlin.
3. Long-haul own-account traffic excluding lorries up to 4 tonnes payload and tractors up to and including 40 kW engine power.

Source: BAG, Köln, Statistisches Bundesamt, Wiesbaden.

Table 2.

GOODS TRANSPORT IN THE EEC ACCORDING TO MODE AND TRANSPORT LINK (MILLION TONNES)
(excluding transit traffic without transshipment)

Mode	Country	Domestic traffic					Shipments from abroad					Shipments abroad				
		1965	1970	1975	1979	1980	1965	1970	1975	1979	1980	1965	1970	1975	1979	1980
Railways	D	242	289	239	266	257	25	36	31	45	38	31	41	36	35	43
	F	187	192	170	167	166	18	20	18	23	22	30	33	26	28	26
	I	26	28	19	17	17	21	24	19	28	30	10	11	10	12	11
	NL	16	12	6	6	6	6	7	5	6	6	5	7	6	9	10
	B	41	41	31	35	35	14	16	11	15	17	8	13	12	18	17
	L	3	5	4	6	6	8	8	7	7	7	4	4	3	4	3
	UK	232	209	174	170	154	-	-	0	1	1	-	-	0	0	0
	IRL	-	-	3	-	-	-	-	0	-	-	-	-	0	-	-
	DK	4	3	3	3	3	2	2	2	2	1	1	1	1	1	1
Road haulage	D	1 629	2 113	2 106	2 521	2 482	16	25	40	54	57	9	17	33	51	53
	F	1 123	1 432	1 357	1 368	1 384	8	17	25	33	36	10	21	26	36	37
	I	743	877				3	6	10			4	7	11		
	NL	256	305	328	334	357	6	12	16	24	24	7	11	17	23	23
	B	216	299	314	286	311	7	14	23	36	35	9	21	30	37	40
	L	9	9	15	18		1	2	5	1		1	1	1	1	
	UK	1 590	1 610	1 602	1 504	1 372	-	-	-	9	9	1	1	4	7	7
	IRL	-	-	-	-	-	-	-	-	-	-	-	-	-	-	-
	DK	-	-	-	-	188	1	2	3	5	4	3	3	4	5	5
Inland waterways	D	98	102	79	84	82	57	76	86	95	92	32	49	51	54	53
	F	58	67	53	51	51	9	13	11	12	12	15	22	22	22	21
	NL	82	93	79	87	89	28	43	44	49	49	60	81	88	103	103
	B	29	34	21	25	25	24	33	34	41	39	15	17	21	27	28
	L	-	-	-	-	-	-	1	2	1	1	-	1	1	1	1
	UK	-	6	4	5	5	-	-	-	-	-	-	-	-	-	-
Shipping	D	2	3	4	5	5	79	106	100	121	114	18	23	28	36	35
	F	9	13	16	15	16	110	169	195	244	235	20	25	41	58	56
	I	26	45	46	55	53	114	201	199	238	225	24	35	30	47	35
	NL	-	-	-	-	-	118	203	243	274	269	29	64	81	85	78
	B	-	-	-	-	-	44	71	50	67	70	21	29	35	38	43
	UK	66	66	70	102	104	157	201	179	160	134	36	49	51	108	118
	IRL	-	2	1	2	1	-	22	19	15	13	-	14	12	5	4
	DK	5	8	7	7	7	23	32	30	36	36	5	7	8	8	8

Source: Statistical Office of the European Communities, Luxembourg.

237

Table 3.

BREAKDOWN OF GOODS TRAFFIC IN GERMANY: MARKET SHARES (PER CENT)

(Short- and long-haul road transport shown separately)

Type of goods	Railways				Inland waterways				Long-distance road haulage				Pipelines				Short-distance road transport			
	1963	1976	1990	2000	1963	1976	1990	2000	1963	1976	1990	2000	1963	1976	1990	2000	1963	1976	1990	2000
Agricultural products	63	46	45	45	18	23	21	23	19	31	33	32	-	-	-	-	49	43	44	45
Food and feed	18	10	11	12	12	16	16	16	70	74	73	72	-	-	-	-	72	62	60	59
Coal	77	78	80	78	21	20	19	21	2	2	1	1	-	-	-	-	30	24	20	17
Crude oil	12	2	1	1	7	1	1	1	0	0	0	0	81	97	98	98	13	1	0	0
Oil products	34	27	27	24	48	49	44	46	18	15	17	18	-	9	12	12	55	54	54	54
Iron ore	58	48	48	45	42	52	52	55	0	0	0	0	-	-	-	-	3	0	0	0
Non-ferrous ores, scrap	65	64	64	63	32	27	27	29	3	9	9	8	-	-	-	-	30	30	30	28
Iron and steel & non-ferrous metals	59	61	62	60	18	16	16	18	13	23	22	22	-	-	-	-	33	24	19	19
Sands and gravels	30	18	18	17	43	43	42	43	27	39	40	40	-	-	-	-	88	89	90	91
Chemicals	57	40	38	37	27	25	23	25	16	35	39	38	-	-	-	-	49	70	72	73
Investment goods	48	31	32	33	3	2	2	2	49	67	66	65	-	-	-	-	52	51	49	48
Consumer goods	34	23	24	25	7	5	4	4	59	72	72	71	-	-	-	-	69	52	49	48
TOTAL	49	35	36	35	27	25	24	25	20	30	32	33	4	10	8	7	67	67	69	71

Source: Deutsches Institut für Wirtschaftsforschung, Revidierte Langfristprognose, 1979, Berlin.

Table 4.

GERMAN DOMESTIC TRAFFIC IN 1980 AND 1972 ACCORDING TO DISTANCE AND MODE

(thousand tonnes)

Distance (km.)	Road haulage(1)		Railways		Inland waterways		Total(1)			
	1980(2)	1972(3)	1980	1972	1980	1972	1980(2) 1 000 t	%	1972(3) 1 000 t	%
Up to 50	1 969 398	1 784 846	110 565	108 509	14 835	19 507	2 094 798	76.5	1 912 862	76.7
51 to 100	215 996	181 491	30 952	29 672	11 975	16 839	258 923	9.5	228 002	9.2
101 to 150	76 272	60 723	20 031	26 652	13 525	15 568	109 828	4.0	102 943	4.1
151 to 200	36 236	26 623	15 581	18 076	10 837	11 182	62 654	2.3	55 581	2.2
201 to 250	24 688	17 960	18 590	19 944	6 596	9 199	49 874	1.8	47 103	1.9
251 to 300	18 971	13 612	14 354	17 085	6 161	7 530	39 486	1.4	38 227	1.5
301 to 400	23 281	16 640	18 503	17 693	10 089	10 476	51 873	1.9	44 809	1.8
401 to 500	14 620	10 704	8 703	10 948	4 209	4 084	27 537	1.0	25 736	1.0
501 to 700	17 326	12 257	14 923	16 523	2 653	2 275	34 902	1.3	31 055	1.3
701 and over	3 473	2 390	4 515	3 338	983	755	8 971	0.3	6 483	0.3
TOTAL	2 400 262	2 126 945	256 722	268 442	81 863	97 413	2 738 847	100.0	2 492 800	100.0

1. German vehicles only.
2. Short-haul road haulage 1978.
3. Short-haul road haulage 1970.

Source: Statististiches Bundesamt Wiesbaden.

Table 5.

COMMERCIAL LONG-DISTANCE ROAD HAULAGE FIRMS(1)

Number of authorisations per firm	July 1966		July 1970		November 1974		November 1978	
	Number	%	Number	%	Number	%	Number	%
1	4 638	43.5	3 774	39.2	3 204	35.0	2 967	32.9
2	2 554	24.0	2 310	24.0	2 145	23.4	2 037	22.6
3	1 247	11.7	1 217	12.7	1 213	13.3	1 176	13.0
4 to 6	1 418	13.3	1 413	14.7	1 551	17.0	1 631	18.1
7 to 10	515	4.8	554	5.8	625	6.8	686	7.6
11 and over	281	2.6	346	3.6	410	4.5	534	5.9
TOTAL	10 654	100.0	9 614	100.0	9 148	100.0	9 031	100.0

1. Including long-distance furniture removal.

Table 6.

NUMBER OF COMMERCIAL SHORT-ROAD HAULAGE FIRMS ACCORDING TO LAND AND SIZE OF FIRM

(as at November, 1980)

Land	Lorries Total	Firms	1	2	3	4	5	6	7	8	9	10	11 and +
			Of which firms with .... lorries										
Schleswig-Holstein	4 808	1 737	836	367	157	110	66	57	47	21	19	13	44
Hamburg	3 972	1 177	534	220	110	65	63	42	26	19	12	20	66
Niedersachsen	12 581	4 019	1 686	840	477	294	207	135	82	67	31	28	172
Bremen	1 712	496	202	103	68	35	13	16	8	5	12	6	28
Nordrhein-Westfalen	35 249	11 339	5 453	2 172	1 111	712	446	354	225	159	122	87	498
of which Westfalen-Lippe	15 193	5 271	2 639	996	515	311	195	172	108	62	54	37	182
Rheinland	20 056	6 068	2 814	1 176	596	401	251	182	117	97	68	50	316
Hessen	10 988	3 878	2 073	649	358	233	156	109	63	50	32	24	131
Rheinland-Pfalz	7 651	3 212	1 747	656	315	150	100	66	42	28	21	18	69
Baden-Württemberg	17 918	7 439	4 243	1 366	691	347	238	132	97	55	46	44	180
Bayern	22 221	8 150	4 060	1 688	905	460	279	195	144	82	56	73	208
Saarland	1 831	813	447	183	72	25	25	18	18	5	4	4	12
Berlin (West)	2 817	738	302	149	102	43	30	27	16	19	3	5	42
TOTAL	121 748	42 998	21 583	8 393	4 366	2 474	1 623	1 151	768	510	358	322	1 450

TOPIC 2A

MANAGEMENT OF FIRMS TO SATISFY TRANSPORT NEEDS

GOODS TRANSPORT BY ROAD

Dr. B. MENZINGER
DANZAS S.A.
Basle, Switzerland

1. INTRODUCTION

It is indeed worthwhile once more to give serious thought to the importance of the transport system in human relations. The subject is certainly as old as mankind, but needs constant rethinking and adaptation to the ever-changing context.

Goods transport is a complex business. Everybody knows something about it, but nobody has a clear overall view. What makes it so hard to grasp but at the same time so fascinating, is the fact that a transport operation never really repeats itself. Something is always different and the possibility that something may be very different means keeping track of all transport phenomena and being ready, when a change does appear, to make an immediate decision about what to do next. Clearly, transport offers plenty of scope for entrepreneurial action and hence for enterprising people.

As a member of the management team of a private transport firm, I was invited to talk about management to satisfy transport needs. Here is a problem we have to face on a day-to-day basis and I am particularly thankful for this task which forced me to think once again about the longer-term prospects for the organisation of private sector transport firms.

The reader needs to know that the writer of this report is in the forwarding business, not road haulage. Although the company does own several thousand vehicles operating in a very decentralised fashion over several countries, it combines both carrying and forwarding functions, with the latter outweighing the former.

The report is too short to present and interpret statistics concerning our own firm, but our comments are based on experience in this firm and on a survey of developments over the whole field.

2. THE ASCERTAINABILITY OF TRANSPORT NEEDS

2.1. Types of transport need and their origins

It is no accident that the papers or even economic reports generally give only global figures for freight transport, which in the final analysis reflect nothing more than the average of individual services. Average figures, however, are silent on the many variants and the range of values covered. It is therefore most important to bear in mind the many dimensions in which freight transport takes place and the complexity concealed by aggregate figures, before embarking upon the detailed consideration of future developments.

Let us therefore consider first of all the different types of transport need. Mr. Binnenbruck's introductory paper has defined the concept of transport needs, so here we can be brief.

The total quantity of goods to be transported plays a part, as does the individual quantity for each transport operation; the nature of the goods in terms of their dimensions, transportability, danger classification, weight, etc. is also important; the duration of the haul and obviously the distance also play a part, but so does the time at which the goods are to be transported; finally, the price to be paid is far from unimportant and both the general economist and the individual entrepreneur know how vital it is to know what transport costs. Transport needs are determined by these factors which, however, are of different relative significance in each individual case. This, finally, is what makes transport operations so complex and hard to understand (and not just for outsiders), namely the multiplicity and complexity of the reasons for a transport need. This is also what makes it difficult to assess transport performance on the basis of overall figures (i.e. average figures) without giving the impression of being too far removed from reality.

The entrepreneur, who has to adapt to existing or emeging transport needs, therefore wants to know first of all whether these needs have been measured anywhere and if so where he can get hold of the relevant information. The answer is that existing transport needs are recorded as global figures in the statistics of a broad range of associations and government departments, but there are seldom figures relating to an individual transport need; emerging

245

transport needs are not recorded anywhere and have to be scouted out and tracked down individually. The consequence of these observations is that monitoring global figures and official statistics may be of considerable interest to the entrepreneur, but if he wants to understand real transport needs he has to depend on virtually daily contact with his customers. Only in this way can he learn something about the emergence of future transport needs and the decline of others.

Transport needs are not created solely by the customer's internal circumstances, however - they are also caused, by external, third-party influences such as a change in quality of the transport infrastructure, or by transport operators when these either introduce new vehicles (technical progress) or make an organisational change to satisfy transport needs.

The origin of transport needs can thus either be a matter of changing existing needs or an actual requirement for new transport services.

Nobody has yet succeeded in measuring and defining the relative importance of all these factors, in total, or for individual markets. To be honest, we have to admit that no transport operation is exactly the same as an apparently similar one because at least one of the vectors in this complicated system will certainly have different values in the two cases.

The first conclusion to be drawn from the above is that firms in the transport sector determine transport needs in the first place from one job to the next on a day-to-day basis: theoretical analyses based on the statistical yearbooks scarcely provide any help for future guidance but are more suited to confirming certain trends after the event or as aids to certain basic decisions.

To give a concrete example, we know of a firm with about 250 employees which makes about 125,000 shipments a year with an average weight of 3.4 tonnes per shipment. This firm makes about 3,500 personal calls on customers each year, i.e. one personal contact for only 36 relatively small shipments. What this means in terms of labour and costs is discussed below.

The circumstances are obviously somewhat different where it is a matter of relatively large individual transport contracts. But even there, it should be emphasized that the real facts behind a transport need can be obtained only on an ad hoc basis and only from the customer.

To take the argument a step further, the satisfaction of transport needs cannot be planned in advance. If we take it that transport is a service for the rest of industry, its task is optimal satisfaction of the transport needs of its customers which means simply that within the realms of the possible an _appropriate_ solution can and must be found for each need. In practice this means that both in the course of time and over the whole geographical range there must exist at all times the full range of possibilities for transport organisation. There may be some constraints resulting from limited infrastructures or restricted investment possibilities (see below). The extreme example is given by conditions in the planned East European economies. Nobody would claim that the transport sector meets customers' transport needs better there than in our "capitalist" system. On the contrary. Where does the main fault lie? It is thought that maximum capacity utilisation of vehicles reduces transport costs - this is certainly correct in the individual case, but is wrong if all the individual cases are considered together, precisely because proper account is not taken of the changes over time in the relative weights of the vectors determining transport needs. Let this be a warning to us not to try to channel transport needs towards supposedly lower freight transport costs through higher capacity utilisation of vehicles. Counted macro-economically the reverse could be true.

We therefore stress that transport needs are subject to constant change and it is the job of the transport industry to react flexibly to these changes. The more flexibly it is able to react, the better it serves the economy as a whole, indeed its degree of flexibility is probably a yardstick for the level of development of the economy concerned.

In order to maintain flexibility it is necessary for a large number of firms to concern themselves with this question because each specialisation needs its own specialist. This is why there are so many firms and so many different types of firm in the freight transport business: big, small, local, national, international, state-owned and private; serving all shippers and serving individual shippers; operating as carriers, forwarders, and so on. This multiplicity is of the greatest importance, but we see three limits to it:

- Infrastructure (availability and costs).
- Vehicle investment costs (depreciation possibilities, service life).
- Rules of the game applying to all participants.

It is the responsibility of associations and the authorities to define these limits, i.e. to construct the context within which transport needs are to arise and be satisfied. The role of the individual firm is to cover the area bounded by these limits and prove itself within them. Here the baseline position must be the same for all and this is only possible in the final analysis if all concerned are subject to the same obligation to balance their books and at least cover costs.

In the following chapter we shall see how private sector firms operate in this context and what internal and external problems they have to overcome in order to adapt with maximum flexibility to the transport needs of the rest of the economy.

3. SERVICE FIRMS IN THE TRANSPORT SECTOR: THEIR PARTICULAR PROBLEMS

Transport sector service firms may be defined as all undertakings offering transport services. In what follows, however, only those firms which operate according to private enterprise principles are discussed, these being mostly forwarding agents and road hauliers.

3.1. Company structures

Service firms in the transport sector are structured in many different ways. A first point is the enormous number of such firms. Furthermore, they are of all sizes: one-man businesses, medium firms and large undertakings. Numerically, the small firms are very much in the majority. It is possibly this complex structure that has so far deferred research institutes and other observers from occupying themselves with this industry as much as with others. In the light of what was said in the previous chapter, we know that the structure has to be what it is and that we should not try to change it too much.

There is no doubt, however, that the trend is towards larger units, for various reasons which will be examined in detail in this chapter.

3.2. Carrier function versus forwarding function

A distinction is generally made in most European countries between firms with carrier functions (vehicle owners and operators) and those with forwarding functions (transport organisers, freight space brokers, special transport services). There have been times and places where there was more competition than co-operation between firms of these two types. The trend in recent years clearly shows, however, that the two functions are being performed in both types of firm with the internal organisation adjusted accordingly. Only the small carriers are unable to restructure in this way and they would be well-advised to intensify co-operation with forwarding agents. In any event, we will constantly meet with both functions, and less and less with parallel company structures. In the longer term this will have its effect on the work of the trade associations.

The carrier function and the forwarding function, in the sense of agent's services, are thus not in opposition, but complementary.

3.3. The importance of terminals

At the end of Chapter 2 we listed available transport infrastructure as one of the limiting conditions. Some qualification is necessary here. Our reference was to the actual network because infrastructure development is not solely a matter of meeting the needs of freight transport, it also serves other purposes so that the decision-makers with regard to extension and development are the political authorities rather than transport undertakings. This is not so in the case of terminals, where the authorities certainly still have their say, but where private initiative is decisive at least in freight transport.

It is clear to everybody that a transport operation cannot be carried out without terminals to allow the goods to be transshipped. Their importance at one time became so great that liner services developed between them. Since the Second World War there has been a great increase in liner services but the development of terminals has obviously not kept pace. There remains a great deal to be done here, in particular as regards the acquisition of land at acceptable prices in places where transport needs it.

In intra-European transport, we know of many cases where the cost of using the terminals is higher than the carriage cost over the link, even over quite long distances. It seems that in the next few years the problem of terminals will come to play an even more decisive role in the quality of transport services and hence the satisfaction of transport needs than has been the case over recent decades.

3.4. Organisation of the bigger firm

The internal structure of service firms in the transport sector has its own quite particular problems in both the carrying and forwarding fields. It is considered that transport is production over a route and not in a particular location, as in the case of other industries. More precisely it could be said that in the case of a transport operation, one-third of the production takes place at the point of departure, one-third on the journey and the last third at the point of destination. These, therefore, are strongly decentralising features. By contrast, investment in vehicles has a centralising effect, because a prime consideration then is concentration in order to achieve maximum return on the purchase price and to minimise subsequent maintenance costs.

As a result, carrier organisations have tended towards centralisation while forwarders have become more decentralised or even "federalistic". Business as a whole has realised in recent years that the great era of concentration is over. At one time units could not be too big and it was believed on all sides that the greatest possible efficiency could be achieved by centralised management. Developments in the EDP field contributed here, as did the advice from management institutes among others.

The forwarding sector was spared this development because, as we have seen, centralisation is counter to its logic and resistance was therefore greater.

This was not the case with carriers, although we would point out that much more can be achieved through a decentralised fleet plus local responsibility for results.

Forms of organisation in service firms in the transport sector will become more decentralised, going as far as local responsibility for business results, although in the carrying sector there will be centralised coordinating functions which will aid sound decision-making in the acquisition of vehicles.

3.5. Technical development and investment

A transport firm's main problem with regard to investment is knowing how far it is possible to have a transport demand busying the facility concerned for the whole of its service life. This, in fact, is the problem with all investment. The particular problem in the transport sector, however, is that profit margins are very narrow which increases the danger of misinvestment. At the same time, technical progress acts as an accelerator and it is clear that, if the replacement value problem is considered, a relatively short depreciation period is essential for sound management.

With the introduction of combined transport in particular, technical development has turned a major corner involving far-reaching changes. There is no doubt at all that in the future individual firms will be forced to invest more than hitherto in vehicles and the main task of the decision-makers will be to strike the right balance between their own and other capacity. Each firm has its own equilibrium in this respect, although this, too, is constantly changing.

As stated in paragraph 3.3, the question of terminals will be of increasing importance. There is scope for entrepreneurial initiative here, but again in the form of further investment.

3.6. Financing

It is impossible to discuss investment without considering its financing.

Recent economic trends and the associated interest rate movements have demonstrated, more forcefully than for many years, how dangerous it can be to finance investment using only borrowed capital. Here again it is necessary to find a certain balance between own and borrowed capital, but in our opinion it is certainly safest to finance vehicles mainly out of own funds. This requirement means nothing less than saying that only in exceptional cases can large fleets of vehicles be built up over a short period - this is fully in line with experience which shows that in the transport sector in particular success cannot be bought with money alone.

In addition to financing investment, the financing of current operations is an important and often underestimated problem. Transport firms are to an increasing extent used as credit institutions by their customers.

3.7. Staffing problems

This is probably the most important factor in the transport sector. We saw in Chapter 2 how complex transport needs are and how necessary it is to react to them flexibly and quickly. This is where staff are the key and not just those who carry out instructions reliably, but also those who react quickly and are prepared to take decisions, in other words, willing to accept responsibility.

Such people cannot be replaced by machines and never will be. It is therefore necessary to recognise and reward their special skill and importance appropriately.

3.8. Technical progress

In these years of increasingly scarce resources, economic growth - and its consequences - is the main topic of discussion and literature. It is interesting that at the same time hardly anyone is in doubt about the need for technical progress. Quite a contradiction!

In the transport sector, technical progress is of great significance in three different areas:

- infrastructure;

- vehicles;
- organisation.

Each of these three areas is developing in its own way and would constitute a subject for study in itself.

In our opinion, the most important developments over the next few years will be:

- infrastructure: improved terminals;
- vehicles: more multi-modal transport;
- organisation: more computerisation.

4. THE GAMBLE OF RESPONDING TO EXISTING OR EXPECTED TRANSPORT NEEDS

In Chapter 2 we tried to describe how imprecise and unclear are transport needs in the eyes of the transport sector entrepreneur. We saw that the customer himself often does not have much advance warning of a transport need and that even where such a need can be foreseen some time ahead, customers rarely inform the transport undertakings who may be interested in sufficient time. It is thus scarcely surprising that it is particularly difficult for transport firms to embark on long-term investment in goods that have to be suitable for flexible use in the short term.

As we saw in Chapter 3, this problem becomes even clearer when the internal structures of transport firms are examined. The whole way in which transport is organised - which after all is the outcome of customers' requirements - produces a tendency to try to maintain short-term flexibility and wherever possible to avoid long-term commitments. Just think of the significance of return loads. Clearly the business can be planned long-term only in a few isolated cases.

And yet the entrepreneur's future is decided at the time when, despite all risks, he decides to meet a specific transport need and commits the corresponding investment. This means, then, that there are two types of firm in the transport sector, those which react only short-term-wise to current transport needs and those which embark on longer-term planning requiring a correspondingly larger investment. There will always be both types of firm because this is the way demand behaves. The firms taking the shorter-term view are mainly small businesses and in this field there will always be a relatively high turnover with new firms springing up and others going out of business.

In what follows we are concerned with transport sector firms adopting the longer-term approach, excluding those with a state monopoly, i.e. forwarding and road haulage firms.

Firstly it must be made clear that a planned approach - i.e. planning for longer-term transport needs not dependent on a single customer - can only be a slow deliberate process. Even large firms, which are really large only because of their geographical extent rather than because they are large in a given location, very often behave not so much as a single planning unit, but rather as the sum of a number of small firms which on the local level tend to think more of the shorter than the longer term.

As already stated, however, businesses can survive only if they do at least a minimum of long-term planning, i.e. at the enterprise level. It is clear that transport firms can and should learn something from the methodology of industrial management - one might say it is a question of "industrialising" planning and management methods in order to be able to satisfy transport needs more satisfactorily in the future.

The big gamble is thus associated in the first place with the response to the longer term.

What are the main considerations here?

4.1. General economic considerations

In future it will be increasingly necessary for entrepreneurs in the transport sector to think about general economic trends.

What is the population trend, how is the purchasing power situation, what are the effects of the energy problem on the economic development of our customers, how important is the pollution problem, what are the probable trends in foreign exchange rates? A very important question is that concerning the value of the goods to be carried. Is it true that finally the function of the developed countries in the world economy will increasingly be to supply services and high-value goods, which in global terms means that the volume of transport in and between developed countries will shrink and also change in composition? And if so, to what extent?

In these and other questions each entrepreneur has to develop a certain intuition. It will be useful to examine each of these questions in turn - not least because the world economic situation shows anything but a clear, unambiguous trend.

4.2. General economic policy considerations

The interrelationship between politics and economics
is well known and intrinsically accepted, though opinions
differ as ever regarding the proper extent of government
intervention. Have private sector transport operators
asked themselves what direct or indirect political influences they are subject to? There are some extremely important influences - the whole transport infrastructure is
decided in the first place by politicians. Is freight
transport always given due consideration in such decisions
or is it not frequently passenger transport which, rightly
or wrongly, determines the direction freight transport
must follow?

In international traffic with countries outside the
OECD area we quickly learn what influence political
changes can have on transport markets. Is it possible to
operate in these markets without previously making some
attempt to assess the risk?

4.3. Considerations at operator level

The most important questions to be answered are those
arising at the level of the individual firm if the aim is
to develop the business and better satisfy customers'
transport needs. We would briefly recall that with this
kind of demand, the carrier or forwarder has to be able to
take short-term action at any time, but at the same time
has to give increasing consideration to the longer term so
that his firm will be able to offer customers longer-term
service arrangements.

The vital questions to be resolved are:

4.3.1. Carrier versus forwarder functions

It should be recalled first of all that private sector transport firms as a rule perform carrier functions as
well as purely forwarding functions. The forwarding function (as traditionally performed by shipping agents) is
geared to the short term while the carrier function requires a longer-term view since it involves investment.

Considering developments in Western European transport and forwarding systems in recent years, it can be
seen that the carrier function has steadily increased,
with a corresponding decrease in the purely forwarding
function. This has happened at all levels and is mainly
connected with the increasing readiness to take responsibility that the customer requires of his transport organiser. It is certainly no accident that this increasing
responsibility is associated with increasing investment on

254

the part of private firms. There is no doubt a two-way effect here.

4.3.2. Size of firm

Since the war we have seen rapid growth in the field of private sector transport undertakings. The first reason is the general economic expansion which went hand in hand with the increasing importance of road transport. Private firms were able to find new scope for expansion in this area and such opportunities were very often taken. Widely differing types of firms grew up and for those which were able to expand to some extent the question now, and particularly for the future, is what is the optimum size. In our opinion the main trend for the future should be for large firms to be organised as a number of small businesses in different places which can be monitored from the centre rather than being a single large concentrated undertaking. Fairly large firms with a decentralised organisation seem to us to be the right formula for the future in order to be able to react flexibly to market changes and to allow the necessary minimum of planning on a higher level within the firm. This of course means that the manager or owner must be more willing than hitherto, and able as well, to share a great deal of the responsibility for the firm with the senior staff.

4.3.3. Market-oriented behaviour

The necessity for this is nowadays very little disputed because it is accepted in other sectors. But what does it mean for transport? It means that transport firms have to analyse market needs much more than hitherto before offering a given service. In the forwarding branch it means that firms will no longer deal with road, rail or air transport in general but rather will specialise in particular country markets, by land, sea and air, or on the other hand there may be greater specialisation by type of freight.

4.3.4. Staff development and training

It is obvious that employees' level of training is crucial when it is a matter of being able to supply the services the market requires. The need to run firms efficiently is increasing, and this concerns all: technical, clerical and driving staff.

Training certainly does not mean merely attending various theoretical courses. We consider practical training at least as important and it is necessary to achieve the right balance between the two.

We would take this opportunity to stress in particular the importance of practical training abroad, for in the transport sector this is the only way to get to know destination markets and thus acquire further specialisation.

4.4. Uninformative official statistics

Before closing this chapter, let us return briefly to the beginning of the report, where we discussed how little help official statistics can really be when it is a matter of assessing transport needs from the transport operator's standpoint. Should anything be changed here? We believe that it is just not possible to produce figures on which decisions can be based. We have in fact seen that transport needs appear at widely differing levels and this variegated picture cannot be reflected in simple statistics. It should be stressed, however, that the furnisher of transport services and transport organisation ideas does not have any meaningful statistics to help his own planning as is the case, for example, with industry.

4.5. Concluding remarks

We hope we have succeeded in this chapter in bringing out just how risky it is for an entrepreneur in the transport sector to commit himself to long-term investment though he can have no exact knowledge of what actual transport needs will be during the depreciation period. And this applies not only to vehicles, but also in the field of office organisation where increasingly large investment is required because of computerisation. The demands on the entrepreneur have risen.

To conclude this chapter, a second assertion can be made: only the front-line entrepreneur will have any chance in future of satisfying customers' transport needs. The future will be no different from the past in this respect. Detailed knowledge, personal contact with customers, expertise and willingness to take risks will continue to be required. Decision-makers in the transport sector cannot - as we saw above - make statistics the scapegoats for their investment decisions. And this is just as well, as it ensures that the necessary flexibility will remain. This again is a precondition for the economy being provided with the necessary quality of transport service.

5. EXAMPLES

After all these theoretical considerations, it will be interesting to try to show, by means of a few practical examples, how the process of continuous adjustment works and how firms endeavour in practice to tailor the services they supply to future transport needs.

5.1. Technical progress

5.1.1. Vehicles

Technical progress in vehicle design continues but no longer at such a rapid rate as in past years. Combined road-rail transport, however, is a technical advance which will bring considerable changes in its wake and is of importance in meeting future transport needs.

The interested reader will be aware of how rapidly this traffic has developed and how it has virtually established a new, third type of transport mode, neither all-road nor all-rail, but truly combined.

The advent of combined transport means new vehicles and rolling stock (railway wagons, semi-trailers, swap bodies, etc.) and hence investment. And new investment means changes in the structures of the firms involved.

5.1.2. Administration

The variety and complexity of production in the transport sector means that it is not easy for outsiders to rationalise procedures in transport firms. There has to be a willingness to delve into detail and there is a certain reluctance to do this so long as there are "easier" projects on hand. This was our judgement on the attitude of computer service bureaux, for example, over many years.

There is now a new attitude however: the opportunities for rationalisation in transport administration is seen as a big market by management consultants and office machine manufacturers and significant developments are now taking place in the sector. The most important are:

- once-only registration of shipments;
- automatic bookkeeping;
- automatic communication with customers and agents at home and abroad;
- automatic scheduling.

EDP is now firmly established in the transport sector, but is only in the initial stages of its development. What is happening here is that unproductive routine

257

work is being taken over by office automation equipment, allowing the employee to use more initiative.

5.2. General economic trends

Over the world as a whole there are certain countries with thriving economies and others experiencing difficulties of varying degrees. A transport entrepreneur has to behave differently in boom conditions in Japan and in the kind of economic stagnation prevailing at present in Western Europe. It would be a bad thing if legal requirements in the service sector were seriously to hamper adjustment to changing outside conditions. Service quality, which is particularly important in times of recession, would necessarily suffer. When the political situation changed in Iran, for example, this had a direct influence on the suppliers of transport services: demand for transport to Iran fell off, meaning that rearrangements had to be made at short notice, and this must always be possible.

Again, there may be a fall in certain traffics because buyers switch to other sources. This is almost a daily occurrence even within Europe. A transport firm must always be able to keep up with its customers and supply the transport service for the goods as quickly as possible.

5.3. Financing investment

As we have seen, the need for investment at firm level is increasing and the problem of its financing has already been raised. Purchasing semi-trailers for combined transport, private railway wagons or electronic data processing equipment is a new requirement needing substantial investment resources. Adequate own-capital formation is a precondition for long-term activity in this sector and many firms have been directing their attention to this problem for many years already.

Increasing capital requirements are also changing the character of firms, however, at least when they come from the forwarding sector: it is becoming less and less feasible to bid for all projects and tenders; a company's entry into the market will not only depend on how skilfully a bid is designed and framed but increasingly on the extent to which adequate own-funds are available to finance the carrying out of the task concerned.

Own-capital resources and skilled staff welded into a team are the foundations of successful activity in this sector. Both requirements can only be met through years of work, so that in our opinion short-term spectacular successes are just not possible or will prove to be illusory.

258

5.4 Terminals

We have already referred to the importance of this question, but now let me quote a practical example. Everybody concerned with European transport knows that Basle occupies a very favourable location and seems ideally suited to be the hub of European surface transport. But does this suffice? Is it enough for Basle not only to be at a suitable distance from the main industrial centres, but also to have good transport links with them? In the final analysis, Basle can become an important transport centre only if terminals are available to enable the goods to be transshipped. The case of Basle shows how the importance of location can be lessened if these infrastructures are not provided at the right time. There needs to be the right balance between them and the transport network. It should be noted however that the network infrastructure is mainly the concern of the authorities while in terminal infrastructures the responsibility of private enterprise is also involved. This is a further example of a situation where the entrepreneur can and must participate in meeting transport needs.

5.5. Sales and marketing

In conclusion, let me give a further example from the sales and marketing area. In Chapter 2 it was already mentioned how difficult it is to obtain orders. After all that has been said, it will be clear to the reader that each transport operation has to be handled individually and that it is hard to work by general, absolute and universally valid rules. This makes it difficult to replace old-style salesmanship by the marketing approach.

The development is under way, however, and cannot be stopped, but we believe that traditional selling will not be replaced but complemented by marketing. To obtain a contract we will still need the individual salesman to convince the customer of the high quality of the service. It is increasingly apparent, however, that marketing is needed in connection with investment decisions, to enable the salesman to cover the market adequately. Marketing will certainly increase in importance.

6. CLOSING REMARKS AND CONCLUSIONS

The subject of this paper is the management of firms to satisfy freight transport needs. We are painfully aware that much more could or should have been said. For example, it would now be interesting to investigate, by means of a concrete example, the different factors influencing a transport firm and what their consequences are.

A further question would be whether trade organisations see their task - as they should - as that of actually helping individual firms constantly to improve their service to customers in greater security, though without removing entrepreneurial risk, while retaining the necessary degree of flexibility.

Many questions still remain, but we believe we have succeeded in first describing the complexity of the situation in private sector freight transport, and above all, showing how few reliable pointers are available to the transport entrepreneur to help him in his business plans and decision-making. In our industry there is a saying, "an example can be found for every possible case" - so that quoting examples does not necessarily constitute proof.

Let me now draw the main conclusions from what has been said.

6.1. Business management

There has been considerable development in the science of management in industry, but much less in the transport sector. This need to catch up now seems to be recognised and we can only hope that what we consider to be the necessary pace is maintained. It should be noted, however, that while there is considerable progress in the carrying sector (transport in the narrower sense) there is virtually none in the forwarding sector. It needs constantly to be brought to the attention of governments, industry and trade that not only transport services as such, but also efficient transport firms are the very basis of a sound business economy.

6.2. Forecasting transport needs

We have seen how difficult it is to foresee the advent of new transport needs. In cases, however, where substantial investment resources are required to extend a transport organisation (whether they concern vehicle purchases or administration), a transport firm can no longer act with maximum flexibility. The customers themselves can alleviate this disadvantage by advising transport firms of any developments in good time.

We have also seen that the gamble of committing oneself to envisaged transport needs is fraught with risk.

6.3. Company structure

We are happy to say that the age of very large and over-large units is past in many sectors. The idea has

certainly spread that the disadvantages of extreme centralisation outweigh the advantages. This also applies in
the case of transport firms.

As in many other spheres, here, too, developments
germinating in industry work through only after a certain
time lag. It is to be hoped that in this case the transport sector will not go through the stage of trying over-
centralisation. We are convinced that federalistic company structure (as regards budget, investment and profit)
can bring about the highest possible standard of transport
services.

6.4. Rationalisation

This is well known as a thorny subject and is quite
justifiably viewed with scepticism in many quarters. It
must nevertheless be stressed that in the transport sector, and particularly in private enterprise, there remain
many opportunities for rationalisation and these must be
taken. It is important to enable employees to adjust to
such developments in good time.

6.5. Financing

The growing need for investment and higher turnover
will increase the need for financing. We believe that on
these grounds alone it is justifiable to require that only
profitable firms stay in the transport sector.

At bottom, keeping unprofitable firms alive, in the
transport sector as elsewhere, is merely putting off the
day when the problem has to be solved. This does not
merely affect the firm itself, there are hidden consequences for its environment, too.

6.6. Staff

The complexity of transport operations and the new
requirements arising daily in performing transport services place considerable demands on employees. In freight
transport it is basically the "man in the front line" who
determines how well the firm is doing. This fact means
that the computer will never replace a good transport
specialist.

A high skill requirement means firstly that employees
need regular further training and second that they must be
given the necessary free rein by their superiors. This
applies not only to independence under a federalistic company structure (see point 6.3), but also applies within
each profit centre to the individual employees.

6.7. Transport policy

Last but not least, an appeal to transport policy-makers. We have seen that for private sector firms (carriers and forwarders) in the transport sector there are really very few reliable basic data on which to plan their activities for optimum satisfaction of customers' transport needs. This is so because the course of a transport operation from the appearance of demand to delivery of the goods at destination comes under so many influences that even with the best preparation unforeseeable changes may be necessary at any moment. Strictly speaking the only fixed datum is the existing transport infrastructure, i.e. networks and terminals. Changes in this area are transparent to everyone, and entrepreneurs are able to adjust to them in good time.

The situation is different in another area which also has a significant influence on the functioning of transport firms, but which is not always clear and visible. The importance of transport policy as a basic datum for all freight transport firms cannot be stressed enough and we believe that in order to achieve sound progress in service quality two things are essential:

1) that there should actually be a transport policy; and
2) that this policy should be lasting.

6.8. Conclusion

Below we summarise the way in which we believe that an entrepreneur in European freight transport can best meet the future transport needs of his customers:

- federalistic, decentralised company structure;
- collaborative style of staff management;
- right balance between own and borrowed capital;
- prudent investment in vehicles;
- refusal to accept frequent repetition of operating losses; and
- introduction of marketing to complement direct selling.

All this will serve the community even better if the firm is able to operate on the basis of a positive, consistent transport policy.

TOPIC 2A

MANAGEMENT OF FIRMS
TO SATISFY TRANSPORT NEEDS

GOODS TRANSPORT BY ROAD

Dr. W. L. VERHOEFF
Nationale Organisatie voor het
Beroepsgoederenvervoer Wegtransport
Rijswijk, Netherlands

SUMMARY

INTRODUCTION

Many factors have to be taken into account by the management of road haulage firms in the pursuit of company objectives. This paper concentrates on one of these, namely social policy.

In doing so it is necessary first of all to delimit the area of interest. In the first place this paper is - on purely pragmatic grounds - confined to internal social policies, i.e. to those aspects of company policy which are concerned with the promotion of staff welfare. Secondly, it should be noted that, as far as can be established, very few studies have been made of social policy in the road haulage industry. This paper is, accordingly, based on:

a) observations in practice;
b) studies of a more general nature on the subject;
c) the situation in the Netherlands.

In view of the social diversity in Europe point (c) may seem excessively restrictive. No two road haulage firms in Europe are the same, their employees do not have the same expectations, and social policy therefore takes differing forms. At the same time, however, it is fair to say of day-to-day employment in the road haulage industry that there are many common or at least similar aspects and problems.

The differences that exist tend to concern such matters as the impact of employers' and employees' organisations on company social policy, political attitudes towards social issues, the level of social provisions, and external and internal company constraints. Attitudes will, consequently, vary with respect to:

1. the place of social policy in company policy;
2. the importance to be attached to social policy;
3. the assignment of responsibility for social policy.

An examination of these questions is important in order to provide an implicit indication of the directions in which social policy will and can evolve.

1. BACKGROUND DATA

Before proceeding to an examination of social policy and the form it takes in individual road haulage firms, some of the main features of the road haulage industry should first be outlined. Further progress in the field of social policy depends not only on the identification of current problems but also on an understanding of the possibilities and limitations peculiar to the industry.

One relevant factor is obviously company size. The survey in the Annex indicates that the industry consists predominantly of small firms.

Approximately 71,000 people are employed by 8,000 firms, of whom 47,000 are drivers; 36,000 of them are payroll employees.

In many of the smallest companies it is quite common for the owner also to work as driver. Once a company employs five or more workers, however, owners generally no longer act as full-time drivers but concentrate on management and administration and building up customers.

The figures on company size are based on the number of vehicles per company; the number of persons working in a company does not, however, follow quite the same pattern. Of the total number of people working in the road haulage industry, 75 per cent work for companies employing ten or more people; in the case of payroll employees the figure is as high as 80 per cent.

Conversely, 70 per cent of the owner/managers and members of their families are accounted for by firms with ten or fewer people. As might be expected, (owner) management and family employees make up 40 per cent on average of such firms. In the case of companies with between 10 and 50 workers, the figure is 9 per cent, while in companies with over 50 workers it is as low as 2 per cent.

A large number of companies are family businesses run by owner/managers. The number used to be even higher. The majority of companies have been built up from these origins in the past 30-35 years. The general pattern is for family businesses to be bought out by third parties, especially as they grow larger, or for the original owner/manager to transfer the management of his business to another member of the family or to "outsiders". In most cases management is transferred to persons with a higher level of training.

The following percentages provide a further broad indication of the nature of the industry:

No. of employees	1-9	10-49	50+
Drivers	83	76	63

of which:

	1-9	10-49	50+
Percent of international drivers	17	28	41
Non-driver staff, including technical, administrative and supervisory staff and store-men/packers	6	17	35
Management	11	7	2

The past 10 to 15 years have seen considerable changes in the educational level of drivers.

Ten years ago, 80 to 85 per cent of drivers had received primary education only. The remainder had received some form of junior technical education, while a mere 2 per cent had completed secondary education. By contrast, the evidence tentatively suggests that of the young drivers entering the industry now, 65 per cent have received some form of junior technical education, 25 per cent have received secondary education and some 5 per cent have even had higher education.

As regards the age structure of the industry, 80 per cent of all employees are under 40, while the average age of drivers and of technical and office staff (with the exception of management) was approximately 33 in 1978 (cf. 31 in 1970). It is clear therefore that there are many young people in the industry. The implications for social policy, or social policy itself, will not be examined at this stage.

By way of comparison, only 60 per cent of the total working population in the Netherlands is aged under 40, and 13 per cent is over 55 (as against 3 per cent in the road haulage industry).

The length of time that workers generally spend in the industry is comparatively brief and this applies even more to the time spent with one company: in the case of drivers the average is five years (cf. approx. three years in 1970), and in the case of technical and administrative staff approximately seven years.

The return on capital is generally low; in recent years it has dropped to the point at which companies have had to draw on their reserves in order to survive.

A recent survey provided some indications of the reasons why people become drivers:

- 50 per cent are attracted by the adventurous nature of the profession;
- 25 per cent cite high earning power as a relevant factor;
- 50 per cent mention more or less accidental factors as having been behind their choice.

2. PLACE OF SOCIAL POLICY

2.1. Formulation of social policy

Social policy, and the form it takes in individual road haulage firms, differs widely, ranging from the absence of any policies at all to their conscious incorporation into company policy. Practice suggests that the attitude of the individual employer has a major bearing on this.

However, it is legitimate to ask whether the adoption of social policies should be purely optional and dependent on the attitudes within the company concerned.

2.2. Company objectives

Each company has its own objectives, even if these are not explicitly formulated. A company makes use of human and material resources to achieve its particular aims. In so doing it will be subject to certain constraints, either of an external nature or as agreed within the company. The clarification of company objectives can itself provide a clear indication of the place of social policy in a particular company.

There are therefore a number of possible variants. One of these would conceivably be for the entrepreneur's own interests to take absolute priority at the expense of the interests of the people working for the company; everything and everyone is subordinated to the interests of the entrepreneur. On account of the external constraints referred to above, this variant is subject to distinct limitations in modern society and is unlikely to be encountered in pure form. To the extent that it does, social policy in the sense of promoting the welfare of the individuals working in the firm is likely to get short shrift.

But even if the company has wider objectives this is still no guarantee of sound personnel policies. In present-day literature, for example, one encounters references to the objective aims of a company as the satisfaction of particular needs in particular markets. A haulage firm working along these lines can easily achieve its aims

268

without any conscious social policies, even to the neglect
of the essential interests of those working in the company
and on whom the attainment of its objectives depends.

At first sight this may seem an implausible proposition. It must however be remembered that:

a) people often fail to formulate or review their own
   interests in explicit terms;
b) there will or course always be social elements
   present, such as wages. In many cases these elements are not decided within the company itself
   but are imposed "from outside", e.g. by the
   government or by collective bargaining agreements;
   and
c) dissatisfaction does not always express itself
   directly in the form of staff turnover.

In this respect it may be noted that the ease with
which people can be replaced, as determined by the nature
of the work (i.e. skilled and unskilled), and the situation in the labour market can often dampen the impact of
inadequate social policies on the actual attainment of the
company's objectives.

A more appropriate and comprehensive formulation of
company objectives might be as follows:

Companies shall seek to satisfy the individual requirements of customers as best as possible within the
general policy orientation of the industry as a whole,
subject to:

1. the consistent payment of a reasonable dividend to
   shareholders;
2. sound inter-personal relationships with and participation by employees, thereby creating scope in
   the company for individual initiative and responsibility and providing employees with legal security and assuring them adequate scope for self-
   development;
3. respect for professional and social standards,
   with the more important coming first where the two
   conflict.

2.3. Duality of company objectives and the objectives of social policy

We have already indicated the major factors of
importance to a company in the pursuit of its objectives.
These include people, material resources (which we do not
intend to discuss) and operational constraints.

The latter reflect interests: the interests of society, of shareholders, of government, and of the people

working in the company - in short interests of a widely-varied nature. In the specific case of a transport company there are all sorts of factors which have a bearing on company management. These include road safety regulations, licensing regulations and shareholders' dividend expectations, to name but a few.

No company can get round these constraints because:

1. a number of them are enshrined in legislation; and
2. failure to satisfy the interests expressed in these constraints will mean in practice that the people whose interests are at stake will turn away from the company in question; financiers, for example, who cease to obtain a return will no longer be prepared to provide finance.

Reference to this complexity of constraints has been deliberately made because many of them have made an indirect or even direct impact on the social policies adopted by individual road haulage firms.

This is because social policy is concerned with the people in a company, with the way they work, the contribution they make to the attainment of company objectives, both individually and collectively, and the welfare they obtain in and through the job. All this however takes place within the larger context of the company as a whole, in which the interests of others also have a bearing. In terms of social policy these interests amount to limiting factors which must be taken into account and which affect the ability to achieve social objectives. These conditions fall into a number of major categories:

a) Conditions with respect to the company's continued existence and its ability to provide employment. Companies can of course lose their ability to fulfil certain conditions, either severally or collectively. The company in question will then cease to exist or will no longer be assured of continuity.
b) A considerable number of the external constraints directly concern the social aspects of a company. These amount to a more or less coercive framework within which social policies can or must be devised. Examples include the wide range of social regulations and legislation drawn up by the government.

Two factors may be noted here:

i) the number of regulations appears to be increasing; and

ii) although the relevant legislation and regulations
apply to large groups of companies and individuals, or even to the business sector as a whole,
they often contain highly detailed provisions.
Other constraints in this context may arise out
of agreements at both macro and micro level between employers' and employees' organisations.
One of the most obvious examples is that of the
collective agreements reached at industry level,
which form a framework for the realisation of
labour conditions within individual companies.
Another example in this context, and one which is
not to be underestimated, consists of the constraints imposed by society, even though these
might not be explicitly laid down in the form of
regulations (e.g. the force of public opinion).

c) The set of constraints to which a company is subject includes elements that either have a bearing
on or are of relevance for both 1. social conditions as such and 2. the implementation of social
policy.

Both of these may be clarified with examples. In the
case of 1. the regulations concerning driving hours are
based both on social considerations and on road safety
factors. It may be asked whether the regulations would
not have been different if they had been drawn up with
social considerations alone in mind.

In the case of 2. there is a clear sphere of interaction and in many cases even of conflict, e.g. between
the required rate of return on company operations (as
pressed for by example by shareholders) and the costs
associated with the implementation of social measures.

It may therefore be seen that the promotion of the
interests of people working in a company occurs in conjunction with - and in certain instances in competition
with - the interests of other parties. This involves a
need for co-ordination, the selection of choices and the
establishment of priorities.

2.4. Who formulates social objectives in a company?

Two questions are of relevance in this respect.

a) who decides what the interests of the people in a
company are?

b) who is responsible for co-ordination, the selection of choices and the establishment of
priorities?

The answer to the first question is closely related
to the views people hold of company objectives. It is
possible to take the view that a company is achieving its

aims if it satisfies the interests of a particular group or individual, e.g. by concentrating exclusively on the maximisation of profits. In this case there will obviously be little if any room for any factors at variance with this aim, unless they are inescapably imposed from outside. Given the evolution in attitudes towards labour as a factor of production in recent decades, however, a subordination of labour's interests of this kind would no longer be feasible. Instead, it is primarily up to the people working in a company to indicate what their interests are. This means that they will also assess whether, subject to the fulfilment of certain other essential conditions, those interests are being satisfied or sufficiently taken into account.

(It may be noted in passing that it was probably the emergence of this sense of self-awareness on the part of labour which was responsible for the belief among hauliers that their employees had become estranged from them, whereas previously they had built up their businesses in a pioneering spirit in close co-operation with their staff. Similarly a certain reserve developed on the part of hauliers towards their staff.)

In practice, however, employees tend not to express or specify their interests, especially in smaller companies. Instead this is often left to others, such as professional associations and the government, especially where collective matters are concerned.

The question then arises whether sufficient account is, or can be, taken of the interests of the individual employees in a particular company or of the individual nature of that company as a community of interests. Seen in this light there will not only be points of correspondence with other companies but also highly divergent elements.

For this reason it is ultimately up to the company itself to discern and formulate the real feelings, aspirations and interests (whether formally expressed or not) of its employees.

Proper insight into these aspects is essential if a company is to pursue social policies. But it is not just a matter of those aspects specifically related to staff; the various aspects referred to earlier as limiting factors are equally as important. These include such matters as the transport company's financial resources; the sectors of the transport market (and there are many) in which the company operates; any specialised knowledge required (e.g. of the transport of the goods in question); the pricing possibilities in that market; the existence of any marked degree of interdependence with the consignor or other haulage firm; and the official regulations to which the company's particular activities are subject.

Information on all these aspects will be required if the company is to assess whether and in what way its objectives can be achieved.

This brings us to the second question, i.e. who is responsible for ensuring that the company is aware of its operational constraints and that these conditions are fulfilled, that the various interests are reconciled, and that priorities are established. Whether the interested party consists of shareholders, staff, the government or society, that party has the right to ask the company whether its interests are being taken into proper account. As shown in practice, this can often be a source of conflict, e.g. between capital and labour or between the firm and its environment. Those responsible for the achievement of a company's aims must therefore also be aware of the interests of the various groups associated with that enterprise. These interests will never entirely coincide, for which reason management will have to be aware of the minimum requirements to be satisfied for a particular group to regard its objectives as having been achieved. This of course has consequences for the style of management. Confining our attention to internal relationships in road haulage firms it may be noted that most companies in the last few decades have been family businesses. The entrepreneur was also the owner and this naturally had its effect on company management.

The process of self-realisation on the part of labour and the increasing number of conditions to which companies are subject have meant that management has increasingly assumed a "buffer" function. While ownership and management are still perfectly compatible, entrepreneurs have become increasingly required to take an objective stance towards the interests which they as owners represent. The same requirement applies in the case of an employee appointed to the ranks of management as a "representative" of labour.

Once it is accepted that the promotion of employees' interests in a company should not be subordinate to other interests but should form an independent aim in their own right, and that the achievement of that aim should form an integral part of any assessment of whether a company is achieving its objectives, it follows that the "independence" of and "objective" reconciliation of interests by management must be assured.

3. SOCIAL POLICY IN THE ROAD HAULAGE INDUSTRY

Once we turn to the road haulage industry in practice, the above considerations may appear to be largely theoretical and to have little practical relevance. As noted earlier the bulk of the industry consists of very small firms in which little or no consideration is given to policy formulation as such. Nevertheless even these firms, to the extent they have payroll employees, are having to contend with:

1. the greater self-realisation of their employees and the latter's interests;
2. the growth in the number of conditions imposed on companies from outside, including with reference to the social aspects of company policy, and the need to adjust to those conditions;
3. the need for a small firm to know what it must offer if it is to attract good quality labour;
4. preventing a pattern of social policy being imposed from outside instead of allowing such policies to evolve in their natural context, i.e. within the company itself.

As noted previously, however, the majority of employees in the industry work for large companies. A change in attitude towards social policy is evident in these companies, and this will inevitably have a follow-on effect in the industry as a whole, forcing small firms to be more conscious of these aspects. Irrespective of its size, every company may be expected to be concerned with the welfare of its employees, i.e. to have social policies. However, whether these policies are deliberately placed in the context outlined above and consciously thought through and formulated in terms of individual company circumstances, will to some extent depend on company size. Hitherto, in what was still the pioneering stage, companies in the road haulage industry were not greatly actuated by policy considerations; running a business was instead largely a matter of dealing with short-term problems and of day-to-day management. On the other hand - partly as a result of the change in management that has occurred - more and more companies are thinking consciously in terms of a structural approach towards and solution of company social problems. In principle the areas of interests are much the same from company to company.

Just how detailed the social provisions made by a particular company are, however, will depend on company size and such related factors as the number of employees, the diversity of functions, the degree to which the entrepreneur is directly involved, the type of work, and the length of lines of communication. These factors will also determine the pressure for social aspects to be taken up, including at managerial level. For these reasons it will come as no surprise that the social policies pursued by individual companies in the road haulage industry are anything but unified. Apart from the substantial variations in company size noted earlier, with the large number of small firms, there are also substantial variations

274

between the sections of the market in which individual companies operate, which in turn affect the nature of their activities and profit potential. Another relevant factor is whether a firm is a family business or not.

At any event a distinction may be drawn between firms on the basis of the level at which management is conducted and the related differences in the way in which the role of social policy in a company is perceived. This diversity, together with need for involvement by government or professional associations in order to get some grip on the situation, have been among the main causes for general regulations to be laid down obliging individual companies to implement social policies. This does, however, mean that the responsibility as described above of both the entrepreneur and the employees in an individual company for promoting the interests of those working in that company is by-passed.

At the same time it must be recognised that the individual approach towards social matters can sometimes be to the detriment of employees or can lead to the distortion of competition in both the labour and the transport market. The fact that employer and employee associations have a role to play in these circumstances does not invalidate the general principle.

4. SPECIFIC AREAS OF SOCIAL POLICY

There are a number of aspects with which virtually every haulage firm has to deal. These include questions to do with pay; the recruitment of good staff; sickness absenteeism; staff turnover; the possibly limited promotion opportunities; working conditions in relation to the company's operating resources, e.g. lorries used, traffic density, lengthy loading or border delays, and lack of flexibility of driving hours, including in social respects; communication possibilities, the importance drivers often attach to driving their "own" vehicle, and job involvement; and availability of work. These aspects come down to the following major categories of social policy: conditions of employment; working conditions; labour relations; the quality of work; and availability of employment. A few of these categories may be examined in more detail.

4.1. Conditions of employment

To begin with we may take the conditions of employment, especially pay. This is not just one of the most basic aspects in employer/employee relations but also one of the most complex. The present-day road haulage industry is no exception. In view of the number of haulage firms and small company size, wages are generally regulated by means of collective agreements. This inevitably means that the increasing desire among companies to tailor conditions of employment to their specific circumstances is by-passed, in that wage agreements are geared to the average transport company (which does not exist) and incorporate understandings concerning major problems (which may not crop up in every company). Although every opportunity is often provided for companies to make their individual views known, the results of these negotiations are often perceived by both individual employers and employees as the imposition of "coercive conditions". This may form part of the reason for the occasional lack of willingness in practice to adhere to these agreements, despite their binding nature for both individual employees and employers. This may be illustrated on the basis of experience in the Netherlands in recent years.

Although collective agreements existed in the industry before 1976, actual rates of pay were often determined independently from company to company. At the very least, the provisions of collective agreements were open to discussion. In the absence of industry-wide guidelines for wage fixation, there arose a great diversity of standards and methods for wage determination in individual companies. Both the form of wage agreements and the maximum and minimum rates varied from company to company. Although the determination of wage rates on an individual company basis might appear normal enough, it meant in practice that:

  i) there were instances of unacceptably low minimum wage rates;
 ii) wage differentials in the order of 20-30 per cent could arise for the same types of work; and
iii) substantial variations in working hours were required in similar jobs in order to obtain equivalent earnings.

These factors prompted the industry to seek a restructuring of the collective agreements. This was based on a system for classifying duties which enabled the relative demands of individual duties to be determined in an objective manner in each company. Alternatively, where this was not required, certain "key" functions were agreed upon as yardsticks. These provisions meant that rates of remuneration were broadly standardized between companies and reflected inherent job differences within companies. The existence of an industry-wide collective agreement also helped ensure that rates of pay bore a proper relation to the nature of work.

Another major consideration is the determination of wage levels for the various categories of functions, as well as their periodic adjustment.

Once again the restructuring of collective bargaining arrangements may be taken by way of illustration. Until 1976, there existed substantial pay differentials for similar categories of work throughout the industry. The restructuring of the collective agreement, however, meant that fresh agreement had to be reached concerning acceptable wage levels.

In doing so the premise was accepted that normal pay should be based on a 40-hour week. This did not lay down the number of hours that were to be worked per week in the industry but established that it should be possible to earn an average income in return for the sorts of hours normally worked in general. Two factors ultimately played a key role in the negotiations between employer and employee organisations concerning the determination of wage levels:

1. the wages paid in practice by road haulage firms (with the highest rates being taken as the index), and
2. wage levels paid in other branches of trade and industry for comparable types of work (on the basis of the system for classifying duties referred to above).

In fact it was the external factors which played a decisive part in the determination of the primary conditions of employment. Each company was therefore required subsequently to make adjustments in line with its particular operating conditions.

One consequence was for example that many individual companies were obliged to absorb a considerable increase in costs. This they had to do in markets where the costs of their competitors were considerably lower, e.g. international transport markets or regional markets where they were up against local hauliers. Much the same process occurs each time the existing collective agreement is renewed.

The large number of firms and the associated requirement for an industry-wide collective agreement, together with the desire to achieve a greater degree of wage standardization throughout the industry, has meant that a substantial area of social policy has been removed from individual company control.

The question arises, however, whether the system of a binding collective agreement in which little or no room is left for adjustment to the circumstances in individual companies is in fact the most suitable method for achieving a greater measure of self-reliance at company level in the field of social policy.

Between 40 and 50 per cent of the costs in the road haulage industry consist of wage costs. Any adjustments in wage rates are therefore bound to have far-reaching knock-on effects on the other limiting factors a company must take into account. These constraints include above all the yield on investment capital and the firm's productivity potential (including the existence of various government regulations).

Apart from the conditions of employment the most vital areas of social policy are working conditions, the quality of work and labour relations. It is however debateable whether the relevant factors which affect these areas and mould the social climate are as yet sufficiently understood; the evidence tends to suggest they are not.

4.2. Working conditions

Drivers obviously occupy a special place when it comes to working conditions in that their working conditions are intimately bound up with the means of production, i.e. the lorry. As such the haulier's main scope for improving working conditions consists of the lorry itself and any mechanical handling aids. Recent years have seen substantial improvements in these areas. In particular, mechanical aids have been continually improved, thereby substantially easing drivers' physical load.

Drivers' dependence on their lorries means however that their working conditions depend heavily on another aspect of company management, namely transport planning.

On the one hand it may be assumed that any demands for the improvement of working conditions will have far-reaching consequences for planning and may even come into conflict with one of the planning objectives, viz. the maximisation of productivity by the best possible transport organisation. On the othe hand transport organisation provides a means for an entrepreneur to eliminate drawbacks and consciously to give concrete expression to the wishes and interests of his employees.

At the same time, however, there are many drawbacks which the entrepreneur can do little to improve. These examples include delays at consignors, border checkpoints and in traffic jams, and the density of traffic in scheduled driving hours. The majority of these drawbacks derive from what were earlier termed external conditions. It may however be asked whether those responsible for the form these conditions take have social implications firmly enough in mind.

One drawback often cited is the length of working hours.

There can be no denying the fact that overtime has to be worked in order to obtain a reasonable level of income in cases where wage rates have lagged behind. In those cases where rates have not lagged behind, however, two observations may be made with respect to the length of working hours.

1. The first of these is that it is in the nature of the business that the length of working hours has to be flexible. It is evident in practice that the job cannot always be satisfactorily carried out subject to the basic hours observed in other jobs.

2. In the second place it is reasonable to ask whether some of the employees in the road haulage industry (especially drivers) do not regard the ability to obtain extra income through overtime as being in their interests. The indications are that they do, although a stage may come at which the number of hours worked can become disadvantageous. Whether this is so, however, requires greater insight into this aspect and it is doubtful whether any universally applicable guidelines can be laid down.

Another by no means unimportant element in working conditions is the status of drivers, or more specifically how drivers are accepted on the job by society. The evidence suggests that they tend to be undervalued. This is not just a matter for improved PR; it is also bound up with the social climate within individual firms, public acceptance of lorries and the inconvenience they can cause to the public, and drivers' own attitudes and behaviour.

4.3. Labour relations

If, for purposes of generalisation, a few principal features had to be singled out with regard to labour relations, one of these would again be the distinction evident in practice between drivers and other employees (generally office staff). In the first place the road haulage industry (often including the big firms) has a number of elements in common with small businesses in general: a simple organisational structure; unstructured consultative procedures; a lack of duty statements; an absence of internal regulations; and close personal contact between management and workers.

Management - especially in the case of an owner/ manager - plays a dominant part right down to the details of individual employees' activities. Depending on the transport sector in which they are working, drivers on the other hand are often required to use initiative and to display a higher measure of self-reliance. Their comparative isolation in respect of the company they work for is

279

undoubtedly one reason for the social cohesion between drivers in their own and different companies. The prolonged absence of drivers can sometimes be regarded as a handicap by companies in maintaining contact (i.e. the problem of management at a distance).

4.4 Quality of work

The quality of work depends not just on working conditions and labour relations but also on a number of other factors.

For a long time many jobs in the haulage industry - especially non-clerical and non-technical jobs - were regarded as unskilled labour. In the case of drivers the main requirements were possession of a driving licence and physical strength for handling of freight. A number of developments have conspired to bring about a change in attitude, although this varies from sector to sector:

1. The nature and quantity of mechanical handling aids have reduced the need for physical strength.
2. Traffic density is increasing.
3. Administrative aspects have become more exacting.
4. There has been a growth of specialisation in the haulage industry requiring greater knowledge of the goods being transported.
5. Changes in internal transport techniques at loading and unloading points mean (or can mean) greater driver involvement.
6. Customer relations and the greater involvement in this respect by drivers.
7. The need for alertness in communications with the company, e.g. in respect of return-loads.

Each of these points indicates that the nature of drivers' responsibility and hence the quality of work is changing.

The consequences have been perceptible, e.g. in relation to the required training. Apart from a shift in favour of a higher level of basic education there is an increasing requirement for supplementary vocational training, both general and specialised. This appears to be related to the greater emphasis being placed on self-reliance in the recruitment of labour.

One of the basic requirements for a driver is the ability to deal independently with such problems as may arise during a protracted absence from base. Examples include the determination of his driving schedule and dealing with technical hitches, organisational problems when loading or unloading, and administrative matters when crossing borders.

280

A haulier's ability to provide constant guidance to his drivers is obviously limited. Increasing stress is likely to be placed on drivers' ability to improvise and to deal with problems themselves - especially as the range of company services grows - but this should at the same time serve to make the profession more attractive.

This does however mean that drivers will have to be adequately equipped. Apart from having the requisite professional skills, they will also be required to have adequate understanding of the way in which their particular firm is managed. To take an obvious example, a driver will be expected to provide those services which his company offers; similarly he should avoid any expenses which were not budgeted for and which could tip the scales as far as the profitability of a particular haulage operation is concerned. In other words drivers bear a clear measure of individual responsibility, and one which can have a decisive effect on operating results.

It was noted earlier that some 50 per cent of drivers chose their profession on the grounds of its "adventurous" nature.

With the odd exception, it is only to be expected that the adventurous element in the driving profession will decline with the requirement for more rigorous and businesslike transport planning on efficiency grounds and the increasing number of government regulations. This factor will then be reduced to the element of self-reliance and individual responsibility. It will then be essential for the precise area of individual responsibility to be very carefully determined, as well as the extent to which individuals can or should be expected to assume responsibility and the impact that this will have on company operations.

Perhaps to a greater extent than in most jobs, a haulier's trading results depend on the efficiency or approach of his drivers. As has been seen, freight rates do not generally make allowance for the sorts of risks that can be encountered in road haulage. In addition it must be borne in mind that drivers are often the visible face of a company and can play a critical role in customer relations.

5. ASSESSMENT OF VARIOUS MAJOR ASPECTS

The prospects for introducing social policies in the road haulage industry depend heavily on the ability and willingness of management to take the full range of interests of their employees into account.

Failure to do so will mean that a haulage company is reduced to a mere source of income, i.e. the most basic form of social policy, even at a time of high unemployment. This situation will moreover give rise to increasing confrontation between workers and management as a result of the process of greater self-reliance on the part of labour, the higher educational qualifications of persons entering the industry, and external developments in the social field and the resultant consequences for individual hauliers.

At all events, it may be expected that social policy will no longer be able to play a subordinate role in the haulage industry as it has often done in the past but that it will come to take its place as an independent element alongside other aspects of company policy.

In that it is concerned with the interests of individuals in the context of the circumstances and constraints in individual companies, social policy is increasingly becoming a matter for companies themselves. Although haulage companies have much in common outwardly, their actual operating conditions can vary considerably, for example because they operate in different sectors of the market. In practice this process of individualisation has encountered a number of problems related to such factors as the number of hauliers, company size, competitive relationships, insolvency, or lack of expertise in implementing social policies.

The determination and implementation of social policies on an industry-wide basis, and certainly in individual companies, is hampered by a number of external constraints or regulations (including in the social sphere). In many cases these regulations are formulated in a way that fails to take due account of the interests of employees in an individual enterprise. Part of sound social policies, therefore, consists of combatting the elements in such regulations which unnecessarily curtail employees' interests.

In this respect it is for example essential for the EEC driving hours regime to be thoroughly revised and adapted to practical realities. This is in no way to suggest that social aspects should be neglected; what it does mean is that the threat posed to the continuity of haulage firms by the present lack of flexibility would be removed and that individual responsibility and initiative among employees would be allowed to come into their own. Any assessment and endorsement of these external regulations will have to take due account of the wide diversity in company size in the road haulage industry and the consequent variations between companies in their ability to formulate their own social policies.

Before social policies can be tailored to the requirements of individual haulage firms, greater understanding will be required on a large number of points concerning the conditions of employment, working conditions, status of workers and the quality of work. A large number of these points will be capable of examination on an industry-basis. The results will, however, have to be translated to individual companies. Both employer and employee associations can play a supporting role in the development of social policies within companies.

The supporting nature of their role should be deliberately stressed because the greater the number of binding regulations imposed on companies with regard to the implementation of social policies (whether negotiated between employer and employee associations or not), the more restricted will their ability be to pursue social policies in the sense of promoting the interests of their employees and improving working conditions as described earlier. Consideration will, however, have to be given to drawing up guidelines for those companies that are less well equipped to implement social policies themselves.

If the road haulage industry follows developments in society as a whole and systematically pays greater attention to the social aspects of running a business, this will simultaneously mean that a start will have to be made in dealing structurally with issues such as productivity (insofar as dependent on staff), sickness absenteeism, staff turnover and the related loss of skills and motivational problems.

On the one hand, there will be a process of clarification with regard to a number of aspects noted earlier in respect of which employees will have a claim on the company; on the other hand, however, there will be a related clarification of the obligations of individual employees in a company with respect to the exercise of their duties and their responsibility for the company's continued existence. Both the rights and obligations of employers and employees alike form an integral part of properly developed social policies.

This will only be possible given a certain openness in policy. Employees must be able to assess whether their company has taken due account of their interests and whether the latter have been satisfactorily reconciled with the other constraints to which the company is subject. Conversely, employers must be able to assess whether employees have been fulfilling their obligations with regard to the company's continued operation. An evolution in this direction will necessarily depend on the existence of a broad consensus and perceived identity of interests, both in individual firms and between the social groupings involved in the formative process.

Developments along these lines are under way in the Netherlands. Employer and employee associations are jointly carrying out surveys into a wide variety of aspects in the fields mentioned above such as the quality of work and legal relationships. These investigations have been based on the question of the requirements that the road haulage industry will have to fulfil if it is to be, and to remain, attractive in the near and more distant future. This is quite clearly a question related to the quality of employment, not just of those already working in the industry but of employment in the future.

284

Number of companies and vehicles in the road haulage industry in the Netherlands as of 31st December, 1980.

No. of vehicles per company	No. of companies
1	2,400
2	1,202
3	833
4	630
5	521
6	405
7	275
8	224
9	195
10	160
11	133
12	131
13	66
14	77
15 - 20	230
20 - 50	343
50 or more	54
Total 29,581	7,879

Source: Central Bureau of Statistics.

TOPIC 2B

MANAGEMENT OF FIRMS
TO SATISFY TRANSPORT NEEDS

INLAND WATERWAY GOODS TRANSPORT

Mr. M. van den BOS
Rotterdam, Netherlands

SUMMARY

PREAMBLE

The plan drawn up for the ECMT's 9th International Symposium on the Theory and Practice in Transport Economics establishes a clear separation of functions between the rapporteurs who have assessed probable trends in transport needs and those who have sought to show how transport undertakings think they can satisfy these needs and what uncertainties or problems may arise. I belong to this second group of rapporteurs and was asked to consider the problem from the standpoint of inland waterway transport.

Before approaching the subject itself, it would seem worthwhile to give a brief overview of the inland waterway transport market in Western Europe, the supply of services on this market, how this transport mode has responded to market trends since World War II and the implications of all these factors in terms of future overall demand for inland waterway transport.

1. BACKGROUND

1.1. The market

It should be pointed out that no common market has as yet been established in the European transport sector in compliance with the Treaty of Rome because it has so far been impossible to set up a uniform legal framework for Europe as a whole.

The system for international traffic - by far the greater part of which is carried on the Rhine - is one of free movement and free competition as established in the Mannheim Act of 1868; the only regulations imposed on Rhine navigation relate to safety and the manning requirements for the different types of craft.

One exception to the freedom of international navigation is the traffic between the Netherlands on the one hand and Belgium/France on the other, where such freedom no doubt also exists in law but in practice certain interested parties have imposed a roster system bound up with the fixing of freight rates.

Inland navigation in the Netherlands, Belgium and France is governed by each country's legislation, under which the governments fix or strictly control rates, while transport operations largely follow a roster system, the rule being that shippers are required to offer their cargoes through exchanges for subsequent allocation, in principle, to the craft available according to the order in which they registered with the exchange.

Finally, in Germany there is a legal fixed rate or fixed margin system; these freight rates are jointly determined under government supervision by shippers' organisations and shipowners' organisations, the shipper remaining entirely free to allocate cargoes to whichever carriers he chooses.

Owing to the different systems outlined above, the market is clearly segmented, though it should be emphasized that the individual markets influence one another. If freight rates are low on the free international market, the number of registrations with roster systems increases; if the free international market is favourable, the number of vessels operating under national roster systems diminishes at once.

In addition to the different operating systems, another factor which segments the market is the size of the navigable waterways; many waterways in Belgium and virtually all the canals in France, for example, are accessible only to barges of 350 tonnes, so that traffic between the Netherlands on the one hand and Belgium and France on the other is largely confined to such vessels. Lastly, another subdivision is obviously the transport of liquid cargoes in tankers.

The conclusion must be that there is no single inland waterway transport market but a great many.

1.2. The supply side and its response to market trends

The outstanding feature of the supply side is the great number of suppliers of inland waterway transport services, mainly owing to the large number of owner-operators in the Netherlands, Germany and Belgium.

Although owner-operators are active mainly on internal markets where there is a roster system, they act as if they were offering services individually. If they are mainly interested in free international navigation, they are for the most part affiliated to marketing associations which obtain cargoes for them. Some of them also conclude fixed contracts with shipping companies.

In addition to these owner-operators there are a large number of inland waterway shipping companies. Once again, these can be subdivided into "industrial" companies - whose role is to meet the transport needs of the group to which they belong - and others which operate freely on the market. Among the industrial companies, moreover, some confine themselves strictly to own account transport, while others are also active on the open market.

Whatever differences there may be in the nature, composition and size of shipping firms, they all have the same objective, i.e. to ensure their own survival in the best possible conditions, which of course also means that they do not consider it their immediate responsibility to worry about whether it will be possible to meet future inland waterway freight transport needs.

Inland waterway carriers are no different in this respect from entrepreneurs in other sectors of the economy in a free enterprise production system, where the first consideration is likewise the survival of the firm.

The entrepreneur therefore has to choose among the various possibilities offered by the market. He has to consider where his best chance lies, whether it be in the roster system, in free navigation on the Rhine, in a subsector of free navigation on the Rhine, such as tankers, bulk cargoes, containers, etc., or in special cargoes, such as chemical products or liquified gas carried by tanker.

By and large, it can be said that the shipping companies have for some years now had a sufficient knowledge of the market and foreseeable trends to be able to choose an appropriate strategy.

This is of course much more difficult for owner-operators, but they are increasingly able to request the assistance of the shipowners' organisations to which they are affiliated.

The point of departure for choosing a strategy for the future is of course in most cases the existing fleet and the existing clientele. The latter often provides an impetus to embark on new ventures alongside the existing ones. To illustrate this last point, we would mention the chemical industry's partial switch from dry to liquid raw materials, which has led to chemicals being carried by specially fitted tankers.

It would no doubt be interesting for the reader to know about the strategy chosen and implemented by the shipping company which the author has managed for many years.

Like many other shipping companies, this one owes its existence to the fact that the import of large and ever-increasing quantities of German coal into the Netherlands induced the importer to seek security of transport through his own fleet. A special subsidiary was accordingly set up and equipped with a large fleet of coal barges and the necessary tugs. The primary function of the shipping company was, of course, to meet the transport requirements of its own group, but its management was also expected to endeavour to obtain the best possible return on the capital invested.

Thus, given the existence of downstream coal cargoes, efforts were obviously made to find upstream cargoes, the main one found being iron ore for the Ruhr steel industry.

Primarily owing to the fact that power stations switched from coal to oil and subsequently to gas, the cargo mix carried by the company changed considerably after World War I, so cargoes suitable for its vessels had to be found elsewhere. The company's range of activities thus expanded to the carriage of all types of freight over the whole stretch of the Rhine between the North Sea ports and Basle. A limited number of motor vessels suitable for bulk cargoes were added to the fleet. In addition, mainly owing to the pressure of the group's subsidiaries along the Rhine, the transport of parcels with a fleet of small motor vessels was undertaken to help the warehousing and transshipment subsidiaries.

Increasing social difficulties were encountered in operating the fleet of towed barges. There were no doubt still enough bargemen, but since the vessel is at the same time the home of the bargee and his family, and children have to be sent to boarding schools - usually to the considerable detriment of family life - more and more problems arose.

There was also an understandable desire for regular time off and holidays at dates fixed in advance. Attempts to resolve these problems by housing the women and children on land and running the vessels with crews relieved at fixed intervals, which guaranteed regular time off and holidays fixed in advance, had little success because this way of life ran counter to long-established traditions.

Considerable difficulties were already being experienced in providing the fleet with crewmen, who were generally housed separately in the bow of the vessel in very cramped conditions and had to cook for themselves. In the mid-fifties, it became clear that operating with towed barges was no longer feasible from the social standpoint or viable from the economic standpoint.

Experience with the fleet of motor vessels for transporting bulk cargoes was not entirely happy either, since the capital invested in the engine was necessarily lying idle during loading and especially unloading, still very lengthy operations at that time. This prompted the shipping company management to turn towards other operating techniques in which separation between the power unit and the cargo space was maintained as with towed barges, but where the social problems inherent in this system of operation could be resolved. It was decided that the answer might lie in operating with pushers on the American pattern but adapted to the conditions on the Rhine. The fact is that unlike towed barges, pushed barges do not need a crew and the pusher crew could be recruited mainly among tug crews who had always sailed without their families on board, so pushers could be maintained in round-the-clock service if the crew was relieved regularly.

After acquiring some experience with a first experimental unit, built for the joint account of four ship-owners, the company continued to invest in pushers and the operating system was improved. After an initial period of navigating solely during the day, there were trials with semi-continuous (18 hours a day) operation which, having proved successful, led finally to continuous navigation (24 hours a day, 7 days a week).

In addition, the loading capacity of each pushed barge was increased from 1,250 to 2,750 tonnes with, of course, a corresponding increase in the engine power installed in the pushers.

At present each pusher has a crew of two watches on board, each of which works 12 hours per 24 hour day; the crew is relieved after 7 days service and has 7 days leave. Under this system each crew member can take four consecutive weeks leave once a year according to a roster system fixed in advance.

In 1968, a strategic decision was taken, whereby the company would no longer operate anything other than pusher flotillas; orders were placed to replace the remaining towed barges by pushed barges, the bulk-carrier motor vessels were sold and the carriage of parcels ceased.

In taking this strategic decision, the company restricted its activities to the bulk cargo market, while the decision also limited the company to the carriage of goods suitable for pusher navigation, i.e. the transport of large quantities over fixed routes.

At the same time, the company adopted the principle of trying to work with other shipping companies that were also important in this branch of transport so as to be able to operate jointly in the most rational way possible. Different associations were set up to facilitate co-operation in different transport sectors.

Each year a plan is worked out for the following three years, covering:

a) the tonnages which companies expect to carry for existing customers; to this end, discussions are held with customers or with partners in the association;
b) the traffic which companies expect to win; this is done by consulting the statistical data and forecasts of transport research institutes and press reports;
c) probable trends in freight rates;
d) probable trends in shipping costs.

On the basis of the data under (a) and (b), a fleet rotation programme is simulated to determine whether the company has too much or too little tonnage. According to the company's assessment of the market, a decision is then made on what traffic can still be won and whether it is necessary to obtain outside tonnage on time or voyage charter.

In parallel with this plan, which is adjusted each year in the light of experience and new forecasts, a pusher fleet renewal programme to 1990 was established in 1973. The strategy takes account of replacement invest-ment and expected lay-ups for the "plan years", as well as the expansion investment deemed necessary in the light of the forecasts of traffic demand. It may be pointed out here that such expansion investment is made only if it has been established with reasonable certainty that the com-pany can count on obtaining the traffic in question.

It is no doubt pertinent to remark here that the planned replacements have hitherto always been made and that the traffic sought with expansion projects has like-wise been won, though sometimes only after a certain delay.

Lastly, the plan takes account of the effects on per-sonnel, the basic approach being that any vacancies are filled through internal promotion from the rank imme-diately below, which means that in practice the company only recruits crew members from outside into the lowest ranks.

In view of the fact that the technical equipment is improving all the time and will continue to do so, the policy of internal promotion means that crew training requirements are very high.

The above description is that of a strategy followed by a firm in its own interest; other inland waterway shipping companies have followed similar or quite dif-ferent policies, but the point of departure has always been the firm's own interest.

1.3. Implications in terms of meeting total transport needs

As we have seen, the inland waterway market is segmented. Every shipping firm defends its own interests on
each sectoral market to the best of its ability without
paying much heed to whether it makes an adequate contribution towards meeting overall waterway transport requirements. In the author's view, this is quite clearly normal
behaviour for entrepreneurs in a free enterprise production system.

It is therefore worthwhile considering whether inland
waterway transport as a whole has been able to meet market
demand satisfactorily, since the answer to this question
would seem to be particularly important insofar as it will
enable us to draw conclusions for the future, which is
what we aim to do at this Ninth International Symposium.
The September 1981 issue of "Zeitschrift für Binnenschiffahrt und Wasserstrassen" (No. 9) provides useful
data on inland waterway freight transport trends in
Germany between 1950 and 1979. These data are particularly interesting because they cover all transport -
both national and international - on the Rhine, Europe's
most important waterway. The most significant data are
the following:

Transport output	1950	1979	Percentage increase 1979/1950
Millions of tonnes	71.9	246.5	241%
Billions of tonne-kilometres	16.7	51	205%

The breakdown of traffic into German internal,
frontier-crossing and transit traffic through Germany is
as follows:

Traffic (millions of tonnes)	1950	1979	Percentage increase 1979/1950
German internal	39.5	83.7	112%
Frontier-crossing	27.2	145.4	435%
Transit	5.1	13.1	157%

Finally, the increase in transport output in tonne-
kilometres per registered tonne of shipping capacity
increased per year from 3,225 T-K in 1950 to 9,417 T-K in
1979, an increase of 192 per cent.

These figures show that in 1979 the inland waterways
trebled their output of 30 years earlier. It is also clear

295

that the expansion is to be attributed not so much to an increase in the fleet as to higher productivity. Aside from improvements to the waterways and faster loading and unloading operations, the higher productivity is largely to be attributed to the motorisation of vessels (switch from towed barges to motor vessels), the use of pushers, an increase in the average size of vessels and round-the-clock operation with the help of radar.

Since the greatest increase is to be seen in frontier-crossing transport, it is tempting to conclude that this is where the steepest rise in productivity has been achieved and that the rise is in fact a direct consequence of the free competition prevailing under the Mannheim Act of 1868.

Be this as it may, it is abundantly clear from the above figures that shipping on the Rhine has proved capable of increasing its transport output very considerably, but this alone does not of course answer the question as to whether it has been entirely able to satisfy the increased transport demand.

In the author's view, however, the response to this question is in the affirmative. During his 26 years of activity in the sector, a temporary shortage of cargo capacity has been experienced on only a few occasions, primarily as a result of low water on the Rhine. During the past 25 years, inland navigation has much more fre-quently been faced with periods of over-capacity, as a result of which freight rates were squeezed to such an extent that it was impossible to obtain an acceptable return on the invested capital. Attempts to remedy this situation have either had little effect or have failed completely. Scrapping rules in Germany and the Netherlands were able to bring about only a temporary improvement.

Since agreement has not been reached at international level, it has not been possible to establish a temporary lay-up system for slack periods on the transport market, although this has been discussed for several years. A plan for overall supervision of capacity by means of a licensing system has so far had no chance of success owing to considerable opposition.

At the time of writing this report, for example, navi-gation on the Rhine and other waterways is again suffering the consequences of substantial over-capacity as a result of the combined effects of a large amount of new building in recent years and an unfavourable world economic situ-ation, as evidenced by trends in freightage on the free international market on the Rhine and, for instance, the Netherlands roster system where waits of 8 days between voyages are by no means exceptional.

1.4. Summary

The above considerations lead to the conclusion that, despite the segmentation of the inland waterway market and the fact that each ship-owner concerns himself only with those sectoral markets which he considers to offer the most favourable opportunities for his own enterprise, inland waterway transport as a whole has admirably succeeded in coping with the enormous growth in demand over the past 30 years.

2. THE OUTLOOK

It is not the author's specific task at the present Symposium to forecast future trends in the demand for waterway transport. Other rapporteurs, unquestionably better qualified, will give their opinion on this subject. I shall therefore confine myself simply to saying that I should be very surprised indeed if the rapporteurs reached the conclusion that there is to be a substantial increase in demand for inland waterway transport.

It has become increasingly apparent in recent years that the high standard of living achieved in Western Europe has seriously weakened the competitive position of our industries on the world market. Relatively simple production processes are increasingly taken over by newly industrialised countries because their much lower living standards enable them to produce more cheaply. It is therefore to be expected that the output of European heavy industry in particular will continue to remain at a level below that of the early 70s, and it is precisely this heavy industry which accounts for such a large proportion of the volume carried by inland waterway transport.

Sands and gravels are other important cargoes which have diminished considerably in volume, the governments concerned having cut back on public works such as the construction of dykes, ports and roads owing to budgetary difficulties. There seems to be no likelihood of any change here in the short term.

One trend on the bulk cargo market to the advantage of inland waterways is that power stations and certain industries (e.g. cement) have begun, and will continue, to switch from oil and/or natural gas to coal. Insofar as power stations are not directly on the coast and cannot receive their fuel directly from sea-going ships, but are located on major waterways within the country, inland waterway transport is the ideal mode. On the other hand, there will be a further reduction in the transport of oil by tankers, which has already diminished considerably.

The carriage of containers by inland waterway craft can also be considered positive. After a difficult

297

beginning, this traffic now shows a steeply rising trend, mainly because of the sharp increase in energy costs for road transport, but also because of the growth of container traffic in general, though it should be stressed at the outset that such traffic provides regular work for only a small number of craft.

As we have seen, inland waterway transport in Western Europe, with the possible exception of some types of craft, such as small barges, has been suffering from a virtually chronic structural over-capacity for many years. It has so far proved impossible to ascertain the precise scale of this over-capacity, mainly owing to the fact that some surplus capacity is necessary in order to ensure that customers get reasonable service even during periods of low water on the Rhine.

However, it is quite clear that there is very substantial over-capacity at present and, if this situation is seen against the rather dismal prospects for the future, it seems quite reasonable to conclude that there is no call to worry about whether inland waterway transport will be able to meet demand over the next ten years. The grounds for such a conclusion would seem to be all the stronger since, as already indicated, inland waterway transport has been able to adjust flexibly to increased supply at an average rate of 7 per cent per annum.

It must be asked, however, whether problems might arise to spoil the reassuring picture painted above, so we shall now briefly examine a few potential problems.

2.1. Energy

It is hardly likely that any viable alternative to diesel engines will be found for the propulsion of waterway craft in the near future, so it must be expected that inland waterways will remain dependant on oil products.

Primarily because oil products have to be imported from regions of the world which cannot be considered among the most politically stable, the possibility of supply problems cannot really be excluded.

The governments concerned in Western Europe would therefore be well advised to consult together to determine priorities in the use of oil products and, in the author's view, the highest priority should be given to freight transport by both waterway and road, since our society cannot function without efficient freight transport.

It is equally important, however, that the engineering industry should do all it can to develop engines which are much more energy efficient. In addition, inland navigation must endeavour to develop types of craft with less

298

hydrodynamic resistance and make use of the residual energy that is at present dissipated in the atmosphere in the form of heat.

The industry is fully aware of these problems and it is reassuring to note that the technical committee of the international association "Verein für Binnenschiffahrt und Wasserstrassen", in co-operation with the "Versuchanstalt für Binnenschiffbau Duisburg", under the direction of Professor Dr. Ing. H.H. Heuser, is taking a very active interest in them.

These factors are of great importance not only from the standpoint of the availability of oil products, but also in terms of their influence on price trends. As we all know, the price of diesel oil for propulsion has risen very steeply since the first energy crisis, and inland shipping companies have therefore had to increase their prices by "fuel supplements", thus further weakening the already difficult competitive position of Western European industry.

Important as this may be, it is still not enough to look for ways of limiting energy consumption in inland shipping. In the interest of both inland shipping itself and Western European industry as a whole, it is necessary to reduce the cost per tonne carried.

2.2. Increasing the size of the unit

The most effective way to reduce cost per tonne is to increase the unit size. Pusher navigation on the Rhine is an eloquent example. Under the regulations of the Central Rhine Navigation Committee in Strasbourg, the unit used on the Rhine may comprise a maximum of a pusher and four barges. At the same time the maximum pusher flotilla lengths and widths are fixed, which means a maximum load per pusher unit of about 11,000 tonnes.

Navigation with six barges has for many years been authorised under certain conditions over the German stretch of the Rhine between Emmerik and Koblenz, so it is here possible to operate with units of 16,000 instead of 11,000 tonnes.

This increased unit size is particularly important for the shipment of foreign raw materials for Germany's heavy industry (e.g. the steel industry), but the Netherlands Government has so far persistently refused to authorise even trial voyages between Rotterdam and the German frontier.

This refusal is based on the view that substantial investment would be required over this stretch in order to ensure safe navigation with six barges. In the author's opinion, this view can be seriously called into question since the investment needs to be made in any event for reasons other than navigation with six barges. The Netherlands Government would therefore be well-advised to waive its objections to trial voyages at any rate.

In addition to increasing the size of pusher units, the cargo capacity of motor vessels should also be increased on waterways that are large enough.

What all this means is that considerable investment is required in inland waterway navigation if it is to adapt to the needs of the age.

2.3. Infrastructure

The existing network of inland waterways offers enough capacity to allow for a considerable increase in traffic without major infrastructural investment. The inland shipping industry is not calling for the creation of new waterways, but it does think that funds should be made available to remove bottlenecks in existing waterways and to enlarge them so that they can take bigger vessels.

2.4. Financing

As in the case of any other firm, an inland shipping company's willingness to invest depends on whether a sound financing method can be found and/or a reasonable return on the invested capital be expected.

Regarding financing, it is unfortunately the case that inland shipping companies generally calculate depreciation on the basis of the purchase price of the operating equipment simply because their operating results preclude the possibility of higher rates of depreciation. Owing to the equipment's long operating life and the rate of inflation over the last 20 to 25 years, the sums written off have generally been insufficient to cover the cost of new operating equipment, which means that a substantial volume of outside funds has to be called on.

The high level of interest rates at the time of writing (late 1981), together with the low rate of return in inland navigation over past years, makes it extremely doubtful whether investment can really be made on the desired scale.

If a better climate for investment is to be established, interest rates will have to fall, while it will also be of the greatest importance to obtain higher rates of return on existing operations.

2.5. Co-operation

Higher returns can be obtained if shipping companies handling sufficiently complementary traffic work together, since fewer unladen trips and shorter waiting times between voyages might be conducive to higher output with the same size of fleet or the same output with a smaller fleet. Such co-operation between shipping companies does not necessarily call for full mergers, since the use of the fleet can very well be rationalised by concluding reciprocal operating agreements. In the case of owner-operators, the conclusion of market co-operation agreements - which already exist in some cases - would seem to be the most appropriate way of improving operating results.

2.6. Crewing arrangements

The increased size of units in inland navigation brought about by the use of motor vessels and increasingly large pusher flotillas, together with increased speeds and round-the-clock operation, have made it necessary to use the most advanced navigational aids.

The standards for navigating crews are therefore high and can only be met by sound training which must be followed by, or combined with, the necessary practical experience.

The training available in countries where inland waterway traffic assumes greatest importance is extremely varied but very good in all cases. In the Netherlands, for example, sole responsibility for training lies with the "Stichting Koninklijk Onderwijsfonds voor de Scheepvaart". This foundation has four schools with boarding facilities which provide a four-year course of basic training. The first two years are mainly devoted to general education, e.g. languages (English and German), maths, natural sciences, technology, commercial training, first aid, swimming, etc. During the last two years the emphasis is on training for inland navigation, e.g. geography and navigable waterways, charts, instruments, theory of navigation, rules and regulations, knowledge of waterway craft, loading and unloading, knowledge of engines and practical maintenance and operation of engines. The theoretical teaching alternates with practical training voyages in the Netherlands or abroad on the foundation's own training craft.

After obtaining the certificate, training can continue in one of two ways:

a) Three years' training at the school of inland navigation and on the Rhine, the last year being devoted to practical work. This path leads to the "skippers certificate" ("Schippersdiploma").

b) The trainee can start working on inland waterway craft immediately on completion of the basic training and follow correspondence courses run by the foundation's "Landelijk Leerlingen Stelsel voor de Rijn - en Binnenvaart". This training leads to the deckhand certificate after which it is possible to follow a course for the "preliminary skipper's certificate", while the skipper's certificate can be obtained as soon as the required number of years of experience have been completed.

In addition to this training there are also special courses for deckhand-mechanics and the radar certificate.

Many young people have been interested in recent years and the boarding schools have been full, but it has unfortunately been found that only a small number of students finally make a permanent career in inland navigation.

Filling vacancies in the lowest ranks is therefore always a major matter of concern to Netherlands' shipping firms. Pusher navigation is less affected than the other branches. As already pointed out, a system of two watches relieving one another in round-the-clock navigation for seven consecutive days is used: after seven days another crew comes on board and the departing crew has seven days leave.

In addition to the two four-man watches, there is always a ship's cook who arranges his work so that crew members always get a good hot meal at the right time in the comfortably-equipped mess. This particular system also allows each crew member to have four consecutive weeks of leave during the summer according to a schedule fixed in advance. The crew have a fixed wage plus a fixed supplement for watch-keeping. Certain motor vessel operators, especially tanker operators, also have continuous (24 hours a day) or semi-continuous (18 hours a day) operation with two watches. These firms also have relatively little trouble in finding crews.

The vast majority of motor vessels operate with a single crew on day work (14 hours a day in summer, 12 in winter). The working conditions are such that a substantial part of the pay is earned by working overtime on top of the 14 or 12 hours mentioned above. This system does not allow time-off to be scheduled in advance.

It seems reasonable to conclude that the need to have well-trained crew members can be met only if a relief system is worked out in order to provide regular time off for this last category too. Steps should also be taken to establish a fixed wage.

MANAGEMENT OF FIRMS
TO SATISFY TRANSPORT NEEDS
INLAND WATERWAY GOODS TRANSPORT

Dr. R. WIJNAKKER
Centre Belge d'Etudes pour la
Navigation Intérieure a.s.b.l.
Ghent, Belgium

SUMMARY

The inland shipping sector in Belgium is currently experiencing a difficult period. I propose to give a brief account of this little-known and often underestimated sphere of economic activity which is nevertheless an essential instrument of production, even in a world governed by technology progressing at such a pace that it is very hard to keep abreast. I shall first examine - briefly of course because the scope of the paper allows for a description of the strict essentials only - the structure of the Belgian dry cargo fleet and its output in Belgium, i.e. on Belgian territory. I shall not discuss the tanker fleet since problems in this sector may be dealt with in a separate study. A description of the Belgian roster system will follow, and I shall then try to throw some light on the strike action by inland waterway carriers in 1973 and 1975 and on its consequences.

Lastly, I shall give a brief account of how the various groups concerned regard Belgian regulations and close with a few comments concerning boatmen and their way of life.

THE FLEET AND ITS OUTPUT

In Belgium, more than in the other countries bordering on the Rhine, a single type of craft predominates in the inland waterways fleet, namely the "spit", a unit 38.5 metres in length whose dimensions match those of the locks of the Freycinet Basin in France and which had formerly been adopted by Belgium for a large part of its own waterway network, including the links with Northern France via the Scheldt and Lys rivers.

As at early 1981 the breakdown of the dry cargo fleet is shown in the following table.

Table 1

	Towed vessels		Self propelled motor vessels		Pushed vessels		Total	
	No.	Tonn-age	No.	Tonn-age	No.	Tonn-age	No.	Tonn-age
25/100t.	-	-	2	156	-	-	2	156
101/150t.	3	439	4	465	-	-	7	904
151/200t.	10	1831	2	375	-	-	12	2206
201/250t.	2	447	6	1351	-	-	8	1798
251/300t.	-	-	18	4941	-	-	18	4941
301/400t.	27	9885	1515	550041	-	-	1542	559926
401/650t.	15	7148	420	223154	9	4938	444	235240
651/850t.	4	2918	98	71718	-	-	102	74636
851/1000t.	5	4730	129	122728	-	-	134	127458
1001/1500t.	17	22978	209	261581	25	33855	251	318414
1501t. and over	11	19678	75	151337	49	112450	135	283466
Total	94	70055	2478	1387847	83	151243	2655	1609145

Source: Ministry of Communications.
Average tonnage in 1981: 606t.

As shown by the following figures, a relatively large tonnage is carried by inland waterways in Belgium:

Table 2

Year	Domestic traffic only (in '000 t)	Total traffic (in '000 t)
1950	17,244	36,279
1960	24,379	61,158
1965	25,778	77,031
1970	31,237	91,565
1974	26,133	106,888
1975	18,477	83,733
1976	21,936	100,284
1977	21,743	100,918
1978	20,113	100,247
1979	21,080	101,400

The following table shows the total output of the Belgian fleet in millions of tonne-km:

Table 3

Year	Domestic(a)	International(b)	Abroad(c)	Total
1965	2,273	2,336	6,791	11,400
1970	2,559	2,313	8,349	13,221
1974	2,002	2,458	8,110	12,570
1975	1,337	1,905	6,821	10,063
1976	1,661	2,266	7,580	11,507
1977	1,597	1,977	7,041	10,615
1978	1,487	2,217	7,625	11,329
1979	1,538	2,197	7,376	11,111

a) Trips starting and finishing on Belgian territory.
b) Tonne-kms in Belgium: incoming, outgoing or transit trips.
c) Trips abroad, including the foreign leg of trips under b) and trips which are entirely abroad.

Source: Ministry of Communications.

Owners of the fleet's vessels fall into three categories: individual owner-operators, navigating and living aboard their craft; other individuals (vessels inherited or bought as an investment which are usually operated by

307

manager-skippers); and shipping companies (or own-account
transport operators) which have a fleet manned by paid
crews. The breakdown in Belgium is as follows:

Table 4

OWNERSHIP OF THE BELGIAN FLEET AS AT EARLY 1981

No. of vessels owned	No. of owners	No. of vessels	Tonnage
- 1	2,059	2,059	1,169,307
- 2	156	312	190,851
- 3	27	81	58,403
- 4 to 5	16	65	70,313
- 6 to 10	8	62	54,835
- 11 to 25	5	76	65,436
Total	2,271	2,655	1,609,145

Table 5

PERCENTAGE BREAKDOWN OF OWNERSHIP OF THE FLEET

No. of vessels owned	No. of owners	No. of vessels	Tonnage
- 1	90.6	77.6	72.7
- 2	6.9	11.7	11.8
- 3	1.3	3.1	3.6
- 4 to 5	0.7	2.4	4.5
- 6 to 10	0.3	2.4	3.4
- 11 to 25	0.2	2.8	4.0
Total	100	100	100

Source: Ministry of Communications.

The following specific trends are to be noted in the
Belgian fleet since 1950: as regards the number of units,
there was a certain stability up to 1960 and a steady
downtrend as from 1961; in terms of tonnage, there was a
very marked increase up to 1967 to reach 2,690,690 tonnes,
which was followed by an appreciable fall. Taking 1950 as
the base year = 100, the index for the dry cargo fleet is
at present 43.9 for the number of vessels and 69.10 for
their tonnage.

The trends since 1950 are as shown in Tables 6 and 7.

Table 6

Year	Towed and pushed craft		Self-propelled motor vessels		Total	
	Number	Tonnage	Number	Tonnage	Number	Tonnage
1950	3,015	1,365,747	3,132	962,970	6,147	2,328,717
1955	1,932	944,795	3,999	1,385,219	5,931	2,330,014
1960	1,254	681,152	4,792	1,806,092	6,046	2,487,244
1965	709	530,241	4,808	2,068,181	5,519	2,598,422
1970	499	393,540	4,660	2,142,052	5,159	2,535,592
1975	328	285,822	3,891	1,905,039	4,219	2,190,861

Table 7

Year	Towed craft		Self-propelled motor vessels		Pushed craft		Total	
	Number	Tonnage	Number	Tonnage	Number	Tonnage	Number	Tonnage
1976	206	177,497	3,548	1,814,435	51	78,619	3,805	2,070,551
1977	164	129,982	3,253	1,717,418	55	88,047	3,472	1,935,447
1978	136	106,026	2,994	1,594,808	60	104,745	3,190	1,805,579
1979	117	88,831	2,763	1,499,827	63	112,724	2,943	1,701,382
1980	105	78,269	2,572	1,412,267	74	134,448	2,751	1,624,984
1981	94	70,055	2,478	1,387,847	83	151,243	2,655	1,609,145

Source: Ministry of Communications.

To complete the statistics, the following tables show the competitive positions of the different transport modes.

Almost 20 per cent of Belgian domestic freight, i.e. freight traffic within the country's frontiers, is carried by inland waterways. This applies in terms of both tonnage carried and output expressed in tonne-kms. In 1979, for example, 101.4 million tonnes out of a total of 517.8 million tonnes were carried by inland waterways, representing 5,908 million tonne-kms out of a total of 30,147 million.

While this percentage may seem relatively high in comparison with the railways 28 per cent of the traffic, it should be noted that in 1970 the fleet accounted for 24 per cent of the traffic while the railways had the same volume of 28 per cent. The first point to be noted is that there is cause for concern about the way in which the inland waterways share of domestic traffic is diminishing.

Table 8

FREIGHT CARRIED BY THE THREE TRANSPORT MODES
(in '000 tonnes)

	1970	1976	1978	1979
Road				
- domestic traffic	298,763	308,851	300,954	286,494
- incoming	16,499	22,658	22,846	24,845
- outgoing	16,499	22,658	22,846	24,845
- transit	4,187	6,293	7,371	6,335
Total	335,948	360,460	354,017	342,519
Inland Waterways				
- domestic traffic	31,237	21,934	20,113	21,080
- incoming	35,638	42,571	44,229	45,198
- outgoing	20,272	31,124	31,370	30,813
- transit	4,418	4,645	4,534	4,309
Total	91,565	100,274	100,247	101,400
Railways				
- domestic traffic	21,646	17,037	17,585	18,181
- incoming	24,143	19,253	18,529	22,107
- outgoing	13,676	12,204	12,993	15,584
- transit	11,404	11,430	13,981	18,007
Total	70,869	59,922	63,092	73,879
TOTALS	498,382	520,656	517,356	517,798

Source: INS.

There is also a downtrend in total output, at any rate since 1975.

It should be noted that in 1979 86.2 per cent of the Belgian fleet's output was abroad, and no more than 13.8 per cent within Belgium itself. More than two-thirds of total output was abroad. The second point is that the Belgian fleet depends largely on foreign traffic and even its output abroad is diminishing.

Table 9

OUTPUT OF THE THREE TRANSPORT MODES
(in millions of tonne-kms)

	1970	1976	1978	1979
Road				
- domestic traffic	9,194	9,300	9,909	9,861
- incoming	1,419	2,103	2,131	2,288
- outgoing	1,419	2,103	2,131	2,288
- transit	837	1,259	1,474	1,267
Total	12,869	14,765	15,645	15,704
Inland Waterways				
- domestic traffic	2,702	1,739	1,609	1,662
- incoming	2,095	2,270	2,255	2,202
- outgoing	1,382	1,476	1,502	1,501
- transit	556	588	569	543
Total	6,734	6,072	5,935	5,908
Railways				
- domestic traffic	1,182	1,051	1,105	1,132
- incoming	3,108	2,355	2,207	2,489
- outgoing	1,404	1,404	1,506	1,787
- transit	2,094	1,825	2,288	3,127
Total	7,777	6,636	7,105	8,535
TOTALS	27,380	27,473	28,685	30,147

Source: INS.

THE ROLE OF THE "OFFICE REGULATEUR DE LA NAVIGATION INTERIEURE"

An analysis of the foregoing figures at once shows that:

1. both the number of vessels and the total tonnage have been diminishing for some years;
2. the average tonnage of units increased, however, from 411 tonnes in 1960 to 606 tonnes in 1981;
3. a very large number of vessels are in the 38-metre class, i.e. units which can navigate Belgian and French canals of the Freycinet type;
4. the fleet's output is also diminishing.

Why is traffic showing such a dramatic downtrend in a country which nonetheless has a very dense inland waterway network? The story dates back a long time, beginning in 1944 when the government decided to set up the ORNI, a clearinghouse for inland waterways freight which, incidentally, replaced the "Centrale Belge de la Navigation Intérieure", established in 1940 during the German occupation. Inland waterways chartering had previously been uncontrolled, in the case of both domestic and international traffic, the rate being subject to the law of supply and demand. Following the economic crisis in the 1930s, available capacity considerably exceeded demand and gave rise to what often amounted to ruinous competition between owner-operators themselves and between owner-operators and shipping companies.

In 1940, with a view to controlling the economy as a whole, the occupying authorities opted for a system of equitably sharing the volume of freight to be carried within the country. This system involved drawing up a list of both available capacity and demand on a regional basis and allocating the transport operations by means of a roster on which members of the "Centrale" were registered. In combination with a system of compulsory rates, this roster system ensured that carriers were equitably remunerated for their services. Chartering vessels for trips abroad of course remained unregulated.

After the liberation of Belgium, the carriers' organisations requested that this system be continued. The Ministry of Public Works, at that time responsible for transport policy, set up the ORNI under a Ministerial Order dated 14th December, 1944, whereby the main lines of the system in force during the war were maintained but, since the system applied to an exceptional situation, provision was made for it to be discontinued when the situation became normal.

Belgium has not apparently experienced a normal situation since that time because the ORNI still exists.

It should also be noted that the ORNI regulations are very liberal insofar as there is no discrimination in Belgium from the standpoint of the nationality of the vessel. Any foreign vessel is authorised to travel within the country (towards the frontier with the country in which it is registered or in any other direction) provided its name is put on the roster.

The following figures show that effective use is made of this freedom: of the 5,908 million tonne-kms of freight carried in Belgium in 1979, 2,172,648 were accounted for by foreign vessels and 3,735,431 by Belgian-owned vessels.

In February 1953 the Inland Shipping Directorate was transferred from the Ministry of Public Works to the Ministry of Communications, which is also responsible for the Belgian National Railways, a major competitor of inland waterways.

Inland shipping has since that time been under both of these Ministries, because the Ministry of Public Works has remained responsible for infrastructures, while the Ministry of Communications lays down the general transport policy and regulations and deals with international issues - a situation that is not calculated to simplify matters.

The roster system is at present organised as follows: in Belgium's inland waterway centres, that is to say in the towns where vessels are chartered, there is an ORNI office which lists, in order of application, the vessels seeking a cargo for shipment from the district covered by the office in question. The requests for cargo space from shippers located in the district are also centralised in this office which holds a daily session during which the tonnages to be shipped are posted up together with the compulsory freight rate and, where applicable, the special conditions imposed by the shipper.

The transport operations are allocated by calling on vessels in the order in which they are listed. The first called has the choice of operations offered provided the vessel is technically capable of handling the operation selected. However, operators are by no means obliged to accept the operation offered to them, whereas shippers cannot refuse a vessel for other than technical reasons. If there are no vessels available for a given operation, it is carried forward to the next session unless the shipper withdraws the offer. A shipper may also propose a rate higher than the compulsory one.

When an operator accepts an operation, a chartering agreement is drawn up by the charterer concerned and submitted for approval to the ORNI which checks to ensure that the relevant conditions comply with the law. If the charterer finds no operator to take the operation after two clearinghouse sessions, he may try to charter a vessel without going through the ORNI office, provided that a number of conditions are met: the freight rate must not be lower than that fixed by law, the rate must be published, and approval by the ORNI remains obligatory.

There have been no major changes in this system since it was introduced in 1944.

STRIKE ACTION BY INLAND WATERWAY CARRIERS

A whole series of events in the post-war period had a profound influence on the transport sector:

- For example, rapid progress was made with motorisation of the fleet, which had already begun prior to World War II. Hundreds of pull-tow craft were fitted with diesel engines and the turn-around speed of the fleet therefore increased considerably. By 1950, 51 per cent of waterway units had been equipped with engines and the figure had risen to 79 per cent by 1960 and to 90 per cent by 1970, so that in 1981 there were only 94 towed vessels out of a total of 2,655 units (dry cargo fleet), i.e. 3.5 per cent.
- New vessels: a good many owners wishing to benefit from the advantages then offered by navigation on the Rhine, sold their 350-tonne vessels in order to replace them with new 1,000 or 1,350-tonne units, the latter tonnage being the European standard introduced by the Community in 1953. Combined with the new units commissioned by newcomers on the transport market, these purchases led to a considerable expansion of the Belgian dry cargo fleet in terms of both the number of vessels and tonnage. Whereas in 1950 the self-propelled dry cargo fleet consisted of 3,132 units totalling 962,970 tonnes, in 1960 there were 4,792 units totalling 1,860,092 tonnes.
- The prodigious expansion of road transport on the strength of the various national motorway construction programmes.
- The switch from coal to oil for the generation of power, thus leading to the closure of Belgian coal mines and the loss of a very important longstanding client of the dry-cargo fleet.
- The pusher system gradually began to develop.
- Labour costs escalated.

The above factors gave rise to a general feeling of disquiet, the effects of which began to be experienced from the mid-1960s onwards. As from 1969 the Belgian fleet began to lose ground and output in tonne/kms within the country diminished. The number of charter contracts under the ORNI system dropped disturbingly, and orders for new vessels became extremely rare. During the years 1970 to 1975, for example, only 60 new units were built in Belgium as compared with 109 in 1965 alone.

The exodus from the profession began: the young no longer wished to continue in the occupation of their parents since they considered that working on a vessel was no longer a paying proposition, or far less so than factory work, while life ashore was easier than aboard small units lacking comfort.

Demands were made for an adjustment of the ORNI rates, while there were protests against what was considered unfair competition from the railways and requests that the roster system be extended to international traffic. The individual operators were poorly organised at that time, being no more than a group of anonymous individuals, and they did not get the desired support from the Minister of Communications.

The first carriers' strike occurred in May 1973. The claims drawn up by the trade union organisation unconnected with the traditional organisations included:

- The general applicatioon of the classification certificate requirement, which was therefore to be extended to cover foreign vessels so as to keep off the market a number of "hulks", some of which were imported into Belgium and put on the roster with a view to benefitting from the advantages of the system.
- A broadening of the role of the ORNI which some felt should not be solely an administrative body but should also have marketing responsibilities.
- Discontinuance of the system of hiring vessels.
- Inclusion on the roster of international transport operations.

Although this strike was not supported by the traditional organisations of Belgian inland waterways carriers, it had a very broad following. Barriers set up at the main intersections and at strategic points on the waterways network stopped all traffic. The strike ended on 22nd May, 1973, a draft agreement being signed between the trade union and the Minister of Communications. Then came the oil crisis with its harmful effects on the economies of the industrialised countries and a sharp drop in demand for transport.

On the Rhine where navigation remained free, freight rates dropped below the 1950 levels, whereas the high rate of inflation was automatically pushing up the cost of labour, repairs, fuel, insurance, etc. Taking 1965 as the base year = 100, in 1975 repair and maintenance costs were at index 210, labour costs at 298 and fuel costs at 171.

The situation quickly became untenable for owner-operators. Since the 1973 agreement had not, moreover, been adhered to by the government, the carriers' trade unions decided in August 1975 to stop traffic once again on Belgium's inland waterways. The same decision was reached in the Netherlands where the fleet was experiencing similar difficulties.

The strike in Belgium lasted until 23rd October when a further draft agreement was signed between the carriers, the Ministry of Communications and the Fédération des Entreprises de Belgique. The main points of this agreement were as follows:

- introduction of a scrapping grant, with a view to reducing fleet overcapacity (breaking up obsolete units);
- recognition of the boatman's wife as a fully-fledged member of the crew;
- retraining grants for boatmen wishing to leave the profession;
- modernisation of the fleet: interest subsidies are provided for loans contracted to buy new vessels or modernise existing units;
- a ban on Sunday operating;
- restrictions on the use of hired vessels for own-account transport;
- control of international chartering contracts;
- introduction of minimum rates and the roster system for trips to France (other than on the Rhine) and posting up of trips to the Netherlands;
- fringe benefits, such as interest-free loans, early retirement, priority treatment when buying or renting community housing;
- organisation of elections to select representatives for duties in certain organisations;
- a study of the problems relating to the education of boatmen's children;
- a study of the problems of intermodal competition;
- with a view to improving the safety of inland waterways, steps were to be taken to refuse access to foreign vessels, make the classification certificate compulsory through EEC channels and have the classification standards for LASH vehicles applied internationally;
- the licence fee paid by boatmen to France was to be reimbursed by the Belgian Government;
- a round table was to be organised by the Ministry of Communications to promote, in collaboration with those concerned, initiatives designed to support and market services provided by owner-operators.

Six years after this agreement was signed, a number of major points have still not been dealt with satisfactorily. The scrapping grant has been introduced and has met with unexpected "success". By the end of 1980 the ORNI had received 539 valid scrapping applications totalling 246,888 tonnes. It should be noted that fleet overcapacity was estimated in 1974 to be 387 vessels totalling 153,540 tonnes at most. This exodus from the profession clearly shows that a by no means negligible proportion of boatmen have lost confidence in it. Sunday operating has been banned to the detriment of shippers. The roster system has been introduced for trips to France (other than on the Rhine) and cargoes for the Netherlands are now posted up. Elections have been held, and the licence fee paid to France is reimbursed. The size of the fleet continues to diminish, however, and this clearly cannot be attributed solely to the scrapping system since, up to 1978, 139 vessels had been sold abroad - mainly to Netherlands' and French operators - and 70 of these units were built after 1951. Very little is said and even less done about modernisation and the fleet continues to age. Lip service is paid to marketing but no practical measures have been adopted.

A NUMBER OF VIEWS ON THE SITUATION

Spurred by the persistent economic crisis, the feeling of disquiet continues to prevail to the present day, since fundamentally no-one can fully accept the existing situation.

First there are the shippers who are not happy with the present system, since they are not for the most part seeking one-off transport operations for 300, 600 or 1,000 tonnes of freight but usually want to deal with people who can undertake to supply transport on a regular overall basis for a period of several months, for example, and amounting to a considerable tonnage at agreed terms. They consider that the regulations governing inland waterways chartering have prevented the carriers from meeting this demand and that the roster system, whereby shippers and carriers are brought together by chance, distorts the fundamental aim of carriers on the roster waiting list, since their aim should be to get a return on their equipment. Not all the carriers on this list would be motivated to respond to the trips offered, so shippers do not in principle have the much needed assurance of seeing their goods arrive at their destination in time. The shippers consider that charterers, as intermediaries in the transport sector, should be able to play the traditional role of providing this assurance. In their view, the ORNI cannot do so because, given its official function of ensuring that chartering takes place in a specific regulatory framework, it cannot perform any functions that would necessarily require it to act outside that framework. Another bone of contention for shippers is the ban on Sunday operating (other than in ports and on rivers subject to tides), and here they meet with a categorical refusal by the carriers' organisations. The shippers, however, see Sunday operating as an efficient means of substantially increasing the productivity of the fleet,

317

especially the modern fleet. They also claim that the
immobilisation of the fleet - and hence inland waterway
transport - under the existing regulations is the reason
why they are losing interest and, in an increasing number
of cases, do not modernise their loading/unloading
facilities and will sooner or later turn to other modes of
transport.

The shippers are not so much calling for the pure and
simple abolition of the roster system but would first like
this system to be made more flexible along lines which
would enable the fleet to be operated in a more rational
and business-like manner.

The same views are held by the shipowners, some of
whom are associated with powerful industrial groups. It
is a fact that the enormous investment made by shipowners
in order to keep pace with technical developments in the
inland shipping sector does not show a fair return under
the existing system. The turn-around rate of vessels
under the roster system is far too slow. The number of
waiting days at the clearing house - about a week in
1981 - is unacceptable for this type of operation and
cannot be supported, moreover, as the shipowners' fixed
costs are too high. It is therefore reasonable that they
should also opt for a change in the ORNI system along the
lines desired by shippers. In the shipowners' view the
concept of "service" is foremost. They are prepared to
match the requirements of those giving the orders but wish
to be able to profit from their own endeavours. Among the
shippers, some firms own their own fleet, manned by
boatmen employed and paid by the firm. These firms were
often in need of additional units, for example when
business was buoyant or in order to cope with peak
periods. Additional units were then hired and, like the
vessels already owned, did not come under the ORNI system,
since own-account transport was not subject to the ORNI
regulations. In 1974 there were 196 units registered
under this own-account system and 79 vessels were hired
for the same type of transport. In that year this
relatively small fleet accounted for 12,192 trips within
Belgium and carried 6,041,000 tonnes of freight as
compared with the 27,452 ORNI trips and 12,894,000 tonnes
carried by all units operating in the industrial transport
sector. The turn-around rate of own-account units is
therefore far higher than that of other vessels (generally
considered to be three to four times higher).

In 1975, however, under pressure from the waterways
carriers' trade unions, the Government abolished the system of hiring vessels for own-account transport and all
shippers were henceforth obliged to deal through the
clearing house, which is clearly to negate the economic
obligation to conduct transport operations or produce services under the best possible conditions.

The owner-operators are not satisfied with the existing system either. Their spokesmen, namely the trade union delegates who acquired this qualification after the 1973 and 1975 strikes, see things differently. Basing their ideas on those of the trade union movement in industry, they usually take the view that the public at large must take priority over the individual and that human interest must come before profitmaking. They accordingly consider that inland waterway carriers as a whole must be able to exercise effective and efficient control over all spheres which even remotely relate to inland shipping, such as the ORNI, chartering, insurance, (group) purchases of materials, intermodal competition. In short, the trade unions want to have their say, participate in discussions at all levels and influence decision-making. They wish to assert themselves on other markets or, at any rate, gain a more important place on markets that remain unregulated. One line of reasoning that is often heard may be summarised as follows: if inland shipping is to be able to meet the demand for transport under all circumstances, provision must be made for reserve capacity, since carriers do not have advance information of peak periods in the supply of tonnage to be carried.

However, inland shipping is expected to be able to respond without difficulty and this view seems to be found quite normal. The sector has simply to accept, moreover, the disastrous consequences of depressed economic conditions.

In periods of low water on the Rhine the reserve capacity can be called on, but what is to be done with this reserve when demand for transport diminishes or collapses?

In the event of a crisis in Rhine shipping, the operators who usually work the Rhine turn towards the domestic markets, which are themselves likewise suffering the harmful consequences of depressed economic activity, so the domestic owner-operators see their chances of obtaining a cargo diminish.

Since the owner-operators cannot push these newcomers back towards their own markets, they endeavour to have the free markets regulated so that the available cargoes may be allocated among a larger number of carriers, namely the owner-operators.

This is an understandable policy which, faced with a hesitant government which does not have a well-defined and well-balanced transport policy, sometimes leads to tangible results, such as having cargoes for France posted up in the clearinghouse or prohibiting the hiring of vessels for own-account transport. Opponents of this policy claim that it is ruinous to inland shipping as a whole insofar as it sacrifices the future to immediate interests.

319

It is a fact that improvements to the fleet have no effect on the level of freight rates and hence on the return of inland waterway carriers.

The situation is partly explained, at any rate where the Belgium/France market is concerned, by the presence in Belgium of many French "spits" which, having unloaded their cargo, wish to make a relatively well-remunerated return trip. All these vessels are therefore taking the place of the scrapped Belgian fleet, so it might be said that the Belgian Government is breaking up its fleet at great expense while at the same time, owing to the liberal ORNI system helping to maintain the fleet of 38-metre French vessels which are just as decrepit as its own vessels if not more so.

INTERMODAL COMPETITION

One of the most difficult matters remaining unresolved since the 1975 strike is the study on problems relating to competition among the three modes of transport. Feelings run high in this connection, moreover, owing to differences in the way in which the modes are subsidised.

Inland shipping does not have to bear the cost of infrastructure itself. Shipping dues, currently amounting to B.Frs.0.05/tonne-km, do not even suffice to pay for the manning of lock services.

On the other hand, the railways finance their own infrastructures but, as in other European countries, they have been operating at a loss for decades and the budget is balanced by the State to the tune of some billions of francs, a sum which cannot be calculated precisely.

The road hauliers, however, cannot claim to bear the cost of road infrastructure, although that does not prevent the struggle between the transport modes from continuing vigorously.

There is no denying that inland shipping has lost a considerable amount of traffic since the 1975 strike, when both road and rail took advantage of this difficult period to supply services to longstanding customers of the inland waterways. The resulting falling away of traffic has still not been fully assimilated.

Moreover, some of the procedures used by the railways are not calculated to pacify. For example, only a few weeks prior to the commissioning of the modernised Brussels-Charleroi canal (1,350 tonnes - inclined plane from Ronquières), the SNCFB lowered its rates with a view to keeping certain traffic which would otherwise certainly have been taken by the inland waterways, so the billions of francs invested by the Ministry of Public Works did not produce the expected returns.

There is also the impression that the various national railways have been conducting a well-organised offensive for some years, one example being international traffic in cereals where rail has managed to take over traffic that has traditionally been reserved for shipping.

While the successes of the railways are spectacular in terms of the size of the contracts seized, it would seem that competition from road transport is a much greater threat. The road hauliers in fact experience the same problems as inland waterway operators: widely dispersed firms, individualistic spirit, and a difficult financial situation owing to the crisis and the very high cost of money. In addition, their equipment wears out much faster than that of their inland shipping competitor. It is not therefore surprising that the number of road haulage firms diminished by 20 per cent in the period 1975-1980. So it is also not surprising that road hauliers sap the very substance of inland shipping's owner-operators: the market for modest cargoes of 200 to 500 tonnes. For example, road transport has taken over all the sand and gravel traffic between the Port of Ghent and Northern France. Traffic totalling several hundreds of thousands of tonnes a year, for delivery to dozens of construction firms, has been lost by inland waterways because the lorry is faster, more flexible and does not oblige the buyer to build up and finance large stocks.

The EEC needs to adopt a position in this connection. A country like Belgium, caught between giants from the standpoint of transport, clearly cannot venture to act alone in establishing a transport policy which, for example, imposes unduly high minimum freight rates. Such an operation is too risky in view of the proximity of the Netherlands' and French ports, since Belgian ports might quickly begin to lose traffic if unregulated rates did not follow the same trend.

Accordingly, only the EEC is in a position to impose on all members a well-balanced policy which enables each mode of transport to be remunerated.

THE BOATMAN AND HIS PROFESSION

Forty years of government supervision have been enough to ensure that some of the inveterate individualists, i.e. the owner-operators, have lost the savour of risk-taking and even the liking for business enterprise.

They have settled in a system which enables them to keep going without too much difficulty but without offering much of a future either, a situation that, combined with dear money and the economic crisis, is the direct cause of the aging of the Belgian fleet to such a critical point.

The question arises as to whether the owner-operator, even the young one, is equipped to struggle successfully for existence in an increasingly hard and complex world which becomes more and more blind to anything outside immediate profits.

Like all the other professions, the boatman's is becoming increasingly demanding and he should today combine the following characteristics:

- self-employed operator: he must know how to navigate his vessel in what are sometimes very difficult and dangerous waters; know the inland waterways' code and the many regulations governing European waterways, as well as social and tax legislation, etc.
- technician: he must have a good understanding of diesel and electric motors, pumps, radio-telephony and all the various kinds of apparatus found on modern units, and he must be able to carry out the necessary small repairs;
- businessman: he must know the various markets on which he works in order to be able to make the most of the scope offered, provide service to his customers and handle the various intermediaries;
- finance manager: he must have what is sometimes an appreciable amount of capital and maximise the returns on it in order to enable his family to have a decent life comparable to that of other citizens;
- skipper: at any rate when he has to have a crew, which is the case for large units;
- husband and father: most of the time occupying a few square metres on a hostile element, i.e. water, with his wife (as an assistant) and children.

The boatman's school education and environment clearly do not enable him to acquire all the necessary knowledge. Accordingly, one of the most urgent matters calling for serious study and a solution at both human and technical levels is that of the education to be given to boatmen's children.

It would seem that the future of the owner-operator, the last of the home workers, essentially depends on two factors:

1. the profitability of the operation;
2. education.

Without profit there will be no modernisation, no new entrants to continue to operate vessels, no motivation to choose a fine profession which gives a man freedom and enables him to achieve self-fulfilment.

Without the appropriate education, the boatman will be unable to measure up, with sufficient chance of success, to the ever-changing technologies and an increasingly complex society.

Ghent, December 1981.

MANAGEMENT OF FIRMS
TO SATISFY TRANSPORT NEEDS
INLAND WATERWAY GOODS TRANSPORT

Dr. H. ZÜNKLER
Rheinbraun Verkaufsgesellschaft mbH
Cologne, Germany

SUMMARY

1. THE GENERAL CONTEXT

The contribution of inland and coastal shipping operators to the optimum satisfaction of transport demand is,
as in other sectors, very much conditioned by economic
policy and the structural environment of the general economy, and is affected by the trends resulting from this
environment. An operator's freedom of action is limited
by these factors and is to be measured against them.

It is therefore important first to make a critical
assessment of the possibilities that coastal and inland
shipping operators actually have to respond efficiently to
transport demand, in order to determine how far the entrepreneur in this sector can go and to what extent he can
act or react in the present increasingly difficult economic situation.

1.1. The basic economic order

The first point is that Western European countries'
economic systems can be described by and large as various
forms of the welfare-oriented market economy, in which the
individual entrepreneur is one market operator among
many. His services are measured against those of competing entrepreneurs; they have to be at least comparable
with those offered by his competitors and need to be constantly improved if he is to hold his own in the market.

This requirement is not altered very much by the fact
that various governments intervene in different ways in
support of their inland and coastal shipping. In international transport, which has always been predominant in
coastal shipping and is now increasingly so in inland
waterway transport, the entrepreneur has to deal with
international demand and international competition though
with differing baseline conditions.

This basic economic policy situation leaves waterway
and coastal shipowners with only one option - to try to
satisfy transport demand efficiently by measures to improve the way they operate. This is, however - as we
shall see - a broad field and a formidable task.

1.2. Demand structure

In the final analysis, each of these measures has to

be demand-oriented, and geared to demand trends, which are sometimes not clearly recognisable, and to react quickly to these trends.

Perhaps more than any other industry, transport is fundamentally involved in the development of all sectors of the economy and therefore trends have to be followed particularly closely. Just as, for example, inland water-ways and coastal shipping clearly benefited from Europe's close economic ties through a substantial increase in border-crossing traffic, they are now confronted with a negative trend which is only to be understood in a world-wide context: the cost of technologically simple large-volume commodities, which provided inland waterways and coastal shipping with bulk traffics, such as pig iron pro-duction or the manufacture of chemical feedstocks, have now become too high in Europe and production is shifting to the developing countries. The resulting trend in Europe towards higher-value, more sophisticated goods tends to favour the other transport modes.

In addition to general trends, it is also necessary to consider those which affect only individual sectors or even individual firms. Thus the falling trend in fertili-zer traffic was foreseeable: the necessary intermediates can be produced at far lower cost in the oil-producing countries than in Europe, where they are burdened from the start with substantial freight costs and in addition, where destined for the developing countries, generally have to be transported back halfway round the world.

Finally, if certain large firms wish to exploit the locational advantages of producing near the coast, for example, this is another trend which needs to be detected early by shipping firms.

1.3. Supply structure

Transport firms, including inland waterway and coas-tal shipowners, have to contend with two forms of com-petition, first with one another (internal competition) and second with other transport modes, i.e. rail and road (external competition). Their room for manoeuvre is therefore limited not only by the economic environment, but also by competition on two fronts.

1.3.1. Competition with other modes

Inland waterways and - to a lesser extent - coastal shipping are in competition with the railways and road transport over virtually all routes. There are relatively few links over which the comparative advantages of water transport are so great that even selective competitive measures by rail or road transport - if in fact possible - have only little effect. Water transport does have such an edge, for example, for traffic between the Rhine estuary and inland Rhine ports and even more so in coastal shipping, for example between the North Sea ports of the European Community, in particular where there is no direct land link. Over all other links, however, inland waterways and coastal shipping have a formidable competitor, namely rail transport which happens to run at a loss in all Western European countries and therefore has to offer special freight rates to defend itself against road transport, the other, very flexible, competitor, thus also indirectly affecting inland waterways and coastal shipping and setting them rigid price ceilings. This upper limit on earnings prevents inland waterways and coastal shipping from being as flexible as deep-sea shipping if costs are to be covered in the medium term.

1.3.2. Inland waterways and coastal shipping

The supply structure in inland waterways and coastal shipping dates back to the beginning of the industrial era, but it has been able to adapt so flexibly to every development (not least in the most recent period through various tax incentives) that any user now finds a wide choice of capable firms to handle any transport requirement and a shipper of large volumes of cargo on a regular basis can find plenty of large operators in a position to provide push-tows - for which the craft have been built at considerable cost - for the rational handling of this traffic.

In coastal shipping, there are efficient companies which in addition to their own substantial capacity can at any time call up additional chartered tonnage for such cargoes. In the case of special traffics such as gases or acids, there are specialised medium-sized firms with the necessary experience to guarantee the safe handling of such traffic. Smaller, occasional cargoes or transport over links served only rarely or where large vessels cannot be used, are the province of the small concern, owner-operators or co-operatives, which in the long term will be able to go on earning a livelihood, even if larger firms have to abandon the field due to their fixed cost structure.

Even though reference is constantly - and rightly - made to the long life of inland waterway and coastal shipping capital stock, the surprising fact is that the fleet has been continually changing over the past thirty years and that all gaps in the supply structure have been rapidly filled.

Towed barges gave way to the self-propelled craft which in turn immediately had to surrender part of their traffic to push-towing. A tanker fleet came into being

329

which was able to handle the booms of the two recent
energy crises virtually without problem, but is now declining with the fall in Western Europe's oil consumption.

With the triumphal advance of the container, container ships and lines came on the scene. In other words,
inland waterway and coastal shipping managements have
always tried to ensure that a full range of services is
available to meet demand, including that for special
services.

Any inland waterway or coastal shipping firm which
gains a temporary competitive advantage through technical
or organisational innovation never remains alone for long
since even in these cases the regulating function of competition soon makes itself felt.

1.4. Economic and transport policies

In addition to the above-mentioned factors inherent
in the economic system and structure, inland waterway
operators and coastal shipowners are also affected by the
objectives, measures and repercussions of current economic
and sectoral transport policy. High interest rates, introduced to combat inflation, severely curtail investment
potential and frequently offset other measures introduced
by governments to encourage shipbuilding. Freight rate
policy decisions, new tonnage quotas and even the deliberate curtailment of waterway facilities, or at least
failure to carry out improvements due to the tight budgetary situation, mean that operators are fighting against a
dense fabric of restrictions.

These few examples will suffice to complete the impression that this first section of the paper is intended
to convey, namely that the possibilities open to operators
in their efforts to meet users' requirements in the best
way possible are severely limited.

2. MANAGEMENT OBJECTIVES

Further limitations stem from the objectives set by
operators themselves or implied by the system. The operator must always be guided by these objectives and it is
against those objectives that he must assess and justify
his performance. Just as the operator has to demand of
his captains that they keep their craft on course in spite
of wind, wave and current, he himself has to keep the
firm's objectives constantly in mind and try to reach them
by the most direct path.

2.1. The basic objective: maximum value added

Whichever way one looks at it, the basic management objective in inland waterways and coastal shipping is the same as in other sectors of a basically free enterprise economy, namely to make a profit and indeed to maximise value added.

After all, it is only if everything - allowing, of course, for all the necessary constraints - is directed at achieving the highest possible value added with the lowest possible use of resources that it is possible to invest in rationalisation and adjustment projects, pay off this investment, create and maintain jobs, properly comply with safety and environmental regulations (of growing importance in shipping as elsewhere), remain competitive and also help shippers who use water transport to remain competitive on international markets.

Though the other aims and objectives of entrepreneurial action and its consistency with the objectives of the economy as a whole may be important and necessary, the basic objective of maximising value added must firmly remain management's central concern and must not be obscured by other tasks if entrepreneurship is not to be doomed to self-doubt and self-abandonment. Even in centrally planned economies, enterprises are assigned goals whereby production implicitly generates value added by comparison with the production factors employed.

In inland waterways and coastal shipping too, where, as we have seen, substantial efforts have had to be made to adapt to changes in demand, and to survive and maintain jobs despite all the difficulties caused by State intervention in transport markets, this goal is and will remain the decisive yardstick for measuring entrepreneurial activity.

2.2. Subsidiary objectives

Further objectives also have to be taken into account without detracting from the basic goal. Their attainment is necessary to achieve this main goal, which is thereby made more difficult and certainly more costly to attain, but in the final analysis nevertheless remains the central aim of managerial endeavour.

2.2.1. Maintenance of industrial peace

The necessity to maintain social harmony in the firm or the less demanding objective of a good working climate or industrial peace is now taken for granted, although currently in shipping this is increasingly becoming a double balancing act.

331

On the one hand, continued technological progress and fierce competition in a time of overcapacity mean that working procedures need to be rationalised to the greatest possible extent in order to utilise the craft to the utmost and maintain employment levels. This means that individual crew members, in particular captains and mates, have to accept increased nervous tension and greater responsibility, while on the other side the physical demands of the job are naturally reduced.

Technical progress has been such that crew sizes could be immediately reduced without causing any difficulties from the technical, organisational or transport standpoints, but in a time of increasing unemployment this idea is hardly greeted with open arms by the unions. It would of course be wrong, however, to continue to insist on traditional manning scales. The example of firemen still employed on electric locomotives on many railways even decades after the last steam locomotive was scrapped is all too pertinent. A considerable sense of responsibility towards the future is demonstrated, for example, by the negotiations which have begun in Strasbourg between the governments concerned and representatives of workers and employers on tailoring manning scales to suit the present technical situation in Rhine navigation.

This development has certainly been helped by the fact that for many years there have been vacancies in inland waterway and coastal shipping and even attractive working and leisure conditions have not been able to correct this labour shortage.

It is true that working on inland waterways or coastal ships means an irregular life and prevents crews from following any leisure occupation on a regular basis as is possible in land jobs, this now being an important factor in the quality of life.

In the field of tension between on the one hand the labour shortage and the offer of attractive working conditions, and on the other the pressure for rationalisation and therefore the need to use a minimum of labour on board, the shipowner constantly has to find new pragmatic solutions to maintain a good working climate.

2.2.2. Safety of transport operations

It is now more important than ever that inland waterway and coastal shipping transport operations should be safe in all respects. The avoidance of accidents here is in the first place a considerable moral responsibility for the firm. In the second place it should be borne in mind that in view of the increasing technicality and automation of working procedures on board, each member of the crew has been through some course of training and to that

extent can be replaced only with difficulty even tempo-
rarily. This is quite apart from the fact that for years,
despite high unemployment in other sectors, inland waterways and coastal shipping have had to contend with a
labour shortage.

In addition to crew safety, particular and increasing
importance is attached to the safety of other craft. Increasingly heavy traffic on waterways, bigger and faster
vessels, have led to considerable additional safety equipment being developed in recent years, in particular ship-
to-ship communications and shipboard radar.

Finally, in the carriage of dangerous goods, for
which both inland waterways and coastal shipping are particularly well-suited, shipping firms have taken special
precautionary measures, which sometimes go far beyond the
official regulations or have led to their further
development.

2.2.3. Environmental protection

It is particularly easy for inland waterways and
coastal shipping to carry goods in a non-polluting and
environmentally conscious fashion. There are simple physical reasons why inland waterways cause less noise and
air pollution than other transport modes.

Operators are not satisfied with these natural advantages, however. Through additional soundproofing, e.g. of
pump motors in tankers, and the introduction of closed
systems for the transport of certain liquids, they ensure
that disamenity is also reduced during loading and discharging operations. The shipowner probably also feels
obliged to treat this as a long-term objective in order
not to impair the attractiveness of waterway transport and
thus imperil his chances of doing business.

3. THE FIELD FOR ENTREPRENEURIAL ACTION

The two preceding sections have shown that inland
waterway and coastal shipping operators' room for
manoeuvre is limited by the existing economic structure,
the economic and transport policy context and by general
and branch-specific managerial objectives. This clarification was necessary to be able to correctly evaluate the
contribution to the optimisation of transport services
made by managements who can move only within a severely
restricted space. There nevertheless remain a number of
opportunities for action at the micro-economic level.
These are described below, certainly not exhaustively, but
under various headings, taking particular account of the
present social, financial and energy-policy constraints.

3.1. Market research

Operators' efforts to satisfy transport demand in the best possible way begin with a careful analysis of the current economic situation and trends and the firm's own position.

3.1.1. Transport demand

In some sectors the demand for transport services is constantly changing. Economic policy or management objectives or structures are altered, locations are shifted or techniques are modified. The operator has to keep a constant watch on these changes and constantly improve the transport facilities he offers.

Of particular importance here are combined traffics, through which, for example, empty return voyages can be avoided and "triangular" traffics organised. Here the operator has an advisory function and has to display considerable imagination and creativity.

3.1.2. Transport supply

The operator must also take into account the plans and strategies of his competitors in his own and other transport modes. This has unfortunately received too little attention in the past; to take one example, temporary boom periods have always led all operators to expect better times and expand their tonnage causing or aggravating general over-capacity. Next to agriculture (the pig cycle), inland waterway transport seems to be the most glaring example of the "cobweb theorem", but because of the long life of craft the effects last much longer.

The only answer, therefore, seems to be that certain guide data on demand and supply trends should be provided through co-operation between operators' associations and the responsible authorities in order to prevent this type of mistake. Some very promising initiatives have already been taken in specific Western European countries and in international bodies. The authorities now simply need to be encouraged to continue along these lines in order to prevent the kind of squandering of national capital which occurs, for example, when first shipbuilding subsidies and subsequent scrapping grants are paid out for the one and the same vessel.

These data are no more than a tool for the operator, however, as in the final analysis the responsibility for any changes in his fleet lies squarely with him, and he would be well-advised to base his decisions on cast-iron prospects. Neither is speculative expansion of any help to shippers: they may certainly benefit in the short term

334

from lower freight rates in a depressed market, but in the medium term they will have to share the cost of the misguided investment.

3.2. The transport chain

Inland waterway and coastal shipping operators' conclusions from observed supply and demand trends have then to be converted into imaginative suggestions to shippers as to the best ways of solving their transport problems. Apart from day-to-day operations which are concerned with providing cargo capacity at the proper time and in the required quantity and quality to handle an existing traffic flow, the supply of water-borne transport always constitutes innovation in a certain sense. Sometimes this may consist in proposing more suitable types of vessel or a transport service schedule better synchronised with production processes. But it may even go beyond the narrow field of inland waterway and coastal shipping and be aimed at offering an optimum solution for the whole complex of transport, handling and storage operations between the producer who may be in a distant country and the user firm.

3.2.1. Terminal hauls

In all inland waterway and coastal shipping single-leg movements, i.e. from a supplier who loads the cargo directly on board and a consignee who discharges it directly from the vessel to his factory, are rare.

In the case of most cargoes, even such low-value materials as sand and gravel, for example, there are terminal hauls in another transport mode, even though they may be very short or within the shipping or receiving firm. In other cases, the coastal or inland waterway leg may be only a minor link in a complete chain of transport and handling operations.

To achieve the most cost-advantageous transport plan, due regard must be given to these essential terminal haul services. The size of vessels and their arrival times should be determined according to the capacity and turnaround period of the terminal carriers. This can reduce rolling stock requirements and possible waiting times which have a decisive effect on the freight and other costs of these services.

3.2.2. Handling and storage

The already very substantial and now increasing imports of coal from overseas are an example of an integrated transport chain including various handling operations in addition to terminal hauls. By the time the coal

335

is loaded aboard an inland waterway craft in a European
port, it has aleady behind it as a rule a rail haul, intermediate storage and transshipment in the foreign port,
the sea crossing and at least one handling operation and
immediate storage in the European port. At the end of the
waterway leg, there is another handling operation, possibly another intermediate storage period, and further
transport by rail to the final destination.

Here the inland and coastal shipping operator,
together with the shipper and the other transport undertakings involved, needs to work on plans for the most
cost-efficient handling of the entire transport operation. This could, for example, consist in making greater
numbers of large-capacity push-towed barges available than
is absolutely necessary for the inland waterway leg, as
this would reduce the intermediate storage and handling
operations in the loading and discharge ports and at the
same time enable the sea leg to use larger and more cost-
efficient vessels than would be possible with restricted
handling and intermediate storage capacity.

The operator's possibilities of getting close to optimum satisfaction of transport needs through a global
logistic approach, sketched in broad outline here, includes a multitude of day-to-day planning and scheduling
measures whose positive effects cannot be rated highly
enough.

Here, I would refer to the handling of ore traffic on
the lower Rhine, where an original solution was reached
through co-operation between the operators concerned, the
Ruhr steel industry and the stevedoring firms in
Rotterdam, which used virtually every possible oportunity
for organisational rationalisation.

3.3. Technological innovations

Finally, the third step in the inland waterway and
coastal shipping operator's systematic approach to the
best possible ways of meeting transport needs is the
choice and definition of the optimum transport technology. In the inland waterways this decision is generally easier than in coastal shipping as in the former the
technology is to a large extent determined by the physical
characteristics of the canals, whereas the predominant
feature of coastal shipping is its versatility in terms of
the variety of routes that can be served.

3.3.1. Push-tugs and self-propelled craft

As will be described by the experts in other sections
of this Symposium, push-towing has brought about a significant cost reduction in the carriage of bulk cargoes by

inland waterways over the last twenty years. Manpower requirements have been reduced and the efficiency of bulk transport considerably increased. These advantages could be exploited even further by increasing the size of push-tows, at least on certain waterway stretches where conditions allow.

Self-propelled barges, which at first appeared likely to be largely supplanted by push-tows have nevertheless secured a place for themselves in the future. Because of their mobility they are unbeatable cost-wise for medium-sized cargoes, provided they approach the maximum size on the larger waterways, or if they are operated in pairs. They are particularly suitable for inflammable liquids or gases, where it is stipulated that the vessel has to be able to manoeuvre at any time during loading and discharging, which means that the power unit has to be present and immediately operable.

3.3.2. Single-hold vessels

Another technological contribution of inland and coastal shipping to more rational traffic handling is the introduction of large or single-hold vessels, which can be loaded and discharged more quickly and thus save handling costs. They are in general stronger as well and thus have lower repair and maintenance costs.

In certain traffics it may also be appropriate to have moveable bulkheads to give the shipper other advantages, such as easy separation of different classes of cargo.

3.3.3. Waterway/sea-going vessels

This means a type of vessel representing a kind of link between inland and coastal shipping, being generally usable for both. Normally, waterway craft are not allowed access to coastal trade, while conversely coastal vessels are very often not suitable for use on waterways because of their size, except for the smaller units, which are in any case uneconomic on the waterways because of their relatively small cargo space and the high cost of their sea-going equipment and crew. Inland waterway craft with the possibility of limited access to coastal trade on the other hand avoid these drawbacks to a large extent and can be used to advantage if they can save the costly trans-shipment procedures in seaports which are sometimes necessary for relatively short coastal movements.

Operators using this type of vessel can solve several of the shipper's transport problems at once - and economically.

337

3.4. Optimum forms of organisation

Once the overall strategy and technology for a specific transport demand are defined, there are many ways of optimising day-to-day operation. These range from economic and efficient voyage scheduling to the rational use of staff, energy and equipment and fully commercial accounting procedures. Two of the most important possibilities are discussed below.

3.4.1. Scheduling

Unlike the overall strategy, which establishes a systematic plan for transport operations, voyage scheduling is mainly concerned with day-to-day deviations from the original plan. The scheduler's job is to ensure the optimum match between cargoes and craft on a continuing basis despite all unforeseeable factors affecting transport operations. The operator therefore needs to provide him with an appropriate information system providing the most complete data as rapidly as possible so that he can adjust the allocation of vessels to the existing situation, adjust operating plans, arrange laydays or slow voyages down.

This last-named, apparently secondary measure, has become of considerable importance in the present circumstances. In various companies engaged in deep-sea as well as in coastal and inland waterways trade, all scheduled or rescheduled transport operations which are not urgent are subject to a "go-slow" order. Running the engine slowly leads to substantial savings on fuel and maintenance costs. The effect on oil consumption is substantial, especially when additional navigating equipment is fitted to ensure that the course is maintained in the most efficient way.

Another substantial and not yet fully researched possibility for optimising voyage schedules is computer-aided optimisation of push-tug and barge combinations so that idle time for craft gives the least cost over the fleet as a whole. Although much research has been commissioned on this topic, so many independent variables have to be taken into account that no economically satisfactory solution is yet in sight.

3.4.2. Order processing

Modern data processing is increasingly penetrating the industry being used for internal accounting, handling orders and invoicing. This development should not be regarded simply as a possibility for rationalising administrative procedures, but rather as a contribution to the accurate and rapid handling of orders. In an up-to-date office, if the scheduler has access to a computer terminal when he receives an order and can request the necessary data about freight rates, other costs, time requirements, this is a help to the customer in his scheduling and placing of orders.

3.5. Training

Finally, a particularly lasting contribution towards achieving the best possible transport service lies in providing aids to people working on the waterways or in coastal shipping to train to their maximum potential, since - being on their own to a greater extent than in many other occupations and having to take responsibility for decisions in unforeseen situations - they need to be in a position to take such decisions making due allowance for the overall situation and, in the end, in the best interests of the customer.

3.5.1. Crews

As regards navigating staff, training should not be limited to knowledge of shipboard work, safety regulations or traffic rules which are all obvious enough, but should include general knowledge about the economic and technical aspects of providing the best service to customers.

Finally, those in supervisory positions should be given particular help with personnel management problems, so that the younger generation are encouraged to take positions of responsibility and the necessary harmony is maintained and strengthened on board.

3.5.2. Administrative staff

The need to train administrative staff may be a little less obvious, but is nevertheless a task which the operator should not lose sight of in the interests of business efficiency and hence the handling of traffic. Sales representatives, clerks and inspectors should all be fully instructed about the general business context in which the company is involved through the links it has with its customers. Only if this is organised in the form of regular information meetings, which call for the maximum of co-operation, can the operator be sure that the work entrusted to individuals will dovetail smoothly into the firm's strategy. Only then can he also expect that customers will be advised and served in the best possible way in their daily business contacts.

4. THE FUTURE OF INLAND AND COASTAL SHIPPING

The following conclusions about the future development of inland waterway transport and coastal shipping are drawn from the above review of the various possibilities open to operators and allow for existing constraints.

4.1. Baseline position

The present situation of these transport modes prompts wholly contradictory findings. While there are good reasons for saying that because of the existing industrial structure, to a large extent organised around waterways, water-borne transport has a secure place in the transport economy, there have also, recently, been not only positive but highly negative developments. The decline in the volume of bulk cargoes connected with the transfer of basic commodity production to the Third World and the continuing escalation in oil prices, which has a particularly serious impact on shipping, are examples enough.

4.2. Opportunities for expansion

If it is nevertheless possible for inland waterway and coastal shipping to face the future with confidence, then this is mainly due to the following points on which operators may orient their policy.

4.2.1. Energy consumption

As compared with other modes, water-borne transport is far and away the most economic user of energy. Operators have various possibilities for reducing energy consumption even further: building new, hydrodynamically more efficient craft, organised "go-slow" operation, computer-controlled piloting and fewer unladen voyages. The measures already introduced are a very promising beginning.

If it is possible to avoid further increases in the price of oil in general, and of that used by shipping in particular, then this will simply increase the latter's advantage over other modes.

4.2.2. Social costs of transport

A further advantage of inland waterway transport and coastal shipping which will increase in importance as time goes by is the fact that they generate lower social costs, i.e. costs which are not borne by transport enterprises,

340

but by the economy as a whole, than any other mode, and road transport in particular.

This is true, for example, of noise and air pollution, but it also applies to the fact that saturated infrastructures cost virtually incalculable amounts of time and money to all concerned.

These costs are a waste of GNP if there are other transport modes less prone to disadvantages of this type. Governments may be expected gradually to convert social costs into internal costs by imposing charges so that they will be reduced through having to be allowed for in entrepreneurial policy. This should further increase the competitive edge of water-borne transport.

4.2.3. Catchment area

Areas served by waterways have always developed more vigorously and achieved higher growth rates than other areas. No further canal construction is to be expected in the near future, but it can be assumed that the service capacity of existing waterways will be improved. This further enhances the locational advantages of the industries they serve, which should in turn increase these industries' transport requirements and that, for the most part, should benefit waterway carriers.

This last argument admittedly takes us many years into the future, but such an outcome may nevertheless be regarded as certain, because a look back over several decades shows the significant contribution that the construction or improvement of waterways makes to the generation of economic and transport activity.

5. OUTLOOK

To sum up, it can be seen that despite the many problems of the day which can be listed as energy shortages, manpower shortages, inadequate public funds for improving waterways and ports and over-capacity as the result of falling volumes of traffic, both inland waterway transport and coastal shipping nevertheless have secure prospects for the future.

This confident statement is based in particular on the fact that despite all the constraints implicit in the present situation and the limitations on operators' scope for action because of the policies decided elsewhere, there nevertheless remain so many possibilities for creative entrepreneurship that they are well able to take the opportunities offered by general development trends in the interests of the optimum, and at the same time lastingly secure, satisfaction of transport needs. This encouraging conclusion is certainly of particular value at a time when other sectors of the economy are faced with major up-heavals and jobs are endangered. Water-borne transport is the oldest of all modes, but it also has unfailing youth and its prospects for the future are assured.

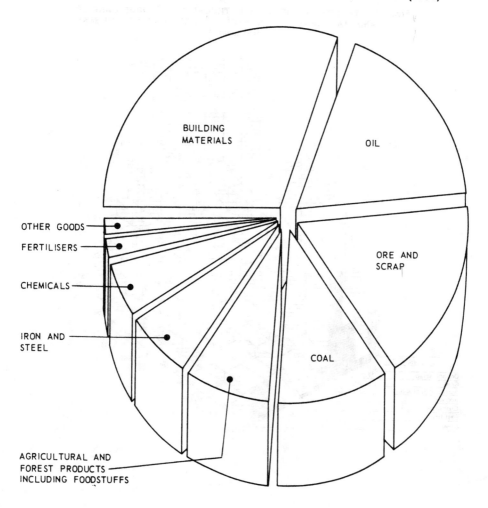

Figure 1 MAIN CATEGORIES OF GOODS CARRIED BY INLAND WATERWAY IN THE FEDERAL REPUBLIC OF GERMANY (1981)

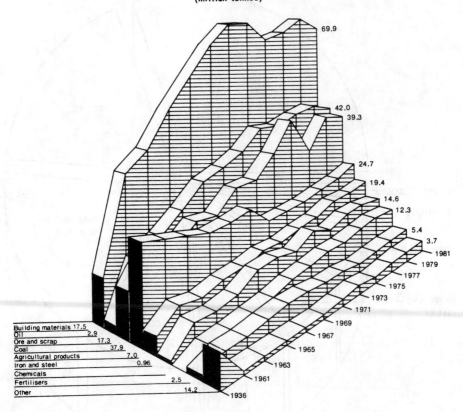

Figure 2 **TRENDS IN THE MAIN CATEGORIES OF GOODS CARRIED BY INLAND WATERWAY IN THE FEDERAL REPUBLIC OF GERMANY**
(million tonnes)

344

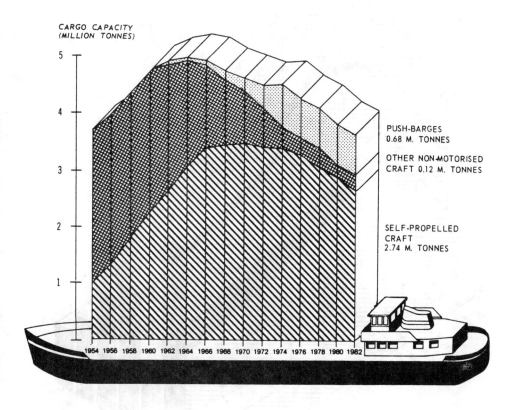

Figure 3 **TRENDS IN INLAND WATERWAY CAPACITY IN THE FEDERAL REPUBLIC OF GERMANY**

CARGO CAPACITY
(MILLION TONNES)

PUSH-BARGES
0.68 M. TONNES

OTHER NON-MOTORISED
CRAFT 0.12 M. TONNES

SELF-PROPELLED
CRAFT
2.74 M. TONNES

1954 1956 1958 1960 1962 1964 1966 1968 1970 1972 1974 1976 1978 1980 1982

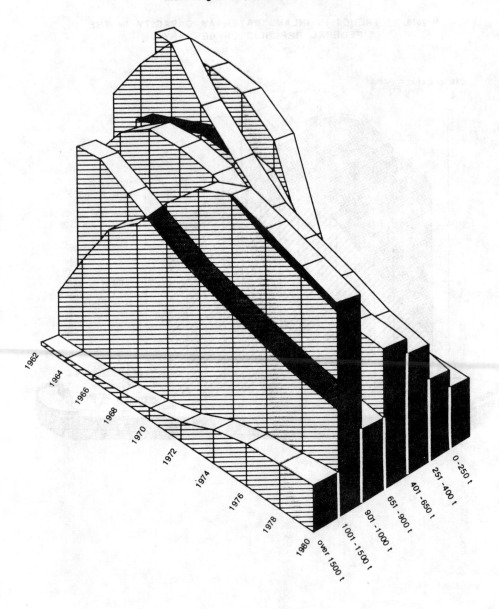

Figure 4 INLAND WATERWAY MOTOR VESSELS IN THE
FEDERAL REPUBLIC OF GERMANY
More large craft, fewer small craft

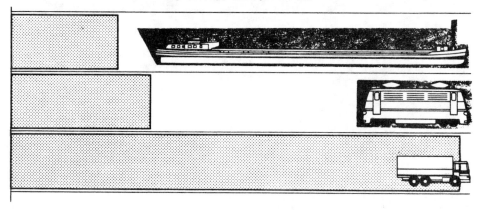

Figure 5· **COMPARISON OF ENERGY CONSUMPTION INLAND WATERWAYS - RAILWAYS - ROAD HAULAGE·**

Comparison based on energy consumption in kg coal equivalent per 100 tkm

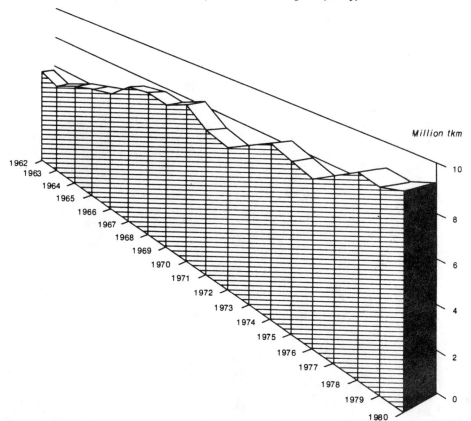

Figure 6 **INCREASING EFFICIENCY OF GERMAN INLAND WATERWAYS**
(tonne-kilometers per tonne deadweight capacity)

347

MANAGEMENT OF FIRMS
TO SATISFY TRANSPORT NEEDS

URBAN AND REGIONAL PASSENGER TRANSPORT

Mr. J.C.F. CAMERON
London Transport
London, United Kingdom

SUMMARY

INTRODUCTION

For the past twelve months the capital city of the United Kingdom, which was one of the pioneers of urban public transport, has been more uncertain than ever before about its policies and plans for the future of its buses and trains.

Some 60,000 people employed by London Transport to serve some six million inhabitants and their visitors have experienced unprecedented changes in policy. Dramatic reductions in fares with an increase in services have been followed within six months by a doubling of fares and a reduction in services.

Throughout the world urban passenger transport undertakings which have been in existence for several decades have experienced changes

a) in costs and in relative costs of
   i) the employment of people;
   ii) energy;
   iii) capital equipment.
b) in the technology available to them,
c) in competitive forms of passenger transport, and
d) in public attitudes towards the environmental impact of transport.

All these changes have added either to the running costs of providing public transport or to the level of new investment needed to reduce these costs.

Authorities responsible for transport in cities have reacted differently to such changes and to increasing demands for funds; some have

a) allowed services to decline with or without higher fares,
b) have invested heavily in new equipment and infrastructure, or
c) have made increasingly heavy revenue payments to augment inadequate income from fares.

Wherever a city has been part of a prosperous economy, the national or local government has been free to take whichever of these courses of action it chooses.

Where a city is part of a troubled economy or where monetary resraint is imposed because the economy is weak or because there is political desire to limit public expenditure, the choice of the appropriate course of action is limited. Failure to recognise such constraints will lead to an increasing proportion of public expenditure being absorbed by urban passenger transport.

DEMANDS FOR CHANGE

Disproportionate allocation of resources to public transport, when there are claims from other sections of the community on behalf of education, health, defence and other public services, leads in turn to an urgent search for alternative solutions.

Transport operators and engineers, "transportants", who for decades have sought after professional improvement or even professional and technical perfection, see their standards threatened.

Transportants in public undertakings, often with little experience of a truly commercial environment or of commercial enterprise, feel threatened: some may despair for the future of the public services which they provide. Their first reaction so often is to say that there are no solutions which will prevent a decline of services.

Members of the community who pay the taxes and rates which have supported services in the past, politicians who have to allocate resources, and the passengers who have become accustomed to transport services at modest fares, refuse to accept that better management by the transportants will not solve this problem.

In the debate which ensues, the superior professional knowledge and experience of the transportant are all that he has to counter the arguments of the far greater numbers of people and the political authority of these other parties. Economists, however skilled and knowledgeable and even persuasive they may be, are of little help to him.

PASSENGER TRANSPORT IN LONDON

In London this debate has been growing steadily over the past ten yeas and rapidly in the past ten months. Neither of the parties to the debate has convinced the other. The transportants fear for their future and for the future of public passenger transport. Many still believe there is no solution but decline.

The others, the politicians, the passengers and the public at large question increasingly the competence of the transportants. As so often in public debates of this kind, the more that is said the less it is heard. The language of the transportants is not the language of their critics: neither understands the other. There is as serious a shortage of listeners as there is of funds.

This paper was invited as a study of the management of urban passenger transport in response to changes in employment, in particular its cost, to changes in the availability and costs of energy and to changes in the attitude of society towards the environmental effects of transport and hence in the cost of meeting its demands.

In London the circumstances, which have also delayed the writing of this paper, have highlighted its relevance. The questions are not now, even if they were a year ago, questions of academic interest alone. They are of crucial importance to all who provide and all who use public transport in London.

In other cities too in the United Kingdom, in Europe and in other continents, public expenditure is being constrained. Public passenger transport, with its heavy investment, its high levels of employment and its use by a great many members of the community whose daily lives depend upon it, is not responsive to sudden change.

Cities and nations with younger urban transport systems than the bus and railway networks of London, and most particularly those now installing new systems, should learn all they can now of the problems that they may face if funds run low.

In London, changes in transport policy, in national, social and economic policy and in the interpretation of statutes which determine transport policies; changes in levels of fares, in the structure of fares, in the levels of services and in the objectives which transportants must pursue, have been greater in 1980, 1981 and 1982 than at any time in the history of its long established passenger transport undertaking.

Most of these factors: policies, fares, service levels and objectives, and as this paper will argue, most importantly the objectives, will have to change again soon and then stabilize before the correct response to the changes listed at the beginning of this paper can be determined and given full effect.

THE MANAGEMENT TASK IN PUBLIC TRANSPORT

One of the reasons why, as claimed above, those who debate public transport economies are at cross-purposes, is their neglect and apparent ignorance of the nature of the management task that has to be performed.

There are four groups of people who are concerned to provide the passenger with the service that he needs. These are:

a) The technicians: the engineers and the operators.
b) The economists: outside and within a transport undertaking.
c) The politicians and other representatives of society at large.
d) The managers, often seen simply as administrators, whose job it is to reconcile the technology, the economics and the political demands.

Technicians have for years "managed" their own technologies. Economists feel sure that they have the key to the decisions which managers, and indeed the technicians and the politicians as well, must make. The politicians and a great many of those they represent are confident that they too could manage public transport effectively if that was their job or if only they were given sufficient "control".

What is this job of management that so many believe they can perform? Is it simply the administration of technology? Is it the implementation of all too obvious actions which sound economic theory shows to be right? Or is it the simple process of effecting a ready response to expressions of political will?

Management includes all three of these tasks. It is not simple even when conditions are stable. When the costs and relative costs of people, energy and equipment are changing; when technology is developing; when other forms of transport are competing even more heavily and when an environmentally conscious society is becoming more articulate, the management task becomes harder.

When all these changes are taking place and, at the same time, there are demands for a reduction in public expenditure, the management tasks become even more difficult. When the transportant has difficulty in understanding what is required of him and when politicians, passengers and the public generally cannot understand what the transportant is saying, the transport manager's task is impossible.

When those transportants whose jobs are predominantly managerial, fail to satisfy the technicians, economists and politicians they are accused of performing badly. When they succeed they are considered not really to have a job at all.

The vast majority of writings, learned and not so learned, which discuss the problems of transport are written by the technicians, by the economists or by those who have political views to express. The technicians write about their engineering and operating achievements, illustrating their papers with photographs of impressive works, modern trains and buses and delights of architectural design. The economists are either transport experts with theories of cost benefit to society or critics of industrial activity with over-simplified views of the transport management task. The politicians make great play of the "control" of public transport, and refer to "responsibility" for public transport or to the "supervision" of public transport as if these were simple administrative tasks.

"Control", "Responsibility" and "Supervision" are part of the language of administrators and of managers alike. Where the transportant's task is quite simply one of running so many trains and buses over so many miles of route, using methods determined by existing technology and continuing to employ the numbers of employees established by custom and practice, control and supervision are straightforward jobs.

Without pressure for economy the aims of the transportant become technical aims. They include the balancing of services to demand, the improvement of safety, the improvement of environmental amenity, investment in capital equipment to eliminate unnecessary maintenance, to collect fares more effectively or simply to show the world what new technology can achieve. In all these tasks technical and professional standards father the aims.

COMPETITION AND COMPARISONS OF PERFORMANCE

Public transport undertakings throughout the world have competed with one another in all these things. With so many urban public transport undertakings being run as monopolies, the only other competition which they have faced has been that of the private car and the pedestrian. Competition between one city and another has not been the competition of enterprise. Until recently, productivity comparisons have been rare.

With each urban transport undertaking located in a different area, with widely differing configurations and widely differing social demands, comparisons have been made only at the two extremes, technical and detailed at one end and political and subjective at the other.

In the earlier decades of this century when few countries had more than one major urban transport undertaking, comparisons in the area of managerial efficiency were invalidated by wide differences in statutory and accounting conventions and by differences in standards of living which confused calculations based simply upon fluctuating rates of currency exchange.

Recent comparisons of levels of financial support for public transport have been complicated by these features. They are, however, the beginnings of recognition of the relevance of managerial performance in the public transport debate. Demands now for reduced public expenditure without any reduction in public service, highlight the importance of the managerial task.

London's 50 years of public enterprise, with only limited investment in extensions of the system or in modernisation, have led to its modestly improving performance indicators being compared very unfavourably with dramatic improvements in productivity in many other areas of the British economy and with the greater efficiency of more modern public transport undertakings in other countries. The professional transportant says these comparisons are invalid. But are they?

Is it sufficient evidence of the necessity for financial support for public transport that all public transport undertakings in major conurbations throughout the world receive subsidies of between 25 per cent and 75 per cent of the income they receive direct from passengers?

Is there anything that can be achieved by more effective management to reduce this dependence upon support? To what extent are the differences in levels of support reflections of differences in the performance of those transportants who are engaged in managerial work?

In London Transport today these questions are being addressed as never before. Some improvements have been made. Steps have been taken and are being taken to lay the foundations for greater improvement. If London Transport Executive's diagnosis of its managerial task and of the preconditions for fulfilling this are correct, significant improvements will result.

Examination of the need for change, that is for management to take over from administration and cause people within an enterprise to respond to demands for change, begins with an analysis of the enterprise and of the behaviour of those people who work in it.

THE CULTURE OF PUBLIC ENTERPRISE

As pointed out earlier, London Transport as a single enterprise will be 50 years old next year. In Britain it predated the main wave of nationalisation of major industries by some 15 years. It had, therefore, developed its own image and traditions and had begun to acquire the culture of a British Public Enterprise well before coal, transport beyond London, iron and steel, electricity, gas and civil aviation were nationalised between 1945 and 1953.

The characteristics of management, the behaviour of administrators and the culture of London Transport as these developed during the 38 years in which it was itself statutorily a nationalised industry, may be peculiarly British, but are not unique. Most British public corporations have revealed similar symptoms. In other countries, in varying degrees, parallels may be detected.

Amongst these characteristics are

a) diminished authority at board level,
b) a self-perpetuating professional senior management whose influence exceeds that of the board,
c) high morale amongst these senior professional managers,
d) depressed initiative amongst the majority of middle and junior managers,
e) a diminished sense of accountability for individual contributions to business objectives,
f) greater interest in professional achievement than in business performance,
g) personal emphasis on status and career progression,
h) subordination of superordinate aims to professional standards,
i) a tendency for the number of professional functions to grow,
j) a tendency for numbers of planners and specifiers to grow,
k) an increasing centralisation of authority and decision-making,
l) ponderous decision-making shared in committees,
m) an increase in bureaucratic processes for the protection of managers from criticism,
n) business objectives confused by conflicting social, economic and political aims,
o) a blurring of distinctions between decisions of policy and rulings on practice, and
p) commercial awareness replaced by theories of worthwhileness.

In an enterprise which has developed characteristics of behaviour of this kind, where the criteria of efficiency are felt by many to be those of professional standards rather than related to business performance,

357

pressure to perform better merely aggravates many of the symptoms. Unless the Board can specify clearly the aims of the enterprise and translate these into businesslike criteria related to managerial accountability, it will be frustrated in any attempts it may make to counter the less desirable features of the culture over which it presides.

It is against this background that the sterile debate about managerial performance between transportants and their critics must be examined. The changes in the costs and relative costs of resources which call for action on the part of transportants and the reductions in expenditure which their critics demand, must be judged against this background.

How does the Board of a public corporation which has developed characteristics of managerial behaviour of this kind bring about the changes that are required? How do the politicians, passengers and the public at large satisfy themselves that all is being done to secure value for money?

There appears so often to be a popular view, reflected in political commentary and in public criticism that all that is needed is for one person, who knows how to manage a business, to tell all its managers what to do. This naive idea assumes first that, even in an enterprise employing more than 50,000 people, it is possible for one person or even for a Board composed of a small number of competent people, to know what should be done by each of the 50,000 it employs. Even when the impossibility of this is comprehended there is a tendency to assume that if broad guidelines are provided, each manager, within his own area of specialism, will respond appropriately.

Many in positions of authority will have experienced the frustration of seeing managers, to whom they believe that they have given perfectly clear direction, fail quickly to achieve the results that are needed. A local or national politician, whose portfolio includes a public corporation, will find all too often that response to his direction is sluggish in the extreme. He may suspect disloyalty or some perverse political objection. He may fail to see the managerial difficulty of changing quickly all the criteria by which managers in a business must perform. In practice very often he is told of emloyee objections whether or not these are paramount.

TRADE UNION OPPOSITION TO CHANGE

If one of the difficulties which is being encountered is the opposition of organised labour to change in working practices, this quickly is identified as the prime obstacle to change. Middle managers may well be very happy to support the impression that employee or trade union opposition is the prime obstacle to change. They are very often uncertain of themselves and, in a corporation subjected to changing policies and political influences, uncertain that what is being called for will be right for the transport undertaking when there is a change in administration.

Where the governing body or political administration is sympathetic to trade union opposition to change this excuse is sometimes acceptable. Managers' failure then to reduce costs may be excused leading to long delays in the adjustment of a public transport enterprise to changes in cost.

Where the governing body is unsympathetic to trade unions, their resistance to change is equally acceptable. By them it is seen, however, as a welcome opportunity for confrontation, preferably by management, with the governing body appearing to be politically resolute but comfortably one step removed. The governing body may then be free to attribute any failure, in the adversarial tactics which it is has provoked, to the inadequacy of management. A governing body, keen to demonstrate its virility, may enjoy the tactic of "tails we win; heads you lose".

The reality so often is not simple. When the culture of the enterprise has developed the characteristics listed above, the conviction of middle managers that change is desirable, notwithstanding trade union objection, is qualified by the preponderance of their concern for professional achievement, career prospects and the correct observance of the mores of the enterprise.

CONFUSION OF MANAGERIAL OBJECTIVES

For example, an engineering manager is expected to perform effectively within a limited budget notwithstanding his professional ambition. His boss's predecessor may well have made his name for masterminding an impressive engineering project. His boss may have an obsession with the develoment of a new technique. The engineering manager is faced with the humdrum tasks of railway maintenance.

a) "they cost far too much" says the Board;
b) "help me to experiment with my new technique", says his boss;

c) "where is the big project that will make you your name", says his ambition?

Who wins? No one. Who loses? The passenger, the taxpayer and the Board.

Unless!? Unless the engineer's boss is clear that business performance is paramount and that creditable and beneficial though a new technique may be, no one wants it regardless of cost. Least of all does the Board want it at the expense of the level of services which effective engineering management with well tried and tested techniques could secure.

New techniques are, of course, to be applauded. Change is essential if costs are to be reduced. There are ways in which everyone can win if the engineer's resourcefulness and skill are motivated to achieve the objectives which the Board is trying to pursue. Engineering ingenuity undirected by business strategy may prove very costly. Engineers who are involved in developing strategy to achieve enduring business aims can work wonders for all.

Countless examples can be found of such conflicts of interest amongst the hundreds of middle managers in a large public transport enterprise. For example, responsibility for changes in systems of fare collection may be shared between the operator, the electronic engineer, the operating manager and an accountant. The appointment of a project manager may appear to resolve the resulting conflicts. But this is so only if the project manager's aim is clear and if all other parties understand what this aim must be and see in achieving it no threat to the achievement of the targets by which they believe they themselves will be judged.

Similar conflicts are found in such ancillary activities as data processing applications; in the design of vehicles or stations, in the use of property, in the allocation of offices to departments, in the organisation of internal catering or internal transport and in the central control or decentralisation of public correspondence. In an elderly undertaking such as London Transport which developed for itself internal support services which in many other undertakings may be undertaken by contractors, there is almost unlimited scope for there to be conflicts of aims. No Chief Executive or Board, however expert, can comprehend all these conflicts or provide a single direction which will resolve them.

It is necessary for the entire undertaking to be structured and directed so that some unity of purpose becomes evident at all these disparate points. Each of the hundreds of managers who have to be employed in a large enterprise must know exactly what are the criteria by which he will be judged. For each the criteria will be a combination of human, technical and economic factors. For

360

each to be most effective the conflicts which a manager may have to resolve for himself must be minimal. Generally the only relatively healthy conflicts will be economic ones of a commercial nature which mathematics or negotiation may resolve. Human and personal conflicts and confusion as to individual managers' aims will be debilitating and detrimental to performance.

TIME FOR ADJUSTMENT TO CHANGE

Equally important in this context is the need for those who determine urban transport policy to recognise the time it must take to train a middle manager. Even an experienced manager, who has to change his approach fundamentally in mid-career, needs help and retraining and plenty of time to adjust. The Board of a public transport undertaking may be able to accept rapidly a change of direction. It could agree at a single meeting, for example, to change its policy from maximising vehicle miles for a given expenditure to minimising the expenditure incurred in providing a given level of service. The implications of this change for all those who allocate vehicles and schedule services, and indeed for all those who have to authorise expenditure for any purpose, would be profound.

A large team of senior managers, set in their ways and sceptical of any change, having seen it all before, will adjust to such changes unwillingly and slowly. Hundreds of junior managers and technicians trained by tradition, steeped in the dedication of their predecessors to the achievement of professional standards, will need years of adjustment to such policy change before it becomes wholly effective. If communication is poor, senior managers unconvinced and trade unions insist on pursuing outdated policies, changes in attitude will be negligible. How much easier for managers to quote trade union resistance, encourage the status quo and leave the trade unions or the Board to shoulder the blame for the costs.

As suggested earlier, many of these characteristics, which become so evident in an enterprise which has been slow to adjust to changes in circumstances, may be peculiarly British. Urban transport undertakings in other cities in Europe and elsewhere may not be aware of such difficulties. In some cities adjustments may have been made to take account of changes in labour costs and attitudes, in the cost of energy and in the greater awareness of the impact of transport on the environment. In some cities the problems encountered in London may become evident as the years go by.

IDENTIFYING THE OBJECTIVES

In London there has been a need to change course towards a more cost effective strategy, certain prerequisites to greater efficiency have been identified. First, it has been seen to be necessary to ask the classical questions as to what businesses London Transport is in. Bus and Rail services have been seen as separately identifiable businesses. Within each, separate markets, geographic and economic, have been identified. In support of these, or ancillary to them, several subsidiary activities are seen now as separate businesses or profit centres. Pricing has supplemented costing and the internal charging practices of commercial enterprise have been introduced.

In turn, such an analysis of a public transport undertaking leads to the identification of many line managers whose accountability can be defined with some precision. As these general managers develop and accelerate their real performance against these objectives, many begin to doubt the need for some of their committees, plans, specifications, rules and standing orders. Initially, costs remain high. Increasingly, as staff work is subordinated to the main task, so the efficiency rises and a new balance in the allocation of resources is developed. Most important, the Board becomes involved once again, as it must have done 40 and 50 years ago in London, in addressing itself to the questions of policy which are its domain. Managers at all levels, deprived of the recognition of their traditional criteria of achievement, demand new and clearer direction.

It is at this point that the insistence by the transportants' critics: the politicians, the passengers and the public at large, upon better performance by the management of a public transport undertaking, receives its due response. What do they want?

Lower public expenditure could be incurred by reducing levels of service or by raising fares. No, the critics will say, we want no reductions in services but merely a reduction in cost.

But, say the transportants, many things have changed and are still changing. To provide the same level of services and to ignore the changes which have occurred, could mean a change in the quality of service or, with an increase in competition, very poor utilisation of vehicles. Significant reductions in cost may be achievable only through major capital investment or by changes in legislation. In London, for instance, there grows a need to legalise penalties for abuse of the fares system and the need to assess the problems of accepting a less heavily manned transport system which could require an increase in the numbers of police.

Even more important is the need, if a real improvement in managerial performance is to be achieved, for the objectives to be communicable to the hundreds of managers upon whom the Board of a major transport undertaking depends. Furthermore, if these hundreds of managers are to continue to perform well and to pursue relentlessly the steady improvements in performance which one might expect in a competitive commercial enterprise, the criteria of performance must endure for several generations of managers. Only thereby will the multitude of local and functional conflicts of motivation touched upon earlier be resolved.

CONCLUSIONS

From these arguments it follows that an urban transport undertaking faced with the changes listed at the beginning of this paper and sooner or later ordered to reduce its demands for public expenditure, should therefore consider four initiatives.

First, it should demand a clear direction from its governing authority of the objectives which it should pursue and of the criteria by which its performance will be judged.

Secondly, it should insist upon a long period of consistency without any reversals of policy or dramatic fluctuations in demand or in financial support.

Thirdly, it should identify clearly for itself the businessess that it is in and any separate markets, discrete accountable management units and subsidiary activities which it must support.

Fourthly, it should define the accountability and criteria of performance of the managers of these business units and train them and develop them to respond to these demands.

Should there be doubt in the minds of members of the Board of a publicly owned transport undertaking as to the ease with which the necessary changes can be brought about, that Board would be well advised to examine its managerial behaviour against the list of characteristics of management in a public enterprise which is provided at the middle of this paper. For as long as these prevail the critics of management in a public enterprise cannot be dismissed.

Conversely, for as long as the critics fail to recognise the importance of defining clearly the objectives which an enterprise must pursue and the importance of

363

decades of consistency in defining these, even if levels of demand and financial support change gradually over the years, so will the Board find it impossible to be sure what business it is in. Even more difficult will it be for the Board to define and communicate its policies and criteria to its managers.

As years go by a public passenger transport undertaking may fail to establish this basis for its performance but try, nevertheless, to respond to changing demands. If it tries to adapt too frequently or too speedily to changes in policy without clarifying its new objectives and criteria of performance for its managers it will waste its resources continuously, as with each change it replaces one inefficiently with another.

MANAGEMENT OF FIRMS
TO SATISFY TRANSPORT NEEDS

URBAN AND REGIONAL PASSENGER
TRANSPORT

Mr. C. ELMBERG
AB Storstockholms Lokaltrafik
Stockholm, Sweden

SUMMARY

FOREWORD

Public transport in larger conurbations is very often a very criticised activity. One American public transport official once said that the reason for this could be traced to the fact that a public transport customer does get the time to read the daily newspaper thoroughly en route to and from work, to discuss editorials and "letters from the readers" on public transport issues with fellow travellers, to compare experiences. Conversely, in one's own automobile such a possibility is not easily at hand.

To manage public transport is to satisfy various demands:

- from the customers who provide the revenues;
- from the employees who provide the expenditures;
- from the politicians who provide the policies and (hopefully) the financial support.

The management's task is therefore to compromise.

Managements of public transport all over the world face essentially the same problems in their efforts to satisfy transport needs. The solutions may differ because of local attitudes to the problems, from sheer neglect to intense interest, often due to financial conditions.

This paper is not meant to solve all these problems, merely to focus attention on some of the more strategic issues that face the managements of public transport undertakings and to relate them to the Swedish conditions and experience. To produce this paper I am very much indebted to my colleagues at the public transport undertakings of the five largest Swedish cities: Stockholm (SL), Göteborg (GS), Malmö (ML), Uppsala (UB), and Norrköping (NL), for their contribution of statistics.

The opinions and conclusions expressed in this paper are entirely my own. Any coincidence with the management's view might be incidental.

Curt M. Elmberg.

INTRODUCTION

In a non-competitive market the management of enterprises providing public transport services in urbanised regions created very few problems. The fares set adequately covered the expenditures, the annual balances showed surpluses. The golden years of viable urban public transport lasted until a competitive transport mode appeared on the scene, the private automobile.

In the competitive market, which arose out of this situation, most managements did not react forcefully in time. Many were caught in the old traditions. Few attempts, if any, were made to market and improve the services and the product. The counter measures consisted primarily of a reduction of service to cope with the changing demand. Managements were caught in a vicious circle: reduced service - reduced passenger volume - reduced revenues - more automobiles on the streets - reduced speed - more vehicles and crews to produce the same service (lower productivity) - further reduction of services to cope with the economic situation - less passengers - more automobiles, etc., etc.

Funds set aside for vehicle and facility replacements had to be used to cover operational expenditures. This resulted in higher maintenance costs to keep outmoded rolling stock in service, as well as old depots and workshops operational. Consequently, the general appearance of many public transport systems decayed.

In a competitive labour market public transport enterprises lost a great deal of skilled employees who had become frustrated at fighting a losing battle against years of neglect and lack of funds available to improve conditions. Other branches offered better working and wage conditions.

The ultimate solution became obvious: public ownership. This also meant a new dimension in the management of public transport. Public transport should be looked upon as a utility for the good of the citizens; public transport became a social factor in urban life.

Public ownership also meant a pronounced political influence in the management of public transport. Two paths of management could then readily be discerned:

- political management;
- commercial management;

and to unite these in a businesslike overall management did, and still does, create difficulties among those who were, and are, trusted to run the business.

The two managements might be defined as follows:

Political	Commercial
Social aspects	Economic aspects
Equity	Productivity
Social level of service	Economic level of service
Social costs	Production costs
Social fares	Market fares
Revenues	Revenues
Financial support	Balance
Balance	

Originally, financial support was provided at local level by the government through taxation. The increasing demands to satisfy transport needs made local governments turn to the national government for financial aid. Different levels of political management were thus created to deal with the same problem. A strong political management might have advantages and disadvantages:

National level	Local level
+ financial support abundant (large funds)	+ support tailored to suit local needs
+ uniformity	+ political changes of less importance
- support less tailored to suit local needs	+ responsibility for productivity
- bureaucratic procedures	- financial support limited
- motivation for productivity less pronounced	

Experiences from countries with a strong national political management of local public transport have verified this, for example the United States and the Netherlands. The greatest risks lie in dependence upon the national government such that a sudden change in national policy might create an unproductive feeling of despair and an unwillingness to make the best of the situation.

With this review of the general development of urban public management elsewhere it is appropriate to analyse the situation in Sweden, where the national support of urban public transport has been, and still is, very limited. Consequently, the political management was at the local level until mid-1981 when a new act formed a joint county and municipal responsibility for urban and rural public transport within the county. During the

1970s, a period of political changes, energy shortage, skyrocketing fuel prices, and a significant inflation, the pressure on the political and commercial managements was considerable. Did they fulfil the expectations to satisfy the transport needs?

SOURCES OF FINANCE

Administratively Sweden is divided into 24 counties and 279 municipalities. The three governments (national, county, and municipal) have the legal right to tax the income of an individual. The tax levied by the three governments combined take a substantial part of the earned income of a Swedish citizen (Figure 1). Local income tax is the main source for financing public utilities, including support of local public transport.

STUDY OBJECTS

It is appropriate in this study to select a few test sites to find what impact, if any, different managements might have had on the provision of public transport services to the citizens. The five largest urban areas in Sweden have been chosen as suitable test sites and some general data are found in Table 1.

POLITICAL MANAGEMENT

In the five selected areas public transport is under political ownership which means that the decision-making body has a political affiliation. There are five political parties in Sweden with an influence in national and local politics. Three of them can be termed right wing and two left wing:

Left wing		Right wing	
Name	Parliament seats	Name	Parliament seats
Communist party (vpk)	20	Centre party (c)	64
Social Democrat party (s)	154	Conservative party (m)	73
		Liberal party (fp)	38
Total	174	Total	175

370

Every three years there are elections to the national parliament and to the county and municipal councils simultaneously. The political parties select their candidates, and the citizens cast their votes for a party, not for an individual. Consequently, on the local scene the distribution of candidates to parties can be different from that on the national scene. Some urban areas exhibit stability regardless of the outcome of the national election, others do not.

Table 2 shows the political management in the five urban areas and its variation with respect to the outcome of the elections 1970, 1973, 1976 and 1979. The political body chosen is the council responsible for the appropriation of funds to support the public transport system serving the area.

SYSTEM CHARACTERISTICS

There are several ways to describe a public transport system and its physical and operational characteristics. In the five urban areas there are different transport modes involved, which are outlined in Table 3. As a market feature "public transport journeys per inhabitant", is chosen and its development in the period 1970-1980 is given in Table 4.

One of the main characteristics of public transport is the fact that a seat produced is consumed at the same moment it is offered to the public, regardless of whether it is occupied or not. The product, the seat, cannot be stored. An appropriate production indicator would be "seat kilometre per passenger kilometre". Unfortunately, passenger kilometre values are difficult to obtain because these require extensive origin-destination surveys, which are costly. The indicator chosen as a production characteristic is "seat kilometre per passenger" (Table 5). A lower value is an indication of a better productivity.

An indicator on transport viability is the "ratio revenues to expenditures" (Table 6).

INVESTMENT POLICIES

An investment policy might be found by the indicator "investment per capita", in which investments are related to a specific monetary value to compensate for the impact of inflation. In Table 7 such an indicator is developed utilising the official production cost index. In addition, the relative burden of public transport investment to other utility investments is also outlined.

Public transport investments do have peaks, primarily because of procurement of vehicles and extension of rail lines. Therefore, a certain caution is required in studying the figures. Left wing political managements are generally more prone to give preference to public transport. This can be seen from the change of political management in Göteborg in the period 1977-1979.

OPERATIONAL POLICIES

From a political point of view there is a conflict between the political and commercial managements. The political establishment is reluctant to raise the fares, even during a period of strong inflation. Table 8 shows the revenues per passenger converted to the 1980 monetary value utilising the official consumer price index. Some managements have adjusted the fares to better cope with inflation.

As was seen in Table 6, financial support is required to operate the public transport system. The relative size of this support compared to other support is given in Table 9.

Among politicians of all affiliations there is a superstitious belief that a low fare policy would attract new customers, preferably the automobile travellers. If the product offered is competitive this might be true. Up until now the cost has been a rather weak factor, more important is service frequency and seat availability. However, rapidly changing petrol prices might alter the traditional way of thinking among confirmed automobile drivers.

The common dilemma for a politician is to defend unpopular decisions in his or her constituency. To reduce criticism of fare increases there has been a tendency to simultaneously introduce various discounts for special categories of passengers, for special categories of journeys, etc. This popular method, to give with one hand and to take with the other, might not produce the revenues expected. The main problem is that there are great difficulties in estimating the market reaction.

TRANSPORT NEEDS

Are transport needs equal to transport demands? All managements must be aware of the transport demands. But there might be groups of citizens whose demands are rarely expressed or exposed to the management, i.e. the demand by

372

those who have difficulties using the regular public
transport system, the handicapped and the elderly. Their
transport needs have been brought into focus in the last
five to ten years.

Sweden has taken a very firm step to satisfy these
needs. Göteborg, being the first city, introduced in 1967
a special door-to-door transport service for handicapped
citizens. This service is operated by the public transport undertaking, acting as a transporting agency, whilst
the responsibility for travel permits lies with the social
authority. Today, the Stockholm and Göteborg public
transport undertakings operate a large scale special service for the handicapped (Table 10).

Furthermore, a new act is due to come into force
requiring public transport vehicles and facilities to be
better adapted to cater for handicapped passengers. The
new act will regulate door step height, door width, size
of letters on destination blinds, location of handles and
location of reserved seats in public transport vehicles
used in urban and suburban services. The crucial issue,
provisions for wheelchairs, has been limited to vehicles
in inter-regional traffic. Most municipalities in Sweden
have an organised transport service for their handicapped
citizens.

The costs of adapting older vehicles to the new regulation as well as supporting the increased production
costs of new vehicles have to be borne by the local
authorities. Consequently, managements will face difficult decisions: how to distribute limited investment
funds to provide both for the large group of "regular"
passengers and also for the reconstruction of vehicles and
facilities to satisfy the transport needs of a limited
group of passengers.

Efforts have also been made to give urban and rural
public transport an improved standard of service by introducing dial-a-bus services, thus directly tailoring transport needs to demand. A very comprehensive experiment,
serving an entire urban and rural area with door-to-door
minibus service for 18 months was conducted in Nynäshamn,
a municipality 75 kms south of Stockholm. The main results from this experiment were that, compared to the
regular route bound system previously in operation:

- The passenger volume increased, in the urban area
  up to 50 per cent, in the rural area up to 20 per
  cent, depending upon the season;
- The need for special taxi services for the handicapped was reduced by 20 per cent, and the taxi
  company encountered a 20 per cent reduction in
  demand;
- The median total travel time, including waiting and
  walking, was reduced, in the urban area from 18 to
  12 minutes, in the rural area from 46 to 31 minutes;

- 70 per cent of the customers in the urban area and 50 per cent in the rural area preferred the dial-a-bus system despite the inconvenience of having to order the service by telephone at least one hour in advance;
- The cost per passenger journey was approximately three times higher.

THE LABOUR DILEMMA

The most precious asset in public transport is the employees. To satisfy transport needs a skilled labour force is essential. To maintain this force it is necessary that working conditions and wages be competitive (Table 11).

The Swedish experience is that a shortage of drivers has plagued the two largest undertakings. The reasons are primarily:

- stressed conditions to manoeuvre large vehicles in automobile crowded streets;
- difficulty in finding suitable housing for the drivers in the vicinity of the depots;
- frustrations of dealing with impatient passengers;
- risk of physical violence directed towards the drivers.

Even in a period of unemployment the working conditions for a bus driver in the Stockholm central area keep many suitable appplicants away despite the fact wages have been raised to a very competitive level, S.Kr.7,000 per month. There are no difficulties, on the other hand, in recruiting bus drivers to work in the Stockholm suburban districts.

A well-trained driver with some years of experience is an investment. A lost driver means re-investment in a new driver. A substantial turnover of drivers does mean that significant sums have to be set aside for training of replacements. A study in Stockholm disclosed that the 1980 cost for training the operating force, bus drivers, metro drivers, ticket collectors, is M.S.Kr.30 (Table 12).

Public transport as a trade is very labour intensive. Out of the operating expenditures the labour cost is significant, (Table 13). Therefore, measures to improve productivity have been directed to:

- elimination of conductors on the vehicles (one-man operation);
- honour fare systems (self-service by passengers);
- larger vehicles (articulated buses, trams);
- larger units (multiple unit operation).

374

Many of these efforts have been counteracted by destructive forces in modern society: vandalism and hooliganism.

DESTRUCTIVE FORCES

Utilising public transport in the larger cities, particularly in the peak hours, does mean crowded conditions and time wasted. In the past years another factor has been added to discredit the branch: the demand for secure journeys.

The growing trend of meaningless destruction of property, i.e. vandalism, of harrassing passengers, of threats and physical violence to the public transport employees on duty have caused managements to counteract directly by:

- employing special guards to patrol facilities and vehicles;
- reducing or discontinuing services at late hours or at trouble spots;
- reviewing vehicle design;
- reconsidering the reintroduction of conductors.

As an example, Table 14 shows the direct costs of vandalism on the Stockholm public transport system. These expenditures could have been used to provide a better service.

The problem is a social one, and it cannot be cured entirely by measures employed by the public transport undertakings. A very active campaign in Stockholm where representatives of the public transport undertaking and of social authorities visit schools and youth centres, informing and discussing openly and informally, has given significant results, but still the situation is unacceptable. It would appear that these problems are far less in countries where the Catholic church has a dominant influence. The Catholic religion puts an emphasis on family unity and the upbringing of children.

Threats to vehicle crews and passengers usually come from persons under the influence of alcohol or drugs. These incidents, of which the more serious ones are rare, make the headlines and reinforce the feeling of discomfort and unease about using public transport. It must be the prime duty of a management to market the product as being a secure one and to train its crews to deal competently with unpleasant situations to restore the customers' confidence.

THE DECISION DILEMMA

Comprehensive investment programmes always require a great deal of thought, particularly in periods when funds are getting scarce. Vehicle replacement or new vehicles require a significant investment. Particularly painful is the case of rail vehicles. Compared to a bus, which can suit a large market, a rail vehicle is often designed for a particular line with unique dimensions, and it is thus tailored for a very small market. A replacement or a supplementary order gives rise to high production costs (Figure 2). Furthermore, the operating life of rail vehicles is normally long, and their replacement would not be envisaged for 20 years or so, and sometimes even longer. To maintain a continuous production awareness for a limited and very specialised market is a dilemma for the industry.

In these conditions there is little doubt that managements in many cases turn to cheaper alternatives: replacement of rail operation by buses. Such proposals are strongly opposed by various pressure groups, primarily on grounds of environmental and energy considerations. The decision makers, irrespective of management affiliation, have to put a monetary price on factors that up to a few years ago were mostly or entirely neglected. To combine factors assigned a fictitious monetary value with factors that can be assigned a true monetary value, has created a great deal of misconception and confusion among decision makers. This is indeed an education process.

Stockholm is in the process of defining "transport standards", in which are included:

- production factors: vehicle kms, crew hours;
- comfort factors: walking distance, waiting time, transfer frequency, seat availability;
- environmental factors: energy consumption, pollution levels.

This sophisticatd approach will hopefully produce a suitable working tool to overcome the decision dilemma.

THE FUNDING DILEMMA

The hesitation of the political management to raise the fares to produce more revenues creates a funding problem when production costs increase due to labour and materials cost increases. Funding the growing gap between expenditures and revenues requires additional sources of income (Table 6). The treasuries, whether national or local, are filled by taxation, but there is also a strong hesitation, not to say a reluctance, to augment the tax burden of the citizens. Consequently, the political management faces a priority dilemma. Is public transport more important than schools, hospitals, social welfare, technical utilities?

To overcome this difficulty the Swedish approach has been to pool the treasuries, i.e. to let the counties and the municipalities jointly assume responsibility for the public transport system within the county. In this manner there are several sources for funding, although there are also limitations. The county treasury can only accept half of the funding, the municipalities within the county the remaining half. One exception is the Stockholm county which assumes the responsibility for all funding, on historical grounds.

The new act leaves the counties to organise public transport services to best suit local conditions in co-operation with the municipalities involved, and the methods adopted have been:

- to create a share holding company where half of the shares are owned by the county and the other half by the various municipalities based upon their population distribution; or
- to create a federation of the county and the municipalities.

The main difference between these two types of umbrella organisations is that the first one operates under the Swedish shareholding act whilst the other operates under the municipal act. In practice, this does very little to achieve the objectives.

To provide the actual services the umbrella organisation purchases these from the local public transport undertakings on a contractual basis. The possibility also exists to acquire the operators, in order to also gain complete control of the operation. This method, applied to its fullest extent, has only taken place in Stockholm, where there is only one operator responsible, the Greater Stockholm Transport (SL). Private and state owned operators have gradually been acquired, both bus and rail. Suburban railway services are purchased from the Swedish State Railways (SJ) in accordance with a treaty which regulates the type and extent of service provided.

CONCLUSION

Satisfying transport needs, in urban and suburban conurbations as well as elsehwere, means having to deal with a number of dilemmas. Managements responsible for policies and for the daily operations of urban public transport have in the past faced, and will in the future be confronted by:

- the competence dilemma: who will run the business, the political or the commercial management?

- the service dilemma: will certain passenger categories get a better service at the expense of other categories?

- the funding dilemma: will political management be forced to accept a better adaptation of revenues to the development of costs?

- the labour dilemma: will labour contracts be competitive to secure a skilled force, yet allow improved productivity?

- the subversion dilemma: will society assume true responsibility to stamp out actions directed against the security of its citizens?

Whether Swedish managements have succeeded better than others in overcoming these dilemmas is not within the scope of this paper. However, public transport has a good reputation world-wide: there is no competition between undertakings to steal customers from each other, with the result there is a willingness to share approaches, to explore ideas, to admit successes and failures. Managements, therefore, do not need to despair of the future.

ROSTER OF FIGURES AND TABLES

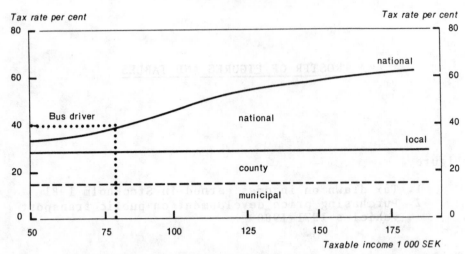

Figure 1   TAX DRAWN ON INCOMES EARNED IN STOCKHOLM 1981

Notes : a. Taxable income is earned income minus deductions.
         b. Local taxes (county + municipal) vary in the country :
             Stockholm = 27.5 %, Göteborg = 30 %, Malmö = 30 %, Uppsala = 28.3 %, Norrköping = 32 %.

Figure 2   PURCHASING PRICE DEVELOPMENT ON PUBLIC TRANSPORT
           VEHICLES 1971 - 1980   (Index 100 = 1976)

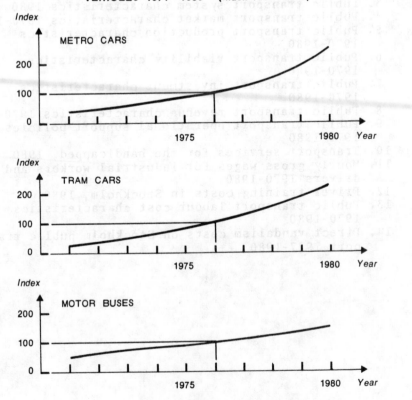

Table 1

URBAN AREA CHARACTERISTICS FOR THE FIVE LARGEST
CONURBATIONS OF SWEDEN, 1980

Conurbation	Land area sq. kms	Population 1,000 inh.	Public Transport	
			Passenger volume million	Journeys per inh.
Stockholm	6 488	1 528	462	302
Göteborg	446	431	86	200
Malmö	154	234	43	184
Uppsala	2 464	146	22	151(a)
Norrköping	1 492	119	17	143
Total	11 044	2 458		
Per cent of Sweden's land area and population	2.7	29.6		

a) Compare with figure in Table 4.

Table 2

POLITICAL MANAGEMENT IN THE FIVE LARGEST URBAN AREAS OF
SWEDEN DURING FOUR ELECTION PERIODS, 1971-1982

Urban area	Number of seats in council							
Period	1971-1973		1974-1976		1977-1979		1980-1982	
Affiliation	Left	Right	Left	Right	Left	Right	Left	Right
Stockholm(a)	73	76	71	78	72	77	73	76
Göteborg(b)	39	42	39	42	41	40	39	42
Malmö(b)	33	28	33	28	32	29	33	28
Uppsala(b)	38	43	38	43	39	42	40	41
Norrköping(b)	46	33	46	39	45	40	47	38

a) County council, responsible for financial support of public transport.
b) Municipal council, responsible for financial support of public transport.

381

Table 3

PUBLIC TRANSPORT SYSTEM CHARACTERISTICS, 1980

	Stockholm	Göteborg	Malmö	Uppsala	Norrköping
Passengers carried					
Total, million	462	86	43	22	17
Suburban ry, %	11%	-	-	-	-
Metro, %	42%	-	-	-	-
Tram, %	1%	56%	-	-	45%
Bus, %	46%	44%	100%	100%	55%
Seat kilometres					
Total, million	21 900	3 096	868	683	251
Suburban ry, %	27%	-	-	-	-
Metro, %	40%	-	-	-	-
Tram, %	1%	51%	-	-	40%
Bus, %	32%	49%	100%	100%	60%
Vehicle kilometres					
Total, million	181	31	11	9	3
Suburban ry, %	17%	-	-	-	-
Metro, %	33%	-	-	-	-
Tram, %	2%	43%	-	-	36%
Bus, %	48%	57%	100%	100%	64%
Vehicles					
Total	3 029	561	236	180	122
Suburban ry	333	-	-	-	-
Metro	884	-	-	-	-
Tram	43	306	-	-	24
Bus	1 769	255	236	180	98
Employees(a)					
Total	10 487	2 391	819	522	388
Drivers, %	64%	57%	74%	79%	64%

a) Number of employees converted to full time working.

Table 4

PUBLIC TRANSPORT MARKET CHARACTERISTICS 1970-1980:

Public transport journeys per inhabitant

Year	Stockholm	Göteborg	Malmö	Uppsala	Norrköping
1970	..	175	123	144	93
1971	..	169	118	150	93
1972	..	170	119	151	109
1973	276	183	125	155	109
1974	285	195	148	168	116
1975	284	191	148	170	117
1976	288	190	149	176	122
1977	285	191	154	184	132
1978	287	183	159	182	133
1979	292	189	173	194	133
1980	302	200	184	198(a)	143

a) The service area population in Uppsala for the
municipally-owned public transport is 112,000 inhabitants
whilst the population within the city limits is 146,000.

Table 5

PUBLIC TRANSPORT PRODUCTION CHARACTERISTICS 1970-1980:

Seat kilometre per passenger transported

Year	Stockholm	Göteborg	Malmö	Uppsala	Norrköping
1970	..	31	21	23	24
1971	..	34	23	25	25
1972	..	34	23	26	21
1973	..	35	23	26	19
1974	..	35	21	26	18
1975	..	36	22	29	18
1976	..	38	22	29	18
1977	46	39	21	28	16
1978	46	40	22	28	15
1979	50	40	20	31	15
1980	47	36	20	31	15

Table 6

PUBLIC TRANSPORT VIABILITY CHARACTERISTICS 1970-1980:
Expenditures(a) covered by revenues, per cent

Year	Stockholm	Göteborg	Malmö	Uppsala	Norrköping
1970	70	68	80	100	71
1971	63	62	77	93	60
1972	57	56	81	89	61
1973	55	52	76	81	60
1974	51	48	71	77	59
1975	50	42	65	74	57
1976	49	42	60	71	54
1977	42	39	59	63	52
1978	42	37	53	65	58
1979	39	38	56	62	59
1980	36	36	53	60	60

a) Expenditures include capital costs (depreciation, interest).

Table 7

PUBLIC TRANSPORT INVESTMENT CHARACTERISTICS 1970-1980:

Left column: Investment per inhabitant in S.Kr.1980 monetary value.

Right column: Ratio: Public transport investments to all investments, per cent.

Year	Stockholm (a)		Göteborg		Malmö		Uppsala		Norrköping	
1970	..	..	193	8	38	1.5	..	1.5	3	0.1
1971	295	34	204	7	56	2.1	..	0.3	2	0.1
1972	354	43	167	7	48	1.8	..	1.0	0	0
1973	302	39	77	4	78	3.7	..	2.4	7	0.4
1974	370	52	64	4	28	1.4	..	4.4	6	0.3
1975	303	43	64	4	16	0.9	..	7.1	24	1.5
1976	246	42	62	4	16	0.9	..	5.6	34	2.3
1977	172	33	83	6	3	0.0	..	5.2	23	1.4
1978	209	33	120	8	22	0.9	..	5.4	17	1.2
1979	112	20	68	5	48	2.2	..	15.9	33	2.1
1980	190	29	26	2	56	2.8	..	4.6	70	5.5
1981(b)	..	26	..	7	..	3.4	..	8.7	..	3.7

a) The Stockholm county council is primarily responsible for financing hospitals and public transport within the county. Municipalities are responsible for financing technical services, schools, social welfare, local streets, transport.
b) Budgeted figures.

Table 8

PUBLIC TRANSPORT REVENUE CHARACTERISTICS 1970-1980:

Revenue per passenger
transported in S.Kr.1980 monetary value

Year	Stockholm	Göteborg	Malmö	Uppsala	Norrköping
1970	..	223	184	198	238
1971	..	221	196	202	211
1972	..	203	208	209	185
1973	220	191	194	200	186
1974	206	170	160	192	174
1975	219	154	158	201	179
1976	226	173	157	205	189
1977	216	171	158	214	178
1978	224	179	145	229	225
1979	212	193	154	232	245
1980	193	181	139	236	235

Table 9

PUBLIC TRANSPORT OPERATIONAL SUPPORT POLICIES 1970-1980

Operational support to public transport in relation to
total operational support to public utilities, per cent

Year	Stockholm	Göteborg	Malmö	Uppsala	Norrköping
1970	..	12.2	..	0.3	4.1
1971	9.1	10.8	..	0.1	3.6
1972	10.4	10.3	..	0.6	3.3
1973	10.8	11.0	..	1.0	3.3
1974	11.4	10.8	..	0.8	3.4
1975	11.1	10.1	..	1.1	2.9
1976	11.0	10.4	..	1.4	3.1
1977	11.6	10.2	..	1.2	3.1
1978	11.4	10.6	..	1.6	3.3
1979	11.9	10.5	..	1.7	3.2
1980	12.1	10.3	..	1.9	3.2
1981(a)	12.2	10.3	..	2.1	3.4

a) Budgeted figures.

Table 10

TRANSPORT SERVICES FOR THE HANDICAPPED, 1980

	Stockholm	Göteborg
Permits issued to be eligible for special transport service	75 967	23 246
Permits per 10 000 inhabitants	497	538
Journeys, 1 000	5 150	1 765
By special vehicle	650	102
By taxi	4 500	1 663
Expenditure per passenger journey		
Handicap service, S.Kr.	68.9	47.9
Regular service, S.Kr.	5.4	5.0
Expenditure coverage by revenue		
Handicap service(a), %	51	34
Handicap service(b), %	20	5
Regular service, %	36	36

a) Including national grant to municipalities providing service for the handicapped.
b) Excluding national grant.

Table 11

HOURLY GROSS WAGE FOR INDUSTRIAL WORKERS AND BUS
DRIVERS 1970-1980 IN S.KR.1980 MONETARY VALUE, S.KR.

Year	Sweden Ind.	Stockholm Ind.	Stockholm Bus	Göteborg Ind.	Göteborg Bus	Malmö Ind.	Malmö Bus	Norrköping Ind.	Norrköping Bus
1970	34	:	43	37	31 1/2	35 1/2	32 1/2	:	:
1971	34 1/2	:	45	38	34 1/2	36	33	:	:
1972	36 1/2	:	47	40	34 1/2	39	37 1/2	:	:
1973	37 1/2	:	46 1/2	40 1/2	34 1/2	40	38	:	:
1974	38	:	45	41 1/2	34	40 1/2	38 1/2	:	:
1975	40 1/2	:	48	43 1/2	35 1/2	42 1/2	39	:	:
1976	41 1/2	:	46	44	36	43 1/2	41	41	43
1977	40	:	43 1/2	42	41	40 1/2	43	39 1/2	46 1/2
1978	40	:	44	42	38	38 1/2	40 1/2	39 1/2	44 1/2
1979	41 1/2	:	47 1/2	43	39	41	42 1/2	41 1/2	46 1/2
1980	40 1/2	:	44 1/2	..	40	..	42 1/2	41 1/2	45

Table 12

DRIVER TRAINING COSTS IN STOCKHOLM, 1980

Training for	Cost per trainee S.Kr.1 000	Total cost S.Kr. Million
Bus drivers	21.8	24.8 (82%)
Metro drivers	18.6	2.1 (7%)
Metro ticket collectors	5.3	3.5 (11%)
		30.4

Table 13

PUBLIC TRANSPORT LABOUR COST CHARACTERISTICS 1970-1980:

Labour cost related to operating cost, per cent

Year	Stockholm	Göteborg	Malmö	Uppsala	Norrköping
1970	..	74	79	57	62
1971	..	77	79	57	62
1972	..	77	79	52	63
1973	..	75	80	52	61
1974	..	72	79	50	67
1975	..	74	80	50	69
1976	60	75	81	49	65
1977	56	74	83	49	68
1978	54	73	83	48	59
1979	53	72	82	51	58
1980	53	71	81	49	58

Table 14

DIRECT VANDALISM COSTS ON STOCKHOLM PUBLIC TRANSPORT
1977-1980 IN S.KR.1980 MONETARY VALUE

Year	Total costs Million S.Kr.	Cost per mode		Cost per passenger	
		Rail pct	Bus pct	Rail S.Kr.0.01	Bus S.Kr.0.01
1977	12.5	64	36	3.4	2.3
1978	12.8	70	30	3.7	1.9
1979	12.3	78	22	4.0	1.3
1980	10.6	77	23	3.3	1.1

MANAGEMENT OF FIRMS
TO SATISFY TRANSPORT NEEDS

URBAN AND REGIONAL PASSENGER
TRANSPORT

Mr. S. ESTRADA
Ayuntamiento de Madrid
Madrid, Spain

SUMMARY

1. URBAN TRANSPORT

1.1. Types of urban transport undertaking in Spain

1.1.1. Definition of urban transport

Land transport in Spain is defined from the legal and administrative standpoint by the Act of 27th December, 1947 on the organisation of motorised transport on main roads.

Article 1 of this Act defines motorised transport on main roads as "the transport of passengers and goods using motor vehicles which operate under fixed conditions outside urban areas". Conversely, transport carried out within urban areas in Spain is considered urban transport and is therefore not governed by the above-mentioned Act of 27th December, 1947.

The regulations implementing this act state that for the purposes of transport and as a general rule, "urban area" means a built-up area in which there are no gaps between buildings greater than 500 m.

1.1.2. Types of urban transport undertaking

Transport carried out in the urban areas defined above are governed in Spain by the Local Government Act as expanded by the regulations for local corporation services introduced by the Decree of 17th June, 1955.

This Act and its regulations set the legal framework for the types of undertaking which can provide local public services.

Summarising these forms or types of undertaking, services can be provided by:

1. Direct management, which includes:

   a) Management by a municipal authority:
      - without a special administrative body,
      - with a special administrative body,
   b) Public service foundation.
   c) Private company with purely municipal or provincial capital.

2. Indirect management

   a) Concession
   b) Contract
   c) Agreement

3. Management through a mixed enterprise

   - a company with both public and private capital.

4. Consortium

   - form of organisation through which the different
     types of service undertaking can be used to re-
     place associated public corporations.

Each of these types of undertaking brings with it exclusive rights to operate services within a fixed area where it has a monopoly position, whether it be a private firm (concession, contract or agreement) or a public undertaking (direct management, with or without a special management body and municipal limited liability company).

Among the private firms existing in Spain there are a certain number with very special characteristics known as "Empresas Laborales" (worker-owned firms). These operate under the indirect management system in the concession category, but the company capital belongs to the workers who are the shareholders and elect the board of directors. Apart from this feature, they operate exactly like any other joint stock company whose capital is in the hands of a fixed and limited number of shareholders.

2. DESCRIPTION OF THE TOWNS WITH URBAN TRANSPORT IN SPAIN AND THE TYPE OF ORGANISATION

2.1. Identification of towns and types of organisation

For this study we have classified Spanish towns according to the number of inhabitants.

Undertakings managed directly by the municipal authority appear in the tables as MU, private firms as PF and worker-owned firms as WF.

Table 1

Population ('000s)	Number of municipalities	MU	WF	PF
> 50	71	-	-	71
50/100	33	1	-	32
100/500	43	8	2	33
500/1000	3	1	1	1
> 1000	2	2		

2.2. Total and average populations served by urban public transport

The population served by urban transport are classi-fied below according to the type of transport undertaking.

Table 2
PRIVATE FIRMS

Population ('000)	Number of municipalities	Population ('000)	Average population ('000)
> 50	71	2,313	33
50/100	32	2,148	67
100/500	33	5,316	183
500/1000	1	620	620
Total	137	10,397	

Table 3
MUNICIPAL UNDERTAKINGS

Population ('000)	Number of municipalities	Population ('000)	Average population ('000)
50/100	1	68	68
100/500	8	2,068	258
500/1000	1	668	668
1000	2	5,171	2,585
Total	12	7,975	

Table 4

WORKER-OWNED FIRMS

Population ('000)	Number of municipalities	Population ('000)	Average population ('000)
100/500	2	459	229
500/1000	1	770	770
Total	3	1,229	

Summarising, the distribution of urban transport undertakings in Spain in 1980 according to type of organisation as defined in paragraph 1.1.2 is as follows:

- Private firms   137   90.13 per cent
- Municipal
  undertakings   12   7.89 per cent
- Worker-owned firms   3   1.98 per cent

In other words, the vast majority of urban transport undertakings are private firms operating for profit. These firms operate in small towns, however, and if we consider the number of people served by the different types of undertaking, we find the following distribution:

Table 5

PRIVATE ENTERPRISES

Type of undertaking	Number of firms	Population ('000)	%
Private firms	137	10,399	53.03
Municipal undertakings	12	7,976	40.58
Worker-owned firms	3	1,299	6.39
Total	152	19,674	100.00

Which means that the private transport firms which make up 90.13 per cent of the total reach only 53.03 per cent of the population served by urban transport.

In 1980, of the total Spanish population of 35,826,125, only 19,606,335 or 54.72 per cent were served by public transport, the remaining 16,219,790 or 45.28 per cent of the population living in small towns and rural settlements with no urban transport.

2.3. Vehicle stock

2.3.1. Distribution of the bus stock in 1980 according to population served and type of undertaking

Table 6

PRIVATE FIRMS

Population ('000)	Number of municipalities	Number of buses	Average buses per municipality	Average population per bus	Average age of buses
50	71	466	6.56	4,964	9.00
50/100	32	591	18.46	3,636	9.02
100/500	33	2,188	66.30	2,429	8.95
500/1000	1	215	215.00	2,888	8.56

Table 7

MUNICIPAL UNDERTAKINGS

Population ('000)	Number of municipalities	Number of buses	Average buses per municipality	Average population per bus	Average age of buses
50/100	1	21	21.00	3,255	8.09
100/500	8	775	96.87	2.669	8.83
500/1000	1	303	303.00	2,205	8.33
1000	2	2,760	1,380.00	1,873	7.27

Table 8

WORKER-OWNED FIRMS

Population ('000)	Number of municipalities	Number of buses	Average buses per municipality	Average population per bus	Average age of buses
100/500	2	139	69.50	3,306	7.42
500/1000	1	259	252.00	3,057	8.26

2.3.2. Distribution of vehicles with one and two-man operation and their capacity according to type of undertaking and size of town

Table 9

PRIVATE FIRMS

Population ('000)	No. of vehicles			Capacity		Average capacity per bus
	one-man	two-man	total	seats	total	
50	367	99	466	16,895	34,235	73.46
50/100	518	73	591	22,242	47,496	80.36
100/500	1,952	236	2,188	80,561	186,823	85.38
500/1000	215	-	215	8,671	18,671	86.86

Table 10

MUNICIPAL UNDERTAKINGS

Population ('000)	No. of vehicles			Capacity		Average capacity per bus
	one-man	two-man	total	seats	total	
50/100	10	11	21	850	1,688	89.94
100/500	493	282	775	32,642	69,642	89.94
500/1000	232	71	303	11,986	24,174	79.69
> 1000	2,171	589	2,760	130,492	257,535	76.06

Table 11

WORKER-OWNED FIRMS

Population ('000)	No. of vehicles			Capacity		Average capacity per bus
	one-man	two-man	total	seats	total	
100/500	139	-	139	5,598	11,120	80
500/1000	70	182	252	10,655	20,935	83.07

2.3.3. The national vehicle stock

The total stock of urban buses has developed as follows:

Table 12

Year	Number of buses	Average annual increase
1970	6,095	
1975	7,240	+229
1977	7,610	+185
1978	7,315	-297
1980	7,710	+197

The distribution in 1980 was as follows:

Private firms	3,460 buses	44.87 per cent
Municipal undertakings	3,859 buses	50.05 per cent
Worker-owned firms	391 buses	5.07 per cent

The age distribution of the bus stock is as follows:

Average age	Number of buses	%
One year	502	6.5
Four years	346	4.48
Seven years	2,871	37.23
Nine years	1,092	14.16
Eleven years	2,899	37.60

The average age of urban buses is 8.3 years, the breakdown according to type of undertaking being as follows:

- average age of PF buses	8.94 years
" " " MU buses	7.68 years
" " " WF buses	7.93 years

3. LABOUR FORCE

3.1. Breakdown of the labour force according to type of enterprise and size of town

Table 13

PRIVATE FIRMS

Population ('000)	Permanent Employees							Average employees per vehicle
	Drivers	Conductors	One-man crew	Inspectors	Mechanics	Administration	Total	
50	154	103	585	10	25	93	970	2.08
50/100	175	263	720	33	125	102	1,418	2.39
100/500	610	965	3,850	105	428	385	6,343	2.89
500/1000		15	494	4	85	22	620	2.88

Table 14

MUNICIPAL UNDERTAKINGS

Population ('000)	Permanent Employees							Average employees per vehicle
	Drivers	Conductors	One-man crew	Inspectors	Mechanics	Administration	Total	
50/100	126	5	54	3	12	6	80	3.80
100/500		425	1,433	65	398	113	2,587	3.33
500/1000		141	715	15	160	125	1,156	3.81
1000	926	1,693	5,963	561	3,770	683	13,596	4.92

Table 15

WORKER-OWNED FIRMS

Population ('000)	Permanent Employees							Average employees per vehicle
	Drivers	Conductors	One-man crew	Inspectors	Mechanics	Administration	Total	
100/500		31	317	23	75	40	486	3.49
500/1000	63	80	528	67	338	88	1,164	4.61

3.2. Total labour force and distribution by type of undertaking

3.2.1. Private firms   9,351   32.91 per cent
3.2.2. Municipal undertakings   17,419   61.29 per cent
3.2.3. Worker-owned firms   1,650   5.80 per cent

4.   TECHNICAL CHARACTERISTICS

4.1. Towns with less than 50,000 inhabitants

There are no municipal undertakings or worker-owned firms.

Table 16

Type of under-taking	No. of lines	Average length of lines (km)	Average No. of stops per line	Average time (min.)	Total services (weekdays)	Total services (holidays)	Average speed (km/h)
PF	364		8.72	23.12	17,444	10,466	12.92

4.2. Towns of 50,000 to 100,000 inhabitants

There are no worker-owned firms.

Table 17

Type of under-taking	No. of lines	Average length of lines (km)	Average No. of stops per line	Average time (min.)	Total services (weekdays)	Total services (holidays)	Average speed (km/h)
PF	201	6.15	10.04		16,808	13,446	13.20
MU	8	4.90	9.40		429	325	13.60

4.3. Towns of 100,000 to 500,000 inhabitants

Table 18

Type of under-taking	No. of lines	Average length of lines (km)	Average No. of stops per line	Average time (min.)	Total services (weekdays)	Total services (holidays)	Average speed (km/h)
PF	522	6.24	12.3	23.54	55,417	41,562	13.10
MU	143	6.33	12.9	29.10	15,727	11,000	13.05
WF	35	6.98	16.4	34.77	3,693	2,585	13.25

401

4.4. Towns of 500,000 to 1 million inhabitants

Table 19

Type of under-taking	No. of lines	Average length of lines (km)	Average No. of stops per line	Average time (min.)	Total services (weekdays)	Total services (holidays)	Average speed (km)
PF	31	10.3	18.50	47.53	5,460	4,445	13.00
MU	43	5.2	12.06	21.71	7,872	5,943	13.26
WF	41	5.3	10.9	24.44	6,825	4,357	13.01

4.5. Towns of over 1 million inhabitants

There are no private or worker-owned firms.

Table 20

Type of under-taking	No. of lines	Average length of lines (km)	Average No. of stops per line	Average time (min.)	Total services (weekdays)	Total services (holidays)	Average speed (km)
PF	294	7.26	18.41	29.52	58,841	48,168	15.16

5. TRAFFIC AND TRANSPORT OUTPUT IN 1980

5.1. Private firms

Table 21

Population ('000)	No. of firms	Total places available	Total passengers carried	Total km.	Percentage occupation	Average
50	71	428,055,000	98,361,450	23,253,256	23	4.23
50/100	32	470,406,500	165,663,183	36,171,191	35.10	4.55
100/500	33	1,635,926,080	508,965,456	119,702,283	31.10	4.26
500/1000	1	164,756,700	68,054,670	12,346,620	41.3	5.51

5.2. Municipal undertakings

Table 22

Population ('000)	No. of firms	Total places available	Total passengers carried	Total km.	Percentage occupation	Average
50/100	1	11,902,635	2,895,341	852,574	24.32	3.39
100/500	8	483,770,000	164,697,526	34,081,605	33.95	4.83
500/1000	1	217,728,400	77,383,210	12,320,651	35.48	6.28
1000	2	1.781.833	715,960,316	144,957,386	40.86	5.14

403

5.3. Worker-owned firms

Table 23

Population ('000)	No. of firms	Total places available	Total passengers carried	Total km.	Percentage occupation	Average
100/500	2	101,187,600	31,974,632	8,605,931	31.10	3.90
500/1000	1	244,708,740	76,780,240	11,547,740	31.37	6.64

6. PASSENGERS, KILOMETRES, EMPLOYEES AND BUSES

6.1. Private firms

Table 24

Population ('000)	No. of towns	Trips per person per year	Buses per '000 population	Km. per employee	Passengers per employee
50	71	38.20	0.20	23,972	91,093
50/100	32	77.12	0.27	25,508	116,828
100/500	33	95.74	0.41	18,871	80,240
500/1000	1	109.76	0.31	19,912	109,764

404

6.2. Municipal undertakings

Table 25

Population ('000)	No. of towns	Trips per person per year	Buses per '000 population	Km. per employee	Passengers per employee
50/100	1	42.57	0.30	10.657	36.187
100/500	8	79.64	0.37	13.173	63.663
500/1000	1	115.84	0.45	10.657	66.937
1000	2	138.35	0.54	9.931	49.051

6.3. Worker-owned firms

Table 26

Population ('000)	No. of towns	Trips per person per year	Buses per '000 population	Km. per employee	Passengers per employee
500/1000	1	74.37	0.30	16.694	70.316
1000	2	99.71	0.32	9.920	65.962

Table 27

Type of undertaking	Trips per passenger per year	Buses per '000 population	Km. per employee	Passengers per employee
Private	79.91	0.33	20.476	88.872
Municipal	107.94	0.48	11.034	55.165
Worker-owned	85.41	0.30	11.886	67.244
Total	91.95	0.39	14.190	67.284

7. COSTS PER KILOMETRE

In order to make a homogeneous comparison of the costs of the different types of firm, they have been grouped according to size; taking the number of buses as the basic unit. The following set of tables give the main characteristics and costs for each size group and type of firm in 1980.

7.1. Private firms

Table 28

No. of buses	No. of employees	Average population ('000)	Smallest no. of buses	Largest no. of buses	Average no. of buses	Total no. of buses	Total no. of employees	Average employees per bus	Average employees per firm	Km per year ('000)	Average km. per firm ('000)
15	34	29	3	12	5.65	192	386	2.01	11	7,191	211
15/25	44	44	16	22	18.35	717	1,739	2.21	40	41,730	948
25/50	41	69	25	43	38.41	1,274	3,556	2.26	86	75,680	1,845
50/100	12	172	54	73	62.31	672	1,727	2.31	144	34,620	2,885
100/250	4	385	102	220	146.10	605	1,943	2.65	485	32,197	8,292

406

7.1.1. Cost comparisons for specific years

7.1.1.1. 1970

Table 29

Size of firm (no. of buses)	Cost/km	Percentage above lowest cost	Percentage above previous group
Less than 15	11.31		
15 to 25	11.45	1.23	1.23
25 to 50	12.50	11.52	9.17
50 to 100	13.52	19.54	8.16
100 to 250	18.23	61.18	34.83

7.1.1.2. 1975

Table 30

Size of firm (no. of buses)	Cost/km	Percentage above lowest cost	Percentage above previous group
Less than 15	21.57		
15 to 25	21.87	1.39	1.39
25 to 50	24.87	21.87	13.71
50 to 100	28.68	32.96	15.31
100 to 250	32.57	50.99	17.05

7.1.1.3. 1977

Table 31

Size of firm (no. of buses)	Cost/km	Percentage above lowest cost	Percentage above previous group
Less than 15	40.68		
15 to 25	41.45	1.89	1.89
25 to 50	47.24	16.12	13.96
50 to 100	54.44	33.82	15.24
100 to 250	56.36	38.54	3.52

7.1.1.4. 1978

Table 32

Size of firm (no. of buses)	Cost/km	Percentage above lowest cost	Percentage above previous group
Less than 15	50.59		
15 to 25	51.60	1.99	1.99
25 to 50	59.49	17.59	15.29
50 to 100	68.52	35.44	17.17
100 to 250	72.04	42.39	5.13

7.1.1.5. 1980

Table 33

Size of firm (no. of buses)	Cost/km	Percentage above lowest cost	Percentage above previous group
Less than 15	64.09		
15 to 25	65.97	1.37	1.37
25 to 50	75.48	17.77	14.41
50 to 100	86.92	35.62	15.15
100 to 250	91.90	43.39	5.72

7.1.1.6. Trends in the differences in costs per kilometre

The variations in costs per kilometre as far as private firms are concerned may be summarised as follows:

Table 34

No. of buses	Year				
	1970	1975	1977	1978	1980
A. Up to 25	Base cost	Base cost	Base cost	Base cost	Base cost
B. 25 to 50	Ax1.10	Ax1.20	Ax1.16	Ax1.17	Ax1.17
C. 50 to 100	Ax1.20 Bx1.10	Ax1.32 Bx1.15	Ax1.33 Bx1.15	Ax1.35 Bx1.15	Ax1.35 Bx1.15
D. 100 to 250	Ax1.61 Bx1.45 Cx1.34	Ax1.50 Bx1.30 Cx1.17	Ax1.38 Bx1.15 Cx1.03	Ax1.42 Bx1.21 Cx1.05	Ax1.43 Bx1.21 Cx1.05

408

7.2. Municipal undertakings

Table 35

No. of buses	No. of employees	Average population ('000)	Smallest no. of buses	Largest no. of buses	Average no. of buses	Total no. of buses	Total no. of employees	Average employees per bus	Average employees per firm	Km per year ('000)	Average km. per firm ('000)
100	6	180	21	94	83	498	1,444	2.90	265	16,613	2,768
100/350	4	426	105	303	168	672	2,379	3.54	560	30,741	7,685
500	2	2,585	940	1,820	1,380	2,760	13,596	4.92	6,798	44,957	72,478

7.2.1.1. <u>1970</u>

Table 36

Number of buses	Cost/km	Percentage above lowest cost	Percentage above previous group
A. less than 100 B. 100 to 350 C. Over 500	24.30 25.63 37.52	5.47 54.40	5.47 46.39

7.2.1.2. <u>1975</u>

Table 37

Number of buses	Cost/km	Percentage above lowest cost	Percentage above previous group
A. less than 100 B. 100 to 350 C. Over 500	43.62 44.12 57.14	1.1 30.99	1.1 29.51

7.2.1.3. <u>1977</u>

Table 38

Number of buses	Cost/km	Percentage above lowest cost	Percentage above previous group
A. less than 100 B. 100 to 350 C. Over 500	71.08 74.00 94.70	4.10 33.23	4.10 28.97

7.2.1.4. <u>1978</u>

Table 39

Number of buses	Cost/km	Percentage above lowest cost	Percentage above previous group
A. less than 100 B. 100 to 350 C. Over 500	86.43 98.01 114.22	13.39 32.15	13.39 16.53

410

7.2.1.5. 1980

Table 40

Number of buses	Cost/km	Percentage above lowest cost	Percentage above previous group
A. less than 100	118.14		
B. 100 to 350	121.02	2.43	2.43
C. Over 500	148.84	25.98	23.54

7.2.1.6. Trends in differences between costs per km

Table 41

No. of buses	1970	1975	Year 1977	1978	1980
A. less than 100	24.30	43.62	71.08	86.43	118.14
B. 100 to 350	Ax1.05	Ax1.01	Ax1.04	Ax1.13	Ax1.02
C. over 500	Ax1.34 Bx1.46	Ax1.30 Bx1.46	Ax1.33 Bx1.27	Ax1.32 Bx1.16	Ax1.25 Bx1.23

7.3. Worker-owned firms

Table 42

No. of buses	No. of employees	Average population ('000)	Smallest no. of buses	Largest no. of buses	Average no. of buses	Total no. of buses	Total no. of employees	Average employees per bus	Average employees per firm	Km per year ('000)	Average km. per firm ('000)
100	2	229	57	82	69.5	139	486	3.49	243	8,065	4,032
100/260	1	770	252	252	252	252	1,164	4.61	1,164	11,547	11,547

7.3.1. Cost comparison for specific years

7.3.1.1. 1975

Table 43

No. of buses	Cost/km	% increase
A. Less than 100	39.14	
B. 100 to 260	57.67	45.80

7.3.1.2. 1977

Table 44

No. of buses	Cost/km	% increase
A. Less than 100	59.96	
B. 100 to 260	90.32	58.56

7.3.1.3. 1978

Table 45

No. of buses	Cost/km	% increase
A. Less than 100	70.11	
B. 100 to 260	109.53	56.22

7.3.1.4. 1980

Table 46

No. of buses	Cost/km	% increase
A. Less than 100	95.40	
B. 100 to 260	139.55	46.27

7.3.1.5. Trends in differences between costs per kilometre

Table 47

No. of buses	Year			
	1975	1977	1978	1980
A. less than 100	39.14	56.96	70.11	95.40
	39.14	56.96	70.11	95.40
B. 100 to 260	Ax1.45	Ax1.58	Ax1.56	Ax1.46

The costs of firms in group B are about 55 per cent higher than those in Group A.

8. REQUIRED AND ACTUAL TARIFFS

Tables showing the tariffs necessary to cover the costs of each type of urban transport undertaking in Spain are given below.

8.1. Private firms

Table 48

No. of buses	1970		1975		1977		1978		1980	
	Cost/km	Tariff required	Cost/km	Tariff required	Cost/km	Tariff required	Cost/km	Tariff required	Cost/km	Tariff required
15	11.31	2.67	21.57	5.37	40.68	9.32	50.59	10.96	64.09	15.09
15/25	11.45	2.71	21.87	5.44	41.45	9.49	51.60	11.18	65.97	15.53
25/50	12.50	2.96	24.87	6.19	47.24	10.82	59.49	12.88	75.48	17.77
50/100	13.52	3.20	28.68	7.14	54.44	12.47	68.52	14.84	86.92	20.46
100/250	18.23	4.31	32.57	8.11	56.36	12.91	72.04	15.17	91.90	21.64

414

8.2. Municipal undertakings

Table 49

No. of buses	1970		1975		1977		1978		1980	
	Cost/ km	Tariff required	Cost/ km	Tariff required	Cost/ km	Tariff required	Cost/ km	Tariff required	Cost/ km	Tariff required
100	24.30	3.56	43.62	7.22	71.08	12.31	86.43	15.20	118.14	20.43
100/350	25.63	3.83	44.12	8.19	74.00	14.80	98.01	19.87	121.02	24.23
500	37.52	6.27	57.14	10.90	94.20	19.25	114.22	23.07	148.84	30.21

8.3. Worker-owned firms

Table 50

No. of buses	1970		1975		1977		1978		1980	
	Cost/ km	Tariff required	Cost/ km	Tariff required	Cost/ km	Tariff required	Cost/ km	Tariff required	Cost/ km	Tariff required
100			39.14	8.59	56.96	14.73	70.11	17.92	95.40	24.55
100/260	33.03	3.55	57.07	7.78	90.32	13.34	109.53	16.22	139.55	22.23

8.4. Comparison of average costs and necessary tariffs for each type of undertaking

8.4.1. Average cost per km

Table 51

Type of under-taking	No.	Year									
		1970		1975		1977		1978		1980	
		Tariff	%	Tariff	%	Tariff	%	Tariff	%	Tariff	%
Private	130	13.58	100	27.35	100	50.76	100	63.90	100	81.57	100
Municipal	12	32.78	241	53.91	197	89.40	176	109.38	172	141.79	173
Worker-owned	3	33.03	243	49.72	182	76.12	150	93.38	147	121.89	150

8.4.2. Necessary tariffs

Table 52

Type of under-taking	No.	Year									
		1970		1975		1977		1978		1980	
		Tariff	%	Tariff	%	Tariff	%	Tariff	%	Tariff	%
Private	130	3.01	100	6.48		11.25	100	13.56	100	18.52	100
Municipal	12	5.53	183	10.12	156	17.90	152	21.83	160	28.36	157
Worker-owned	3	3.55	117	8.02	124	13.75	122	16.20	123	22.08	120

416

8.4.3. Total cost per kilometre of the sector and required and actual tariffs according to the National Institute of Statistics

Table 53

	1970	1975	1977	1978	1980
Average cost per km.	22.31	41.39	70.55	86.35	112.50
Average tariff required	4.22	8.53	14.71	17.72	22.72
Average actual tariff	3.23	6.90	10.72	12.31	15.61
Average tariff deficit	0.99	1.68	6.01	5.41	7.11

Table 54

Year	Municipal undertakings			Worker-owned firms			Private firms		
	Loss per passenger (ptas.)	% Tariff	Deficit million (ptas.)	Loss per passenger (ptas.)	% Tariff	Deficit million (ptas.)	Profit per passenger (ptas.)	% Tariff	Profit million (ptas.)
70	2.51	77	2,027	0.35	10	39	0.20	6	163
75	3.04	44	2,961	1.02	15	142	0.31	4	263
77	7.00	65	6,732	2.85	27	323	0.40	4	342
78	9.42	76	9,067	3.80	31	421	0.43	3	400
80	12.69	81	12,199	7.18	46	777	0.52	3	439

417

- Actual tariffs have been very similar in all urban transport undertakings regardless of the type of organisation.
- Tariff changes to offset cost increases have always occurred only after a long delay in Spain, which in the case of municipal undertakings and worker-owned firms has resulted in an enormous financing burden, since the municipal authorities which are legally responsible for making up deficits in no case have in their budgets the funds necessary to cover them.
- The private firms had reduced their profits from the legally authorised 15 per cent to about 3 per cent by the end of the 70s and furthermore had run down capital by not being able to replace vehicles as they should, so that the average age of buses is now nine years.
- There can be no doubt that if Spanish urban transport undertakings amortized vehicles at replacement cost the result would be:
  a) increased losses for municipal and worker-owned undertakings;
  b) the average private firm would show a loss.

9. TARIFF CHANGES

9.1. Legal provisions in Spain

Between 1973 and 1976, tariff increases were regulated by a decree-law which stated that bus and trolly-bus fares could be regulated on a sector-wide basis.

The system in force during this period was as follows:

a) The National Urban Transport Association carried out an economic study of the sector in which, according to the cost increases, it indicated the percentage fare increase required. These studies included a supplementary fare increase based on demand elasticity.

b) This study was submitted for consideration by the National Price Council, which informed the Government which finally issued a decree automatically increasing fares over the whole country.

In 1977, the Government handed over the power to authorise fares increases to the civil governors of the provinces, subject to a binding report by the municipal authorities and a subsequent non-binding report by the Provincial Price Council.

This system was very prejudicial to all urban transport undertakings as the municipal authorities virtually always refused fares increases. In 1977 and 1978 undertakings had to run down capital which meant increased subsidies to the municipal and work-owned undertakings and made investment impossible for the private firms.

In 1979, faced with the consequences of the previous years, the Government produced a decree in which the power of the municipalities was altered as follows:

a) its report on fares was non-binding;
b) if the municipal report was not produced within a fortnight it was considered to be positive.

This decree represented an improvement on the 1977 position for transport undertakings.

In 1980, the Government reverted to producing a sectoral decree, authorising a nationwide percentage increase according to a polinomial formula:

$$\Delta T = \frac{55 \, \Delta L + 12 \, \Delta F + 10 \, \Delta V + 8 \, \Delta CP}{85}$$

where

ΔT = percentage fare increase
ΔL = percentage increase in labour costs
ΔF = percentage increase in fuel prices
ΔV = percentage increase in vehicle prices
ΔCP = percentage increase in consumer prices

The polinomial formula allows a fares increase permitting up to 15 per cent profit.

In 1981, undertakings requiring fares increases obtained them under the conditions of the decree of 1979 establishing a maximum recommended by the General Transport Directorate to the civil governors.

From 1981, responsibility for fares has been delegated by the national government to the autonomous governments, starting with the Basque country, Catalonia and Galicia, the civil governors being relieved of this responsibility.

There is no doubt that for the management of transport undertakings, sectoral measures are much more convenient since individual requests by undertakings give rise to the following difficulties:

Municipal authorities are very sensitive to urban transport fares increases and therefore always oppose them or in the best of cases reduce them and delay their implementation. Finally, it may be pointed out that if there is no single percentage criterion, there could be undertakings with higher fares than others with equal costs.

The basic cause of these difficulties stems from the fact that urban transport in Spain is the only type of public transport which does not come under the Ministry of Transport, not even technically.

10. FINANCING URBAN TRANSPORT

10.1. Present situation

In view of the difficulty of establishing self-financing tariffs, for the reasons described above, financing possibilities are undoubtedly a serious preoccupation for all undertakings. Their situation with respect to this problem differs according to their legal status.

10.1.1. Municipal undertakings

These undertakings, whose board of directors is in the control of the municipal authorities should have their losses, if any, covered by the municipality, which logically ought to make the necessary provision in their budgets. Nevertheless, this does not happen in the case of any municipal undertakings and the sums necessary for their survival are obtained from public or private bank loans, the interest on which increases the said losses and, what is more, since they always arrive late, this is prejudicial to good management planning.

10.1.2. Worker-owned and private firms

These firms operate as concessionaires, a system designated in the present Local Government Act as indirect management.

The regulations governing local corporation services in Article 127, Point 2.2 states that the municipal authority has to maintain the economic viability of the concession, being obliged according to the Act and its implementing regulations:

a) to compensate the concessionaire for any modifications it may order to be introduced into the service and which increases costs or reduces income; and

b) to revise tariffs and subsidies when, even without modifications in the service, unforeseen circumstances arise which for any reason cause a loss of economic viability for the concession.

This Article 127 is one of the most widely-ignored in Spanish legislation, since it has virtually never been put into practice.

10.2. Urban transport financing bill

10.2.1. Background

The unstable situation of all types of urban transport undertaking obliged the Government in early 1981 to prepare an urban transport financing bill, giving priority to legislation being drafted for transport in metropolitan areas.

The basic provisions of this legislation are as follows:

a) Tariffs should be self-financing, i.e. should cover all costs;

b) In the exceptional case where tariffs were not sufficient, the municipal authority could impose a tax known as the "municipal tax to finance the deficit of surface public transport". This tax would cover the losses, whatever the type of undertaking, whether public or private;

c) At the beginning of the year the transport undertakings would automatically revise their tariffs in line with their budgets and according to a polinomial formula;

d) The criterion for liability to this tax would be use of a dwelling in the municipal area, the occupant having to pay. The tax base would be the rateable value and the maximum would be 0.5 per cent;

e) Metropolitan areas would be authorised to set up consortia and reach agreement with neighbouring municipal authorities on the distribution of the tax.

10.2.2. Opposition to this bill

When the government made public this bill which was admitted by the plenary session procedure and published in the official journal of the parliament on 24th June, 1981, there were a number of objections, which may be summarised as follows:

a) Federation of residents' associations

At the XIth national congress of residents' associations held in Valencia in June 1981, the citizens' movement passed a resolution against the bill which obliged residents to bear the losses of urban transport through paying a tax.

On 10th June, 1981, the Provincial Federation of Residents' Associations of Madrid showed its opposition and even attacked the bill as "anti-constitutional".

The reaction was similar all over Spain.

b) Official Chambers of Urban Property Owners

At the end of June 1981, the Chambers of Urban Property Owners together with the Chambers of Commerce protested to the administration and expressed their total disagreement that it should be home owners who would have to bear the deficits of urban transport.

10.2.3. Support for the bill

a) Urban transport operators

All are in favour of a standard method for regulating finance, above all if it establishes technical and administrative conditions giving the possibility of long-term funding such as the polinomial formula for revising fares which set the month of December each year for applying this formula to cover the financial needs of the following year.

10.2.4. Report of the treasury committee of the parliament

10.2.4.1. Amendments

There were two total amendments to the bill - one from the Catalan minority and the other from the Communist party - and 51 partial amendments.

10.2.4.1.1. Catalan minority

This minority claims devolution because the bill does not resolve the problem of Barcelona since it does not include the suburban railway and, what is more, the 0.5 per cent maximum tax surcharge would not cover Barcelona's urban transport deficit.

It is proposed that the path to self sufficiency should be that of improved management efficiency.

10.2.4.1.2. Communist Party

The Communist Party accepts that 45 per cent of the cost, and in exceptional cases more, should be covered by subsidies from the municipality, territorial authority and state with local authorities recording a higher deficit being penalised through the establishment of a scale of tariff coverage starting at 55 per cent, with the local authority contribution falling from 70 to 50 per cent and the state or autonomous region share increasing progressively from 30 to 50 per cent i.e. equal shares for the local authority and state or autonomous region when the tariff coverage reaches 50 per cent.

The local authority contribution would be paid out of the following tax surcharges:

- 30 per cent on residence tax and plus values;
- 20 per cent on the property tax, without tenants being affected;
- 50 per cent on the modified road tax.

10.2.4.1.3. Partial amendments

These can be summarised as follows:

a) Before imposing a tax it must be demonstrated that the deficit does not result from bad management;
b) The law should include the polinomial revision formula;
c) The tax should be imposed for one year only. In the second year it should be the local authority who resolves the problem and if the deficit persists the service should be put up for tender to private firms;
d) The tax should be imposed for a maximum of three years;
e) The tax should cover a maximum of 25 per cent of the cost of the service;
f) There should be a surcharge on company tax and personal income tax to form a national fund asssigned to the Ministry of Territorial Administrtion;
g) The taxable value of premises and shops should be increased;
h) A period of five years should be allowed for imbalances to be corrected and if they still exist after this period the concession should be put up to public auction with the Ministry of Transport fixing fares;
i) A transitional arrangement should be set up through which local authorities whose undertakings are recording losses should receive with respect to the specific deficit in 1980 the following percentages in current pesetas:

```
1980        50 per cent
1981        40 per cent
1982        15 per cent
```

10.2.5. The Treasury Committee's report

The Committee rejected all the amendments and modified the tax base by adding to the utilisation of dwellings that of premises devoted to commercial, industrial,
service and professional activities within the municipal
area. It also included two temporary provisions:

The first stated that "local authorities whose public
urban land transport undertaking whether run by concessionaires or municipal services have recorded deficits in
successive years will receive from the state the following
percentages in current pesetas with respect to the 1980
deficit:

```
1980        50 per cent
1981        40 per cent
1982        15 per cent
```

The second temporary provision states that "the tax
provisions and regulations for municipal taxes will come
into effect from the 1982 fiscal year, so that they should
be approved by the local authorities within two months of
the publication date of the present act, unless an exceptional request for a revision of fares has been made
within the said period".

This report was published in the official journal of
the parliament on 11th December, 1981.

This urban transport financing Act has nevertheless
been removed from the agenda of the plenary session of the
congress five times through lack of parliamentary support.

In view of the difficulties faced by the Act, in
September 1981 the socialist opposition party presented a
new bill, a variant of that presented by the communists,
which may be summarised as follows:

a) It accepts the principle that fares should be
   self-financing and that a polinomial fares revision formula should be used with requests for and
   authorisation of such revisions at the beginning
   of each year;
b) In the exceptional case where fares are not self-
   financing the deficit could be covered by
   contributions from state and municipal resources;
c) If fares cover 60 per cent of operating costs, the
   state will cover 50 per cent of said deficit from
   its general budget;

d) The municipalities will cover the remaining 50 per cent of the deficit through the following procedures:
   - surcharge of up to 50 per cent on the urban land tax;
   - surcharge of up to 25 per cent on fiscal licence fees and property tax;
   - surcharge on road tax up to the legal limits;
   - municipal tax on bank clearings (a newly created tax).
e) 50 per cent of the deficits for the years 1980 and 1981 would be covered in the 1982 general state budget and the other 50 per cent through contributions from the local authorities to whom the local credit bank would grant loans;
f) Municipalities not covering 60 per cent of the cost of urban transport would conclude contract programmes with the state to reach the said level within a period to be determined.

In order to overcome the difficulties presented by the bill, an expert committee was convened and after studying the bill and its predecessors issued the following report, made up of comments and conclusions.

Comments

The tax on dwellings and business premises identifies all the inhabitants of the municipality as being the indirect beneficiaries of urban public transport.

The tax has little flexibility as regards the configuration of its base. As a result it is insufficient in the case of Barcelona.

The bill has not used financial instruments created to support a transport policy favouring public modes.

It is not known how it will fit into the future taxation structure of local tax authorities.

The municipal tax on bank clearings has exactly the same negative features, aggravated in this case because being an indirect tax it has the disadvantage of more opportunities for being passed on, which is very much counter to the basic principle of internalising costs.

Conclusions

1.   The urban public transport deficit has three characteristics:

   a) it is limited to municipal and worker-owned undertakings;

425

b) municipal resources are insufficient to cover it;

c) it has been virtually stable over the last two years.

2. The deficit may be due to the following causes:

a) deliberate municipal policy;

b) disagreement in the process of determining tariffs and other modes of finance;

c) management shortcomings.

The financing system should allow:

a) the existence of a planned deficit;

b) definition of responsibilities in fixing tariffs;

c) establish bases which make it possible for the consequences of inefficient management to be fully assumed so that there is every incentive to correct this situation.

3. The deficit should be covered in the first place at the expense of the municipal budget and therefore with revenue from local taxes. For reasons of equity and efficiency it is accepted that the cost of urban public transport should be internalised at the local level, this coinciding with the area occupied by the direct and indirect beneficiaries. To make this criterion effective, it is necessary to expand and adjust the taxation possibilities of local authorities so that between them tariffs and local taxes ensure the necessary financial cover.

The tax surcharges proposed by the expert committee are as follows:

- 1 per cent on urban rateable values;
- 50 per cent on the present revenue level for road tax;
- surcharge of 1 peseta per litre on gasoline sold within the municipal area concerned;
- increase of 50 per cent on actual licence fees for business and professional activities;
- municipal income tax equivalent to 1 per cent of the taxable incomes of the residents of the municipality.

Actual urban transport deficits and the proposed additional taxes are shown in the following table.

Table 55

Town	Urban surface transport deficit in the last three years			Estimated annual revenue for each of the proposed additional taxes				
	1979	1980	1981	1% on rateable values	50% on road tax	1 pta/litre on gasoline	50% on licence fees	1% on income tax
Almería	33.4	45.5	50.0	36.5	42	18	35.3	
Barcelona	6,905.9	6,828.0	(7,000.0)	880.0	685	298	(580.0)	(6,200)
Burgos	52.3	65.1	65.5	53.2	48	19	127.3	
Córdoba	0.0	154.9	272.0	61.9	114	47	77.0	
Gijón	40.3	40.2	60.6	117.2	83	43	70.3	
Huelva	111.0	141.3	217.5	40.0	42	22	74.9	
Madrid	3,928.7	3,464.8	3,450.0	1,420.0	1,016	641	903.0	
Málaga	215.3	224.6	231.8	167.9	145	84	123.9	
Mieres	20.1	20.3	21.3	6.5	13	6	6.9	
Palma de Mallorca	41.0	64.1	(85.0)	188.0	167	70	103.2	
Las Palmas	264.5	323.6	414.0	87.5	209	-	110.0	
Santander	92.1	55.0	62.9	77.0	52	27	63.7	
Sevilla	375.2	664.9	(850.0)	226.0	206	109	(142.5)	
Valencia	701.2	724.3	(950.0)	328.6	305	129	(200.0)	(660)
Total	12,781.0	12,816.6	13,730.6					

The figures in brackets are estimates.

1. Million pesetas.
2. This figures has been estimated taking into account the whole metropolitan area.

Source: Report on transport financing drawn up by the Government-PSOF Committee.

427

According to the data on deficits and tax revenues:

Barcelona and Seville would have to pay five taxes;
Madrid and Huelva would have to pay four taxes;
Córdoba, Valencia and Las Palmas would have to pay three taxes;
Almería, Burgos, Málaga and Mieras would have to pay two taxes;
Gijón, Palma de Mallorca and Santander would have to pay one tax.

4.   The use of existing forms of tax are recommended before the creation of new ones.

5.   Once the previous point is accepted, the following order is proposed for the choice of indirect beneficiaries considered relevant:

a) tax on the value of urban property;
b) municipal tax on vehicles;
c) unification of existing types of tax such as road tax, fuel tax, parking fees;
d) fiscal licence fee;
e) municipal income tax.

6.   As we saw in conclusion 3, even in such municipalities as Barcelona and Seville the deficit is covered with the application of all taxes.

7.   During the period of transition from the centralised model to that of multiple financing, the support of the Central Treasury is recommended.

8.   This Treasury aid would consist of:

A loan equivalent to the 1980 and 1981 deficit plus a figure equivalent to the 1981 deficit to cover that of 1982.   Interest on this loan would be at the expense of the State and the principal - 39,327 million pesetas - would be the responsibility of the local authorities.

Between 1983 and 1985, the central Government would subsidise transport services to the extent of a certain percentage of the revenues which the local authority would have obtained initially by means of using the tax reserves described above specifically to cover the transport deficit.

Whenever the sum of local authority and State finance does not cover the deficit, the municipality would be obliged to increase its taxes or introduce new ones from the range available to the extent required to cover the deficit.

Transport fares should be eliminated from the concept of official prices.

The local authorities concerned were in broad agreement with this report, describing it as technically good and proposing the following modifications to its conclusions:

Extension of the period of interest-free loans to 1983, the 1983-85 subsidies to be put forward to 1984-86. This would mean increasing the initial loan to 50,000 million pesetas. The loan conditions should be improved (15 year repayment and constant amortization) and the subsidies in the transition period should be 100 per cent for 1984, 66.6 per cent for 1985 and 33.3 per cent for 1986.

As a provisional measure, the Government has granted a loan of 12,000 million pesetas in the 1983 budget to local authorities with municipal or worker-owned undertakings in deficit, although since 6,500 had already been received, the fact is that they will receive only 5,500 million pesetas.

The private firms have requested their local authorities and civil governors for an increase in tariffs according to costs. At the same time they have pointed out to the Government the injustice of using State funds to aid municipal and worker-owned undertakings only.

Conclusions of the study

1. In the group of towns with less than 100,000 inhabitants, urban transport is operated entirely by private firms, but for one single exception. The number of non-private undertakings increases with population size.

Private firms carry out their activities in small and medium towns, though there are important exceptions: Zaragoza, Bilbao, Vigo, Alicante, La Coruna.

2. The average number of inhabitants per bus falls as population increases, from 4,964 inhabitants per bus in towns of under 50,000 to 1,873 per bus in towns of over 1,000,000 inhabitants. It is clear that the need for motorised transport increases with the size of the town.

3. The buses owned by private firms are older than those in non-private undertakings, both overall and within each town size group. The best situation as regards vehicle age is in the municipal undertakings in Madrid and Barcelona and the worker-owned undertakings in Almería and Palma.

4. The percentage of seats with respect to total passenger accommodation is higher in municipal and worker-owned undertakings than in private firms.

5.   Of the total labour force in the sector, 75 per cent
are drivers or conductors, 19 per cent work on maintenance
and 6 per cent in administration.

As the size of the undertaking increases, the number
of maintenance staff increases from 3 per cent in the
smallest firms to 28 per cent in towns of over 1,000,000.

The relative weight of administrative staff falls
with population size from 10 to 5 per cent between the two
extremes.

For the same size of town, municipal and worker-owned
undertakings have a higher percentage of workshop and administrative staff than the private firms.

The total percentage of one-man operation is 88 per
cent, with 93 in the worker-owned undertakings, 89 in
municipal undertakings and 86 in the private firms.

The overall average number of employees per bus is
3.7, with considerable differences between the private
firms who have 2.7 employees per bus and the municipal
undertakings with figures of over 4. This figure increases with the size of firm regardless of the type of
organisation.

The differences are less in the number of drivers per
bus. The annual average is 2.2, with 1.9, 2.4 and 2.3 for
private, municipal and worker-owned undertakings
respectively.

The number of trips per inhabitant per year grows
with population size. The supply of buses per thousand
inhabitants increases with population size and occupation
rates also increase.

6.   The private firms have much higher transport output
per employee than non-private undertakings, the difference
being greater expressed in km per employee than passengers
per employee.

If the output indicators are calculated per driver
the difference between private firms and municipal and
worker-owned undertakings is greatly reduced.

7.   The overall average unit cost of municipal undertakings in 1980 was 1.74 times that of private firms.
Worker-owned undertakings were between the two. Unit cost
per employee in municipal undertakings is almost double
that of private firms. There are two reasons for this:
first, a relatively slight difference of 10 per cent in
labour costs per employee per year and second, more importantly, output per employee is 1.8 times higher in private than in municipal undertakings.

This does not apply to output per driver. It is only 1.3 per cent higher in private than in municipal undertakings. Nothing very definite can be said about productivity, because there is no breakdown of the working day into normal and overtime hours.

8.   From the data in this study it seems that there are clear diseconomies of scale. To analyse this the following variables and ratios have been selected from all those calculated in the study.

    a) number of buses in the undertakings;
    b) population (thousands) served by the undertaking;
    c) total kilometre covered per year by the undertaking.

There is no doubt that all these factors depend on the size of the undertaking and are not influenced by the type of organisation.

Taking cost per kilometre (t) as the dependent variable, we have grouped the private firms on one side and municipal and worker-owned undertakings on the other and for these data have calculated a multiple linear regression using the least squares method, which fits a linear equation:

$$t = a + bx + cy + dz$$

where the coefficients of regression a, b, c and d are calculated using the Gaussian elimination method.

Applying this multiple linear regression fit to the group of private firms and municipal and worker-owned undertakings, with:

t_i = cost/km as dependent variable;
x_i = number of buses;
y_i = population served;
z_i = annual kilometrage per undertaking;

we obtain the following results:

Private firms

$$t_i = 60.43 + 1.35\ x_i + 1.5\ y_i - 0.62\ z$$

R^2 = 0.98 = coefficient of determination
R = 0.989 = coefficient of correlation

Municipal and worker-owned undertakings

$$t_i = 93.67 + 0.64\ x + 0.05\ y - 0.01\ z$$

R^2 = 0.96 = coefficient of determination
R = 0.979 = coefficient of correlation

Results of the multiple linear regression analysis

1.   From the values of the coefficient of correlation, which are virtually 1, it can be seen that there is such a strong linear correlation between the variables that it can be regarded as perfect.

2.   The value of R^2 - coefficient of determination indicates that the total variation of t is completely explained except for 2 and 4 per cent for private and non-private undertakings respectively.

3.   If the independent variables are taken as zero, the constant values are:

Private	Municipal and worker-owned
$K_1 = 60.43$	$K_1' = 93.07$

Which means that "without going out to work" there are costs of about 60 and 93 ptas/km respectively for private firms or municipal undertakings, which is very much in line with the ranges of 5.65/146.10 buses in private firms and 69.5/1,380 buses in non-private undertakings.

4.   The coefficient of regression of the value of the variable x_i (number of buses) has the following values:

- Private firms $t_i = 1.35 \, x_i$
- Municipal undertakings $t_i = 0.64 \, x_i$

Holding the other two variables (population and kilometrage) constant, unit costs per bus increase more in the private firms than in public undertakings, i.e. the number of buses has less influence in municipal than in private undertakings.

5.   The population size has an influence in private firms, its increase being virtually nil in the linear equation fitted to the non-private undertakings.

6.   In both equations, the number of kilometres covered per year does not have any influence on variations in costs per kilometre.

11. REGIONAL TRANSPORT

11.1. Background

At the 44th Congress of the UITP in Dublin, the Regional Transport Committee of this body pointed out the difficulty of defining regional transport, specifying that this term should include "non-urban" transport of a public nature serving passengers outside urban areas.

In Spain, passenger transport is divided into urban and inter-urban and there can be no doubt that regional transport is included in the latter.

11.2. Regular regional transport in Spain

Regular passenger transport is governed by various Acts on the regulation and co-ordination of land transport. The Act regulating motorised transport on main roads confers the nature of public service on any transport carried out for hire or reward, establishes a system of concessions for regular public services on main roads and permits prior official authorisation for occasional services. The Act allows free access to the road transport market, and this has produced an increase in transport supply in this field based on very small firms. At the same time, the Act on the co-ordination of land transport protects rail transport by means of as a rule not authorising regular public transport by road over routes served by rail, concessions in favour of railway managing bodies for those services whose routes do coincide and the possibility of railway undertakings substituting transport by rail for transport by road.

In addition, there used to be a levy on parallel routes which provided for the transfer of certain funds of parafiscal origin collected on top of the road transport fares and transferred to the railway undertaking.

The legal situation described establishes the following conditions:

- Regular lines are operated by private companies, subject to the granting of an administrative concession. Such concessions are of unlimited duration but can be revoked by the state without compensation after 25 years.
- Occasional and special services are also in the hands of private firms who serve tourist traffic or run special services for workers, school children, etc.

11.2.1. Description of regular (regional) road services in Spain

The data describing these services in Spain in 1981 are as follows:

- Number of firms operating bus services   1,431
- Total number of lines   2,715
- Total number of routes, including branches   4,442

433

- Number of buses   10,577
- Total seats available   447,187
- Average vehicles per firm   7.4
- Average seats per firm   333.5
- Number of towns linked by regular services   23,152
- Total population with regular services   30,263,000
- Average seats per vehicle   45.11
- Passengers carried   604,740,117
- Total trips   15,115,600
- Passenger kilometres   11,560 million
- Kilometres covered   439,590,166
- Average passengers per trip   40.01
- Average distance per passenger (km)   16.74
- Receipts per km (ptas)   54.07
- Income per passenger (ptas)   39.30
- Tariff (ptas/passenger/km)   2.292
- Total income (ptas)   23,769 million
- Kilometres per bus   41,560

Staff and ratios:

- Drivers   11,670
- Other employees   16,161
- Employees per bus   1.5279
- Drivers per bus   1.1540
- Kilometres covered per employee   27,201
- Kilometres covered per driver   37,646
- Passengers carried per employee   37,419
- Passengers carried per driver   51,788

12. CLASSIFICATION OF FIRMS

12.1. By number of vehicles

Following the criteria of the Transport Institute,
the firms are divided as follows:

- Small firms: up to 5 buses;
- Medium firms: between 6 and 20 buses;
- Large firms: over 20 buses.

12.1.1. Distribution of lines between small, medium and large firms

Table 56

Number of lines

Number of buses	Number of firms	%	1	%	2	%	3	%	4	%	5	%	6-10	%	11-15	16-20	20
<5	1,028	71.83	818	89.80	165	65.48	32	28.82	3	6.12							
6-20	310	21.66	89	9.65	76	30.16	65	58.55	40	81.63	20	68.97	20	38.46			
>20	93	6.51	5	0.55	11	4.36	14	12.63	6	12.25	9	31.03	32	61.54	11	2	2
	1,431	100.00	922	100.00	252	100.00	111	100.00	49	100.00	29	100.00	52	100.00	11	2	2

12.1.2. Distribution of vehicles according to number of seats between small, medium and large firms

Table 57

Number of seats per bus	Small	%	Medium	%	Large	Total	%
<30	340	22	557	17	889	1,786	16.68
31-50	936	60	1,540	47	2,221	4,697	44.41
>50	285	18	1,173	36	2,636	4,094	38.71
	1,561	100	3,260	100	5,766	10,577	100.00

435

12.1.3. Breakdown of firms according to the number of buses and concessions

Table 58

Number of firms	%	Number of buses	%	Buses per firm	Number of seats	%	Number of lines	%	Seats per bus
223	15.58	223	2.10	1	8,509	1.78	223	8.21	38.16
387	27.04	772	7.30	2	30,992	6.48	430	15.83	40.04
197	13.76	594	5.62	3	24,484	5.13	243	8.95	41.85
140	9.78	560	5.29	4	25,003	5.24	220	8.10	44.65
84	5.87	425	4.02	5	18,631	3.90	141	5.19	43.84
171	11.94	1,307	12.35	7.59	58,100	12.17	350	12.89	44.42
136	9.50	1,936	18.30	14.23	89,041	18.65	493	18.16	45.97
53	3.70	1,467	13.87	27.67	64,867	13.59	294	10.82	44.37
15	1.05	734	6.94	48.93	36,087	7.56	112	4.12	49.16
13	0.91	916	8.66	70.46	42,686	8.94	124	4.57	46.60
4	0.27	344	3.13	86.00	18,160	3.80	22	0.81	52.79
6	0.42	796	7.53	132.00	37,288	2.81	40	1.47	46.84
2	0.14	504	4.76	252.00	22,892	4.79	23	0.85	45.42

This table shows the predominance of small firms in transport concessions. 1,031 firms, i.e. 72 per cent of those holding concessions, have a maximum of five buses and hold 1,257 concessions, or 46.3 per cent of the total, these being operated by 2,574 buses, which is only 24.34 per cent of the total number of buses.

93 firms, or 6.8 per cent of the total, have over 20 buses and control 615 concessions or 22.65 per cent of the total, which are operated with 4,762 buses, or 45.02 per cent of the total.

12.1.4. Distribution according to province

The Spanish provinces have been classified in four groups, according to population:

a) Those with over one million inhabitants, in decreasing order of size: Madrid, Barcelona, Valencia, Sevilla, Vizcaya, Alicante, Asturias, La Coruna, Málaga and Cádiz;

b) Population between 500,000 and one million: Murcia, Pontevedra, Zaragoza, Granda, Las Palmas, Córdoba, Guipúzcoa, Santa Cruz de Tenerife, Baleares, Badajoz, Jaén, León, Tarragona, Santander and Navarra.

c) Population between 300,000 and 500,000: Vallodolid, Toledo, Cuidad Real, Gerona, Castellón Cáceres, Huelva, Orense, Almería, Lugo, Salamanca, Burgos, Lérida and Albacete.

d) And finally provinces with less than 300,000 inhabitants, Alava, La Rioja, Zamora, Huesca, Cuenca, Palencia, Avila, Teruel, Segovia, Guadalajara and Soria.

Total incomes are as follows:

- 50.48 per cent, 11,999 million pesetas for the 10 provinces with over one million inhabitants;
- 32.9 per cent, 7,820 million pesetas for the 15 provinces with 500,000 to one million inhabitants;
- 12.37 per cent, 2,240 million pesetas for the 14 provinces with 300,000 to 500,000 inhabitants;
- 4.25 per cent, 1,009 million pesetas for the 11 provinces with less than 300 million inhabitants;
- 100 per cent = 23,768 million pesetas total income.

It can be seen that 25 provinces account for 19,819 million pesetas, or 83 per cent of the total, while the remaining 25 provinces receive only 17 per cent of the total. 64.22 per cent of the firms operating concessions are concentrated in the first 25 provinces. These circumstances are explained by the great difference in population and population density.

437

Table 59

Type of province	Population (thousands)	Inhabitants per km	Area (km)	Roads (km)	Per capita income (thousand ptas)	Firms	Lines	Buses	Seats	Passengers (thousands)	Income (thousand ptas)
(a)	1,946.3	273.10	8,166.5	3,053.4	392.87	53.2	94.3	424	18,881	31,923	1,199.0
(b)	684.6	110.20	9,743.7	2,708.1	299.00	32.2	57.4	247	11,071	12,775	521,333
(c)	413.8	39.29	13,466	3,698.5	289.34	25.23	44.92	140	6,629	3,532	210,000
(d)	188.2	25.27	10,153	2,582.2	328.58	15.45	25.54	63	2,837	977.6	91,727

438

12.2. Tariff-fixing for regular transport services

In November 1975, the government authorised a polinomial formula for revising the fares of regular road passenger transport services:

$$K = 0.40 \, \frac{A_1}{A_0} + 0.15 \, \frac{B_1}{B_0} + 0.30 \, \frac{C_1}{C_0} + 0.15 \, \frac{D_1}{D_0}$$

where:

A = national labour cost index;
B = index based on the official price for diesel;
C = index of the changes in heavy vehicle prices authorised by the government;
D = index of consumer prices published by the National Institute of Statistics

In addition to this annual tariff revision as a function of the four parameters mentioned, there is in practice an automatic fares increase whenever fuel prices rise.

The government also authorises a tariff supplement for vehicles fitted with air-conditioning.

The polinomial formula for revising this supplement is:

$$K = 0.5618 \, \frac{E_1}{E_0} + 0.1151 \, \frac{F_1}{F_0} + 0.3231 \, \frac{G_1}{G_0}$$

where:

E = index based on the depreciation of the equipment;
F = index of maintenance and repair costs;
G = index based on fuel prices.

Authorisations for fares increases since the publication of the polinomial formulae have been as follows:

Table 60

AUTHORISED TARIFF INCREASES FOR REGULAR TRANSPORT SERVICES

General tariff increases			Increases in diesel prices			
Authorisation	Authorised increase (ptas/km)	Reasons	Authorisation	Price (ptas/l)	Increase (ptas/l)	Per cent
OM 17 Nov 75	0.032(1)	Diesel	OM 14 Nov 75	14.00	1.50	12.00
OM 29 Mar 76	0.21	General costs				
OM 17 Mar 77	0.22	General costs				
OM 26 Jul 77	0.05	Diesel	OM 23 Jul 77	16.70	2.70	19.28
OM 10 Mar 78	0.23	General costs				
O. communicada 11 July 78	0.08	Air conditioning				
OM 18 May 79	0.18	General costs				
OM 18 May 79	0.015	Air conditioning				
OM 9 Jul 79	0.09	Diesel	OM 1 Jun 79	19.00	2.30	13.77
			OM 3 Jul 79	21.00	2.00	10.52
OM 24 Jan 80	0.072(2)	Diesel	OM 7 Jan 80	26.00	5.00	23.82
OM 27 Mar 80	0.255(2)	General costs				
OM 27 Mar 80	0.03	Air conditioning				
OM	0.042	Diesel	OM 6 Jun 80	30.00	4.00	15.38

1. The average tariff for the sector is considered to 1.00 pesetas per passenger/kilometre.
2. 12.43 per cent.
OM = Orden Ministerial (Ministry Order)

The average fare for regular road public transport services between 1975 and 1980 was as follows:

Year	Average fare (ptas/km)
1975	0.957
1976	1.160
1977	1.430
1978	1.660
1979	1.930
1980	2.292

The additional fare for using air conditioned vehicles is at present 0.225 Ptas per kilometre.

12.3. Low-traffic regular services

There is in Spain a very dense network of regular regional services which, as will be seen in the detailed study below, serve areas whose traffic has diminished as a result of the dramatic increase in car ownership and the migration from agricultural areas to urban centres.

This situation is so serious that many firms have decided to relinquish their concessions, thus creating a serious problem for the country, since in addition to passengers, these transport concessions also carried parcels by road.

The government has made provision for aiding such services, defining eligible low-traffic services according to the following criteria:

a) They must be essential for communications between the population centres served;
b) There must be no more than 300 people per route-kilometre over the whole area served, excluding the population of the largest urban area served;
c) There must be no more than 6 vehicles employed on the service.

The advantages are as follows:

- authorisation to reorganise routes, trip frequencies and timetables;
- access to official credit sources for renewing the vehicle stock;
- subsidies for feeder traffic;
- compensation for fare reductions which the concessionaire is obliged to grant because of legal provisions;
- tax benefits in the case of mergers;
- possibility of an annual subsidy based on operating results.

Instead of the above definition of low-traffic services, the National Association of Transport Operators proposed a much simpler one to the government: low-traffic services are concessions or parts of them which do not link provincial capitals or towns of over 100,000 inhabitants and whose route serves a population with an average of less than 600 per kilometre, excluding the population of the biggest town.

This definition greatly simplifies classification and has been used in what follows.

12.4. Classification of regular lines in Spain

In 1980, 2,715 regular service lines with 1,727 branch routes were being operated, but these figures include services of very different natures. For the purposes of the study we have classified concessions in five groups:

Group I.   Normal-traffic regular lines;
Group II.   Low-traffic regular lines;
Group III. Regular suburban lines with 15-30 trips a day;
Group IV.   Regular suburban lines with over 30 trips a day;
Group V.   Regular lines which link towns with railway stations.

The characteristics of each group are described below.

12.4.1. Normal-traffic regular lines

These lines fulfil the condition of linking provincial capitals or towns of over 100,000 inhabitants and the population served along the route averages over 600 inhabitants per kilometre, excluding the biggest town.

Number of lines	146
Average length (km)	101.53
Average trips per year	4,786
Passengers per trip	122.38
Average kilometres per passenger	98.96
Total kilometres	70,947,630
Total passengers	85,514,629

These lines have 89 branch routes and the average length is weighted average of all routes as is the average of annual trips.

Further characteristics of these concessions are as follows:

```
Number of lines                                        146
Number of vehicles                                   1,995
Number of drivers                                    1,987
Number of other employees                              693
Total employees                                      2,680
```

The main ratios characterising these lines are:

```
Vehicles per concession                              13.66
Drivers per concession                               13.60
Employees per concession                             18.35
Drivers per vehicle                                   0.99
Employees per vehicle                                 1.34
Kilometres per driver                               35,562
Kilometres per employee                             26,462
Daily return journeys per concession                     6
Average tariff (ptas per passenger
  kilometre)                                          2.301
```

Costs

The costs of these concessions are as follows:

Item	Total cost (million ptas)	Cost per km (ptas)
Labour	1,906	26.86
Fuel and lubricants	865	12.59
Equipment	44	0.62
Repairs	244	3.44
Sundry	96	1.35
Total	3,156	44.48

The average pay per employee was 711,306 Ptas, including social security.

The total income of these concessions was 3,343 million pesetas or 47.13 pesetas per kilometre.

12.4.2. Low-traffic regular lines

These lines, which total 2,193 with 1,426 branch routes, are those which fulfil the conditions described at the beginning of the section. The data are as follows:

```
Number of lines                                      2,193
Average length (km)                                  44.38
Average trips per year                               2,020
Passengers per trip                                  41.72
Average distance per passenger (km)                  38.95
Total kilometres                               199,707,835
Total passengers                               187,734,992
```

The average length and average number of trips are the weighted averages of main routes and their branches.

The other characteristics are as follows:

Number of lines	2,193
Number of vehicles	3,808
Number of drivers	4,168
Number of other employees	400
Total employees	4,568

Ratios

Vehicles per concession	1.51
Drivers per concession	1.90
Employees per concession	2.08
Drivers per vehicle	1.09
Employees per vehicle	1.20
Kilometres per driver	52,442
Kilometres per employee	43,718
Return trips per concession per day	3
Average tariff (ptas per passenger kilometre)	2.298

Costs

Item	Total cost (million ptas)	Cost per km (ptas)
Labour	3,511	17.58
Fuel and lubricants	2,699	13.51
Equipment	277	1.39
Repairs	326	1.63
Sundry	207	1.03
Total	7,020	35.14

Average income per employee, including social security is 768,744 pesetas.

The income of these concessions was 7,331 million pesetas or 36.71 ptas/km.

12.4.3. Regular suburban lines

Suburban lines are defined as regular lines which link population centres, basically medium and large, with their peripheral areas.

Their main characteristics are as follows:

a) there are a great number of trips per day;
b) the average distance covered is small;

c) in the peak commuter traffic periods there are a great number of extra trips which means that a large fleet of vehicles must be available;
d) a substantial proportion of the route is within the urban area, so that there is a conflict of interest with urban public transport lines;
e) according to the legislation in force in Spain, buses are allowed to carry standing passengers in these areas, so that virtually all the vehicles used are similar to urban buses;
f) the number of trips per day is not the same since services are most frequent on work days from Monday to Friday and are reduced by 30 per cent on Saturdays and 50 per cent on Sundays.

The lines of this type are classified according to the number of trips:

1. Over 30 trips a day;
2. Between 15 and 30 trips a day.

There are a number of short routes which also connect population centres with the periphery, but because they have only a small number of passengers and trips per day, they are included with the low-traffic services.

12.4.3.1. Regular suburban lines with over 30 trips a day

Their main characteristics are as follows:

Number of lines	228
Average length (km)	16.95
Average trips per year	39,342
Passengers per trip	34.03
Average distance per passenger (km)	12.87
Total kilometres	152,096,880
Total passengers	305,316,535

Route length and number of trips are the weighted averages of main routes and branches.

Other parameters, ratios and costs are as follows:

Number of lines	228
Number of vehicles	4,260
Number of drivers	4,764
Number of other employees	2,108
Total	7,216

Ratios

Vehicles per concession	18.68
Drivers per concession	20.89

445

Employees per concession	31.64
Drivers per vehicle	1.12
Employees per vehicle	1.69
Kilometres per driver	31,926
Kilometres per employee	21,077
Return trips per concession per day	54
Average fare (ptas per passenger-km)	2.291

Costs

Item	Total cost (million ptas)	Cost per km (ptas)
Labour	6,551	43.080
Fuel and lubricants	2,541	16.71
Equipment	356	2.34
Repairs	912	6.01
Sundry	851	5.59
Total	11,211	71.73

Average income per employee 907,924 pesetas.

Total income of these concessions 11,886 million pesetas or 78.19 pesetas per kilometre.

12.4.3.2. Regular suburban lines with 15/30 trips a day

The main characteristics are as follows:

Number of lines	116
Average length (km)	17.44
Average trips per year	8.020
Passengers per trip	32.26
Average distance per passenger (km)	12.78
Total kilometres	16,229,850
Total passengers	30,021,426

The length and number of trips are the weighted averages of main and branch routes.

Other parameters, ratios, costs and incomes are as follows:

Number of lines	116
Vehicles	481
Drivers	726
Other employees	283
Total employees	1,019

Ratios

Vehicles per concession	4.14
Drivers per concession	6.25
Employees per concession	8.78
Drivers per vehicle	1.50
Employees per vehicle	2.11
Kilometres per driver	22,355
Kilometres per employee	15.92
Return trips per concession per day	10
Average fare (pesetas per passenger-km)	2.289

Costs

Item	Total cost (million ptas)	Cost per km (ptas)
Labour	783	43.93
Fuel and lubricants	195	12.58
Equipment	35	2.18
Repairs	116	7.25
Sundry	65	4.06
Total	1,114	69.60

Average income per employee 690,239 pesetas.
Total income of these concessions 1,167 million pesetas.
Income per kilometre 72.93 pesetas.

12.4.4. Regular lines linking population centres with railway stations

In this study of concessions these lines are treated separately as we believe that they are of a special nature providing an indispensable social service.

Number of lines	32
Average length (km)	15.06
Average trips per year	2,687
Passengers per trip	13.41
Average distance per passenger (km)	10.06
Total kilometres	866,627
Total passengers	1,153,045

The average length and number of trips coincide with those of the routes because there are no branches.

The other parameters, ratios, costs and incomes are as follows:

```
Number of lines                          32
Vehicles                                 33
Drivers                                  32
Other employees                           0
Total employees                          32
```

Ratios

```
Vehicles per concession                        1.03
Drivers per concession                         1.00
Employees per concession                       1.00
Drivers per vehicle                            1.96
Employees per vehicle                          0.96
Kilometres per driver                        27,144
Kilometres per employee                      27,144
Return trips per concession per day               3
Average tariff (pesetas passenger-km)         2.245
```

Costs

Item	Total cost (million ptas)	Cost per km (ptas)
Labour	19	22.49
Fuel and lubricants	10	12.03
Equipment	0.860	0.99
Repairs	1	1.32
Sundry	0.989	1.14
Total	31	37.97

Average income per employee, including social security 593,750 pesetas.
Total income 36 million pesetas or 40.67 pesetas per kilometre.

12.4.5. Summary of data

From Table 61 it can be seen that:

a) The two types are regular suburban lines which cover 39 per cent of the kilometres, carry 55 per cent of the passengers, run 45 per cent of the vehicles and finally receive 50 per cent of the income of regular lines in Spain.
b) These suburban services which account for roughly 50 per cent of transport output of regular lines are run by 344 concessions or only 12.67 per cent of the total.

Table 61

Type of line	Kilometres	Per cent	Passengers	Per cent	Buses	Per cent	Cost (million pesetas)	Per cent	Income (million pesetas)	Per Cent
Normal traffic	70,947,630	16.12	85,514,629	14.05	1,995	18.80	3,156	14.01	3,343	14.07
Low traffic	199,707,835	45.48	187,734,992	30.85	3,808	36.00	7,020	31.16	7,331	30.85
Suburban > 30	152,096,880	34.56	305,316,535	50.17	4,260	40.28	11,211	49.80	11,846	49.93
Suburban 15-30	16,229,850	3.69	30,021,426	4.93	481	4.55	1,114	4.94	1,167	4.91
Railway feeder	865,627	0.20	1,153,045	0.19	33	0.31	31	0.14	36	0.15
Total	439,847,822	100.00	608,587,758	100.00	10,577	100.00	22,532	100.00	23,763	100.00

12.4.6. Summary of ratios

Table 62

Type of line	Vehicles/concession	Drivers/concession	Kilometres/driver	Average fare (pesetas per passenger-km)	Cost/km (excluding depreciation)	Income/km
Normal traffic	13.66	0.99	35,562	2,301	45.08	47.13
Low Traffic	1.51	1.08	52,442	2,298	35.14	36.71
Suburban > 30	18.68	1.12	31,926	2,291	71.73	78.19
Suburban 15-30	4.14	1.50	22,352	2,289	69.60	72.93
Railway feeder	1.03	0.96	27,144	2,245	37.97	40.67
Total						

The following conclusions emerge from these figures:

a) The cost per kilometre of regular suburban lines
   is extraordinarily close to that of urban lines.
   A government decree ensures that the fares of regular suburban lines cannot be lower than those of
   corresponding urban lines.
b) The costs of normal and low-traffic lines are
   lower than those of regular suburban lines although here again the concessions with more vehicles have higher costs per kilometre.
c) The difference between costs and revenues amounts
   to 1,200 million pesetas which, together with the
   9,451 million a year required at current prices to
   renew the road passenger transport vehicle stock
   means that this sector is in a serious crisis
   situation.
d) Looking at this situation for the different types
   of concession we find:

Table 63

Type of line	Difference between cost and income (million pesetas)	Annual cost of replacing 10 year old vehicles	Per cent
Normal traffic	187	1,596	11.72
Low traffic	311	3,046	10.21
Suburban 30	675	3,400	19.85
Suburban 15-30	53	384	13.80
Railway feeder	5	25	20.00
Total	1,231	9,451	12.73

It can be seen that on average the 2,715 concessions
cover their costs but by an amount which is on average
only 12.73 per cent of the cost of replacing vehicles at
current values.

e) These average values show the present situation of
   the concessions.

The reasons for this crisis situation in regular
lines area basically:

a) Illegal competition from lines which operate without complying with the obligations of regular
   lines;
b) Competition from legal special lines of a frequent
   and seasonal nature;
c) The development of car-ownership in Spain which
   has been spectacular since 1965;
d) Migration from the country to the town;

e) The lack of protection for regular suburban lines which do not benefit from measures which have been developed in the cities such as bus lanes, etc. There are lines which run 400 trips a day without there being any bus lanes which would enable them to increase their commercial speed. We do not know of a single measure in Spain established to protect regular suburban lines despite the fact that they carry 305 million passengers a year;

f) Finally, we would point out that in order for this sector to cover:

1. costs;
2. depreciation at replacement value;
3. industrial profits of 15 per cent;

the average fare in 1980 would have had to be 3.6852 pesetas per passenger/kilometre instead of only 2.292 although some limitation on variations from this means would be required.

BIBLIOGRAPHY

- Ministerio de Transportes y Comunicaciones
  Libro Blanco

- Direccion general de transportes terrestres
  Memorias y Datos Estadisticos
  Guia

- Instituto de estudios de transportes y communicaciones
  Memoria

- Fenebus
  Asociacion nacional de transportes regulares por
  carretera.
  Asociacion nacional de transportes urbanos.

- Instituto nacional de estadistica
  Anuarios Estadisticos

- UITP
  Informes de la comision internacional de transportes
  regionales

- Comision GOBIERNO-PSOE para estudiar la Ley de
  Financiacion de Transportes Urbanos.

- Los Transportes Urbanos en Espana. Senda-3.

- Jornados sobre gestion y financiacion de los transportes
  urbanos
  Los Transportes Publicos Urbanos en Madrid.
  Juan Claudio del Ramón.
  Los Transportes Urbanos desde el punto de vista de las
  empresas - privadas de transporte. Gonzalo Alvarez
  Arrojo.

MANAGEMENT OF FIRMS
TO SATISFY TRANSPORT NEEDS

URBAN AND REGIONAL PASSENGER
TRANSPORT

Mr. D.W. GLASSBOROW
National Bus Company
London, United Kingdom

SUMMARY

INTRODUCTION

This report will be directed mainly to the problems
of regional passengers since my colleagues will be dealing
effectively with local urban transport problems.

The main management problems of finance and manpower,
however, show many similarities, whether the undertaking
to be managed provides local urban or regional services.
The differences between urban and regional management
tasks are more of emphasis and degree than of kind. It is
probably true, however, that the differences from country
to country for regional transport are greater than for
urban transport. For urban services the size and population density and historical growth of the continuous urban
area has a marked effect on the scale and degree of difficulty of the problems to be tackled in the fields of
finance and labour supply. In the case of regional transport more specific differences of history and geography
are the source of the greater variation in the present
situation from country to country.

Since collective passenger transport services in
most, if not all, of the member countries of the European
Conference of Ministers of Transport have had a worsening
economic foundation in the last twenty-five years, requiring financial assistance to maintain adequate services,
the development of political opinions has had a major influence on the success or otherwise of public transport
operators in maintaining the services the public needs.
In general political attitudes have developed more favourably for urban operators than for regional ones.

1. WHAT IS REGIONAL TRANSPORT?

The term regional public transport service is not easy to define, as a study of reports presented at successive congresses of the International Union of Public Transport makes clear. If the purely local services provided in the main urban areas, on the one hand, and the long distance services provided by national railways, internal air services and road transport, on the other, are excluded, there is left a wide variety of services catering for a great diversity of travel needs. The journeys undertaken on these services vary in length but are typically in the range of 10 to 30 kilometres. Individual passengers may repeat their journeys daily, weekly or monthly or make use of the services only rarely and with no regularity. A particular feature of regional travel is that in many areas the passenger flows are not dense enough to support, on their own, a frequent service and the passenger is obliged to conform to a timetable and adjust his other activities accordingly. This is an important difference from services inside major urban areas which can often be used on the spur of the moment. Since the journey lengths are well short of those which are tiring to the car driver, the use of a car instead of the regional service is particularly attractive.

It is important to draw a distinction between rural public transport and regional public transport, although they have a number of problems in common. Journeys of the length typical of regional transport will normally pass through both town and country. Where the region is mainly urban, the regional service may often be a railway one. Given the journey lengths, there is a need for a journey speed which is only attainable if the distance between stops is greater than is typical of urban bus services or metropolitan railways. In country areas this will often coincide with the needs of rural travellers.

It is this ability of a regional service to cater for the needs of some rural travellers on part of its route which lies behind the desire of some political authorities to have it diverted to serve a small community which would otherwise not be served. This apparently attractive solution to rural transport problems is achievable only at the expense of the travellers on the regional service, and simply encourages them to use private cars instead.

On the other hand it is possible to find routes on which are operated public transport services whose main justification is to provide for short distance local passengers. In other cases the route may be one where the service is primarily one for long distance travel. Regional passengers will find it convenient to use these services if the stops are in the right places. In some instances the economics of the service are improved by its fulfilling the additional role. The situation is, however, much more difficult if a modification of the service to improve it for the regional traveller would reduce the quality of service for the other travellers.

There are to be found in some European countries local railway networks outside the ownership of the national system. The aggregate route mileage of such railways has diminished in the last ten to fifteen years. At one time the operators of these networks thought that their economic and financial problems might be alleviated by replacing some or all of their services by buses. It was clear that operating costs could at that time be reduced and services could be made more convenient to communities which had developed away from the existing railway stations. What was not adequately appreciated at the time was that the replacement bus services were also declining in profitability, being affected by the same social and economic developments that were undermining the basis of other bus services.

Some of these local railway networks carry a substantial volume of freight traffic. This can make a significant difference to the overhead costs which have to be met by the passenger services. It does mean, however, that the managers of these undertakings, though clearly engaged in regional transport, are not in charge of regional passenger transport narrowly defined.

It is clear that nearly every operator of regional services is engaged in transport activities beyond those which meet the needs of regional travellers. It is thus much easier to define the function of a regional passenger service than to identify undertakings whose business is wholly or mainly the provision of such services. Many transport undertakings which are mainly suppliers of urban services also cater for the needs of regional travellers and the national railways in many countries are major operators of such services. Within these undertakings there are however managers whose main responsibility is regional transport and it is possible to identify aspects of the task of such managers which are characteristic of regional transport.

2. REGIONAL PASSENGER TRANSPORT - THE POLITICAL ELEMENT

In any one industry the difficulty of the management task varies from one enterprise to another. The reasons why one is more successful than another include, as well as the ability of the managers, the historical, geographical and political elements in its situation. In the case of regional transport, the main financial problems are made more difficult to resolve because of the political constraints on the courses of action open to the management of the undertakings supplying the services. It may be noted that operators whose main activity was regional transport were relatively successful in the late 1950s and early 1960s when urban public transport and the national railway systems were unable to prevent a serious deterioration in their finances. There remains a widespread belief that regional services ought to be able to manage with much less support than is given to urban services and to national railways.

In consequence of the inability of urban services to make ends meet, large sums are accepted as being needed to support city public transport undertakings - recent events in Great Britain may point to an exception to test the rule. Similarly the long history of railway unprofitability has led national governments both to remove many inherited financial and social obligations from the national railway systems and to compensate them handsomely for those which remain. This practice is now enshrined in EEC Regulation No. II9I/69, which seems to have been applied in a way which guarantees that the forecast total deficits, including losses on their commercial operations, will be covered. It does not appear that there is a disinterested summation of the costs borne by the railway undertakings as a result of the conscious imposition by governments of social obligations.

One of the provisions of the Regulation was that its application would be extended to include other operators of public transport within three years. Little progress has been made towards this end. This has had particular bearing on the position of regional railways not part of the national systems. More generally the absence of a common and consistent political approach to the provision of all public transport services has an all-pervading influence on the manpower and financial problems of the transport managers concerned.

It may be noted that the urban transport undertakings which operate in conurbations often have an advantage over the operator of regional transport services in that the majority of them are effectively owned by the governing authority and in consequence the financial support needed for the continued operation of the services is more or less automatically provided. I will not, however, deny

458

that the professional operators of such undertakings suffer disadvantages from the detailed political intervention and, in some instances, changes of direction which a change in political control can bring. The sufferings of the management of London Transport and their passengers are topical at the time of writing. It should not be thought that London Transport or even Great Britain is alone subject to such problems.

It is nevertheless true that the lack of a one to one relationship between the undertaking and the competent local authority or central government does create particular problems for many regional transport undertakings. It is from time to time suggested that a solution is to restructure the existing transport undertakings in a region so that the areas of their operations coincide with those of the relevant government authorities. This is a course which has obvious superficial attractions, particularly to the tidy-minded. A major condition for the success of such an action is that the existing structure of government in the country concerned is a sufficiently close match to the natural geographic operating areas of the public transport networks concerned.

I also think that there is a great need for national transport policies to take account of the consequences for efficient operation of local services of changes in the structure and composition of the firms engaged in the business. In their Report to the 1979 Congress of the International Union of Public Transport, members of its Regional Transport Commission representing ten European countries stress the consequences of small undertakings being absorbed into larger ones. In that Report Herr Elliger, the Director of the Westfälische Verkehrsgesellschaft of Münster/Westfalen, in particular refers to the need to ensure that employees can take a personal pride in belonging to a new group as they did to the company to which they belonged before it was merged. This will not happen unless positive steps are taken to bring it about. As Herr Elliger points out, the geographical area to be covered by the manager of a regional transport undertaking makes it more difficult for him to meet and know all the men and women in the company than it is for the manager of an urban undertaking with the same numbers of staff but a smaller area of operations.

Some fifteen years ago I argued strongly, and I believe correctly, against a proposal to subject public transport in Great Britain to the straightjacket of a structure of local government which bore no relation to the natural catchment areas for local transport networks. It seemed to me then that the degree of public financial support required by efficiently managed undertakings was small enough not to require such a close identity with the political authority for it to be made available. I also believed that the associated political intervention which such a relationship would bring with it would itself increase the financial support needed to maintain a given standard and quantum of service. I think that the initial performance of the management of the newly created passenger transport executives in Great Britain serves to support my first contention while later experience for most of them confirms the second.

The level of financial support now needed to maintain an adequate service to the public is now much greater, particularly for regional transport. I do not now disagree so strongly with the idea of matching the structure of regional transport with that of local or regional government. I believe, however, that elected local government should exercise very great self-restraint over their desire to intervene in the management of public transport operations and that such self-restraint should be supported by national laws that define clearly and closely the powers of local government to intervene. There is a great need for much better understanding among all concerned of the separate roles of government and management. It is probably better for the line to be drawn slightly in the wrong place than for it to continue not to be drawn.

A particularly harmful form of political intervention in public transport management is in labour relations. It is much to be regretted that this is an area where some large elected local authorities have intervened with serious consequences for the efficient and economic use of manpower in the transport undertaking directly concerned and with wider repercussions for management in other public transport undertakings. Its immediate effect is to give the employees relatively high wages and easy conditions of work at the expense of higher taxation or higher fares for people of the area.

It is right that local or national governments when, as now seems inevitable, they provide substantial financial support to public transport should have some say in the general level of fares to be charged, even if this is confined to setting general criteria for their determination. It is also right that the same authorities should set standards for the scope and quality of the services to be provided. A question of considerably greater doubt is in what detail the government body should intervene with the aim of ensuring managerial efficiency. I myself do not think it possible for government at any level to intervene in management without causing a loss of efficiency.

I believe the right role for government is to seek to regulate operations in the interests of safety and so to provide financial support that fair and equal treatment is given to all operators, national and local railway and bus operators in all areas. Currently most national transport policies fall well short of achieving such a situation.

460

This inequity bears most hardly on regional transport services not provided by national railways.

3. <u>CURRENT ECONOMIC PROSPECTS FOR REGIONAL TRANSPORT</u>

There is little doubt that with a continuation of the current level of financial support within the present framework of government intervention in the travel market regional transport services generally can expect a fall in passengers. Although the long-term rate at which national incomes are growing has clearly slowed down and there will not be a return to the days when oil supplies were expanding at a falling real cost to the user, there still remains scope for an expansion of car ownership and use. The advantage of the private car over public transport is so great for regional travel in general that there are few cases where an improvement in the quality of the service can slow down or reverse a trend towards the greater use of cars.

It is possible to specify advantages to the community as a whole which would accrue from the greater use of public transport in satisfying certain travel needs. It is rare to find cases where this applies to the individual motorist. The use of a car for journeys of the length which would otherwise be performed by regional transport incurs fewer disadvantages in traffic congestion delays and terminal parking problems than are to be faced for local urban travel, while the reduction in journey times and the increase in convenience of not being tied to the public transport timetable is much greater. This is in contrast to the use of public transport on some much longer distance routes where journey times in some cases are reduced and travel fatigue can be less if the car is abandoned. Where this is the case the level of fares can become the decisive factor.

There is little scope for the reduction in the cost of regional transport services other than by the elimination of those services which are provided at a high additional cost to the network. Very considerable reductions in costs have been achieved over the last twenty years by the increasingly efficient scheduling of vehicles and crews, by improvements in maintenance procedures and by the reduction of administrative overheads. More recently service networks have been comprehensively replanned to reduce costs of the peak operations with the minimum loss of passengers. Such steps inevitably bring with them criticisms from some passengers, usually regular daily travellers, who find that the change of a few minutes in departure or arrival times needed to reduce the driver and vehicle complement is a source of unacceptable inconvenience to them.

Changes in the specific departure times of a ten minute interval service cause little trouble. The better regional transport services with headways of thirty minutes or an hour permit little scope for switching without inconvenience to an earlier or later departure when the times are varied by a few minutes. The basic economic reality for regional public transport services is that there are seldom the mass traffic flows which can support a frequent service and there are few routes where throughout journey speeds can be acceptably close to those of the normal car user.

A question which needs to be answered is whether the loss of many regional transport services in the next ten years or so is acceptable on social or economic grounds. If it is not, what steps can best be taken to preserve essential services at the least cost to the community?

The reasons why public transport services are socially necessary have been recounted many times. Some of these reasons relate more to the quality of life in a modern society which people in general expect to be able to enjoy, rather than to the true necessities of life. Others are linked to the provision of education and health services, social welfare and shopping facilities, which have become increasingly centralised to reduce the costs of their provision, such costs excluding the additional travel costs which many have to incur as a consequence of such centralisation.

The need to increase the present level of financial support to regional passenger transport services if the present networks are to be maintained leaves national governments with a number of choices. They can decide not to increase the amount of financial support and thereby increase the numbers of citizens who neither have the use of a car nor of a public transport service. They can decide to reduce the need for public transport by restoring essential facilities to small local communities, maintaining present services in the interim period. They can plan to set up a coarser network of regional transport services with an assured future so that those without cars can locate themselves with access to it, thus making it possible for them to have better services at a lower overall cost in terms of financial support. They can decide to support broadly the existing transport networks, whatever the cost.

Obviously the choices available to government are much less simple than that. The immediate problem for many public transport operators, including those providing regional services, is that they lack any assurance that they will receive the financial support necessary for the maintenance of the services they will be expected to provide. Such is the political and economic environment within which the management of public transport undertakings have to plan their future services.

4. FINANCIAL PROBLEMS OF REGIONAL PASSENGER TRANSPORT

The management of a regional passenger transport service undertaking, like the management of any company supplying goods or services, has to meet the day to day costs of being in business and, if the undertaking is to have a future, also to meet the additional costs of staying in business.

The costs of being in the business of regional passenger transport include paying the wages and salaries of those employed and meeting the related costs which governments impose on employers, buying fuel and other necessary stores and spares for running and maintaining the vehicles and other plant and machinery, paying for postal and telecommunication services, for water supply and heating, official fees for licensing and certifying as safe vehicles and services, meeting insurance premiums or otherwise covering risks, paying the rent or maintenance costs of buildings and paying the taxes imposed by both local and central government.

The additional costs of continuing in business include all the costs related to the assets employed in the business not already listed, such as the servicing and the amortisation of loans, and the costs of renewing or replacing the assets. Vehicles become worn out with use or become obsolete and have to be replaced, buildings in the course of time become unsuitable for continued use, because of their location, because of national legislation concerned with working conditions, because of changes in customers' or management needs. From time to time major expenditure may be required to refurbish them. Stations and workshops may need modification to accommodate new types of vehicle and the related plant and machinery may need to be replaced.

The management and statutory accounts of the undertaking will include provisions for depreciation or amortisation of these assets. Such provisions are conceptually an estimate of the costs which need to be met out of current income if new assets are to be bought as required for the continued operation of the business in future years.

The continual erosion of the value of money by inflation makes annual provisions based on the original costs of the assets concerned and on estimates of their useful lives inadequate to finance the replacement of the assets. A major current problem for management is to estimate the proper provision to make to take account of inflation. The method currently in favour in Great Britain in the accountancy profession still leaves problems for general management.

For a small undertaking which does not buy new vehicles each year, the funds provided in a year of no intake will need to be invested so that they grow in step with inflation if they are to make an adequate contribution to the costs of new vehicles when the time arrives. Where the existing assets have been financed by a loan the provisions need not currently take account of inflation but must be enough to repay the loan when due and to meet the associated interest charges. The decision whether to continue in business then turns on the feasibility of a fares increase to meet the servicing charges on the new loan needed to buy the more costly new assets.

In a larger undertaking which customarily replaces a part of its fleet each year, management is continuously faced with the need to decide whether to replace assets or to use the related provisions to redeem loans or for investment in other activities. The opportunity to make such decisions depends on the undertaking having obtained enough cash from one source or another. This question of the proper provision for replacement is a source of much argument between operators and government authorities when the amount of financial support is being decided.

If management can expect to obtain in the next few years sufficient income from one source or another to meet all expenses properly chargeable to revenue account, they will be justified in setting in hand a capital expenditure programme for the next few years sufficient to maintain the size of the business. They will be able to finance the programme out of the total depreciation provisions provided that these are calculated each year on the current replacement cost. It may be added that the reinvestment each year in new vehicles of the replacement depreciation provisions effectively ensures that the depreciation fund grows at the rate of inflation assumed. The difficulty for management is that a significant proportion of their annual income lies in the hands of politicians who may not continue to accept that replacement costs should rank for financial support.

Some public transport undertakings have inherited from the past a capital debt carrying interest and redemption liabilities which has to be serviced. This can be regarded as a legitimate obligation for a business in a purely commercial activity. It does, however, create serious difficulties for management in the political jungle in which public transport often has to operate.

The above simplified description of the financial task of management in a regional transport undertaking could apply, mutatis mutandis, to most business activities. The special financial problems of public transport lie in the fact that operations are necessarily exposed to political intervention, which intervention is influenced by a variety of public attitudes and expectations. A common feature is the belief that anyone not engaged in public transport could easily manage the business much better.

For regional public transport this can be particularly burdensome. Past experience has led many people to accept it as natural that heavy support should be provided to national railways out of national tax revenues. Equally it is regarded as right and proper for the passengers on city services to bear only a moderate share of the costs of the services, the remainder being charged to the city government or in some cases shared with national taxpayers. In the case of regional transport the relatively small part of the costs not borne by the user in the past has led to the belief that the services can and should be provided in the future with little or no support. If support is needed the national government tends to argue that this is properly a local responsibility, while the local authority claims that it is up to central government to bear at least an equal share of the support required. At a time when cuts in government expenditure are being sought in many countries, the newly discovered needs of regional passenger transport are greeted generally with a lack of enthusiasm and, in some cases, with hostility.

The ever-present source of financial problems for regional transport management is thus the uncertainty whether financial support from government will be adequate first to enable them to meet their budgeted operating costs for the next year and, in the longer term, to enable them to plan their services and their capital expenditure some years ahead with sufficient assurance that their finance from all sources will match their commitments.

There is now a recommended standard form for preparing and publishing the accounts of public passenger transport operators in Great Britain. It is not in practice generally complied with. It is therefore very difficult to obtain comparisons of the degree of public support given to different operators which go beyond broad estimates. At the international level it is doubtful if any reliance can be placed on the figures. There is, however, little doubt that the management of a public transport is highly efficient - or operating in exceptionally favourable circumstances - if on the widest definition of costs it meets 85 per cent of them out of passenger revenues. An operator may be said to be favourably treated if he receives more than 50 per cent of those costs in financial support from all sources.

There are a number of ways in which financial support is made available to operators. It can come through the revenue account by making good losses on individual services or groups of services or the whole of the networks. Compensation for reducing fares to particular groups of passengers can only be classed as a form of support if the

465

compensation is more than the actual loss to the operator from the fare reduction. It can come from the government relieving the operator of some or all of the taxes which he would normally bear, either general taxes applicable to all businesses or taxes paid by that mode of transport in general.

It can come through the capital account, by assistance in financing the provision or replacement of assets, if this is not covered by revenue account support.

A question of importance to management is whether the support is agreed in advance based on forecast needs or paid after the event whatever the out-turn. Capital account support can be provided in advance by grants to meet some or all of the cost of new assets or after the event by taking over some or all of the capital liabilities of the undertaking if it is unable to meet the related charges in full. Revenue account support can be agreed in advance on the basis of forecast results for a future year or a guarantee can be given that the losses for that year will be reimbursed. It will be appreciated that any system of revenue support will include an element of automatic coverage of the loss, to the extent that provisions for depreciation of assets and charges for interest are included in the assessment of the loss.

In principle, the preferred solution for maintaining managerial efficiency is to relieve public transport of its tax burdens. This was the first step taken in Great Britain for regional road passenger transport which received a rebate of tax levied on road users of diesel fuel. This enabled operators to continue the process of cross-subsidy between services, since relief was given whether the services were currently profitable or not. Inevitably the decline in passengers continued until the overall profitability of the operators could not be assured, even with the tax being rebated in full. Relief of the tax became insufficient to prevent a reduction in the size of networks and the frequency of services and an increase in the level of fares in real terms.

Next to be preferred is the provision of grants for the purchase of capital assets. An advantage is that this does not necessarily entail continuous intervention in the affairs of the undertaking; it does not need financial justification to be provided beyond what management must have for its own needs but this does not seem in practice to prevent government from seeking it. Its major disadvantage is that it can encourage manufacturers of the assets to raise their prices. This is particularly likely if the grant is a fixed percentage of the cost of the assets. In some cases governments set design standards which themselves cause an escalation in costs.

A decision by government to take over capital debts of the operator gives immediate relief to management. It usually has adverse consequences for the future relationship between the management of the undertaking and the government authority concerned. It raises the question how the future purchase of capital assets will be financed and it will obviously have been preceded by an investigation of steps the operator might have taken to continue to meet his liabilities, including increases in fares and reductions in services. It will have been agreed that those steps would not have been politically desirable. The scene will, however, have been set for greater intervention in the role of management - even though it may well have been that past intervention was a major factor.

How new or replacement capital assets should be financed is at the heart of the difficulty faced by operators and government authorities in assessing how much revenue support is needed. It would be very helpful if this source of dissension could be avoided. Unfortunately the total relief which could be given from tax rebates, relief of interest and other capital charges and full reimbursement of capital expenditure falls short of what is needed for regional transport operators in general to continue to provide adequate services at an acceptable level of fares. For a large British operator in 1980 full relief of interest charges on its capital debt, full rebate of road fuel duty and external grants to meet in full the necessary provision for replacing its assets would have covered only some 15 per cent of its costs including such charges.

There is, in my view, no way of escaping from the need to go beyond general tax reliefs, capital grants to cover the full costs of replacement of assets and the removal of inherited capital liabilities if adequate regional public transport services are to be provided at reasonable fare levels. Given that the political will exists - which is not always the case - this still leaves considerable scope for disagreement between the operator and the relevant government authority.

First of all, what should the level of fares be? Since the short-term elasticity of local transport fares is low - according to most estimates it is of the order of -0.3 - there is usually scope for reducing any loss by increasing fares. Certainly that is the likely immediate effect. In some areas the local authority may wish to keep down fares for political reasons. In others the local authority may ask for fares to be raised against the commercial judgement of the operator in order to reduce the financial support needed. Little has been done to determine objectively what is a socially desirable level of fares. It is obviously difficult to derive suitable criteria for general application.

Another problem area is determining the proper size
and density of the network and the frequency and timing of
the services. No public transport network can be equally
convenient to all users and it is a matter of judgement to
decide whether a reduction in inconvenience to a group of
passengers justifies the additional cost of the change in
the service to the community as a whole. There will always be a tendency for the political power to argue that
the operator is exaggerating the costs of any change the
politicians want.

From the point of view of the public the support
given to public transport operators should be provided in
such a way that the risk of reducing efficiency is
minimised. The operator, looking at the other side of the
coin wants the support to be given in the way which imposes on him the least additional burden of negotiation
and of attempted outside interference in the proper role
of management. There is a sense in which managers and the
public have the same aim.

It is, however, inevitable that the political desire
to minimise the cost of financial support will generate,
from time to time, claims that the operator is inefficient
and that by better planning of services and better management of staff and vehicles, including a reduction in the
number of administrative staff, the financial results
would be better.

It is, of course, one of the duties of elected members and their officials to ensure that money raised in
taxation is no more than is needed. It is, however, inevitable that their efforts to satisfy themselves and the
electorate in this respect will place on the public transport manager and his financial staff in particular an
additional burden, making them use up time and effort
which is needed for running the business. If he does not
then add to his establishment, other management matters
will be neglected and efficiency will decline. If he does
recruit more staff, additional costs are unavoidable.

It is, therefore, the responsibility of both the
political authority and the management to ensure that the
procedures for carrying out this public audit restrict its
scope to the essential minimum. This can be made more
difficult if the members of the political authority
believe that they are capable of managing a public transport service. There is no a priori reason to believe that
the background training and experience of elected members
or their officials gives them this ability. They should,
however, be able to judge whether the manager has the
political arts and the dedication to public service which
are needed in addition to his professional expertise.

Public transport management thus needs today to be
able to provide financial information in a way which gives

the political authority all the facts it can reasonably require without inviting interference in the management of the business. The manager also needs to be able to show that he is in touch with changing passenger needs and is capable of responding to these by quickly and economically replanning the services.

Passenger survey and service planning techniques which are not expensive are now well-established for the simpler case of high frequency urban operations. The cost of surveying passenger movements in towns where large numbers of travellers have similar origins and destinations is not high in relation to the likely fare revenues. There are well-tried applications of computer programmes for the efficient scheduling of vehicles and crews to high frequency services on urban routes.

In the regional scene the problem is often more difficult. First, the passengers are more scattered and have a greater variety of travel needs and destinations. The proportion of passengers and potential passengers which has to be surveyed becomes much higher. Secondly, it will be rare for a driver or vehicle to be allocated to a single route, if an adequate part of their time available is to be usefully employed. It may also be necessary for a route to be shared between two depots and a change in this share can have repercussions for the whole network.

The cost and difficulty of using computer-based techniques is therefore much greater for a regional transport operator and the result of having to make simplifying assumptions if they are to be used at all is that they provide solutions which are more expensive to use than those produced by more traditional methods. The use of computer systems is even less advanced for the replanning of networks of services directly from the information about passenger origins and destinations.

Data about actual passenger carryings on individual services on a route has become increasingly expensive to obtain, partly because the traditional methods of analysis are very labour-intensive and partly because the increase in use of pre-paid tickets and a variety of multi-journey and multi-route and season tickets have made the analysis of ticket issues unsuitable for the purpose. Such data will be needed both by management and by the political authority. It is fortunate that the use of micro-computers on vehicles for recording ticket issues and for validation of pre-paid tickets and passes of all kinds now makes it feasible to have this information at an acceptable cost. This can form part of an integrated data processing system using common codings throughout the business. By the use of such a system management can promptly have the basic data for decisions about services and the likely results of such decisions.

There is a widely held belief that it is possible to calculate the costs of a bus service within sufficiently narrow limits for it to be possible to say whether it is profitable to operate it or not. Many political authorities find it difficult to accept that this is not the case. Most systems of costing for public transport services are founded on apparently reasonable allocations of costs which are overhead to the business or common to sets of services or sets of routes or to a number of depots. For example it may appear reasonable to apportion the cost of a driver between services in proportion to his driving time on each of them. There is, however, no reason to suppose that these allocations of costs provide a close approximation to the effect on the total costs of the business of not running the service and replanning the residual network in the most efficient way. In the case of regional transport services, the proportion of the total costs of the business which are common to several services is generally high and the margin for error is wide. In consequence the use of a costing system which involves the full allocation to individual services of costs that are common to the whole network will produce figures that are usually misleading. On the other hand, if the immediately avoidable costs of a service are alone brought into the reckoning, very few individual services of a network will appear to be unprofitable.

It is possible that the time is approaching when it will be feasible to provide a manager with a financial model of his business so that the revenue consequences and the cost consequences of any change in the service provided can be forecast with sufficient precision at minimal cost. This will undoubtedly require the use of a high capacity computer system. It will be the task of the financial manager of the regional transport undertaking to introduce such a system. He will need to be able to collect and process data for all management purposes and ensure that the figures provided are compatible. In doing so he will have to get rid of many traditional practices and attitudes. Although the hardware and software currently available is not as trouble free as the suppliers will suggest, the costs of installing such systems are continuing to fall and their reliability and running costs have greatly improved. There is little doubt that capable and confident financial managers will in the end succeed in giving management and the political authorities the required basis for their decisions.

Even though it should become easier for the management to provide the political authority with an estimate of the revenue and cost consequences of their choice of the networks which they believe the public requires, this will only remove one of the causes of friction. Proper financial discipline will be promoted only if the financial support needed is assessed in advance and some means needs to be found for establishing the proper fares level

and structure. Once it is accepted that a large proportion of the costs will not be borne by the passenger it is
no longer appropriate to base the fares on the costs of
the services. There is a need to develop other criteria
which can command public acceptance.

Since manpower is such a large factor in determining
the costs of public transport, the political decision to
support public transport has a major impact on the relationship between management and labour in regional
passenger transport.

5. LABOUR PROBLEMS OF REGIONAL PASSENGER TRANSPORT

Relations between management and labour in all sectors of industry are greatly influenced by history. For
regional passengers the inheritance from the past is on
the whole a beneficial one.

These benefits come from the nature of the services
in regional transport, which requires the individual to
act much more upon his own initiative than in many other
transport businesses and in other sectors of industry.
They are also the result of the traditionally small size
of the undertakings. It is also important that profits
have never been easy to earn in regional transport, compared with the urban operations of the 1950s. These
aspects of the relationship between management and staff
are well described in the Report to the 43rd Congress of
the International Union of Public Transport, entitled Man
in Regional Public Transport: Evolution and Perspectives.

Also in that report reference is made to the increasing problem of management, as small undertakings have been
merged in response to the movement of political opinion to
favour large transport communities, which far exceed in
size and geographical area the typical regional transport
undertaking. Only by a deliberate policy of appointing
high quality managers to local operating units and consciously giving them large responsibilities and effective
authority is it possible to overcome the disadvantages of
large size. Even so, once a large organisation has been
created, the political pressures from outside upon the
central directing body to intervene in local management
are not always resisted.

Good local labour and management relations depend on
the belief that the local manager has the authority and
the desire to exercise it, so that all grievances, well-
founded or not, can be and are promptly dealt with. All
restrictions on his freedom of action from outside either
directly or through the management line are potentially
harmful; there can be some occasions when they can be used
to support a decision.

In all industries questions of pay and hours of work are the major issues, brought into even greater prominence by continued inflation and by expectations of higher living standards. The desire of some national governments to limit inflationary pay settlements generally and to use direct action in the case of public employees is a constraint on regional transport managers in perhaps the most important aspect of their managerial role.

There is, furthermore, the possibility that the local authority which provides the financial support will wish to intervene in wage settlements, in view of the very important effect that such settlements have on the costs of the operator and hence on the amount of financial support needed. Intervention by the political authority is equally harmful whether the power is in the hands of a party of the left or of the right - or of the centre.

Reference may be made to the suggestion which has been put forward, apparently seriously, that bus operators should be required to return to two-man operation, on the grounds that this would be a means of giving employment to some of the unemployed at no great cost to the community since the increased costs of the operator to be borne by the taxpayer would be largely offset by the reduction in direct payments to the unemployed. It may well be that the quality of service to the passenger can be improved substantially on some services by the restoration of the second member of the crew. I myself believe it was a mistake in Great Britain when urban services were converted to one-person operation before suitable ticket issuing systems were introduced to avoid increased delays at picking-up points. Nevertheless management efforts to improve productivity and efficiency would be undermined by such action by the political power to conceal the existing level of unemployment. This is an extreme example of a problem management might face as a result of political intervention.

As has been mentioned earlier, the importance of excessive size of the undertaking as a source of staff problems cannot be stressed too greatly. If a change is made throughout the undertaking which produces unsatisfactory results in one area and the area manager has no authority to put it right, the local staff will tend to regard the area manager as a nonentity and the remote top manager as a fool. It may be that for all other areas the central decision is perfectly logical, but the necessary respect for the competence of management is weakened.

Currently it is fashionable to talk about the unsocial hours which public transport employees have to work and to put this forward as a justification for a relative increase in their wages. The difficulty of recruiting staff willing to work such hours in regional transport is often exaggerated and those who are attracted by a pay

472

differential alone do not stay for long. Those engaged in regional transport have always had to work such hours and the longer serving employees seem to prefer the varying shifts needed to cover the needs of the public. Public transport managers who are temperamentally suited to the job do not complain about the long and irregular hours of work required - and their families come to accept the situation.

It is of course true that the contrast between the weekly hours of operation of public transport services and the normal week in the manufacturing industry has been enhanced in recent years with the widespread introduction of the five day week and the shortening of the working day. This has also had an impact on the demand for public transport as the times of the journeys to and from work have changed. Equally the changes in social habits have greatly reduced the demand for public transport in the evenings and at weekends. Many public transport employees are quite content to work at times when the majority of the population are at leisure and their services are needed. It is, however, quite another matter if they are running services at those times and carrying hardly any passengers.

So long as the community expects public passenger services to be provided at such times for very few and widely scattered passengers regional transport managers have to find ways of dealing with this problem. A variety of different ideas for providing evening services have been developed. Most of them require a departure from the practices which have been agreed with the staff over a long period of years and are still appropriate to the operation of the full daytime services on normal working days. If management and staff are allowed to get on with the task of agreeing the new arrangements without the hindrance of well-meaning offers of assistance from others, this will be achieved sooner rather than later.

Among the difficulties faced by management in their task of maintaining and improving the effective use of manpower in regional transport are the regulations to control the working hours of drivers. The only justification for such government control is to ensure that safety standards are adequate. There is however no evidence that the reductions in the permitted hours of driving in EEC countries in the last twenty years have been needed for safety reasons. The flagrant cases of excessive hours have been in breach of all the limits which existed. The regulations tend to be so tightly drawn that they make it impossible to cover the needs of the public, particularly for morning and evening travel during the normal working week, and at the same time to schedule efficiently the working time of the drivers employed. The existence of these regulations unnecessarily restricts the scope for new agreements between management and unions, since there

is no point in reaching an agreement, however sensible
from the point of view of efficiency, safety, economy and
satisfaction for the driver, if it would only be legal to
work if the regulations were to be changed.

Both management and staff face an increasingly troubled future from the increase in vandalism and violence to
staff. Regional transport, often operating in areas where
and at times when police and public-spirited citizens are
not easily to be found is particularly vulnerable. The
installation of two-way radio systems so that help can be
summoned is less effective if the nearest help is at least
ten minutes away. The development of systems of fares
with a large element of pre-payment can reduce the sums of
money carried on the vehicle and make theft a less likely
motive for an assault on a driver. Management and staff
are taking all the steps within their own resources to
cope but in the end it is for society as a whole to tackle
this social evil and enable public servants to do their
job in reasonable safety.

In most of regional public transport there remains a
good tradition of mutual respect between managers and the
rest of the staff. Provided that good communications are
maintained inside each undertaking and political intervention in management is successfully resisted, this tradition can be kept alive and well. This requires a conscious effort to limit the size of the operating units, to
handle any amalgamation with this in mind and to maintain
local management autonomy. If this is achieved, the only
serious labour relations problems will be due to a failure
of the public to provide through their elected representatives the level of financial support needed to keep in
being the services the public regards as socially
necessary.

6. ENVIRONMENTAL AND ENERGY CONSIDERATIONS

This report has reviewed the situation of regional
public passenger transport with particular reference to
financial and manpower problems, on the assumption that it
will be unacceptable on social and political grounds for
such services to disappear, perhaps an insecure assumption. History does not suggest that governments are as
concerned to conserve regional transport as they are to
keep in existence urban services and the national railways. Certainly in many countries much larger sums have
been provided to support the latter than to help keep in
being regional services, taking account of the relative
sizes of the operations. Indeed the continued existence
of many regional networks is the result of two factors,
good management and the protection provided by licensing
systems. The latter have enabled many services which

would otherwise have been withdrawn to be supported by cross-subsidy.

Regional transport undertakings would find it impossible to maintain networks of services without greatly increased direct financial support if the opportunity to cross-subsidise were to be removed by changes in or the abandonment of licensing. It is difficult to obtain figures showing the general importance of cross-subsidy; one or two studies in Great Britain have indicated that it may provide some three or four times as much to keep the services as is provided by direct support. This ratio may be unfair to passengers on the profitable services but it would seem foolish to give it up entirely. Once a method is found for determining what is an equitable level of fares its application would also deal with the equity of cross-subsidy in a broad sense.

The social needs of people without cars do not make up the whole case for supporting public transport services. It is argued with considerable conviction that without public transport cities would be unable to function. It may not be true that the growth of car ownership makes it necessary to subsidise public passenger services in and into cities, but in many countries it appears to be politically more acceptable to do so, rather than to seek to limit the use of cars on urban roads by a combination of price and regulation.

It is more difficult to see what justification there is for subsidising national railway passengers, other than those on railway services which perform a regional or urban function. The case on environmental grounds of increased road congestion seems weak. The wider case for keeping in being national railway systems on energy conservation grounds - and ultimately as an insurance against the exhaustion of fuels suitable for road transport - is questionable. It may be remarked that financial support for railways at its present level is hardly a cost effective means of conserving energy. The predominance of road transport in most European countries suggests furthermore that the insurance cover provided is far from adequate.

The case for preserving regional passenger transport on road congestion or energy conservation grounds is a very uneven one. It varies widely from one area to another. Qualitative judgement would suggest that it is not negligible. The potential direct contribution of regional transport to energy conservation may not be large, because fuel consumption rates for road vehicles outside the major built-up areas are relatively low and in total energy consumption for regional travel is probably a small part of a country's energy needs. A transfer from car to bus does not reduce petrol consumption as much as a similar transfer for a short distance urban journey.

Increases in the real price of diesel fuel would not cause severe problems for regional passenger services. The cost of fuel is a very small part of the cost of running a regional service and would be offset by a small rise in load factor, quite likely in a period of rising petrol prices. Growing fuel supply problems need not be a hindrance to greater use of regional services. Experience has shown that difficulties in obtaining petrol rather than its price is the cause of a switch to public transport for some journeys.

The main uncertainty for regional passenger transport management is the political one. Once that has been resolved it will be possible to achieve a financial balance at an agreed level of service. There is no reason to believe that manpower problems more difficult than those which have to be faced by employers generally will be encountered provided political interference in management can be resisted. There are good grounds for believing that national transport policies should include the provision of support for public transport and there is no reason for excluding regional passenger services.

MANAGEMENT OF FIRMS
TO SATISFY TRANSPORT NEEDS

URBAN AND REGIONAL PASSENGER
TRANSPORT

Dr. W. PÄLLMANN
Hannoversche Verkehrsbetriebe (ÜSTRA)
Hannover, Germany

SUMMARY

1. INTRODUCTION

Urban and regional public transport has become an essential part of the infrastructure of our towns and communities. Its significance has considerably increased in recent years as a result of greater public awareness of environmental problems and the critical energy situation. In towns, and particularly in town centres, public transport is the main factor enabling the area occupied by private cars to be kept within limits; it creates the necessary conditions for developing large, integrated pedestrian precincts and reduced-traffic residential areas without jeopardising the operability of the urban structure. Public transport also performs essential tasks for the community as a whole: even in countries with high car ownership levels, well over half the population does not or does not at all times have access to a car. These people rely on public transport to meet their mobility requirements. In rurally structured areas in particular, the character of the public transport services is an important factor in determining the quality of life. There, admittedly, the centralisation that is nearly total in many spheres and on all planes has quite definitely brought many advantages, but on the other hand it has also caused in some cases considerable difficulties for many citizens in such matters as reaching community and recreation facilities or even meeting their daily needs.

The close connection between public transport and housing patterns has naturally always existed. So long as public transport operation and its economic framework was to a large extent automatically regulated by supply and demand, there were no particularly significant problems for the management of public transport undertakings. The picture changes completely, however, if the self-regulating mechanism of the market is judged - and that judgement depends on historical, social, economic or aesthetic standpoints vis-à-vis the town and its functions - not to be running properly. All the basic influences affecting the town and its components also affect public transport; major changes in the social and economic environments inevitably affect public transport.

All this is admittedly not new, but it is extremely topical. The public till is empty, environmental pollution is verging on the intolerable and energy is costing more and even too much for many, and is sometimes even scarce. Public transport is now more or less directly

479

affected by all these factors and there is little likelihood that this will change in the foreseeable future. The range of tasks facing the management of public transport undertakings and possible approaches to a solution can be seen very clearly from the current situation. So long as there are no difficulties, managing any kind of enterprise is relatively easy. It is only when serious problems have to be overcome that the essence of management tasks and whether or not a particular approach is right become apparent.

2. <u>CASE STUDY - HANNOVER</u>

I have not chosen the example of Hannover to explain some selected aspects of modern public transport management simply for the obvious reason that it is the example I know best; quite generally Hannover seems to me ideal as an illustration of public transport management problems and opportunities. The town is known far beyond its own regional boundaries for being skillfully planned and having a comprehensive system of community facilities. The town is associated with the name of Rudolf Hillebrecht, one of the most important urban planners of the period after World War 2. The main public transport undertaking in the Hannover area is the Hannoversche Verkehrsbetriebe AG, known as ÜSTRA, an abbreviation of its earlier name Uberlandwerke und Strassenbahnen AG". ÜSTRA was the last big private tram and bus undertaking to operate in Germany (up to 1970). In its 90-year history this company went through all the stages of technical and organisational development characterising public transport in large towns.

With its 1.1 million inhabitants, Greater Hannover is one of Germany's large conurbations: it has a distinctly monocentric structure and covers an area of about 2,300 km^2. About 50 per cent of the population of Greater Hannover live within the boundaries of the Land capital itself (the central area), about 20 per cent in the peripheral area and the remaining 30 per cent in the outskirts at a distance of about 15 to 30 km from the centre. The distribution of jobs is roughly 75 per cent in the central area, 10 per cent in the peripheral area and 15 per cent in the outskirts. This typical imbalance in the distribution of homes and jobs creates the commuter traffic which largely determines the pattern of public transport in Hannover.

3. <u>THE POLITICAL DIMENSION</u>

Although trams and buses had long held an important place in Hannover town life, until the very recent past

contacts between the transport undertaking and the local
authority had been confined to a few technical traffic
questions and financial matters. Whereas elsewhere the
changeover to de facto absorption of urban transport by
the local authority has been a largely smooth and progressive process, the time of the event in Hannover can be
pinpointed exactly.

In 1969, the ÜSTRA had to increase its fares again in
order to be able to meet expenditure. Surprisingly enough
the company was still operating more cheaply than most of
the other transport undertakings which had long been receiving government subsidies, but this time the normally
placid and not easily provoked Hannovarians nonetheless
took to the streets. The fare increase was probably just
the last straw after a long period of irritation caused by
a certain indifference on the part of the local authority
towards public transport and the consequences of that indifference. In any event, there were day-long blockades
of urban transport, scuffles with the Land police, mobi-
lisation of voluntary private transport associations in
the form of "Red Spot Action" and much more. The demon-
strations and actions in Hannover set a precedent and many
similar events followed all over Germany. Ever since,
urban transport has been a central topic of local government policy in Germany, and rightly so in my opinion.

In Hannover, ÜSTRA as it then was and the town authorities had to merge and at last make public passenger
transport their common concern. The town immediately
bought out the carrier, set politically acceptable fares
and covered ÜSTRA's shortfall in income by subsidies from
the town's tax revenue. Responsibility for urban transport policy decisions was thus transferred to the town
- but not for long. Since the ÜSTRA transport network was
of importance for the whole Hannover area, it was only
natural to hand it over to the "Greater Hannover Association" (Verband Grossraum Hannover), a political and administrative body created a few years earlier covering the
whole area. In 1970 the Association acquired ÜSTRA and in
1971 made it a subsidiary of the "Versorgungsund
Verkehrsgesellschaft Hannover mbH". Another event in 1970
was the setting up of "Grossraum Verkehr" - a transport
corporation covering all the urban and regional public
transport undertakings in the area. It was in fact the
second largest transport corporation of its kind in
Germany after Hamburg. Public transport services in virtually all German conurbations are now controlled by such
corporations and organisational structures suitable for
country areas are now being tried out.

The age of more or less independent private enterprise public transport policy was thus definitively over
in Hannover. Instead of a small number of carriers making
largely independent decisions there is now a complicated
structure of local politicians, undertaking managers and

administrative experts. The problems of such structures are familiar. They have become an important part of the activities of those responsible for urban transport services and this is not likely to change in the foreseeable future. The close liaison with and firm implantation in the local government scene now accounts for a good 50 per cent of management time. Obviously it does not always seem that the time is employed usefully and effectively enough. One often wishes that decision-making processes could be shorter and organisational structures simpler.

Thus there may now and again be some hankering after the "good old days" of largely independent decision-making; but this is no longer compatible with the nature and function of public transport in the German Länder. An urban transport manager's role is now and will in future be determined by the tensions between the partly contradictory tasks of running a business undertaking and being responsible for one of the essential facilities provided by the local authority; he has to be capable of both business and political thinking and the more he succeeds in harmonizing these two basically contradictory tasks the better he is at the job. Now and for the foreseeable future he is in fact in a relatively advantageous position, as some important problems with which local authorities are having to contend argue in favour of public transport. Summarised, these are: the space requirement of the motor car, environmental pollution, energy problems.

Priority for public transport has been an undisputed objective of all local government planning activities in Germany for many years already. Under the pressure of the most recent developments, promoting public transport is now also a focal point of Federal Government transport policy statements, even though under the German federative constitution urban public transport is in principle the concern of local government. The Federal Government is involved only to the extent that the Federal railways and post office themselves provide local transport services.

Needless to say, the formulation of objectives and basic transport policy statements alone do not achieve much in local government programmes. At best, they provide a useful platform for implementing measures in accord with those policies. Implementation itself requires continuing activity at all levels, ranging from the lowest local planning level to the Federal or national level.

One of the most important tasks of the urban transport manager is and will be personally and directly to promote, through transport associations and political representatives, the interests of his own undertaking and of local passenger transport generally and tenaciously to force through his own ideas in the power game of interests. It would amount to criminal neglect of duty simply to live in the pious hope that the intrinsic good of public transport will prevail in the end because of the magnanimous understanding of the representatives of conflicting interests. The financial situation of urban and regional transport undertakings in Germany could be improved by tough negotiation at Federal level to win relief in such forms as:

- compensation for public transport services of benefit to the whole economy (e.g. Federal Railways local services);
- compensation for transport in the education field, for the benefit of the whole economy;
- compensation for the free transport of the severely disabled;
- tax relief (turnover tax, road tax; fuel tax, unfortunately this relief has again been reduced as from 1981).

A particularly important and again topical example of the need for active involvement far beyond the direct context of the individual undertaking is the present debate in Germany on Federal investment aid under the Law on the Financing of Local Transport (Gemeindeverkehrs-finanzierungsgesetz - GVFG).

In 1961 the Federal Government set up a committee of experts to work out principles and measures for the future structure of transport in towns and communes. The report produced in 1964 ended with a number of practical recommendations aimed equally at Federal, Land and local governments, industry, transport undertakings and even the individual citizen as a transport user. Improving public transport was one of the main priorities. It was established that the existing problems were not to be solved without considerable construction work at the local level. An appeal was made to the different levels of government to work together to make the necessary resources available.

The Federal Government subsequently accepted its share of responsibility for implementing the required measures. A new source of finance was created by an amendment to the tax laws whereby fuel tax was increased provisionally by 3 Pfg/l and the extra tax yield earmarked for transport infrastructures at local level. At first 40 per cent was allocated to urban and regional transport. Eligible projects were almost exclusively fixed metro and S-Bahn installations. It then took protracted and tough negotiations between Federal, Land and local governments - with the not inconsiderable involvement of urban transport operators - before the GVFG came into force in 1971 and the law on transport financing in 1972. The public transport share was raised in steps from 40 to 50 per cent and the Länder were given permission to redirect first 10 then 15 per cent of their road fund appropriation to public transport investment measures. About

6 Pfg/1 of fuel tax revenue is now made available for these purposes. In addition, Federal participation in eligible measures has been increased from 50 to 60 per cent and the list of eligible measures has been enlarged.

Since that time an annual average of DM.1 billion of GVFG funds (DM.1.3 in 1981) has flowed into urban and regional public transport investment. By 1981, Federal, Land and local governments and transport undertakings had invested about DM.25 billion to improve local public transport. This would not have been achieved without the superhuman efforts of leading figures in public transport undertakings.

Today the much-discussed changed economic and social conditions give further grounds for the persistent defence of the interests of public transport in this connection in order to ensure that the required investment resources will be made available by the authorities in sufficient quantity.

Under the pressure of drastically increased oil prices, consumption in Germany has fallen substantially in recent years. This in itself is certainly to be welcomed, but as a result of the direct connection, under the GVFG, between oil consumption and investment resources, the planned financing of certain projects is now at risk. Hence the paradoxical situation that, at the precise moment when energy policy calls for the development of public transport, the necessary investment resources are becoming scarcer. This fixed connection still applies although it goes back to a time when the energy situation was fundamentally different. It may seem entirely logical that account should be taken of the changed situation, but it is by no means obvious that this will automatically happen, not least because there is after all an important sector of the economy involved, i.e. municipal road building with its own jobs and perfectly legitimate interests to defend. Once again therefore intensive effort is needed on the part of urban transport undertakings, and above all the personal commitment of management. In this connection, at its 1981 annual conference, the Association of Public Transport Undertakings (Verband öffentlicher Verkehrsbetriebe - VöV) made a number of proposals to the Federal Government for improving the financing of urban public transport projects. It requested, for example, that:

- at least 1 Pfg/1 of fuel tax revenue should be additionally earmarked for GVFG resources;
- the GVFG allocation scale should be altered substantially in favour of public transport;
- the possibility of transfers from road building to public transport should be considerably enlarged.

The question of extending the list of eligible investment is also being discussed. Inclusion of operating control systems seems to be imminent and assistance with rolling stock investment is also in the air; so far only the Länder have committed themselves, and to very differing extents.

Each business has a wide range of possibilities and requirements in the defence of its own interests; a basic task of public transport management today is to take advantage of those opportunities to build maximum stability into its own basis.

4. OPERATION

Within the general external context of public transport, but which public transport can itself influence, the manager of an urban transport undertaking must strive to exploit every public transport possibility and opportunity that will benefit his town and the transport business he runs.

The emphasis in promoting public transport has so far been on building rail-based rapid-transit systems in large towns and conurbations. Hannover with its pre-metro system comes under this category. The planned extension of the Hannover pre-metro network meant an investment between 1965 and 1981 of about DM.1 billion on infrastructures (tunnel in the town centre, new permanent way, interchange facilities) and stations and about DM.300 million on rolling stock. For the next few years the estimated annual investment will be about DM.130 million for further track and DM.30 million for rolling stock, i.e. a total of about DM.160 million. After allowing for the Federal and Land contributions, ÜSTRA still has to find about DM.50 million a year. To be able to shoulder this financial burden, the ÜSTRA has had to increase its capital in stages from DM.24 to 132 million over the past few years.

This kind of development and such expenditure is of course only possible and politically feasible if the investment produces tangible results. The undertaking will have the necessary economic staying power only if the investment pays off in terms of increased traffic and hence increased income. Finally, the subsidising authorities can be persuaded to continue only if the investment concerned as far as possible continually produces direct results. Particular attention was paid to this aspect in extending the Hannover pre-metro. The relevant objectives were achieved. Growth in the number of passengers carried makes this clear, particularly when compared with public transport trends for Germany as a whole (see Table 1). The positive trend in Hannover is all the more remarkable

486

as car ownership - also shown in Table 1 - increased considerably over the same period.

A household survey carried out in 1978 in the first metro line (line A) catchment area proved the correctness of the design in a number of interesting ways:

- the modal split, which was roughly 40:60 (public transport: car) for the town area as a whole was reversed in the direct metro catchment area;

Table 1

TRENDS IN PASSENGERS CARRIED (ÜSTRA AND GERMAN AVERAGE) AND CAR OWNERSHIP IN HANNOVER

Year	ÜSTRA Hannover		All urban and regional transport	Car ownership	
	Number of passengers carried	Growth in %	%	Cars per thousand population	Growth in %(*)
1969	98,311.000	100.0%	100.0%	219.7	100.0%
1970	105,431.000	107.2%	104.6%	236.1	107.5%
1971	107,530.000	109.4%	107.4%	244.6	111.3%
1972	107,704.000	109.6%	108.4%	253.2	115.3%
1973	112,476.000	114.4%	111.1%	260.4	118.5%
1974	114,312.000	116.3%	112.8%	239.4(*)	109.0%(*)
1975	109,576.000	111.5%	113.1%	256.8(*)	116.9%(*)
1976	114,245.000	116.2%	109.4%	279.0(*)	127.0%(*)
1977	120,666.000	122.7%	108.2%	291.1	132.5%
1978	123,086.000	125.2%	108.4%	307.0	139.7%
1979	130,763.000	133.0%	110.4%	322.4	146.7%
1980	137,087.000	139.4%	113.3%	336.5	153.2%

*) Not strictly comparable with earlier years due to the local government reform of 1st March, 1974.

- 50 per cent of all persons with full access to a car nevertheless used public transport in these areas when travelling to the town centre;
- 78 per cent of all trips to the town centre were made by public transport;
- 91 per cent of informants were of the opinion that the money spent on the metro was a good investment.

This last finding would no doubt have been different if the investment had not brought such obvious and substantial advantages to the citizens and town as a whole.

These results doubtless explain why the ÜSTRA has up to now managed to attract a considerable share of GVFG resources to Hannover and thus create the necessary conditions to tackle other very important transport policy tasks.

5. TARIFF POLICY

Every economic service has to be paid for and this is just as true for public transport services as for the products of trade and industry. Quality of service is one of the decisive criteria in price formation, both with regard to the price structure - i.e. the tariff system - and the level. Improvements in service generally justify a higher price.

Urban public transport is also subject to market forces. Responsible management has to endeavour to exploit local transport market potential in setting prices. In the final analysis, in paying the market price the passenger is confirming the value that the transport service represents for him. The upper limit is reached when passengers are no longer willing to pay the price asked and increasingly switch to their own transport or make more trips on foot. From the transport policy standpoint there is no case for charging fares that are too high, i.e. higher than what the market will take, and incurring even greater losses of custom. Experience has shown that with keen competition from other modes, in particular the car, once traffic is lost by public transport it is very difficult to win it back.

In German transport undertakings, the principle of adjusting fares at fairly short intervals (e.g. yearly) in line with the general trends in incomes and prices has proved its worth over a long period. Moderate, regularly spaced price increases are much better accepted by the population than the large jumps at irregular intervals that used to be tariff policy practice. The reason for this mistaken policy was often reluctance on the part of policy-making bodies to ask people to pay the proper price for the service offered. For some time, however, there have been increasing signs that because the economic situation of towns and communities is becoming critical the local governments are trying to make fares unduly high. These efforts must be emphatically resisted by transport management. Now, particularly, it is quite indefensible to urge people to make more use of public transport and at the same time have a pricing policy which acts as a deterrent and erodes the present and potential public transport market. Such a policy of overcharging would also nullify the results achieved, particularly in the very recent past, through the constant improvement of urban public transport services.

In its "Konzept '76" the Federation of Public Transport Operators (Verband öffentlicher Verkehrsbetriebe - VöV) were already calling for more freedom of decision for urban transport undertakings within the limits of their legal responsibility. Management independence and the shouldering of responsibility are still too often paralysed by the exercise of political influence. Urban public transport can be optimised for the general economy only if it is operated as a commercial undertaking, with the public service obligation as an integral part. For public transport, the management objective is not to maximise profits as it is in trade and industry, but to cover costs. In this context, on the income side, fare receipts need to be supplemented by payments in compensation for the relatively numerous public service facilities which transport undertakings have to provide. These services arise out of the basic obligations which give carriers the right to the title public transport undertakings. The obligations relate to operation, timetables, carriage and fares but also to steps taken which are not justifiable on commercial grounds but are dictated by general economic, social and cultural needs. Examples are a deliberate low-fares policy, "social" fares of all types, including those for schoolchildren and students and the conserving of uneconomic lines and a standard of service not warranted by the traffic in slack periods. These services are quantifiable, they can be worked out in advance and given a price. They should be fully compensated by the authorities who require them to be provided. This is a claim that must be made by transport undertakings. It is not rational (because in the final analysis it is uneconomic) for deficits to be met, after the event, by general subsidies as this means that the decision-makers often fail to account to themselves early enough for the financial effects of their measures.

Because of the relation of tension between market-governed fares and a fares structure aligned on educational, social and structural policy objectives, a reasonable minimum has to be decided for the percentage of costs to be covered by operating revenue. The unanimous opinion of the German Congress of Towns and the VöV in 1976, was that the degree of cost coverage should depend on the type of area served and the services provided, and not fall below the following:

- 80 per cent in country areas with buses operating scheduled services;
- 70 per cent for buses in small and medium towns;
- 60 per cent for metros or trams and buses in large towns and conurbations.

As shown in the following table, ÜSTRA has been able to meet about two-thirds of its costs out of own income in recent years.

Table 2

ÜSTRA PERCENTAGE COST COVERAGE FROM 1970 TO 1980
(FROM 1977 INCLUDING STATUTORY GOVERNMENT COMPENSATION FOR
CONCESSIONARY SCHOOL FARES)

1970	1971	1972	1973	1974	1975	1976	1977	1978	1979	1980
87.6	74.1	69.0	64.4	59.5	59.5	59.2	66.3	65.8	67.5	67.0

6. EMPLOYMENT

Investment creates and secures jobs, but in the first
instance mainly outside the transport sector. Successful
investment, however, has positive effects on job security
in transport too and job security is no doubt one of management's most important tasks and obligations in any
business enterprise. It is no news that this obligation
is not exactly easy to meet at the present time.

If costs have to be cut to improve the trading position, but not to the detriment of the job situation, then
because of the high percentage of labour costs in transport undertakings' total costs (about 60 per cent on average) this can generally only be done if services can be
made more attractive, thus leading to gains in productivity and higher revenue, without any increase in workforce. In addition, transport undertakings - like all
other businesses - are obliged to explore all rationalisation possibilities within the existing social legislation. Meanwhile, however, the scope for rationalisation
measures has shrunk and progress can now usually be achieved only through heavy investment.

Thanks to its systematic investment policy, ÜSTRA
increased its productivity (capacity(1)/kilometres per
employee) by 34 per cent between 1970 and 1980 (see
Table 3). The share of labour costs in total expenditure
has also fallen to a comparatively low figure as can be
seen in Table 3.

Job security obligations and opportunities in and via
public transport extend far beyond the sector itself however. A stable, attractive public transport supply is now
a decisive factor in attracting jobs to a region. Rail-
based systems are known to be particularly effective. A
rapid-transit station with a favourable position in the
network - above all with good connections to the centre -
is an extremely important factor. Trends in land prices
along new rapid-transit lines is a reliable indicator of

---

1. million passenger places.

Table 3

EMPLOYMENT, LABOUR COSTS AND PRODUCTIVITY IN
ÜSTRA

Number of Jobs

1970	1971	1972	1973	1974	1975
2,015	2,081	2,142	2,172	2,207	2,192
1976	1977	1978	1979	1980	
2,181	2,099	2,153	2,158	2,197	

Labour Costs as a Percentage of Total Costs
(excluding pension reserves)

1970	1971	1972	1973	1974	1975
57.1	61.7	62.6	63.8	64.5	61.7
1976	1977	1978	1979	1980	
57.0	58.1	57.0	57.6	56.8	

Productivity (million passenger places/kilometres) per
employee

1970	1971	1972	1973	1974	1975
1.56	1.55	1.55	1.55	1.57	1.61
1976	1977	1978	1979	1980	
1.86	2.00	1.94	2.06	2.09	

this, though it must be interpreted with caution. While
for decades urban transport networks have followed building development, including that of trade and industry, it
is now increasingly playing its much more logical role of
component part of development infrastructure, and precondition for growth and restructuring, as was generally true
in many places in the early days of urban public transport
towards the end of the 19th century. This again is an
important aspect of the local government policy dimension
of urban transport management tasks at the present time;
awareness of this and active participation in it is, in
the final analysis, another important requirement in improving the situation of the individual transport undertaking. This is primarily true of metro-type facilities,
but with systematic exploitation of the potential for bus
operation quite similar results are possible.

7. ENVIRONMENT AND ENERGY

Public transport is basically more energy-efficient and environment-friendly than private transport, or at any rate than the car. This fact strengthens the public transport case and has been generally recognised by the public. In the latest of the sample surveys carried out by the VöV every two years, German citizens gave considerably better marks to urban transport for being "energy-saving" (77.6 per cent) and "environment-friendly" (75.1 per cent) than to the car (14.6 and 18.7 per cent respectively). As compared with earlier surveys, this shows a continued upward trend in favour of public transport. Absolute fuel consumption and emission figures also argue clearly in favour of public transport: public transport modes use about one-quarter of the energy per passenger used by the car. These figures and the satisfactory picture they paint do not mean that we can sit back however - there are still plenty of reasons and opportunities for making further improvements in public transport. Many of these opportunities are beyond the capabilities of the individual undertaking, however, and need a concerted effort by the whole industry. As a rule, such effort, in its turn, can only reflect the resolve and energy of the executives in charge and is thus again a typical present-day management task.

In its "Aktionsprogramm für die 80er Jahre", the VöV logically enough focussed on these two subjects: environment and energy. The following activities were mentioned under the heading of long-term security and mobility through energy conservation:

- calculation of capacity reserves by each transport undertaking as a basis for capacity planning for short-term increases in demand;
- formulation of short and medium-term strategies to increase capacity in emergency situations;
- exploitation of potential for recovering braking energy in rail-borne vehicles and in buses;
- co-operation in developing alternatives to the present diesel engine and testing them in real operating conditions.

A priority in environmental protection is to reduce noise emission to which the following should contribute:

- initiatives and active co-operation in the development and testing of low-noise rail-borne vehicles (metros, S-Bahns, trams) and road surfaces for urban transport;
- stimulation and support for university-level research on the theory of noise generation in rail-borne vehicles and VöV cooperation in empirical investigations;

- sound-deadening of engines in all VöV buses and support for research into the reduction of rolling noise;
- formulation of general guidelines on noise protection in public passenger transport based on research on motor vehicles and infrastructures.

While the energy savings achieved through increased use of public transport can certainly make a considerable impact on the overall energy balance, technological measures to reduce the energy consumption of urban transport vehicles themselves cannot have very much effect. In total the diesel consumption of all the buses in the VöV area accounts for only about 1 per cent of aggregate oil consumption.

Energy accounts for only 4 to 8 per cent of urban transport running costs but economies are still possible. For example, with new developments in power electronics it will be possible to recover the braking energy of rail-borne vehicles. ÜSTRA utilised this possibility when extending the pre-metro and in co-operation with the manufacturers developed the Hannover railcar, fitted with a new type of thyristor control which improves comfort through smooth starting and stopping and makes substantial savings through the recovery of braking energy. Measurements carried out in actual operation point to an average energy saving of 20 per cent, equivalent at the moment to a saving of about DM.1 million a year on electricity.

Speaking personally, I have some reserves about the "disaster scenarios" discussed from time to time with regard to the oil supply situation and the role envisaged for urban public transport or the demands which might be made on it. I do not think that urban transport undertakings should take potential crisis situations as a guide for their activities. As a rule, and in all fields, emergencies can best be met if the normal position is one of strength; i.e. the best way to prepare is to have the best possible supply, to improve the services offered by one's own undertaking in order to develop its potential. Oil price rises alone have produced only minor shifts to public transport. Appeals on environmental grounds help even less; everybody agrees in principle but leaves it to the other fellow to actually do something. So far as it is in their power, urban transport undertakings have to try to increase the use of public transport by improving their own services. Generally this will make the most direct contribution to energy conservation and environmental protection. Examples are the systematic extension of the urban transport network and the many possible measures that can be taken to facilitate bus movement; special bus lanes, lane segregation, priority at light-controlled intersections, etc. The smoother flow and hence more efficient use of the engine, can of itself produce fuel savings of up to 30 per cent. Further conservation potential

lies in the higher commercial speed and the improvement
this makes to capacity utilisation. ÜSTRA has for years
given particular attention precisely to this aspect, and
with considerable success.

8. ADVERTISING, PROMOTION, INFORMATION, DESIGN

So long as urban public transport supply and demand
balanced themselves largely automatically and management
tasks were those of a private service enterprise, it would
have been perfectly understandable for carriers to adver-
tise their product intensively. Once urban public transport more or less became a public service, a cessation of
advertising could have been regarded as entirely logical
- nobody advertises hospitals, kindergartens, sewers,
etc. In actual fact the sequence was reversed. Up to the
early 1970s advertising in Germany for urban public transport was practically non-existent; it was regarded as
superfluous whereas now, as a management task and instrument, it is here to stay.

In Germany, intensive advertising by individual
undertakings has for some years been combined with successful joint advertising at three levels:

- improving the image of urban public transport in
  general;
- increased involvement of individual undertakings in
  the advertising of local services;
- persuasion of other institutions to support public
  passenger transport.

Quite apart from the many specific advertising media
- posters, hoardings, press, radio, etc. - the biggest
advertising potential, at least to my mind, is in the
overall image the public has of the public transport
undertaking and the measure of confidence the passenger
has in the service.

As already emphasized, public transport is a basic
urban function; it should present itself clearly and
attractively as such. ÜSTRA has been particularly
attentive to this and has for years pursued the aim of
clothing all its urban transport facilities in a standard
livery. In co-operation with famous specialists ÜSTRA
strives to give the whole enterprise a unified and aesthe-
tically right appearance. This makes it easier for passengers and employees to identify with "their" buses and
trams and adds in a positive way to the image of the
town. The design is extended to everything, vehicles,
depots, surface and underground stations, ticket offices,
the information system, long-distance coaches, type and
style of advertising and many other details including
employees' uniforms.

494

Even in the underground stretches of the pre-metro the Hannover authorities and ÜSTRA have specifically striven to develop a new standard of urban architecture both in the interests of their own image and in the awareness of their responsibility for the image of the town as a whole. Instead of the old tram stops in the centre there are now underground stations with accesses and footbridges which are some of the loveliest structures in Hannover. All in all, this means that urban transport is in fact a patron of contemporary architecture; it contributes in a positive way to the town's image and thus imprints itself in a favourable light on the minds of the population.

These too are aspects of modern urban transport management whose importance is all too often neglected. Providing a technically and operationally faultless service is understandably what passengers and the community have a right to expect but only a positive image, the satisfactory provision of information and forceful promotion of what the transport undertaking does can lay the necessary foundations for winning over potential passengers in addition to the captive market.

9. RESEARCH AND DEVELOPMENT

Constant improvement of the services provided in as many respects as possible is obviously the maxim for any manager of a business. To an increasing extent today this means making use of scientific and technological advances. Here too, progress has not come of itself or by chance. In the present situation, R & D in urban transport is to a large extent no longer regulated by the market alone; the necessary resources can rarely be found within the transport enterprise to finance research by institutes or research firms. In R & D, as in other fields, individual undertakings have to join forces.

The introduction of new technologies is rarely free of friction. Individual undertakings have to be prepared to accept some of these teething problems, otherwise no progress will be possible in urban public transport as a whole. But readiness to co-operate and take risks in this area can have direct positive effects on individual undertakings. Participation in R & D projects requires and supports - at least to some extent - the presence of a team of qualified people who are, however, also available for the routine side of things, i.e. they can help to ensure that the appropriate skilled planning and preparatory work can be done for all operational aspects.

ÜSTRA has for some time been involved mainly with development work in the field of operations control systems. The first project, in 1974, with assistance from the Federal Ministry for Research and Technology, was to develop and test a computer-controlled, operating system for the pre-metro. The main object was to achieve the optimum service in terms of punctuality and regularity. The experience gained to date shows that these goals are achievable and have to some extent been achieved already.

In addition to ÜSTRA's development work, the Greater Hannover Association has been testing a dial-a-bus system and carrying out research and testing work in the field of operation control technology. In 1979, ÜSTRA and the Greater Hannover Association combined their activities in this field, concentrating on a scheduling system for urban public transport. The main objective of this activity is to develop a computer-controlled system which can meet present and foreseeable future requirements both for scheduled service operation and dial-a-ride facilities. Thus intensive, generally significant work is being promoted and performed both for town conditions and those found in the semi-rural areas of the surrounding region.

10. RESUME

The range of tasks for public transport undertaking managements in both town and country is at present dictated by the conflicting requirements of having to run the undertaking as far as possible like a private business and bearing the political responsibility for one of the essential services and an important one at that. This explains the particular problems, but also gives the job its particular attraction. Technology and operation are no longer the be-all and end-all of urban transport, but are the necessary preconditions for fulfilling requirements demanding far more than those associated with the traditional representation of a public transport undertaking.

A feeling of political responsibility and commitment - though not in the party politics sense - are now essential; understanding for and experience in all aspects of a modern business enterprise are all necessary in qualified and successful management. The fact that all present and foreseeable developments - whether they be increasingly scarce financial resources or environmental and energy problems - argue in favour of public transport certainly help the manager, but he cannot and should not expect success to follow more or less automatically. Using potential crises as a means of getting demands accepted does not appear to be a very useful approach to the job. Continual and active improvement in the services supplied is the only effective answer in the long run. Readiness to take investment risks, an understanding of the problems involved in presenting transport systems as an important part of urban development and the commitment to R & D are some aspects of the "job description" for today's public transport managers; this will not change very much in the foreseeable future.

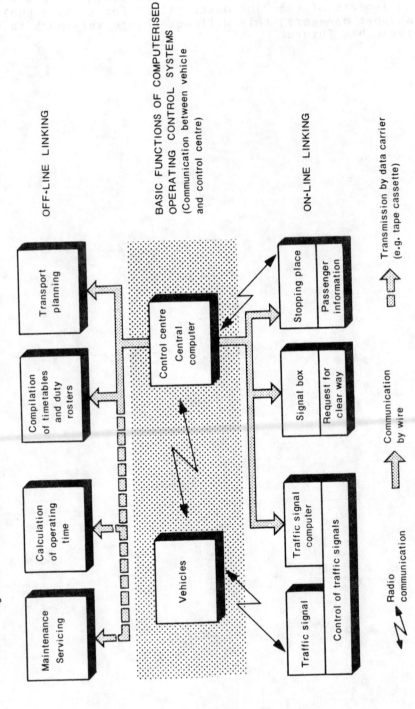

Figure 1 MANAGEMENT SYSTEM FOR PUBLIC TRANSPORT, FUNCTIONAL STRUCTURE

OFF-LINE LINKING

Maintenance Servicing

Calculation of operating time

Compilation of timetables and duty rosters

Transport planning

BASIC FUNCTIONS OF COMPUTERISED OPERATING CONTROL SYSTEMS
(Communication between vehicle and control centre)

Control centre Central computer

Vehicles

ON-LINE LINKING

Traffic signal — Control of traffic signals

Traffic signal computer

Signal box — Request for clear way

Stopping place — Passenger information

Transmission by data carrier (e.g. tape cassette)

Communication by wire

Radio communication

Source : ÜSTRA Hannoversche Verkehrsbetriebe AG.

498

BIBLIOGRAPHY

- VöV-Konzept '76
  Öffentlicher Personennahverkehr für die
  Gesellschaft von heute und morgen Zielvorstellungen
  und Wege zu ihrer Verwirklichung
  Herausgeber: Verband öffentlicher Verkehrsbetriebe
  (VöV) im Jahre 1976

- VöV-Aktionsprogramm für die 80er Jahre
  12 Ziele zur Verwirklichung eines
  fahrgastfreundlichen öffentlichen
  Personennahverkehrs
  Probleme, Lösungswege, Aktivitäten,
  Rahmenbedingungen
  Herausgeber: Verband öffentlicher Verkehrsbetriebe
  (VöV) im Jahre 1980

- Fahrpreise im öffentlichen Personennahverkehr
  Herausgeber: Deutscher Städtetag
  Verband öffentlicher Verkehrsbetriebe
  (VöV) im Jahre 1976

- Dieter Eisfeld
  Stadt und öffentlicher Nahverkehr
  Der Fall Hannover (1852 bis 2000)
  Herausgeber: ÜSTRA Hannoversche Verkehrsbetriebe
  AG
  im Jahre 1980

- ÜSTRA-Geschäftsberichte für die Jahre 1970 - 1980

MANAGEMENT OF FIRMS
TO SATISFY TRANSPORT NEEDS

RAILWAYS

Mr. O. ANDRESEN
Danish State Railways
Copenhagen, Denmark

SUMMARY

INTRODUCTION

When one speaks of future prospects, it is implied that the problems with which we struggle today will either multiply or become more complex. But the future can also bring the possibility of new, unconventional ways of thinking which can prevent today's problems from becoming future problems.

Today we are very preoccupied with finding solutions to acute problems caused by, among other things, the tight economic situation and the demand for conservation of energy resources.

But what are, then, the prospects for the future? The Danish State Railways (DSB), are now trying to come as close as possible to the real problems of the future through their long-term planning.

AN IDEA OF TRENDS IN THE FORESEEABLE FUTURE

The future is not known. We have a reasonable idea of what we today believe we have responsibility for, but we all feel that we encountered sudden surprises in the past. In spite of this, some of the general features of social development which, in all probability, will set the framework for future railway operation, are presented here.

Great changes can be expected in the international political situation; conflict will dominate over co-operation; the southeast corner of the globe will become the dominating growth centre, with Japan as its leading country; competition from the new industrialising countries will increase.

Society's economic development will still be characterised by the type of economic growth, but the prognoses show only a very small growth. Inflation will increase.

Unemployment will increase. The productive apparatus will no longer function. The processes of production and the work force will still be too costly in relation to the compensation which will be offered through the so-called new technology.

Today's cut-backs in the public sector will become more and more comprehensive and will result in a limiting of the public sector. At the same time private and joint ventures will become increasingly common. A focusing on production improvement and increased effectiveness will become a reality, not least within the public sector.

Another of the controlling factors in our surroundings will be the development in the area of energy. There will be an uneven distribution of resources to the advantage of the energy sector and at the expense of, among others, the transport sector. Collective traffic will not, however, be the sector of society which will be hit hardest by the cut-backs. A continuous adjustment to the rising real prices of oil will be required. In addition to vigorous energy conservation, a transition to new energy forms will be demanded. New propellants for automobiles and buses can be expected.

The consequences of the introduction of so-called new technology is another of the future working conditions. It is a fact that this workforce and/or energy saving technology is now becoming inexpensive and will quickly be introduced into our industries and concerns. Developments in electronics will be interesting, mainly applied to the combination of data processing and telecommunications/ telematics, computer development, together with a very strong development in Office Automation Systems.

Ability to compete will depend greatly upon if and when the new technology is introduced. We know from previous experience that the "new" will first be introduced in industry, and after that in administration.

Technological development will be so comprehensive that there will be talk of "The Technological Revolution" in many walks of life. Completely new possibilities will present themselves for, among other things, localisation of production. Why have large places of work when one can equip homes with terminals and so on? Why continue personal service when one can automise? Why perform tasks in countries with the highest wages when, in principle, there are no restrictions for performing work in the countries with the lowest wages? Etc, etc.

In the technological field the energy-saving car, electrically propelled car and low-noise aircraft will be developed and put into operation.

Some of the other tendencies and probable occurrences which now are becoming apparent can be mentioned:

There are clear tendencies towards a continuing increase in leisure time through reduction in the number of workdays per week, the number of hours per workday, earlier retirement, plus a lengthening of holidays and an increase in the number of public holidays. More people will get variable working hours and better opportunity to choose their holiday periods.

The labour market's demand for effectiveness and productivity will grow.

The tendencies towards morning-shift and afternoon/evening shift in the labour market will increase. De-industrialisation will give a new outlook on the labour market and its capacity for work. We will have a division of the labour market: those who are necessary for the application of data technology, and those who will be replaced by it. The difficulties will be great for public concerns to establish a quantitatively relevant labour force.

The development towards more corporate organisation is strong. The opportunities for change will be in the hands of the large organisations. Perhaps in the future unions will seek to prevent the implementation of policies, rather than influence the drawing up of policies.

Implementation of democratically made decisions could be prevented by unions delaying and prolonging the decision making process if they feel that they do not have enough influence on complex decisions.

There is nothing in the area of traffic policy which supports a reduced effort in collective traffic. The international development of traffic policy will be the strongest competition controlling factor in the future. The balance between commercial/economic and social/economic considerations will be a very likely dilemma.

Changes in people's values are, in the long run, probably one of the strongest controlling factors. It will be a characteristic of the future that we will be more likely to have sharp differences rather than agreement in our values and opinions. Our well-developed democratic society will - instead of experiencing a renewed agreement on past dominating values or quick acceptance of new values - be marked by a division of values. The changing values of the population will show a sharp contrast between the value priorities of the youngest and oldest generations.

We will have a generation gap between the old, who value economic and material security highest, and the young, who give all non-economic conditions the highest priority. Strong demands for the limiting of noise levels, in traffic safety and so on, are changes which will affect the railway traffic of the future.

DSB'S DEVELOPMENT UP TO THE PRESENT TIME

The problem areas sketched here do not come out of the blue. They are the results of the geographic and social conditions under which the DSB must work, and of the observed development and the development which the DSB believes then will be in the short- and medium-range view.

It would probably be useful for a better understanding of the managerial challenges which the DSB face to take a look at the conditions under which the railway is operated in Denmark.

A DESCRIPTION OF PAST EVENTS

Denmark lacks, to a large degree, the natural prerequisites for a rational, modern railway operation.

Geographically, the Peninsula of Jylland (Jutland) and the many islands mean that Denmark has a long coastline, which is a natural advantage for transportation by sea, domestically as well as internationally (see Figure 1). The geographic conditions also mean that there is a need for many ferry routes between parts of the country and to neighbouring countries.

This favours private motoring as well as lorry traffic, since the only railway ferry crossing between parts of the country is between Kørsor on Sjaelland (Zealand) and Nyborg on Fyn (Funen). There are, for example, 448 km of railway from Copenhagen to Denmark's fourth largest city, Ålborg, in the northern part of Jutland, while one needs to drive only 200 km in an automobile.

Denmark's geography also favours air traffic, and Denmark has therefore the world's densest domestic network. This is felt strongly by the DSB in the profitable business travel market. With respect to the geographic distribution of the population, Denmark is dominated by Copenhagen which, with its surrounding area, contains about 40 per cent of the country's population of approximately 5.1 million. Since Copenhagen literally sits on an island in one corner of the country, with no other population concentrations to counterbalance her dominance, there is an uneven distribution of both long-distance passenger traffic and freight traffic, in the same way that Copenhagen demands a considerable commuter traffic. This traffic is characterised by its very uneven capacity utilisation, and high costs.

In addition, Denmark lacks the raw materials which traditionally constitute a considerable part of the railway's bulk freight transports. The conditions for the running of relatively inexpensive block trains therefore do not exist.

The lack of raw materials also means that Denmark's trade structure lacks the concentrations of large industrial companies, normally good railway customers. 93 per cent of the country's enterprises have fewer than 500 employees, which means a great number of customers despatching small amounts of goods. In addition, a large proportion of these goods are in an advanced manufactured state, which means that the transport price's share of the total product price is modest, which is to the particular advantage of the road hauliers.

Nevertheless, the DSB has a railway network of 2,463 km, of which 469 km are exclusively freight railways. Add to this 13 private railways with a total of 328 km.

In 1981, the DSB transported 132 million travellers by train, compared to 86 million in 1975. 112 million of the passengers in 1981 were commuter traffic in the Copenhagen area and the region east of Storebaelt (the Great Belt) and 8 million were long-distance traffic. The DSB's freight traffic is more modest. In 1980, 7.5 million tons were transported, made up of 1/3 transit, 1/3 import/export and 1/3 domestic goods.

In contrast to passenger traffic, freight traffic has fallen in the last few years.

It is obvious that such a large increase in passengers as experienced by the DSB gives a number of managerial problems unlike those which the DSB faced in the seventies.

The main problems in the seventies were how to manage in a society which was increasingly directed towards the needs of individual traffic and which demanded of the DSB efficiency, comfort, speed and business-like results, without the DSB actually receiving the competitive prerequisites for these demands.

To channel the demands imposed by this situation, and to set goals for the cuts in the DSB which occurred in the seventies, five-year planning was introduced.

This started in 1975 with "Plan 1990", a plan of how everything would look in 1990 if the DSB had its way. The DSB did not have its way. One of the reasons was because social development took another course than had been anticipated at that time. Today, halfway through the plan's period, it is still of interest because it demonstrates how difficult it is to predict a course of development over a 10-year period. And it is, of course, quite

Figure 1

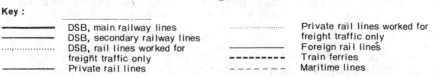

Key:

─────── DSB, main railway lines	············ Private rail lines worked for freight traffic only
─────── DSB, secondary railway lines	─────── Foreign rail lines
············ DSB, rail lines worked for freight traffic only	─ ─ ─ ─ ─ Train ferries
─────── Private rail lines	─ ─ ─ ─ Maritime lines

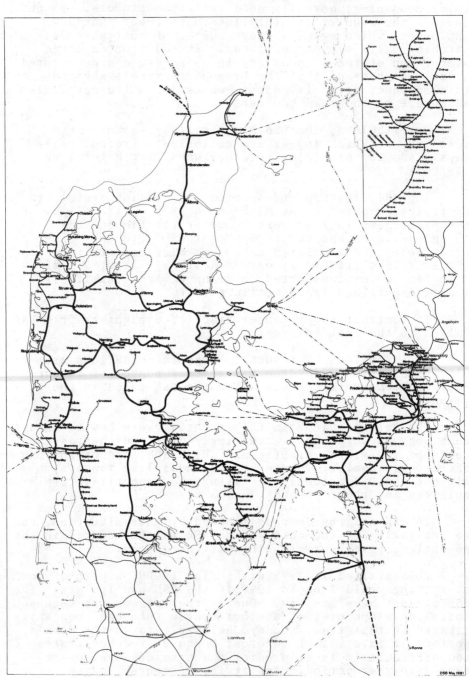

irritating when one thinks of the life expectancy of our great investments.

Plan 1990 was followed by 5-year plans which were sent out annually for the following period. Thus, the latest plan sent out covers the period 1984-88.

But not even the 5-year planning procedure is static. In the initial years, the 5-year plan was the basis for the budget, which the DSB as a State department forwarded to the Minister of Finance for the following year plus the subsequent three years, when it then became a part of the total State budget.

But as the State's financial situation became tighter, a closer co-ordination between the 5-year plan and the budget became necessary, and today one has to say that importance has shifted from the planners to the bookkeepers.

It is possible that this is because the planners and technicians do not think: "what can we get for the money we have?" but rather "which solution is the best?".

It is also possible that the sudden large passenger increase resulted in the most important task being to find room for all the new passengers and at the same time cope with a tightening of the State's economy, requiring a number of immediate solutions which helped at the time but which were not optimum with respect to planning. An example of this was the continued building of existing types of passenger coaches, although technical developments indicated a new and improved type to be more suitable.

It must be expected that the economic framework for investments for the remainder of the eighties will become tighter than was previously visualised, partly because interest and payments of the State's domestic and foreign debt will grow, partly because the rise in real income in Denmark will fall. And partly because operational costs, the result of large investments in physical facilities in the social, health and educational sectors in the sixties and seventies, will take up an increasing share of available public funds.

This is, of course, not an ideal situation for the DSB, especially since the economic changes in society bring with them a departure from individual to collective transportation, which demand considerable investments from the DSB in rolling stock as well as infrastructure.

It is therefore essential to adapt the economic means at our disposal to the best of our ability so that the consumers' needs are fulfilled as much as possible.

This demand for the fulfillment of needs has been a motivition for our plans till the present time without our being aware of its full extent. But the combination of economic tightening on the one hand and the increase in passengers combined with the desire for better results in freight traffic on the other, make it increasingly necessary to base our planning upon needs.

To this end it is a requirement that the necessary infrastructure be in place and in such a condition that personnel productivity is high and that equipment can be used in the most economical way.

One of the conditions for this is the electrification of the most frequented lines. It is unnecessary to mention here the advantages of electrification, which are well known to all.

This project, which covers 1,065 km, is to be completed before the year 2000. This is quite a long time span, but for a concern the size of the DSB it represents a considerable contribution of capital and personnel. Financing is partly secured through an index-regulated extra appropriation from the State of D.kr 100 million annually. It is characteristic of the difficulties in consistent planning that the first thing to happen was that the DSB was requested to cut back 15 of the 100 million during the initial years, a decision which has resulted in delaying the first stages of the project by a couple of years.

Procurement of electric locomotives also raises more general problems, since we are at a technological crossroad between chopper technology and triple phase asynchronous traction motors. To make the correct choice between the well-known and the untested, but promising, technology, when a system is to be built from scratch, is a managerial decision that is not without consequence.

In addition to the purely railway-operational assessments, there are some factors which are presumably well known to most railways, namely top-level political considerations such as industrial and employment policies.

From a purely railway-operational point of view, such external factors can be felt to be burdensome. No matter what their legal position vis-à-vis their governments, the railways are, or are at least perceived as, belonging to the State. It is thus logical that the politicians also wish to have a certain influence over the high-level decisions of the railways.

It is inappropriate to complain about this, and there is little doubt that it apportions the railways a good deal of goodwill when the politicians can identify with "their" railway.

THE FERRY PROBLEM

Another illustrative example of a complicated managerial problem with wide-reaching consequences is the building of a tunnel or a bridge route across Storebaelt or
Øresund (the Sound), and the ensuing problems which are
created for the DSB's ferry operation.

The decision to build a bridge over Storebaelt has
been postponed for the time being; it will be discussed in
the Danish Parliament in 1982 or 1983, and the uncertainty
with respect to a permanent connection over Øresund is now
even greater.

Since the ferry sector is characterised by very sizeable periodic investments of long duration, it is obvious
that conditions for decision making have to have a solid
and clear basis which is economically, technically and
operationally sound. For example a modern ferry costs
approximately D.kr.250 million and a ferry berth with the
necessary landing facilities costs about the same. Both
have an operating life of 25-40 years. Another dimension
of the problem is that the DSB's annual average reinvestment requirement in ferries alone is D.kr.250 million.
With such a reinvestment requirement, there are some extremely consequential decisions to be made.

The ferry problem has an international dimension
since one of the main lines, "Fugleflugtslinien (As-the-
bird-flies line)" affects two ferry crossings, namely
Rødby-Puttgarden, which is operated together with the
German State Railway (DB), and Helsingør-Helsingborg,
which is operated together with the Swedish State Railway
(SJ). The quality of transportation on "Fugleflugtslinien" is, for the time being, insufficient because the
ferries are too small and cannot, for example, transport
piggyback wagons. An improvement of this transportation
quality, which would put the railways in a much better
position compared with lorries, requires the introduction
of a new ferry system on Østersøen (the Baltic Sea) and a
new ferry route on Øresund, which in turn means an
investment from the Danish side of up to D.kr.1,000 million. If it is decided not to build a permanent connection over Storebaelt, there will be a need for investment in new car ferries on Storebaelt with a possible
joining of railway and car ferry routes, at the same time
as carrying out the reinvestments mentioned above.

Investments of this size far exceed resources which
the state can be expected to put at our disposal in addition to the normal appropriations.

What are we to do, then? It will be a first-rate
management solution for the eighties, namely the optimum
combination of that which can be accomplished politically,

that which is desirable in traffic and that which is possible economically.

WHAT ARE "TRANSPORT NEEDS"?

The so-called "transport needs", under which today's transportation systems operate, originate not so much from the basic needs of people, but are rather a necessary result of the built-up social structure. Cause and effect interchange: for example, the physical social structure has given a certain accessibility, which in turn has created a specific transport need, and at the same time this accessibility, which the transportation system makes possible, creates a part of the physical social structure which we have today.

In other words, to move from one place to another is only rarely an end in itself, but rather a means to achieve something else, for example the need to participate in some social activity. It is, however, not so easy to say that the knowledge of human need for activity is enough by itself in the decision to use the transportation system. For example, the continuing development of transportation systems gives a high degree of accessibility, which has made possible a different localisation of activities, This is, to all appearances, a paradox: the use of transportation facilities depends on the localisation of activities, which in turn depends on present transportation facilities. This seems to be the classic case where supply creates its own demand.

As a starting point in society's functional organisation, one can imagine a theoretical "transport need", which can be described as the transport patterns which arise if there are no restrictions on the use of the transportation system: in other words, if one could travel wherever and whenever one desired with no time consumption or cost.

The individually limited human resources reduce this "transport need" to a "transport demand".

The difference between "transport need" and "transport demand" is that the latter concept implies participation in activities which most often necessitate travel sacrifices in terms of time, money, etc.

Transport demand is therefore a variable which depends upon a number of "demand factors". These factors can be "positive" or "negative", based on whether they tend to increase or decrease demand.

512

The number of persons served by the transportation system, together with their incomes and automobile owner- ship are usually positive factors. The same is true for the number of activities served.

The negative factors include in the first instance the sacrifices or "costs" which are a part of the trip itself: time, price, discomfort, uncertainty, etc. There can be positive aspects to the trip, but the trip is not usually an end in itself.

Demand for a certain alternative, for example a cer- tain means of transportation, depends not only on the fac- tors which characterise this means of transportation, but depends just as much on the factors which characterise the possible alternative means of transportation. The number of trips made by train depends in this way on what service and price the competing means of transportation, auto, bus and airplane, offer.

Transport demand is therefore a complex function of many variables.

In the future it will be of decisive importance to clearly define which human activities can function satis- factorily only by situating demands for transportation. When should there be collective traffic? Which types of transportation will be necessary and desirable for trans- portation concerns to supply? Such decision-making is urgent since society tends towards a development charac- terised by an increased demand for transportation, for example the expected increased number of economically active persons, increased educational and course activi- ties, centralising of services, the possibility of pendu- lum travel over longer distances, the impact of energy development on price competition between motoring and col- lective traffic, and so on.

One can postulate very broadly that future possibili- ties for transportation, in other words the established accessibility, can create transport needs which in turn, when economical and other limits are applied, generate a demand for, among other things, railway transportation. Therefore, the development of the railway, through its transportation supply, will also in the future contribute to the satisfaction of, as well as the creation of, trans- port needs. A question for the future is: shall we con- tinue with this?

SOME FUTURE MANAGEMENT PROBLEMS

The most certain thing about the next ten years is that they will be full of uncertainty. On almost every aspect of the future there is deep disagreement among experts and laymen alike. Living with uncertainty will be one of management's biggest challenges, which will require great flexibility. And flexibility will often be risky and difficult in an environment conditioned by the bureaucratic rigidities of governments and the sometimes conflicting demands of powerful trade unions, pressure groups, and so on.

Therefore the DSB will in the future operate in an environment which today is characterised by general uncertainty, change and the unknown. The only help we get is a recommendation to develop the concern with maximum flexibility. Can this be done with such a heavy system as a railway operation? The answer today must be: it is imperative that we do it.

The types of management problems which today the leaders of the DSB, among others, can expect to face are:

- The general uncertainty of social development makes it difficult to establish a course of action based on the long-term prognoses. It is difficult to set up long-term goals for the management of the concern.
- The difficulties in working towards a future where the railways' role is not clearly defined. In which market should the railway operate?
- The accentuated demands for production increase in the public sector.
- The dramatic changes which will occur at all levels of the concern because of the technological development in electronics.
- The unequivocal demand for a changeover of operation because of a new attitude to energy consumption.
- The possible revised view of public concerns, increased privation and the subsequent economic resource problems.
- The sensitive balancing act between the concern's economic effectiveness and social considerations.
- The large problems of establishing a qualitatively and quantitatively relevant work force.

All this, and more, must, of course be seen in the context of the complex management situation in which the leadership of the DSB already finds itself. For example, the complexity of seeing the individual decision-making problems as part of a larger and more long-term whole: to continuously have a general view of the consequences for the respective products within the concern, as well as for the DSB as a whole; the demands for optimum performance. At the same time, one must have personnel motivated to achieve decisions and to get the unions' support for the implementation of suggestions, etc.

And all this in a situation where strategic leadership is not something which can be accomplished with the help of a few simple technological tools or techniques. And in a time when perceptions of the optimum type of management and organisation are very varied: Is decentralisation better than centralisation? In which activities and to what degree should one establish joint ventures or leave them to private enterprise?

SOME SOLUTIONS AT MANAGERIAL LEVEL

So what solutions do we have for the sketched-out future management problems? The answer in short is that, just as turbulence and change characterise the surrounding society's development, management theories are evolving into something new and unknown and therefore there are no patented solutions. The only thing we can do in this "waiting position" is to build on the so-called flexibility with all the means at our disposal, plus projecting as far as possible into the future so that we can know the worst as early as possible.

Because of the great importance and impact which the DSB's service and system have on Danish society, it is necessary that the DSB's planning and operation satisfy and at all times take into maximum consideration the new demands and challenges which the transportation sector will face in the future.

The need for early warning is of the greatest importance for a concern such as the DSB, which is characterised by heavy investments which must meet projected demands and situations from the moment the investment decisions are made.

Furthermore, a part of the answer is that the long-term plans, which the earlier managements used as support, no longer apply in the times we are entering now.

Today, long-term plans are no longer made with the same enthusiasm and certainty as they were in the 70s, when we mostly made prognoses and lived in a society of continuing development. We knew what the problems of the future were, we were to be a little better, a little bigger, have more products, and so on.

But now, in these changing times, it is not a matter of solving the problems "more correctly, but of solving the correct problems". This means that large sections of the foundation of traditional planning must be revised.

Previously the DSB made much of its long-term goal, setting discussions in connection with work involving Plan

515

1990. With fixed long-term goals, which could be put into operation in steps, in policies and in active programmes, a foundation for the business-like management of the DSB was established. The DSB's supreme management instrument was planning: purposeful development in the long-, middle- and short-term.

This planning was the basis for the DSB's management instrument. It included all activities and tasks, both in breadth and depth, short- and long-term, internal and external.

Future management instruments are, however, different. Environmental uncertainty makes planning which is closely tied to the launching of long-term goals unusable. A complementation is required in the form of a discussion of the concern's real future problems. The ability to react quickly will also be necessary. Established plans must be flexible and adaptable to drastic changes in the environment, and so on.

All in all, the new situation may open the way for new content and methods in planning. Long-term planning will be less and less planning which ties us to definite actions somewhere in the future. Planning will to a decreasing degree be the making of refined consequential calculations in conditions which become more and more uncertain. Planning must increasingly occupy itself with current and continuing analyses which can give a more correct diagnosis of the problems which arise. Its task will be less the formulation of unfinished solutions than the implementation and management of processes.

The most important task for a planner will not be to obtain some refined technical tool, but to acquire an understanding of the processes in society which have an effect on his planning area.

How will the DSB handle these extreme demands for flexibility and quick reaction in an uncertain future? The main method of management is still continuous planning, although the knowledge content is somewhat different. At present we are trying to achieve new knowledge by looking into the far future and finding so-called external indications about social development together with the probable influence of these developments on the DSB's operation. This must be considered as an accentuated external orientation and should be seen as complementing the known problems and intended decisions - in other words, the so-called internal indications. When these indications are combined, the management has the possibility of evaluating the DSB's future problems.

It is now imperative for managerial considerations to establish a strategic indication system, which continuously keeps the DSB management up to date with

516

internal as well as external developments. It is, generally speaking, from the following conditions that the indications should be taken and maintained.

EXTERNAL INDICATIONS

- the market's qualitative and quantitative demands and tendencies;
- the competition's present and future strengths and plans;
- production factors' accessibility, costs and development;
- political directives and legal aspects.

INTERNAL INDICATIONS

- the concern's internal technical-economic status and possibilities;
- personnel welfare and contentment.

The goal of a strategic indications system such as this is to contribute to the optimum flexible management of the concern by:

- making possible a reduction of the concern's total reaction time;
- making possible a general view so that the entire concern has the best possible common foundation for planning and decision making;
- using the early indications in relation to present DSB products to improve and accomplish activities which make use of the negative as well as the positive market trends;
- making possible changes in the original projected conditions on which new products, 5-year plans, etc., are based.

This first small attempt to take all of these things into consideration and reach these difficult conclusions is made in the DSB's case in a so-called perspective planning process. For example, at the moment we are receiving imminent external indications from the following areas:

- work-time development;
- labour market development;
- area application and environmental quality;
- population development;
- energy resource development;
- trade development;
- union development;

- conditions for competition in the future;
- human evaluation;
- introduction of new technology;
- political development;
- traffic policy development;
- educational development;
- the development of unconventional means of transportation;
- economic development.

The aim is to secure as high a degree of flexibility as possible, in that the activities which are completed in the short-term are seen as a background for a common foundation of attitude and in this way fit in with the probable development tendencies which the future has to offer.

CLOSING COMMENTS

It is difficult to express precise concluding views on this very large and comprehensive problem area. When one looks at a very uncertain future, it is problematic to postulate standpoints which can be conceived as a step on the way to that future.

The following can be postulated about, in the short-term and long-term, as a summation of some thoughts which are discussed in this paper:

- Denmark is and will remain a country which lacks the condition for a rational and modern railway operation;
- in the short-term, the DSB will be faced by difficult economic problems in a time when the conversion from individual to collective traffic will accelerate sharply;
- the problems are large when it comes to the conversion from short-term to long-term development. Solutions to pressing problems are difficult to find in the long-term perspective;
- the railways' environment will be characterised by great uncertainty and change, which makes the railways' market, future transport needs, etc. very uncertain;
- the railways' role in the "new society" is as yet undefined. Lack of clarity with respect to the future goals of the railways makes management difficult;
- a comprehensive external orientation will become much more important;
- a planning solution must be able to keep abreast of development, both short and long-term, internal and external;

- all means should be used to create flexibility and an ability to react quickly;
- a common attitude as a framework for future development is more important for management than long-term plans.

And in the end we all know: that crisis spells opportunity!

TOPIC 2D

MANAGEMENT OF FIRMS
TO SATISFY TRANSPORT NEEDS

RAILWAYS

Mr. D.J. COBBETT
British Railways Board
London, United Kingdom

SUMMARY

1. INTRODUCTION

It is over 150 years since railways first became agencies of public transport and during this whole period they have seen development and change of great consequence and significance. In the technological field, progress has been exciting and far reaching but it is interesting to note that although steel wheel on steel rail has stood the test of time, the changes in traction types, signalling and communications, safety and comfort make modern railways, overall, very different from their ancestors. Equally important and far reaching have been the changes in the demand for railways and the conditions in which they operate.

From its inception the railway was so vastly superior to any other form of transport that there was no comparison and, certainly, no competition. Early legislation was related to ensuring that sufficient funds were available to build the railways that were proposed and protect the interests of shareholders (some people would see that as not dissimilar to present day financial problems), to prevent monopoly exploitation (governing the common availability of railway transport to all comers, avoidance of undue preference being given to favoured customers and to control the level of railway rates and charges) and - rather belatedly - to ensure safety of operations for passengers, staff and property.

This "Golden Age" of railways lasted for about one hundred years until the emergence of the motor lorry and the motor bus as a direct result of the 1914-1918 War, which had presented an opportunity for the technical development of the internal combustion engine, revealed the flexibility and capacity of road transport for certain operations and produced men of character and individualism who were determined to make their own way, using the motor vehicle as the opportunity. Unfortunately, railway management, failing to recognise the challenge, did not change their ways and persisted in trying to be all things to all men. The railways tried to continue all their activities, but in a more up to date form and clamoured for legislation to protect them. The Second World War clouded the issue further. There was a huge need for transport and diversion of technical development to war purposes. The railways were in great demand and were seen as indispensable parts of the war effort. The lessons of the thirties were forgotten and the railways were run down into exhaustion in the great struggle.

After the war, victors and losers alike set about
rebuilding their railway networks with various forms of
financial assistance and making use of surplus war
stocks. Fundamentally, it was a case of replacing the old
order. Although new forms of traction and other technical
equipments were introduced, there was a second failure to
recognise clearly the growing strength of the opposition,
which was, now, not just the motor lorry and the motor
bus, but increasingly the private car, for which a whole
new manufacturing industry had emerged. The growing
strength of organised labour and the increasing significance of environmental attitudes were other new factors.
The world had seen enough destruction and wished to preserve and develop its heritage. Running parallel was the
tendency to take railways into national ownership, which
was beginning to introduce a new concept for the provision
of services - that of social need and benefit rather than
the commercial gain of the operators and private shareholders. Services not suitable for the creation of profit
were increasingly seen to be needed as lifelines to communities, which would be seriously deprived without adequate transport. The common factor being a low level of
revenue potential because demand was low - either due to
the availability of private transport or the basic low
level of population - which had to be balanced by external
funds. These are called "subsidies" in conventional terms
and by people who wish to denigrate the policy, or
"support", which is more correct when the transport agency
is operating a public service deemed to be essential, is
best provided by that form of transport and is something
which the operator would not choose to do if his remit was
purely commercial.

Post Second World War years have been marked by an
acceleration in the pace and nature of the changes, which
affect railways and, for the first time, the basic question of the survival of railways has become an important
issue. Survival, absorption of new technology and the
associated changes in working practices and productivity,
increasingly powerful trade unions, response to competition, increased national ownership, recognition of the
real role of the railway in the national economy, inflation and the effects of environmental pressures have all
played their parts and we see very different railways now
from those, which existed even when most present senior
managers started their careers - or, for that matter,
politicians started out on their roads to fame.

What faces us at this conference is the need to recognise the changes that have occurred during our involvement with the transport industry so that we can identify
the forces which have been at work and sort out the real
role for railways in the future. We must concentrate on
our strengths both in the commercial fields and also in
the area of social benefit where rail can provide a necessary service better than other providers. We must eschew

all else, forgetting the "glorious traditions of the railways" and the "divine rights" which are so comfortable and comforting, but so pernicious, and concentrate on an effective and efficient railway able to earn its keep, support its future by sensible replacement policies, and develop its potential for the common good by investing in profitable new techniques and business ventures. In this way the railway will survive as a useful and essential part of social and economic life and it will be supportable politically. It is not the duty of politicians to support the railway - or even transport - unquestioningly and as an act of faith, but it is their duty to support an essential and efficient section of the national economy, which is making an effective contribution. There is clear evidence of failure on both sides of this equation, both now and in the past, and a better balance has to be struck. This conference, assessing as it is society's transport needs and the management of transport to satisfy those needs can make a major contribution to that balance. It can do so by recognising that comprehensive national transport plans are needed, truly reflecting needs and the appropriate contribution from each different form of transport and expressing this in clear objectives backed up by sensible financial policies.

The purpose of this paper is to consider how railways are, and should be, managed to provide a satisfactory and effective supply of their form of transport and it must be read in conjunction with the other papers, which are dealing with the transport needs of society. However, to be complete, it is necessary to spend a little time on the question of needs - described as demand - so that the reasons for management decisions and action on supply (to use the economists' term) can be seen in context. Having discussed demands, this paper will then talk about the proper objectives for railways and the organisation and management style appropriate to implementing those objectives. This will be supported by comments on what is an effective railway, how that railway should be managed financially, the implications on labour relations including productivity of manpower and physical assets and the increasingly important aspects of energy availability and consumption. The emerging question of private sector involvement in national industries will then be dealt with and, finally, international aspects will be discussed.

2. THE DEMAND FOR TRANSPORT

2.1. People

The needs of people are paradoxical. They require independent personal mobility for which they are prepared to pay quite highly, often at the expense, in national terms, of unreasonable importation of energy or material goods. They also insist on the general availability of public transport to meet the marginal requirements of those who have motor cars so as to avoid the purchase of a second or even a third vehicle. They also want transport on the widest possible terms and at the lowest possible cost for those who have no car or cannot use one because of age or infirmity, and for their own use in exceptional circumstances, such as adverse weather, or exceptional shortages of fuel. Should this situation properly be met by public transport? That it can be is certain but only at an unreasonable cost to the public purse. Socially, economically and politically it is expected that public transport will do so but only at a reasonable cost. Thus managers must use their ingenuity dexterously. They must recognise the basic role of their transport agency and reflect this in the standard pattern of their operations so that base costs are covered and that a reasonable level of marginal capacity remains with sufficient flexibility to take on excessive overloads or unusual diversion into other demand areas without an unbearable burden. Success in doing this depends on identifying the real basic role of railways and then interpreting it in local terms. It is suggested that the nature and capacity of railways makes them most suitable for the following activities:

  a) Inter-City long distance travel.
  b) Travel in some rural areas.
  c) Dense commuter operations around large cities.
  d) Leisure opportunities.

Inter-City - because traffic flow levels are likely to be acceptably high and of sufficient journey length to offer opportunities for stimulation by marketing devices. A network of inter-city services creates cohesion within a nation and the flexible mobility, which generates commercial opportunity, social stability and quality of life, which are the foundations of a civilised and thriving community. The ease and convenience of planning a journey with a timetable provide commercial opportunities, which offer prospects for managing such a network on a business-like basis against an objective of viability.

Railways are suitable for meeting travel needs in some rural areas where volumes are likely to be more than can be coped with by bus, or where opportunities for integration with longer distance rail journeys are more conveniently met by inter-train connection. In a number of cases the existence of a railway forms the basis for a transport network and it is a more effective use of capital or operational financial support to use and develop it rather than to build new roads and provide new buses. A variation of this situation occurs in many very isolated areas where branch railway lines exist upon which the train services provide essential services at all times and are "lifelines" in certain adverse circumstances. In such

526

cases it is not difficult to show that even quite high levels of support are cheaper than closing the railway and allowing the rural community to wither and force individuals into adopting very low standards of isolated living or uprooting themselves and moving into unaccustomed towns. Such population movements are always accompanied by the need to build houses, schools, roads, utility supplies, hospitals, employment opportunities at much greater cost - financially and in human terms - than supporting the continued operation of a rural railway. Management implications are clear in the widest terms and the cheapest way of operating the line must be found. This means using the least track, signalling and rolling stock facilities to the greatest possible extent and shaping the pattern of service offered to reflect the need, but with greater regard to production efficiency than would be the case in a railway operated on a commercial basis or a more intensively used social service.

Throughout the world, railways are recognised as efficient carriers of <u>commuters</u>. They are seen to be the only answer to the dense flows of passengers every morning and evening, which make it possible for large city units to be effective and produce their recognised business advantages without being unbearable places in which to live. This area of railway operations is, undoubtedly, difficult for management. No commuter network in the world pays for itself, let alone makes money, and there are about as many different ways of squaring the financial circle as there are separate commuter systems. It is highly unlikely - perhaps undesirable - that one simple financial system will be found that meets all needs. What, in fact are those needs? Some of the factors from which the needs of each individual city area will emerge are as follows:

a) The function of the city. Is it a local market, a regional or national centre, or somewhere of international importance?
b) How big is the subordinate area? A short train ride or as much as 100 kilometers?
c) Is the subordinate area purely a dormitory or has it industry and commerce in its own right? Do these train services have to meet a multiple purpose?
d) Is it in the national interest that people should commute long distances or could this be regarded as a waste of resources?
e) Is it sensible - nationally or in lower level economic terms including the finances of the railway - to adopt different fare policies for different types of travellers, e.g. peak-period regular travellers, short- and long-distance journeys; work and leisure travel?

527

f) Is the best overall interest met by maximising the use of the train services by fares and service level policies, or producing the best railway financial results and lowest call on public funds by maintaining high fare levels?

g) How are railway service and operational plans to be meshed in with other social, economic and environmental plans to produce the best balance over the whole area?

h) Who benefits from the train services? Is it just the commuter or is it the wider community, the employers, commerce or entertainment industries, people who enjoy less congested roads, those who have opportunities for a more cultural life or better education? How should these other beneficiaries pay for their gains? Or should travellers alone bear the whole burden?

i) Are the existing facilities in good condition or are they worn out or old fashioned? Should replacement be on a like-for-like basis or the opportunity taken to provide for the future? How are the costs to be met? Are there reserve funds available? Should present-day users meet all the costs or should loans be taken so as to spread the costs over the whole operational life of the assets? What is the correct relationship between revenue account costs and capital costs?

j) How significant and conflicting are local and national political interests? Do the structures of government at all levels permit the successful development of integrated transport policies and - most importantly - their financing? Should the various governing bodies have executive authority or be advisory only. Who is to be their supremo? What powers will he have?

Managing a railway to meet the appropriate combination of these factors in any particular area is a complex task. It calls for acceptance that the railway alone cannot decide; it cannot trample through the delicate fabric and balances of society and economic life guided only by its own interpretation of its duty. And yet it cannot stand back and allow the complicated relationships of the area in which it operates to produce a pattern of demand and resulting operating costs, which are contrary to other statutory duties that may have been imposed upon it. It certainly cannot allow the local situation in any commuter area to dominate the interests of the national network, of which even the largest commuter areas form only a subordinate part. What must management do? It must never lose the initiative. It must have its own plans, which it feels are the correct answer to its overall duty. It must be unceasing in its efforts to ascertain the needs of its customers and the other interested parties in the area and to absorb them into those plans, making adjustments where necessary. It must strive to improve its efficiency and thus its costs, thereby easing pressures on fares levels and financing needs. It must seek understanding with the political bodies who have influence in the area and try constantly with them to create a framework of consultation, co-operation, and integration of planning which allows acceptance of plans and policies to be dynamic - evolving harmoniously into effective services, equitable fare levels, maximum use of the assets and adequate reflection of indirect benefits in supporting financial policies. Above all, it must never lose control and whilst encouraging the maximum involvement of "outsiders" in the creation of policies, it must retain to itself sole responsibility for implementing those policies in a professional but accountable way.

Leisure Travel can sometimes be viewed as a social necessity - probably increasingly so as working hours become shorter and it becomes more and more important to provide opportunities for using the increased leisure time available - but in the context of managing railways for the reasonably foreseeable future it needs to be seen as a marketing opportunity for filling up the capacity of services already provided to meet the basic role of the railway. People's needs in this area reflect many strands of life - a break from tedium, visiting friends and relations, having a holiday, pursuing hobbies and education, sporting activities. None are sufficiently great in themselves or even together to justify services in their own right but all are important to the quality of life. All are opportunities to be grasped by railway managers for making better use of services and improving financial results.

2.2 Freight

It would not be true to say that the movement of freight can be regarded entirely as a commercial activity. There are questions of environmental benefits or disbenefits created by the actual choice of transport - heavy lorries in villages and on popular motor car routes; industrial development and employment policies, which can be powerfully affected by the availability of transport, are examples of this. Nevertheless, for most practical purposes these can be set on one side and for the management of a railway it is acceptable to regard freight traffic as having to conform to commercial rules, and thus allow the selection of traffic flows and operating methods to be governed by the strength of the railway system and the prices which can be achieved in the market. If the rate per tonne which is available against the competition is above the cost per tonne, i.e. the direct cost plus a reasonable contribution to indirects, the traffic flow is suitable. If it is not, it should not be considered unless operating costs can be forced downwards to the appropriate level. This is a powerful incentive to efficiency if the railway system or route involved is volume hungry. As a general rule, and there must be local exceptions although they should be very few in number, the following types of freight traffic flows are good for railways:

a) Bulk products.
b) Bulk created by containerisation.
c) Production line movements between works.
d) High value "distribution" type goods.
e) Express parcels.

This selection reflects the suitability for rail of bulky traffic - either in its natural form or combined by container into train load sizes - which can enjoy the superior economics of the train load rail haul. Combining this with the flexibility and economy of road transport over short distances avoids the intermediate handling of small consignments and the expensive and time consuming shunting and tripping arrangements, which are associated with other than train load working. Certainly, length of haul has a part to play in the calculations, but it is quite wrong to generalise that everything under a certain distance is right for road movement and above it is suitable for rail. There are many cases where very short hauls of sufficiently large volumes can be highly suitable for rail - the key factors are size of trains, capacity of individual wagons, rapid loading and unloading facilities and maximum productivity of rolling stock, traction units and train crews. It goes without saying that such movements on rail give very high environmental benefits from the heavy lorries kept off the roads. In this situation a combination of interest and determination by the producer of the traffic, the transporter and the receiver is necessary. If one or more have reservations, there may well be a case for external non-commercial financing help to overcome an obstacle, e.g. access arrangements, terminal facilities or provision of rolling stock so that the total benefits available are secured.

Obviously, there is a limit to the traffic, which is naturally bulky and thus ideal for rail. Few, if any, general purpose railways can expect their total requirements for freight volume to be met from this source; all should be seeking ways of breaking into wider markets to obtain fresh areas of operation or acquire traffic to use up the marginal movement capacity available in the infrastructure - and, occasionally, manpower, traction and rolling stock. It is important not to go too far and take on flows which do not fit the natural strengths of railways or could move better by other forms of transport. They may provide temporary benefit but are, probably, part of the slippery slope to ruin if carried on for too long.

The traffic flows which are likely to be suitable are those which move in containers - and can be bulked into train loads by cranes at concentration depots fed by road vehicles - and moderate sized consignments between originating point and destination, which can be loaded in wagons forming sections of through trains not requiring intermediate marshalling. Such flows will not be numerous or large-scale, but careful selection, marketing and service planning can develop a significant sector of business, which makes a worthwhile net contribution to railway finances and to the national economy. Frequently the movements form part of a production process and can command high charges reflecting the savings in inventory costs, etc., which would otherwise be incurred.

At the other end of the market are the express parcels movements, which are a very important sector of freight transport needs. The traffic concerned is of high value, urgent and often perishable and unsuitable for bulking into container or wagonloads. That there is a market is obvious from the large numbers of providers of such a service. Railways can secure an important segment of this business as a marginal activity associated with the network of passenger trains - mainly inter-city, but sometimes advantageously linking with more rural services. It is important to recognise that the railway strength ends at the station door. Once collection and delivery activities are involved costs escalate and quality of service and reliability disappear. A well managed railway meets this particular freight need by providing a station-to-station service only - and invests considerable sums and managerial effort in it.

3. THE OBJECTIVES FOR RAILWAYS

In most countries, railways were brought under national control many years ago in very different circumstances. Thus, the controlling statutes have become unsuitable for current activities and almost without exception, amending legislation, capital reconstructions, new support systems etc. have been introduced. However, the updating of statutes has not always been along modern business lines, nor has it always reflected changing financial and economic circumstances, nor the changing role of the railway in the modern social, economic and competitive climate.

This is neither fair to railway management, nor effective in terms of securing a transport plan within which the railway system can give of its best. The fact that railways are nationalised means that there will be political direction and influence, but it does not mean that it should be biased or dictatorial. The general political interest is best served by enabling the influences of professional operators, users, those who benefit indirectly, local authorities, trade unions representing the interests of railway staff, and social, financial and economic factors to come together in a mature and balanced way allowing flexible and efficient interpretation by railway managers. The task of the politician is not to obstruct this process, but rather to create a mechanism and climate in which it can operate and then to fashion the results into a practical shape. He will, almost certainly, have to reconcile conflicting interests. He should ensure that everyone understands the relationships between benefit, costs and revenues and, at the end, he must draw the line at what can be afforded, deciding the balance between operating revenue and external support and between the financing of revenue and capital expenditures. He must express all this in terms of objectives which the operating authorities can meet and for which their activities can be accountable. The politician must judge results and take any necessary corrective action either with the operating management or in the form of amendments to the objectives. Above all, the politician, whether at national or local level, must not be involved in actual operations. He should stick to his last, which is to identify and reconcile the wider factors within which transport and railways are to act and to provide any financial support necessary, and leave it to the professionals to do the job to his requirements.

There is a variety of ways in which objectives can be structured and expressed and different national and local situations call for different treatments. Thus a country possessing an intensive railway system, handling passenger and freight traffic may want quite different objectives for its railway than its neighbour, which is of different size and economic structure. In each country the national objectives, whilst they cannot be in conflict with subsidiary area objectives, must be sufficiently flexible to accommodate variations. It follows that national objectives should be expressed broadly and should spell out the role of the railway and the part that it should play in the national transport plan. They should be heavily related to the strengths of a railway as a form of transport, but if there is a requirement for it to perform tasks not ideally suited to it, because no other form of transport can do them as well in the particular circumstances of the case, the fact should be recognised and adequate compensatory arrangements made.

The more detailed expression of these requirements would be written out in the subordinate sets of objectives drawn up for sub-sectors of the railway business or geographical locations, thus there should be no attempt to describe operations precisely. The objectives should be expressed at a high level, leaving the operators free to interpret them as best meets their reading of market requirements and their duties. At the lower level, it would be necessary to integrate the objectives of different transport agencies so that co-ordination occurs where it is most important to the user, e.g. bus and train connections.

A note of warning should be sounded. Broad high-level objectives are not vague objectives. Care must be taken to ensure that what is required is practical as far as operation is concerned. The operators should be involved so that realism is reflected - opaqueness will cause poor discernment of problems and definition of the answers. It could also lead to misdirection of political decisions often tending towards treatment of the signs of a problem rather than the causes, e.g. money may be directed to improving comfort to relieve overcrowding when the real problem is one concerning operations, which causes unreliability and cancellation of trains.

4. ORGANISATION, MANAGEMENT STYLE AND IMPLEMENTING THE OBJECTIVES

This paper is not a vehicle for a detailed treatment of various types of organisation, which might be suitable for a railway. Again, no one single solution would suit all countries and all circumstances. What is of the greatest importance is to recognise that organisation structures and management styles must be flexible to reflect changes in the role of the railway and the objectives which it is set. Reorganisation is difficult and disruptive but is often essential. The more flexible the structure the more it can bend, adjust and absorb changes in requirements without painful upheaval.

Assuming that proper high-level objectives are set by superior authority, it is the responsibility of management to convert them into aims for achievement by the subordinate levels. Those aims should always be relevant to the main objectives and should be expressed in terms which are appropriate for the recipient whether he is the head of a technical department, a business sector or an operations manager. All the aims must be internally consistent and the common thread has to be financial results on a net basis. The task is to "manage" and not simply to "run" the railway and there is a wealth of difference between them.

The major problems with a railway organisation are the wide geographical spread of activities, the volume of traffic handled, revenue earned and costs incurred and the great extent to which infrastructure facilities are shared and costs are joint. Attribution of costs (and to some extent revenues) has to be employed in any organisational shape which is to be workable and this is difficult to control. Nevertheless, the bringing together of costs and revenues in an appropriate number of separate business sectors, which match revenues and their associated costs will ensure the tightest possible control of financial results and will limit the extent to which responsibilities can be clouded. It will ensure that judgement-type decisions are kept to the minimum.

Such a "net revenue responsibility" type of organisation can be made to fit the different types of activity which the railway is required to undertake, e.g. freight, passenger, commercial or social, and facilitates the setting of objectives, which are meaningful to management. It reduces the problems which arise with organisations where line functions cross geographical responsibilities at numerous places and lessens the risk of wrong decision or no decision at the points of intersection - the points of indecisiveness.

It is worthwhile giving some thought to whether the management structure of a national railway should be as a government department, a separate statutory Corporation or even as a quasi-private sector operation. A government department is bound to be dominated by broad political factors and will tend to use the railway as part of the mechanisms of State, often subordinating transport and railway interests to wider economic and social issues. It is proper - and indeed, most desirable - that the railway should limit its activities to those at which it is good, and it would be wrong to force it to continue inefficient operations as a means of propping up an ailing industry or economic sector. This would be distortion and would cause the proper decisions not to be taken. This risk is reduced - if not completely avoided - if the railway is a statutory corporation, having financial duties and objectives, related to tasks for which it is most suitable. A quasi-private sector structure would be suitable if the main or major task of the railway was commercial and there were no social objectives for it to meet. In most developed countries this would be an unusual situation and such a pattern of organisation is unlikely to be attractive except for very small and discrete areas of activity. This would not be such a strong argument in the less developed countries and the system should be kept in mind, especially if it ensured that essential railway transport - provided or supported by aid, for example - was kept clear of political or other risks.

The style of management must always be relevant to the objectives and subsequent aims. In any modern economy, money is always a crucial factor and this is especially true in a national railway. Very important in its commercial activities, where it must work to a net profit if it is to survive, but no less so in its social benefit services where the Government is both the customer and the banker. The use of public money is a very sensitive matter calling for very clear accountability from both the user of that money - is he doing so efficiently? - and also the provider - is he making the best use of it? But how can it be judged and by whom? The financial results should give a good idea provided they are presented in a form which can be identified with the activities in question - and in a manner which is relevant to managing the business. All too often financial figures are presented in a way suitable for the annual accounts, as required by other areas of legislation, but not for managing the business. Perhaps both are necessary and, if so, the cost of producing them must be faced. As likely as not, however, the ultimate measurement will reflect public opinion or political expediency and the management style of the railway must be one which keeps in close touch with the views and needs of its customers and also the political atmosphere. Railway management must know what is going on and must adopt stances, which help it to sense and influence the political "wind". Normal marketing activities are an important part of managing a railway to meet the needs of people and freight, but equally important is close contact with press, television and politicians and involvement in general public affairs.

An organisation pattern and management style which is based on sectors of business rather than geographical areas, achieving effectiveness through a small number of managers responsible for the net financial results must have short lines of communication, well defined information systems, clear duty specifications and few overlaps. It requires minimum management and much supervision. In other words, responsibility for thinking and developments beyond the daily task of providing services, obtaining business and achieving planned financial results should rest with as few people as possible and the main task of the organisation must be to implement the plan. This is not to say that lower levels should not produce plans and budgets and contribute to longer-term policy, but everyone in that sub-level need not be involved and even those that are should be under strict control and work to a short time horizon. Managing a busy operating railway requires much daily attention and most of its staff should not be concerned with longer-term issues.

However, such issues do have to be faced because they will affect the objectives of the railway and its finances. Most issues of real importance to a railway are macro and are the consequences of changing national - or even world - economic and social conditions. Railway management must also, therefore, operate in large-scale, long-term and strategic terms and assess the ways in which they will come to bear a long way ahead. Twenty or so years forward is a proper horizon for this sort of consideration because it is in that time scale that the effects will work through the political and economic system. It is also an appropriate time scale for making changes in the physical structure and traction and rolling stock equipment of a railway and, equally important, the pace of change in conditions of service of employees. Human beings do not like change and nobody more so than trade unions. Gradually and slowly are the ingredients for changing working practices, which are seen as having been hard won in the past (generally true) and not to be given up easily or too quickly. Changing the established attitudes of trade unions demands trust, confidence and patience and these can only be developed over a long period and are only possible if future events are seen far enough ahead to enable their coming effects to be anticipated and gradually worked into the system.

The management style must link together the strategic view, the planning processes, which bring together all the separate activity and business plans within a medium-term programme and the budgets, which convert plans into action and present the picture upon which judgements and decisions can be made. This provides cohesive management and calls for a measure of centralisation - logical when it is realised how much of the infrastructure and activities of the railway have an underlying long-term commonality - but short-term results can be allocated to separate management. The important matter is time scale - short-term, say two years, for business sector management, medium-term, say five years, for corporate planning and budgeting as parts of one overall process, and beyond that for strategic thinking. Planning and strategy should be two interlinking parts of another overall process.

The subject of organisation and management style cannot be left without reference to the need for training and development. All areas of railway activity have changed immeasurably over the last thirty years and none more so than the responsibilities of managers. They have had to cope with technological change, industrial relations problems - which are now markedly different from the military style conceptions of servants, duties, responsibilities and adherence to orders of the past - political attitudes, new roles, withdrawal from old activities and above all else, the concept of financial control and value for money. Thirty years ago, very few railwaymen questioned costs or had any idea of the worth of traffic or areas of activity. The railways had operated in such a manner for one hundred years and that was quite good enough. Nowadays, managers have to see things differently and generally enjoy doing so, but it does mean that they must possess or develop different skills. There will always be a place for the disciplined, thinking, practical man provided he is aware of the cost and relevance of what he is doing but, more and more, railways must build on the skills of engineers, accountants and economists. They must be developed into practitioners rather than theorists, who can use their art to develop an effective railway producing good financial results in commercial and social terms. There is no room for the theorist who finds the railway wanting within his terms of reference and, therefore, rejects it out of hand. The selection of managers, their training at business schools and special courses and their development on the job is a highly professional activity and railway management style must embrace it wholeheartedly.

5. AN EFFECTIVE RAILWAY

The underlying theme of this paper on managing a railway to meet the transport needs of people and freight is that the railway should only be expected to do those things at which it is good. This represents a perfect situation, which is unlikely to apply very often, particularly in the complicated societies of modern nations. Thus, there is the area of the social railway, where the railway, although not entirely suitable, is better than any alternative. This is probably only a temporary situation as it reflects the fact that a railway already exists and keeping it going and providing operating support is cheaper than introducing an entirely new system with all the capital costs involved. It is very unlikely that many new rural passenger railways will be built and, even now, increasing problems are being experienced when present structures and rolling stock require heavy repairs or renewals.

The strengths of a railway system lie in its possession of a private right of way, the disciplined control of movement over it, the efficiency of the steel wheel on the steel rail in moving heavy loads at speeds and the superior economics of the rail line haul provided the unit of movement is big enough. The last point is of the greatest importance, and reflects the biggest weakness of a railway - the cost of creating a big enough load to take advantage of the long-distance line haul economics. A small country or one with few major industries or sources of bulky raw materials will have great difficulty in finding an effective role for railways at a worthwhile financial result. If freight train loads have to be put together from a number of separate traffic sources by a complicated tripping and shunting process, it is unlikely that it will be an effective and profitable operation. If the train load so constructed moves for a short distance only before being broken up again, the situation is made worse. Far better, in such circumstances, to use other forms of transport. A similar situation applies with meeting the transport needs of people. In the early days of railways, when most people did not move at all or did so by horse, the railway was a stupendous development, which was worth a great deal of effort to use. Nowadays, it is quite unthinkable to walk several miles to a station or to use a car or bus to get there if only a short rail journey is involved. Thus, the railway is weak in the areas of low volume and short-distance people movement. However, as with freight, if bulk movements of passengers can be developed at railheads and longer-distance movements encouraged by fast regular services, the strengths of the railway system are being employed and an effective role for the railway has been found.

Railway management must build on these strengths and provide services, which take advantage of them in terms of speed reliability and economy. Unless specially asked by Government to operate services in their weaker areas, and properly remunerated for so doing, they should seek to withdraw from them. If they are required to operate rural passenger services, for example, they must develop the simplest possible operations with minimum staff and equipment and tailor the service pattern to the "just adequate" at the lowest possible cost. The possibilities of connectional journeys via other services are very important and this applies equally to rail operated services and to any bus substitution which is introduced. In future, many rural railway lines must be replaced by the private motor car, mini-buses or conventional buses, perhaps operating as part of a total rail service pattern, if a properly integrated and effective transport plan is to be developed. The difficulties lie in persuading public opinion that this is the correct action; in making the alternative systems as comprehensive, available, reliable and cheap as the present for users and overcoming the resistance of trade unions to the reduction in jobs and the apparent - but not real - diminution of the railway system. As in other things, it will be a long process and the sooner it starts, the better.

Once management has succeeded in creating the proper role for railways in national transport policies based on these strengths and has developed (or has plans for) a network of services, which can secure the maximum amount of traffic, which can be handled effectively, its tasks are three fold. First, to invest in infrastructure and traction and rolling stock, which can take advantage of the rail line of communication with speed and economy. Secondly, to provide services, which reflect these advantages and can be operated productively and, lastly, to market those services to potential users in such a way that they are worth the highest possible rate that can be charged. Marketing is not selling. It requires far more understanding of the customers' production and distribution processes, of reasons for and patterns of travel of the people; it requires flexible railway services to fit in with users' requirements; it calls for deep financial understanding of the revenue and capital costs involved on both sides; it requires a knowledge of spare capacity available and the marginal costs of putting it to advantage; it needs an understanding of the effects of national costs on railway costs and vice versa.

Thus, regarding the strengths and weaknesses of a railway and converting them into an effective transport agency calls for many skills in railway managers, which are very different from those needed in the early days. Transport man, financier, economist, politician - all in one makes the modern railway manager and enables him to influence the nation into selecting the proper role for his industry and setting the correct objectives.

6. FINANCIAL MANAGEMENT

This paper deals with the management of a railway to meet transport needs and has shown the importance of proper objectives and financial management. Financial management can be defined simply as the supply and control of the money which passes through the business. Earlier sections have differentiated between commercial and social benefit activities, but they can be seen as being controlled in a similar way financially if Government support and fares income are taken together as a market rate for the social railway product. Commercial businesses depend upon costs, including the replacement of assets, being lower than revenues, competitiveness maintained, new developments introduced, new or expanded markets tackled and interest paid on borrowings. Social benefit activities require that costs are kept as low as possible and fares and charges do not drive away traffic but bring in sufficient revenue so that the consequent gap with costs is not beyond the level at which the nation deems the railway service to be worthwhile. Alternatively, maintenance of a predetermined level of traffic could be an objective set and varied by Government through a fares policy.

The commercial business area thus requires a tight control of costs, but gives railway management freedom to adjust prices to market levels and use this mechanism to maximise use of capacity with net financial benefits. Spare pockets of capacity in rolling stock, train loadings and infrastructure must be identified so that they can be marketed to greatest advantage or removed if that would produce the best financial result. The financial management of this sector is similar to a private sector company which has a statutory duty to continue in business and avoid bankruptcy.

The social services sector and its financial management present much greater complication. It begins with the initial decisions that such services are worthwhile and how much it is worth paying for them, followed by subordinate judgements about what level and quality of service, how much the users should pay, and whether all should pay the same amount. The first decision rests upon social cost/benefit assessments (which are notoriously difficult to make and will vary with circumstances), environmental benefit considerations, social and economic (job creation) opportunities and often - although probably not really very relevant - traditional practices. The subordinate decisions are more difficult and, generally, of greater significance. Often, the decision to provide socially necessary services is easy, can be seen to be correct and be accompanied by support levels, which are not high in terms of national finances. The second level is subjective and emotional as it brings the matter down to a scale, which is comprehensible and where the difference of a few millions in money terms has a meaning. Frequency of service, quality of the rolling stock, conditions of stations, efficiency of communications are all tangible items which generate forceful opinions. In this detailed area railway management must have sole responsibility for decisions guided by the high-level objectives and backed by an overall limit to the amount of financial support available from Government.

EEC regulations permit support of social railway services through the Public Service Obligation compensatory payments, which can be seen as a contract with railway management for the provision of services considered to be socially necessary. Inevitably, there is an element of political expediency about the obligation but given a clear understanding of what is required, i.e. the need, how that need is to be met, how much it is worth and how the costs are made up, a workable relationship between Government and railway management will be possible. It will never be free of tension and disagreement. It cannot be, because there will, inevitably, be a degree of generalisation in the scope of the services to be covered in the PSO and, because of joint use of assets, there will be attributions of costs and revenues, which present opportunities for disagreements. An overall PSO covering a large number of social services and, possibly, some, or all, of the commercial services is an imprecise instrument with many weaknesses. As far as possible the PSO should be expressed in segments clearly reconciled with the financial results of properly identifiable groups of services. Management organisation, style and information flows should reflect this.

Normally, a PSO payment is revenue account based, and this leaves an area of difficulty around the replacement of physical assets. Maintaining them is clearly a matter of current operations and rightly within the PSO, but replacement, or the provision of new equipment, raises many problems especially when having to take inflation into account. Should the PSO be large enough to cover all reasonable and proper items? Should all capital expenditure be outside it? Should capital expenditure be separate from operating costs and revenue and funded by special grants? If so, how should such grants be justified and who should provide them? How should they be controlled by Government against its original judgement that a certain level of social service at a certain cost to public funds is worthwhile? If they are kept separate from the PSO how should they be funded? Against the current fashion of controlling the financing of national industries by External Financing Limits this could be difficult because there may not be sufficient headroom to absorb these requirements of the social services as well as the capital needs of all other activities. It may be perfectly acceptable to borrow money to finance worthwhile investment in commercial activities, but these borrowings would be in competition with the needs of social services within a fixed EFL. Who is to make the choice - Government or railway management?

There are no clear answers to this conundrum at the moment and it is a matter requiring urgent resolution because until it is resolved, the physical state of the assets of social railways and the ability of commercial services to develop and prosper are in jeopardy. What does seem clear is that efficiency will be enhanced if all genuine operating costs, including the normal maintenance of fixed and rolling equipments should be covered by revenue. This would leave renewals, life extensions and improvements in quality and extent of service offered to be met by separate capital grants. The level of these and their funding should rest with Government taking the advice of railway management about the most cost effective investments and relating their decisions to the national economic and social position and the implications of the investment on the overall objectives they have set railway management. They must not require railway management to make decisions between conflicting objectives in the areas of vital investments.

A few important, but smaller, points need to be made in concluding this section on financial management. First, it is very important to identify the full benefits stemming from railway services and all those who enjoy them. They are rarely, if ever, solely the users and there are many individuals, business activities, communities and local authorities, who benefit indirectly from the existence of railways. Since local prosperity in terms of employment opportunities, quality of life, education amenities, etc., is raised because the railway provides the opportunity and the impetus, these beneficiaries must provide some responsive finance to enable the services to continue and to avoid excessive costs falling on travellers and national exchequers. The question of wider contributions is inadequately answered at the moment and if tackled properly will be found to provide helpful answers to the problems of finance.

Financing changes in railway operations is an increasing problem. Many systems are wearing out; many need to change to grasp an opportunity or to reflect new social and economic conditions created by outside processes; many just need to get up to date and get rid of old-fashioned ways. All require funds to replace assets or buy out working practices but cannot afford to spend the limited money available in this way because other opportunities provide better returns, or the consequent burden in terms of higher fares would be intolerable for present users. Ways must be found to cut these knots and make additional money available now for these worthwhile improvements. Transition grants - accounted for separately - provide an answer. They should be interest free, or at low rates, if the project is essential socially or to remove outdated impediments, or over long periods if there is likely to be a worthwhile return a relatively long time ahead. They are investments to increase efficiency and not subsidies to prop up bad practices.

7. LABOUR RELATIONS

Railway operations are very human activities and rely heavily on intelligent and dedicated work by individuals performing on their own with little or no supervision and few opportunities for consultation and receipt of advice. High-quality staff with high involvement and morale are, therefore, essential. This must be reflected in pay levels which, in turn, demand good productivity.

In their early years, railways were the advanced technology of the time and attracted the best type of workman, who was used to a highly disciplined relationship between master and servant. This was fostered by early railway management and was valuable in inculcating the traditions of reliability and efficiency that were necessary to ensure an effective railway service operating over a wide geographical area. The less than reliable new technologies in the hands of inexperienced men called for much local initiative and dedication.

These qualities are still required today, although technological developments and communications have taken away much of the unreliability and uncertainty. These developments have been accompanied by changes in human nature, where men and women are not prepared to be taken for granted; expect to be consulted and to be allowed to make a contribution; and require fair and improving conditions and remuneration. This is reflected in the rise of organised trade unions and the increasing part which railway staff insist on playing in the management of their chosen occupation.

This is a most valuable development, which must be fostered and encouraged - but directed into productive channels. Management has a duty to educate and train its staff and develop their initiative in the technicalities of their work, in the new and changing role of the railway, its relevance to national affairs, the economics of industry and the railway itself and the relationship between input and reward. The fact that little or nothing put in means little or nothing coming out is not always clearly understood. Management must ensure that over the years - and it will be a very long task - these lessons are learned and that every employee has the opportunity to become acquainted with the business facts of the railway. There are few, if any, secrets that really need to be kept and facts must be revealed and staff encouraged to become involved.

It is unlikely that the trade unions will wish to become directly involved in the management processes as to do so would inhibit their prime duty of seeking to improve the conditions of their members. However, they must be involved in the objectives and results, the national scene and the way their railway fits into it. In this area they have as much responsibility and as many duties as management and must be given the facts and kept in the know. This can be accomplished through a consulting style, where management and trade union leaders sit around a table as equals to receive results, discuss problems and consider developments in a corporate way. Thus, they become partners and can see conditions of service, remunerations, productivity, efficiency, traffic levels, revenue, investment, support, etc., as part of a balance sheet and can make their decisions in an informed and constructive way. This requires trust and knowledge and accumulated confidence. It will not be achieved overnight but will develop over time with the application of patience and understanding on all sides, which includes Government as well as management and trade unions.

8. ENERGY

Recent years have seen concern about the availability and cost of energy now and in the future and, quite properly, a great deal of attention has been given to the likely problems. They concern national economies to the greatest extent but transport, as part of those economies and businesses in their own right is caught up with them. Availability and cost of fuel are the two main factors with the latter as the more important. There will always be fuel - if it is not oil, it will be a substitute - but the cost will increase in real terms. No-one can be positive about how much, but it will be significant. We should not be misled by the current apparent stability in crude oil prices. This is the result of the recession which is gripping the world and the consequent lack of bargaining power of the oil producers. As the slump recedes, oil becomes more difficult to recover and when substitute processes are developed the price will rise.

The transport industry must heed the warning and make every effort to become fuel efficient. Research and development programmes must concentrate on this aspect of costs and management must strive for more fuel efficient operations. The basic requirement is to ensure that each form of transport is used only where it is most effective - where it can operate on its strengths and with the largest possible loads. As this coincides with the fundamentals discussed under the headings of objectives and financing no additional problems arise. Within this requirement the technical question of the best form of fuel becomes important. With railways the issue is between diesel oil and electricity for traction.

It is difficult to determine whether, or not, electric traction produces primary energy savings as the overall energy conversion processes for electric and diesel traction are similar, but diesel has the disadvantage in that it must carry its own power plant and fuel, which is a significant weight (and energy) penalty. In services where it is commercially desirable to achieve a high level of performance, the weight penalty of upgrading or providing diesel traction capable of achieving the same level of performance as electric traction could incur a primary energy penalty of up to 30 per cent. In practice, an electrified railway is operated at higher speeds than diesel, because the marginal costs of providing such extra performance with electric trains is small. The optimum commercial result is to provide a faster more attractive service giving better resource utilisation. Insofar as the theoretical savings possible are translated into an improved service little, if any, overall saving in primary energy will occur with conversion to electric traction but the improvements in the quality of the service for a given level of price could attract traffic to rail and, to the extent that this would be a transfer from air or road travel which, at typical load factors are less energy efficient modes of transport, there would be some primary energy savings overall.

More specifically, electric railways reduce national dependence on oil, which can be very important in national economic and financial terms if oil has to be imported. Most countries are planning to reduce their total oil consumption in the future by, typically, some 5 per cent and increasing the extent of electrified railways will make a worthwhile contribution to this. The ability to reduce a nation's dependence on oil for transport - and make it available for other more important uses - by replacing it by electricity, which has the flexibility to be generated from the most appropriate or readily available fuels, must be reflected in management activity in the next few years. There must be at least one form of national transport that is independent of the oil pipeline. The fact that it will also be cheaper to operate and more efficient and attractive to customers is an additional bonus, which railway managers must represent clearly and forcibly at all times until the goal of widespread electrification in the national interest is attained(1).

9. NATIONAL INDUSTRIES AND THE PRIVATE SECTOR

With a few exceptions, developed countries have mixed economies - national industries and utilities exist, compete and work alongside privately owned counterparts and live with them effectively as many are customers of each other, either transporting their goods or buying their products. It is very important that this should be so and vital that the expertise of each sector should find mutual support and opportunities.

Railways can obtain help in many ways. In the Board Room or highest levels of management where experience and judgement forged in different fires can be valuable aids to decision making; combining the skills of scientists and technicians in mutually valuable research and development programmes is fruitful; entrepreneurial marketing, which keeps private businesses alive, is increasingly necessary to railways seeking to build on their strengths by integrating their transportation processes with the production lines and distribution patterns of industry; joint training programmes for managers, accountants, economists and financiers teach both sides a great deal; and there are other areas of joint co-operation, which need to be fostered.

A most important area of involvement concerns the availability and provision of capital funds for essential renewals and developments. Inevitably, because they are part of the national economy, railways are subject to the wider policies of Government and in times of financial stringency they must take their share of restrictive measures. These are generally applied as a reduction of financing limits, which affects the money available for investment. This is particularly true in times of heavy inflation, and is logical as it is the inflation itself which is the basic cause of the difficulties. In these conditions railway management must seek ways and means

---

1. This chapter is based on the Review of Main Line Electrification - a joint study by the British Railways Board and the Department of Transport. Published in 1981 in London by HMSO.

of replacing the restricted national funds from other sources so as to prevent the deterioriation of their assets and ensure that they will be properly equipped to take advantage of the opportunities as the difficulties disappear. This is a responsible thing to do provided there is no risk of fuelling the causes of inflation or consuming funds, which could be put to more valuable use in other parts of the economy. In these circumstances railways should be seeking to invest in capital projects which will increase efficiency, reduce costs and utilise otherwise underused production capacity. There are opportunities for railways and their supplying industries, which Governments should encourage, where possible.

A development of great significance concerns the actual transfer of parts from a national industry to the private sector. This may be because of current political policy, or because there is no real logic in the activity being part of the industry or as an expedient to obtain access to fresh sources of funds and/or managerial ability. Whatever the reason, it can be encouraged if positive benefits will accrue either to the national industry or the business sector in which it operates. The only proviso should be that if the ultimate intention is to retain the industry in a nationalised state nothing should be done which will prejudice its main activity and nothing should be permitted which distorts the terms of competition, trading or investing funds - neither national industry, private business nor investor should gain any special benefit.

10. INTERNATIONAL FACTORS

Since the Second World War there has been a great increase in international co-operation, co-ordination of activities and sharing of knowledge and experience. This is particularly true of railways, especially in Europe and is not really surprising because the national systems have been connected for more than a century and as the raison d'être of railways is to provide mobility of people and goods there is no real reason why frontiers should intervene.

Although it is true that nations have different characteristics it is always noticeable that whenever railway people get together (it is probably just as true in other walks of life) they have many common interests, attitudes to problems and similarity of answers. There is clear recognition that a transit system must be treated as a whole so that the benefits of widespread connections, long hauls, improved use of resources, larger marketing opportunities and shared research can be exploited. UIC and ORE are examples of this, and other developments within the EEC are bearing fruit on a more local basis.

A recent comparison of the performance and policies of ten European railways has put together a mass of valuable information, which is proving to be a spur to greater or differently directed effort which will be increasingly useful. It should be kept up to date and widened in scope. Among the items covered, the study revealed the importance of international traffic within the total activities of the railways concerned. It ranged from 2 per cent for BR through just over 20 per cent for DB and SNCF to over 60 per cent for FS and NS. There is a clear indication in these figures that the sea barrier between BR, SNCF and SNCB is a major impediment. The Channel tunnel is obviously a vital necessity offering long-distance transits by rail, which will be a great benefit to the finances of all European railways and to the economies of Europe.

The building of tunnels under water or mountain barriers; the closure of gaps in and between systems; cut off and spur lines to reduce distances; combined technological research and development and the wider availability of investment funds will enable railways to expand their services, improve their quality and reduce their costs so that they can be more competitive with other forms of transport and stimulate movement where none exists now. Passenger and freight traffic will increase and financial results improve. International railway co-operation is of great importance.

11. CONCLUSION

Railways can play a major part in meeting transport needs to the benefit of the national economy.

They can do so effectively only if they are selected to undertake those transport tasks for which they are best suited and given clear objectives against which to perform.

Those objectives can be both commercial and social and must always reflect the financial constraints which are to apply. They should be expressed at a general level leaving railway management to determine their detailed implementation.

The financial mechanisms which relate national interests and railway management performance should be consistent with the objectives and should not confuse revenue and capital factors.

They should be sufficiently flexible to permit access to adequate capital funds outside the public sector whenever such a course would be beneficial.

The increased involvement of staff in the policies, finances and operation of the railways on a partnership basis is of growing importance.

Electricity is the preferred form of traction as it combines efficiency of operation with economy and energy effectiveness. Adequate funds should be made available for electrification in the years ahead.

International co-operation, technical development and traffic growth through improved links such as the Channel tunnel are important factors for the future.

TOPIC 2D

MANAGEMENT OF FIRMS
TO SATISFY TRANSPORT NEEDS

RAILWAYS

Mr. G. VÁZQUEZ CÁBEZAS
Ingenieria y Economia del Transporte, S.A.
Madrid, Spain

1. INTRODUCTION

The management or administration of an undertaking involves running the institution and ordering, allocating and organising its resources. Railway management objectives can be summarised as the production of supply balanced as to the volume, quality and pricing required by demand, with the aim of achieving the optimum socio-economic benefit. On the last point, the views of the undertaking and of the community may well not coincide, and where this is so, and where the railways are unable to provide services under competitive conditions such as to ensure a positive return on operations, the general interest can be made to override the specific interests of the undertaking, provided that doing so promotes the greatest social benefit and that the clearest possible view is gained of the consequences involved in each policy choice.

This report begins with a reflection on the pressures by Spanish society on transport demand, and an analysis of the current major issues affecting the railways which serve it, expanding into a detailed critique of current planning and the enumeration of some basic factors in securing maximum utilisation in furtherance of the final benefit to society.

2. DEMAND CONSTRAINTS

Albeit briefly, before focusing attention on the current major issues and the future of the railways, it appears appropriate to consider the trend in passenger and freight demand in order to investigate the cause and history of behaviour patterns, the root causes underlying demand patterns and, before reaching the necessary conclusions, to pinpoint the desired characteristics of railway supply in order thereby to render its role more suitable in catering for each type of activity in which it may be used, whether alone, in competition or in co-operation with the remaining modes, with the policy instruments it has available, and also those which may lend themselves to the purpose.

2.1. Trend in mobility

The tables in the attached statistical annex (Table Nos. 1 to 3) attempt to set forth the basic parameters situating Spanish society today. It can be gathered from them that a radical change has occurred in the national economy, and a glimpse can be gained of the substantial changes in its social structure and in the indicators of its behaviour.

The geographical location of the population has indeed undergone one substantial change in evolving from a rural society to an urban one. This process has been under way alongside, and has effectively supported the expansion of the most significant components of the economy, as reflected in the trend in incomes and in gross domestic product. Hence, when considering macro-economic measurements, the low population density, of some 73 inhabitants per square kilometre, the heavily-accidented mountain conditions which affect both mobility and transport supply characteristics, place Spain today in a mid-field position, in the group of the less developed countries amongst the Member countries of the ECMT. The phenomenon of urbanisation runs parallel with industrial concentration and increased production.

All this leads to increased mobility of passengers and goods and to certain changes in their behaviour patterns which it might perhaps be useful to recall, since it is these that underlie some of the factors behind the railways' situation. Their enumeration could be useful in classifying railway services in an approach from the angle of adaptation to demand constraints and hence, in defining rational criteria for improved management.

With regard to the population, the increase in the number of journeys which is a feature of all upward trends in family income has been affected in the main by three identifiable trends in primary activities:

- the reduction in the working day, in weekly hours worked and in working days in the week, and the increase in holiday periods;
- the predominant role played by education as a fundamental activity of society;
- the interrelationship of the various industrial sectors, the specialisation of manufacturing industry and the expansion of markets.

Hand-in-hand with the new profile of activities come substantial changes in the pattern of mobility:

- the shorter working day frees more time for leisure and purchases;

  . it concentrates urban and suburban journeys over five days in the week,
  . it affords scope for long journeys, including

journeys abroad, with regular changes of residence during holiday-times.

- the boom in university-level education makes for
  considerable inter-city movements although the
  greatest impact of this is felt in an urban context;
- the extension of trade, the interdependence and
  complexity of industrial links, the predominance of
  commercial and marketing activities lead to further
  inter-city business travel.

There would be no presumption in considering that
this tranformation of habits and attitudes would be un-
imaginable or would have proceeded at a much slower rate,
if it had not coincided with the general spread and con-
solidation, even the supremacy of new modes of transport.
Furthermore, the improvement in supply has boosted the
concentration of activities in urban areas to such an extent that on the one hand a rash of property speculation
has broken out, with the result that high-density dormitory suburbs have been built, and on the other, the quality of urban life has degenerated, a trend which finds
its counterpart in the low-density residential areas on
the outskirts of cities.

Apart from the Madrid industrial zone and some isolated points inland, the major manufacturing centres are
located on the periphery of the peninsula: hence imports,
which are substitutes for home manufactures, are virtually
carried to their destination by sea. However, from the
standpoint of mobility of goods, various points can be
made which, while affecting the intensity of traffic or
the quality of goods, impose precise requirements upon
supply:

- preferential location of industrial centres at the
  periphery of the country, despite the inland location of some centres of development, cause the
  approximation of production sites to consumption
  centres;
- coal consumption in coal-fired power stations located near mine-heads;
- the significance in volume terms of petroleum
  products;
- the expansion in the production of manufactured
  goods;
- the regulation of crop surpluses, particularly
  cereals;
- the boom in the construction and chemicals
  industries;
- the expansion of fruit and vegetable crop
  production.

In this way, on the basis of a general raising of
production levels and the more frequent handling of goods
at the various processing stages, the shorter journeys

553

gain ground on the longer journeys, the sizes of shipments
between a given shipper and consignee diminish, with some
exceptions, and a network of industrial and trading links
becomes consolidated, calling for considerable agility and
swift response to its transport needs in the endeavour to
rationalise stock levels, having regard to the high cost
of financing them.

2.2. Trend in demand

In very direct relationship with the socio-economic
variables referred to, demand for transport has been constantly increasing, while at the same time calling for new
qualities in the supply, which has tended towards diversification. Quantitative trends will be discussed first of
all, then the basic changes underlying shifts in behaviour
patterns as evidenced by the shift of priorities in the
evaluation of supply characteristics.

2.2.1. Volume and quality

On a 1955 base, while overall passenger transport
demand has increased 12-fold, demand for goods alone has
increased fivefold, both components at a more rapid pace
than production which, at market prices, has only increased 3.3 times (see Tables 4 and 5). With regard to
passenger mobility within the national territory, the most
significant fact is that 92.7 per cent of the increase in
demand has been absorbed by roads for which the car has
become the leading factor in this respect, a fact which
should cause no surprise if it is noted that from a car
ownership index of four private cars to 1,000 inhabitants
in 1955, the figure increased to 23 cars in 1965 and
reached over 200 in 1980, with a slight increase in passenger-kilometres travelled by private cars over the same
period, in spite of the incidence of oil price increases
on car use.

If the aforementioned trend is indisputable, it is
also true of air transport, of which the competitiveness
on a national scale will be touched upon in paragraph 3.2.2., reflected in a sharp fall in the share of
railways in the modal split for demand, it is no less certain, and at times it is taken for granted, that the latter has seen its own demand increase 1.51 times over the
same period (1.69 times in the case of RENFE)(1).

Having established this point, while per capita income has risen 2.5 times and railway staffing levels have

---

1. The lack of homogeneity in the figures available,
commented upon in the Annex, prevents the true value being
obtained which, on the same basis of calculation, would
lie around 2.2 for RENFE.

fallen to just above half over the same period, other causes would in consequence be investigated (not just the trend in traffic) while the present major issues would be examined from the standpoint of existing difficulties, in order to achieve the hoped-for equilibrium.

Concerning freight transport demand, progress over the last 20 years has been similar to passenger transport demand, with fairly low rates of increase, though with comparable behaviour to that of the road sector. Excluding coasting traffic, which is important in Spain, since links with island provinces are dependent upon it, it can be estimated that 94 per cent of the increase has been cornered by road traffic, while railways alone have increased their traffic by 24 per cent (33 per cent for RENFE), with their share of freight traffic being reduced from 33 to 8 per cent.

Nevertheless, on the basis of limited data for 1975 which it was impossible to change to relative levels to take account of the boom in the coal sector, the crisis in construction and the differing extent to which the economic paralysis may have affected the various sectors, the pattern of demand calls for comment, and Tables 6 and 7 have been compiled accordingly, whence the following deductions can be made:

- 49.86 per cent of demand in tonnes is carried for distances of less than 50 kilometres;
- 83.23 per cent of demand is for an average carrying distance of less than 100 kilometres;
- only 9.45 per cent of demand is carried for average distances greater than 150 kilometres and 10 groups travelling over more than 200 kilometres assume not more than some 2.71 per cent of total demand;
- out of all those classes of goods of which the percentage carried exceeds 1 per cent of total demand only in four, equivalent to 8.28 per cent of demand, does the average distance carried exceed 100 kilometres and in no case does it exceed 200 kilometres.

All this would be incomplete without the corroborative evidence (in Table 8) that 91.8 per cent of transport demand has undergone an average of 2.8 interchanges between its production site and the centre of consumption.

The expansion of passenger incomes and the increase in value added of manufactured goods have led in both cases to a lower incidence of cost of transport on the market price of consumer products (labour, leisure, etc., or goods as such).

555

2.2.2. Supply requirements

Taking account of the volumes and types of demand referred to in the previous section, each area of operation in primary activities makes demands upon supply which in this section are presented in the form of characteristics.

Passenger transport demand can be set forth as follows, albeit only broadly outlined:

Demand	Requirements of supply	Features required of supply
Suburban	. capacity	. high capacity at peak periods
	. regularity	. high frequency at peak periods
	. co-ordination	. pace of services (availability) in off-peak periods
	. flexibility	. rapid penetration into city centres
	. speed	. interchange with the urban and suburban transport system
		. competitive fares or combined fare systems
Intercity	. convenience	. matching of timetables (availibility)
	. rapidity	. high speed for daytime travel
	. regularity	. capacity which can be aggregated on certain specific days
	. comfort	. additional facilities (countryside, meals, magazines, music, etc.)
		. prices commensurate with the standard of service

Regarding goods traffic, from the results of a survey in 1978 of 960 industrial locations, covering a sample of 45 per cent of domestic production in tonnes, any further implementation of plans is rendered unnecessary in view of the order in which the following factors affect modal choice (see Table No. 9):

- Price is a major influencing factor, being considered first in 37 per cent of replies received,

although its frequency falls to 24 per cent if the
three first factors mentioned by each interviewee
are considered.
- Delivery time is the foremost factor for some
22 per cent of those interviewed.
- However if all factors in some way relating to time
are considered together, rather in the sense of the
expiration of delivery times than of their duration, the percentage of those who place this first
rises to 42 per cent and to 49.5 per cent for the
first three factors taken together.
- Door-to-door service is a characteristic of supply
which is increasingly taken into account by demand
in making the modal choice. On the other hand, the
physical safety of consignments is of declining
concern and distance alone is only considered in
very few instances when making the choice.

3. CURRENT MAJOR ISSUES AND THE FUTURE

The railways in Spain, with a consolidated network
under RENFE (Red Nacional de los Ferrocarriles Espanoles)
of a wider gauge than the European network, a complex of
narrow-gauge lines, often discontinuous, consolidated
under the FEVE (Ferrocarriles de vía estrecha), various
lengths of competing narrow-gauge track within the province of the Autonomous Governments of the Basque Country
and of Cataluna and some private, basically mining, railways (see Annex, Table 10 and Figure 1) have for ten years
been experiencing considerable economic as well as financial difficulties which have become more acute in recent
years. The marginal nature of the railway undertakings
not consolidated under RENFE, although they may contribute - and have in fact done so - their share to the reduced market which they serve, it would be advisable to
focus attention on examining RENFE - although without excluding provision of some additional data on the other
railways.

The major issues covered in this chapter arise from
an etiology which underlies the nature of the railways,
the configuration of the network, the structure of the
undertaking, and the management and operating techniques,
but is not bound by these limits, being included in the
regulatory forces of the transport market, and in the
final analysis the social domain it serves. Examination
of this item will therefore proceed in two sections, of
which the first considers endogenous causes and the second
exogenous causes. From their correlation should be deduced those measures that should be proposed to promote the
more efficient use of the resources set aside by society
for the railways to secure optimum returns for society's
benefit.

3.1. Endogenous causes

Looking at the national RENFE network from outside, the characteristic feature of its situation is the chronic deficit of many years' standing which is making it ever more doubtful whether it can be made to reach an economic break-even and gives grounds for considering, in some quarters, the option of cutting back its activity as the only way to deal with the problem.

However, the foremost concern of undertakings must undoubtedly be the financial difficulties, which do not arise exclusively from internal management results but are related rather to the public finance situation in a way that will be analysed in detail.

A rapid review of other points determining the characteristics of the network will enable us to come closer to understanding how this state of affairs arose, bringing us to the point where it can be explained internally, as well as enabling us to grasp the pattern of the Gordian knots, which it is management's prime task to untie, in order to improve the balance and be forearmed to face the challenge of the future with the appropriate means.

The first point to be tackled, in a logical exposition of the problem, should be that of the major issues as reflected in expenditure followed by those issues arising from insufficient revenue, and then an examination of the factors working against a break-even.

3.1.1. Issues reflected in expenditure

For purposes of analysis, we shall break down total expenditure into the three conventional components:

- operating expenditure (staff, energy, equipment and sundries);
- depreciation;
- finance.

It might be very interesting to tabulate the major parameters for 1969 and 1980 in order to observe the trend in operating expenditure as shown in the table on the following page.

From an analysis of the results obtained, the following conclusions can be drawn and behaviour patterns established:

- The increase in operating expenditure is identical to increases in output and incomes. Therefore not all improvements in technical productivity have been reflected in economic productivity.

558

REAL TRENDS IN THE MAJOR COMPONENTS OF THE ECONOMY

Item	1969(1)	1980 (2)	Ratio of (2) to (1)
Per-capita national income (1980 Pesetas)	275,505	378,576	1.374
Production (million train-kilometres)	168,000	175,000	1.042
Operating expenditure (1980 Pesetas million)	84,000	121,702	1.432
Staff expenditure (1980 Pesetas million)	53,271	83,206	1.562
Per-capita staff costs (1980 Pesetas)	604,100	1,174,400	1.944
Energy expenditure (1980 Pesetas million)	8,843	7,970	0.901
Expenditure on equipment and sundries (1980 Pesetas million)	21,029	30,526	1.452

Source: RENFE and author's compilation.

- Offsetting the increase in energy prices, an improvement in the energy-dependency position is observable in absolute and relative terms. Such a development should not be understood as resulting from greater efficiency, at equal levels, in primary energy consumption, but rather as the consequence, to a large extent, of the electrification plans and of contracts with electricity suppliers. The capacity of railways to respond to the rise in oil prices can be noted in any case.
- The increase in expenditure on equipment and sundries implies a further increase in the revenue spent in labour itself related to the causes of the financial difficulties on this account which RENFE is experiencing. The delays in payment of more than six months, and the high cost of money allow one to suggest that roughly 10 per cent of this component actually corresponds to financial costs.
- On the basis of objective data which would deserve to be contrasted with similar positions in other undertakings in the sector and in the national economic situation, all increases in productivity and improvements in management, as well as a sizeable proportion of the increase in subsidies have worked back to staff in the form of direct wages and social security costs.

The immediate causes of this trend, which was partly maintained throughout staff reductions over the 1969-1973 period, can be pinpointed as:

- initially low wage costs;
- a sizeable increase in real income;
- political pressures on management during this period;
- the continued existence of an operating structure which will be examined in paragraph 3.1.3.

Depreciation

Depreciation cannot be examined without considering assets and also in this case the rate of investment. Table 12 was compiled for this purpose (see Annex) making for further conclusions:

- Depreciation comes to 4 per cent of capital invested at current prices, i.e. assets for year n, plus investment, less depreciation. Capital investment is therefore a summing of non-homogeneous items which is of no significance.
- Fixed assets, following recent estimates, amount to roughly Pesetas 1 billion at 1980 prices. Depreciation at replacement cost should amount to some Pesetas 40,000,000, at similar rates of depreciation, and to some Pesetas 50,000 million on periods closer to the real average working life of railway asset investments. Given that Spanish legislation does not provide for tax concessions on the revaluation of assets or depreciation at replacement cost, the profit and loss accounts have suffered distortion and the negative balance shown on them should be increased by between Pesetas 30,000,000 and Pesetas 40,000,000 for the 1980 financial year.
- Average annual investment for the period under review was Pesetas 47,500,000 from which it can be deduced that between 63 and 84 per cent of this was set aside for replacement investment, which may improve the quality though not the quantity of supply. There are reasonable indications that this percentage should be greater since preservation of some items can be catalogued as maintenance costs.

This practice leads to a steady decline in the capital stock of the railway network and seriously compromises any investment programme, especially where no preservation balances are explicitly formulated.

Interest

The increase in interest has been far more rapid than the increase in operating expenditure, and is sufficiently similar to the total deficit on this item for it to be closely correlated. Interest charges do indeed bear a direct relationship as matters stand to the central government's delays in paying its share of the costs and the inability to meet investment needs from central government funds. In essence, this increase occurs as the consequence of recourse to credit for:

- investment;
- satisfying cash requirements in the very short term;
- covering exceptional deficits not forecast in the original estimate, and therefore not included in central government estimates.

As indicated earlier, the financial costs of suppliers are included as expenditure where they are embodied in purchase or assistance contracts on the basis of prudential provisions for services.

3.1.2. Effects on income

There must obviously be some relationship between specific demand and the fare system, although it is no less obvious that demand cannot be defined on a piecemeal basis in absolute values. Rather, an identical variable should be included for the other competing modes of transport and the remainder of the characteristics of multimodal supply, as well as those of overall demand, in order to arrive at a satisfactory explanation. However, to view matters from within the undertaking, reasons may be found to account for the real fall in fare income.

Furthermore, an examination of the following table confirms that real receipts have fallen, by 13.7 per cent for passengers and by 6.7 per cent for goods. Taking into account actual increases in traffic between both dates, an apparent fall in fare-levels can be deduced, by 48.4 and 33.1 per cent respectively. If, for basic fares, this reduction was smaller, the final result per unit carried is changed by:

TREND IN REAL INCOME
(1980 ptas. million)

Category	1969	1980
Passengers	33,365	28,800
Goods	34,426	32,128
Mail	3,655	4,474
Other	7,073	10,392
Total	78,519	77,794

- the introduction of concessionary passenger fares, for individuals and groups, on specified days in the year;
- an increase in suburban demand on trains at lower fares than those for long-haul journeys;

- the existence of concessionary fares for certain
  kinds of freight traffic (mineral ores, cereals,
  etc.) under constraints which are exogenous in
  character;
- internal transfers of demand from the more expensive services to the cheaper services;
- fares for the greater part of full-wagon traffic
  are governed by agreements between RENFE and its
  clients on a reduced-fare basis.

However, undoubtedly, given the number of services
available with average occupancies virtually never greater
than 60 per cent, more demand might be taken on than actually is, the reason being that the quality of such services is generally poor on account of the structure of the
network itself and for reasons of internal arrangements as
evidenced by the fact that(2):

- only five suburban lines have frequencies greater
  than or equal to five trains per hour at peak
  periods and four other lines have a frequency of
  four trains per hour;
- only on one neighbourhood line are combined fares
  available for use on part of the connecting urban
  services;
- there are very few daytime inter-city services with
  distances of less than 350 to 400 km and they are
  generally of poor frequency(3);
- the service speeds for these daytime services are
  very low, not exceeding some 80 kilometres per hour
  until 1980(4), and still lower in relation to other
  transport modes when distances between two points
  are considered;
- the carriage of goods by full wagon-loads does not
  guarantee delivery-time, and acceptable quality of
  service is only achieved when assignments are sent
  in complete trainloads;
- sending consignments piecemeal by the full wagon-
  load makes for considerable dispersion in the dates
  of delivery at the point of destination;
- goods wagons are not available, through lack of
  flexibility on occasions, to satisfy unscheduled
  demand.

---

2. Elsewhere in this paper some of these reasons will
be related to other causes, both structural and exogenous
to the railway undertaking.
3. 1980-81, work began on the remodelling of some of
these services which are having to cater for an increase
in demand of some 7 per cent.
4. In 1981 services were introduced with service
speeds of up to 110 km/h. for certain inter-city routes
and up to 98 km/h. over 1,100 km.

3.1.3. Difficulties in improving the income/expenditure ratio

It would probably be presumptuous, and we shall refer to this further on, to seek to make a national railway network break even, designed as it is with the limitations and purpose of service which are common to the railway networks operating in Western Europe. Nevertheless, within the framework of the case analysis in this report, separate well-grounded reasons can be identified as tending to make the desired object still less attainable. In this paragraph we go on to state the internal reasons which, in my view, have major repercussions.

a) Network structure

From the structural point of view, the Spanish railway network, both by its pattern and by its characteristics, fails to match accurately the majority of the trends in the pattern of industrial and urban development, since:

- the railway network is markedly radial in character, given that residential and industrial locations occur at the periphery with the exceptions of Saragossa, Valladolid-Valencia, Puertollano and above all, Madrid. It is therefore a network designed to cater for radial routes but not transversal ones: of the latter only the Valencia-Barcelona-Port Bou section is suited to the requirements of demand and on the former, the considerable difficulty involved in crossing mountain ranges has to be coped with. There are important production sites such as those located in the Cantabrian heights which are not linked directly by broad-gauge railway;
- the radial layout of the network, along with the existence of mountain ranges surrounding the central uplands - which are also broken up in places by mountains - cause the distances along radial routes by railway to be greater than the corresponding distances by road in most cases. Where it is necessary to make a connecting journey on the railway, the ratio of distance by railway to distance by road is between 2 and 5, while if there is a direct link between points of departure and destination, the ratio varies from 1.08 for short distances to 1.20-1.4 for 200 to 400 kilometres falling thereafter to 1.1 from 700-800 kilometres onwards;
- the profiles of the various lines, with steep gradients restricting the speed of trains and some 38 per cent of the track being curved, of which 15 per cent with radii of less than 500 metres, make high service-speeds difficult to attain, although the condition of the track could be a major reason;

563

- the percentage of dual track line (16 per cent) is very small compared with the total network, and also compared with the length of the basic network. Alongside this, the absence of adequate signalling systems on single-track sections makes it necessary for some stations to be maintained for operating reasons;
- there are no true networks designed to provide suburban-line services in the major metropolitan areas;
- approximately 9,000 level crossings cause a high proportion of staff to be assigned to supervision of most of them.

b) Management

Management of RENFE is subject to the pressure of change, as can be gathered from the fact that in the last 12 years, six Chairmen and five Directors-General have been in charge of the undertaking, the former having at some time undertaken an executive function in the railway plan. Four Chairmen and one Director were Ministers in various administrations, while others were counsellors and held high office in the undertaking. There is therefore indubitably a correlation between management of the railways and the ascent to the highest échelons of national politics. To speak with conviction though with respect, the management structure of the railway network has enabled the country to be steered on an even course through obviously trying times, although it has made the RENFE's activity sluggish:

- by making provisional arrangements the rule in the organisation of the undertaking, which was in the habit of changing with each change;
- by blurring the borderline between the political and managerial échelons and between the échelons of state official and expert, at the expense of professionalism;
- by making management potential subordinate to the possession of political muscle and to relations with the authorities;
- by concentrating most of the decision-making at the top, particularly for decisions involving expenditure even where this is insignificant, making for loss of efficiency;
- by weakening and reducing cohesion between central agencies and those on the periphery.

Nor, besides, does the management appear to rely in its decision-making on clear, complete and true information as can be gathered from outside contributions in which it is surprising to note that, by changing one method for calculating satisfied passenger demand, this goes down by some 25 per cent while the average length of journey per passenger however, has remained unchanged at 81 km for eleven years, nor have the values of wagon-loading cycles, availability of stock, etc., shown any change.

c) Staff

The trend in the RENFE establishment has already been set out earlier, and staffing-levels have contracted considerably, and are now beginning to be considered inadequate, especially for the servicing of traffic and maintenance. We have preferred to avoid compiling ratios for comparison with other networks just for the sake of giving an opinion on the matter, since no comparable situations exist: extension of the network, signalling, railway stock, traffic types and structure, frequency of services, operating systems, state of maintenance of track, plant and rolling stock, agreements entered into, supply quality, etc., make impossible any attempt at homogeneity. While the Spanish railway are apparently capable of matching their establishment, distributed uniformly between zones, by function, to the real needs based on the volume and quality of service required by society, they must cope with certain constraints such as:

- the high proportion of staff costs to total expenditure;
- the proportions attained by the unemployed in the labour force (approximately 14 per cent);
- the political problems involved in closing lines and stations;
- the significance of its being the largest undertaking in the country, and therefore to a considerable extent influencing income and employment policies nationally.

d) Operation

The operation of Spanish railways is faced with problems stemming from the network structure, capacity and state of maintenance of track, actual availability of rolling stock, etc., although along with commercial policy and with constraints external to management, surpassable techniques and practices are being maintained, probably out of concern for safety rather than for any other reasons. It is certain that the works raise problems of maintenance three or four years after delivery, that there is scant overhauling of rolling stock, and that there are more than 2,000 km of lines clearly running at a loss which there is pressure to maintain and operate because the undertaking is not vigorous enough in its efforts to close them down, or because of government opposition to their closure, that 9,000 km of the network would afford a direct service to more than 80 per cent of goods traffic and a still greater percentage of passenger traffic, while it is no less certain that:

- traffic programming schedules and superfluous pre-
  cautions are being maintained which make for journey times some 15 to 25 per cent greater than those
  which could be offered;
- virtually 50 per cent of the locomotive fleet is
  set aside for servicing piecemeal batches of full-
  wagon-load traffic (some 25 per cent of freight
  traffic), with these locomotives being allocated
  equivalent segments of manpower and track, as well
  as serving the majority of marshalling yards;
- traffic of little significance occupies a significant proporition of track, rolling stock and staff;
- optimum capacity utilisation is not achieved on
  sections of dual track equipped with automatic
  blocks and override braking.

e) Commercial

RENFE cannot be said to lack a commercial policy in
its strictest sense since the new passenger services, the
attractive and, at times, bold fare-concessions show some
evidence of drive. It must also be noted, however, that
there are not, to our knowledge, any medium- to long-term
development programmes, perhaps because of the uncertainty
regarding the fulfilment of investment plans and the ability to improve services, on account of the gradual whit-
tling-down of commercial objectives for actual services as
and when these are modified in the programming process and
also during successive episodes of internal reorganisation. Thus, situations arise which defy comprehension,
such as the following:

- A very comprehensive commercial organisation covering the whole of the national territory, which
  could achieve noticeable savings in the operation
  of the overall transport market, but is devoted
  exclusively to catering for railway demand alone,
  which is highly concentrated as shown in the table
  below, both in terms of stations and when it is
  noted that 55 clients account for 87 per cent of
  full-wagon-load traffic and for 90 per cent of its
  income, this being represented by 98 per cent of
  all movements of freight and 75 per cent of income
  from freight.
- The average price per tonne-kilometre of
  full-wagon-load traffic paid by the major clients,
  i.e. those who tend to dispatch goods more in
  block-booked trains or complete train-loads than in
  isolated wagon-loads. This may be the result of a
  pricing policy based on quality of service although
  flagrantly at variance with real production costs.
  On the other hand, services have also been
  introduced at lower fares than those in existence
  which have led to internal transfers of traffic
  while securing new custom.

TRAFFIC STRUCTURE BY STATIONS

Traffic	Number of stations accounting for the percentage of traffic			
	25%	50%	90%	100%
Passengers	3	18	130	1.006
Goods dispatch	4	23	157	1.695
Goods traffic	4	45	260	1.695

- Thinking along the same lines, average and overall values can lead to error, since the average price for these clients is considerably influenced by its being applied to the carriage of petroleum products, and if extended to all complete wagon-loads, it would improve the network's operating coefficient from 1.57 to 1.19. Moreover, the persistence of such a policy has led the Petroleum Monopoly to construct a network of pipelines which on entering into operation has depressed goods traffic while coal imports have substantially increased(5).
- Consequently, traffic is operated on a piecemeal basis - part-loads - using a costly procedure of low energy efficiency, with lower economic returns than those for roadways.
- The minimum 10 km charge is maintained for suburban traffic, with the charge on the excess rounded in 5-kilometre steps, which gives bus networks the advantage. For goods, the minimum charge on 25 and 50 kms makes it difficult to secure custom for short-haul carriage of large volumes of goods.

f) Investment and finance

Until 1977, 90 per cent or more of investment in the network was covered by RENFE out of its own funds, obtained in most cases through loans on the domestic and foreign capital markets. Out of these quantities (see Table 13) virtually 80 per cent or more was set aside for replacement of assets with slight improvements in quality though not quantity. From 1979 onwards, the central government, through the Ministry of Transport, Tourism and

---

5. This network is warrantable from the commercial point of view but not from the national point of view when considering the resultant disinvestment or under-utilisation resulting in the railway network.

Communications, was given responsibility for a major share of infrastructure investment which has already reached 30 per cent of earmarked capital. The rate of investment - which, by all accounts, has not enabled the track and stock to be maintained in perfect condition - has been maintained through recourse to long-term debt, at a level now close to Pesetas 70,000 million. This problem, with multiplier effects on interest and equipment suppliers, also affects investment itself, since the budget proposals include provision for potential financial costs of delays in payment. Thus unit costs of works in Spain are very high, while within two years of delivery the tracks are damaged, the tension-regulated catenaries cannot cope with speeds of 120 kms/h, etc.

3.2. Exogenous causes

In addition to the set of problems listed above, there are other problems external to the railway undertaking which partly explain those problems, and of which the fundamental reasons can be grouped together in two categories: the economic and social situation and inter-modal competitiveness.

3.2.1. The economic and social situation

This is characterised first of all by a slackening in the rate of growth of gross domestic product which went down from 7.5 per cent in the 1960s to 3.91 per cent in the 1970s and 2.08 per cent in the period from 1975 to 1980. This situation is reflected in transport demand, highly correlated with the two variables mentioned, and sets limits to any attempt to improve management through reductions in variable costs, with fixed costs increasing through investment.

The second, and the more serious, factor is a staggering increase in unemployment in both absolute and relative terms. Today there are 1.5 million fewer persons in employment than in 1975. During this period it has not been possible to cope with new job applications resulting from the natural growth in the labour force nor has there been any success in maintaining the jobs of those actually in employment. Since construction and civil engineering are one of the sectors most affected, it is no surprise that:

- there is mounting tension involved in the shedding of staff and/or tight constraints on any possibility of reduction;
- questionable works contracts are being made with firms which are going through difficulties, aimed at alleviating their position.

The third characteristic phenomenon in recent years is the fall in savings, privately, in business and by public administrations. The Government deficit appeared in 1979 and forecasts for 1982 show that it will reach $8,000 million of which only a small part will be set aside for investment. The indebtedness to the Bank of Spain is reaching the $13,000 million mark, and is growing at a rate which appears irreducible with the established forces at work. Government resources for investment in railways are limited and the government's lack of liquidity makes for delays in budgetary payments leading to spiralling interest charges as already mentioned.

On the other hand, the deficit in the foreign trade balance, of some $9,000 million in 1980, although partly offset by tourist receipts, points to a delicate situation and calls for further increases in exclusively exported production. Panic exports of capital, which cannot be accurately calculated, tax evasion which is estimated to be correspondingly high, and a rate of inflation of about 14 per cent per annum give the broad outlines of the national economic situation which does not exactly favour stability in the transport system.

3.2.2. Inter-modal competitiveness

Expenditure items included in the output costs of the separate modes of transport are not homogeneous and the fare-systems derived from them do not therefore reflect the cost structure.

Thus, market distortions arise which affect the modal split for demand and the financial results for subsectors. I will attempt to set forth briefly the fundamental differentiating features:

- Virtually all railway infrastructure investment is apparently, as stated earlier, carried out by the undertaking itself whereas no other transport mode has included such investment at the level of service undertakings, with the result that:

  . highways, apart from turnpike roads, are financed from government funds, and tax pressure is very high on cars (thanks to fuel taxes) and very low on heavy goods lorries.
  . the national airport network, built and maintained by the government, is loss-making and has no income from the national airlines in respect of airport taxes.
  . the majority of the national ports, built and maintained by the government, return an operating deficit and virtually never cover their depreciation costs.

- Although oil is the cause of, and governs, the growing crisis, pricing policy has not been the same in all sectors:

  . electricity is much cheaper for railways which pay for fuel at the same prices as those charged for road transport.
  . petrol is heavily taxed, while the tax on gas oil does not allow the costs of maintaining the road network to be covered.
  . while energy in other modes is heavily taxed, aviation fuel is sold at approximately what it costs to produce.

- Compared with behaviour patterns predating the situation due to the energy crisis, the railways have obviously shown more capacity to react than the remainder of the modes as is normal since it consumes 2 per cent of the additional energy in the sector and satisfies 8 per cent of demand. Nevertheless, services are offered which have energy yields lower than those afforded by competing modes, e.g.:

  . part-load consignment services
  . single full wagon-loads
  . complete lines usually in the form of branch lines, with occupancy rates of less than 20 per cent of supply.

- The working day is shorter in aviation than on the railways and is unregulated on roadways for the self-employed who account for more than 80 per cent of supply in the sector. From the expenditure point of view, the cost structure here is one in which the weight of staff costs is reduced by dint of increasing the working day.
- The road sector is highly competitive, even to the extent of prices being ridiculously low as has been confirmed in various surveys(6) although on average, they secure custom at rates some 40 per cent higher than railway freight transport rates. Nevertheless, domestic fares(7) in the airline sector do not enable the production costs of airlines to be covered, let alone satisfy airport taxes and charges for air navigation, and this sector only achieves a balance with the profits from the international market(8).
- Lastly, it is obvious that there is another series of costs, grouped together under the heading of social costs, which are not included in returns by

---

6. Costes del transporte por carretera por cuenta ajena. Ineco-RENFE, 1975.
7. Domestic traffic.
8. Análisis del sistema tarifario. Ineco - 1979.

the transport system, and in which railways have a much smaller share than any of the other modes except pipelines. Land use with its ominous characteristics in cities, air and noise pollution and accidents are items not written up to the profit and loss account, and these might alter it substantially.

3.3. The problem of balance(9)

Within the frame laid down by the co-ordinates set forth in the preceding paragraphs, it is no simple task to bring the undertaking close to a breakeven, which is probably impossible to reach within the usual terms of economic theory. With the necessary simplifications which must be taken into consideration in a more thorough analysis, the production-expenditure function for Spanish railways was of the type represented as I in the early 1960s, i.e. with relatively low fixed expenditure and very high marginal costs on account of certain limitations of productive capacity, the interval of which may be defined by band 1 (see figure 2). To get out of this deficit situation, it was decided to make an adjustment by transforming function I into II, reducing the marginal cost through investment to improve equipment and manpower, all this being on the assumption that specific demand increases, as GNP has, at a 7 per cent rate, also assuming that the production band should move up to 2. Nevertheless fixed costs have risen despite forecasts (ΔD_o compared with ΔD_0) and variable costs also underwent a greater increase on account of salary increases and the failure to fulfil commitments on energy prices so that real aggregate production changed to III and, given the high competitiveness of road transport, the production differential only moved up into band 3. From the foregoing, it can be deduced that the present condition of railways is qualitatively and quantitatively worse than was the case immediately beforehand, as reflected in Figure 3 which shows the cost-benefit functions.

During the period under review, the railway administration forecast some results defined by curve (II) in the estimated breakeven segment (a) corresponding to a production/expenditure function II and demand situated in the production differential band 2. However, the fact that the conditions of competition are not fulfilled, as already stated, caused these functions to move into (b) in (II) so making for nil profits, and taking into account that traffic also failed to reach forecast levels, cost of

9. The theoretical reflection in this paragraph was developed in 1977 by Professor Roa in some considerable detail and was published in the July-August issue of the ALAF magazine.

production increased, so that curve (II) went into position III taking the railways further at each step from the estimated breakeven under the conditions stated.

With this prospect in view, the railways are faced with only two options. The first would be to apply once again the principles of the 1970s, so that the production function would be IV, provided that the production zone should always start at least at interval A. The second option would involve reducing variable costs without increasing the fixed costs, in order to reach production V while maintaining the production zone or, better still, increasing it, e.g., to band 5. Either option would give rise to cost-benefit curves as shown in (IV) and (V) with no possibility of improving the labour zone c, on account of fare controls and the displacement of (II) and (III), to C_{IV} and C_V respectively.

Taking into account that the economic climate in the decade 1970-1980 can reasonably be expected to consolidate itself and be maintained during the present decade, it is evident that in the labour areas defined by market prices, which are the room management has for manoeuvre, RENFE will continue to run a deficit without managing to cover the considerable fixed costs of its investment in fixed assets. The only way open with this prospect in view is to include "community costs" greater than market price and cost price, so that functions (IV) and (V) would be able to grow in value terms until the ordinate is greater than the abscissa, at which point a positive final balance is returned. In fixing this price and setting up the relevant services, the problem is met of making the railway networks break even in the future. Given that the services themselves are the preserve of political decisions, the railways must be given the ability to provide immediate response by adjusting their price, whatever supply options may occur.

4. CURRENT PLANNING

As with all the other transport modes, the basic objective of the railways is to provide a service to man and society as a whole, by meeting the latter's requirements through optimum use of the means available at the lowest production cost ensuring that peak periods are covered. Clearly, if the requirements call for the railways to perform a social service, thus modifying the above conditions, operating at a profit is a contradictory objective. Such is the present situation, and there is every evidence that it will continue in the medium term.

However, difficulties arise not only in achieving a balance owing to the impossibility of reconciling requirements with conflicting objectives. Financial problems, which appreciably raise production costs and create very serious cash-flow tensions, will not be overcome so long as the public finance deficit and lack of liquidity or payment delays remain. Consequently, from his critical standpoint, the reviewer feels it is legitimate to call on the authorities to examine this essential sector for maintaining national economic activity, and to clarify the scope of the proposed objectives.

With this in mind, the chapters below briefly review the objectives set in the basic government policy paper(10), the railways' response to it and the author's view that both should be supplemented with a few additional proposals.

4.1. General framework for the future

The general framework which is to incorporate future railway management should consist of the policies - so long as they remain in force - laid down in the White Paper, which was drawn up in order to define general guidelines with the basic objective of achieving "the establishment and effective operation of a comprehensive transport system". The basic principles of this policy would be as follows:

- Government transport policies should be harmonized with economic and social policy;
- the State should set up the basic infrastructure required for the separate transport modes, whether directly or through concession;
- public and private enterprises should operate in competition;
- the State should ensure that users have access to a good quality service on at least one of the possible links provided by the various transport modes;
- a plan will be drawn up for transport infrastructure and public services to ensure efficient use of available resources;
- in a comprehensive transport system, each mode should cater for the traffic for which it is best suited, and consequently the railways will be promoted in the following areas:

  - suburban traffic in large cities;
  - bulk and long-distance freight transport;
  - passenger transport in high-population density corridors.

---

10. The White Paper on Transport was presented to the public by the Ministry of Transport and Communications in early 1979.

Finally, the following points are made concerning the railways:

- the need for long-term planning;
- bringing the railways in line with the other modes as regards infrastructure and operating costs;
- raising standards up to those achieved today by other European railway systems on their established lines;
- meeting the public service requirements imposed on the railways on grounds of public interest and payment of compensation by the authority that has imposed such requirements.

4.2. General Railways Plan

In order to carry out the above tasks, within the limits laid down by the White Paper, a General Railways Plan has been drawn up which, according to the paper setting out its Basic Principles, requires "long-term planning following the main guidelines approved by the Legislative Chambers, the Government being responsible for implementing this plan for shorter periods through the budget and programme-contracts". It is impossible to summarise a document containing 40 pages of basic principles within the short space available in this report, but it would be pointless and tantamount to encroaching on the railways' own future plans to comment on the basic features without first describing them.

4.2.1. General Plan for 1980-1991

The basic points are:

- Investment of Pesetas 1,200,000 of which 400,000 will be allocated for maintenance in re-tracking, laying double-tracks and purchasing equipment.
- Daily inter-city services for runs of less than five hours in radial links, with trains running at 120 km/h every two hours at the most and an increase in traffic of at least 300 per cent.
- Overnight services with better equipment and a 5 per cent growth in traffic.
- Travelling time on regional services reduced to two-thirds of the present level and more than four daily services per link with an 80 per cent growth in traffic.
- More infrastructure for suburban services, with trains running at the most every five minutes at peak periods and not more than thirty minutes during slack periods, with a 250 per cent increase in traffic, park-and-ride facilities, urban and suburban links and combined tariffs.
- Door-to-door service for full-wagon loads with the

supply of private shunt lines, the guaranteed
delivery time being reduced to 50 per cent of the
present level, and promotion of private wagons and
specialisation with a 3.5-fold increase in traffic.
- Increase in the number of container terminals and,
  where possible, separation of parcel services from
  passenger ones, while promoting part-load consignment services.
- Planning and operation of services supplementing
  and replacing the railways.

4.2.2. The network and its facilities up to the 1991 Horizon

The structure of the network should be as follows:

- 5.901 km of basic network, more than 70 per cent
  double-track, with trains running at 160 km/h on
  30 per cent of the network;
- 519 km of double-track suburban lines, specially
  designed for this type of service, with automatic
  blocks;
- 7,124 km of other types of line;
- adjustment of rolling stock;
- administrative integration of narrow-gauge railways
  forming a global operating unit;
- 55 per cent rise in the labour force to 111,900.

4.2.3. Achievements and results

In order to meet the above objectives, it will be
necessary to undertake a number of major engineering and
modernisation projects. Under the programmes outlined,
the operating balance, which will remain steady up to
1984, will become positive as a result of increased traffic, the profit margin reaching the same volume as the
present deficit, i.e. Pesetas 62,000 million (at 1979
Pesetas) in 1991 including depreciation and interest.

The funds required to implement the General Plan
amount to about 2 to 3 per cent of the overall State
budget.

4.2.4. Railway management

Railway management will be governed by the following
general principles:

- managerial autonomy and private enterprise status;
- flexible tariff system adjusted to the market situation and governed by the national interest;
- State control;

- expansion of activities to include complementary services;
- professional status of governing bodies and executive boards;
- autonomous assets;
- maximum use of present infrastructure in urban areas;
- increased technological research and external technology transfer;
- labour terms fixed by agreements;
- improved staff training.

4.2.5. Financial policy

The following budget arrangements are laid down in accordance with financial policy:

- non-management costs, public service liabilities and others not protected by this condition will be financed in accordance with the rules laid down by the EEC;
- for transport over short distances, participation of local bodies will be established provided the tariffs cover most of the production costs;
- investments for other types of traffic will be financed by RENFE under its own budget;
- for the construction of special facilities official credit will be available;
- analytical accounts will be drawn up by line and service;
- the enterprise will be given an adequate cash flow, and any additional financial requirements will be financed by the State in accordance with the needs arising from the development of the network's working capital policies.

4.3. Weak points of the Plan

The first and most important weakness in any planning process is undoubtedly the uncertainty as to its implementation and, in this case, it is highly probable that the basic requirements for meeting the proposed objectives are not met. Indeed, one of the Plan's best features was that it required approval by the Legislative Chambers, but the step failed and it was not even possible to obtain approval by the executive powers for the entire period, with such support as there was from an agreement made by the enterprise's own management board, 18 months after the theoretical starting date for the Plan, and an agreement by the Council of Ministers on investment during the 1982-84 period. It could be said that the General Railways Plan has no official backing outside RENFE.

The second point concerns the proposed investment:

although during 1969-80 investment reached almost
Pesetas 600,000 million, the state of both rolling stock
and track markedly deteriorated and also maintenance costs
rose in real terms, so that it does not seem likely that
Pesetas 400,000 million would be sufficient to maintain
the entire fixed assets under adequate production conditions during a similar period and with much heavier traffic. Therefore there is a serious risk that maintenance
costs will be much higher than predicted, thus posing a
serious threat for breakout investment.

The third point to be considered is the outcome of
the diagnosis on which the Plan is based, namely that the
Spanish railways are operating practically at full capa-
city(11), hence the need to make breakout investments as a
matter of priority to expand double and four-track lines
and construct major variations in layout. While accepting
the general statement, it is not however possible to agree
upon the causes, which in my opinion are as follows:

- poor state of rolling stock and track;
- poor train diagram based on standards favouring
  track occupation;
- continuation of inadequate freight services designed to compete with road transport so that rolling stock and track that could be used by other
  services are unavailable,

although this does not preclude the near-saturation of all
types of railway service in various specific local
areas(12).

Having reached the verdict to be deduced from the
initial diagnosis, i.e. breakout investment, there is a
further weak point in the Plan, which can be illustrated
by the following example: investment estimates for one of
the major variants totalled between Pesetas 25,000 and
45,000 million at 1979 rates. The more detailed analysis
of alternatives now being carried out and a comparison
with other similar projects suggest that measurements more
closely adjusted to the projected level might yield values
almost twice as high as the previous average limit.
Although this conclusion cannot be generalised to the remainder of the major variants, which estimate investments

---

11. "Largely because of their own structural
conditions, but perhaps also because of the economic and
trading context, the Spanish railways are operating at a
level very close to real capacity...". 1980-91 General
Railways Plan. RENFE.
12. The type of rolling stock encourages such situations. The latest locomotives to be purchased cannot
pull more than 1,000 tonnes on slopes of more than 15 per
cent, hence an increase in traffic in mountain areas.

at Pesetas 300,000 million, the cost of maintenance plus investments and the construction work entailed might possibly swallow up the total budget under the Plan.

Although agreeing with the basic planning arrangements for passenger services, it is unlikely that the demand for inter-city day services can increase to cumulative annual rates of more than 12 per cent during the entire period. As for freight traffic forecasts, there are groups such as liquid fuel transport where the decisions made to construct the pipeline network and the consumption forecasts under the National Energy Plan forestall the possibility of any rise in traffic, although this has been estimated at more than 40 per cent. The effects that the confirmation of excess traffic forecasts might have on the calculation of results would undoubtedly contribute to worsen the economic and financial situation in the railways and would increase society's misgivings regarding the ability of the latter to meet present and future challenges.

Out of a total of 1,600 passing tracks accounting for 73 per cent of total freight traffic, 100 generated and attracted about 80 per cent of the traffic concerned. Major production centres in Spain, which can make up full train loads, have the facilities but sometimes do not use them. Thus the problem lies not with the number of tracks, which is undoubtedly excessive, but with the service offered, which requires a radical change in order to adjust to demand requirements, and all the implications of this problem have possibly not been analysed.

The operating system under the Plan and the traffic estimates require a 55 per cent increase in the labour force by the end of the Plan's implementation period. In spite of the fact that such a staff for the traffic volumes under consideration might seem reasonable in the light of the staff size of other European railway undertakings, this might be the most important variable of all those dealt with in the Plan, and this without ensuring the network maintenance programmes. If so, failing a policy balancing employment requirements with adequate distribution of value added produced, this would have been a major step towards ruining the railways' opportunities for competing with road transport by controlling labour conditions in the latter, through the effect of higher fuel prices and a probable increase in taxation.

These seven points, which concern the major aspects of current planning, together with a few proposals put forward in the following section are sufficient to arouse serious misgivings about the viability of the programmes established for meeting transport requirements and to confirm the deep concern for the economic and financial future of the railways.

4.4. Basic factors for adjusting the railways to future requirements

Through their total assets, in terms of property and staff, the energy savings provided for certain types of traffic, the lower accident risk, land-use, low pollution effects, production costs in some cases and potential production costs in others, the railways undoubtedly have a role to play in meeting transport demand requirements for some groups and in given geographical areas. To this end, especially at first, the railways ought to make the actual situation quite clear by supplying accurate information to the public and defining the following responsibilities:

- policy constraints, national requirements and public service obligations

  . Maintaining lines open to traffic where demand is met by a daily bus or truck service under official pressure at various levels and for the purpose of national defence;
  . Providing unnecessary services as a superfluous option in many cases;
  . Transporting a number of types of traffic with compulsory tariffs under government decision;
  . Exclusive supervision of more than 4,000 level crossings and participation in engineering work to do away with them;
  . Repaying interest on investment loans or bridging loans to cover any delays in meeting Public Finance contractual obligations;
  . Concluding engineering and equipment contracts at excessively high prices owing to strictly economic considerations for enterprises in the sector and as a result of employment policy;
  . Being at the forefront of government policy in labour matters;
  . Suffering the constant reshuffling of top management posts whenever the political situation swings around.

- Effects of railway management as such

  . Providing inadequate information for taking decisions on a subordinate basis for the public;
  . Providing inadequate services for meeting demand requirements;
  . Maintaining operating systems that do not make maximum use of fixed assets;
  . Allowing the gradual deterioration of fixed assets with unsuitable conservation and/or maintenance policies;
  . Commissioning engineering work and equipment that does not fulfil the conditions required as to theoretical specifications and purchase costs;
  . Establishing mutually competitive services.

579

Once this first step has been taken, implementation
programmes will have to be drawn up on the basis of the
following principles:

1. Convincing outside decision-making bodies, i.e. the
    Government and Parliament in particular, that the
    present financial situation is unacceptable and that
    it is necessary to bring it back to normal as quickly
    as possible so that budgeted payments can be speeded
    up and to exercise the utmost prudence henceforth in
    managing credit on the capital market whilst reducing
    this practice to a strict minimum.

2. Encouraging the Government and Parliament to debate
    what service thresholds should be maintained or set
    by the railways in order to meet demand requirements
    by proposing the corresponding economic evaluation
    for each option, taking into consideration accurate
    costings for infrastructure conservation and equip-
    ment maintenance to get the most out of both, and
    taking account of the social costs of the railway
    solution and of alternative transport modes. Never-
    theless, it should be noted that transport services
    do not seem to be the most suitable tool for imple-
    menting either an income redistribution policy or one
    subsidising industrial activities.

3. Reducing the length of line operated, should similar
    standards be adopted to those in Western Europe advo-
    cating balanced goods transport operation and major
    coverage of suburban and inter-city services. To
    this end, types of traffic should be investigated
    which, from the community standpoint, might be better
    served by other transport modes; this would probably
    entail cutting out 2,000 to 4,000 km of low-traffic
    network, provided the latter is not necessary on
    logistic grounds for bridging gaps in the remainder
    of the main network. The labour and equipment
    resources released as a result of this policy would
    be used under the new operating plan suggested above,
    both for providing new traction and for running
    maintenance programmes.
    In any case, if so required in the local, regional or
    national interest, suitable financing agreements
    should be drawn up to face the foreseeable operating
    deficits and the corresponding items of depreciation
    at replacement cost. It would be essential to estab-
    lish analytical accounts by line and service to
    achieve strict control of the agreements and to
    strengthen the initially outlined clarifying measures.

4. To draw up agreements with the department responsible
    for road construction and maintenance and with the
    relevant provincial or municipal autonomous bodies,
    covering the construction of level crossings and
    maintenance of protected level crossings.

5. As already mentioned when examining the problem of
    making the railways break even, given the present
    national and international economic situation and the
    prospects for the outcome of the crisis, circum-
    stances are such that it is inadvisable to conduct
    production-cost-reducing policies - it should be re-
    called that actual transport service output is equi-
    valent to real consumption or demand - by means of
    large increases in fixed costs and by reducing the
    variables, since demand does not usually reach these
    production thresholds and supply components might
    well tend to increase. There should also be some
    measure of control over the final amount of invest-
    ments accumulating as fixed capital. To this end
    management should channel its efforts towards main-
    taining infrastructure, facilities and equipment in
    perfect running order and to have these in sufficient
    quantity and quality for the services planned, with
    greater flexibility in adjusting to demand trends
    rather than constructing major projects to be
    written-off over an uncertain length of time.
    This does not mean that such options should be exclu-
    ded from those to be taken into consideration. The
    disparity in the quality of the service, insofar as
    the capacity of the latter may have a substantial in-
    fluence on the outcome of modal choice at demand
    level, is due more to new technology bringing with it
    high-speed passenger transport (more than 200 km/h
    compared with the current 80 km/h and the target of
    120 km/h in the General Railways Plan) and in the
    ultimate features of the freight transport service,
    which certainly does not require similar speeds.

6. The heading for required infrastructure investments
    includes those relating to suburban railways in such
    major metropolitan areas as Madrid and Barcelona,
    which finds justification in repeatedly updated eco-
    nomic and social profitability studies, and delays in
    their implementation are preventing specific oper-
    ating programmes from being launched to ensure the
    mobility of large sectors of the population under
    acceptable conditions, not only by rail but also by
    bus and private vehicles. Likewise other specific
    points or stretches of the network might be the
    subject of changes or adjustments, provided strict
    economic/social profitability studies indicate they
    are necessary, through the decisions and in the form
    indicated under Heading 3.

7. Meeting the needs of passenger transport demand in
    suburban areas by constructing specific
    infrastructure with lines running into or through
    urban centres, with adequate signalling systems and
    suitable links with urban transport networks in

high-density areas and outer urban and inter-city areas. Providing high train frequencies at peak periods and staggered services in off-peak ones using special high-speed and high-capacity equipment, priority being given to the latter at times where demand is more intensive. Agreeing with complementary transport modes on combined tariffs encouraging customers to choose the railways in penetration and cross-movements, where access road capacity and various urban networks are saturated and there is no sufficient space for expanding the services, by a fair sharing formula based on adequate control of demand and of output costs and specifying relevant compensation by mutual agreement with the competent authorities. It will be necessary to establish analytical accounts for this purpose. In these areas top priority will be given to setting up single transport authorities at metropolitan level.

8. Focusing all efforts to increase the commercial speed of inter-city services on improving transport equipment and its availability at full capacity, ensuring that both track and overhead lines are in perfect working order to achieve maximum efficiency, and in the immediate future, on finding methods for drawing up theoretical graphs. In this way it should be possible to have service-speeds of between 100 and 120 km/h on most inter-city links even without resolving the problem of greater distances between cities compared with other transport modes, owing to the special maximum limits on slope gradients required for mixed passenger-freight railways. This need not prevent alternative investment from being made within the limits laid down under Headings 3 and 6 or any extension in the radius of individual curves in order to reduce the distance and improve train speeds both in absolute terms and compared with other transport modes. Any routes with suitable signalling for maximum capacity requiring conversion to double-track because their scope as single-track routes has been exhausted, may be converted by means of the work indicated.

Services must supply at least four trains per day, suitably timed in accordance with the results of demand surveys as and when permitted by the availability of equipment. More services should be laid on for links of less than four hours' travelling time (450-500 km) than for longer ones and additional services provided to reduce travelling time subjectively. Tariffs will be fixed in accordance with market conditions, with such savings as are allowed by those conditions, and will be aimed at supplying revenue to cover all output costs pertaining to such services.

9.   The demand for door-to-door services is steadily rising in freight transport and also for more reliable
storage times over a reasonable period until invoicing for a specific destination is completed. If
this could be achieved for the railways, the selling
price could be increased by about 50 to 60 per cent
on average, improving competitiveness with road
transport(13), all the more in view of the bullish
trends of this sub-sector.
Thus the objective of marketing policy is to offer
door-to-door services and that of operational policy
is to organise traffic as simply as possible so that
the former objective can be met at minimum production
costs. Along these lines, the new principles imply
using all freight traffic exclusively by making up
and running block trains or complete train-loads from
departure to destination, regardless of whether or
not they are unit trains or regular services, where
possible under a rigid system (hence suitable for
planning) and at the same time a flexible one open to
new demand requirements where adjustment can be made,
as is nearly always the case with RENFE.
This type of action entails major changes in the output structure, turning into further advantages for
the undertaking and/or users. For example:

-    the most extensive and comprehensive marketing
     network that any transport body could provide to
     meet demand, conversion into transport operators
     by using market economies for the benefit of the
     entire community;
-    by allowing the network itself to select the most
     suitable transport mode, transport times will
     become entirely reliable and shorter than those
     offered at present;
-    there will be no need for marshalling or trailer
     trains - with the accumulation of delays in
     freight transport in turn affecting passenger
     transport and motor units unavailable because they
     are being used for shunting - railway operation
     becomes simpler, there are fewer risks of train
     itineraries not being completed and fewer trains
     are required;
     it will be possible to take advantage of the bene-
     fit of automatic signalling and capacity increases
     to improve productivity as well as safety.

10.   In a first stage, operation in block trains as prac-
ticed by RENFE (25 million tonnes) could be maintained, and the following might be added:

_____

        13. This conclusion is drawn in the study entitled
"Estudio de los costes de transporte de mercancías por
carretera por cuenta ajena". Ineco-RENFE 1975, in an
elasticity analysis of both transport modes.

- about 100,000 tonnes by aggregating separate consignments in programmed block trains;
- a further 2.7 million tonnes by means of temporary
groupage of currently scattered consignments either
at stations or in sidings.

In order to do this it would be necessary to programme trains with the agreement of customers concerning the possible expansion of loading, unloading
and storage facilities at the point of origin and/or
destination, and also to study the programming of
empty wagons in closed-circuit routing so as to improve rotation, and to study the design of two- or
three-purpose wagons to improve overall space filling.
The second stage would consist in operating the remaining full wagons on an isolated basis and part-
load consignments as a marginal activity from the 20
or so concentrated traffic stations between which
regular services would be programmed twice monthly,
weekly, every other day, daily, etc. The user would
be offered full transport with a specific delivery
day for each destination, from each point of departure and/or passing the goods over to road transport
if the customers' requirements cannot be met. These
trains would be made up of full wagons, containers,
part-loads and empty wagons as necessary to maintain
the fleet located where necessary. During this stage:

- the stations mentioned would be constructed or
adjusted;
- marshalling yards would be shut down or converted
into sundries depots;
- about 300 stations and many sidings would be shut
down;
- about 450 stations would no longer be used for full
wagon traffic;
- the secondary routing plan would be deleted;
- above the threshold of 400,000 hours per train,
marshalling and shunting activities would not be
carried out;
- reduction of approximately 3 million train-km and
800,000 hours per train for the same traffic volume;
- removal of almost 200 main-line locomotives plus
part of the freight locomotives used exclusively
for shunting;
- creation or subcontracting of groupage and dispersal networks by road; and
- extension of the marketing network and forwarding
agents.

The part-load consignment plan would also be cancel-
led as it is highly uneconomical to run in terms of
energy, with occupation rates of about 10 per cent,
while the express parcel service would be maintained
since it brings in marginal income without disrupting
passenger traffic.

Tariffs would be fixed in relation to market conditions so as to achieve self-sufficiency. It is recalled in this connection that the sector is not suitable for cross-subsidies which might also lead to incorrect use of available means.

11. Like other railway undertakings, RENFE has the opportunity of tailoring its staff size. Any variation in the present number of railway employees will have to be justified in accordance with the foreseeable effects of the proposed measures, which in no case should give the impression of supporting a cutback in existing traffic but on the contrary, an increase with improved use of resources. In this respect, a close watch should be kept on the possibility that productivity increases, arising from improved organisation and operating methods, might be mostly channelled mainly towards wages rather than being used to balance the trading results arising from the normal operation of market forces.
An employment boosting policy, whether or not it is conducted at the same time as a reduction in working hours, should be included in a national solidarity agreement with no effect on the structure of production costs apart from reducing the impact of unemployment compensation payments as a maximum limit. Furthermore, any drop in unemployment should never be allowed to occur if it is to impede the development of conservation and maintenance programmes for track, rolling stock and facilities.

12. It is necessary to separate policy decisions from the practical ways in which railway management can meet society's requirements as expressed through the representation channels. To this end, it is essential to attempt to clarify the information on the network's results and profitability by providing an instantaneous "snapshot" view of them. Hiding or failing to account for the process of decapitalisation of the railways by "window-dressing" the accounts will speed up the process of destruction. Consequently, it is essential to obtain permission to revalue assets - except land - on an annual basis or to depreciate at replacement cost.

FIGURES AND STATISTICAL ANNEXES

Figure 1

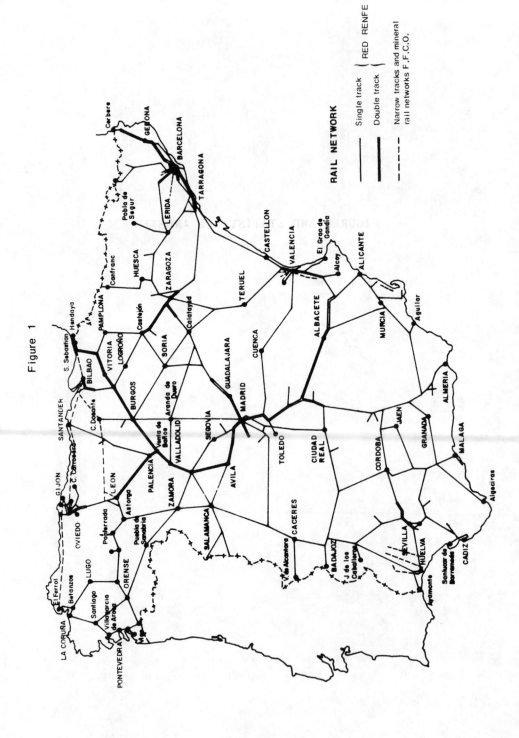

RAIL NETWORK

Single track } RED RENFE
Double track }

Narrow tracks and mineral
rail networks F.F.C.O.

588

Figure 2

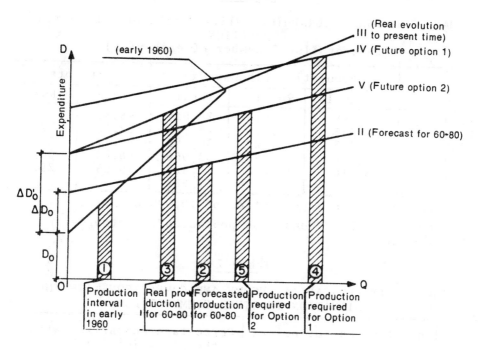

Figure 3

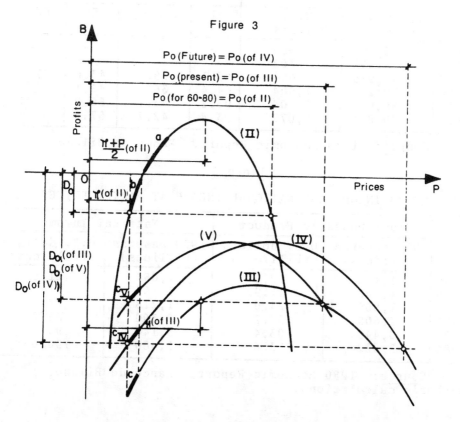

Table 1

CHANGES IN THE GEOGRAPHICAL DISTRIBUTION OF THE SPANISH
POPULATION
(Date at 31st December of each year)

Year	Population (Thousands)			% of total	
	Urban(1)	Rural	Total	Urban	Rural
1940	12,698	13,316	26,014	48.81	51.19
1950	14,643	13,475	28,118	52.08	47.92
1960	17,363	13,220	30,583	56.77	43.23
1970	22,576	11,380	33,956	66.49	33.51
1975	25,916	10,611	36,527	70.95	29.05
1981			37,682		

1. Towns with a population of 10,000 or more.

Source: INE. "Censos de población". Author's
calculations.

Table 2

CHANGES IN PER-CAPITA INCOME AND COMPARISON WITH THE
SITUATION IN OTHER COMMUNITIES

Year	Income at market prices		Percentage comparison with the situation in:			
	1970 Pesetas	U.S. Dollars	Italy	Germany	EEC	OECD
1955	35,692	393	-	-	-	-
1960	38,387	362	-	-	-	-
1965	53,915	695	67.1	38.4	43.6	37.1
1970	70,267	1,004	64.4	36.1	45.1	38.1
1975	88,932	2,704	93.2	43.1	56.0	54.4
1980	90,851	5,077	93.4	42.7	57.6	60.4

Source: 1980 Economic Report. Banco de Bilbao.

Table 3

TRENDS IN GDP AND NATIONAL INCOME AT MARKET PRICES

Year	Gross Domestic Product		National Income	
	1970 pesetas (billions)	U.S. dollars (billions)	1970 pesetas (billions)	U.S. dollars (billions)
1955	1,142	12.6	1,054	11.6
1960	1,262	11.9	1,163	11.0
1965	1,866	24.0	1,718	22.1
1970	2,605	37.2	2,360	33.7
1975	3,449	103.4	3,148	95.7
1980	3,822	213.6	3,400	190.0

Source: 1980 Economic Report. Banco de Bilbao.
Author's calculations.

Table 4

TRENDS IN DOMESTIC PASSENGER TRANSPORT BY MODE OF TRANSPORT
(in billions of vehicle-kilometres)

Year	Railways			Road				Air	Cabotage	Total
	RENFE	Narrow-gauge	Total	Bus	Car	Motorcycle	Total			
1955	8.0	1.3	9.3	3.4	2.6	n.a.	6.0	0.2	n.a.	15.5
1960	7.3	1.5	8.8	7.9	12.2	n.a.	20.1	0.4	n.a.	29.3
1965	12.2	1.7	13.9	11.2	23.8	4.0	39.0	0.9	0.5	54.3
1970	13.3	1.7	15.0	20.9	61.0	3.5	85.4	2.0	0.8	103.2
1975	16.1	1.5	17.6	26.9	99.3	2.7	128.9	3.9	1.5	151.9
1980	13.5(1)	0.5	14.0	33.3	130.3	2.1	165.7	6.0	2.1	187.8

1. This value results from using a new method of calculation from 1979 onwards. It reflects a 6.8 per cent increase in traffic in the last year.

n.a.: data not available.

Sources: RENFE, IETC, Gen. Dir for Highways, Gen. Dir. for Ports, Campsa, the Civil Aviation Subdivision. Author's calculations.

Table 5

TRENDS IN DOMESTIC FREIGHT TRANSPORT DEMAND BY MODE OF TRANSPORT

(in billions of tonne-kilometres)

Year	Railways			Road	Air	Cabotage	Pipelines	Total
	RENFE	Narrow-gauge	Total					
1955	8.2	0.8	9.0	5.4	-	12.8	-	27.2
1960	7.1	0.9	8.0	13.1	-	15.9	-	37.0
1965	8.5	0.7	9.2	31.7	-	20.0	-	60.9
1970	9.7	0.6	10.3	51.7	0.1	24.3	0.7	87.1
1975	10.7	0.4	11.1	76.5	0.3	28.1	2.1	118.1
1980	10.9	0.3	11.2	94.8	0.3	32.5	3.0	141.9

Sources: RENFE, IETC, Gen. Dir. for Highways, Gen. Dir. for Ports, Campsa, Civil Aviation Subdivision. Author's calculations.

Table 6

CATEGORIES OF COMMODITIES ACCOUNTING FOR
MORE THAN 1 PER CENT OF DOMESTIC DEMAND IN 1975

CSTE code	Category	Demand tonnes '000s	Percen- age share	Average distance carried (km)
5	Cereals	18,371	1.64	100
7	Fresh fruit and vegetables	21,476	1.91	166
10	Animal feeds	14,881	1.33	85
12	Drinks	25,859	2.31	88
17	Wood and cork	23,522	2.10	95
21	Sand and gravel	248,143	22.12	53
22	Mineral ores	331,734	29.58	10
23	Iron ore	21,704	1,93	17
27	Coal and agglomerates	26,187	2.33	39
30	Petroleum and petroleum products	75,609	6.74	47
43	Lime and cement	31,122	2.77	62
44	Construction materials	95,620	8.52	38
46	Processed iron and steel works	29,766	2.65	124
52	Other transactions	23,311	2.08	152
	Total	987,265	88.01	46
	National Total	1,121,756	100.00	48

1. The survey used here for road freight traffic has often been criticised. The traffic recorded in this survey accounted for 65 per cent only of the demand set out in Table 5, itself established on the basis of data on the volume of traffic on the national road network as a whole. Aside from under-estimates due to incorrect assessment of lorryloads, the error would also appear largely attributable to short-haul freights.

Sources: Second national survey on road freight transport, 1975: INE(1). RENFE statistics on full-wagon-load traffic, 1975. Cabotage: The Central Shipping Bureau (OFICEMA). Author's calculations.

Table 7

CATEGORIES OF COMMODITIES CARRIED OVER AN AVERAGE DISTANCE OF MORE THAN 200 KM IN 1975

CSTE code	Category	Demand tonnes '000s	Percentage share	Average distance carried (km)
2	Meat and meat products	3,929	0.20	216
4	Fish and fish products	3,496	0.31	234
9	Sugar	2,059	0.18	203
18	Paper pulp	1,375	0.12	251
33	Animal or vegetable oils and fats	2,495	0.22	203
34	Chemicals and chemical compounds	7,605	0.68	218
37	Plastics and synthetic resins	980	0.09	274
38	Sundry chemical products	3,986	0.35	231
41	Paper	4,471	0.40	218
47	Non-ferrous metals	1,757	0.16	256
	Total	32,153	2.71	224.2

Sources: Second national survey on road freight transport, 1975, INE. Statistics on full wagon-load traffic, 1975, RENFE. Cabotage: Central Shipping Bureau (OFICEMA). Author's calculations.

Table 8

PRODUCTION AND TRANSPORT OF COMMODITIES

CATEGORY	Production and import (tonnes '000s) (1)	Tonnes carried (2)	(1)/(2)
Cereals and derivatives	14,208	18,371	1.29
Fresh fruit and vegetables	8,312	21,476	2.58
Meat, fish and derivatives	8,692	7,425	0.85*
Sundry foodstuffs	868	5,269	6.07
Drinks and oils	6,905	33,003	4.78
Wood and cork	9,210	23,522	2.55
Fertilisers	6,448	17,677	2.74
Sand, gravel and ores	168,505	608,723	3.61
Solid fuels	14,003	27,691	1.98
Petroleum, gas and petroleum products	42,699	81,743	1.91
Chemicals	16,634	21,775	1.31
Cement	23,970	31,122	1.30
Construction materials	33,910	95,620	2.82
Metals	11,644	35,293	3.03
Total	365,908	1,028,710	2.81

* A large proportion of fishery catches are landed directly at canneries.

Source: Short-term plan for the optimisation of energy consumption in the freight transport sector, INECO, Centro de Estudios de la Energía, 1978.

Table 9

FACTORS INFLUENCING MODAL CHOICE FOR FREIGHT TRANSPORT AND THEIR DEGREE OF INFLUENCE

	First reply	%	First 3 replies	%
1. Cost of transport	336	37	577	24
2. Transport time	205	22	495	20
3. Door-to-door service	76	8	309	13
4. Safety of consignment	70	8	298	12
5. Supply opportunities	43	5	130	5
6. Reliability of service	33	4	162	7
7. Flexibility of service	28	3	103	4
8. Methods of loading and unloading	28	3	111	5
9. Distance carried	25	3	66	3
10. Capacity available	14	2	78	3
11. Commercial relations	7	1	30	1
12. Other	42	4	65	3
Total	907(1)	100	2,424(2)	100

1. In 53 cases no reply was given to this question.
2. Some replies referred to one or two factors only.

Source: Short-term plan for the optimisation of energy consumption in the freight transport sector. INECO. Centro de Estudios de la Energia, 1978.

596

Table 10

LENGTH OF SPANISH RAILWAY NETWORKS BY COMPANY

Network	Not electrified			Electrified			Total
	Single track	Double track	Total	Single track	Double track	Total	
RENFE	8,016	53	8,069	3,255	2,218	5,473	13,542
FEVE	1,297	70	1,367	120	21	141	1,508
Private companies(1)	224	-	224	71	-	71	295
Operators coming within the province of regional authorities	89	-	89	228	70	298	387
Total	9,626	123	9,749	3,674	2,309	5,983	15,732

1. Does not include the mining railway of the Spanish Rio Tinto Mining Company and the Railway from Ribas to Nuria.

Sources: Annual reports of the railway operators. Annual report of IETC. Author's calculations.

Table 11

RENFE TRADING RESULTS
(millions of Pesetas at current prices)

Year	Income	Operating expenditure	Operating results	Depreciation	Interest	Deficits offset by the State
1965	15,097	16,252	-1,155	-1,705	-623	-3,483
1966	15,557	16,754	-1,197	-1,947	-645	-3,789
1967	16,743	19,181	-2,438	-2,236	-739	-5,413
1968	17,131	20,217	-3,086	-2,389	-429	-5,904
1969	17,829	19,299	-1,480	-2,613	-561	-4,644
1970	19,329	19,462	-133	-2,871	-656	-3,660
1971	21,834	21,857	-23	-3,130	-693	-3,846
1972	24,540	23,035	+1,505	-3,860	-752	-3,107
1973	28,665	25,651	+3,014	-4,410	-1,025	-2,421
1974	33,631	31,765	+1,866	-4,532	-1,761	-4,427
1975	38,150	44,227	-6,077	-5,064	-2,557	-13,698
1976	47,689	57,094	-9,405	-5,682	-3,521	-18,608
1977	56,549	74,749	-18,200	-6,385	-5,610	-30,195
1978	66,552	88,632	-22,080	-8,557	-7,328	-37,965
1979	72,182	101,231	-29,049	-10,024	-7,388	-46,461
1980	77,794	121,702	-43,908	-11,350	-9,173	-64,431

Source: RENFE Annual Reports. Author's calculations.

Table 12

TRENDS IN RENFE INVESTMENT AND DEPRECIATION

(Millions)

Year	Investment(1) Pesetas at current prices	1980 Pesetas	Depreciation 1980 Pesetas
1969	8,850	38,975	11,508
1970	9,824	40,937	11,963
1971	11,971	46,064	12,044
1972	15,356	54,575	13,718
1973	14,572	46,470	14,063
1974	18,502	51,029	12,499
1975	28,053	66,121	11,936
1976	23,100	46,292	11,387
1977	29,864	48,141	10,293
1978	24,888	33,474	11,509
1979	39,950	46,182	11,588
1980	50,840	50,840	11,350
Total		569,100	143,858

1. Includes State-financed investment.

Sources: RENFE Annual Reports. Author's calculation.

CLOSING SPEECH

by

The Secretary-General of the ECMT

The topic you have been invited to discuss - "Transport is for People" - might seem to be an unnecessary truism, and one might think that there was really no need to have a symposium on the subject.

After all, transport, as a service, is by definition essential to the smooth running of life.

And, to borrow from Aldous Huxley, transporting matter from one point on the earth's surface to another is really what human activity is all about.

In fact, the purpose of the symposium is not so much to endorse a self-evident truth - although it sometimes does no harm to remind ourselves of it - as to look at what its implications and applications are in practice.

It was, furthermore, eminently necessary to hold this exercise at this time, for our societies are now faced with the need to reconsider both the nature and the importance of the factors contributing to their growth.

Transport's response to this new situation is especially important, not to say crucial, to the smooth running of people's lives in a difficult economic and social context the constraints on which sometimes call for conflicting solutions.

The task before us is to reconcile all the different requirements, those bound up with firms' productivity and profitability, those stemming from all the sociological and social aspirations of populations and those connected with the concerns of government.

In short, while transport will more than ever be for people, the conditions and ways in which it is organised and operated will be different from those of the decades in which we enjoyed economic growth.

I cannot go back over all the aspects of the discussion, which the General Rapporteur of our Symposium will sum up better than I. What I want to do is to try and pick out the points that have to do with the framing of transport policy for the future.

All the preparatory reports and indeed the statements contributing to the discussion have shown that:

1. We are in the presence of social change whose scale and whose effects on the future organisation of transport cannot be anticipated, far less measured.
2. This means that when political authorities and transport operators have to take decisions regarding the development of the activities for which they are responsible they no longer have at their disposal, as they had during the earlier period of growth, information enabling them to determine in advance, with a fair measure of certainty, what strategy to follow in order to adjust transport supply to demand.

On the first point - the changing economic and social situation - the following observations can be made:

First of all, the restructuring of production and trade underlying the current depressed state of activity - and proceeding in spite of it - may be expected to lead to a growth of international trade with the implications this will have for goods transport. However, this growth will take place in a different context from the past in terms of the volume and nature of the goods transported and in terms of European domestic traffic flows. The shares of the different modes in this traffic will be affected accordingly.

A similar situation will no doubt arise in connection with personal mobility which will continue to be a prominent feature of our societies. It may be that the substantial advances that will inevitably be made in information technology will have an impact on conventional forms of transport by the end of the next decade. But, for the time being at least, these conventional modes will continue to have to handle the carriage of individuals. Requirements will, of course, vary and policies and measures will have to be differentiated according to purpose, e.g. tourism, business or routine travel, such as commuting. Because of this, the problem cannot be looked at or dealt with in the same way for international, regional and local transport.

The present crisis has also made it clear that the way in which transport will be organised in the future will depend to a great extent on its responses to the problems of energy consumption in the transport sector, and to what is decided, among other things, about investment in infrastructure developments, how they are put into effect and the conditions in which they are used.

Allowance will also have to be made for changes in technology designed to improve vehicles from the standpoints of consumption, safety and the environment, and consequently from that of the new opportunities this will afford the different modes as regards their share of goods and passenger transport.

Environmental protection and land-use planning will feature more and more prominently in decision-making.

The social aspect of the transport problem will also need to be taken into account, i.e. conditions of employment and work and social progress generally in a sector which is to a great extent labour-intensive and whose workforce accounts for a high percentage of total dependent employment.

The financial difficulties facing all nations will, furthermore, greatly constrain transport policy options, particularly at a time when it is also necessary to fight both inflation and unemployment.

Account will also have to be taken of all the cost aspects of transport and this cannot be done by drawing on the past. The cost at individual and firm level will be only one of the components from which costs to the community can be assessed for the purposes of finding ways to reduce those costs.

To sum up, as one of our rapporteurs has stated: "It will be difficult to reach a balance between commercial considerations, on the one hand, and socio-economic considerations, on the other".

All modes of transport are facing the problems of our time but they are affected by them in different ways, as I have said, as regards trade, quality of service, and the overall economic and social implications of their activity.

For the railways the problem is to find a way of adapting their organisation and activities, in terms of the services they can provide, to meet traffic requirements from two standpoints: economic viability and the provision of the public service that may be asked of them.

The current financial difficulties of railway companies must not be allowed to obscure the part that this mode will continue to have to play in meeting transport demand.

The present economic context may also prompt some enquiry into the position held by road transport in overall transport activity, and into ways and means of switching part of the traffic to other modes, as circumstances permit.

In fact, it is not easy to reason in terms of a choice of alternatives.

As one of the rapporteurs has stated, when emphasizing the limitations of a scientific approach to model-building in today's circumstances, we can no longer reason in terms of a simplistic relationship between production and transport. Industry will base its choice of transport on many other criteria.

Clearly, we are in the presence of a change that will lead these manufacturing industries to study, in the light of the economic situation, as it is or may become, the best possible means of answering their problems, taking into account all the factors affecting their decisions. There is plenty of room for road transport in this scenario.

The waterways will also have to adapt to the problems of today.

They hold a number of valuable cards which will help them to satisfy the requirements and conditions of transport demand over those traffic routes where they offer a service.

They have made, and are continuing to make, a great effort to increase productivity but they still have the problem of types of transport demand which are not always favourable to them, given present trade and goods transport conditions.

In the end, the utilisation of the different modes will continue to depend largely on users' choice, but this will depend in its turn on how transport undertakings are able to cope with demand.

At the general level the issue is that of the liberalisation of transport with all its problems, now being posed in a new context, and more especially that of international transport, because of the reactions of countries which are having to cope with extremely dense foreign traffic on their territories. Clearly this means that the objective of the complementarity of modes, which has hitherto always been the affirmed objective, now assumes far greater relevance. This is demonstrated, among other things, by the efforts made to optimise the use of transport.

Without encroaching on the conclusions of the General Rapporteur of the Symposium, I believe it may reasonably be said to be essential, both from the standpoint of the political authorities and from that of operators and businesses in the transport sector, to devise strategies that will accommodate the greatest possible flexibility.

On the government side, while the forward-looking approach should not be discarded, from now on the planning instruments which shaped the course of action in the past will have to be regarded as simply providing reference data needing to be adjusted in the directions indicated by a careful monitoring of developments.

The approach that is taken to problems will need built-in flexibility to allow a change of heading in the light of events in every possible field, political, economic, monetary and social, and on the world or national scale, which could abruptly or indirectly invalidate a course of action envisaged.

One thing is certain; we shall no longer be able to forecast the future by extrapolating from the past.

Firms in the transport sector are battling with the implications of this same truth.

The discussion at this Symposium has shown that they are fully aware of their responsibilities which call, on their part, for risk-fraught choices putting their very existence in the balance.

One of the problems which, in the end, faces everyone is the need for co-ordination between public and private sectors and for action serving the common interest, in this case to ensure the smooth running of the societies of today.

In fact, whilst the commercial slogan "the customer is always right" need not be taken as the absolute rule, it is clear that transport cannot play its part unless it really is run as a service to its users. Transport, in other words, is for people, and it has to bring people the goods they need in the right quantity and quality and provide the facilities they need to organise their private lives.

*

* *

I cannot express how valuable your discussions at this Symposium have been to the ECMT.

However, by way of summing up what we have achieved here, I shall turn to the OECD "Interfutures" project, the transport section of which was presented to the ECMT at its last Symposium in Istanbul in 1979.

The title of the report was "Facing the Future" and its sub-title was:

"Mastering the probable and managing the unpredictable".

I believe that your contributions to this Symposium will enable transport problems to be tackled along these lines.

Clearly, the study of how transport should be organised in the years to come can no longer be an exercise in
futurology. Instead all the incipient trends in the present economic and social situation need to be identified
and then taken into account in government and business
decision-making.

The findings reached at this Symposium will help to
establish the ways in which the transport sector should
develop so that it can best perform its role and negotiate
the narrow and difficult path it is now having to follow.

*
* *

And now, finally, I come to the most enjoyable part
of my task.

I should like to extend, on behalf of everyone here,
warmest thanks to Mr. Gamir-Casares, Spain's Minister of
Transport, Tourism and Communications, first, for making
it possible for his country to take responsibility for one
of the ECMT's most important events and, second, for having handled the arrangements so very efficiently, thereby
ensuring the success of our Symposium.

And I shall always remember the warmth of the welcome
extended to us.

With the Minister's permission, may I also express
our gratitude to Mr. Jorge Hernando, the Director General
of the Institute of Transport and Communications Studies,
who, with his very wide knowledge of transport problems,
his experience of the international milieu, and his diplo-
macy, courtesy and sense of organisation, has made this
such an excellent Symposium.

Our thanks also go to Mr. Luis Imedio, Mr. Isidoro
Gonzalez-Costilla and all the representatives and
officials of the Ministry of Transport and the Institute,
for the work done by the Spanish Delegation; without them
nothing would have been possible.

Our thanks, too, to the rapporteurs for the excellent
quality of their presentations, and to the chairmen and
members of the panels for their efficiency in leading the
discussions. Thank you all for your constructive
statements.

Finally, we thank the interpreters for their excellent work.

I wish you a safe return to your countries, but also
a happy stay in Spain for those of you who are taking up

Mr. Hernando's suggestion in his opening address and staying on for a few days in this beautiful country which has been such a generous host to us.

SUMMARY OF THE DISCUSSION

Mr. J. JOUTSEN
Ministry of Communications
Helsinki, Finland

SUMMARY

Topic 2A

Topic 2B

Topic 2C

Topic 1A

ASSESSMENT OF SOCIETY'S TRANSPORT NEEDS - MOBILITY OF PERSONS

THE REPORTS

The definition of mobility, a precondition for its assessment, proved to be somewhat elusive to both panel members and participants alike.

Recognised as an important factor of human behaviour by Cerwenka (Cerwenka, page 9), the boundary between quantity and quality cannot be clearly drawn. "Overall mobility is the resultant of a very complex and hard-to-grasp interplay of human wants (demand for mobility), constraints (land use, spatial distribution, time, money), and technological and economic potential for bridging space (transport supply)" (Cerwenka, page 11).

In everyday speech, mobility is perceived as the ability to move. However, in transport economics, the concept is not always uniformly defined. One definition is the following: "...mobility is readiness and ability to bridge the distances between the fixed predetermined locations of different functions..." (Cerwenka, page 13). The minimum indicators necessary for the understanding of mobility are (1) trip frequency, (2) trip length, and (3) trip duration, or, speed. Several specifications for considering the results of mobility surveys were presented, the conclusion being that "the constant increase in speed through technological progress has greatly extended the radius of action while travelling time has remained the same". The greatly simplified definition of mobility may therefore be "finally reduced to the dimension of speed" (Cerwenka, page 48). In this regard, mobility is seen as a product of speed, the use of which must be continuously held rationally in harness.

Rühl, Baanders and Garden seek to describe alternative methods usable for establishing the transport needs of society, the goal being the attainment of "improved understanding of individual needs which in turn would raise further questions about inequalities in society arising from the unequal satisfaction of travel needs" (Rühl, Baanders and Garden, page 58).

The merits of alternative means of establishing needs are considered through the adoption of a series of examples. The purpose of understanding phenomena relating to needs is limited, as "knowledge of needs will only be relevant insofar as it increases understanding of the way in which demand [for transport] will change". As economics presupposes need as a given determinant of demand, "other sciences should be used to determine what the needs for transport are" (Rühl, Baanders and Garden, page 61).

The conclusions of the paper state that the market should continue to be permitted to satisfy needs "providing the economic cost of doing so is borne by the users". However, "many needs are likely not to be satisfied when the market is left to work on its own...". and "...public transport services could be provided where the market did not justify [laissez-faire] in order to guarantee the sufficient supply of [transport]" (Rühl, Baanders and Garden, pages 90-91).

The suggestion put forth by the paper is that policies should be based more on information about the needs of individual people or groups of people, requiring a highly differentiated level of information gathering. Mentioned as specific subjects in need of further investigation are:

1. the needs of the handicapped, people living in isolated areas or lacking access to certain transport modes;
2. the investigation of minimum levels of provision related to important activities for e.g. isolated areas and off-peak periods in suburban areas;
3. transport needs for children; and
4. travel patterns and needs associated with particular household structures, e.g. the single parent family.

In conclusion, the authors state that "...a combined effort of commitment and imagination is required in order to realise the objective of relating policies to the needs of individuals in society" (Rühl, Baanders and Garden, page 91).

THE DISCUSSION

The Chairman of the session outlined the structure of the discussion by dividing the topic into four parts as follows:

The first issue is to define the problem, i.e. what is the distinction between need and demand, on the one hand, and mobility and accessibility, on the other? Can the question of the definition of mobility be reduced to a question of speed? Is a more suitable definition, perhaps, the ability to be able to travel relatively freely to prearranged destinations?

The second area is the need to know what has happened and will appear to happen to the level of transportation availability. The question can be asked whether mobility has increased similarly for different groups of the population. Further, one can ask if there exists some natural limit to mobility.

The third issue is to state the objectives for transport policy. One of the reports presented three ways for defining needs, and the applicability of these methods should be discussed. In particular, it should be questioned whether the reference group approach is a sensible way in which to assist in the selection of objectives for transport policy.

The fourth task is to identify a framework for policy application. Can information be presented in a way which is operational? If transport services are in effect produced in response to the forces of the market, is it correct procedure to use the aforementioned information, particularly regarding different groups, for the application of internal subsidies and external insertion of subsidies, and, also, for limiting entrance into the transport market?

Defining needs for transport

Transport need is essentially a personal concept and does not so much depend on the supply of transport. What it depends on more heavily are customs and habits. Only in the context of an understanding of these customs and habits then is it possible to begin to define what the needs are. The determination of needs must, in effect, be done analogically.

The need for transport thus reflects human desires which are just as real as the desire for other goods. If man has freely at his disposal a means of transport to satisfy that need, then the rational course of action would be to use it. There is no contradiction between this way of approaching the concept of need and the practical definition of mobility as determined, albeit in a greatly simplified manner, by speed.

There is, of course, some danger of becoming excessively preoccupied with the characteristics of transport supply such as speed. In pondering practical solutions

for transport, one must inevitably concentrate on
physical movements (as perceived by observed transport)
rather than the underlying desires which generate the
transport needs. But differing activity markets produce differing needs for physical movements, i.e. transport. The transport provision, however, in all its
diversity, still remains only as a way of satisfying the
desires and should not be treated as though it defines
the desire itself.

An important conclusion follows from this distinction. Invoicing choice (that is to say, observing statistics for e.g. passenger fare receipts) is not helpful
in determing transport needs as it does no more than indicate the level of service that it has proved profitable
for the market to supply in a given historical and institutional situation. Therefore, one should centre on the
reasons which make us travel, and this is not a mobility
problem but a social structure problem. The conclusion
is that inferring need is not possible solely from observing behaviour. Looking at other forms of communication
than passenger transport will make it evident that need
is not contained in observed transport alone.

Determining needs for transport

One approach to the determination of need is by
means of analytical studies of human behaviour, and the
determination of policy objectives, themselves political
in nature, should be based on analytical discussions.
Asking people about their needs for transport is here a
common procedure although the level of transport possibilities would very probably influence perception of need.
Nevertheless, some policy implications emerge from survey
results which give evidence of which trips are considered
more essential than others.

Are there limits to mobility?

It was argued that certain descriptive magnitudes
should be agreed upon which are relevant for political
actions. This course of action involves avoiding the
moral description of mobility and limiting the definition
to a descriptive one. In this sense, it can be asked if
there is any necessary limit to the need for mobility,
e.g. in travelled km/year given that a further increase
in mobility would be produced by an increase in speed.
The factors which might limit the increase of mobility,
thus defined, might well be physiological, psychological,
technical and economical.

Another speaker argued that no practical upper limit
may be set for mobility by those in charge of the implementation of transport policy. Theoretically, therefore,

the demand and the need for transport may become infinite
although in practice the limitation of needs is based on
personal experience. The difficulty lies in being able
to establish what the needs for transport are in different instances. Some help in establishing what such
needs are may be found in studies of the activities at
the destinations, but the possibilities for the utilisation of such information are also limited.

It was noted in passing that, simultaneously with
the holding of the symposium, man was circling the globe
at a speed of 30,000 km/hour. In this respect, the
limits to personal mobility as defined by speed will certainly continue to be exceeded in the foreseeable future. The pertinent question is how the amount which
people travel should really be measured, as the perception of time is highly variable. One must ask why people
travel and how people travel, and be very careful of definitions. Comparisons between countries, in this respect, are only beginning to emerge.

Evidence indicates that a tendency exists for a
higher portion of the population to have access to the
technical ability to travel. Referring to British studies, it was suggested that growth of car ownership and
its use has had little dependence on the general growth
of available income in recent years. Although improvements in road conditions have, in the last two decades,
greatly affected the amount of travel performed by the
population, the general conclusion (in reference to Great
Britain) is that those who do own cars are not now driving very much further per year. This seems to point to
the idea that within a given mode, there is a suggestion
towards a limit of physical mobility.

What do people need?

Regarding the distinction between needs and wants in
transport, it was lightheartedly observed that if people
actually need transport services at a frequency of one
service per hour, and are offered these services at a
rate of one every ten minutes, they will still desire
them at a rate of one every five minutes. The task for
the decision-makers regarding the financing of transport
in general, then, is to decide what is needed and not
what is currently supplied.

Due to the general availability of transport facilities, the question of "what is needed regarding mobility"
is very difficult to answer. New transport infrastructure and, indeed, new services often trigger new needs.
These needs are inevitably met by new constraints.

A further contributor suggested that the phenomenon
of mobility must be looked into separately for different

modes of transport and for the different activity patterns of people. The opinion was expressed that (in the Federal Republic of Germany) it is evident that leisure and holiday traffic are increasing, while professional transport will very likely stagnate in the foreseeable future due to changes in locational structure, among others. The usable definition of mobility should be pursued by going into details regarding the activity patterns of people. No enormous increase in leisure and holiday travel will occur in the foreseeable future, but new techniques and ideas will almost certainly evolve, providing new transport possibilities for the future.

Converting transport needs into a policy framework

It was suggested that policy action involves the allocation of money to certain purposes. But needs have no value automatically attached to them by the market and hence it is not possible to seek an optimum situation in the transport market aggregating the value of the needs satisfied. In this respect, comparing alternative solutions with specific goals would be a more desirable course of action than simply seeking an optimum solution to satisfy needs.

The measuring of transport needs, particularly in urban areas, is essential for policy considerations. However, the way in which people use transport is not always based on real needs. The difficulty lies in determining who is authorised, in turn, to determine the difference between needs and wishes. Of acute importance is the evolution of the wishes of today into the claims and rights of tomorrow. Another speaker offered a different approach to policy making.

Theoretically reargued, the transport market is very close to the principle of natural selection existing in nature. But democratic policy strives not only to satisfy the desires of the majority, but also the needs of minorities. In a democratic political system, the decision-maker should know as much as possible of the alternatives and the consequences of possible action.

Great emphasis should be placed on allowing the little we know of the situation in the transport market to be available to all the people. In this sense, experts should also be honest in differentiating between knowing, desiring to know and pretending to know relevant information relating to needs for transport for policy framework considerations.

An important policy problem raised in the discussion concerned the relationship between the "commerical" and "non-commercial" aspects of public transport policy. If operators are making their decisions on commercial grounds how can we integrate the satisfaction of "needs" into the system in a way which gives appropriate indications to government and to operators on the disposition of resources? Clearly there is a danger of waste in having a separate provision for pure needs-based transport (e.g. hospital services, etc.) but there is equally a failure so far to integrate, institutionally or conceptually, the satisfaction of quite different kinds of transport needs.

THE CONCLUSIONS

The essential statement made during the course of the discussion is that once a need for transport is made into a right, then it is for the government to come up with the technical and financial means which must be employed for the attainment of the right to the transport in question.

As new forms of living such as telecommunications are developed for the benefit of mankind, their effects on development of transport and mobility should be observed. It is difficult to estimate the effects of such development on needs. An example is that of the development of the telephone, as this did not reduce the need for physical transport, but rather increased it.

The original dilemma of the physical need for communication, i.e. the question of whether the provision of mobility is limited or whether it is a question of marginally increasing speed, has not been answered.

One must consider the groups for which transport information needs are important. Such knowledge is useful in order to anticipate needs in the future. It is very much in the interest of public authorities to know the needs of the users of transport, e.g. in order to develop transport infrastructure in accordance to the needs of the community.

A number of characteristics can be identified regarding the definition of mobility:

- need is personal, a "felt need";
- need does not depend on supply;
- need depends on customs. These in turn are a social base for the interpretation of what is needed.

The use of transport varies greatly. Evidence of stability of the time-budget holds at the aggregate level, but large differences occur at the disaggregate level. The conclusion, therefore, is that, in need, a variation exists.

Mobility must also be defined qualitatively, as different qualities of transport exist for different purposes.

A pertinent question for decision makers is whether more is being supplied than is actually needed, as a lot appears to be wanted.

Regarding the trends and the future in mobility and the need for mobility, we must ask ourselves if some natural boundary for mobility does exist. Today, it appears that the average distance travelled by car is levelling off, and we may assume that the expansion of car ownership must also even out. In total therefore it appears that some boundary for mobility must exist for a given mode of transport. Though for an individual, a multitude of ways exists to use time, an individual is unlikely to use an unlimited amount of time for transport.

We must ask whether it is the aggregate or the average which is at the centre of our interest, or is it our use of the supply of transport. Whilst we may appear to be approaching a boundary of mobility, this boundary is shifting due to technology, location of economic activity, and changes in social taste.

In respect to the selection of objectives, the function of scientists as presenters of information should be to describe and not prescribe solutions. Scientists should give a summary of evidence for decision makers so that these in turn are able to identify problems and procedures, i.e. how to resolve the problems of society.

The mobility of people is a result of people's decisions, and as such is traded off against some other form of activity. The dwelling place, one's access to work, etc. are choices which individuals are always making which involve such trade-offs. Low levels of mobility exist where such activities are locked into social structure, the environment, etc. One should attempt to identify where mobility has declined in particular sections of society, not because of their own decisions, but because of action taken by society or those in charge of transport infrastructure and undertakings. In this respect, a wide range of definitions of need is necessary for policy makers.

An important question concerning the provision of mobility of persons is whether we are able to integrate a needs approach into public sector policies on the distribution of funds to operators of different types of transport. Alternatively we must ask ourselves if there should exist a non-market sector specially for "needs" transport. A precondition would be that certain requirements (e.g. hospitals, education etc.) needing particular intervention be taken out of the market. But this may

involve great cost as it is very difficult to separate
such requirements from the provision of economically
based services, and this would very possibly entail the
wasteful provision of services. In certain countries, it
has been recognised that large scale provision of public
transport for specific needs has led to inefficient provision of transport.

It was agreed that transport planning should be more
sensitive to needs. It is very difficult, however, to
understand what the needs are. We can attempt to do so
through sample studies aimed at a variety of needs,
rather than presenting uniform standards of provision.
The data requirements of this are enormous, and it is
very easy to overstep the possibilities by forgetting the
costs involved. The standards of information desired by
politicians are difficult to provide, and very often
these same standards of information are difficult to accept by politicians due to the changing needs of society.

Topic 1B

ASSESSMENT OF SOCIETY'S TRANSPORT NEEDS - GOODS
TRANSPORT

Two introductory reports were prepared for this
topic. Due to the different nature of these reports, and
indeed of the ensuing discussion [the first report(I)
deals with environmental effects of goods transport by
road, the second report (II) deals with economic models
and the structure and future of goods transport], these
shall be dealt with separately in this general report; in
the actual discussion both were dealt with simultaneously.

THE REPORT (I)

The first preliminary paper for this topic was written by Haigh and Hand. Giving a broad overview of recent
trends in the development of road freight, the report
concentrates on presenting environmental effects caused
by lorries, advocating the radical limitation of road
transport in order to limit damages to the environment.

This paper is both abrasive and provocative, as indeed it was very likely intended to be. Recognising the
inadequacy of studies on environmental constraints, the
authors nevertheless maintain that such constraints are
already at work, and "to ignore them will not only result
in increasing damage to the environment but will result
in the pursuit of transport policies and of more general
economic policies which time will prove to have been misguided" (Haigh and Hand, page 95).

The paper puts forth the idea that there exists a
"lorry problem" and then endeavours to quantify the components of this. The "lorry problem" referred to in the
paper is made up of a series of problems. However, the
incorporation of any assessment of lorry-based negative
effects into a single lorry nuisance figure is recognised
to be impossible to achieve. In addition to noise,

negative effects of lorries are seen as being vibration, accidents, air pollution, visual intrusion, damage to buildings, delay and frustration, and miscellaneous social costs.

The conclusive remark of the paper is that "In the absence of a refined indicator of [environmental] effects [caused] by lorries we can, in the meanwhile, state more crudely that vehicle-kilometres of the heaviest lorries should be stabilized" (Haigh and Hand, page 130). As a primary tool for intervention to stabilize the growth of long distance road transport, the authors advocate the use of the artificial raising of the price of transport oil products.

THE DISCUSSION (I)

In accusation of the lorry

The central point at issue is how different social groups perceive the lorry, and are disutilities experienced by large portions of the population. A survey was mentioned which shows that of some 700 urban areas in the United Kingdom with populations of 500 to 150,000 inhabitants, only some 25 per cent have by-passes, a rough indication of the amount of people affected by the negative effects of lorries.

Of the harmful effects of lorries, it was felt by the rapporteurs that noise is perhaps that which could most probably be dealt with by technical means. It was noted that, in 1977, the Council of Ministers of the European Community (EC) set a target of 80 decibels to be met by lorries in 1985. However, this target cannot be met, as lorry users and the lorry industry have not, it was maintained, done what they can to reduce the noise level. It was further brought out that, if this cannot be dealt with, then it is hardly possible to tackle the other, more difficult, environmental problems caused by lorries.

In relation to passenger transport forecasts, which indicate a saturation level, goods transport forecasts were seen as appearing to have no saturation level at all, thus seeming to go on forever. It was asked what the environmental effects will be if the forecasts for the end of the century are indeed met.

In defence of the lorry

To be practical, one must ask how it is possible to go about formulating legislation prohibiting further deterioration of the environment. Although it is very easy to put forward such a thesis, lorries also have a function in society.

All arguments defending lorries would most certainly stand up in a court of justice, were the use of lorries brought to court because of their environmentally damaging effects. This is very important in view of practical measures to be taken, and what is left, due to the impossibility of judicial measures, is a difficult pathway. This would very likely encompass measures for alleviating the situation in specific instances, such as in densely populated areas, etc.

Although certain hostility to the long vehicle may be characteristic of certain groups of the population, it is nevertheless true that the economy cannot possibly function without the use of the heavy lorry. The main point is that one should attempt to visualise the problems which an administration faces when seeking rational solutions to the problems involved.

In a specific intervention, it was agreed to that the anti-lorry viewpoint presented in the report is perfectly respectable and reasonable, but that a critical analysis should be taken of the arguments put forth in this introductory report.

In reference to the accusation presented in the report stating that one reason for the large increase in heavy lorry traffic is that these do not pay their full track costs (Haigh and Hand, page 100), the speaker referred to a study published by British Rail eight years ago which dealt with track costs. In this study, it was brought out, though drawing broad conclusions, that lorries of competitive size operating over competitive routes with the railways were, at that time, in fact paying between one-third and one-half of their track costs. Currently, the allocations which in the same country are made to the individual categories of vehicles are far beyond what is statistically available for making such allocations. In effect, all available figures today show that the lorries, in general, are broadly speaking paying their full track cost.

The next point with which the speaker disagreed was that the report maintained that entry into the road haulage industry has always been easy. The cost of setting up a road haulage firm today, which is certainly quite high, is in itself an indicator of the difficulties involved in entering the transport market.

The discussion was referred to (Haigh and Hand, page 102) which stated that the relationship of the decrease in tonnage lifted does not correlate to GDP. The speaker asked why such a correlation should indeed exist. In many cases, with modern goods, the lorry, properly used, is full before it is loaded to sometimes even a quarter of its load limit. This is very relevant when taking into account the characteristics of today's freight which have a much greater proportion of high value and low weight goods than has previously been the case.

Furthermore, it was asked if all the damage caused to houses (referred to on pages 112-113 of the report) is indeed caused by vibrations from road traffic? A probable cause may be variations in temperature which buildings are not designed to withstand.

Coming to the accusation that greater damage is done by vehicles with a greater weight, it was argued by the speaker that a comparison of the damage done by e.g. two simple axles, each loaded to five tonnes, as compared with a compound axle loaded to ten tonnes, showed that the compound axle loaded to ten tonnes does far less damage. As a historical perspective to this question, the speaker referred to a newspaper clipping, seen in a cathedral in London, from the London Times in the year 1926, which quoted someone as saying that, because of the increase in size of vehicles which were then found on London streets, inevitably the buildings in London would fall down within five years.

In conclusion, it was said that the by-passes, which road hauliers have wanted to be built as much as anyone else, should have been built. However, why should the road hauliers be blamed for the shortcomings of the government and the communities which they serve? The rational thing to do is to build these by-passes and not be so critical of the development of the road haulage industry which has done so much to save a great deal in transport costs, and also has contributed greatly to the growth of modern society.

In another intervention, an invitation was made to anyone interested in environmental protection to visit one or another of the West German vehicle manufacturers to appreciate the efforts which have been undertaken for many years, not without success, and to also appreciate how difficult it is to keep below the noise level fixed by the Common Market authorities. It is very hard indeed to go below these levels. It was suggested that, in many urban areas, the noise which most people find to be most irritating is not so much that caused by lorries, but by the continuous noise coming from construction sites in the big cities.

A point of clarification was given by another speaker to the contribution previously made in criticism of the report on environmental effects caused by lorries. In reference to the assumption, made in the report, that heavy lorries have the lion's share of the market because they do not cover all the infrastructure costs, it was said that it is very obvious that one type of transport which does not cover its infrastructure costs is the railway.

According to studies carried out by the Spanish Institute for Transport Studies of infrastructure charges, one can deduce that, even if all road users covered infrastructure costs daily, the heavy lorries do not cover all the costs for which they are responsible. In the Spanish case, however, the maximum differences between infrastructure cost charged to the users and fiscal charges paid by the users does not exceed Pesetas 200,000, which is far less than US$2,000 a year per vehicle. If an average mean is given for the use of a road haulage vehicle, the cost per tonne-kilometre is less than 20 centimos, the case precisely of a 3-axled vehicle of 18 tonnes. This was indicated as hardly influencing competition in transport.

In rebuttal: environmental effects of lorries

In reply to the arguments presented against the views expressed in the report on environmental damage caused by lorries, it was replied from the panel that there should be no difficulty in drawing up precise legislation explicitly enforcing heavy lorry quotas for the purpose of protecting the environment. Referring to the possibility of reducing the noise level of lorries, the point to be made, it was said, is that this is a technological challenge which is capable of a technological solution. It was also stressed that, at least in Great Britain, government figures for the end of the year 1981 showed that the heaviest lorries are not paying their full track costs and had not done so for a number of years. On vibration, it was pointed out that the effect is not fully known, and there should be research on this. The road haulage industry should be generating pressure for it, it was stated from the panel, and not leave it to the environmental bodies.

THE REPORT (II)

The second of the two introductory reports, written by Quinet, Marche and Reynaud, concerns itself with:

1. the structure and development of goods transport volume;
2. goods traffic modelling; and
3. trends in transport organisation.

The report, which is based mainly on French findings, recognises the historical close link between goods transport and economic activity. The trends in continental transport show an increasing share for road transport and stagnation since 1970 of railway and waterway traffic. Quoting trends for e.g. transport for own account and the development of complete trainloads in rail transport, the questions were put forth, firstly, how much (of the change) was due to changes in the make-up of the goods to be transported and, secondly, what was the influence of changes in the quality of service? In the case of the French railways it was noted that, in the 1970s, "a higher quality of service through shorter transport times led, in the case of wagon groupings, to a substantial decrease in the ordinary service to the benefit of the rapid service" (Quinet, Marche and Reynaud, page 153).

The influence of distance on the rail/road modal split reflects the influence of transport costs. However, due to the difficulties of interpreting modal split as a function of transport prices (it is difficult to assess the actual price of transport, and the quality of service has an effect), the authors find it likely that the development of these types of models "will need in the future to adopt a dissaggregated approach based on sample shipments, these being placed in the logistic chain" (Quinet, Marche and Reynaud, page 163).

Several types of models for goods transport are given. The authors present results and depict the limitations of the use of the demand models, the supply and demand equilibrium models, and the individual behaviour models illustrated (Quinet, Marche and Reynaud, pages 164-170).

Finally, it is indicated that logistical policies are appearing now in firms which are also recognising the transport chain logic. Also, it is shown to be evident that more attempts are being made to control the shipment of products.

Giving a rough overall estimate of the transport share in intermediate consumption as approximately 10 per cent (the figure ranges from 2 to 20 per cent, depending on the sector), the authors state that a logistic policy can both reduce the cost of transporting goods and accelerate the turnover of capital.

It is recognised that economic reasons exist justifying specialisation in goods transport. Among specialisation factors in international transport are the knowledge of the practices and regulations of other countries, and the existence of durable commerical contracts guaranteeing the continuance of the transport chain. Regarding the diversification of activities into

e.g. areas controlled by trading partners, a certain
limit to the extent to which these can be pursued by
transport firms seems to exist. Survey results show that
diversification of activities rarely exceeds 25 to 30 per
cent of turnover.

THE DISCUSSION (II)

The function of models

Models should try to picture an abstraction of reality, pinpointing certain highlights. In this respect,
they can only reflect an image of reality. A choice must
therefore be made between the phenomena that are relevant
for the purpose of making a highlight, and here value
judgements must be introduced. For this reason, models
are not always exclusively analytical, but have an assessing or even political character.

One shouldn't envision, for either goods transport
or passenger transport, universal models for the purpose
of explaining everything. All models are not necessarily
explanatory in nature, as some models are drawn up in
accordance to some target.

Framework conditions

A prime objective is to better understand how transport will use the different transport chains. With a
view to the total volume of transport and the transportable volumes, there is always a relation between an economic activity globally or by sectors, together with the
quantities transported. Changes will occur in the structure of the various products to be transported and also
in the geographic structures. When forming sectorial
models, there can be a change in the structures of the
products, as in the geographical location or in the market. Those changes are not necessarily the same, whether
we are concerned with a considerable or low growth rate,
or even a recession. Globally, many problems still occur
in linking the quantities to be transported with the economic activity.

The difficulties encountered

Quantities transported are often little known in
both road transport and in international transport, as
statistics in different countries are not always cohe-
rent; better statistical information is available regarding rail and shipping. Rail transport (which is connected to international transport) accounts for

approximately 40 per cent of international transport, a very big figure. On the whole, however, we have a lack of information as regards the quantity of transport as well as the costs of transport. Time of transport, the feasibility of transport, and the function of transport are not well known from a statistical point of view. This general "lack of adjustment to statistical observations" perhaps explains the difficulties encountered in quantitative models, these being either macro-economic or micro-economic.

Macro-economic models

Macro-economic models are used to forecast total tonnage or tonne-kilometres in a given country or region within a given time period. This forecasting and the corresponding models are rather traditional and they aim at explaining the tonne-kilometres transported in relation to economic activities. These models can be presented either globally for the whole of the economy or for a sector of the economy. Globally, these models do not really reproduce reality. Recent structural upheavals in economic activities have indicated that the global links between the whole of economic activity and the total volume of the amount of goods transported are no longer as strict as was the case immediately after the Second World War.

Micro-economic models

Micro-economic models are those aimed at expressing the choice for a firm or group of firms according to a geographical area. These models, of which many have been tested, are hindered by a lack of statistical data. The choice of mode involves the cost and the quantities transported, but also other elements which statistics do not explain globally, such as the size of the consignment and the nature of the item transported.

The modal choice can only be understood in a complete analysis of the policy of the firm as regards storage, distribution and handling. The statistical elements we have available are very restrictive. Furthermore, micro-economic models are essentially static and do not explain trends in a time sequence. The point of departure which is essential regarding the awareness of strategic trends is that goods transport is an instrument of the activities of economic agents, and one has to place this phenomenon within this set of activities.

Individual behaviour models

The authors base these models on behaviour assumptions and, additionally, on "proven principles". It was

629

asked what evidence exists for the principles to be taken as proven? As stated in the report, these types of models ecompass the possibilities to put in more factors than for instance transport time and cost. Unfortunately, in the results discussing elasticities, only transport cost factors are included. (Author's note: Might an answer be "Time is money"?).

Individual behavioural models are concerned with the behaviour of industrial entrepreneurs, shippers or loaders, or those who delegate the decision-making to the heads of these firms. The idea to be retained is to situate transport from the point of view of the physical routing, the chain to be used by successive means of transport, and to replace this transport within a framework of production organisation and distribution. This results in a logistical approach to transport, and in this sense we are obliged to take up the point of view of the shippers and the loaders and to consider case by case, a micro-economic approach.

Success controls of models

With models, one can only make forecasts under the conditions of development, and very rarely does one endeavour to undertake success controls. With the scientific approach, and to improve our argumentational basis, success control is absolutely necessary and should be carried out periodically. It is doubtful, however, whether politicians will be very understanding about this.

In goods transport, model results have been less than perfect in the past. In this respect, we shall see in the future what actually occurred vis-à-vis the forecast. What we will retain are the tonne-kilometres and the cost of transport, and when attempting to analyse the causes for error, since these global volumes are closely linked to the economic activities and structural changes, it is obvious that the inaccuracies one might have made would depend to a great extent on the forecast one has made of the economy itself. The difficulty in forecasting transportable potential lies in forecasting the trends of economic activity.

As to which would be the best formulation from the point of view of modal split, it was acknowledged that not many models have been sanctioned by experience. The extrapolation of the modal distribution has been based on the past because, precisely, it has not been possible to introduce explicitly which variables intervene (the goods cost variables and service quality variables). A balance should be found between the statistical population, which is rather numerous, so that not just the case of a few firms is considered. Also, rational analysis presupposes

sufficiently homogenous goods. Micro-economic or behavioural models would have to consider each firm case by
case, as a logistical approach exists for each firm. One
must find a way of reasonably representing reality, with
a picture which would not be too grim, but which would
include the logistical problems of the firm.

Prospects for the future

It was put forth that the demands of society in the
future would always lead to a higher use of the lorry
vis-à-vis rail. The portion of rail transport could be
diminished not only in percentage, but also in absolute
figures. It was maintained that this evolution should be
sought in the emergence of a multi-polar economy with a
growing importance of third world countries, entailing
substantial changes in geographical distribution.

The access to the areas producing large quantities
of raw materials will have a bearing on bulk transport,
and multinational companies will have an effect on this
development and will show a more decentralised structure
than at the present time. More multipolarity will come
about in the flow of certain goods, with the flow of
goods becoming more and more diversified with a tendency
towards more reduced volume.

In the future, therefore, we are counting on models
with higher flexibility, showing better modes of access.
Additionally, more dispersed and demanding models are
needed as to quality of service, and a higher emphasis on
the reduction of costs. However, the choice of transport
mode will not depend solely on cost, but on e.g. length
of haul, personal contacts, and demands for specialised
services.

Forecasts showing a greater proportional increase of
road goods transport over rail were criticised for several reasons. In view of considerations regarding the
increase in the transport of goods from third world countries through European ports, it was argued that railways
have excellent potential, both technological and economical, to participate in this activity, particularly dealing with containers.

It was argued that Common Market studies (no specific studies were referred to) show that heavy lorries are
far from paying full track costs, and an increase of
25 per cent should be levied on the charges to these
vehicles in certain EC-countries (no reference was made
to the track costs of railways).

It was said that the drivers of heavy lorries often
drive for 60 to 80 hours a week, inferring that serious
road safety problems are ensuing from this. Referring to

631

statistics, it was suggested that heavy lorries, which account for approximately 20 per cent of the traffic, are involved in twice as many of these accidents than other forms of traffic.

Some countries are seeking to favour the use of railways for transit traffic due to the congestion on the roads. Finally, it was brought out that competition between road and rail only occurs after a certain distance. As a large amount of road traffic is carried out within a radius of 50 or 60 kilometres, there is no competition for this traffic on main traffic lines. It was suggested that a more accurate analysis should be made of transport statistics before concluding that road wins over rail.

THE CONCLUSIONS

1. Effects on the environment

The Chairman concluded that any assessment of efforts concerning the effects of transport on the environment will always remain subjective. The nuisance caused by long vehicles depends on the volume of traffic and on individual appreciation. Long vehicles and the nuisance caused to the environment are only two aspects; sometimes other modes of transport cannot offer the same means of service without an increase of transport costs.

The detrimental effects of lorries can to some extent be decreased through technical means in the future. Participants are not in favour of an artificial drop in goods transport by heavy vehicles, as they prefer to stress technological improvement in heavy lorries within certain limits and we should arrive at a better physical distribution. One should endeavour to seek a harmonization of the different modes of transport instead of stressing competition between transport modes.

2. Models and prospects for the future

The Chairman ended the discussion with the comment that the issues at hand had been discussed in a highly lively and sometimes controversial manner, and that it was very difficult to arrive at a common conclusion.

The target of the model is to build and develop a picture, in time, which is as complete as possible regarding future developments within the transport sector. A sure fact is that many restrictions are involved in modelling, although experts always make a considerable effort to improve models and thus to improve the results which emerge from them.

The results of models are used by those concerned with decision making and they therefore must be informed of the limitations of these models so that they are not considered infallible. One should not lose sight of the relativity of models, and this is true the longer the period covered by the model.

We are living in a society with a slow down growth or 0-level growth with occasional stagnation, coupled with increases in unemployment and inflation. The quantitive development of transport is behind us, and mobility will increase more slowly for goods as well as passengers.

Transport flows are more and more dispersed and variable. We can expect a reduction in transport resulting from the decentralisation at the world level of industrial activities. The different modes of transport are obliged to adjust to these new developments. This implies that the future is less pessimistic for modes of transport which are flexible and which offer a high quality of service.

International transport has, as in the past, risen at a rate higher than national transport, and one can expect that this development will continue in the future. In a context with slow down growth and increased competitiveness on national and international markets, the rationalisation of transport operations, storage and handling appear as a new source for increasing productivity and is therefore a competitive factor. It is within this context that we have to include combined transport as well as integrated transport.

Finally, it is with diversification of means that we can meet the future, a more accurate adjustment to demand. It shows the link existing between transport and economic activities, a passage from quantitative to qualitative aspects which characterises the current period, and this is also found in the field of transport.

Topic 2A

THE MANAGEMENT OF FIRMS TO SATISFY TRANSPORT
NEEDS - GOODS TRANSPORT BY ROAD

THE REPORTS

Three introductory reports were prepared for this
topic. In the report by Binnenbruck, the topic is looked
upon from a market economy standpoint in view of transport demand trends and emphasis on transport needs. An
assessment is made of the tasks and problems for firm
managements, and alternative ways and means are presented
for meeting the need to adjust to general economic
conditions.

Referring to transport trends for the Federal Republic of Germany, it was pointed out that 43 per cent of
the amount of goods carried by rail are shipped over distances less than 50 km, although this volume is considerably less than that compared to local goods transport by
road. Pointing out that the internal relations of town
delivery have as yet been little researched, it is maintained that "the overall trend is for transport to increase over shorter distances [in relation to total
transport volume]" (Binnenbruck, page 199).

The different categories of requirement for goods
supply, which is seen as a logistic problem, are listed
in the report (Binnenbruck, pages 206-207). It is
brought out, however, that "the total road haulage system
has not yet been comprehensively and intensively analysed
from the standpoint of the logistic requirements of the
economy as a whole"; specifically, there is a lack of
knowledge of the organisational and institutional links.
Therefore, "a transport management system is to be developed which will facilitate the necessary linkages and
make possible the necessary institutional arrangements"
(Binnenbruck, page 210).

Goods delivery and pickup in large towns and conurbations is becoming increasingly difficult due to e.g.
traffic limitation regulations and several other

reasons which are listed (Binnenbruck, page 212). The more unfavourable traffic conditions become, the greater the need for rationalisation of transport operations. However, it is maintained that "...transport supply does little to further rationalisation where it is most urgently needed...", i.e. in local goods transport (Binnenbruck, page 214).

Structural weaknesses of transport firms are brought out as being mainly connected to their small size, which limits the range of action of management due to organisational factors. Among others, the weaknesses of transport firms lie in the internal organisation and in "the lack of a fully developed cost and production accounting system, and lack of a selective marketing concept" (Binnenbruck, page 221). Also, legal conditions enforce constraints on the activities of transport firm management.

Finally, certain ways and means of meeting the need to adjust to general economic conditions are presented. It is pointed out that "managements have clearly not yet exhausted the possibilities of co-operation as a policy instrument" (Binnenbruck, page 228). Also, "management has to recognise and exploit the right innovations... Scheduling in particular needs computer support..." and "...information transmission and processing systems extending beyond the [transport] firm need to be developed" (Binnenbruck, page 230).

The second report, written by Menzinger, is presented from the point of view of a representative of the forwarding business. The point emphasized is that, if an entrepreneur wishes to truly understand real transport needs, this can only be achieved through virtually daily contact with his customers.

In dealing with the particular problems of service firms in the transport sector, only those firms which operate according to private enterprise principles are discussed, these being mostly forwarding agents and road hauliers. It is pointed out that "...There is no doubt...that the trend is towards larger units..." (Menzinger, page 248). A distinction is made, referring to the European situation, between firms with carrier functions (vehicle owners and operators) and those with forwarding functions (transport organisers, freight space brokers, special transport services). However, these two functions are being increasingly performed in both types of firms, and the view is presented that "...Only the small carriers are unable to restructure [internal organisation accordingly] and they would be well advised to intensify co-operation with forwarding agents" (Menzinger, page 248).

The particular problem of the transport sector is pointed out as being narrow profit margins, while

635

technical progress is simultaneously an accelerator. The conditions for sound management therefore include a relatively short depreciation period, as "...in the future, individual firms will be forced to invest more than hitherto in vehicles and the main task of the decision-makers will be to strike the right balance between their own and other capacity" (Menzinger, page 250).

The third report, written by Verhoeff, deals with the social policy considerations for transport firms. Pointing out that social policy is but one of the many factors to be taken into account by management, some of the main features of the road haulage industry are outlined, on the basis of data from the Netherlands, as a background for the examination of the subject.

The place of social policy in individual road haulage firms was dealt with by first asking whether "it is legitimate to ask whether the adoption of social policies should be purely optional and dependent on the attitudes within the company concerned". It was pointed out that "the clarification of company objectives can itself provide a clear indication of the place of social policy in a particular company" (Verhoeff, page 268).

Social policy is defined as being "...concerned with the people who work in a company, with the way they work, the contribution they make to the attainment of company objectives, both individually and collectively, and the welfare they obtain in and through the job" (Verhoeff, page 270). It is brought out that "it is primarily up to the people working in a company to indicate what their interests are" (Verhoeff, page 272).

As a word of warning, however, it is pointed out that "the individual approach towards social matters can sometimes be to the detriment of employees or can lead to the distortion of competition in both the labour and the transport market. The fact that employer and employee associations have a role to play in these circumstances does not invalidate this general principle" (Verhoeff, page 275).

Mentioned as specific areas of social policy are conditions of employment, working conditions, labour relations, and quality of work. In an assessment of the major aspects it is held that the failure of management to take into account the interests of their employees will, among others, "...give rise to increasing confrontation between workers and management as a result of the process of greater self-reliance on the part of labour, the higher educational qualifications of the people entering the industry, and external developments in the social field and the resultant consequences for individual hauliers" (Verhoeff, page 282).

Transport for own account

The view was presented that transport for own account was somewhat overlooked in the reports, despite the fact that this plays a highly important role in goods transport. Although the ideas expressed by the rapporteurs are very creative, the conclusions which were drawn only concern transport for hire and reward. However, about 40 to 50 per cent of the volume of transport comes under own account, as does about 15 to 20 per cent of the tonne-kilometres.

It has been estimated that approximately 60 per cent of goods transport in Ireland is done for own account, the reasons for this, in the eyes of the panelist, being that difficulty exists to persuade the drivers and staff of the own account firms to switch over to road haulier firms, possibly due in part to trade union pressures. In theory, it could very well be government policy to move towards a more professional transport system, but in practice, creating such a system by the means of transferring the non-professional transport employees of firms conducting transport for own account over to professional road hauliers would be a very difficult task to accomplish.

According to Irish studies, approximately 28 per cent of the decisions made by the customer regarding what mode of transport to use for goods transport have been based on price, the situation being one where customers are to a great extent dictating the prices to the hauliers. In Ireland, the structure, in the main, is of small road haulier companies. The latest report to hand, by a consultative commission on road frieght transport, recommended broader use of quality controls only, and no increased use of quantity controls limiting the operation of road hauliers.

An oligopoly?

It was asked whether the tendency to operate with a logistical principle will have an effect on the goods transport market structure. The speaker maintained the existence of a tendency towards concentration; one reason for a modal split-up in the transport market is that technological development has caused transport capacity to become specialised, causing difficulties in specific capacity being transferred into different areas. In this respect, more concentration on logistical services will also contribute to this type of split-up of the transport market, creating risks for an oligopolistical situation appearing in the transport market sector in the future (due to functionally and regionally oriented monopolies). If this were to occur, the market structure would become a more political issue.

The problems of distribution, if they are given economic solutions, will probably lead to an oligopolistic situation. This is, however, a trend of the integrated transport chain. It is not possible, at this time, to determine the effect of this process on small transport companies. Nevertheless, logistics can give a certain economic dimension by means of market segmentation. Big companies can also be endangered by this technique, but perhaps free competition will decide which is the best solution. In road transport, society needs pluralistic organisational and managerial structure as well as flexibility. The survival rate of goods transport by road will depend in the future on the elasticity of the road transport system.

Transport policy should ensure the continued existence of the positive aspects of small-scale road haulage firms, such as the ability to flexibly react to changes in demand. In fact, it was underlined that it is not so much the individual small transport firm which is flexible, but, rather, it is the small business system which is flexible. For this reason, the speaker felt that transport policy should endeavour to develop and stimulate the small-scale business system in road haulage, rather than developing transport management.

Comment by the IRU

In an observation from the International Road Union, a more flexible use of the means available was advocated, e.g. by reducing the number of empty return trips through the multinational utilisation of bilateral returns for destinations other than the country of origin. It was suggested that improvement of staff productivity does not provide many improvements of productivity in short-haul goods transport because of the incidence of intermediate and terminal operations. For long-hauls, the increase of co-operation between rail and road must be explored.

It was brought out that the time has past when marketing and sales managers insisted on offering maximum service to all people, regardless of their locations and the profitability involved. In this approach, where transport is one element of logistics, five key decision areas were indicated, which together constitute what can be considered the "logistic mix":

1. facility decisions;
2. inventory decisions;
3. communications decisions;

4. utilisation decisions; and
5. transport decisions.

These five areas together constitute the total cost
of distribution in transport for a company, where a decision taken in one area will often affect decisions in
other areas. For example, the closing down of a depot, a
facility decision, will affect not only transport costs,
but also the inventorial location and, probably, that of
operational processing costs. Distribution, therefore,
is not only transport, as transport is only one, vital,
element among the five sectors.

In the future, the relative importance of the transport element in its most comprehensive sense, will become
even more important in relation to the other four. For
this reason we must continue to make efforts to seek,
promote and invent new solutions for new transport
combinations.

Credit needs

The problems of operational financing in transport
are often underestimated. The problem of access to capital for small- and medium-sized road haulage firms has
been looked into recently, and the results indicate the
importance of investment in vehicles and material which
amount to over three-quarters of total investment of road
haulage and passenger transport firms. However, the credit needs of small- and medium-sized transport firms in
some European countries are today not properly covered.

Despite the large number of banking circuits which
deal with transport firms, and taking into account the
number of funds and financial trust actions which it is
possible to undertake, leasing etc., small- and medium-
sized transport firms do not have the means available to
acquire needed capital to operate in a sufficiently efficient manner. A lack of own account finance is typical
of these firms, i.e. they are operating to a great extent
on borrowed capital.

The very nature of the structure of small transport
undertakings, i.e. the fact that their capacity for profit making is small, makes them more and more dependent
on their bankers and suppliers. Since the beginning of
the present economic crisis, a lack of funds for these
firms in particular has become evident, resulting in an
increase in their degree of short-term indebtedness and
in the hindering of investments. The situation is thus
expressed by increased obsolescence of the fleet and by
the increase of energy costs. It can be noted that over
two-thirds of small- and medium-sized road transport
firms have difficulties in acquiring their own funds, a
very serious situation.

Added to this difficulty is the lack of interest on
the part of many banks in small- and medium-sized
transport firms despite official encouragement from
governments. The reason for this is partly due to the
fact that road haulage firms are considered as rendering
a service. They are, however, also part of the
production and dis- tribution process. This situation is
even more difficult to cope with today due to the high
level of interest rates and to the low level of capital
availability.

A proposal for equity funds

It was suggested that among others, equity funds
should be made available and, also, financial and fiscal
measures should be provided by the government or public
authorities.

In contradiction to the above mentioned proposal,
disagreement was voiced to the proposition made for subsidising small-scale firms through the use of equity
funds. It is not a good long-term policy to prevent companies from gathering sufficient company-owned capital
over time. Favouring small-scale transport companies
would be unwise, as there are many such companies in
which the owner-drivers are far removed from the questions of amortizing investments, creating company-owned
capital, knowing when to replace vehicles, etc. This is
a question to be tackled by governments and financial
experts.

Leasing equipment - a current issue

Lorry investments are short-term duration investments which influence considerably the budget of the
firms and the owner of a vehicle fleet is sometimes in a
situation of over-capacity or under-capacity. The leasing of lorries, which is becoming continuously more developed in some countries, is in other countries faced with
many restrictions. The speaker maintained that healthy
development for road hauliers is to be observed in countries where the hiring of lorries is possible, and that
this therefore meets a need. In countries where such
authorisation does not exist, however, the needs exist
nevertheless. In a time when firms are striving to rationalise all aspects of their economic behaviour, it
would be wise if they could have recourse to hiring or
renting their lorries and related equipment.

Supplying information

The difficulties in drawing together meaningful information are both technical and institutional.

Although the wish can be recognised on the part of industry and commercial organisations to maintain freedom
of action and to be involved in a minimum of outside commitments, a distinct reluctance exists on the part of
industry to provide information on which their operations
depends to government officials. Indeed, many of the
firms which would be providing this information are in
competition with one another in their respective modes of
transport. Therefore, when calling for positive and consistent transport policy, all parties involved need to
co-operate in assuring the flow of the necessary information to public officials.

Licensing for environmental protection - A proposal

The use of licensing for the purpose of environmental protection purposes was advocated. It was suggested
that the common transport policy of the EC is one of its
less successful aspects, and as a result of the impasse
which has been reached, the European Parliament has recently decided to take the Council of Ministers to the
European Court for failure to act on various proposals
forming part of the common transport policy. The most
important one of these, in the view of the speaker, is
the proposal which would eventually require the liberalisation of road freight transport, and therefore the abolition of licenses. It was asked of the panelists
whether they would care to comment on the aspects which
would occur were the aforementioned proposals to succeed
and, in particular, whether it could be envisioned that
licensing could be used as a new tool for environmental
protection.

In reply to the above mentioned proposal, it was
strongly suggested that governments should have a very
definite goal for licensing systems, but that the use of
licensing for solely environmental protection purposes
would be a crude measure indeed. Environmental problems,
it was pointed out by the panelists, are specifically
located in certain urban areas, but a licensing system
permits a vehicle or a firm to cary out specific operations all over the country or in a specific geographical
area. In this perspective, it was not understood how
pollution, emissions, noise etc. in a particular conurbation could be stopped through a licensing system, and
that such a measure would therefore be very inefficient.

Effects of liberalisation - Recent experience

Commenting on an assertion presented that the own-
account transport sector is too large in comparison to
the professional road haulage sector, it was observed
that in countries where the licensing system is fairly
liberalised, the transport for own-account sector is

normally much smaller than in countries where the associated controls are fairly strict as to access to the
market, etc.

It was mentioned that Sweden has developed its system of licensing from one of fairly strict controls to
one which is fairly liberalised, and during the transition period, transport for own-account decreased
considerably and professional road haulage firms simultaneously gained control of a larger slice of the market.

It was noted that the situation in Sweden is different from that of the Federal Republic of Germany, for
example, where the own-account sector is very large,
coupled with strict controls and an elaborate licensing
system.

What should be done?

Conditions in the freight transport market are
affected by the operations of three different parties:

1. the transport firms;
2. the shippers; and
3. the government.

It was brought out that a clearer distinction should
be made between the activities proper to each of these
parties.

In order to achieve more efficient transport services, the pertinent questions to be answered are the
following:

1. What could transport firms do?
2. What could shippers do?
3. What could and should governments do?

A number of sound suggestions about what to do were
presented in the introductory reports, but the role of
the shipper has perhaps been overlooked to some extent.
Very important is the development of the role of logistics, or materials administration, as it is also sometimes called. Here, the speaker felt that shippers could
do much more than is being done today. What was mentioned earlier in the discussion concerning logistics was
perhaps stated in too narrow a sense, in that it referred
only to the logistics of road freight transport, and not
to freight handling as a whole. Cargoes should not be
lying idle in various transshipment points, as is today
the case, such as in terminals, ports, airports, or in
warehouses. Capital is tied up, and interest must be
paid on inventory.

The proper role for government has not been clearly

stated. It is well known that a good number of restrictions exist for the road haulage industry. In many countries, government officials decide which firms may have access to the market. In many instances, government officials decide to what extent companies may expand their fleet of vehicles, e.g. with one or two vehicles, etc. Restrictions exist on the types of commodities transport firms are allowed to carry, and on the geographical areas in which the firms are allowed to operate, and so on.

It can be asked whether this is in the interest of the road haulage industry. If dynamic and efficient transport firms must always have to go to a government agency to ask for a license, expansion etc., it would be very interesting to hear what representatives of road haulage firms have to say about the many things which could be abolished in order for road haulage firms to become more efficient.

The key element is for the government to prepare a stable policy. The most modest request to be put forward is that the transport policy imposed by the government should be as stable as possible so as to allow the road haulage industry to know what to expect. The speaker felt that any kind of transport policy is better than no transport policy at all.

Social policy considerations

It was stated that the implementation of social policy in the road haulage industry appears to be a relatively simple task, but that, in reality, it is rather comprehensive and difficult to carry out.

Roughly speaking, social policy in the past concentrated on two points, wages or conditions of employment and, secondly, on the interest the entrepreneur showed in the personnel. Moreover, in reality, conditions of employment were drawn up by employees' and employers' organisations, and not by individual road hauliers. It was therefore significant that social policy determined at the industry level had to be forced on entrepreneurs and their personnel. It should further be noticed that this is, in some instances, still the case.

A number of reasons were presented for the lack of consideration of social policy by road hauliers in the past. Among these were the problems of day-to-day management (instead of a long-term social policy within the firm), the lack of knowledge in dealing with the social aspects of business contracts, and fear of anti-social feelings within the individual companies. On the other hand, the diversity of the road haulage industry (the number of firms of different size, organisations and turnover that operate in more or less the same market) makes it desirable to ensure that, amongst other things, fair competition and conditions of employment are of a similar level in all those firms.

Regarding the transport firms themselves, social policy will have to be accepted as both an integrated and independent part of total company policy. In order for this to be realised, several conditions must be met. If there is a conflict of interest between shareholders and personnel, the interest of the shareholders should not prevail, as those of the employees are preponderant. Secondly, a change must occur in the position and quali- fications of the entrepreneur, as management should in- creasingly become an objective buffer between groups of personnel, shareholders and financiers, i.e. one who will reconcile their interest, as they alone are capable of voicing their own opinions on matters of concern to them.

Very important is that road haulage firms should have at their disposal knowledge of all social aspects concerning business conduct, whether these are conditions of employment, working conditions, labour relations, quality of work, or availability of employment. However, many firms in the road haulage sector are not always equipped to collect the necessary knowledge and instru- ments with which to solve these problems by themselves.

Here lie the tasks for the employers' and employees' organisations. The goal should be, as a minimum, to pre- sent entrepreneurs and employees with a framework for social policy, but no more. Obviously, for the organisa- tions to be able to put this idea into effect, they will have to work in harmony.

Finally, the effect of the outlined social policy on the government was indicated. Governments, it was poin- ted out, have a tendency to regulate things. These regu- lations have a direct or indirect influence on road haul- age firms and are often laid down by law. These laws and regulations must therefore be revised so that they do not hinder the effectiveness of social policy considera- tions. Customs problems, for instance, have a negative influence on social policy. They result in long hours in waiting at the border, and here the example of the neces- sity for regulations for rest periods was presented as an example of proper social policy action.

It was emphasized that one does not wish to give the impression that there is no good social policy in trans- port. At an international level, the International Road Union has created conditions which are pragmatic for the driver, who, due to unfamiliarity with the conditions in different countries, is unaware of what may happen to him in international traffic. Time is today more easily calculated for the driver, and vehicle manufacturers have made efforts to improve his work conditions. There is a plan for a human work place, and this plan has been complied with. However, conditions are not so good regarding restaurants, rest areas etc. In loading and unloading areas, in particular, the driver often encounters unacceptable conditions.

Today, pressures exist for extending the two-year period of training for drivers to three years in order to allow for better and more solid experience. The driver must gain experience, which cannot be learned at training centres, but on the road. A final point refers to working hours, as the driver must be able to stop his vehicle in negative situations, e.g. due to poor weather. Allowing the driver to make decisions concerning working conditions should be made possible through co-operation with the unions.

THE CONCLUSIONS

The Chairman thanked both panelists and participants for the many stimulating ideas put forth, directed to governments, trade unions and firms alike.

The Chairman pointed out that no reasons seem to exist which would hinder the creation of a transport policy allowing for the development and co-existence of firms of different structures in the transport market.

Work remains to be done in eliminating step by step obstacles at border crossings, as problems still exist here in relation to firm productivity and social policy considerations.

Transport is an element of logistics. In developing company management, the use of automatic data processing facilities will continue to play an increasing role in the rationalisation and the further integration of the firms in the road haulage industry.

Further attention should be given to the development of terminals and the influence they may have on the improvement of speed and service.

In general, evidence seems to suggest that larger road haulage undertakings may often improve productivity through the decentralisation of management.

The need exists for taking into consideration the independent social policy expectations of the employee, while making possible the formation of social policy into an integrated part of company policy. The co-operation of company management, trade unions and governments is necessary for the attainment of this goal.

MANAGEMENT OF FIRMS TO SATISFY TRANSPORT NEEDS - INLAND WATERWAY GOODS TRANSPORT

THE REPORTS

Three introductory reports were prepared for this topic: by van den Bos, Wijnakker, and Zünkler. The reports and the subsequent discussion centred on aspects of inland waterway goods transport as regards primarily the situation in Belgium, France, the Federal Republic of Germany, the Netherlands and, to a certain extent, in the Nordic countries.

Van den Bos, in his report, emphasizes ways in which transport undertakings attempt to satisfy needs. Giving a background to the present situation, attention is drawn to the fact that inland navigation in the Netherlands, Belgium and France is governed by each country's legislation, under which the governments fix or control rates, while transport operations largely follow a roster system. In the Federal Republic of Germany, a legal fixed rate or fixed margin system is in effect. Van den Bos concludes that "...the market is clearly segmented... there is no single inland waterway transport market, but a great many" (van den Bos, page 290).

Inland waterways have, in the rapporteur's view, as a whole been able to meet market demand satisfactorily (certain figures are given; see van den Bos, page 295). However, it has not been possible to establish a temporary lay-up system for slack periods on the transport market, although this has been discussed for several years, nor has a plan for overall supervision of capacity by means of a licensing system been successfully implemented due to severe opposition.

No substantial increase in the demand for inland waterway transport is envisioned for the near future. In view of this outlook, potential problems are brought out relating to energy considerations, increasing the size of the unit, removing bottlenecks in the infrastructure, financing, co-operation between shipping companies, vocational training and crewing arrangements.

The second of the introductory reports, by Wijnakker, emphasizes the reasons for the exodus from this profession during the last decade. It is, in the view of the rapporteur, clear that "a by no means negligible proportion of boatmen have lost confidence [in this profession]" (Wijnakker, page 317).

Giving the reasons behind this development, it was pointed out that shippers consider the regulations governing inland waterway chartering as preventing the rational method of meeting demand, and that the roster system does not ensure that shippers will see their goods arrive in time or that carriers will receive an adequate return on their equipment.

The immobilisation of the fleet in Belgium on Sundays is seen by shippers as one reason for a lack of interest in the modernisation of loading/unloading facilities. Shippers and shipowners alike, in the view of the rapporteur, would like to see the roster system become "more flexible along lines which would enable the fleet to be operated in a more rational and business-like manner" (Wijnakker, page 318). However, owner-operators and the trade unions are stated to be in favour of the roster system in order to "exercise effective and efficient control over all spheres which even remotely relate to inland shipping..." (Wijnakker, page 319), and to maintain surplus provisions for meeting future increases of demand for inland waterway transport.

In clear disagreement with the view of the owner-operators and trade unions as expressed above, the author sees that inland shipping has sufficient reserve capacity with which to be able to respond to demand without difficulty, and that "the sector has to simply accept the ... disastrous consequences of depressed economic conditions" (Wijnakker, page 320).

The regulation of domestic markets for the purpose of allocating cargo among a larger number of carriers is seen as having tangible results, but it is pointed out that "the opponents of this policy claim that it is ruinous to inland shipping as a whole insofar as it sacrifices the future to immediate interests"; it is furthermore pointed out that "it is a fact that improvements to the fleet have no effect on the level of freight rates and hence on the returns of inland waterway carriers" (Wijnakker, page 320).

The third report, by Zünkler, discusses management objectives and the field for entrepreneurial action in inland waterway transport. The author sees the basic economic situation as leaving shipowners with only one option: "to try to satisfy demand efficiently by measures to improve the way they operate" (Zünkler, page 324).

The demand structure has changed in recent years due amongst other factors to the shifting of the production of raw materials to the developing countries and the trend of light weight and higher-value goods being transported by other modes of transport. Regarding the structure of transport supply, rail transport is seen as having favourable competitive advantages over inland waterway and coastal shipping by the fact that railways are running at a loss in all Western European countries and therefore have "to offer special freight rates to defend [themselves] against road transport...thus also indirectly affecting inland waterways and coastal shipping and setting them rigid price ceilings. This upper limit on earning prevents inland waterways and coastal shipping from being as flexible as deep-sea shipping if costs are to be covered in the medium term" (Zünkler, page 329).

The future of water-borne transport is seen as somewhat secure due to, for example, the organisation of existing industrial structure around waterways, despite the decrease in transport volume and reduction of both fleet and personnel. Reasons for optimism regarding the future are seen as the favourable consumption of energy per unit transported, and the increasing importance assigned to generating lower social costs, i.e. costs borne by the economy as a whole (pollution, noise, etc.). The author proposes that "governments may be expected gradually to convert social costs into internal costs by imposing charges so that they will be reduced through having to be allowed for in entreprenurial policy. This should further increase the competitive edge of water-borne transport" (Zünkler, page 341).

THE DISCUSSION

A rapporteur quoted the words of an Englishman who once said: "Shipping is the most complicated way of losing money." Although this could be more or less true, this is a job which is not only interesting but very important. The major problem is over-capacity. A system must be introduced for scrapping vessels and to take measures so as to permanently and globally supervise capacity in the future.

Over-capacity: The basic problem

It was stated de facto that, globally, over-capacity does exist, but that to deduce from this that one should

restrict investments, within Europe, of fleets and infrastructure is going too far. Decisions related to infrastructure investment are taken in many countries, as
put forth by a panelist, without sufficient input-output
or cost-benefit analysis on which to base such decisions,
the main considerations for or against these investments
being mainly political.

The definition of over-capacity does not equal that
of seasonally conditioned over-capacity, but only that of
structural over-capacity which arises due to the elimination and deletion of important sub-markets. There is
only one correct answer to the problem of over-capacity,
though very tough socially speaking, and this is to scrap
obsolete vessels with the help of grants from the government and maintain only the most modern vessels with full
employment. Any other action would entail total costs to
society which would completely outweigh the benefits to
limited groups of people.

The profitability of the undertaking was seen to be
crucial regarding the possibilities of boatmen to continue in their profession, as profitability is a precondition for the modernisation of the fleet. Among others,
the existence of suitable opportunities for vocational
training, on the one hand, and the improvement of living
conditions on board, on the other, were felt to be necessary in order to motivate people to enter the industry.

The drop in employment

An essential aspect of inland waterway navigation is
the dramatic trend of employment, which has dropped from
approximately 80,000 in the year 1965 to approximately
40,000 people today for ECMT countries. For this reason,
it was pointed out, the productivity of the industry has
undeniably improved, coupled with the modernisation of
vessels. However, the independent boatman does not have
an optimistic picture of the future.

In Europe, governments have invested in a modern
inland waterways transport infrastructure during the
1970s, but the tonne-kilometres have remained more or
less constant for the last few years. If the trend remains the same over the next few years, the speaker felt
that a portion of rail transport should be given to the
inland waterways, taking into consideration the larger
amount of infrastructure costs necessary to accommodate
the use of the railways in comparison with inland waterways, as depreciation costs for inland waterway infrastructure are much lower than for the railways.

The drop in employment by 50 per cent over the last
17 years was primarily seen to have been due to the
modernisation of the fleet. Considerable amounts have

been invested in the inland waterway fleet in the Federal Republic of Germany and in the Netherlands, whereas in Belgium, the amount of investment in vessels has been relatively small over the same period. Despite the radical drop in employment being regrettable, one panelist nonetheless saw it as being necessary in order to compete with other modes of inland transport.

Restraints on the entrepreneur

Possibilities for action by the entrepreneur in inland waterway and coastal shipping can only be evaluated if one is conscious of the many restraints put on the transport entrepreneur. The trend of bulk transport on European waterways is declining due, amongst other things, to the increasing location of the production of raw materials in the third world countries. Furthermore, the boatman must adapt to fluctuations in the demand for products composing important shares of the cargo transported by vessels, e.g. iron and ore products, mineral oil, etc.

The inland waterway entrepreneur must compete with other modes of transport, and thus be able to adapt technically to long-term trends of development, e.g. the former prevailing weight of barges has decreased and that of self-propelled vessels has increased, and these are now being replaced by the push-tow barges, the most modern means of navigation.

The roster system: Pro and con

A panelist felt that the roster system in Belgium, although to a certain extent ensuring the operations of the owner-operator by an even distribution of freight over vessels listed on the roster, does not promote motivation for investment. It was felt that fixed rates would better ensure employment on the inland waterways. However, the problem of over-capacity was agreed to be an international problem in need of international solutions which particularly relate to a continuation of the discussion of possibilities for international scrapping funds.

A participant asked panel members to explain the true meaning of the roster system, which was seen by the speaker as being the only really useful method of ensuring cargo to the small shippers who do not have the opportunity, as do bigger undertakings, of using for example agents in the search for cargo. Additionally, panel members were asked whether they had any ideas why equivalent measures to the roster system work quite well for the private road haulage industry, but not for inland waterway transport.

In response to the above mentioned questions, it was stated from the panel that small shippers understandably do not have the same means at their disposal to operate as bigger shipowners do. It was felt that, despite being applicable to small shippers, the roster system is not adequate since it does not encourage motivation for improvement of transport services. The roster system was seen as simply a new distribution of poverty, as the entrepreneur is not able to actively search for cargo, but must queue in order to receive freight at a given (and possibly unsatisfactory) rate.

A proposal: Commercial authorities for boatmen

The proposal was put forth that self-employed boatmen should in the future become organised under systems of commercial authorities similar to the roster system in order to survive. It was envisioned that such commercial organisations (referring to France) might form contracts per tonnage on a roster system and also issue payment to the self-employed boatmen who would be members of this grouping. This grouping would receive financial assistance from the government in order to make possible advance payment to the boatmen and also to allow for compensation for empty carriers, for the modernisation of ship-pools, and by favouring the entry of the young into this sector by means of an early retirement programme for older boatmen.

Container traffic

It was noted that the trend in development of container traffic on inland waterways is fairly recent, i.e. within the last few years. Referring to the Port of Rotterdam, only about 50,000 tonnes of container cargo passed through this port to inland waterways a few years ago, now this figure has increased more than three-fold. The reasons for this delay in development in inland waterways were seen to be many, the primary factors being the lack of sufficient loading and unloading installations at inland ports, and also to the slow reaction of the management of shipping companies.

The late development of container transport on the inland waterways was seen to be not entirely due to a lack of infrastructure in inland ports, as the corresponding facilities and equipment were in fact under-employed for many years. However, bottlenecks did occur, and sea ports offered more favourable conditions than inland navigation. Secondly, referring specifically to the Rhine, the speaker maintained that the shipment of

containers by means of waterway transport was discriminated against by renting conditions which were unfavourable
to inland waterway transport and worked to the benefit of
road transport. Today, however, the transport of containers is increasing on the Rhine, and at least three
big shipping companies are engaged in this activity.

Future outlook

It was envisioned that the major portion of inland
waterway transport would continue to take place on the
Rhine, where the current volume is approximately 250 million tonnes per annum. This, together with the traffic
on the other West German waterways, is perhaps the lion's
share of the West European inland waterways.

For these two markets, the predominant transport
policy of the future will very possibly continue to be
quite liberal. The speaker, referring to findings of the
Rhine Commission, among others, felt that no impelling
reasons speak in favour of government intervention in the
situation on the Rhine, where there has never been
government intervention, even though prices in other West
German inland waterways were not totally free as they are
on the Rhine. In these other inland waterways, prices
are always fixed in agreement with the forwarder, but
here also no plan exists for having a subjective licensing system.

Inland waterway transport does not pollute the environment to any great extent, is able to carry large loads
of bulk goods, and has an infrastructure which is far
from being saturated. In this respect, measures should
be discussed to optimally include this mode of transport
in the transport chain.

Inland waterway transport between East and West

It was brought out that the Eastern European operators of vessels are subsidised by their respective
States, and that this will cause difficulties for Western
shippers to compete with them on the limited international coastal and inland waterway markets. One possibility would be to allow the transport in question to be
completely handled by East European shippers, with the
ensuing flow of Western currency to these countries, and
allow the sub-markets to be subsequently monopolised.
The other possibility would mean a certain degree of subsidisation of Western European shippers by their respective governments.

The fleets of Eastern and Western Europe are governed by totally diverging market systems. The major
difficulties of co-operation in this area of transport

lie mainly in the reliance of free acquisition and purchase by the West, while in the planned economy countries
distribution of cargoes are based on macro-level plans.
In the West, cost-oriented prices exist for inland waterway goods transport, while in the planned economy countries, this is not the case.

It was maintained that the efforts of the COMECON
countries to enter the West European inland waterway market are nevertheless legitimate, and that the only link
is over the Rhine: from whence access to the canals to
Poland and Czechoslovakia. Today, only Poland takes advantage of this waterway, and traffic between West
Germany and Poland, on the basis of a bilateral agreement, is approximately 1 million tonnes per annum. Other
links could be established to the Danube, allowing links
between several ECMT countries. In this area, Austria,
Yugoslavia and the Federal Republic of Germany would be
in competition with the planned economy countries.
Although currently limited problems on the Danube will
undoubtedly increase in quantity and quality with the
opening of the Rhine-Main-Danube connection, regulations
and measures have been worked out by West European
governments in order to make the transition as smooth as
possible. The questions relating to capacity control
(and avoiding the dumping of prices) will be handled by
bilateral agreements between the governments concerned.

THE CONCLUSIONS

The Chairman summarised the discussion by stating
that a range of problems beset decision-makers regarding
inland waterway transport. Of particular importance are
over-capacity, the roster system, the different points of
views confronting the anticipated increase of inland
waterway transport between the Eastern and Western European countries, and specific problems related to employment and social policy considerations.

Over-capacity exists in inland waterway transport
over and above the spare capacity necessary for flexible
reaction to changes in demand. Vigorous action was proposed to adapt measures for scrapping obsolete vessels.
Also proposed were the limitation of capacity, limitation
of traffic on certain days of the week, and the limitation of working hours, all designed to do away with surplus capacity. However, the prevailing situation for the
different countries must be taken into consideration
where among others the degree of modernisation of the
fleet and the structure of vessel ownership may vary considerably. Therefore, although one may be aware of the
existence of over-capacity in the various sub-markets, it
is very difficult to come up with the appropriate
measures to remedy the situation.

The roster system, a form of regulation, is felt by some people to be the main problem of inland waterways, while others find the system necessary and are very much in support of it. Obviously, different interests exist here, and there is a great deal of tension among the various groups involved in the trade. On the other hand, nothing appears to have been said in the way of constructive proposals to do away with the negative effects of the roster system, apart from the wish to make it more flexible in the future.

The picture one has of the small craft with the skipper and his family living and working onboard is about to disappear, as the development of new techniques and innovations in vessels and in ways of running the business are rapidly overtaking the traditional boatman.

Optimistic suggestions were put forth with regard to possibilities of doing something about the future of inland waterway transport, particularly on the international scene and the scope for improving the transport chain. A very strong plea was presented during the symposium for international organisations to do what they can to remedy the severe drop in the employment of those working in inland waterway transport in Europe.

Inland waterway transport is very advantageous from the point of view of energy consumption, environmental protection, and the use of infrastructure.

Forming commercial organisations for small shippers would assist them in obtaining advantages similar to the bigger undertakings of the trade. The discussion also referred to the great importance attached to the improvement of vocational training possibilities for crew members.

Although interesting information was given dealing with aspects of inland waterway transport between Eastern and Western Europe, no conclusions were drawn concerning this delicate and important question.

Topic 2C

MANAGEMENT OF FIRMS TO SATISFY TRANSPORT NEEDS - URBAN AND REGIONAL PASSENGER TRANSPORT

THE REPORTS

The first report, by Cameron, indicates the different reactions by city authorities to far-reaching changes in costs, available technology, competition with other modes of transport, and public attitudes towards the environmental impact of public transport. The results have been, to a varying degree, either individually or collectively the following (Cameron, page 351):

- a decline in the standard of service;
- a reduction or increase of fares;
- heavy investment in equipment and infrastructure;
- having to make increasingly heavy revenue payment to augment inadequate income from fares.

In listing the demands for change, the author maintains that the expertise of the manager of the public transport firm is the single means at his disposal to answer the arguments presented by the public and politicians. In this task, "economists, however skilled and knowledgeable and even persuasive they may be, are of little help [to managers]" (Cameron, page 352).

The tasks of management are presented as including:

1. the administration of technology;
2. the implementation of economically sound measures; and
3. reacting in response to political decisions.

It is pointed out that "demands now for reduced public expenditure, without any reduction in public service, highlight the importance of the managerial task". Indicating the variance in the subsidisation of public transport undertakings in the world's major conurbations, which range from 25 to 75 per cent of income, the question is raised whether "anything...can be achieved by

655

more effective management to reduce dependance upon [public financial] support?" (Cameron, page 356).

Seeking an answer to the above mentioned question, an extensive list of characteristics of London Transport, as perceived by the rapporteur, is presented. In analysis of these, the author states the following: "Unless the Board [of Directors] can specify clearly the aims of the enterprise and translate these into businesslike criteria related to managerial accountability, it will be frustrated in any attempts it may make to counter the less desirable features of the culture over which it presides" (Cameron, page 358).

In conclusion to the presentation of several arguments common in day-to-day management of public transport undertakings, four initiatives for change are put forth for consideration (see Cameron, pages 363-3649):

1. Management should demand a clear direction, from its governing authority, of the objectives to be pursued and of the criteria by which its performance will be judged.
2. Management should insist upon a long period of consistency under stable conditions.
3. Management should identify clearly for itself the businesses that it is in and any separate markets, and the varied accountable management units and subsidiary activities which it must support.
4. Management should define the accountability and criteria of performance of the managers of these business units and train and develop them to respond to these demands.

In the second of the reports, written by Elmberg, attention is focused on strategic issues relating to Swedish conditions and experience. In reviewing operational policies, the rapporteur refers to the "superstitious belief", commonly found among politicians, that a low fare policy could attract private motorists to public transport. This is rarely seen to be the case, but higher petrol prices in the future might change this situation. The practice of introducing fare discounts for special categories of passengers involves the difficulty of estimating market reactions.

The rapporteur sees several ranges of problems facing the public transport manager:

- the competence dilemma (who is in charge, the politicians or commercial management?);
- the labour dilemma;
- the service dilemma (the allocation of service to different passenger categories);
- the funding dilemma;

- the subversion dilemma (will society assume responsibility to eliminate vandalism and
  hooliganism?).

The third introductory report is a case study of
urban and regional transport in Spain, written by
Estrada. A comparison of public and private passenger
transport undertakings is conducted by means of statistical and mathematical analysis.

The fourth report, written by Glassborow, asks the
question: what is regional transport? Although not easy
to define, regional transport is seen as a wide range of
services, typically within the range of 10 to 30 kilometres, between local urban transport, on the one hand,
and long-distance services, on the other. Several distinctions of regional services are given (see Glassborow,
page 456).

It is maintained that the reasons why some public
transport enterprises are more successful than others are
attributed, in addition to the ability of the managers,
among others to the historical, geographical and political elements in its situation. "In the case of regional
transport, the main financial problems are made more difficult to resolve because of the political constraints on
the courses of action open to the management."
(Glassborow, page 458).

The rapporteur argues against subjecting public
transport to the administrative boundaries of local
government, as these seldom resemble the natural catchment areas for local transport networks. Also, excessive
political intervention in the management of public transport "would itself increase the financial support needed
to maintain a given standard and quantum of service"
(Glassborow, page 460). In this respect, the intervention by politicians into the management of public transport should, in the view of the rapporteur, be supported,
defined, and limited by law, and, moreover, "...It is
probably better for the line to be drawn slightly in the
wrong place than for it to continue not be be drawn"
(Glassborow, page 460).

An overview of current economic prospects for
regional transport is given, followed by an axiomatic
presentation of the financial problems involved with the
management of regional transport. One conclusion drawn
is the following: "Once it is accepted that a large portion of the costs will not be borne by the passenger it
is no longer appropriate to base the fares on the costs
of the services. There is a need to develop other criteria which can command public acceptance" (Glassborow,
page 471).

The fifth and final report, by Pällmann, refers to the case study of Hannover. Initially, public transport is pointed out to have an essential place in the community as a whole, as "even in countries with high car ownership levels, well over half the population does not or does not at all times have access to a car" (Pällmann, page 479).

Indicating that public transport has been given priority in urban planning in the Federal Republic of Germany for several years, the rapporteur points out that "the formulation of objectives and basic transport policy statements [by the government] alone do not achieve much in local government programmes. At best, they provide a useful platform for implementing measures in accord with those policies... One of the most important tasks of the urban transport manager is and will be personally and directly to promote, through transport associations and political representatives, the interests of his own undertaking and of local passenger transport generally and tenaciously to force through his own ideas in the power game of interests." To do otherwise and hope that "...the intrinsic good of public transport will prevail in the end..." would amount to "criminal neglect" (Pällmann, page 483).

Giving a review of the political dimension of public transport in Hannover, problems are presented which relate to operation, tariff policy, employment, environmental considerations and energy constraints. Further tasks for public transport management are advertising and promotional activities aimed at the public, as well as research and development for the constant improvement of services by means of scientific and technological advances. The rapporteur states that "continual and active improvement in the services supplied is the only effective answer in the long run. Readiness to take investment risks, an understanding of the problems involved in presenting transport systems as an important part of urban development and the commitment to R & D are some aspects of the 'job description' for today's public transport managers; this will not change much in the foreseeable future" (Pällmann, pages 496-497).

THE DISCUSSION

The basic objectives

Public transport management is striving to offer public transport so as to satisfy the demands of the major portion of the population. Political authorities, with regard to the definition of objectives, have borne in mind new factors of public and collective concern,

these being urban congestion, employment, energy, environmental protection, etc. These have been and still
are motivating factors for the development of public
transport.

The question of major concern was presented as the
relationship and the appropriate role of the political
authorities vis-à-vis the commercial management of public
transport.

A review of recent developments in London Transport

It was pointed out that London Transport, in less
than three years, has had two total reversals in policy.
The situation has moved from high fares and limited services to low fares and increased services. Within the
same period, three chairmen have been appointed, one of
them reappointed four times. Fares have been doubled,
and after six months, services reduced to match the reduced demand.

The performance of managers

It was stated by a rapporteur that we now know more
about transport economics than we know about the behaviour of those whose job it is to manage transport. The
result is that many of the figures upon which economic
theories are based are themselves capable of being changed by changing the performance of managers. The performance of managers, moreover, is influenced most strongly
by the direction which is given to them by statutes and
by the politicians to whom they must report. Naturally,
politicians are reluctant to accept any clear dividing
line between their own prerogatives and the area of dis-
cretion which they accord to managers. Without such a
clear distinction, however, managers cannot perform
well. Ultimately, especially when funds are short, both
managers and politicians will fail.

If the objectives which managers have to pursue are
clear, and their performance criteria well understood,
good transport managers must succeed, and only thus will
the politicians succeed.

The following are essential factors and related
problems have a bearing on the role of the public transport manager:

- for the decision-making process: objectives
- for the necessary funds: scarcity
- for the staff: loyalty
- for energy: availability

The main problem of public transport managers today is to work out objectives together with the political decision-maker, and in so doing, to separate certain social obligations from strictly operational or managerial ones.

Political stability has a fundamental effect on the smooth management of public transport. The relationship between political decision-makers and public transport management is a learning process which is interrupted by the intervention of political elections; in planning operations, the manager needs to know what to expect in the form of directives from political decision-makers. Funds are often ear-marked by political decisions for what, from the point of view of the public transport manager, are unproductive obligations to the public. Words such as "profitability" and "effectiveness" become meaningless if the managers are denied the possibility to direct the path of development.

A panelist felt that the management of transport is not intellectually too taxing a task, and a surplus of intellectual power can never be a substitute for relevant knowledge. Here, the word "relevant" was emphasized. In particular, it is the aforementioned lack of awareness on the part of the public and of the political establishment which makes the situation so difficult for transport managers, who have quite enough to do dealing with the day-to-day problems of management which occur in all forms of business life.

The speaker also felt that it is the same lack of awareness, as mentioned previously, which is primarily responsible for the "silly ideas" which often gain currency in political and, regretfully, academic circles, in the field of measurement of transport performance, of the organisation of supervisory bodies to plan services, to co-ordinate investments, and to integrate road and rail, i.e. metro and bus.

A proposal for working relations between managers and political authority

It was suggested that if professional operators wish to have more stable relations with the politicians, then a certain distance should be put between these two parties: their dealings should be placed more on a business footing so that such relationships as do exist will become more of a contractual kind. Such practices, indicated the speaker, should therefore lead away from the trend of a further municipalisation of public transport, a trend advocated by certain political bodies.

The second suggestion put forth relates to the style of management: if operators recognise that there are strong needs which do not arise as a commercial demand and which form the basis of some kind of public financial support, they must themselves identify those arguments for support and convert them into operational criteria. It is then for the politicians to amend these needs. Hence, the large public transport undertakings should view (what Cameron referred to being) the roles of the economist and the politician to be actually part of the responsibility of the manager, rather than separate from it and conflicting with it.

The manager: experienced or a political appointee?

The public, in addition to the politicians and their advisors, do not seem to value, probably because they are not fully aware of its importance, the knowledge and understanding which can only be acquired by years of practical experience inside a transport business, and the great importance to any one of those transport businesses of those who have made that undertaking their career. Not all managers acquire these "crumbs of wisdom", but the speaker who pointed out this truth insisted that no one from outside these undertakings is in a position to acquire any of them.

A panelist agreed in principle to the importance attached to the distinction between the role of the politicians and public transport management being based upon statutes, but doubted whether this would be sufficient to ensure better management.

The real problem, as presented by Mr. Glassborow, a Rapporteur, is that the appointment of those to run the public transport undertaking is made by the politician; if the appointee wishes to get or, later on, to keep his job, or wishes some specific favour from the politician, then, inevitably, the chairman of the undertaking will often give way to the politician in a future matter of principle.

This, to the speaker, is the dilemma: in many cases, a man of strong principle will not be appointed as manager, and the man who is appointed will not resign when asked to do something by the politician which goes beyond his standards. The real problem then is one of power, and this problem is not solved by institutions, but only by democratic morality which, in the view of the panelist, is not entirely in the system at the present time.

Mr. Elmberg noted that he works with the same politicians within two different organisations, one is a public transport undertaking where the political body makes all decisions which have to do with social obligations, the other body operates under the Swedish shareholding act. The same politicians are present in the Board of Directors of the latter undertaking, but must now look at all things in a business-like manner; the speaker found it amazing that they really do so.

What should a manager do?

Transport managers should use any argument available to market public transport, e.g. that public transport is able to produce a service more cheaply than is the case with the private automobile. An example was given of a bus company which joined forces with car rental agencies to persuade people to use public transport between Mondays and Fridays, and to use a rented car on Saturdays and Sundays, at a discount price.

The influence of trade unions on management

It was stated by a rapporteur that trade union influence in certain decision-making situations is today paramount. In Sweden there is a law which states that all major decisions must be discussed beforehand with representatives of the union attending the session. In certain public transport enterprises, union representatives are now associate members of the Board of Directors, albeit with no voting power, but with the right to voice their opinion. Because Board members are elected to defend the interests of their constituency, i.e. the users of public transport, whereas union representatives defend the interests of the union members, difficulties may well arise as to the interpretation of the term "service". In such a clash, firm management may well serve as the moderator.

Financing public transport: The Federal Republic of Germany

The level of investments and granting of loans to public transport in the Federal Republic of Germany are coupled to the amount of oil consumed by transport; as this oil consumption has decreased in recent years, so have the funds granted for investment. It was claimed that the revenue deriving from transport oil consumption should be allocated more purposefully by enhancing the funds for public transport.

It was brought out that the tax-exemption of buses will be done away with at the beginning of 1983, after which bus taxes will no longer be refunded to the public transport enterprises. This is to say that the politicians have moved in exactly the opposite direction by directing taxation revenue, previously ear-marked for public transport, to the public treasury. One effect of

this, in addition to abolishing the tax-exemption of public transport, is to cause road transport as a whole,
public transport included, to become more conscious of
energy consumption.

Adaptation to demand

Referring to adaptation to demand, it is worthwhile
to remember that market surveys tend to show that people
travel by bus not because it is the best of the possibilities open to them, but simply out of habit. Things one
does by habit are easy to do, whereas things one has to
think about are more difficult. If a public transport
undertaking readapts its services too much, travelling
habits are also broken up, resulting in the loss of the
passengers which the undertaking thinks it is serving.

The role of small-bus operators

A small operator might be able to better serve the
real transport needs of given social groups than the bigger bus companies, which were seen as rather inelastic in
adapting their services to the actual situation.
Demand-responsive bus-taxi-type transport was a case in
point, as was the example of the community-operated bus
and, also, the combined use of resources, i.e. the use of
the vehicles in question for different purposes at
different times of the day. In addition, it was asked
whether a form of subsidisation such as today exist in
general for the railways might not allow several small
private bus companies operating in the rural areas of
many countries to continue operating, and in this way
cater for the transport needs of individuals living in
isolated areas, etc.

In answer to the above, it was agreed that a role
does exist for the small undertaking both in urban and in
rural areas, and that it can often provide a service that
is not possible for the more organised large undertaking. Indeed, one of the problems of the large public
transport companies is that the public expects more from
the large undertaking than it does of the smaller ones.
This is particularly so with respect to coverage at difficult times of the day.

Demand-responsive services

Demand-responsive services have been tried out from
time to time, but appear to be more satisfactory to the
passenger than to the subsidising authority. Studies on
demand-responsive services have shown that the amount of
money required, other than revenue from the passengers,
increases greatly in proportion when compared to

conventional bus services. If the local or regional authority is prepared to pay the extra money, then the passengers will evidently be pleased. However, it is necessary to have some means for deciding what in effect is the best way of allocating the scarce funds available.

Community-operated buses

Community buses do work in some places, often in co-operation with the local authority. The community bus is run by volunteer drivers. The real problem here is a managerial one, as it is necessary to have a large enough number of volunteer drivers who will be willing to go out and do the job. What is needed is to have someone with the interest and the ability to organise the drivers, as the maintenance of the vehicles and matters of regulation can be entrusted to somebody else. This, however, is the key to the problem: if the organiser and the drivers are available, the only problem left is whether the vehicle which is provided is in fact good enough to do the job. A bus which is driven by a large number of drivers develops faults which a bus driven by only one driver does not.

Arguments in criticism of public transport

A speaker felt that it has been shown many times in international studies undertaken in the last few years that public transport has very high labour costs, these being sometimes as much as 85 per cent of total operational costs. As public transport capital is very labour intensive, labour costs are going up at a rate faster than prices in general. Because public transport is very labour-intensive, public transport prices are therefore going up faster than the cost of living; recent figures (for Great Britain) show a faster annual price increase for public transport (3 per cent) than for private transport.

With respect to the energy situation, it was pointed out that the private motor vehicle can adapt very quickly to a serious reduction in available energy. Public transport, however, is at a disadvantage in not being able, as easily as is the case for private vehicles, to scrap old vehicles and acquire new ones in order to adapt to e.g. energy constraints.

In addition to the above mentioned two disadvantages of public transport, the speaker saw having to bear the costs of a system of management as a third argument speaking against public transport and in favour of the use of the private motor vehicle. The speaker pointed out that he could choose where to go in his own car without having to consult anyone else than perhaps his wife, whereas, with public transport, enormous numbers of people are involved in decisions related to the purchase of vehicles, time schedules, etc.; this is a cost that the public transport system has to bear. Therefore, the speaker felt that improving public transport presupposes the reduction of the number of people involved in making a decision, the improvement of the ability to adapt to energy constraints, and a reduction in the labour intensity of public transport. Because the amount of people who wish to become involved in deciding what to do with public transport seems to be growing, the only solution would be to separate the points concerned into different decision areas.

It was felt that unless there is public support for public transport, it will deteriorate. Such a deterioration is made worse by the inadequacy of the directives stating what the objectives of public transport management should be.

The car: The oasis of the city?

Were it politically possible to limit the use of the private automobile within urban areas, this would greatly improve the service standards of public transport. In effect, motorists do not simply "choose to use the car", but actually reveal a preference for the use of the car, in comparison to public transport service which can be made available, despite the congestion on the city streets which it creates. In this respect, the private automobile, often referred to as the "oasis of the city", is an instrument of free personal choice to those who have the opportunity to own and use it. However, a large portion of the population will continue to rely on public transport as the primary, and to many the only, available means of transportation.

A closing comment

In a final comment, Mr. Cameron wished to elucidate that what is being advocated is not a large subsidy to public transport undertakings, but rather that a political decision should be made to make it quite clear what subsidies should be provided, which should be as consistent as possible, and for the objectives of the undertaking to which the subsidy is paid to be perfectly clear. Nowhere (in the report or elsewhere) has there been a plea for a larger subsidy to public transport. As for London Transport, all that would be necessary for a profit to be made would be to eliminate all the buses, as the ensuing traffic jams in the streets of London would allow London Transport to charge what they like on the underground!

THE CONCLUSIONS

The Chairman summarised the main points which arose in the discussion:

A compromise should be found between contradictory positions. A need exists to reconcile entrepreneurial management of a commercial nature and political authority, and to keep political objectives clear. The relationship between the management of public transport undertakings and political authority must be clear and trustful.

Proposals for the improvement of public transport should be made in all fields of this sector, even if the final decision lies with the political authority.

The need to have general objectives for public transport undertakings, within a transport policy, may well find expression in the form of a kind of "contract" or understanding between political authorities and public transport management; indeed, such a "contract" might well exist and function among political authorities only.

The efficiency of public transport may well be improved through a decentralisation of the management of large public transport undertakings.

MANAGEMENT OF FIRMS TO SATISFY TRANSPORT
NEEDS - RAILWAYS

THE REPORTS

Three introductory reports were presented: by Andresen, Cobbett and Vazquez Cabezas. In the report by Vazquez Cabezas, a detailed overview of the situation on the Spanish railway system is presented, and suggestions are put forth for adjusting the railways to future requirements in Spain.

Andresen foresees that the public sector in general will be the target of cut-backs in the future, but that collective transport will not be the hardest hit by these measures.

Regarding the tasks of management, the author states that "it is now imperative for managerial considerations to establish a strategic indication system which continuously keeps [railway] management up to date with internal and external developments" (Andresen, page 516). A list of several of these indications is given (see Andresen, page 517). In conclusion, however, the rapporteur points out that "...a common attitude as a framework for future development is more important for management than long-term plans" (Andresen, page 519).

In the report by Cobbett, a summary of the objectives for railways is presented. Because of the nationalisation of the railways, the author points out that "there will be political direction and influence, but it does not mean that it should be biased or dictatorial" (Cobbett, page 531). The primary task of the politician, in the view of the author, is to "fashion the results [of the interpretation of railway goals by railway management] into a practical shape. He will, almost certainly, have to reconcile conflicting interests ... Above all, ... the politician must not be involved in actual operations" (Cobbett, page 532).

In discussing organisation, management style and the implementation of objectives, it is pointed out that "re-organisation is difficult and disruptive but is often essential" (Cobbett, page 533). In particular, it is emphasized that the "style of management must always be relevant to the objectives and subsequent aims ... Normal marketing activities are an important part of managing a railway to meet the needs of people and freight, but equally important is close contact with the press, tele-vision and politicians and involvement in general public affairs" (Cobbett, pages 534-535).

Taking into consideration the range of problems be-setting European railways, the author maintains that the real problems of the railways are due to changing econo-mic and social situations. Because of this, it is felt that railway management must operate on a scale of simi-lar long-term duration. "Twenty or so years forward is a proper horizon for this sort of consideration because it is in that time scale that the effects will work through the political and economic system. It is also an appro-priate time scale for making changes in the physical structure and traction and rolling stock equipment of a railway and, equally important, the pace of change in conditions of services of employees" (Cobbett, pages 535-536).

In conclusion, the rapporteur maintains that the railways can play a major part in meeting transport needs, but ..."can do so effectively only if they are selected to undertake those transport tasks for which they are best suited and given clear objectives against which to perform" (Cobbett, page 547).

THE DISCUSSION

What customers look for

The passenger market offers more possibilities for the railways than does that of freight transport. Here, the passenger looks for accessibility to the train, for speed, safety, comfort, frequency of schedule, reliabi-lity and for a fair price. In terms of types of busi-ness, a railway is strong in long-distance fast movements between cities and in commuting. In these areas, the railways have many social benefits to contribute, such as allowing people to live in less crowded suburban areas, alleviating traffic congestion, etc. The belief that people want faster and more frequent trains was contra-dicted: it was argued that what people really want is reliability, i.e. that trains arrive on time and do not break down.

The demand for goods transport and passenger transport is different for the railways. The first requirement of the customer is that goods transport should be reliable, secondly that it should integrate with the production and distribution pattern, and thirdly that the price that the railways ask is in correct proportion to the market price which the manufacturer can obtain for his products.

A needed definition

It is necessary to put forth a definition of the proper roles of transport based on the strengths of the different modes of transport. As most railways are nationalised in Europe, governments can well give a lead by requiring the railways to concentrate on activities in which they are strong and prevent them from competing in areas where they are weak. However, railway management should be reasonably aggressive and not allow the government to force obligations on them to operate transport activities unsuitable for the railways.

The railways should concentrate on their strengths: railways should concentrate on bulk traffic, and trains should be in blocks, with a minimum amount of marshalling. Also, to a certain extent, railways are seen to be able to compete quite well in the container transport market.

A high level of capital is required in order to make possible the special infrastructure and rolling stock provisions of a mass movement agency such as the railways. This is particularly true where such investments will enable the railways to be more efficient in terms of productivity of labour and machines, but also in the use of energy.

Railways should continuously strive for increased productivity, as the deficits of the railways are severe. In this area, the necessity for an increasing contribution from the trade unions was emphasized.

A continuous status quo?

In several comments from the participants, it was advocated that the railways close down such activities which can be better and more cheaply provided by other means of transport services. The idea presented is that the railways do not have a value on their own, but must prove their existence in their stronger areas of activity.

The deficit: A link between management and government

The deficit of the railways was proposed to be considered as a link between railway managers and the State. Regarding the deficit, it is possible to advocate two extreme positions:

1. management for budgetary equilibrium, i.e. a position which places the tax-payer in a more favourable position than the user; and
2. a system which justifies all excesses in expenditure.

One aspect of the deficit of railways is a long-term aspect, namely the historic law which states that there is a relationship between the deficit of a transport undertaking, on a long-term basis, and the level of obsolecence of the system. When a transport system has a long-term deficit, there are always good reasons for not financing the modernisation of the system, one being that subsidies for investment are made at the cost of operations. Such long-term aspects, however, are quite contradictory to short-term aspects, as an increase of the deficit in the short run goes against the notion of obsolecence. By increasing the deficit, and through subsidies, one can modernise the system. There is, therefore, a contradiction between these short-term and long-term financing aspects of railways.

It is more important to have a long-term investment programme for the strongest activities of the railways, guaranteeing a satisfactory future, than for money to be spent on trying to maintain every single line.

There is no use in discussing the future of the railways unless governments are quite clear in making a commitment in deciding on long-term investment.

A proposal: Introduce private financing

The question was asked why governments could not envision bringing in private finance in assisting in the financing of railway investments. Despite the obvious difficulties involved, the speaker felt that this is not beyond the bounds of possibility. The reason why more has not been done about this is because we are nervous about giving a long-term commitment to the main railway network. If governments were to make a clear commitment to improving the main railway network over e.g. the next twenty years, then private capital would surely be very much interested in participating in the finance of the more profitable activities, e.g. electrification.

It was also asked whether it would be advisable to shift the ownership of the railway infrastructure over to the government and charge the railways for its use, as is the case for roads and waterways. It was suggested that perhaps the answer to this question would facilitate a constructive relationship between government and railways.

Separating infrastructure from the assets of the railways and charging the railways for its use was argued against. Today, there is a great deal of mixed use of railway infrastructure. Several different types of traffic are run on the same track, and in many countries, different statutory remits from the government exist for each type of traffic. Also, many railways work under the control of public service obligations which require the railways to be socially-minded in their activities. For these reasons, it was deemed impossible to maintain a proper balance between the different responsibilities of the railways unless railway management was in complete control of all its assets and able to decide how the money which is available both on revenue and capital accounts should be spent, and what is the best technical and economical means of operation.

The importance of labour relations

The attitude of railway staff was emphasized as an essential aspect of the smooth running of the undertaking due to the relations which railway workers have with the customers and the public in general. Because of the influence of public opinion on the railways, and in order to increase staff motivation, the participation of staff representatives in managerial decisions was advocated.

The aims of "aggressive management"

Among the options available to the railway manager, aggressive behaviour obviously plays a central part, hence the proposal for aggressive pricing policy (by Cobbett). Doubts were raised whether an aggressive pricing policy would induce the railway management to go beyond the objective of producing transport services economically. The aim of aggressive price policy is to chase the competition from the market or to close the access to the market. This in turn shows a tendency towards monopolisation.

It was felt that the railways are well able to implement an aggressive price policy, not because they are a strong company, but because they are simply not subject to the risks of the private sector. The consequence of not being eliminated from the private market due to mistakes in management decisions causes the railways to in fact become immortal.

The dangers involved in the creation of "immortal" railways are:

1. the evolution of price monopolies;
2. additional needs for controls and regulation of the transport market (which one today wishes to do away with); and
3. the triggering off of additional taxation and contributions to cover the deficit.

For the above mentioned reasons, the speaker felt that the slogan of aggressive price policy from the railways should be deleted from the vocabulary of transport policy. Instead, a suggestion was made for a "dynamic price policy", in which pricing policy would be based on motivation and the factors of the market.

A goal for decentralisation

A decentralisation of management in effect gives large numbers of local managers the opportunity to make decisions, both good and bad, but on a small scale. This gives the local managers a degree of freedom to make mistakes, on which progress is in effect ultimately founded. The alternative is to have a small group of central managers who either take bad decisions on a large scale, or no decisions at all, which is often an even worse situation.

Several speakers advocated a decentralisation of railways management. Such a scope would make all the problems which seem to be so daunting when viewed from the central management point of view quite feasible to handle when they are seen at the local level. If these problems are handled by local management, this would be a step in the right direction towards solving the basic problems, in particular labour management and productivity problems. It may be that it would be necessary to create what is often lacking in the railways, that is the local manager on the spot, someone very desirable from the point of view of the customer. It was felt, in answer to the suggestion that there is a limit to how far the railways can indeed go in decentralisation, that once the railways begin to be decentralised, the further away that limit would actually be.

THE CONCLUSIONS

The Chairman summarised the main conclusions as follows:

Railways must in the future prove their existence in the market.

The essential tasks of the railways need to be defined.

Railways must adapt their structure to future external and internal changes (which derive from production and demographic conditions etc.).

Railway management must be creative and risk-minded.

A decentralisation of management was suggested; in effect, this would amount to giving the local manager a balance sheet and profit and loss account to work towards.

Proposals were made for the use of private funding of railway investments. However, these were seen to limit the ability of management to control railway assets, a precondition for proper management.

OECD SALES AGENTS
DÉPOSITAIRES DES PUBLICATIONS DE L'OCDE

ARGENTINA – ARGENTINE
Carlos Hirsch S.R.L., Florida 165, 4° Piso (Galería Guemes)
1333 BUENOS AIRES. Tel. 33.1787.2391 y 30.7122

AUSTRALIA – AUSTRALIE
Australia and New Zealand Book Company Pty. Ltd.,
10 Aquatic Drive, Frenchs Forest, N.S.W. 2086
P.O. Box 459. BROOKVALE, N.S.W. 2100

AUSTRIA – AUTRICHE
OECD Publications and Information Center
4 Simrockstrasse 5300 BONN. Tel. (0228) 21.60.45
Local Agent/Agent local :
Gerold and Co., Graben 31, WIEN 1. Tel. 52.22.35

BELGIUM – BELGIQUE
Jean De Lannoy, Service Publications OCDE
avenue du Roi 202, B-1060 BRUXELLES. Tel. 02/538.51.69

BRAZIL – BRÉSIL
Mestre Jou S.A., Rua Guaipa 518,
Caixa Postal 24090, 05089 SAO PAULO 10. Tel. 261.1920
Rua Senador Dantas 19 s/205-6, RIO DE JANEIRO GB.
Tel. 232.07.32

CANADA
Renouf Publishing Company Limited,
2182 ouest, rue Ste-Catherine,
MONTRÉAL, Qué. H3H 1M7. Tel. (514)937.3519
OTTAWA, Ont. K1P 5A6, 61 Sparks Street

DENMARK – DANEMARK
Munksgaard Export and Subscription Service
35, Nørre Søgade
DK 1370 KØBENHAVN K. Tel. +45.1.12.85.70

FINLAND – FINLANDE
Akateeminen Kirjakauppa
Keskuskatu 1, 00100 HELSINKI 10. Tel. 65.11.22

FRANCE
Bureau des Publications de l'OCDE,
2 rue André-Pascal, 75775 PARIS CEDEX 16. Tel. (1) 524.81.67
Principal correspondant :
13602 AIX-EN-PROVENCE : Librairie de l'Université.
Tel. 26.18.08

GERMANY – ALLEMAGNE
OECD Publications and Information Center
4 Simrockstrasse 5300 BONN Tel. (0228) 21.60.45

GREECE – GRÈCE
Librairie Kauffmann, 28 rue du Stade,
ATHÈNES 132. Tel. 322.21.60

HONG-KONG
Government Information Services,
Publications/Sales Section, Baskerville House,
2/F., 22 Ice House Street

ICELAND – ISLANDE
Snaebjörn Jónsson and Co., h.f.,
Hafnarstraeti 4 and 9, P.O.B. 1131, REYKJAVIK.
Tel. 13133/14281/11936

INDIA – INDE
Oxford Book and Stationery Co. :
NEW DELHI-1, Scindia House. Tel. 45896
CALCUTTA 700016, 17 Park Street. Tel. 240832

INDONESIA – INDONÉSIE
PDIN-LIPI, P.O. Box 3065/JKT., JAKARTA, Tel. 583467

IRELAND – IRLANDE
TDC Publishers – Library Suppliers
12 North Frederick Street, DUBLIN 1 Tel. 744835-749677

ITALY – ITALIE
Libreria Commissionaria Sansoni :
Via Lamarmora 45, 50121 FIRENZE. Tel. 579751/584468
Via Bartolini 29, 20155 MILANO. Tel. 365083
Sub-depositari :
Ugo Tassi
Via A. Farnese 28, 00192 ROMA. Tel. 310590
Editrice e Libreria Herder,
Piazza Montecitorio 120, 00186 ROMA. Tel. 6794628
Costantino Ercolano, Via Generale Orsini 46, 80132 NAPOLI. Tel. 405210
Libreria Hoepli, Via Hoepli 5, 20121 MILANO. Tel. 865446
Libreria Scientifica, Dott. Lucio de Biasio "Aeiou"
Via Meravigli 16, 20123 MILANO Tel. 807679
Libreria Zanichelli
Piazza Galvani 1/A, 40124 Bologna Tel. 237389
Libreria Lattes, Via Garibaldi 3, 10122 TORINO. Tel. 519274
La diffusione delle edizioni OCSE è inoltre assicurata dalle migliori librerie nelle
città più importanti.

JAPAN – JAPON
OECD Publications and Information Center,
Landic Akasaka Bldg., 2-3-4 Akasaka,
Minato-ku, TOKYO 107 Tel. 586.2016

KOREA – CORÉE
Pan Korea Book Corporation,
P.O. Box n° 101 Kwangwhamun, SÉOUL. Tel. 72.7369

LEBANON – LIBAN
Documenta Scientifica/Redico,
Edison Building, Bliss Street, P.O. Box 5641, BEIRUT.
Tel. 354429 – 344425

MALAYSIA – MALAISIE
University of Malaya Co-operative Bookshop Ltd.
P.O. Box 1127, Jalan Pantai Baru
KUALA LUMPUR. Tel. 51425, 54058, 54361

THE NETHERLANDS – PAYS-BAS
Staatsuitgeverij, Verzendboekhandel,
Chr. Plantijnstraat 1 Postbus 20014
2500 EA S-GRAVENHAGE. Tel. nr. 070.789911
Voor bestellingen: Tel. 070.789208

NEW ZEALAND – NOUVELLE-ZÉLANDE
Publications Section,
Government Printing Office Bookshops:
AUCKLAND: Retail Bookshop: 25 Rutland Street,
Mail Orders: 85 Beach Road, Private Bag C.P.O.
HAMILTON: Retail Ward Street,
Mail Orders, P.O. Box 857
WELLINGTON: Retail: Mulgrave Street (Head Office).
Cubacade World Trade Centre
Mail Orders: Private Bag
CHRISTCHURCH: Retail: 159 Hereford Street,
Mail Orders: Private Bag
DUNEDIN: Retail: Princes Street
Mail Order: P.O. Box 1104

NORWAY – NORVÈGE
J.G. TANUM A/S Karl Johansgate 43
P.O. Box 1177 Sentrum OSLO 1. Tel. (02) 80.12.60

PAKISTAN
Mirza Book Agency, 65 Shahrah Quaid-E-Azam, LAHORE 3.
Tel. 66839

PHILIPPINES
National Book Store, Inc.
Library Services Division, P.O. Box 1934, MANILA.
Tel. Nos. 49.43.06 to 09, 40.53.45, 49.45.12

PORTUGAL
Livraria Portugal, Rua do Carmo 70-74,
1117 LISBOA CODEX. Tel. 360582/3

SINGAPORE – SINGAPOUR
Information Publications Pte Ltd,
Pei-Fu Industrial Building,
24 New Industrial Road N° 02-06
SINGAPORE 1953, Tel. 2831786, 2831798

SPAIN – ESPAGNE
Mundi-Prensa Libros, S.A.
Castelló 37, Apartado 1223, MADRID-1. Tel. 275.46.55
Libreria Bosch, Ronda Universidad 11, BARCELONA 7.
Tel. 317.53.08, 317.53.58

SWEDEN – SUÈDE
AB CE Fritzes Kungl Hovbokhandel,
Box 16 356, S 103 27 STH, Regeringsgatan 12,
DS STOCKHOLM. Tel. 08/23.89.00
Subscription Agency/Abonnements:
Wennergren-Williams AB,
Box 13004, S104 25 STOCKHOLM.
Tel. 08/54.12.00

SWITZERLAND – SUISSE
OECD Publications and Information Center
4 Simrockstrasse 5300 BONN. Tel. (0228) 21.60.45
Local Agents/Agents locaux
Librairie Payot, 6 rue Grenus, 1211 GENÈVE 11. Tel. 022.31.89.50

TAIWAN – FORMOSE
Good Faith Worldwide Int'l Co., Ltd.
9th floor, No. 118, Sec. 2,
Chung Hsiao E. Road
TAIPEI. Tel. 391.7396/391.7397

THAILAND – THAILANDE
Suksit Siam Co., Ltd., 1715 Rama IV Rd.
Samyan, BANGKOK 5. Tel. 2511630

TURKEY – TURQUIE
Kültur Yayinlari Is-Türk Ltd. Sti.
Atatürk Bulvari No : 77/B
KIZILAY/ANKARA. Tel. 17 02 66
Dolmabahce Cad. No : 29
BESIKTAS/ISTANBUL. Tel. 60 71 88

UNITED KINGDOM – ROYAUME-UNI
H.M. Stationery Office, P.O.B. 276.
LONDON SW8   5DT. Tel. (01) 622.3316, or
49 High Holborn, LONDON WC1V 6 HB (personal callers)
Branches at: EDINBURGH, BIRMINGHAM, BRISTOL.
MANCHESTER, BELFAST.

UNITED STATES OF AMERICA – ÉTATS-UNIS
OECD Publications and Information Center, Suite 1207,
1750 Pennsylvania Ave., N.W. WASHINGTON, D.C.20006 – 4582
Tel. (202) 724.1857

VENEZUELA
Libreria del Este, Avda. F. Miranda 52, Edificio Galipan.
CARACAS 106. Tel. 32.23.01/33.26 04/31.58.38

YUGOSLAVIA – YOUGOSLAVIE
Jugoslovenska Knjiga, Knez Mihajlova 2, P.O.B. 36. BEOGRAD.
Tel. 621.992

Les commandes provenant de pays où l'OCDE n'a pas encore désigné de dépositaire peuvent être adressées à :
OCDE, Bureau des Publications, 2, rue André-Pascal, 75775 PARIS CEDEX 16.

Orders and inquiries from countries where sales agents have not yet been appointed may be sent to:
OECD, Publications Office, 2, rue André-Pascal, 75775 PARIS CEDEX 16.

67048-10-1983

OECD PUBLICATIONS, 2, rue André-Pascal, 75775 PARIS CEDEX 16 - No. 42555 1983
PRINTED IN FRANCE
(75 83 05 1) ISBN 92-821-1083-4